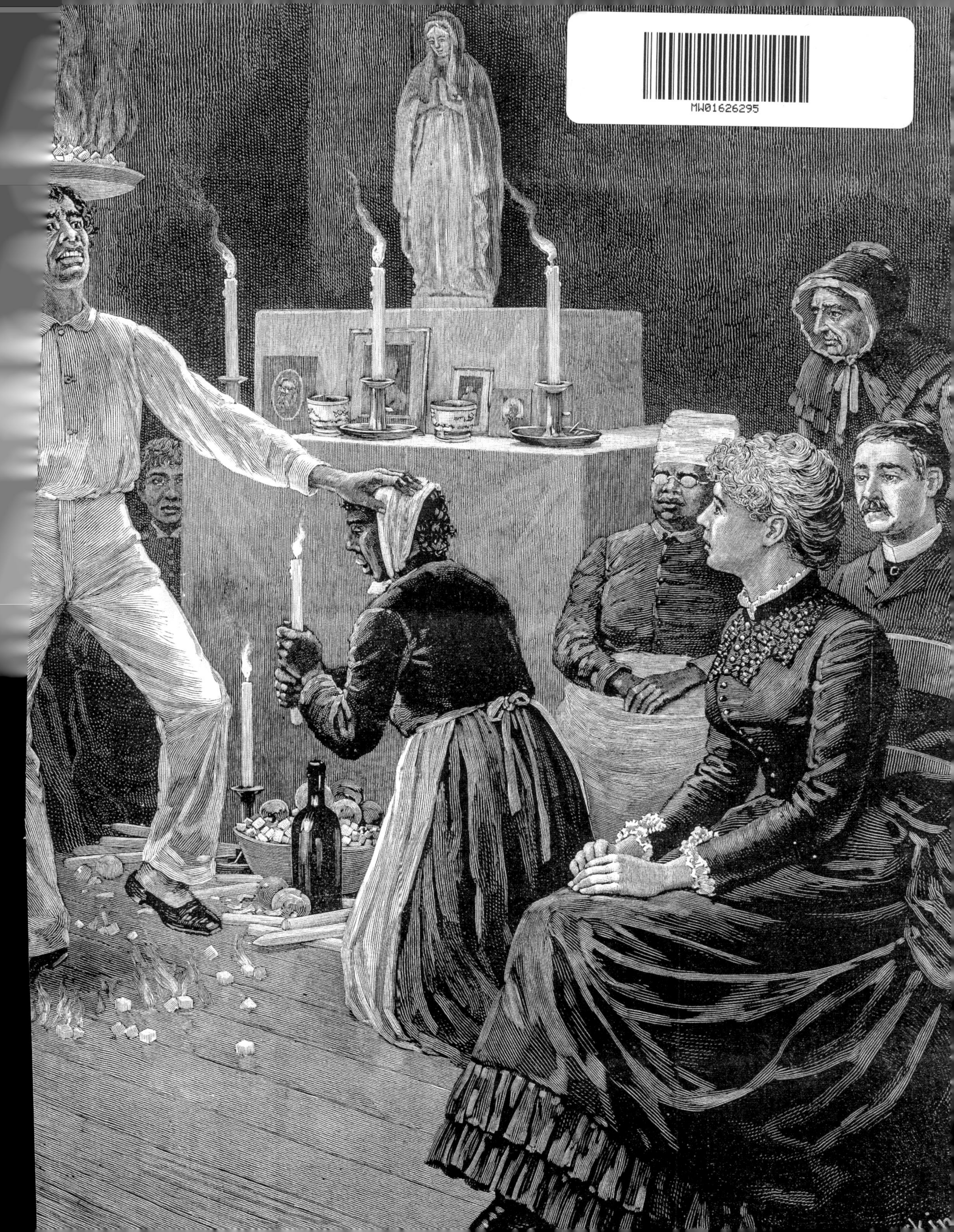

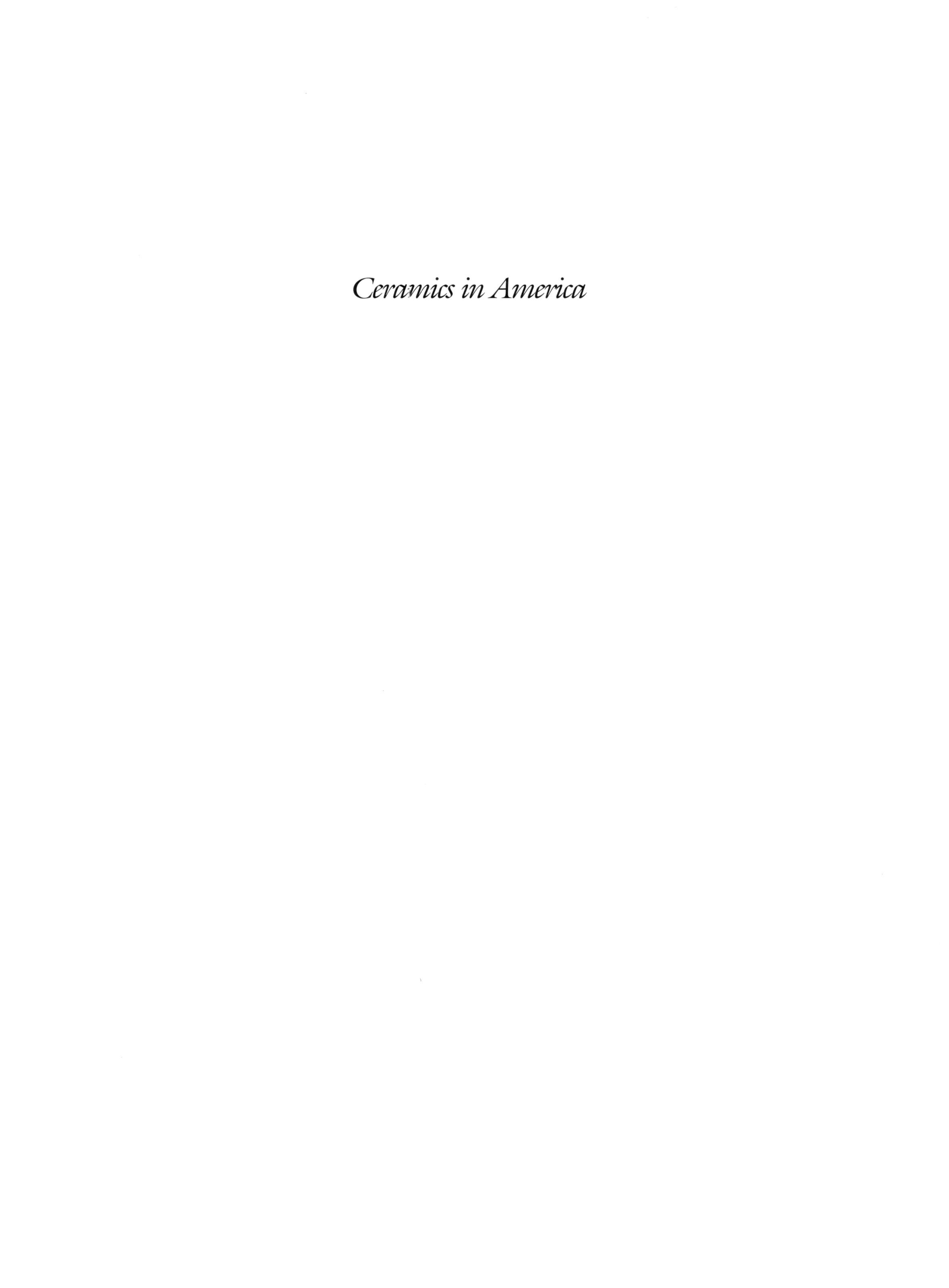

Ceramics in America

CERAMICS IN AMERICA 2023

Edited by Robert Hunter and Ronald W. Fuchs II

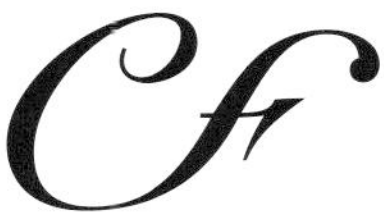

Published by the CHIPSTONE FOUNDATION

Milwaukee

Distributed by Casemate Academic

EDITORS
Robert Hunter
Ronald W. Fuchs II

PHOTOGRAPHER
Gavin Ashworth

Cover Andrew Hopkins, *Dr. Peter Davis*, New Orleans, Louisiana, 2017. Acrylic on board. 16 x 20". (Courtesy, Robert Hunter.)

Endpaper "The Blackville Gallery,—No. IV," *Leslie's Weekly*, January 20, 1898, pp. 40–41. Copyright by Knaffl & Bro., Knoxville, Tennessee, 1898. Photogravure. 22 x 16". (Courtesy, Robert Hunter.)

Design and production Wynne Patterson, VT
Copyediting Mary Gladue, CT
Permissions Angelika Kuettner, VA

Published by the Chipstone Foundation
www.chipstone.org
Distributed by Casemate Academic
1950 Lawrence Road, Havertown, PA 19083

Printed in the Czech Republic
ISSN 1533–7154
ISBN 978–1–737715–2–2

Contents

Editorial Statement VII
Robert Hunter

Introduction IX
Robert Hunter

Southern Hoodoo and the Dr. Peter Davis Ring Bottle 2
Robert Hunter

At the End of a Rope: A Stoneware Jar and Political Frustration 36
Elyse D. Gerstenecker with Robert Hunter and Kurt Russ

John Wesley Carpenter (1842–1913): Tradition, Innovation, and Adaptation in the Post–Civil War South 50
Stephen C. Compton

Geochemical Investigation of a Ceramic Snuff Box—A-Marked English Porcelain Attribution Confirmed 90
W. Ross Ramsay, Howell G. M. Edwards, Errol Manners, and Ashley Howkins

"From Death to Life": Slavery and Emancipation in the British West Indies as Revealed on a Child's Plate 113
Daniel S. Sousa

Hidden Histories: The Case of Elijah Lovejoy and the Production of Anti-slavery Ceramics 124
Neil Ewins

A Chelsea Keramic Art Works Vase with a Portrait of William Lloyd Garrison 134
James D. Kaufman

Earth, Fire, and the Abolitionist: The Emancipation of Clay for Social Change 139
David Mack

Souvenirs of Fantasy: George Ohr's Clay Tokens 150
Ellen J. Lippert

English Delft for Colonial Tavern Tables in King William County and Williamsburg, Virginia 162
Elizabeth Donison, Ned Rose, and Angelika Kuettner

A Tale of Two Chinese Porcelain Punch Bowls 170
Amanda Creekman Isaac and Captain Charles T. Creekman

Family Reunion: The Clay Sculptures of Babette Wainwright 196
R. Ruthie Dibble

Index 215

Editorial Statement

Ceramics in America is an interdisciplinary journal intended for collectors, historical archaeologists, curators, decorative arts students, social historians, and studio potters. We seek articles on the broad role of historical ceramics in the American context, including essays on ceramic history, archaeological research, technology, social history, studio pottery, and collecting. Further information about this process can be found at the Chipstone Foundation's website, www.chipstone.org. Authors are encouraged to contact the editors before submitting materials.

The Chipstone Foundation offers significant honoraria for full-length manuscripts accepted for publication, and reimburses authors for photography that is approved in writing by the editors.

If an article is accepted for publication, the author should submit photocopies of the title page and copyright page for all cited published sources. Authors are encouraged to provide digital files for all images, along with permissions to reprint. Low-resolution digital images or photographs of poor quality will not be accepted for publication.

Questions and comments from readers and authors are welcome.

Robert Hunter
Editor, Ceramics in America
P.O. Box 401
Yorktown, Va. 23690

Ronald W. Fuchs II
Co-editor, Ceramics in America
P.O. Box 3785
Gettysburg, Pa. 17325
rfuchsceramics@gmail.com

Robert Hunter

Introduction

▼ WITH THE PUBLICATION of the 2023 volume of *Ceramics in America*, this will be my last introduction to it. After twenty-two years I am stepping down as editor and passing the ceramic baton to my co-editor Ron Fuchs, who will shepherd future volumes. For the near future, my time will be occupied with other research and writing assignments related to projects that I started along the way but shelved in deference to the annual demands of *Ceramics in America*.

It seems like only yesterday that I met with David Knox, CEO and chairman of the Chipstone Foundation, and its executive director, Jon Prown, to pitch my idea for a journal devoted to ceramics made and used in America. I have benefited greatly from their counsel, trust, and support through these many years. The journal was modeled on Chipstone's highly successful *American Furniture*, created by my friend and mentor Luke Beckerdite to whom I owe so much. In those early discussions we envisioned a publication that would build bridges between the fields of archaeology, the decorative arts, and contemporary craft and the legions of collectors with an interest in the field. I will let others gauge the level of success we have had. After thousands of pages of articles, photography, short new discoveries, and book reviews, it is my hope that history will be kind.

I am indebted to the many contributors and advisers who have made this journey such a joyful personal achievement for me. My friend George Miller has been a constant source of advice and has provided a steadying hand at times. For many years Merry Outlaw, editor of New Discoveries, and Amy Earls, editor of Book Reviews, helped round out the offerings of *Ceramics in America*. The brilliant design and production work of Wynne Patterson has made our volumes lasting works of art. The genius photography of Gavin Ashworth set the highest standard for illustrating ceramic topics. The incisiveness of our irreplaceable copy editor Mary Gladue has helped bring clarity, distinction, and cohesion to the journal. Behind the scenes, Peggy Scholley has proofread final pages. My colleague Angelika Kuettner, now curator of ceramics and glass at Colonial Williamsburg, has assisted with arcane references and last-minute requests for tracking photographs.

I am deeply blessed to have had the support and insight provided by my partner, ceramics artist Michelle Erickson, whose significant contributions to understanding historical ceramics technology have been featured in many of our articles. So much of what I have learned about the mechanics of the ceramic craft has come from watching and listening to this master potter at work.

Looking back over the twenty-plus volumes is like revisiting a road trip from long ago, a mental shoebox filled with snapshots, roadside souvenirs, and somewhat hazy recollections of random encounters along the way. Although each journey had its own intended destination, the unexpected detours stand out as the most memorable. The 2023 volume is no exception, underscoring how ceramic history can inform us about the past and the present in unique ways.

Among the twenty-first-century tools that have transformed our field are the Internet, search engines such as "Google," and the phenomenon of social-media networks. In 2017 an important Southern stone ring bottle coming up for sale was brought to my attention via a Facebook message indicating that inscribed on the base was "Dr. Peter Davis" and the date "1888." A subsequent Facebook post by researcher Corbette Toussaint identified Dr. Davis as a "root doctor" in Columbia, South Carolina. Eventually I was able to study the ring bottle in its role in the context of Southern hoodoo. Among many fortuitous encounters along the way, I met Andrew Hopkins, a New Orleans folk artist, who drew on his considerable knowledge of nineteenth-century material culture to produce an "imagined" portrait of Dr. Davis with the ring bottle. I am delighted that it serves as this year's cover image. Highlights from the ongoing journey into this often sensationalized topic are presented in this year's opening article, "Southern Hoodoo and the Dr. Peter Davis Ring Bottle."

The catalyst that continues to drive the research and publication of ceramics histories is the unexpected discovery of previously unknown ceramic specimens. One might think we have completely mined the reserve of such treasures, but they continue to be unearthed in old collections, estates, sales rooms, and even in the back corners of museum storerooms, overlooked or neglected by their custodians. Some of these discoveries defy all expectations. If you had told me that a stoneware jar was made in Richmond, Virginia, at the onset of the Civil War and decorated with the initials C.S.A. (Confederate States of America) along with iconography related to the Union and images of Abraham Lincoln and Jefferson Davis, I would have laughed. But in 2017 such an object surfaced (or resurfaced) in a dealer's collection, having been out of sight for many years. It was explored in a paper presented at the Museum of Early Southern Decorative Arts' Summer Institute by Elyse D. Gerstenecker, and we are fortunate to be able to publish an updated version titled, "At the End of a Rope: A Stoneware Jar and Political Frustration," with contributions by Virginia stoneware scholar Kurt Russ and me. Although the subject matter of the illustrations on the jar is harsh, it reflects the tumultuous themes of racial and political divisions, many of which of course continue to be prevalent in our modern social and political discourse.

More has been written about the history of North Carolina's pottery than that of any other state in America. In his article "John Wesley Carpenter (1842–1913): Tradition, Innovation, and Adaptation in the Post–

Civil War South," author Steve Compton reminds us that there is still much to learn. Although Carpenter was an extremely prolific potter, the full story of his life and his stoneware has never been told. He produced both alkaline-glazed and salt-glazed stoneware, much of it quite distinctive and beautiful. Throughout much of America, the making of pottery was a family business, the production secrets passed down through marriage. Steve takes on the task of documenting the multi-generational history of John Wesley, and his brothers and their connections to other potting families of the Catawba Valley. Beyond the pottery, the importance of the article is enhanced by the poignant portrait of John Wesley, and his struggle to pursue his craft and to overcome the harsh economic realities of the post–Civil War South .

One of the most cherished of American ceramics origin stories is the encounter with a raw source of kaolin clay from the backcountry of the Carolinas in the early eighteenth century. It became known as "Cherokee Clay," its source being in the mountains of the Cherokee Nation. The material had been specified in a 1744 London patent calling for the use of a particular clay—"an earth, the product of the Chirokee nation in America, called by natives unaker." In 1937 British ceramics historians recognized a group of English-made porcelains thought to have been made from samples taken from this fabled kaolin source in the Carolinas. The group was designated "A-marked" because of an incised "A" that appeared on the various examples. Scientific analysis of the most recent member of this group is presented in "Geochemical Investigation of a Ceramic Snuff Box: A-marked English Porcelain Attribution Confirmed" written by authors W. Ross Ramsay, Howell G. M. Edwards, Errol Manners, and Ashley Howkins.

The history of slavery and its ultimate abolition in Great Britain, the West Indies, and America is complex and interrelated. The ceramics produced by various American and British potters to promote the abolition of slavery lend themselves to such questions as who designed and commissioned them, what audience were they made for, and ultimately did they have their intended effect. In his article "'From Death to Life': Slavery and Emancipation in the British West Indies as Revealed on a Child's Plate," curator Daniel Sousa uses a nineteenth-century Staffordshire plate recently acquired by Historic Deerfield as a springboard into that international narrative.

In the next article, British ceramic scholar Neil Ewins examines another printed nineteenth-century Staffordshire plate in "Hidden Histories: The Case of Elijah Lovejoy and the Production of Anti-slavery Ceramics." The printed pattern references the martyrdom of the Reverend Elijah Lovejoy (1802–1837), the proprietor of an abolitionist newspaper in Alton, Illinois, who was murdered by a pro-slavery mob on November 7, 1837. Ewins re-examines the origins of this plate design, previously thought to have been produced to support the cause of abolition in America. Ewins instead uncovers the true tale of the New York ceramics dealer and importer Thomas F. Field, who appears to have commissioned the design for his "Abolition China Store," and proclaims Field a hero of the abolitionist movement.

Turning from the relatively unknown social champion Thomas Field, we are introduced to a rare if not unique American-made ceramic vase created to memorialize William Lloyd Garrison, the most acclaimed white abolitionist of the nineteenth century. This recent ceramics discovery is presented by collector James Kaufman in his "A Chelsea Keramic Art Works Vase with a Portrait of William Lloyd Garrison." Garrison was a founder of the American Anti-Slavery Society and editor of *The Liberator*, a newspaper he published in Boston from 1831 until the end of slavery in the United States in 1865 and one of the nation's leading anti-slavery publications. Although many examples of abolition-themed English ceramics were made in the eighteenth and nineteenth centuries, only a few seem to have been created by American makers.

In the next article, we are privy to the art and firsthand commentary of working ceramic artist David Mack. Born and raised in Baltimore, Maryland, David had an atypical path in his career. He served in the military, retiring with the rank of Lieutenant Colonel. He was a highly successful athlete and coached cross country and track and field for many years. He also studied and taught ceramics early in his life. In his essay, "Earth, Fire, and the Abolitionist: The Emancipation of Clay for Social Change," David illustrates his sculptural work undertaken in the past twenty years that has been inspired by the American heroes of the nineteenth-century abolition movement. We are excited to present his three-dimensional portraits depicting Harriet Tubman, Martin Luther King Jr., Sojourner Truth, and Frederick Douglass. Today, David remains an ardent champion of Black ceramic artists, both living and dead, and recently his essay "Enslaved and Freed African American Potters" was published in *Ceramics Monthly* (2020). His current work includes sculptures of Vice President Kamala Harris and Supreme Court Justice Kentanji Brown Jackson.

The name George Ohr is readily recognizable to students of twentieth-century American ceramics history. Ohr was a master potter but also excelled at promotion and hyperbole, billing himself as the "greatest potter in the world." His highly imaginative and sensually contoured glazed earthenwares command enormous sums in today's market, but in his own lifetime his work was largely ignored. In "Souvenirs of Fantasy: George Ohr's Clay Tokens," author Ellen J. Lippert examines a group of clay tokens that have received little attention by scholars and collectors. Certainly created as trinkets, these tokens contained unexpected explicit and suggestive sexual messages, objects to giggle at perhaps when presented to unsuspecting bystanders. Ellen suggests that beyond psychological markers of Ohr's unique personality, the tokens foreshadowed the trends of the so-called American funk movement, where ceramics became a medium for expressing shocking and lowbrow humor.

Ceramics have always been an essential tool for archaeological dating and understanding the function of sites. As result, much has been written on the chronology of ceramics and the study of ware type in particular by archaeologists and decorative arts scholars. In their article "English Delft for Colonial Tavern Tables in King William County and Williamsburg, Virginia," authors Elizabeth Donison, Ned Rose, and Angelika Kuettner combined their approaches to contextualize a delft plate found at an eighteenth-century tavern in Virginia. The fragmented plate, decorated with a fanciful Chinese-inspired scene, has parallels in several museum collections as well as a related tavern in Williamsburg that not only provide a firm date but give us a snapshot of prevailing style and taste chosen to grace the tables of Virginia tavern patrons.

For the penultimate article, authors Amanda Creekman Isaac and Captain Charles T. Creekman present "A Tale of Two Chinese Porcelain Punch Bowls." The subjects of their study are two highly decorated Chinese porcelain punch bowls that are linked to George Washington and the American naval hero Thomas Truxtun. The authors note that the gifting of punch bowls was a time-honored practice among the power brokers of late-eighteenth-century Anglo-American politics and commerce. Tracing the journeys of the bowls from the time of their commissioning in the Chinese port of Canton, Isaac and Creekman contend that they were created as political gifts to promote the establishment of the U.S. Navy during a time of uncertainty in the founding years of the United States government.

We opened this year's journal with an article offering a glimpse into the topic of "hoodoo" as it was practiced in the nineteenth-century American South. In our concluding article, we encounter Haitian Vodou, an active spiritual practice alive and well in both the Caribbean and the United States, one of the various aspects of that culture that informs the ceramics of Wisconsin artist Babette Wainwright. Ruthie Dibble's essay, "Family Reunion: The Clay Sculptures of Babette Wainwright," journeys into the artist's deep and intensely personal work, which is imbued with Haitian aesthetics, spirituality, religion, architecture, and history.

If I had any prediction about the next twenty-three years of this journal, it would be that the history of ceramics made and used in American contexts will continue to be of great interest to a wide audience. Upcoming volumes are already well underway, with topics that include eighteenth-century Philadelphia slipwares, the important stoneware of New York's Black potter and abolitionist Thomas Commeraw, and many wide-ranging new discoveries. I sincerely thank our readers for their attention and continued interest in *Ceramics in America*. Microphone drop.

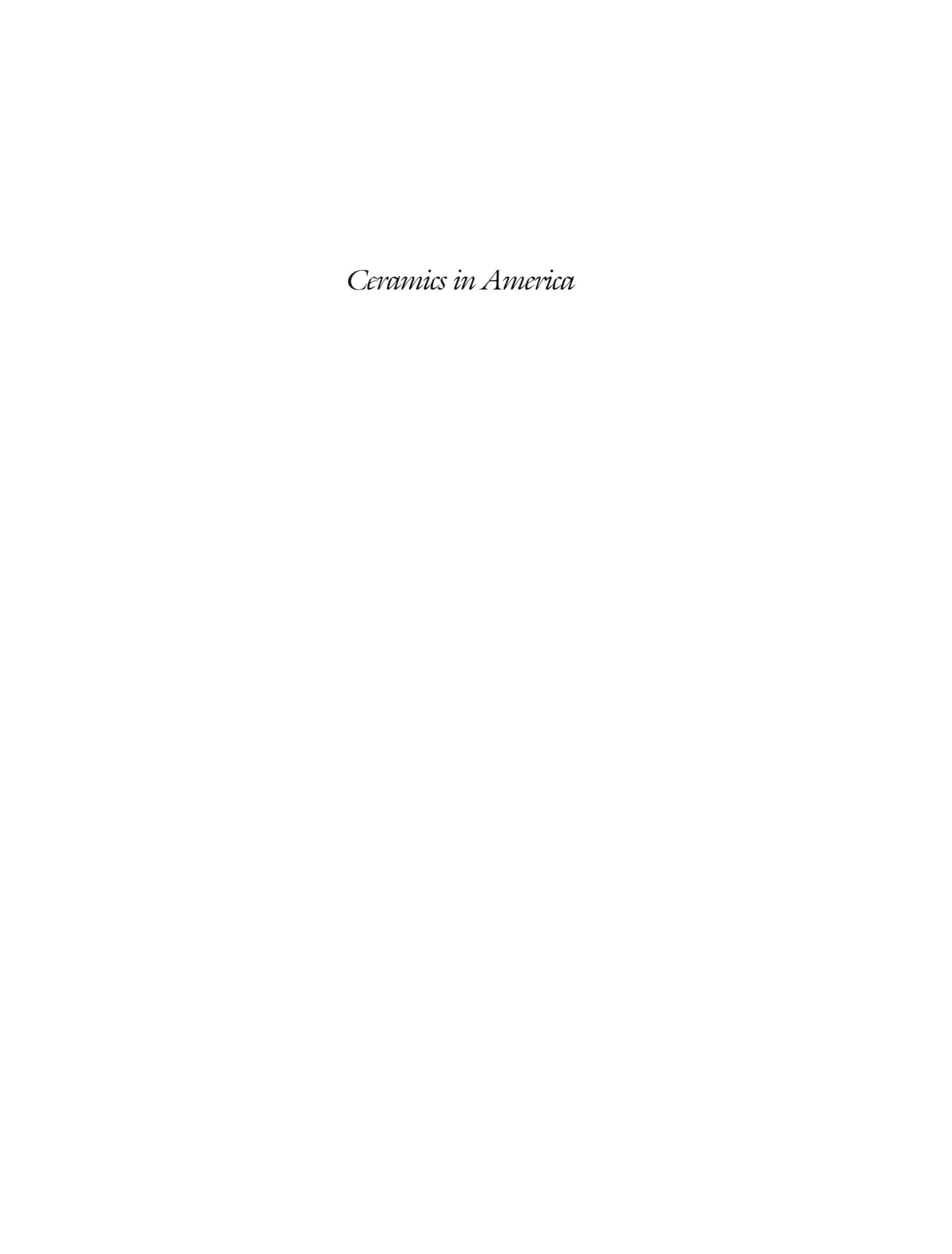

Ceramics in America

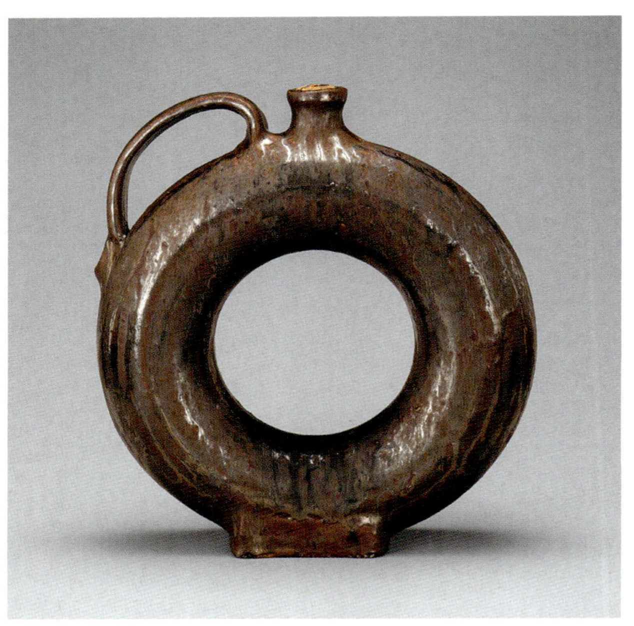
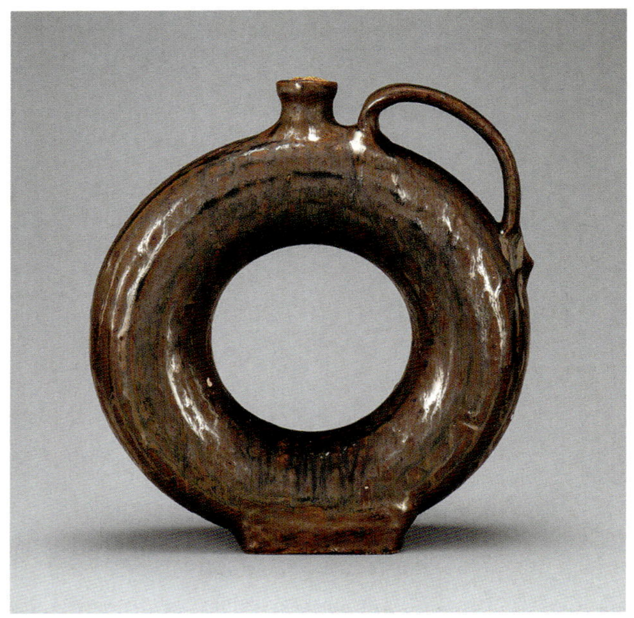

Figure 1 Ring bottle, attributed to Edward and Robert Stork Pottery, Columbia, South Carolina, 1888. Alkaline-glazed stoneware. H. 10". (Chipstone Foundation; all photos by Robert Hunter unless otherwise noted.) The hollow ring that forms the body was thrown on the wheel from a single ball of clay. The neck/mouth was thrown in a separate operation. The solid rectangular base was molded by hand. These components were assembled at the leather-hard state of the clay. The handle was pulled separately and attached to the body.

Robert Hunter

Southern Hoodoo and the Dr. Peter Davis Ring Bottle

"Dr." Peter Davis . . . a cross between a gorilla and a badger and a lineal descendant of one of the witches of "Macbeth."[1]

—"The Hoodoo Doctor," *Camden* (S.C.) *Chronicle*, November 10, 1893, p. 1.

▼ WHEN THE AUDIENCES OF William Shakespeare's *Macbeth* (ca. 1606) first heard the Three Witches recite their famous lines "Double, double toil and trouble / Fire burn and cauldron bubble," the inner workings of witchcraft and sorcery were well embedded in the Jacobean zeitgeist. King James I himself had already published *Daemonologie*, his treatise on "black magic," in both Scotland (1597) and London (1603), and his subjects knew him as a staunch opponent of the practice.[2] To counter bewitchment, various apotropaic or protective magical spells incorporating the use of talismans, amulets, potions, bones, and powders were in vogue in all ranks of British society. Shakespeare may have drawn directly from well-known conjurations circulating in the populace when he included "Eye of newt and toe of frog" as ingredients in the witches' brew.[3]

Gonna sprinkle ding 'em dust all around her door. . .

Some four hundred years later in America, another mysterious charm was delivered to listeners of Bessie Brown's music when she sang the lyrics to her composition "Hoodoo Blues" (1924):

> Gonna sprinkle ding 'em dust all around her door
> Gonna sprinkle ding 'em dust all around her door
> Put a spider in her dumplin', make her crawl all over the floor
> Goin' 'neath her window, gonna lay a black cat bone
> Goin' 'neath her window, gonna lay a black cat bone
> Burn a candle on her picture, she won't let my good man alone.[4]

American blues musicians had become the troubadours of "hoodoo," a tradition of magical thinking in the quest for supernatural interventions. Variously called conjuring, rootwork, and often conflated with the term *voodoo*, hoodoo has been of great interest to chroniclers of American social history. Traces of its material-culture component are scarce; much of its history is documented through newspaper accounts, oral histories, and archaeological research. What follows is a tale worthy of Shakespeare: the finding of an American Southern stoneware object that provides both a physical and metaphysical portal into the history of American hoodoo.

The Discovery

On October 10, 2017, a nineteenth-century American stoneware ring bottle came up for sale in a midweek auction in Columbia, South Carolina (fig. 1).[5] The ring bottle (sometimes called a jug or flask) was a somewhat common Southern vessel form made in a number of regional potteries from the late eighteenth century onward. The example presented at auction, however, was distinguished by the addition of a graceful handle and a sturdy rectangular base so that it could stand upright. The bottle was covered in a streaky, iron-rich slip glaze generally characteristic of the Columbia area. It was brought to my attention because the unglazed base was inscribed "Dr. Peter Davis" along with the date "1888" (fig. 2). That elevated an attractive but not particularly unusual Southern ceramic form to one of considerable rarity, since inscriptions of this type are generally not found on surviving antique examples. No other historical information was offered at the time of the sale.

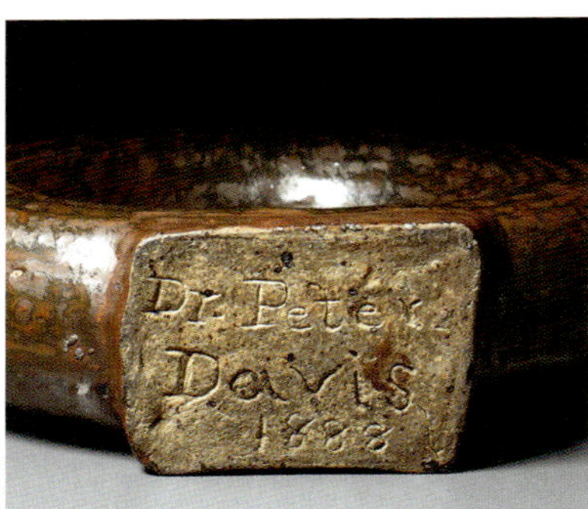

Figure 2 Inscription on the base of the ring bottle illustrated in fig. 1: "Dr. Peter / Davis / 1888"

The Columbia auction house was a small, regional business dealing in household liquidations and estates. Not so long ago its offerings would have reached a relatively limited audience, yet all that has changed in the age of the Internet and social media. Someone in the cadre of Southern pottery collectors had spied the bottle, and before long its existence was known throughout the network of Facebook groups that seek such finds. I reached out to my colleague Phil Wingard, who lives within an hour and a half's drive of the auction house. After discussing the object's merits, Phil agreed to travel the distance to preview the bottle and to buy it at that evening's sale. When he arrived, Phil found the bottle nestled among the boxes of household bric-a-brac slated for the auction block—and, to his dismay, a veritable who's who of Southern pottery collectors in the audience. Undeterred, Phil and I settled on an aggressive bid. We were outbid by a considerable factor, however, and a local collector, to the astonishment of the midweek attendees accustomed to spending tens of dollars not tens of thousands, took home the prize.

Several days later, the ring bottle became the focus of a Facebook specialty group with many admiring "likes" and congratulations for the new owner. As is often the case in such groups, the owner was soliciting insight from the collective minds of stoneware aficionados: "Any info on Dr. Peter Davis would be great. . . . .I think maybe Union SC. . . . .but not sure." One of the respondents was Corbett Toussaint, a collector and historical researcher of the nineteenth-century South Carolina stoneware industry. Her first observation was "I see a 'Dr' Peter Davis in the Columbia newspaper in the 1890s who was arrested for performing 'Hoo Doo' on other people."

That comment hit me like a bolt of lightning. My interest in the ritual use of Southern ceramics has percolated for nearly thirty years, first as an archaeologist investigating the meaning of African-American charms and ceremonial objects recovered from historical contexts, and later in the proposition that the antebellum Edgefield face jugs were associated with African spiritualism and conjure.

A subsequent dive into various newspaper accounts further described Dr. Davis as "colored" and an active "root doctor," "herbalist," "conjuror," "hoodoo doctor," and "voodoo doctor," depending on the source. Beginning in 1893 and continuing into early 1894, Dr. Davis's legal troubles were reported in South Carolina newspapers and in nationally distributed papers as far away as Hawaii.[6] The ring bottle took on new significance as the only verifiable American ceramic object directly associated with nineteenth-century American hoodoo.

Southern Hoodoo or Conjure

The practice of hoodoo is one of many overlapping folk traditions that combine ritual and materials to connect with external cultural or spiritual forces. At its most basic, I think of hoodoo as "wishful thinking."

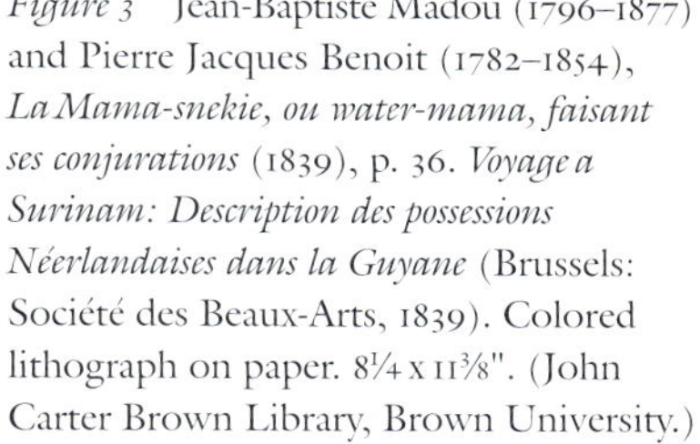

Figure 3 Jean-Baptiste Madou (1796–1877) and Pierre Jacques Benoit (1782–1854), *La Mama-snekie, ou water-mama, faisant ses conjurations* (1839), p. 36. *Voyage a Surinam: Description des possessions Néerlandaises dans la Guyane* (Brussels: Société des Beaux-Arts, 1839). Colored lithograph on paper. 8¼ x 11⅜". (John Carter Brown Library, Brown University.)

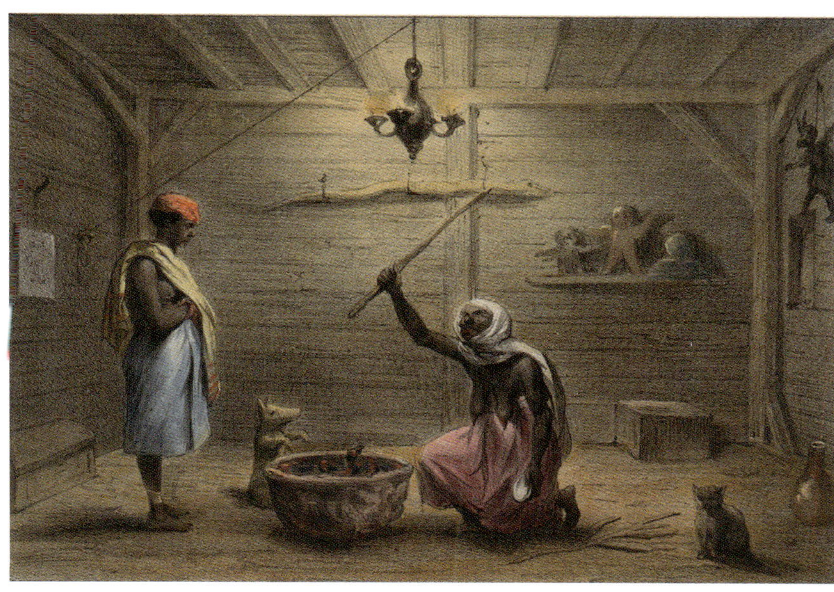

Figure 4 Unknown artist, *Obeah Man*, probably Jamaica or Barbados, ca. 1830. Oil on mahogany panel. 7¼ x 5¼". (Private collection.)

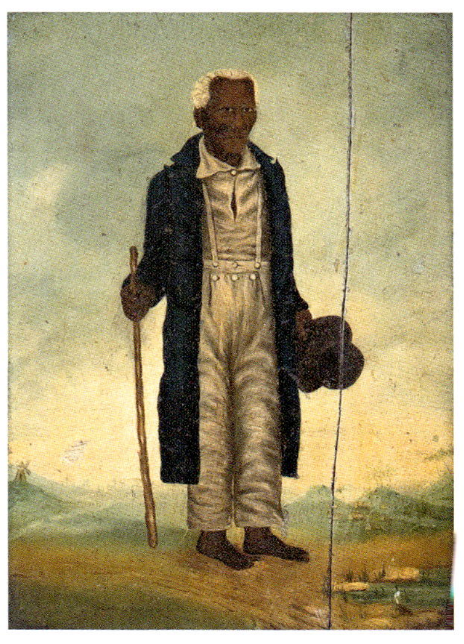

For example, blowing out birthday candles and making a wish could be described as a simple folk-magic ritual. On a larger historical and cultural level, however, defining hoodoo is anything but simple.

Hoodoo is not a religion, but it is informed by underlying African, Christian, and Native American religious beliefs. The term *conjure* is often used interchangeably, particularly before emancipation. The practice, which incorporates rituals, objects, and a wide range of natural oils, herbs, plants, roots, salves, and powders, is an integral part of the African-American historical fabric from the early days of slavery to present times.[7]

Other magical traditions often are conflated or confused with American hoodoo, such as Obeah and Vodou.[8] *Obeah* is a term for a system of spiritual and physical healing that developed among West African–enslaved populations of the West Indies (figs. 3, 4).[9] *Vodou* or *Voodoo* refers to religious rites and beliefs that evolved in Haiti between the sixteenth and nineteenth centuries as new African immigrants arrived. The term *voodoo* is more commonly used in the American South, usually associated with New

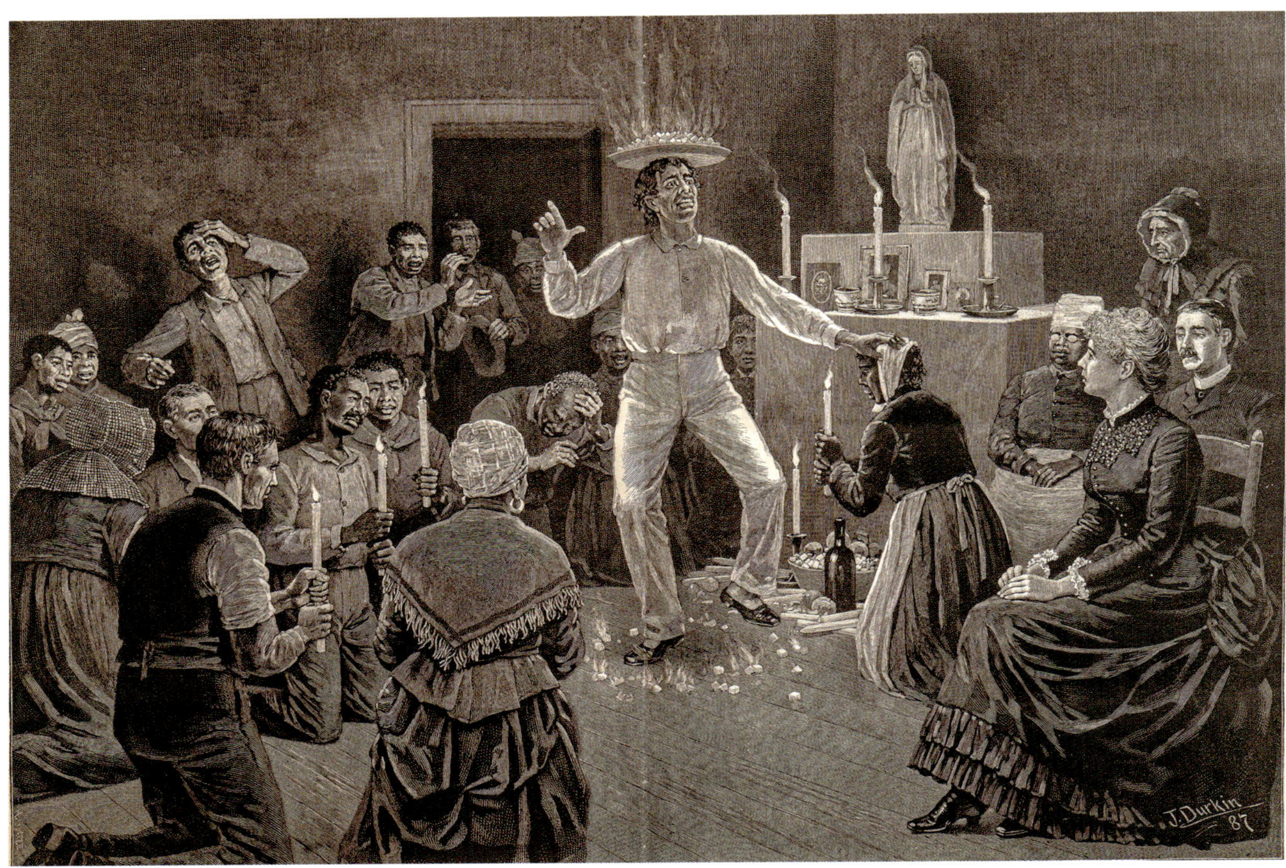

Figure 5 "A Voudoo Dance," drawn by John Durkin, *Harper's Weekly*, June 25, 1887, pp. 456–57. Uncolored engraving. 16 x 22". (Private collection.)

Orleans (fig. 5).[10] *Powwow*, also called "*Brauche*" in German or "*Braucherei*" in Pennsylvanian Dutch, is a system of herbal remedies and magic that developed among the German immigrant populations of North America.[11]

The evolution of what is now called hoodoo in America begins with the influx of enslaved Africans directly from Africa and those influenced by Caribbean religions. Prior to emancipation, conjuring was central to the lives of the enslaved populations, particularly those serving on plantations.[12] Nineteenth-century texts known as "slave narratives" demonstrate the power that the conjurer held over both the enslaved communities and, at times, the white oppressors.[13] Historian John Blassingame contends that "the conjurer had more control over the slaves than the master had."[14] One writer, Henry Walton Bibb (1815–1854), an American author and abolitionist who was born a slave in Kentucky but escaped to Canada in 1842, observed that "conjuration, tricking, and witchcraft" were indispensable to enslaved plantation workers. Bibb identified specific ingredients and prescriptions: "The remedy is most generally some kind of bitter root; they are directed to chew it and spit towards their masters when they are angry with the slaves. At other times they prepare certain kinds of powders, to sprinkle about their masters' dwellings."[15]

Another account was written by William Wells Brown, who was born into slavery in Montgomery County, Kentucky, but fled to Ohio in 1834 at the age of nineteen. He ultimately became a prominent advocate and author in the cause of abolitionism. In his writings, Brown claimed that "nearly every large plantation . . . had at least one [conjurer], who claimed to be a fortune-teller, and who was regarded with more than common respect by his fellow-slaves."[16]

Famed abolitionist and former slave Frederick Douglass (1818–1895) wrote of his solicitation for protection against harsh beatings.[17] The conjurer, whom Douglass identified as "an old advisor" and a "genuine African, [who] had inherited some of the so called magical powers, said to be possessed by African and eastern nations."[18] While remaining skeptical, Douglass acquiesced to carry the prescribed "root of the herb" in his pocket and ultimately acknowledged it had offered some defense against excessive whippings.

Often overlooked in the rush to investigate African-American supernatural rituals was the medicinal value of conventional herbal remedies.[19] Enslaved men and women served as caregivers and health practitioners for their communities, drawing on African, Caribbean, European, and Native American folk pharmacological knowledge using herbs, minerals, plants, and roots.[20] Faith in the sacred was vital in the success of the root doctor, not just a knowledge of the natural world. Sharla M. Fett, in her book *Working Cures*, underscores that the work of the root doctor was equally "spiritual and practical."[21]

With the advent of emancipation, hoodoo was transformed into what Katrina Hazzard-Donald calls "old tradition black belt Hoodoo," a folk system of spiritual belief, medicine, and control.[22] It was in this era that the word came into everyday usage. A lengthy three-part article that appeared in the *Memphis Daily Appeal* on October 25, 1868, is the first published discourse on the topic:

Vaudooism
African Fetish Worship Among The Memphis Negroes
A Little White Girl the Victim

> The word Hoodoo, or Vaudoo, is one of the names used in the different African dialects for the practice of the mysteries of the Obi (an African word signifying a species of sorcery and witchcraft common among the worshippers of the Fetish). In the West Indies the word "Obi" is universally used to designate the priests or practices of this art, who are called "Obi" men and "Obi" women. In the southern portion of the United States—Louisiana, Alabama, Mississippi, South Carolina and Georgia—where the same rites are extensively practiced among the negroes, and where, under the humanizing and Christianizing influence of the blessed state of freedom and idleness in which they now exist and are encouraged by the Freedmen's Bureau, the religion is rapidly spreading. It goes under the name of Vaudooism or Hoodooism. The practicers of the art, who are always native Africans, are called hoodoo men or women, and are held in great dread by the negroes, who apply to them for the cure of diseases, to obtain revenge for injuries, and to discover and punish their enemies. The mode of operations is to prepare a fetish, which being placed near or in the dwelling of the person to be worked upon (under the doorstep, or in any snug portion of the furniture) is supposed to produce the most dire and terrible effects upon the victim, both physically and mentally. Among the materials used for the fetish are feathers of various colors, blood, dog's and cat's teeth, clay from graves, egg-shells, beads, and broken bits of glass. The clay is made into a ball with hair and rags, bound with

twine, with feathers, human, alligators' or dogs' teeth, so arranged as to make the whole bear a resemblance to an animal of some sort. The person to be hoodooed is generally made aware that the hoodoo is "set" for him, and the terror created in his mind by this knowledge is generally sufficient to cause him to fall sick, and (it is a curious fact) almost always to die in a species of decline. The intimate knowledge of the hoodoos of the insidious vegetable poisons that abound in the swamps of the South, enables them to use these with great effect in most instances.[23]

The Southern Workman, a monthly journal distributed by the Hampton Institute in Virginia, published African-American and Native American folklore beginning in 1872. Those essays represent some of the first attempts in which Black Americans recorded and classified their own culture's conjure rituals.[24] What might be the earliest listing of spells appeared in 1899 in the *Southern Workman and Hampton School Record*, written by an anonymous Hampton student:

> Get grave-yard dirt and put it into the food or sprinkle it around the lot. It will cause heavy sickness. Have a vial, put into it nails, red flannel, and whiskey. Put a cork in it, then stick nine pins in the cork. Bury this where the one you want to trick walks.[25]

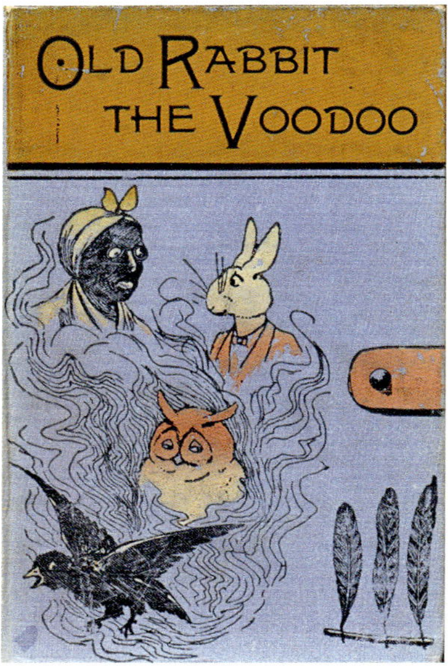

Figure 6 Book cover, *Old Rabbit, the Voodoo, and Other Sorcerers* by Mary Alicia Owen, illustrated by Juliette A. Owen and Louis Wain (London: T. Fisher Unwin, 1893).

In 1893 Mary Alicia Owen (1850–1935), a white writer, published *Old Rabbit, the Voodoo, and Other Sorcerers*, stories based on her experiences with Native American and African-American conjurers in her hometown, St. Joseph, Missouri (fig. 6).[26] She wrote using customary albeit stereotypical Southern Black dialect.[27]

Articles on hoodoo, conjure doctors, and rootworkers appearing in newspapers through the 1920s were often sensationalized accounts that underscored prevailing and disparaging racial stereotypes. Indeed nearly all accounts are of African-Americans, although occasionally white hoodoo doctors appear.[28] The stories generally portray these figures as tricksters, hucksters, and charlatans, and typically refer to their clients as victims.[29]

African-American folk magic became the subject for serious investigators beginning in the early twentieth century. Born and raised in Mississippi, for example, Newbell Niles Puckett (1898–1967) developed an interest in the local African-American culture, which led to his research focused on the belief systems of African-Americans in the South. He conducted fieldwork by interviewing residents of Lowndes County, Mississippi, about spiritual songs, graveyard decorations, conjuring spells, and various folk-medicine recipes. In 1926 Puckett published *Folk Beliefs of the Southern Negro*, an expanded version of his doctoral dissertation. He also created a remarkable photographic archive of conjurers, root doctors, and related paraphernalia that is now maintained by the Cleveland Public Library.[30]

Another influential ethnographer and prolific writer was Zora Neale Hurston (1891–1960), who was born in Notasulga, Alabama, and raised in Eatonville, Florida.[31] Trained in anthropology at Barnard College and Columbia University, Hurston is regarded as the most important Black writer to collect firsthand accounts of conjure and rootwork. Her lengthy article "Hoodoo in America," published in 1931, includes tales of Marie Laveau and firsthand interviews with contemporary hoodoo doctors. She even took lessons in hoodoo, learning the materials and rituals for spells such as "Business Success," "Court Scrapes," "Love," and "To Kill."[32] Her 1935 book *Mules and Men* focuses on her excursions to New Orleans and Alabama to record African-American stories, songs, superstitions, and detailed descriptions of the hoodoo practice.

A massive archive of hoodoo and conjure spells recorded by Harry Middleton Hyatt (1896–1978) from African-American informants resulted in a 4,666-page, five-volume publication, *Hoodoo–Conjuration–Witchcraft–Rootwork*.[33] Hyatt was an ordained Anglican priest but had a passionate interest in African-American folklore.[34] Published in 1970, the archive consists of 13,458 separate magic spells, folktales, and anecdotes that come directly from practitioners in twelve different states (fig. 7). Hyatt observed that "hoodoo is an amorphous body of rites and substances continually changing. . . . Its conglomerate nature made it difficult to grasp as a whole."[35]

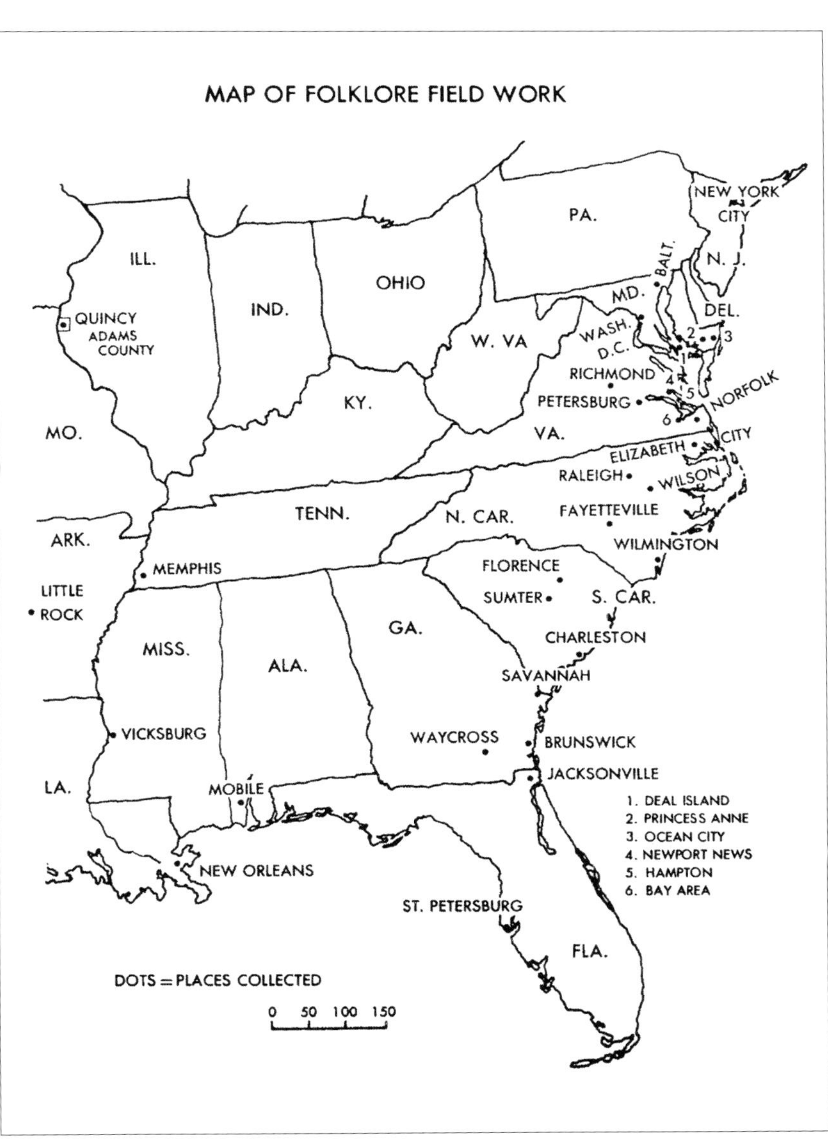

Figure 7 "Map of Folklore Field Work," from Harry Middleton Hyatt, *Hoodoo—Conjuration—Witchcraft—Rootwork: Beliefs Accepted by Many Negroes and White Persons, These Being Orally Recorded among Blacks and Whites*, Memoirs of the Alma Egan Hyatt Foundation 5: frontispiece ([Hannibal, Mo.]: Printed by Western Pub., 1978).

Twenty-first-century scholars continue to explore the topics of hoodoo, conjure, and rootwork.[36] The bibliography for such studies is extensive, and spans the fields of anthropology, archaeology, folklore, social and religious histories, African-American studies, ethnography, and musicology.[37] The practice also remains very much alive, as evidenced by the large body of how-to literature, conjuring supplies, and vast Internet and social media resources.[38] A prolific writer and supplier is Catherine Yronwode, who runs an online business, the Lucky Mojo Curio Company (luckymojo.com), a maker and distributor of hoodoo and conjure supplies.[39]

Southern Ring Bottles

Ring bottles are an iconic Southern ceramic form, produced in both earthenware and stoneware by many different potters from Texas to Virginia. The form originated in classical antiquity, and later appears in medieval and modern Europe (fig. 8). The small number of the American-made examples that survive inscribed with initials and dates suggests that ring bottles held special significance for the makers as well as the end users (fig. 9). The ring bottle remains a staple of Southern folk potters and continues to be a prized production item.[40]

A ring bottle of the same general form as the Dr. Davis example is owned by the Charleston Museum, where it is attributed to the ca. 1850–1880 Linneaus Landrum Pottery of Richland County, South Carolina; another is in the collection of the Chipstone Foundation (fig. 10).[41] The Landrum Pottery was first established by Abner Landrum in the second quarter of the nineteenth century, and after his death in 1859 was owned by his son Linneaus.

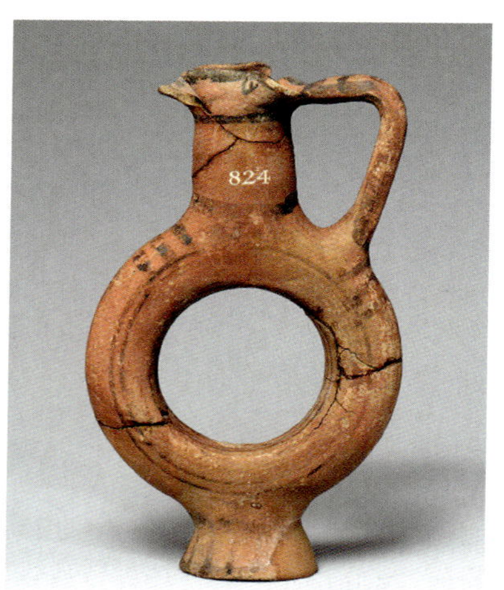

Figure 8 Ring flask, Cypro-Geometric III–Cypro-Archaic I, 850–600 B.C. Terracotta. H. 6¾". (Metropolitan Museum of Art, The Cesnola Collection, Purchased by subscription, 1874–76, 74.51.651.)

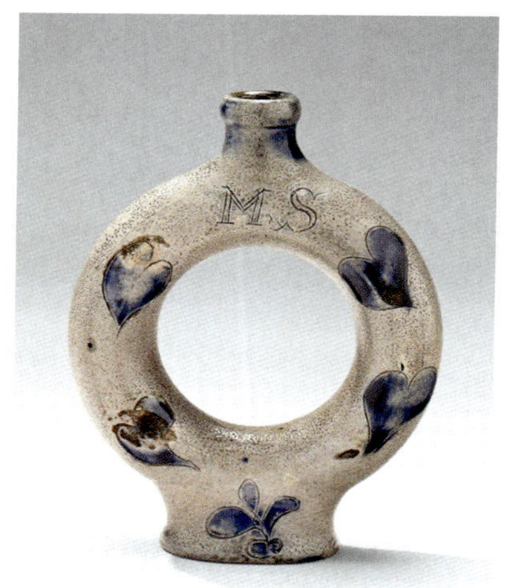

Figure 9 Ring bottle, New York, New York, ca. 1800–1830. Salt-glazed stoneware. H. 6½". (New-York Historical Society, Purchased from Elie Nadelman, 1937.579.) It is decorated with incised hearts, fish, birds, and the initials "M.S."

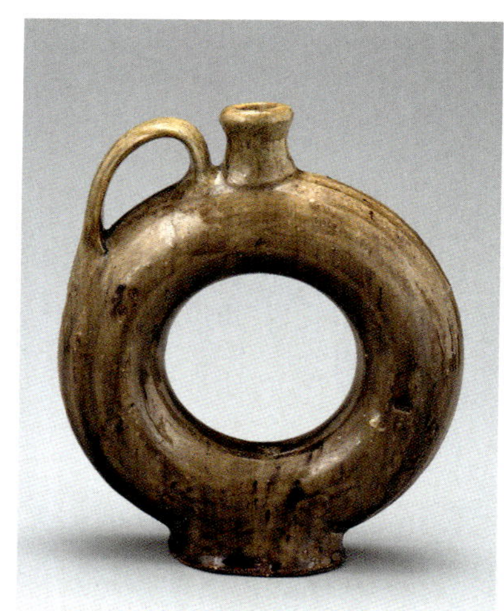

Figure 10 Ring bottle, attributed to the Landrum Pottery, Richland County, South Carolina, ca. 1870. Alkaline-glazed stoneware. H. 10⅛". (Chipstone Foundation.)

Figure 11 Archaeological fragment of ring bottle, John Stork Pottery, Columbia, South Carolina, ca. 1880. Alkaline-glazed stoneware. Inscribed on ring, "John J. Stork" (Courtesy, South Carolina Institute of Archaeology and Anthropology.)

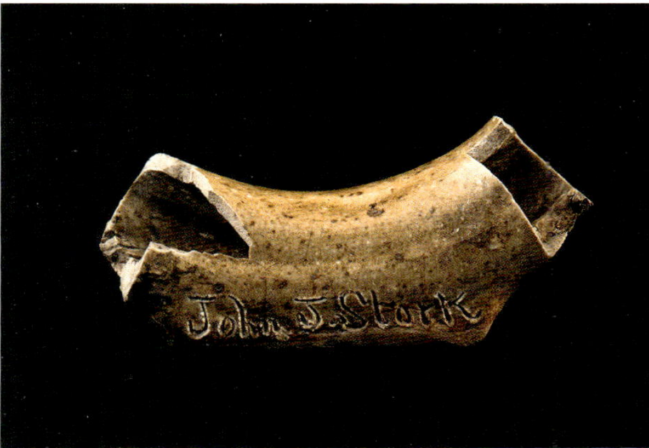

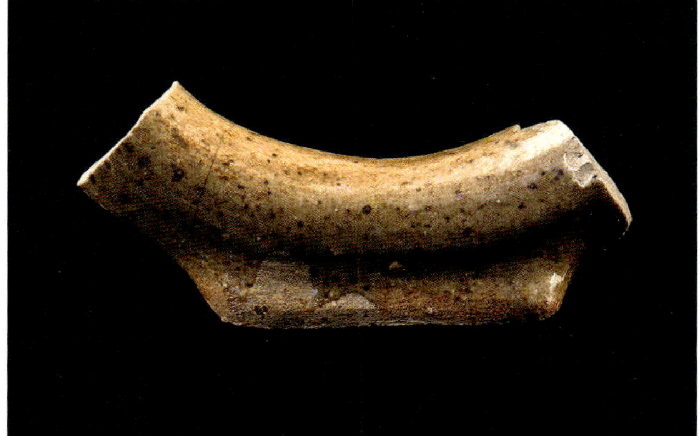

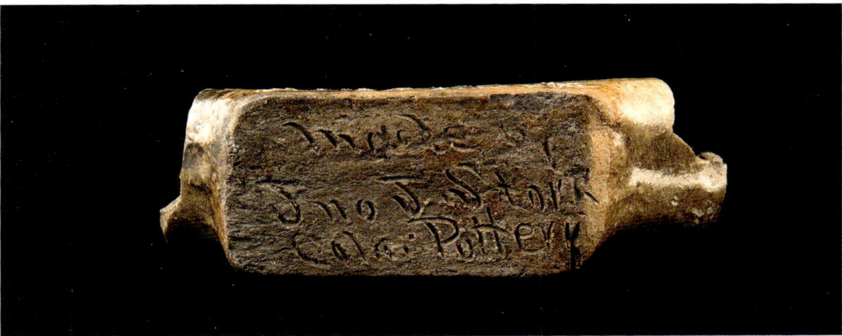

Figure 12 Detail showing the base of the ring bottle fragment illustrated in fig. 11. Inscribed "made by / Jno J. Stork / Col. Pottery"

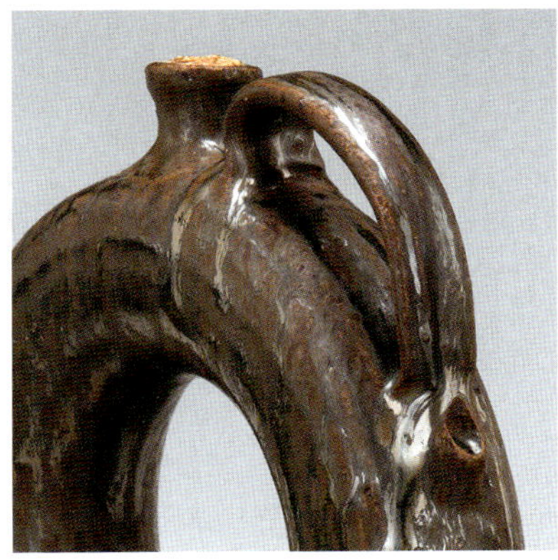

Figure 13 Detail showing the dark, iron-rich glaze of the ring bottle illustrated in fig. 1.

Archaeological fragments of a similar ring bottle have been found at the Landrum Pottery site; they are inscribed "John J. Stork" and "Made by / Jno J. Stork / Col. Pottery" (figs. 11, 12).[42] John J. Stork was the son-in-law of Abner Landrum and worked at the pottery. Stork later operated his own pottery in the Dentsville community just outside of Columbia. There his sons Edward Leslie and Robert Manning transitioned from the lighter color ash and lime glaze to a dark, almost black iron-rich glaze (fig. 13).[43] The 1888 date on the Dr. Davis ring bottle corresponds with the Stork sons' tenure at the Dentsville pottery. Edward left that pottery around 1900 and

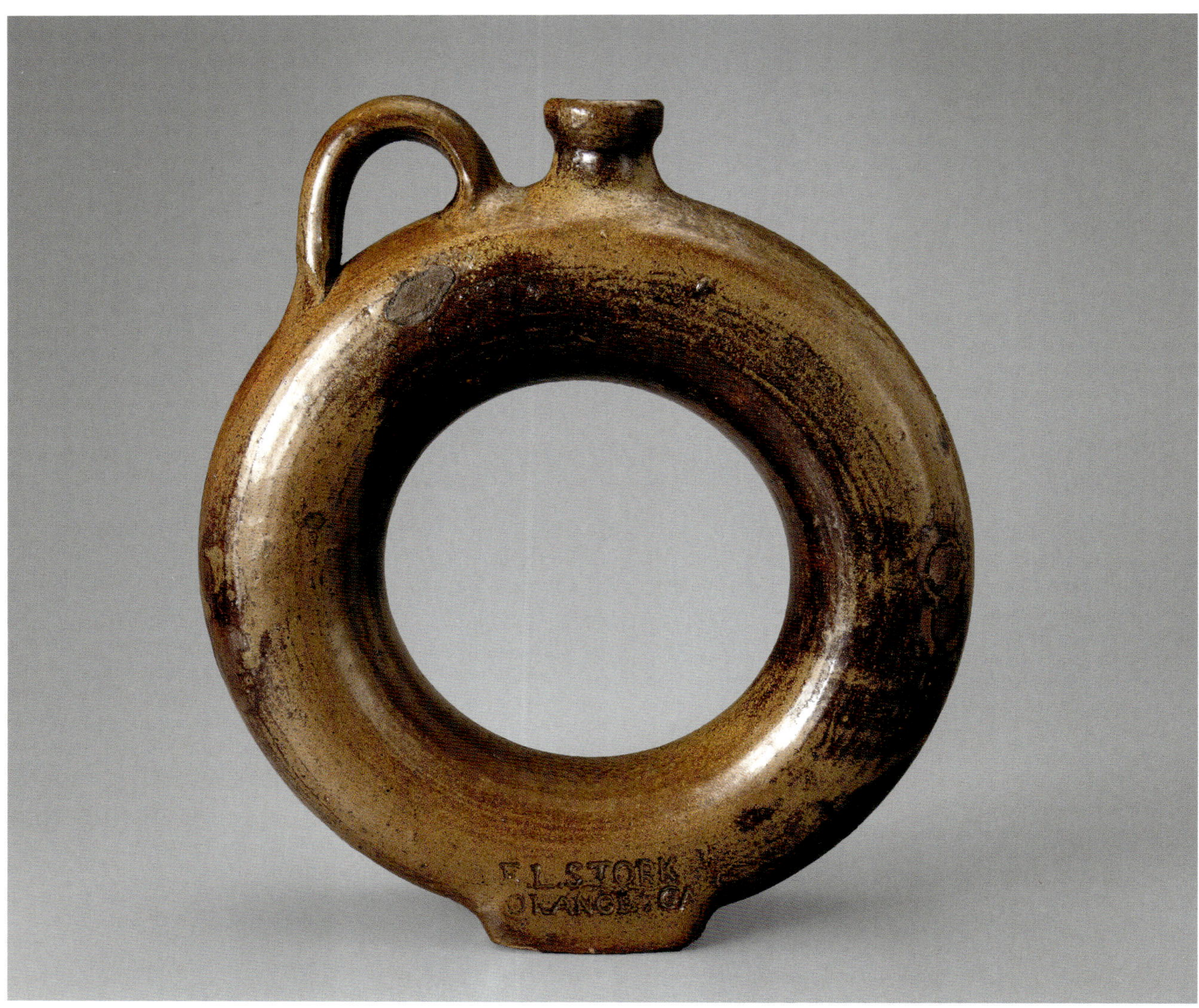

Figure 14 Ring bottle, Edward L. Stork, Orange, Georgia, ca. 1909. Alkaline-glazed stoneware. H. 10½". Impressed: "E.L. STORK / ORANGE, GA." (Courtesy, William C. and Susan S. Mariner Private Foundation.)

worked at several different potteries in Alabama, Mississippi, and Georgia. By 1909 he had established his own workshop in Orange, Georgia, where apparently he continued to produce the form (fig. 14).[44]

Who Was Dr. Peter Davis?

A full biography of the man has yet to be written; what we know is based on a few legal records and a rather large number of newspaper accounts published from New York to California in the 1893–94 period. Census records show that Peter Davis (1812–1911) was born in South Carolina around 1812 (figs. 15, 16).[45] There is no indication whether he and/or his parents were enslaved and we know that Columbia did have a small community of free Blacks.[46] His wife, Jane, is listed in the 1880 census as age 59, and her occupation as "Keeping home." Peter is listed as "Farmer," even though he resided in Columbia's 3rd Ward, a developed urban setting outlined in figure 17.[47] He signed the 1882 voter roll with his "X" mark, which suggests that he was illiterate. No children are recorded.

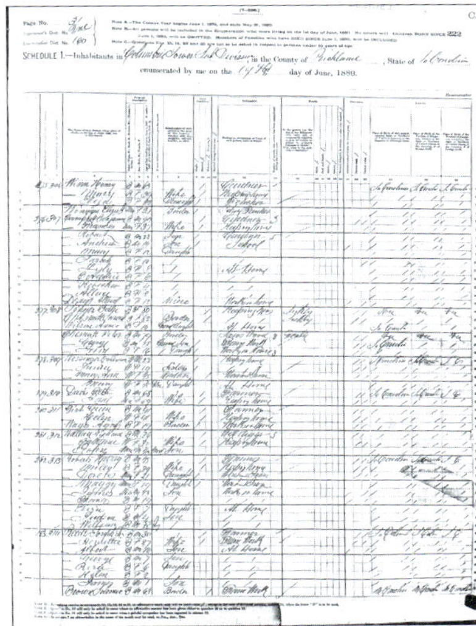

Columbia served as the state capital beginning in 1786 and grew steadily; when it was chartered as a city in 1854, it had the largest population in the Carolinas. With an economy based on the processing of cotton, available records show that 1,500 enslaved people were in residence in 1830, and by 1860 that number had risen to 3,300. After emancipation, this large, predominantly enslaved African-American population transformed itself into a community of social, political, and economic power.[48]

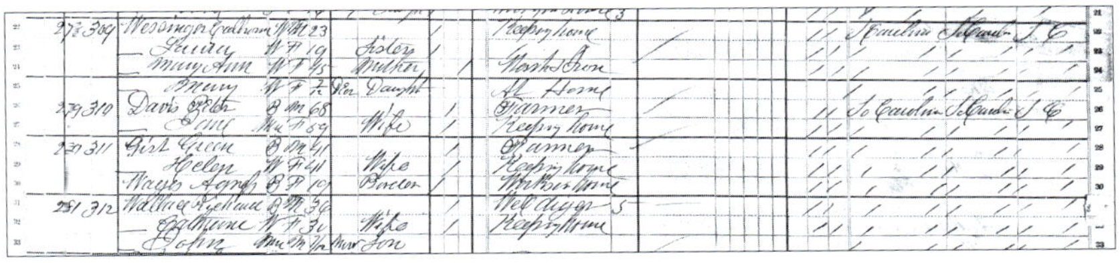

Figure 15 1880 Federal Census, "Inhabitants in Columbia Lower Sub Division in the County of Richland, State of South Carolina, June 14, 1880."

Figure 16 1880 Federal Census entry for Peter Davis as a Black male, age 68, occupation farmer, and listing his birthplace and that of his parents as South Carolina.

Figure 17 C. N. Drie, *Bird's Eye View of the City of Columbia, South Carolina* (Baltimore, Md., 1872). Colored lithograph on paper. 21¼ x 27½". (Library of Congress, Geography and Map Division, Washington, D.C., 2008675451.)

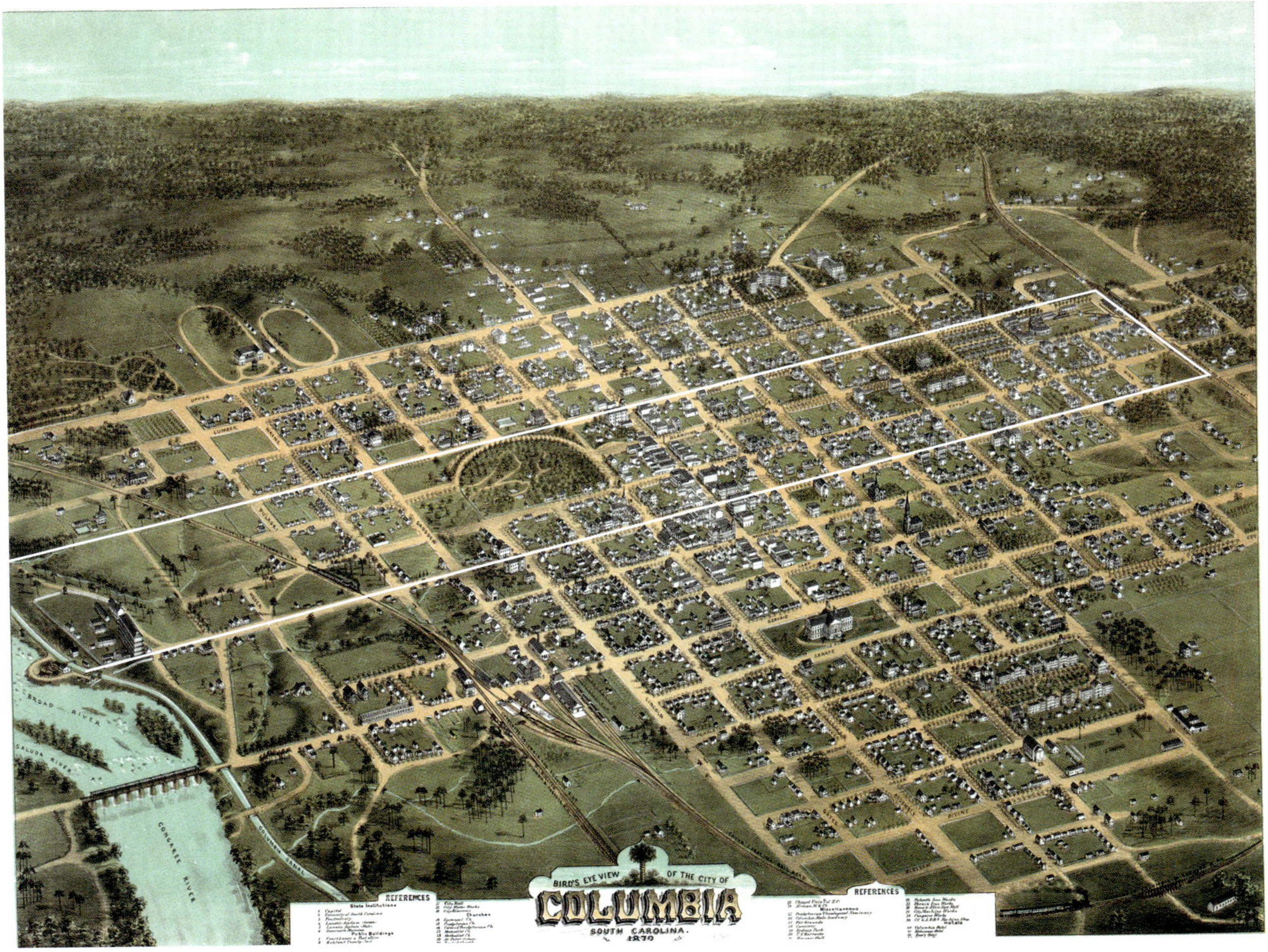

PETER DAVIS, M. D., COLORED.

HE SUSTAINS HIS RIGHT TO THE TITLE IN OPEN COURT.

COLUMBIA, S. C., Aug. 2.—An old negro named Peter Davis was recently graduated in medicine for the second time in open court. In 1874 there was a statute on the books of South Carolina which prohibited any one from practicing medicine in this State who was not a graduate of a medical college, but a proviso permitted one who had practiced for seven years without a diploma to continue to practice if that fact could be certified by a practicing physician or three responsible citizens, one of whom was empowered to administer an oath. Davis had practiced in the rural districts for years, and in 1873 he was called upon to attend a young man in Kershaw County, on the border line of this county, who had been a long sufferer from an eating sore on one of his legs. The father of the young man declared that a number of physicians had exercised their skill upon the diseased limb without success, and he offered to pay Davis $300 if he could effect such a cure that the young man could dance as well in the future as he had been capable of previous to his affliction. Davis accepted the offer and took the case in hand. In time he accomplished all that had been required and presented his bill for services. Payment was refused and Peter placed the account in the hands of Monteith & Bausektt, attorneys at law in this city, for collection. The attorneys obtained a certificate from an apothecary of Columbia, that he had sold Peter Davis medicines to be used in prescriptions for 20 years before the suit was entered, and other witnesses for the plaintiff were at hand. When the case was called at the Spring term of the Court of Common Pleas for this county in 1874, Judge R. B. Carpenter presiding, the attorneys for the defendant weakened, and asked for time to consult with the attorneys for the plaintiff, with the view to a compromise. Time was granted. The plaintiff had the law and the testimony on his side and $275, including the costs, was the result of the compromise in favor of the plaintiff. Thus Peter Davis, M. D., colored, was graduated in medicine in open court.

Ten years passed, and at the recent term of the Court of Common Pleas for this county, Judge J. S. Cothran presiding, Dr. Peter Davis instituted suit for the recovery of a fee of $50 for medical services rendered the wife of a citizen of this county. The partnership of Monteith & Bauskett, attorneys at law, had been dissolved between the time of Dr. Peter's first suit and the one last mentioned, but Mr. Bauskett was retained by Peter Davis, M. D., and, strangely enough, Mr. Monteith was the attorney of the defendant. The defendant's attorney relied upon the law compelling practitioners in medicine to register as the means for tripping Dr. Peter Davis in his suit. But the attorney for the plaintiff, in anticipation of this defense, had taken the precaution to see that his client enrolled himself on the register in the Clerk of Court's office as a practicing physician. When the trial came on it was proved that the plaintiff had complied with the law regarding the registration of physicians; that he had previously recovered at law a fee for medical services, and that his practice had extended over a great number of years. The plaintiff for the second time recovered a fee at law, and was for the second time recognized as Peter Davis, M. D., by a judicial tribunal. Dr. Davis certainly cannot be charged with "ratting" the fee bill.

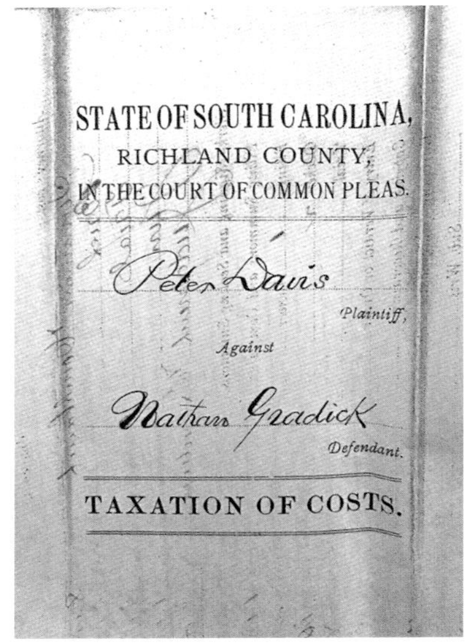
STATE OF SOUTH CAROLINA,
RICHLAND COUNTY,
IN THE COURT OF COMMON PLEAS.
Peter Davis
Plaintiff,
Against
Nathan Gradick
Defendant.
TAXATION OF COSTS.

Figure 18 "Peter Davis, M.D., Colored. He Sustains His Right to the Title in Open Court," *New York Times*, August 3, 1884, p. 7.

Figure 19 Peter Davis vs. Nathan Gradick, Taxation of Costs, State of South Carolina, Richland County, in the Court of Common Pleas, July 21, 1884.

An 1884 *New York Times* article—"Peter Davis, M.D., Colored. He Sustains His Right to the Title in Open Court"—recounts a Columbia court case where Davis was suing for the "recovery of a fee for $50 for medical services rendered the wife of a citizen of this county" (fig. 18). In preparation for this article, researcher April Hynes undertook a review of the legal documents pertaining to the case, which showed that Dr. Davis was successfully awarded $50.00 plus $33.70 in court costs (fig. 19). From the *Times* article we also learn that Dr. Davis had no formal medical training but, through some legal maneuvering by his lawyers, had been previously awarded legal recognition of his title "Dr." in 1873.[49] His name was subsequently included in the 1884 list of licensed physicians for Richland County, which credits him as having a diploma but conspicuously leaves blank the columns for "Date Issued" and "By Whom Granted" (fig. 20).[50]

Presumably, "Dr." Davis continued to practice unimpeded until 1893, when he appears in a series of newspaper accounts about legal charges brought against him, this time by Adolph (sometimes Adolphus) Holuv

Figure 20 "List of Licensed Physicians and Surgeons of the State" (Richland County, South Carolina), *Reports and Resolutions of the General Assembly of South Carolina, at the Regular Session Commencing November 23, 1886, Vol. 2* (Columbia, S.C.: Charles A. Calvo Jr., State Printer, 1887), p. 262. Available online at https://www.carolana.com/SC/Legislators/Documents/.

RICHLAND COUNTY.
LIST OF PHYSICIANS AND SURGEONS.

NAME.	POSTOFFICE ADDRESS.	AUTHORITY FOR PRACTICING.		
		DIPLOMA OR LICENSE.	DATE ISSUED.	BY WHOM GRANTED.
J. J. Durham	Columbia	Diploma	March 1, 1882	Central College of Tennessee.
B. W. Taylor	Columbia	Diploma	March 1, 1858	Medical College of the State of S. C.
Peter Davis	Columbia	Diploma	....	
George Howe	Columbia	Diploma	June, 1870	South Carolina University.
John A. Keith	Adams Cut	Diploma	March 5, 1881	Medical College of the State of S. C.
D. S. Pope	Columbia	Diploma	March, 1875	Jefferson Medical College, Phila.
W. T. C. Bates	Columbia	Diploma	June 28, 1868	South Carolina University.
A. A. Sylvester	Columbia	Diploma	March 1, 1861	University, Nashville, Tennessee.
Frank Green	Columbia	Diploma	Feb. 28, 1873	Louisville Medical College.
H. D. Heinitsh	Columbia	Diploma	M'ch 11, 1875	Jefferson Medical College.
A. N. Talley	Columbia	Diploma	March, 1850	Medical College of the State of S. C.
J. L. Thompson	Columbia	Diploma	March, 1880	Medical College of the State of S. C.
P. E. Griffin	Columbia	Diploma	March, 1855	University of Pennsylvania.
L. K. Philpot	Columbia	Diploma	March 4, 1875	Atlanta, Georgia, Medical College.
D. B. Miller, Jr.	Columbia	Diploma	March, 1874	Bellevue Hospital Med. College, N. Y.
S. W. McKenzie	Gadsden	Diploma	March 1, 1860	University of Pennsylvania.
J. D. F. Lever	Columbia	Diploma	March 1, 1860	Jefferson Medical College, Phila.
E. S. Abney	Columbia	Diploma	Feb. 24, 1870	Phila. University of Med. and Surg.
C. H. Suydam	Congaree	Diploma	March, 1861	College of Physicians and Surgeons, Medical Department of Columbia College.
R. G. Elliott	....	Diploma	March 5, 1881	Medical College of the State of S. C.

262

"What Fools These Mortals Be."

The Columbia Evening Journal says that about a year ago a German named Adolph Holuv and his wife went to that city from Orangeburg and, in company with "Dr." Peter Davis, colored, well known there as a root and herb Doctor, went to Mr. John Bauskett to get him to draw up a contract between "Dr." Peter Davis of the first part and Adolph Holuv of the second part, in which Davis agreed to protect Holuv, his family, cattle and crops from sickness, drought, storms and pestilence, in fact make him prosper in spite of his own shortcomings. For and in consideration of the same Holuv was to pay Davis in the fall the sum of $50, with interest, he taking a lein on Holuv's crop to secure the payment of the same. This done, the poor German and his "frow" departed happy in the thought that the sun of plenty, peace and happiness was to shine upon them most abundantly. But, alas for human expectations! The balance of this remarkable story is told by the Journal as follows:

"Too delighted with the prospect of success beyond the measure accorded to his neighbors, he began to tell some of them what he had done and how he was to be blessed. Seeing that he had been duped, they told him so. This caused him to grow dissatisfied and he returned to Mr. Bauskett and asked him to change the nature of the contract, making it read that Davis should conjure away all storms, droughts, pestilence, sickness, etc. This was done and again he departed. After a similar stay, he returned, claiming that Davis had failed to carry out his part of the contract; that his sister-in-law was then lying critically ill; that he had lost eighteen hogs by sickness; that his cow, which had a fine udder and looked like she would give gallons of milk, would only give about a quart; that his neighbors' hogs were fatter than his, while he fed his in greater abundance; that his crops were suffering and a multitude of similar complaints, all going to show that "Dr." Davis had not done his part by him. Davis was sent for and the contract was withdrawn, Holuv saying that Davis might keep about $17 which he had paid him on account if the contract was forfeited. This was done. Later he appeared again, complaining that "Dr." Davis had conjured his family, stock and crops, and sought some means of redress, but found no encouragement along this line. He departed. He claimed that there was an old witch in Orangeburg county who said that she could relieve his people and cattle but for the fact that Davis had them conjured and was stronger than she. After leaving here he went to many of the Trial Justices in Orangeburg to try and secure the arrest of Davis, but none of them gave him any satisfaction until he found one who told him that the United States commissioner at this place was the proper person to prosecute as the State had no jurisdiction over witchcraft. So Mr. Holuv came here and had a warrant sworn out before Trial Justice Stack charging "Dr." Davis with obtaining money under false pretenses, and it is on this charge that he will be tried.

Figure 21 "What Fools These Mortals Be," *The Times and Democrat* (Orangeburg, S.C.), July 19, 1893, p. 8.

CHEATING FOREIGNERS.

Where there is a Will There is a Way—How a Negro Fooled Some Strangers.

The Columbia correspondent of the News and Courier tells this story:

Here is a pretty "how-de-do" as they call it. It's Governor Tillman's hand, and shows how he can act when he makes up his mind to do a thing. The facts as given and without color or prejudice are: A family of Bohemians in some way made an agreement with a negro, Peter Davis, who claims to be a veterinary surgeon and is popularly classed as a vodoo or hoodoo doctor. He was for fifty dollars to keep the cattle and poultry on the place in good condition. The foreigners claimed that after the alleged doctor had been paid seventeen dollars he had the evil spirits to kill all the poultry and cattle. The agriculturists then thought that the hoodoo doctor had worked a miracle and killed their cattle. They wanted to prosecute the doctor and tried in vain to get a warrant in Orangeburg County and from one or more justices in Richland.

The parties then went to State Treasurer Bates and had him to write a note to Trial Justice Stack to investigate the case. He did so, and Mr. John McMaster represented the negro. The case was dismissed on the ground that there was no law covering the case. The warrant charged "receiving money under false pretences." The "doctor" was released. Then the foreigners sought an audience with Governor Tillman, and finally succeeded. Governor Tillman sent for Trial Justice Stack to come forthwith to his office. Mr. Stack was busy at the time, but later went there with Trial Justice Clarkson, who had previously declined to issue a warrant in the case.

Governor Tillman said that he did not want the idea to get out that foreigners did not receive justice here and demanded that the "doctor" be rearrested. Upon these orders Trial Justice Stack issued a new warrant and the case is now in the hands of Solicitor Nelson, Davis having waived an examination. There is no new evidence or facts since the case was first dismissed by the trial justice.

It is said that Governor Tillman made it plain that if the negro was not rearrested the trial justice would be dismissed.

Figure 22 "Cheating Foreigners," *The Laurens* (S.C.) *Advertiser*, October 10, 1893, p. 4.

(sometimes Hulob, Hublov, or Hohler), variously described as a "farmer," a "German," a "Dutchman," and a "Hungarian" of Orangeburg, South Carolina. An article published in Orangeburg's *Times and Democrat* on July 19, 1893, shows the charges to be "receiving money on false pretenses" (fig. 21). Holuv's complaint was that after contracting with Davis to "conjure away all storms, drought, pestilences, and sickness, etc." from his farm, the doctor had not lived up to the terms of the agreement, and by way of evidence offered that "his sister-in-law was then lying critically ill; that he had lost eighteen hogs by sickness; that his cow, which had a fine udder and looked like she would give five gallons, would only give about a quart." He also claims that "Davis had conjured his family, stock, and crops" in retribution for Holuv's complaints that the conjures had not worked.

Progress of the case appeared in South Carolina's *Laurens Advertiser* on October 10, 1893 (fig. 22). The Holuvs are not mentioned by name but are described as a family of "Bohemians." Dr. Davis claims to be a "veterinary surgeon and is popularly classed as a voodoo or hoodoo doctor."[51]

Peter Davis Re-arrested.

Last night, upon a warrant issued by an Orangeburg trial justice, old Peter Davis, the negro herb doctor who was discharged by Trial Justice Stack, afterwards rearrested and sent to the Court of General Sessions where the charge of hoodooing a couple of cranky old foreigners was thrown out, was once more arrested upon the charge of obtaining money under false pretenses. This is the third time that he has been arrested on the same charge and for the same offense.

Figure 23 "Peter Davis Re-arrested," *The State* (Columbia, S.C.), October 25, 1893, p. 8.

In October 1893 *The State* described the accused as "old Peter Davis, the negro herb doctor" (fig. 23) and pointed out that "this is the third time that he has been arrested on the same charge and for the same offense."[52] By then Davis's case had gained considerable attention as it continued to heat up in South Carolina newspapers. The *Camden Chronicle* best summarizes the details of the case against Dr. Davis and is transcribed in its entirety here:

> THE HOODOO DOCTOR
>
> Trial Justice C. P. Brunson was engaged all day last Friday in the preliminary hearing of the State against "Dr." Peter Davis, of Columbia, a cross between a gorilla and a badger and a lineal descendant of one of the witches of "Macbeth." The charge upon which the defendant was arraigned being "voodoism." The prosecutor was a Hungarian of the Knott's Mill section, named Adolphus Hulob [Holuv], who testified as follows: That owing to the sickness of two of his horses, and the death of one, he consulted a neighbor as to the best course to pursue toward getting the animals well. This neighbor advised him to consult the defendant. Soon afterward he went to Columbia and called on "Dr." Peter Davis, and asked him his advice. Deponent said by signing a contract agreeing to pay him (Davis) $55 he would give him medicines etc., that would not only cure his horses, but also keep his family and all his stock in perfect health. Hulob paid the doctor $17 for which he received roots and different kinds of medicines, which he gave his family and stock according to direction. Nine days afterward he lost 27 hogs, and his wife and sister-in-law were made very sick. At his next visit to the skillful doctor he received a loadstone for which he paid $5. This he was to put whiskey on once a week, while doing which, he was to raise one hand and open and shut the fingers thereof. The effect of which ceremony would keep away the enemy who was poisoning his horses. At one time he was presented with a gourd two feet long. He was to cut off the necks and scatter about his yard at 12 o'clock in the night the seed of the gourd. This would prove a most effectual sanitary measure for his chickens, geese, and jackasses. He was also the recipient of some loadstone powders, which after being put in the gourd and moistened, were to be rubbed on the faces of Hulob and his family, also as a sanitary measure. At his next visit to the eminent M. D. Hulob received 3 pieces of load-stone which he was to carry in his pocket for nine days, after first wetting them with a strong smelling liquid very easy to obtain. This was to neutralize malaria and make witches keep at a distance. Davis was put in jail to await trial in default of $200 bond. *Orangeburg Enterprise*.—[53]

Yet another retelling of the case appeared on November 15, 1893, in the *Charlotte News* with the incendiary title "A Dutchman Hoodooed: A Wily Negro 'Doctor' Pulled Up in a South Carolina Court" (fig. 24). That version included new details of the case, notably that Peter Davis had given

A DUTCHMAN HOODOOED.

A Wily Negro "Doctor" Pulled Up In a South Carolina Court.

The famous hoodoo doctor, Peter Davis, colored, of Columbia, has had a preliminary hearing before Trial Justice Brunson on the charge of fraud and obtaining money under false pretenses. The victim was a Dutchman named Hohler, who farms several miles from here.

The examination was very interesting and quite amusing, Mr. Charles G. Dantzler representing the Dutchman and Mr. Henry H. Brunson of the firm of Izlar, Lathrop & Brunson appeared in behalf of the hoodoo. Hohler appeared to be completely disgusted with the treatment of hoodoos. In his testimony he said among other things that Peter had given him "graveyard dirt" to distribute around his farm, telling him that he would make a large crop by using the mystic dirt freely. Hohler used the dirt, "but," said he, "your honor, I plant 15 acre and make only one bale cotton."

Peter at another time sold the Dutchman some "dead men's powder," which was guaranteed to make Hohler's somewhat poor, but not sick, mule lively. "Your honor," said the very mad Dutchman, "after I gif mit him de medicine he lie down in de road wid me and my wife on de way home, and he neffer been such a mule as he vas pefore ven I bot him from Henry von Ohsen." Hohler got a gourd and some powders from old Peter on another occasion. These he was to use for the general all round health of his family. He was to scrape the seed from the gourd at 12 o'clock one night, and at 12 o'clock the next night he was to sweep his yard clean and sprinkle the seed around the house. The gourd was to be filled with 13 drops of water of a peculiar hoodoo kind and some other fluid, then hung up in the house.

In summing up his testimony Hohler said that "Doctor" Peter had robbed him of his crop, made his mule lie down in the road when he promised to make the mule lively, and had made all his "family sicker than dey vas pefore dey took de medicine." Such was about the gist of the complaints that the Dutchman had to make against the hoodoo. Peter was put under a bond of $200 to appear at the next court of general sessions for this county.—Orangeburg Cor. Charleston News and Courier.

Figure 24 "A Dutchman Hoodooed: A Wily Negro 'Doctor' Pulled Up in a South Carolina Court," *Charlotte* (N.C.) *News*, November 15, 1893, p. 3: "Peter had given him 'graveyard' dirt to distribute around."

Holuv (spelled Hohler here) "graveyard dirt" to spread on the farm, which would encourage a bumper crop of cotton. Holuv testified that he used the graveyard dirt as directed, complaining to the judge, "your honor, I plant 13 acres, and make only one bale cotton."

Versions of the case with slightly different accounts of the testimony continued to appear in national newspapers well into 1894.[54] Somewhat anticlimactically, and in spite of all the public interest in the case, the Orangeburg Court of General Sessions indicated that the solicitor never obtained an indictment and the case was dismissed on January 8, 1894.[55] Presumably Dr. Davis continued to practice his profession.

The last public mention of Dr. Davis is his death record, which indicates he died from "Senile Exhaustion" on December 21, 1911, at the age of 99. He was buried in an unmarked plot at the so-called Colored Asylum Cemetery in Columbia, now called the South Carolina State Hospital Cemetery for African Americans.[56] The cemetery was established as a segregated burial ground exclusively for Black patients from the now-defunct State Hospital for the Mentally Ill, which operated on Bull Street from 1828 through the 1980s. Between 2,000 and 3,500 African-Americans were buried in this historic cemetery until 1922, when the hospital designated a new burying ground for Black patients on Slighs Avenue.[57]

Figure 25 Bartmann or Bellarmine bottle, Frechen, Germany, ca. 1650–1680. Salt-glazed stoneware. H. 8⅝". (Courtesy, Pitt Rivers Museum, University of Oxford, 1910.18.1.) This vessel was recovered in 1904 during excavations in Westminster, London, and donated to the Pitt Rivers Museum by Edward Warren. Once sealed with a cork, its contents suggest it was used as a "witch bottle." For more information, see http://objects.prm.ox.ac.uk/pages/PRMUID25735.html.

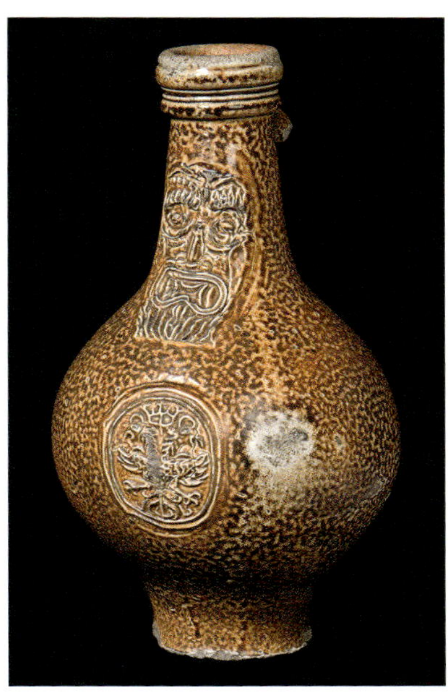

Folk-Magic Practices and Containers

Of course one wonders how Dr. Davis's ring bottle functioned within his practice. No direct information about the vessel is known other than the inscription on the base. Was it a special presentation piece, perhaps from a grateful client? Or was it something Dr. Davis simply ordered for himself?

I introduced this article referencing the phenomena of witchcraft and sorcery in seventeenth-century Great Britain. During that period, proscriptive texts for the preparation of so-called witch bottles as counter spells to evil are well documented. The container of choice for such protective charms was a stoneware bottle form known as a Bartmann (Ger. "bearded man"), so named for the decorative bearded face mask on its lower neck. More colloquially, it is called a Bellarmine. An example of period instructions for making these counter-magical charms comes from Joseph Glanvill (1636–1680/1) in *Saducismus Triumphatus: or, Full and Plain Evidence Concerning Witches and Apparitions*.[58] Instructions given to a man who thought his wife had been possessed were to fill a bottle with his wife's urine "together with Pins and Needles and Nails," cork it, then place it in a hearth fire.[59] Examples of such witch-bottle charms are often found buried in areas associated with hearths and chimneys (figs. 25, 26).

Archaeological specimens found in North American excavations suggest that witch bottles were being used in the eighteenth, nineteenth, and well into the twentieth century.[60] Widely available glass containers, such as wine bottles, medical bottles and phials, and ointment jars became the favored receptacle for those charms. Like their English counterparts, they were intentionally placed near hearths or doors to protect the house and ward off evil. The earliest identified example, a mid-eighteenth-century

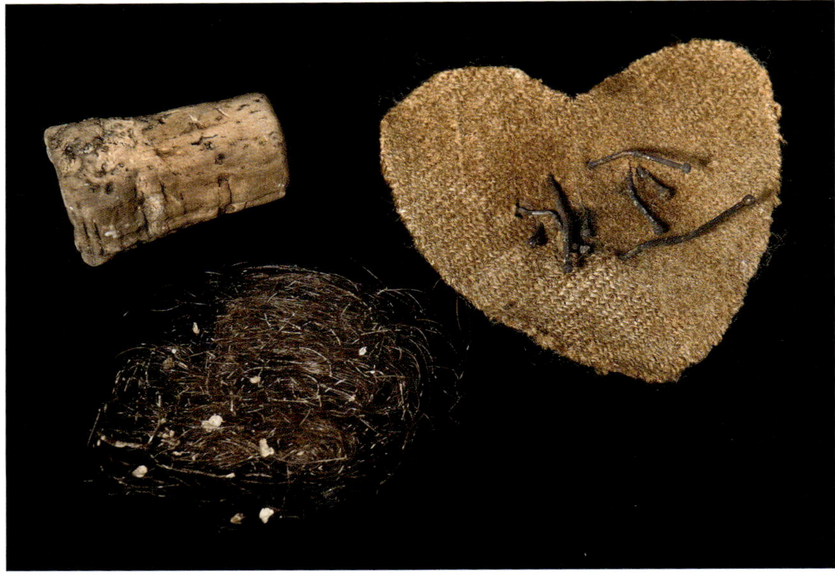

Figure 26 Contents of the bottle illustrated in fig. 25, which include a coarse-fabric cloth heart stuck with straight pins, human hair and fingernail clippings, and a cork stopper. (Courtesy, Pitt Rivers Museum, University of Oxford, 1910.18.2–4.) For more information, see https://www.museumoflondon.org.uk/discover/sorcery-display-witch-bottles.

English wine bottle containing six brass pins and sealed with a wood stopper, was found near the base of a house's chimney in Delaware County, Pennsylvania.[61]

Since the publication of that find, dozens of other glass witch bottles have been identified in archaeological deposits in America.[62] Figure 27 illustrates a fragmentary black-glass English wine bottle, also of the mid-eighteenth-century, that was recovered adjacent to a brick hearth from a mid-nineteenth- to early-twentieth-century tenant-house site in Maryland's

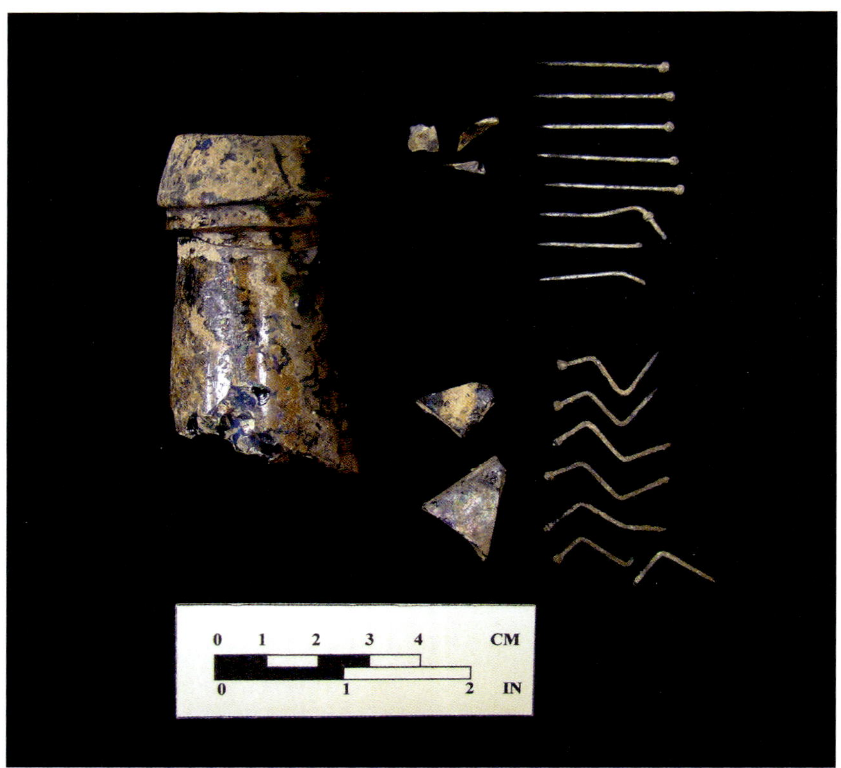

Figure 27 Fragmentary glass wine bottle and associated contents. (Courtesy, Maryland Archaeological Conservation Lab, Jefferson Patterson Park and Museum.) An example of an eighteenth- or nineteenth-century witch bottle burial was found at the White Oak site in Dorchester County, Maryland. A wine bottle neck, horseshoe, bottle glass sherds, and bone fragments were beside a brick hearth. Several straight and bent pins had been inserted into a solid stopper in the bottle neck, both on the inside and outside of the bottle.

Dorchester County.[63] Although the bottle was broken, seven copper-alloy pins were found stuck in its cork.

The most celebrated ceramic vessels associated with spiritual or magical practices are the mysterious stoneware face vessels made by enslaved African-American potters in the Edgefield District of South Carolina in the mid-nineteenth century. Various theories suggest that they served as powerful ritual objects used in conjuring.[64] The connection between Edgefield face vessels and African-American magic is circumstantial, as the evidence comes primarily from oral histories, yet physical evidence does appear on several examples, which could shed light on their use.[65] The face jug on the left in figure 28 has traces of red pigment, possibly ocher or even brick dust, that was placed in the pupils and over the kaolin teeth at some point (fig. 29). This red pigment has a long history of use in conjure and for protection against evil.[66] The jug on the right in figure 28 has a circular hole in the bottom that might have served a supernatural function. A number of

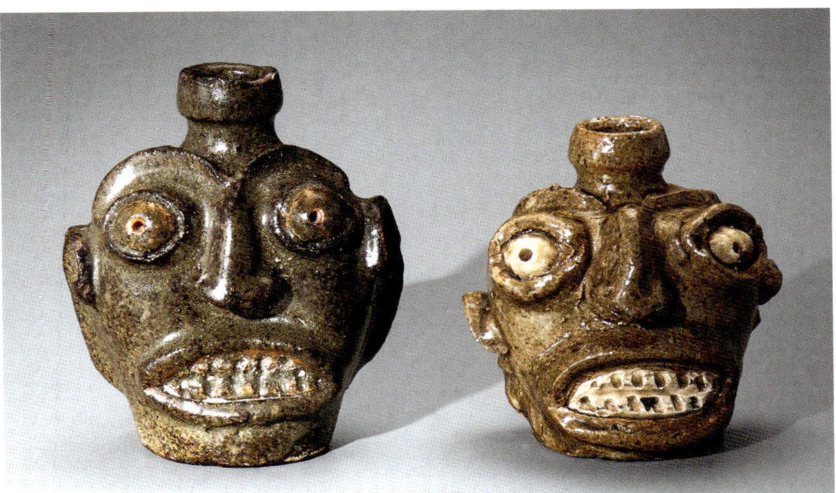

Figure 28 Face vessels, Edgefield, South Carolina, ca. 1850–1860. Alkaline-glazed stoneware. H. of the tallest 5½". (Private collections.)

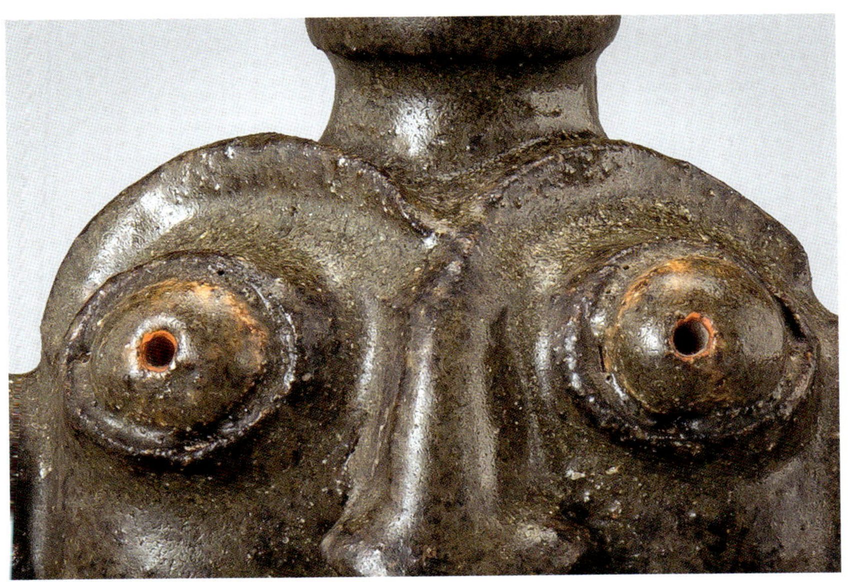

Figure 29 Detail of the face vessel illustrated on the left in fig. 28 showing traces of red pigment for the eyes and pupils.

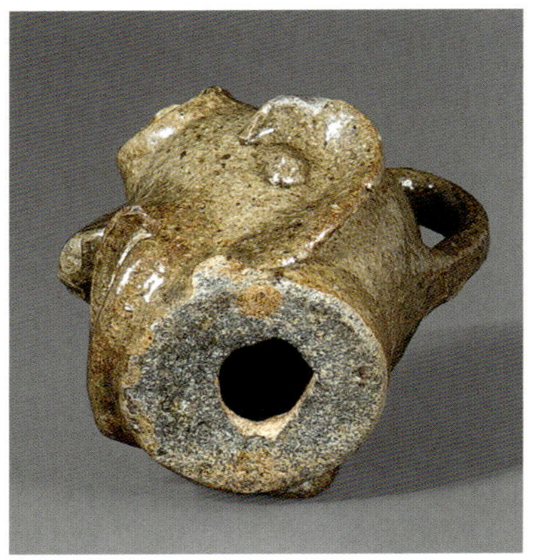

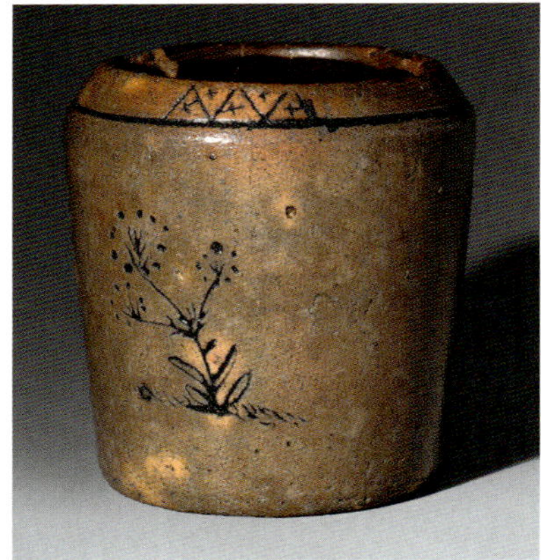

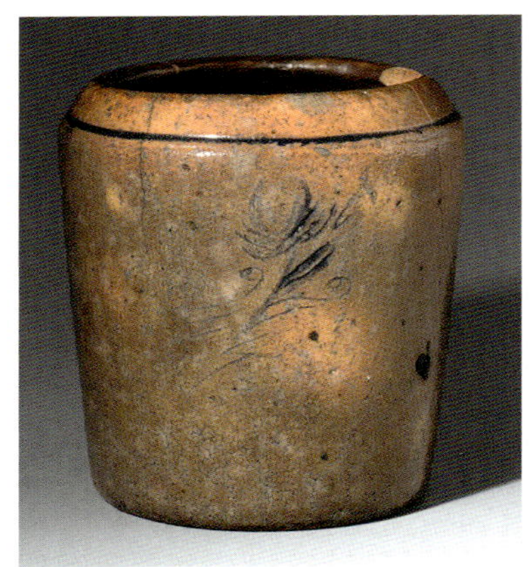

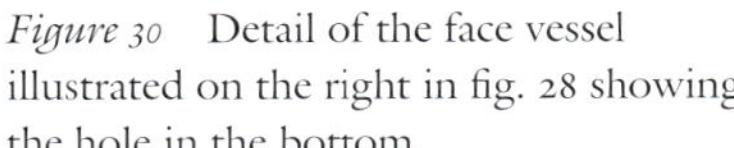

Figure 30 Detail of the face vessel illustrated on the right in fig. 28 showing the hole in the bottom.

Figure 31 Ointment or salve jar, possibly Virginia, Maryland, or Pennsylvania, ca. mid-nineteenth century. Salt-glazed stoneware. H. $3\frac{3}{8}$". (Courtesy, William C. and Susan S. Mariner Private Foundation.)

glass and ceramic vessels retrieved from African-American graves in many Southern cemeteries have been ritually "killed" by having their bottoms broken out (fig. 30).[67] John Vlach has observed that this was a practice rooted in African belief systems, based on writings by ethnologist E. J. Glave who wrote about grave decoration with "crockery, empty bottles, old cooking pots, etc., etc., all of which are rendered useless by being cracked or penetrated with holes."[68]

In 2017 a fascinating salt-glazed ointment jar appeared in a social-media feed and was later acquired by my colleague Curtis Rice. The jar was inscribed with representations of two plants, along with a series of incised triangles and crosses on a portion of the rim (fig. 31). It was once in the collection of the late Dr. Stephen Leder, a Yale professor of medicine and a serious stoneware collector who had written on Bennington, Vermont, stoneware, but little other history is known.[69] Based on the characteristics of the clay color and the interior dark-brown clay slip, the jar was thought to have been made in or near the Valley of Virginia, perhaps around the mid-nineteenth century. Given this likely geographic origin manufacture, it was thought to have been used in immigrant Germanic folk medicine rather than Southern conjure.[70]

One of the plants was thought to be garden angelica (*Angelica archangelica*), and the other a type of thistle plant (fig. 32). Both plants have a long history of medicinal use.[71] Angelica is commonly used for protection against evil spirits, as well as healing.[72] It has been designated one of the "lunar herbs," and it is possible that an incised figure on the jar's body represents the so-called man in the moon (fig. 33).[73]

In 2018 a small stoneware flask was brought to my attention by Rick Meech Burchfield, a collector of stoneware flasks (fig. 34). Rick was asking for an opinion on the vessel's origin. The bottle has a flattened shape and a reed neck seemingly of the early nineteenth century. Both sides are decorated in a snakelike ribbon of cobalt. More significant to me at the time was the rolled-up fragment of printed paper that had been found inside the bottle. Close examination revealed that it had been torn from a King James Version of the Bible, retaining partial verses from the book of Romans (figs. 35, 36). The Bible is often cited in hoodoo spells; in fact, many agree

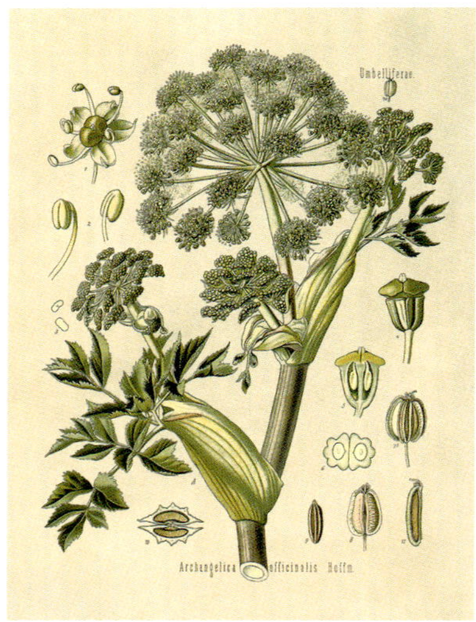

Figure 32 Illustration of *Angelica archangelica* (*Archangelica officinalis*), commonly known as garden angelica or wild celery. Chromolithograph on paper. 8 x 10". From *Köhler's Medicinal Plants*, by Hermann Adolph Köhler, edited by Gustav Pabst (Germany: Köhler, 1887). (Author's collection.)

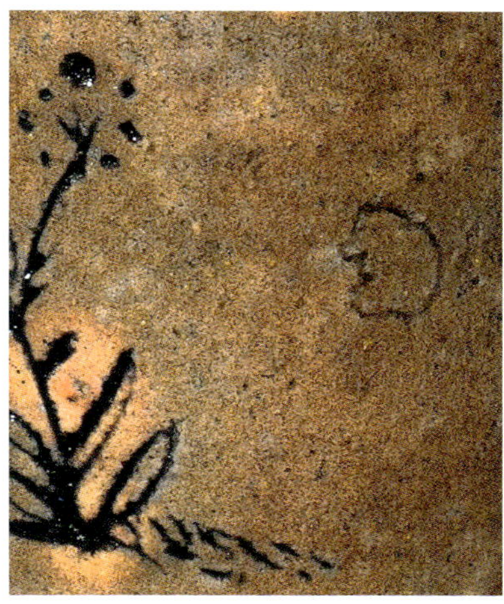

Figure 33 Detail of the jar illustrated in fig. 31.

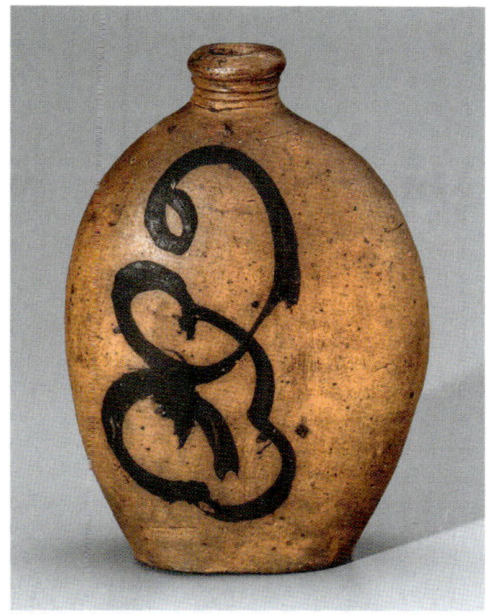

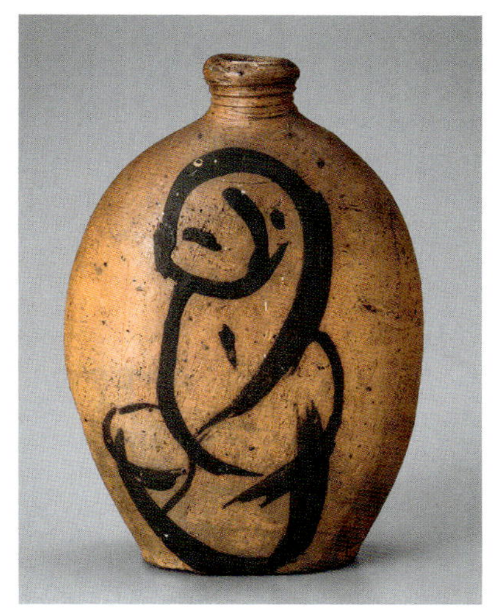

Figure 34 Flask, American or possibly Asian, nineteenth century. Stoneware with cobalt decoration. H. 5¾". (Courtesy, Rick Meech Burchfield.)

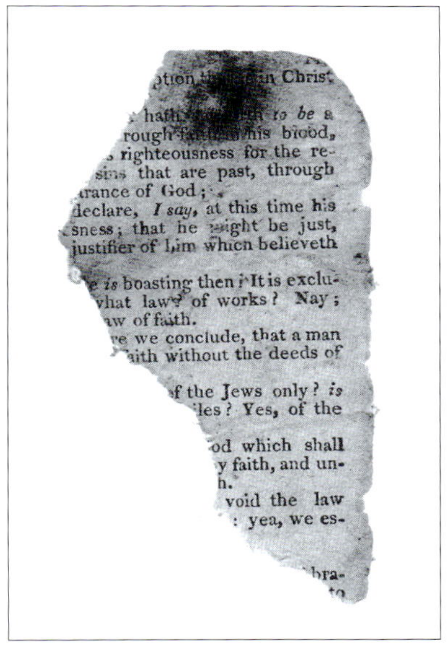

ption in Christ
hath to be a
rough his blood,
righteousness for the re-
sins that are past, through
rance of God;
declare, *I say*, at this time his
sness; that he might be just,
justifier of him which believeth

is boasting then? It is exclu-
what law? of works? Nay;
aw of faith.
re we conclude, that a man
aith without the deeds of

f the Jews only? *is*
les? Yes, of the

od which shall
y faith, and un-
h.
void the law
: yea, we es-

bra-
to

Figure 35 Fragment of a page from a King James Bible, probably nineteenth century. It contains partial verses from Romans 3:25–31.

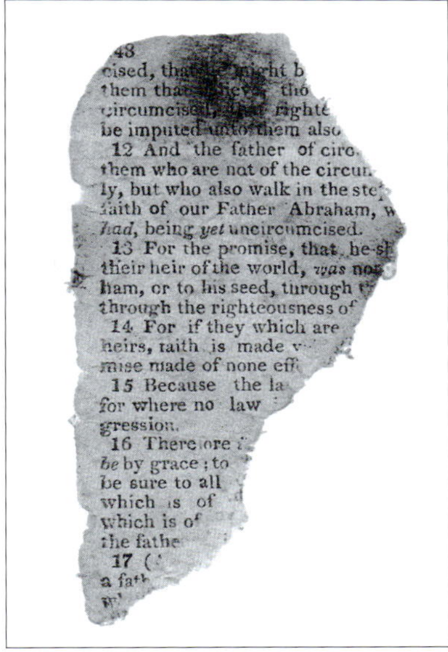

48
cised, that he might b
them that believe, tho
circumcised; that righte
be imputed unto them also
12 And the father of circ
them who are not of the circu
ly, but who also walk in the ste
faith of our Father Abraham, w
had, being *yet* uncircumcised.
13 For the promise, that he sh
their heir of the world, *was* no
ham, or to his seed, through
through the righteousness o
14 For if they which are
heirs, faith is made v
mise made of none eff
15 Because the la
for where no law
gression.
16 Therefore
be by grace; to
be sure to all
which is of
which is of
the fathe
17 (
a fath

Figure 36 Reverse of the page fragment illustrated in figure 35. It contains partial verses from Romans 4:11–17.

that it is "the greatest conjure book in the world."[74] Harry Middleton Hyatt, among others, recorded the use of torn pages of scripture in many conjure and hoodoo spells.[75] Contemporary practitioners of "Bible Magic" discourage the tearing or defacing of Bibles, opting instead to write out by hand the specific verses on paper and using that instead.[76]

From the review of the preceding examples, it is clear that ceramics and glass vessels have a long history of use in the creation of supernatural charms and spells. But the question of how the ring bottle may actually have functioned in Dr. Davis's Columbia, South Carolina, practice remains open to speculation and further investigation. At the very least, it probably held whiskey or another distilled spirit—always cited as the single most universal ingredient in conjure and rootwork prescriptions (fig. 37). Alternatively, it could have contained specific "waters" or potions concocted by Dr. Davis. One might imagine these liquids being ceremoniously dispensed from such an imposing container.

Figure 37 Detail of the 1893 *King of the Voodoos* engraving illustrated in fig. 39. This 1893 detail emphasizes the use of whiskey as one of the primary ingredients in a variety of hoodoo rituals.

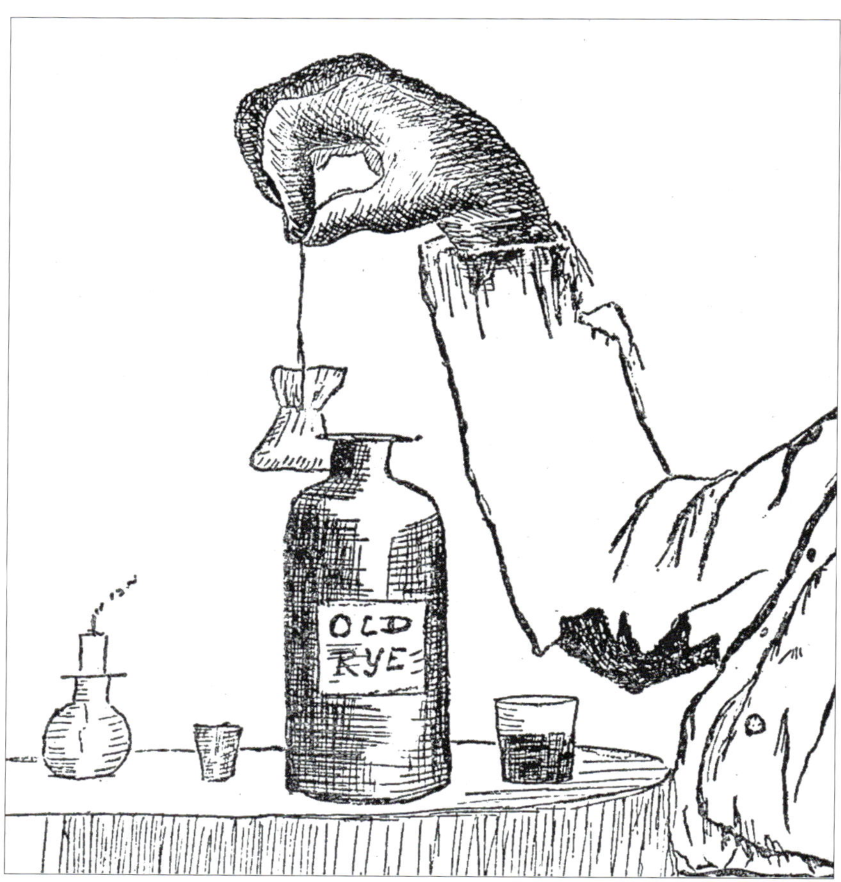

Figure 38 *Immagine del manoscritto Zoroaster Clavis Artis*, MS. Verginelli-Rota, Biblioteca dell'Accademia Nazionale dei Lincei, Roma, 2:18 (1738). (Photo, The Picture Art Collection / Alamy Stock Photo.)

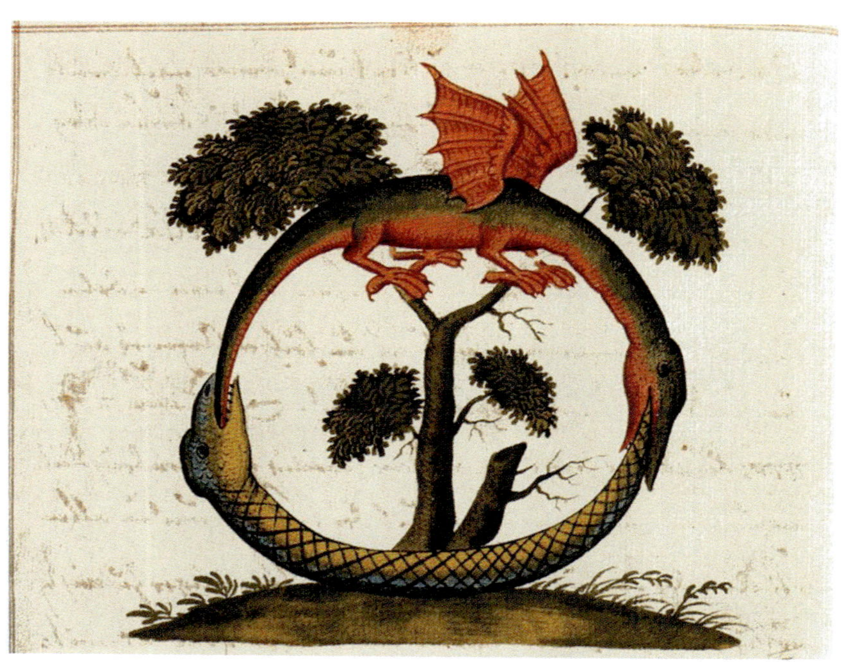

Like a shaman's staff or a fortune teller's crystal ball, the ring bottle conceivably represented a symbolic "power" object, possessing energy for protection, luck, and good intentions beyond its physical existence. The ring has symbolic meanings much like the *ouroboros* did for the ancient Egyptians and Greeks (fig. 38). The *ouroboros* represents a snake or a dragon eating its own tail and serves as a symbol for eternal cyclic renewal or a cycle of life, death, and rebirth. Psychologist Carl Jung observed that "One symbol of original perfection is the circle. Allied to it are the sphere, the egg, and the *rotundum*—the 'round' of alchemy."[77]

The ring bottle's contents have remained undisturbed, sealed with a cork. X-ray analysis might prove fruitful for deciding the next step in the investigation. I have spoken with several conservators about determining its contents, but I have been advised by more than one person of the potential adverse reaction if the bottle is unsealed. Jack Montgomery, who grew up in Columbia and has studied and written on magical healing, was particularly excited about the find but cautioned: "sounds like you might have a 'trap.' Enjoy it, but do be careful. Sounds like that root-doctor was quite accomplished."[78]

Imagining Dr. Davis

No visual record of Dr. Davis has yet been discovered. From newspaper descriptions we have a few disparaging comments, such as "a cross between a gorilla and a badger," which are consistent with historical accounts citing distinctive physical characteristics that set both male and female conjurers and rootworkers apart from others. This phenomenon is seen in other cultures where shamans are often those who have physical abnormalities that signify a person who might have a special relationship with the spirit world. As Newbell Niles Puckett has commented: "In Africa, the witch-doctor is usually selected because of some physical or mental peculiarity which shows him to be possessed of a spirit. I have noticed that the American witch-doctor is also possessed of unusual mentality and often shows physical peculiarities as well."[79]

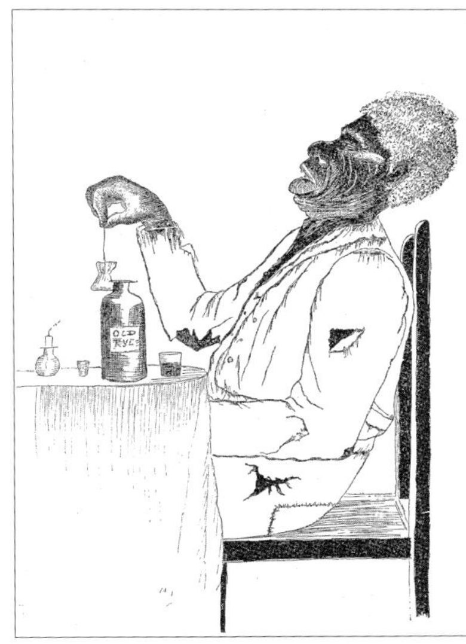

Figure 39 Louis Wain, "King of the Voodoos," in Owen, *Old Rabbit, the Voodoo, and Other Sorcerers* (1893), p. 172.

An early visual rendering of an American hoodoo doctor is found in Mary Alicia Owen's chapter "Luck Balls," in which she describes her interactions with "King Alex—a Voodoo doctor or cunjurer of great powers and influence."[80] The illustration of King Alex shows him "charging" a mojo bag, or luck ball, with a dose of "Old Rye," a process that Owen witnessed firsthand (fig. 39). Her description of his physical appearance is matched only by the rendering, which serves as the frontispiece for the chapter as well as the book:

> His eyes were snaky, his narrow forehead full at the eyebrows but shockingly depressed above. His nose was broad and with a flatness of nostrils emphasized to the perception of the beholder by the high, bony ridge that divided them. His chin was narrow and prominent; at first glance, it seemed broad by reason of the many baggy folds that surrounded it after the fashion of a dew-lap. He was far from beautiful when his features were in repose, but the time to fully realise that he was a self-chosen disciple of his Satanic Majesty was when he unclosed his great rolling lips in a silent laugh.[81]

In 1898 *Leslie's Weekly* published "Fortune Teller Reading the Palm of a Society Lady," a large, two-page spread showing a Black woman in front of her hearth reading the palm of a white female client (fig. 40).[82] By the early twentieth century, the telling of fortunes was an important part of conjuring, which included white professional fortune tellers catering to

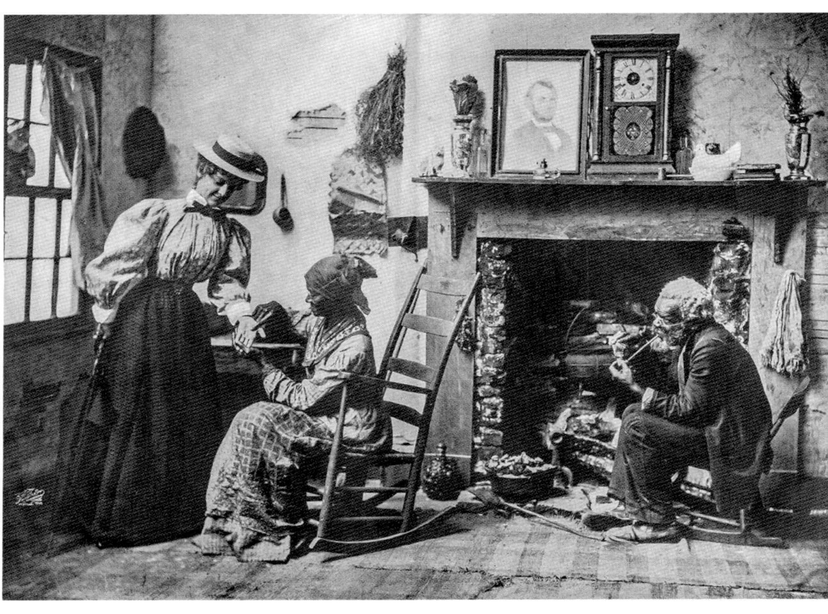

Figure 40 "The Blackville Gallery,—No. IV," *Leslie's Weekly*, January 20, 1898, pp. 40–41. Copyright by Knaffl & Bro., Knoxville, Tennessee, 1898. Photogravure. 22 x 16". (Author's collection.) The image shows a fortune teller reading the palm of a society lady as the fortune teller's partner smokes a long pipe next to the fireplace. The caption under the title reads, "A Blackville Fortune Teller,"—"Lawd, Chile! Yo Gwine to Marry Rich."

privileged clientele throughout America.[83] The photograph is particularly valuable, however, for the wealth of material culture in the scene, including what appear to be herbs and a so-called memory jug on the hearth.[84]

Several compilations of photographs of male and female root doctors can be found in published works and online repositories.[85] Most important is the image collection by folklorist Newbell Niles Puckett, who photographed African-American conjure doctors in his native Mississippi and South Carolina as part of his research (fig. 41).[86] Included in this archive, which is maintained by the Cleveland Public Library, are images of his sources and various paraphernalia associated with conjuring, such as mojo bags, charms, amulets, and "magical" plant material (fig. 42).

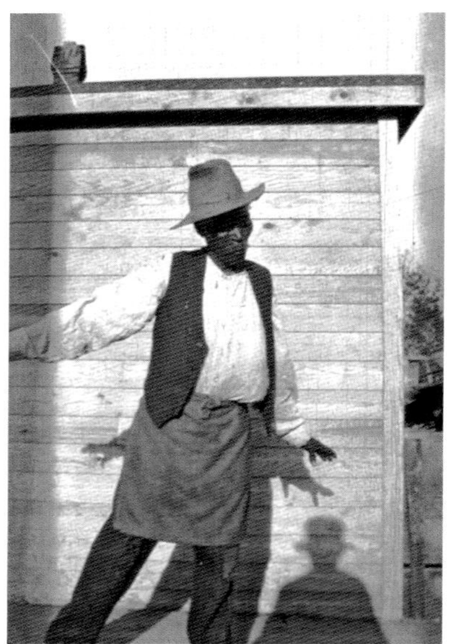

Figure 41 "Mississippi Hoodoo Doctor," 1920–1940. Gelatin silver print. From Photographs from the Puckett Collection: Folk Beliefs of African Americans in the Southern United States. (Cleveland Public Library, Fine Arts and Special Collections Department; photo, Newbell Niles Puckett.)

In the absence of a visual image of Dr. Davis, I invited New Orleans artist Andrew Hopkins to create an imagined portrait incorporating the ring bottle in the scene.[87] Andrew is well known for his interest in the creole cultures of southern Louisiana, particularly the architecture and interior furnishings of the late-eighteenth- and nineteenth-century domestic environments of New Orleans. He has made many portraits of Marie Laveau (1801–1881), who is the most famous voodoo priestess in all of America.

I provided Andrew with what background information I had at the time on Dr. Davis, but with very little instruction, leaving the end result up to his artistic vision. The resulting portrait offers a respectful rendering of the man, dressed in a formal suit with a pleated shirt, cravat, and vest (fig. 43). He is seated at a cloth-covered table, the stoneware ring bottle in

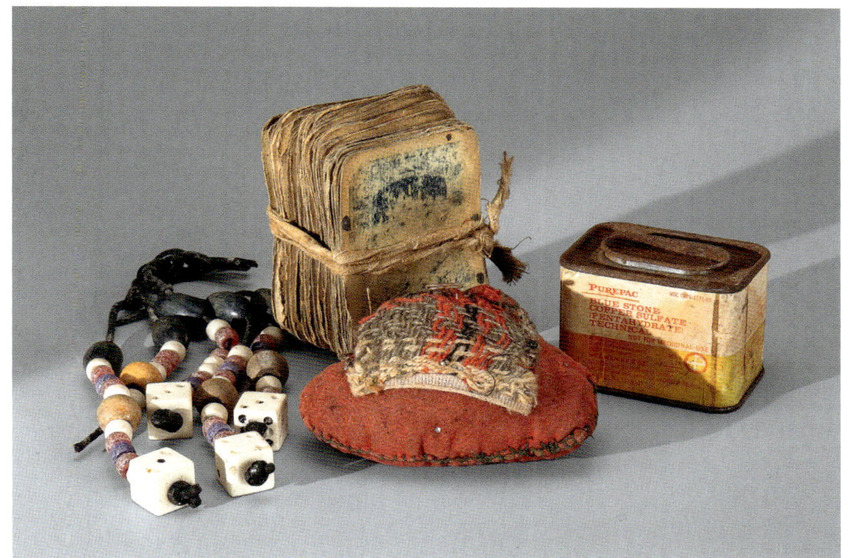

Figure 42 Conjure objects from the practice of Mrs. Mamie Wade Avant DeVeaux of Savannah, Georgia, mid-twentieth century. (Mamie Wade Avant DeVeaux Archive.) The objects include a string of beads and dice, playing cards, a heart-shaped mojo bag, and a container of "Blue Stone" (copper sulfate.) Bluestone is a traditional magical substance used for making mojo hands and luck balls for protection and good luck.

the foreground painted to scale, with some herbs and a pile of powder, perhaps graveyard dirt or a concoction of salts. In his hand, he holds a root.

In homage to the deep-seated connections of Black American rootworkers, Andrew created a companion portrait of Marie Laveau (fig. 44).[88] Her appearance is based on a ca. 1837 oil painting that depicts a New

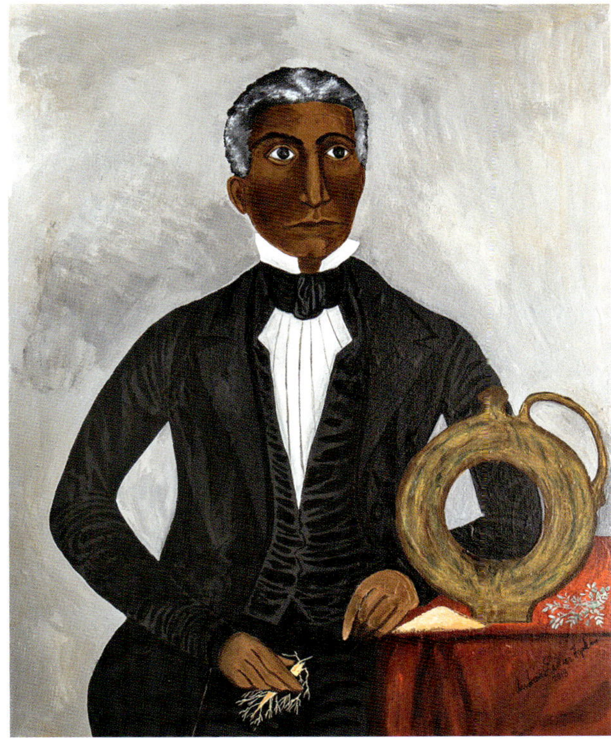

Figure 43 Andrew Hopkins, *Dr. Peter Davis*, New Orleans, Louisiana, 2017. Acrylic on board. 16 x 20". (Author's collection.)

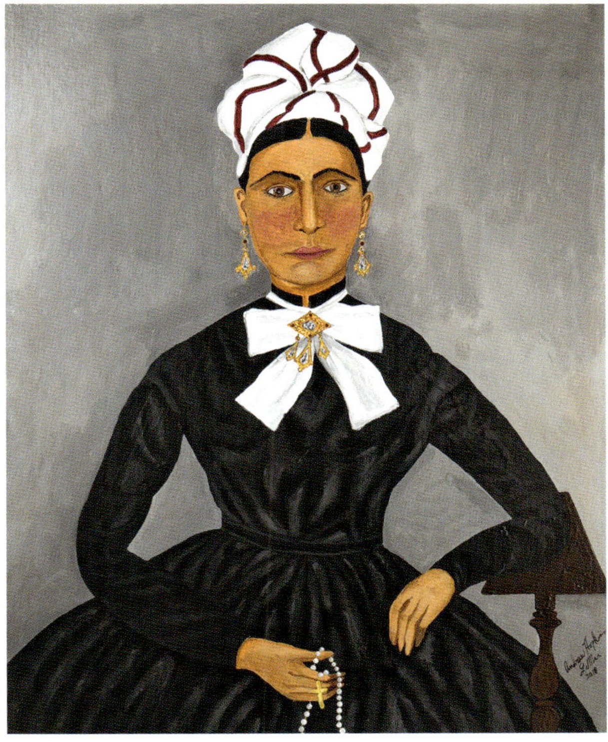

Figure 44 Andrew Hopkins, *Marie Laveau*, New Orleans, Louisiana, 2017. Acrylic on board. 16 x 20". (Author's collection.)

Orleans free woman (identified by the tignon she wears, which was legally mandated to identify free women of color) who supposedly is Marie Laveau.[89] Much has been written about her life and her exploits, though most of it highly sensationalized fictional accounts.[90] Despite the legends of her wild voodoo ceremonies and malevolent behavior, she was a devout Catholic who ministered to the sick and poor. She is depicted in Andrew's portrait wearing a tignon and holding a rosary made of white beads.[91]

Re-creating Dr. Davis's Medical Bag

In her 1935 collection of Southern Negro folktales, *Mules and Men*, Zora Neale Hurston included an appendix of "Paraphernalia of Conjure." Even though thirty-eight lengthy entries of various oils, powders, candles, medals, and natural herbs, roots and other materials are given as examples, Hurston concedes: "It would be impossible for anyone to find out all the things that are being used in conjure in America. Anything may be conjure[,] nothing may be conjure, according to the doctor, the time[,] and use of the article."[92]

My initial plan was to re-create the specifics of Dr. Davis's "medical cabinet" from the various newspapers between 1893 and 1894 which listed a number of common hoodoo substances. I developed what might be described as a shopping list of the paraphernalia and ingredients cited. The list includes:

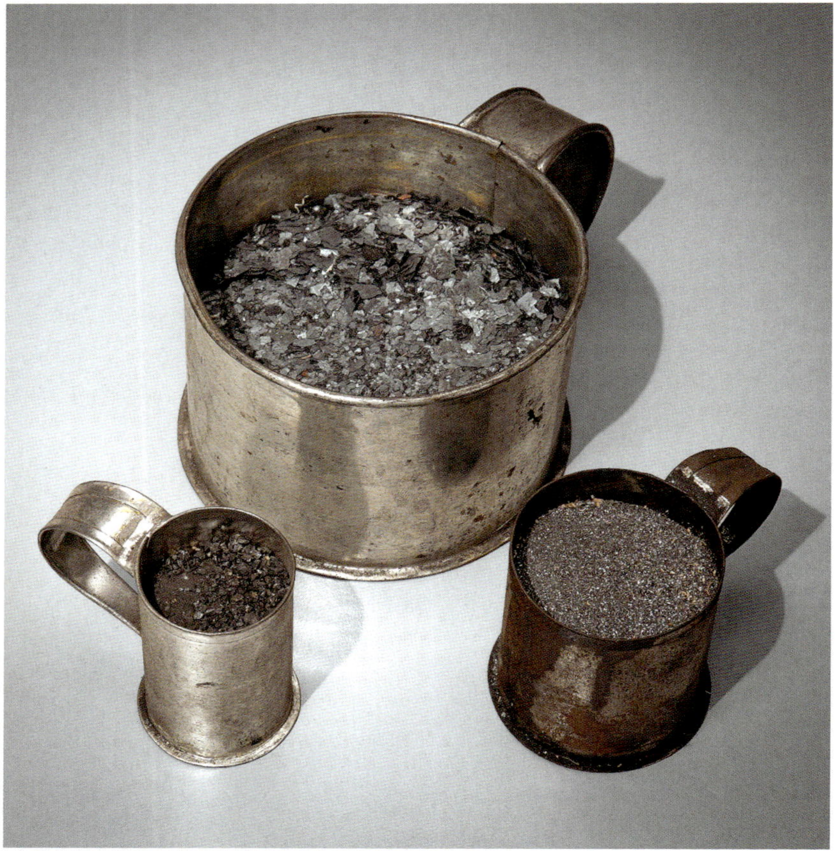

Figure 45 Anvil dust sourced from Colonial Williamsburg's blacksmith shop. Anvil dust, the metallic residue created during the blacksmith's forging process, figures prominently in the practice of conjure and hoodoo. The 1928 Ma Rainey tune "Black Dust Blues" is a classic tale of "goofering," a synonym for hoodooing. In it, Ma Rainey sings "Black dust in my window, black dust on my porch mat / Black dust's got me walking on all fours like a cat."

HOODOO WATER. These waters are prescribed for protection, cleansing, and blessing. These waters go by various names include Florida Water, Floor Wash, Moon Water, Indigo Water, and War Water.

GRAVEYARD DIRT. One of the essential ingredients in hoodoo and rootwork is the soil taken from the burial shaft of a human grave. Used in rituals and spells, graveyard dirt conveys the powers of the dead over the living.

DEADMEN'S POWDER. Most often referred to as "goofer dust," this powder can contain a mixture of graveyard dirt with salt, cayenne or black pepper, gunpowder, sulfur, ground bones, and anvil dust (fig. 45).

LODESTONES. Used for centuries in magic, lodestones are natural magnets that "charge" spell items and "power" mojo bags and gris gris bags. They are said to attract good luck, healing, and more.

WHISKEY. Whiskey, or sometimes rum, is used in conjunction with many other ingredients to activate the power of a charm. Mojo bags are routinely feed offerings with whiskey.

GOURDS. These inedible, hard-rinded fruits are often used as containers for various conjure ingredients such as roots, graveyard dirt, and powders, that might otherwise be found in a mojo or conjure bag.

ROOTS. Many common culinary and medicinal herbs are used in rootwork, conjure, hoodoo, and other healing practices, among them mint, jimson weed, sassafras, various peppers, and milkweed, as well as strange-sounding roots such as High John the Conqueror, five-finger grass, and devil's shoestring (catgut).[93]

I had wanted to visit the Columbia area to see what I could purchase from the half dozen modern-day emporiums categorized as spiritual, occult, herb, holistic healing, or metaphysical supply stores. With fitting names like Belladonnas, Seven Rays Book Store, Rose Marie Spiritual Gifted Reader & Advisor, Sphinx Paw, Solomon's Temple, and St. Francis Catholic Shop, these businesses are located today within just a few miles of where Dr. Davis had lived and worked.[94] Due to travel issues related to the Covid-19 pandemic, I turned to what most of us had done during that time

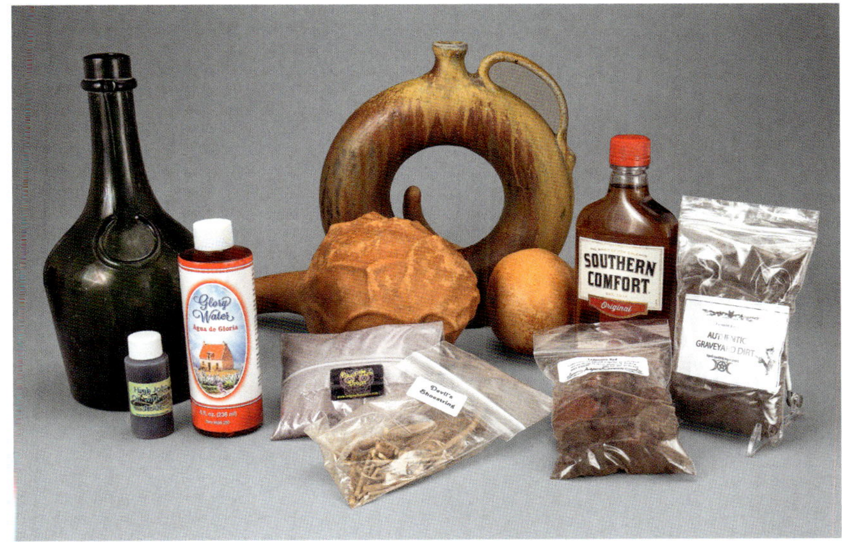

Figure 46 Modern-day hoodoo materials—including hoodoo water, graveyard dirt, deadmen's powder, lodestones, gourds, and "roots"—alongside a replica of Dr. Davis's ring bottle. Those ingredients were used in the "treatment" of Adolph Holuv and his family as gleaned from the newspaper accounts of Dr. Davis's 1893 court proceedings. (Private collection.)

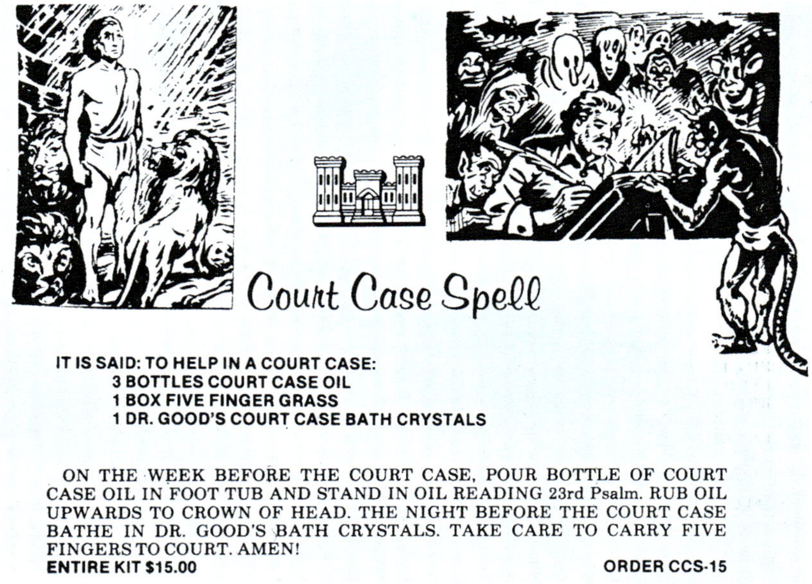

Court Case Spell

IT IS SAID: TO HELP IN A COURT CASE:
3 BOTTLES COURT CASE OIL
1 BOX FIVE FINGER GRASS
1 DR. GOOD'S COURT CASE BATH CRYSTALS

ON THE WEEK BEFORE THE COURT CASE, POUR BOTTLE OF COURT CASE OIL IN FOOT TUB AND STAND IN OIL READING 23rd Psalm. RUB OIL UPWARDS TO CROWN OF HEAD. THE NIGHT BEFORE THE COURT CASE BATHE IN DR. GOOD'S BATH CRYSTALS. TAKE CARE TO CARRY FIVE FINGERS TO COURT. AMEN!

ENTIRE KIT $15.00 ORDER CCS-15

Figure 47 "Court Case Spell" (Order CCS-15), *Ritual Supplies Mail Order Source Occult Supplies!*, ca. 1960–1970. (Mamie Wade Avant DeVeaux Archive.) A page from a catalog for Miller's Rexall Drugs, 87 Broad Street, S.W., Atlanta, Georgia, 30303.

of restricted personal contact and explored my online options. Amazingly, within a half hour or less of electronic browsing through eBay, Etsy, and Amazon, plus the magic of second-day shipping, I was able to replicate key components of Dr. Davis's medicine cabinet (fig. 46). Remarkably, these ingredients and the recipes for their use appear to have remained unchanged since the late nineteenth century, when written accounts were first compiled.

Concluding Thoughts

When a newspaper correspondent in November 1893 characterized Dr. Davis as a "lineal descendant of one of the witches of 'Macbeth,'" the writer was acknowledging the universal belief in the invocation of supernatural powers to craft changes in the human condition through the intercession of magic.[95] Unlike Shakespeare's dramatis personae of the Three Witches, Peter Davis was not a fictional creation. He lived, breathed, and practiced folk magic in nineteenth-century Columbia, South Carolina. Rather than using the witches' ingredients of "eye of newt" and "toe of frog," Dr. Davis relied on "graveyard dirt" and "dead men's powder" for his conjurations.

While we are limited in our knowledge of the full range of Dr. Davis's skills, we can surmise that his clients/patients sought out the typical hoodoo cures for illnesses, charms for protection and good luck, and perhaps fortune telling. The ethnic identity of Davis's disgruntled client Adolph Holuv as "German," a "Dutchman," and a "Hungarian" corroborates Jack Montgomery's study of South Carolina's folk healers which suggests that German-speaking settlers, in the so-called Dutch Folk area of the Columbia area, were predisposed to powwow and other magical alternatives.[96] His observations imply that those practices overlapped in the African-American and Germanic communities; hence, Dr. Davis's services would have been a natural outreach for Holuv.

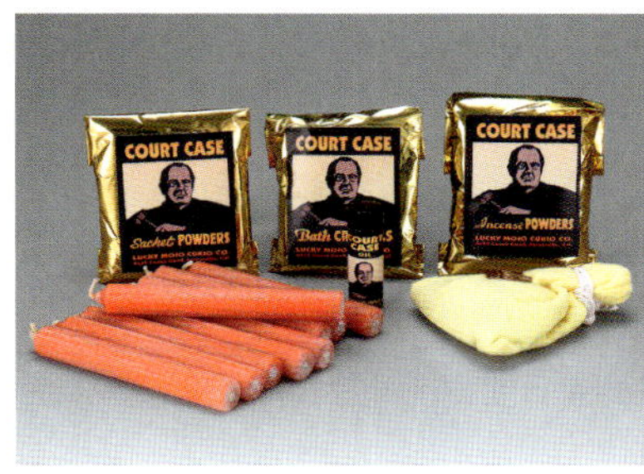

Figure 48 Court Case Spell Kit, Lucky Mojo Curio Co., Forestville, California. Powders, oil, mojo bag, and nine candles. (Author's collection.)

Among the most widely documented services of nineteenth-century hoodoo doctors were intercessions for successful outcomes in legal proceedings and court cases. We know that Dr. Davis interacted with the court system on several occasions both as a plaintiff and as a defendant. As Jeffrey Anderson observed, during the Jim Crow era "African-Americans required all the legal help they could get," and the hoodoo doctor provided those who believed in magic with spells to sway judges, juries, and law-enforcement officials.[97] Other writers go so far as to proclaim that hoodoo doctors were considered the poor man's lawyers in the Black communities that were denied professional legal services (figs. 47, 48).[98] Readers may recall the scenes in John Berendt's 1994 novel (and its subsequent 1997 film) *Midnight in the Garden of Good and Evil*, in which the Savannah, Georgia, root doctor Minerva chews the root and employs graveyard dirt in her spells during the murder trial of antiques dealer Jim Williams, seeking a favorable outcome.[99]

Perhaps like many readers, my feelings about hoodoo were conditioned somewhat by stereotypes that developed from exposure to gothic novels, visiting tourist voodoo shops on Bourbon Street, and watching Hollywood horror films. In most cases, those sources left the impression that hoodoo was primarily intended as "black magic" for curses and nefarious outcomes. Other perceptions of hoodoo were, and still are, associated with fraudulent scams, with psychic 'healers' simply taking money from unsuspecting clients. Nineteenth- and twentieth-century newspapers are replete with tales of gullible "clients" giving their hard-earned money to fortune tellers, root doctors, and spiritual advisers.[100] And while there is no question that an exploitative component exists in many transactions, "real" hoodoo is intended to promote the well-being of a person's spiritual and physical life.

After emancipation, thousands of male and female rootworkers in African-American communities in the South and the North were active in the "old tradition black belt Hoodoo."[101] Using herbs, roots, minerals, and other natural resources, the rootworker was an alternative for those denied access to formal medical care or who simply did not trust the system. In the twentieth century the practice was codified in the music of the American blues, although many today who sing along to the "Hoodoo Man" song have only a vague understanding of the historical depth and significance of its lyrics. An active commercial market for hoodoo supplies developed, targeting African-American consumers throughout the country. Today, hoodoo doctors offer advice, counsel, and spiritual interventions to their clients using Instagram and Facebook, and can be paid via PayPal.

Although countless men and women were engaged in conjuring and rootwork within their respective communities, most remained nameless. By virtue of the widespread newspaper reporting of his legal woes in 1893, Dr. Davis may represent one of the most recognized hoodoo doctors of his time. Furthermore, no other nineteenth-century object, and certainly no ceramic vessel, has ever had such firm association with a specific hoodoo doctor. For example, despite the notoriety of New Orleans's Marie Laveau, no artifacts associated with her life have been identified.

The Peter Davis stoneware ring bottle provides a physical and tangible link to an under-interpreted practice of African-American folk magic that was part of Southern culture from the early days of colonization and slavery and continues into the present day. It is an object with great symbolic power and it possesses a remarkable tactical quality, and almost magnetic resonance, when handled in person. With a little imagination, it can transport you into an enigmatic realm of mystery and intrigue. It is one of the most important Southern ceramic artifacts to come to light in recent history.

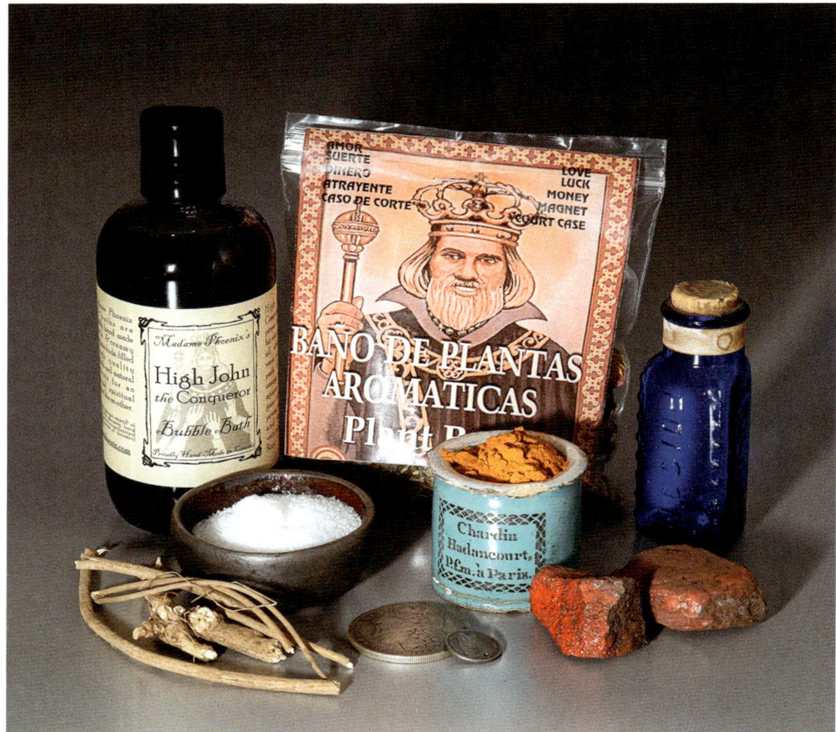

Figure 49 A group of hoodoo objects and ingredients mentioned in "Folk-Tales and Conjure," *Southern Workman and Hampton School Record* 28 (March 1899): 112. (Author's collection.) The "Remedies to Cure Conjuration" include High John the Conqueror plant bath, salt, cayenne pepper, devil's shoestring roots, red lodestone, and nineteenth-century

After opening this article with some lines from the most oft-quoted magical instructions in Western literary history, I would like to conclude with one that is not as well-known but certainly would have been in Dr. Davis's grimoire as a countercharm against conjuration. Published in 1899 in *The Southern Workman and Hampton School Record*, it may prove useful to readers in the unfortunate position of having had someone place an ill-intention spell on you (fig. 49).

Remedies to Cure Conjuration.

> If the pain is in your limbs, make a tea or bath of red pepper, into which put salt, and silver money. Rub freely, and the pain will leave you. If sick other-wise, you will have to get a root doctor, and he will boil roots, the names of which he knows, and silver, together, and the patient must drink freely of this, and he or she will get well. The king root of the forest is called "High John, the Conqueror." All believers in conjuring quake when they see a bit of it in the hand of anyone.[102]

ACKNOWLEDGMENTS I am very grateful to a number of people who facilitated the research into the history and significance of the Dr. Davis ring bottle. Thanks to Phil Wingard and the late Frank Williamson for making the acquisition of the bottle possible. Jon Prown, director of the Chipstone Foundation, subsequently acquired this important object for the collection in Milwaukee, Wisconsin. Dr. Corbett Toussaint was the first to recognize the identity of Dr. Davis and provided newspaper references to the history of his practice in Columbia. April Hynes undertook courthouse research and provided copies of documents related to Dr. Davis's legal proceedings. Luke Beckerdite contributed his insights into *Obeah* and provided the oil portrait of the Jamaican *Obeah* man. Carl Steen and Saddler Taylor made available fragments of ring bottles from the Stork pottery in Columbia. Dr. Bernard Means undertook scanning of the bottle and created 3-D replicas at Virginia Commonwealth University's Virtual Curation Labatory. Michelle Erickson reproduced several examples of the ring bottle, using a number of iron-rich glaze formulas to better understand the technical aspects of its manufacture. The glazes were created using anvil dust provided by Ken Schwarz and Stephen Mankowski of Colonial Williamsburg's blacksmith shop. Dr. Jane Przybysz, director of the McKissick Museum in Columbia, South Carolina, facilitated some important last-minute research with records at the South Carolina Department of Archives & History. Patricia Samford and Rebecca J. Morehouse of the Maryland Archaeological Conservation Lab provided photographs and information about the glass witch bottle found in Dorchester, Maryland. Rick Meech Burchfield shared the discovery of his stoneware flask containing the remnants of a "Bible Spell." Curtis Rice was instrumental in the acquisition of the stoneware ointment jar. Angelika Kuettner assisted with locating some important images for the article. I owe a special thanks to New Orleans artist Andrew Hopkins, who was willing to undertake the imagined portrait of Dr. Davis and the companion rendering of Marie Laveau.

1. William Shakespeare, *Macbeth*, act 4, scene 1 (Ware, Eng.: Wordsworth Classics, 1992), p. 75.

2. *Dæmonologie, in forme of a dialogue, divided into three Bookes*, https://www.bl.uk/collection-items/king-james-vi-and-is-demonology-1597.

3. Shakespeare, *Macbeth*, p. 75.

4. Bessie Brown, *Hoodoo Blues*, July 3, 1924.

5. Sale, October 10, 2017, Ballentine Auction and Estate Services, Columbia, South Carolina.

6. "A Dutchman Hoodooed," *Honolulu Advertiser*, January 13, 1894, p. 2.

7. Trudier Harris, "Conjuring," in *The Companion to Southern Literature: Themes, Genres, Places, People, Movements, and Motifs*, edited by Joseph M. Flora, Lucinda H. Mackethan, (Baton Rouge: Louisiana State University Press 2002), pp. 182–84.

8. Trudier Harris, "Voodoo," in *Companion to Southern Literature*, pp. 948–49.

9. Joseph John Williams, "Origin of Obeah," *Voodoos and Obeahs: Phases of West Indian Witchcraft* (New York: Dial Press, 1932), pp. 108–41; Nathaniel Samuel Murrell, *Obeah: Magical Art of Resistance in Afro-Caribbean Religions: An Introduction to Their Historical, Cultural, and Sacred Traditions* (Philadelphia: Temple University Press, 2010), p. 231.

10. Blake Touchstone, "Voodoo in New Orleans." *Louisiana History* 13, no. 4 (1972): 371–86.

11. Jack Montgomery, *American Shamans: Journeys with Traditional Healers* (Hector, N.Y.: Busca, 2008).

12. Walter Rucker, "Conjure, Magic, and Power: The Influence of Afro-Atlantic Religious Practices on Slave Resistance and Rebellion," *Journal of Black Studies* 32, no. 1 (September 2001): 84–103.

13. Christopher S. Lewis, "Conjure Women, Root Men, and Normative Visions of Freedom in Antebellum Slave Narratives," *Arizona Quarterly* 74, no. 2 (2018): 113–41.

14. John W. Blassingame, *The Slave Community: Plantation Life in the Antebellum South*, rev. and enl. ed. (New York: Oxford University Press, 1979), p. 110.

15. Henry Bibb, *Narrative of the Life and Adventures of Henry Bibb: An American Slave* (New York: Published by the author, 1849), p. 12, available online at https://docsouth.unc.edu/neh/bibb/bibb.html.

16. William Wells Brown, *My Southern Home: or, The South and Its People* (Boston: A. G. Brown & Co., 1880), p. 70.

17. Alicia M. Simmons, "The Power of Hoodoo: African Relic Symbolism in Amistad and The Narrative of Frederick Douglass, an American Slave," *Oswald Review* 2, no. 1 (2000): 41–47, available online at https://scholarcommons.sc.edu/tor/vol2/iss1/5.

18. Frederick Douglass, *The Life and Times of Frederick Douglass, Written by Himself* (Boston: De Wolfe & Fiske Co., 1892), pp. 170–71.

19. Glenda Sullivan, "Plantation Medicine and Health Care in the Old South," *Legacy* 10, no. 1 (2010): 17–35, available online at http://opensiuc.lib.siu.edu/legacy/vol10/iss1/3; Michele Elizabeth Lee, *Working the Roots: Over 400 Years of Traditional African American Healing* (Oakland, Calif.: Wadastick Publishers, 2015); Sharla M. Fett, *Working Cures: Healing, Health, and Power on Southern Slave Plantations* (Chapel Hill: University of North Carolina Press, 2002).

20. In Herbert C. Covey, *African American Slave Medicine: Herbal and Non-Herbal Treatments* (Lanham, Md.: Lexington Books, 2007); David McBride, "'Slavery as It Is': Medicine and Slaves of the Plantation South," *OAH Magazine of History* 19, no. 5, Medicine and History (September 2005): 36–39; Jerome S. Handler, *Slave Medicine and Obeah in Barbados, Circa 1650 to 1834* (Netherlands: KITLV Press, 2000) [originally published in New West Indian Guide /Nieuwe West-Indische Gids 74, no. 1/2 (2000): 57–90].

21. Fett, *Working Cures*, p. 36.

22. Katrina Hazzard-Donald, "Crisis at the Crossroads: Sustaining and Transforming Hoodoo's Black Belt Tradition from Emancipation to World War II," *Mojo Workin': The Old African American Hoodoo System* (Chicago: University of Illinois Press, 2022), pp. 84–115.

23. *Memphis* (Tenn.) *Daily Appeal*, October 25, 1868, p. 3.

24. Catherine Yronwode, "Source Materials on Hoodoo, Rootwork, and Conjure: African-American Folk Magic and Spirituality" (Yronwode Institution for the Preservation and Popularization of Indigenous Ethnomagicology, 2019), http://www.yronwode.org/hoodoo-bibliography.html; Alice M. Bacon, "Folk-Lore and Ethnology: Conjuring and Conjure Doctors," *Southern Workman* 24, no. 11 (November 1895): 193–94.

25. Anonymous Hampton student or student-teacher, "Folk-Tales and Conjure," *Southern Workman and Hampton School Record* 28 (March 1899): 112–13.

26. Mary Alicia Owen, *Old Rabbit, the Voodoo, and Other Sorcerers*, illustrated by Juliette A. Owen and Louis Wain (London: T. Fisher Unwin, 1893).

27. Biographical information for Mary Alicia Owen can be found at https://historicmissourians.shsmo.org/mary-alicia-owen.

28. "James Ellis, (Dock) the white hoodoo doctor and preacher has been arrested and is in Spartanburg jail, charged with rape," *The Gaffney* (S.C.) *Ledger*, September 12, 1899, p. 2.

29. Jeffrey E. Anderson, *Hoodoo, Voodoo, and Conjure* (Baton Rouge: Louisiana State University, 2005), pp. 93–96.

30. "Mississippi Hoodoo Doctor," in *Photographs from the Puckett Collection: Folk Beliefs of African Americans in the Southern United States*, Cleveland Public Library, https://cplorg.contentdm.oclc.org/digital/collection/p4014coll9/id/37/rec/7.

31. Wendy Dutton, "The Problem of Invisibility: Voodoo and Zora Neale Hurston," *Frontiers: A Journal of Women Studies* 13, no. 2 (1993): 131–52.

32. Zora Hurston, "Hoodoo in America," *Journal of American Folklore* 44, no. 174 (October–December 1931): 317–417.

33. Harry Middleton Hyatt, *Hoodoo–Conjuration–Witchcraft–Rootwork; Beliefs Accepted by Many Negroes and White Persons, These Being Orally Recorded among Blacks and Whites*, 5 vols. (Hannibal, Mo.: Western Publishing, 1970).

34. Michael Edward Bell, "Harry Middleton Hyatt's Quest for the Essence of Human Spirit," *Journal of the Folklore Institute* 16, no. 1/2 (1979): 1–27.

35. Hyatt, *Hoodoo–Conjuration–Witchcraft–Rootwork*, 3:xv.

36. Yvonne Chireau, "Conjure Magic and Supernaturalism in Nineteenth-Century African American Narratives," in *Voodoo, Hoodoo and Conjure in American Literature: Critical Essays*, edited by James S. Mellis (Jefferson, N.C.: McFarland & Co., 2019).

37. Laurie A. Wilkie, "Secret and Sacred: Contextualizing the Artifacts of African-American Magic and Religion," *Historical Archaeology* 31, no. 4 (1997): 81–106; Aaron E. Russell, "Material Culture and African-American Spirituality at the Hermitage," *Historical Archaeology* 31, no. 2 (1997): 63–80; Christopher C. Fennell, "Conjuring Boundaries: Inferring Past Identities from Religious Artifacts," *International Journal of Historical Archaeology* 4, no. 4 (2000): 281–313; S. K. Moses, "Enslaved African Conjure and Ritual Deposits on the Hume Plantation, South Carolina," *North American Archaeologist* 39, no. 2 (2018): 131–64.

38. Denise Alvarado, *Voodoo Hoodoo Spellbook* (San Francisco: Weiser Books, 2011); Hoodoo Sen Moise, *Working Conjure: A Guide to Hoodoo Folk Magic* (San Franciso: Weiser Books, 2018).

39. Catherine Yronwode, *Hoodoo Herb and Root Magic: A Materia Magica of African-American Conjure* (Forestville, Calif.: Lucky Mojo Co., 2002).

40. John A. Burrison, *Brothers in Clay: The Story of Georgia Folk Pottery* (Athens: University of Georgia Press, 1983), pp. 58–62.

41. Cinda K. Baldwin, *Great and Noble Jar: Traditional Stoneware of South Carolina* (Athens: University of Georgia Press, 1993), p. 46.

42. I thank Carl Steen and Phil Wingard for making me aware of these fragments.

43. Baldwin, *Great and Noble Jar*, p. 119, citing notes from an interview with R. M. Stork on file at the Charleston Museum, South Carolina.

44. Burrison, *Brothers in Clay*, pp. 172–73.

45. Federal Census, Inhabitants in Columbia Lower Sub Division in the County of Richland, S.C., June 14, 1880.

46 "Slavery at South Carolina College, 1801–1865: The Foundations of the University of South Carolina" (https://web.archive.org/web/20140722215524/http://slaveryatusc.weebly.com/urban-slavery-in-columbia.html).

47. His voter attestation in 1882 lists him as "Dr. Peter Davis," a resident of Columbia's Ward 3. *Stolbrand vs. Aiken*, Papers and Testimony in the Contested Election Case of C. J. Stolbrand vs. D. Wyatt Aiken, from the Third Congressional District of South Carolina, printed January 10, 1882, p. 34 (Washington, D.C.: GPO, 1882). Available online at https://archive.org/details/unitedstatescon7560offigoog/page/n46/mode/2up.

48. George Brown Tindall, *South Carolina Negroes 1977–1900* (Columbia: University of South Carolina Press, 2003).

49. "Peter Davis, M.D., Colored.; He Sustains His Right to the Title in Open Court," *New York Times*, August 3, 1884, p. 7.

50. *Judgment*, July 15, 1884, Ledger, August 5th, 1884, Book "D", p. 77, Richland County Court of Common Pleas.

51. *Laurens* (S.C.) *Advertiser*, October 10, 1893, p. 4.

52. "Peter Davis Re-arrested," *The State* (Columbia, S.C.), October 25, 1893, p. 8.

53. "The Hoodoo Doctor," *Camden* (S.C.) *Chronicle*, November 10, 1893, p. 1.

54. *The Charlotte* (N.C.) *News*, November 15, 1893.

55. Orangeburg County Court of General Sessions, Journal L3806S, 1890–95, pp. 593, 595, January 8, 1894, 275KoI.

56. South Carolina State Hospital Cemetery Survey Index, Walker Local and Family History Center, Richland County Public Library, p. 51 (https://localhistory.richlandlibrary.com/digital/collection/p16817coll12/id/64).

57. https://www.findagrave.com/memorial/120905946/peter-davis. Michael Trinkley and Debi Hacker, "Dealing with Death: The Use and Loss of Cemeteries by the S.C. State Hospital in Columbia, South Carolina" (Columbia, S.C.: Chicora Foundation, Inc.), January 17, 2001 (https://www.historiccolumbia.org/tour-locations/2091-slighs-avenue).

58. Joseph Glanvill, *Saducismus Triumphatus:* OR, Full and Plain EVIDENCE Concerning WITCHES AND APPARITIONS. In TWO PARTS.

The First treating of their POSSIBILITY, The Second of their Real EXISTENCE.

By late Chaplain in Ordinary to his Majesty, and Fellow of the Royal Society.

With a Letter of Dr. *HENRY MORE* on the same Subject.

And an Authentick, but wonderful story of certain *Swedish* Witches; done into English by *Anth. Horneck* Preacher at the *Savoy*.

LONDON: Printed for *J. Collins* at his Shop under the *Temple*-Church, and *S. Lownds* at his Shop by the *Savoy*-gate, 1681. https://quod.lib.umich.edu/e/eebo/A42824.0001.001?view=toc

59. https://quod.lib.umich.edu/e/eebo/A42824.0001.001?rgn=main;view=fulltext.

60. Henry M. Miller, "Buried Bottles" (https://www.hsmcdigshistory.org/clues-to-early-maryland-8-buried-bottles/).

61. Marshall J. Becker, "An American Witch Bottle," *Archaeology* 33, no. 2 (1980): 18–23.

62. M. Chris Manning,"The Material Culture of Ritual Concealments in the United States," *Historical Archaeology* 48, no. 3: Manifestations of Magic: The Archaeology and Material Culture of Folk Religion (2014): 52–83.

63. Rebecca Morehouse, "Witch Bottle," Maryland Archaeological Conservation Laboratory, Curator's Choice 2009 (Maryland Department of Planning, Jefferson Patterson Park & Museum, August 2009), https://jefpat.maryland.gov/Pages/mac-lab/curators-choice/2009-curators-choice/2009-08-witch-bottle.aspx; Martha J. Schiek and Edward C. Goodley, "Archaeological Site Examination: 18DO129, Dorchester County, Maryland" (Newark, Del.: Mid-Atlantic Archaeological Research, Inc., 1984); Rebecca Morehouse, "Witch Bottles and Bottle Charms," *The Magic and Mystery of Maryland Archaeology*, Maryland Archaeology Month, *Maryland Archaeological Conservation Laboratory* (April 2019), p. 6. http://marylandarcheology.org/MAM2019/2019_MAM%20Booklet.pdf, p. 6.

64. See Regenia Alfreda Perry, *Spirits or Satire: African-American Face Vessels of the 19th Century*, exh. cat., Gibbes Art Gallery, Charleston (Charleston, S.C.: Carolina Art Association, 1985), pp. 7–10; Claudia A. Mooney, April L. Hynes, and Mark M. Newell, "African-American Face Vessels: History and Ritual in 19th-Century Edgefield," *Ceramics in America*, edited by Robert Hunter (Hanover, N.H.: University Press of New England for the Chipstone Foundation, 2013), pp. 2–37.

65. Two other nineteenth-century Edgefield face vessels recently surfaced with histories of ownership by the family of Mrs. Mamie DeVeaux (1906–1983), a successful root doctor from Savannah, Ga. It is thought that those face vessels descended through her father, a nineteenth-century doctor. See "Voodoo Slave-Made Edgefield Face Jug Smiles for $72,000 at Slotin," November 13, 2017, https://www.antiquesandthearts.com/voodoo-slave-made-edgefield-face-jug-smiles-for-72000-at-slotin/.

66. "Documenting Southern Indigenous & African-based Cultural Traditions in the 21st Century," *Hoodoo & Conjure Magazine* (December 22, 2010), https://conjureartquarterly.wordpress.com/2010/12/22/find-us-on-facebook/.

67. John M. Vlach, *The Afro-American Tradition in Decorative Arts* (Cleveland, Ohio: Cleveland Museum of Art, 1978), pp. 139–47. Vlach noted that the objects found on graves included not only pottery, but also "cups, saucers, bowls, clocks, salt and pepper shakers, medicine bottles, spoons, pitchers, oyster shells, conch shells, white pebbles, toys, doll heads, bric-a-brac statues, lightbulbs, tureens, flashlights, soap dishes, false teeth, syrup jugs, spectacles, cigar boxes, piggy banks, gun locks, razors, knives, tomato cans, flower pots, marbles, bits of plaster, [and] toilet tanks."

68. Ibid., p. 142, citing E. J. Glave, "Fetishism in Congo Land," *Century Magazine* 41 (1891): 825.

69. Steven B. Leder and Fred Cesana, *The Birds of Bennington* (Hamden, Conn.: Stoneware Publications, 1991).

70. Robert Phoenix, *The Powwow Grimoire* (Lemoyne, Pa.: self-published, 2017).

71. David L. Cowen, "The Folk Medicine of the Pennsylvania Dutch Pharmacy in History," *American Institute of the History of Pharmacy* 55, no. 2/3 (2013): 88–95.

72. Yronwode, *Hoodoo Herb and Root Magic*, p. 30.

73. Aurora Kane, *Moon Magic: A Handbook of Lunar Cycles, Lore, and Mystical Energies* (New York: Quarto Publishing, 2020), pp. 50–55.

74. Hurston, *Mules and Men*, p. 287; Anderson, *Hoodoo, Voodoo, and Conjure*, pp. 4–5; Theophus H. Smith, *Conjuring Culture: Biblical Formations of Black America* (New York: Oxford University Press, 1994), p. 32.

75. Hyatt, *Hoodoo–Conjuration–Witchcraft–Rootwork*, 5:4051, entry 10708. Hyatt records several "spells" that make use of torn Bible verses; one informant from Fayetteville, North Carolina, prescribed the following for success in job hunting: "Tear Leaf From Bible—In It Wrap Up Salt And Red Pepper—Pray Over—Boss Likely To Give Job." Ibid.

76. Miss Michaele and Professor Charles Porterfield, *Hoodoo Bible Magic: Sacred Secrets of Scriptural Sorcery* (Forestville, Calif.: Missionary Independent Spiritual Church, 2014), p. 21.

77. Carl Jung, *The Origins and History of Consciousness* (Princeton, N.J.: Princeton University Press, 1973), p. 8.

78. Personal communication via Internet, January 23, 2018; Montgomery, *American Shamans.*

79. Puckett, *Folk Beliefs of the Southern Negro*, p. 201.

80. Owen, *Old Rabbit, The Voodoo*, p. 173.

81. Ibid.

82. "The Blackville Gallery, — No. IV," *Leslie's Weekly*, January 20, 1898, pp. 40–41.

83. Henry Carrington Bolton, "Fortune-Telling in America To-Day. A Study of Advertisements," *Journal of American Folklore* 8, no. 31 (October–December 1895): 99–307.

84. The interior, which might have been staged for photographic effect, is very similar to the oil paintings of Harry Herman Rosewell (ca. 1867–1950), an American genre artist who made a series of portraits of African-American fortune tellers in the late nineteenth and early twentieth centuries. See Rena Tobey, "Harry Roseland: Reading Tea Leaves," July 2, 2013, New Britain Museum of Art (https://nbmaa.wordpress.com/2013/07/02/harry-roseland-reading-tea-leaves/).

85. See online images Denise Alvarado, "Conjure Doctors & Spiritual Mothers," https://www.conjuredoctors.com/conjure-doctors.html; and Tony Kail, *A Secret History of Memphis Hoodoo: Rootworkers, Conjurers, and Spirituals* (Charleston, S.C.: History Press, 2017).

86. https://cplorg.contentdm.oclc.org/digital/collection/p4014coll9/id/19.

87. John Berendt, "Artist Profile: Conjuring a Creole Past," *Magazine Antiques* (March 7, 2022) (https://www.themagazineantiques.com/article/artist-profile-conjuring-a-creole-past/); and https://www.nytimes.com/2020/01/16/arts/design/Andrew-LaMar-Hopkins-New-Orleans-winter-show-.html.

88. The definitive biography of Marie Laveau remains Carolyn Morrow Long, *A New Orleans Voudou Priestess: The Legend and Reality of Marie Laveau* (Gainesville: University Press of Florida, 2006).

89. Manny Mareno, "'Her strength is haunting and unparalleled': Painting Once Thought to Portray Marie Laveau Sells for Nearly $1 million," in *The Wild News: Pagan News & Perspectives*, May 29, 2022 (https://wildhunt.org/2022/05/her-strength-is-haunting-and-unparalleled-not-marie-laveaus-portrait-sells-for-nearly-1m.html).

90. Samantha Mast, "Marie Laveau's Gumbo Ya-Ya: The Catholic Voodoo Queen and the Demonization of New Orleans Voodoo," *Voces Novae* 9, no. 1 (2018), article no. 4 (https://digitalcommons.chapman.edu/vocesnovae/vol9/iss1/4).

91. Long, *New Orleans Voudou Priestess*, pp. 20–21.

92. Hurston, *Mules and Men*, pp. 284–87.

93. Carolyn Morrow Long, "John the Conqueror: From Root-Charm to Commercial Product," *Pharmacy in History* 39, no. 2 (1997): 47–53.

94. Google search for spiritual shops in Columbia, South Carolina.

95. "The Hoodoo Doctor," *Camden Chronicle*, November 10, 1893, p. 1.

96. Jack Montgomery, *American Shamans: Journeys with Traditional Healers* (Hector, N.Y.: Busca, 2008), pp. 52–55.

97. Jeffrey E. Anderson, *Conjure in African America Society* (Baton Rouge: Louisiana State University Press, 2005), p. 152.

98. Kail, *Secret History of Memphis Hoodoo*, p. 49.

99. John Berendt, *Midnight in the Garden of Good and Evil* (New York: Random House, 1994).

100. Carolyn Morrow Long, "Perceptions of New Orleans Voodoo: Sin, Fraud, Entertainment, and Religion," *Nova Religio* 6, no. 1 (2002): 86–101.

101. Hazzard-Donald, "Crisis at the Crossroads," pp. 84–115.

102. Anonymous Hampton student or student-teacher, "Folk-Tales and Conjure," *Southern Workman and Hampton School Record* 28 (March 1899): 112.

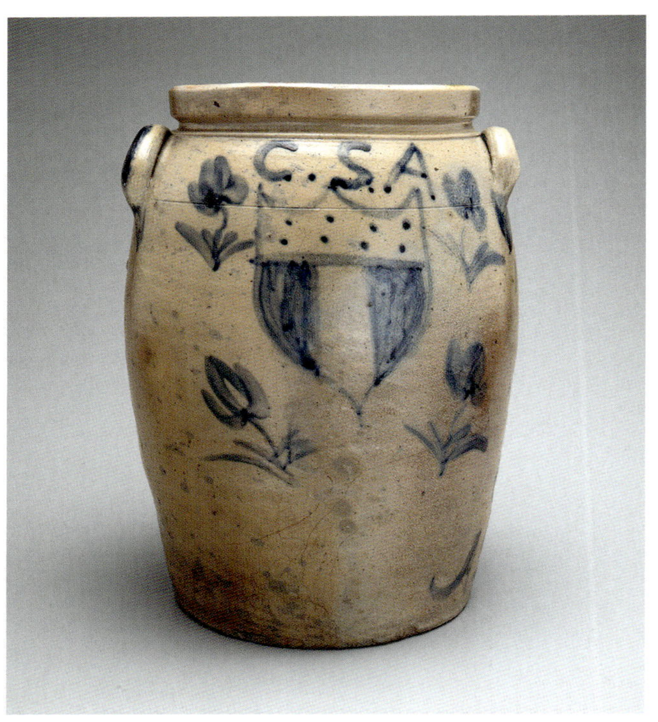

Figure 1 Jar, attributed to the Keesee & Parr Pottery, Richmond, Virginia, ca. 1861. Salt-glazed stoneware jar with cobalt decorations. H. 17½". (William C. and Susan S. Mariner Private Foundation; photo, Robert Hunter.)

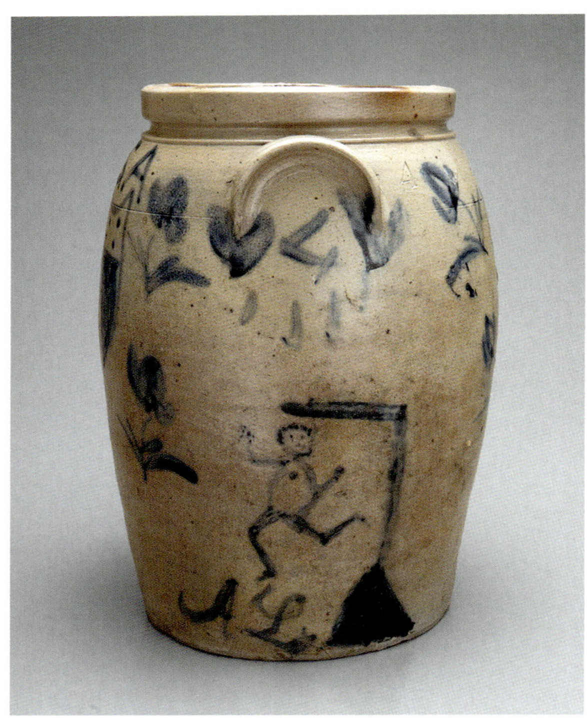

Figure 2 Second view of the jar illustrated in fig. 1. Inscribed: "4" (four gallons). (Photo, Robert Hunter.)

Elyse D. Gerstenecker with Robert Hunter and Kurt Russ

At the End of a Rope: A Stoneware Jar and Political Frustration

▼ NINETEENTH-CENTURY salt-glazed stoneware manufactured in the lower James River Valley has been collected and studied for more than half a century. Recent research has combined new archaeological information with intensive analysis of surviving pieces in public and private collections.[1] Although the vast majority of the stoneware products served utilitarian functions in both domestic and commercial contexts, a surprising number were decorated with well-developed pictorial statements, ranging in themes from comic to political. One such embellished example is a newly reattributed four-gallon salt-glazed stoneware jar from the Keesee & Parr pottery in Richmond, Virginia, that offers a rare glimpse into a perspective on the outbreak of the American Civil War.[2] Contrary to the sectionalistic or nationalistic political editorials that we often glean from the period, the jar's cobalt decoration suggests that someone, either the decorator or a client, was decidedly displeased with all sides.

Viewed from one side, the jar looks like a paean to the Confederacy—it is marked "C.S.A.," the initials for the Confederate States of America, and is decorated with a shield with three bars and eight stars, all surrounded with four tulip-like flowers (fig. 1). Turning the jar clockwise, the enthusiasm for Confederate victory becomes more violent, with a ghastly image of a figure hanging from gallows above the initials "A.L." painted near the base (fig. 2). Coupled with the initials, the figure's distinctly long, thin legs and hairstyle suggest that it represents Abraham Lincoln. The Confederate shield and Lincoln's fate align, fitting into a growing iconography for the Confederacy. However, further turning the jar clockwise muddles the matter a bit.

Opposite the side showing the CSA shield is a different one, with stripes, also surrounded by four tulips (fig. 3). The word at the top of the shield has faded, probably during the firing process, but the beginnings of "Union" remain visible. Rotating the jar once more completes the confusing narrative, as now a different figure is shown hanging above the scrawled name "Jeff D..." (fig. 4). The key to comprehending the jar, we contend, lies in the face painted under the lug handle above this figure (fig. 5). Eyes narrowed and teeth bared, it conveys frustration, perhaps from the pressure to choose a side, and anger, directed equally toward the leaders of the Union and the Confederacy.

Although surprising, given Virginia's outsize role during the Civil War, the divisiveness of political views in the commonwealth in this period suits both the jar's attribution and its fractious decorations. Significantly, Virginia did not immediately secede from the United States along with South

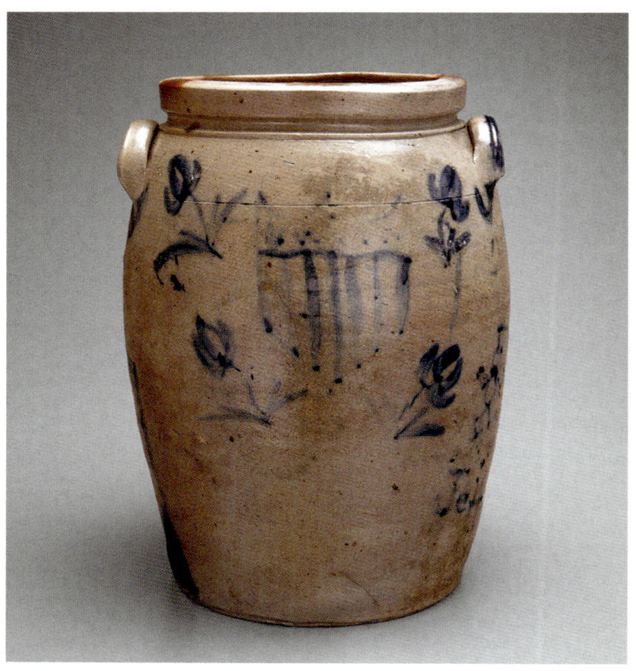

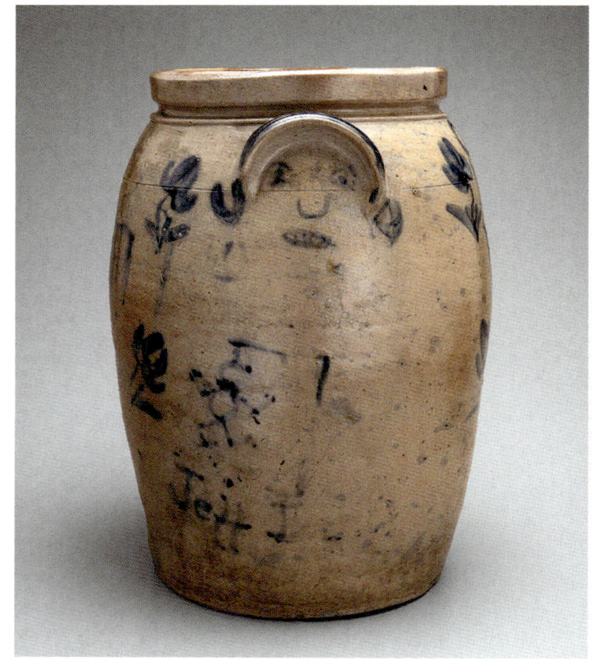

Figure 3 Third view of the jar illustrated in fig. 1. (Photo, Robert Hunter.)

Figure 4 Fourth view of the jar illustrated in fig. 1. (Photo, Robert Hunter.)

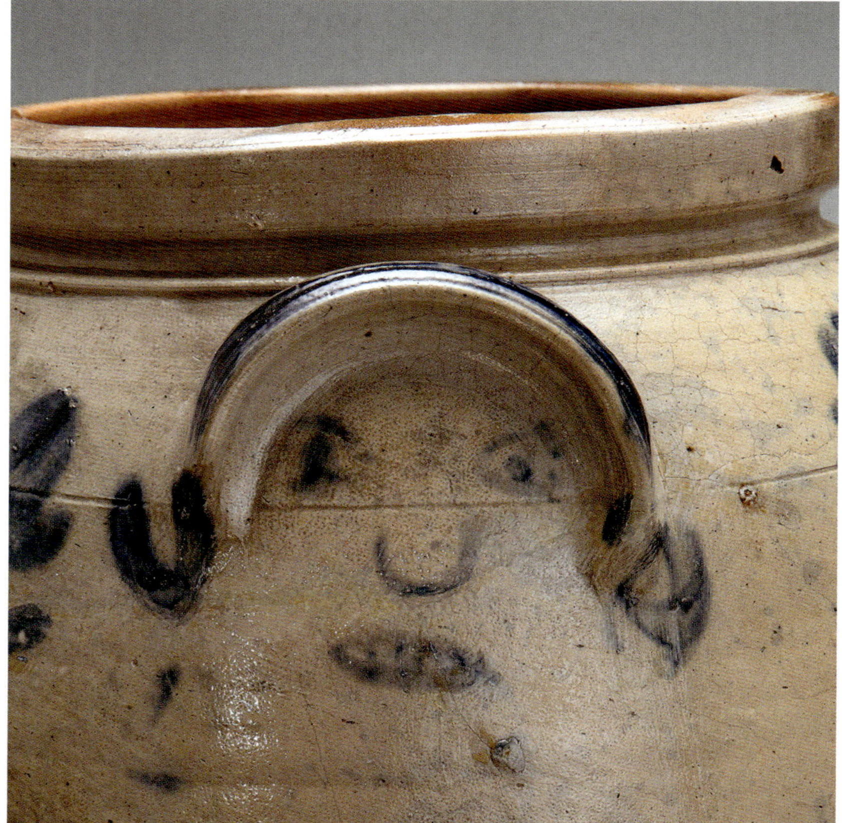

Figure 5 Detail of the decoration under the handle of the jar illustrated in fig. 4. (Photo, Robert Hunter.)

Carolina, and the highly charged discourse surrounding secession in the months leading up to its ultimate departure in April 1861 reveals the multiplicity of political views in the state at that moment in time. Few Virginians in the public sphere made arguments against white supremacy or the institutions of slavery, to be sure, but many fought against the idea of leaving the Union as the only means to preserve them.

In January 1861, a Richmond-area legislator warned his constituents about "disunionists" who wished to bring about secession, claiming that "This Union, which, if our internal dissensions can be allayed, is destined, in glory, in wealth, and in power, to outstrip all other Governments can be preserved, intact—can be maintained with equal rights to all the parties to it if Virginia will pursue a determined, but yet considerate course," and presciently warning that "Disunion is a remedy for none of the ills Virginia has to deal with; its effect on her and the other border States would be particularly disastrous."[3] Even as late as April 4, 1861, two-thirds of Virginia's secession convention voted against a secession ordinance.

In addition to its reluctance to leave the United States, Virginia had a significant internal fissure with which to contend. Slavery's central role in secession was not lost on contemporaries, pitting enslavers in the eastern regions of the commonwealth against westerners who were far less invested in it. Westerners resented the enslavers' firm grip on political power, perceiving that it put them at far greater risk of harm than those in the east who were pushing for secession. As one assemblyman stated during deliberations over sending representatives to the secession conference in South Carolina in 1860, "It was useless to talk of secession without war. The Ohio river would be a blaze of fire in 30 days after the Union was dissolved, and he [Mr. Haymond, of Marion] thought he was as much interested . . . as gentlemen living far from what would be the seat of war."[4] Ultimately, the events at Fort Sumter, South Carolina, brought about Virginia's secession, but not as an intact state. The western portions seceded separately, and eventually formed West Virginia in 1863.

Reframing this stoneware jar within the particular context of political fracture in Virginia, the number of stars atop the Confederate States' shield becomes especially meaningful. Unlike the official "stars and bars"—which first numbered seven, reflecting the initial states to secede, and then nine, after Virginia and North Carolina joined in the spring of 1861—this shield is topped by eight stars. That could have been a simple mistake on the decorator's part, but the specificity of the remainder of the jar's decoration suggests that the number is intentional. Eight stars would mark the occasion of Virginia's entry into the Confederate States. The decorator's violent treatment of both leaders also becomes more explicable given the context of the bombardment at Fort Sumter. To avoid appearing as an aggressor, President Abraham Lincoln sent supplies, not troops, in response to the requests for additional support by the fort's leaders. The Confederate States' newly elected President Jefferson Davis accurately believed that other slave states, especially Virginia, would secede from the Union and join the cause if war broke out, and he launched the attack on the fort that Lincoln anticipated.

If decorator (or a client) of this jar were a politically astute pro-slavery Unionist, it would not be a stretch for them to conceive of Virginia's position in the war as a tug-of-war between two treasonous gamblers deserving of identical fates.[5]

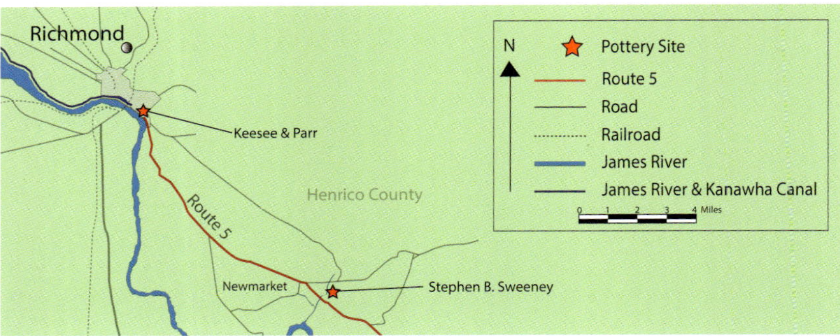

Figure 6 Map of the Richmond area of Virginia, showing the locations of the Keesee & Parr stoneware pottery and the Stephen S. Sweeney pottery.

Richmond Stoneware

Regardless of the idiosyncrasies of Virginia's secession-era politics, attributing the jar to a specific decorator in a particular Richmond pottery is something of a challenge, due to the numerous anonymous craftsmen working in these quasi-industrial firms. According to the U.S. Manufacturers' Census for 1860, there were two "pottery ware" manufacturers in Henrico County: the Keesee & Parr stoneware pottery in the Rocketts neighborhood of Richmond, and Stephen B. Sweeney's pottery on his farm in the eastern part of the county (fig. 6).

Each pottery was listed in the census as employing ten males.[6] At these potteries the men created utilitarian wares in substantial batches. Laborers could move from pottery to pottery, and worked in varying capacities. There is a distinct possibility that the individual who formed this jar on the wheel was not the one who created the lug handles, and it is highly likely that someone else applied the cobalt decorations.[7]

As seen with many of the potteries along the James River in the nineteenth century, the Keesee & Parr and Sweeney potteries' stoneware objects share common stylistic characteristics, and discerning between the two can be difficult. Moreover, after Stephen B. Sweeney's death in 1862, the entire property was sold at auction, where David Parr purchased many of the supplies and materials. Thus, stamps and other identifiers were used at both locations.[8] Further demonstrating the potential for exchange between the potteries, Watt Green, a free Black man who was listed in the 1850 census as working at Sweeney's pottery, is listed in the 1869 Richmond city directory as an employee at the Keesee & Parr pottery.[9]

Some of the political perspectives of the "hands" at Richmond potteries can be ascertained from the activities that were documented in newspapers and other records. Many at the Keesee & Parr pottery were members of the David Parr family. Formerly a china dealer in Baltimore, David Parr relocated to Richmond around 1852, with the support of David Maulden Perine, a manufacturer of salt-glazed stoneware in Baltimore.[10] In 1857 Parr

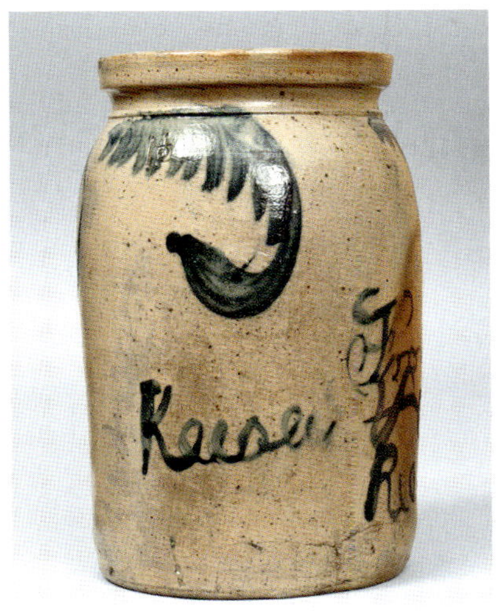

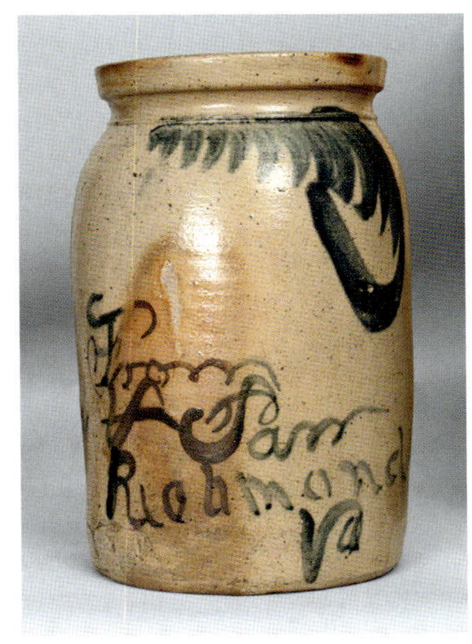

Figure 7 Jar, Keesee & Parr Pottery, Richmond, Virginia, 1860–1865. Salt-glazed stoneware. H. 14". Capacity: 3 gallons. Inscribed in cobalt: "Keesee & Parr / Richmond / Va" (Courtesy, The Valentine; photo, Crocker Farm Auctions.)

entered into a partnership with auctioneer Thomas Keesee, which lasted until 1862, when Parr brought his sons David Jr., John L., and James into the partnership (fig. 7).[11]

Although previous scholarship has suggested that the Parrs were Quakers and therefore pacifists and possibly abolitionists, contemporary accounts in newspapers suggest that by the mid-1850s the Parr family was deeply involved with the Methodist Episcopal Church in Rocketts.[12] They also were not opposed to the institution of slavery. In 1853 David Parr Sr. advertised that a man named Billy Holmes, whom he had rented from Captain Thomas Atkinson, had self-emancipated from his pottery at Rocketts, and Parr offered a reward for his return.[13] Furthermore, it appears that at least one of the Parr sons fought for the Confederate States, as David Parr Sr. placed an advertisement in Richmond papers, to be copied in national publications, requesting information about Private John L. Parr, taken prisoner at Front Royal, Virginia, on August 10, 1864.[14] However, Keesee & Parr employed potters of a range of political persuasions. Allowing for a little conjecture, it is easy to imagine a decorator or potter placing this jar in the kiln, anti-Confederacy images turned away from peers' eyes, and hiding it among all of the other stacks of jars, churns, and chamber pots.

David Parr wrote on behalf of a Quaker man, Tilighman Vestal, who had been imprisoned in Richmond for objecting to his enlistment in the Confederate Army due to his pacifist beliefs; Vestal subsequently worked at the Keesee & Parr pottery for several years.[15] Joseph B. Ramey, another Richmond-area potter who may have worked for the Parrs, enlisted in the Confederate Army in 1862 and was injured in 1864.[16] Most important, Parr's employees also included George Newman Fulton, an Ohio native who enlisted in the Union Army in 1862.

George N. Fulton was born in Loudoun County, Virginia, in 1834, but by 1835 the family had moved to Fultonham, Ohio, located in Muskingum County.[17] George learned his trade from his father, James Fulton, who was a local potter. During the 1850s George worked as a brick maker and bricklayer, but by 1856 he had moved to Richmond to work in the pottery shop of David Parr. There he is known to have made a massive twenty-gallon, salt-glazed beer or water cooler signed and dated "MAY 15 1856." Fulton continued to work in the Parr shop until he enlisted as a private in the Union Army on July 23, 1862, with Company E of the 9th West Virginia Volunteer Infantry Regiment. In November 1864 he transferred to Company B of the 1st West Virginia Veteran Volunteer Infantry Regiment. A family tradition says that George Fulton was taken prisoner by Confederate forces at White Sulfur Springs, West Virginia.

After his discharge on June 14, 1865, Fulton eventually founded potteries on the western side of Virginia, first in Alleghany County, then possibly in Botetourt County. Extant works from these potteries are covered in elaborate, expressive brushwork decorations in cobalt and manganese, often helpfully paired with a very large signature (figs. 8, 9). We believe the

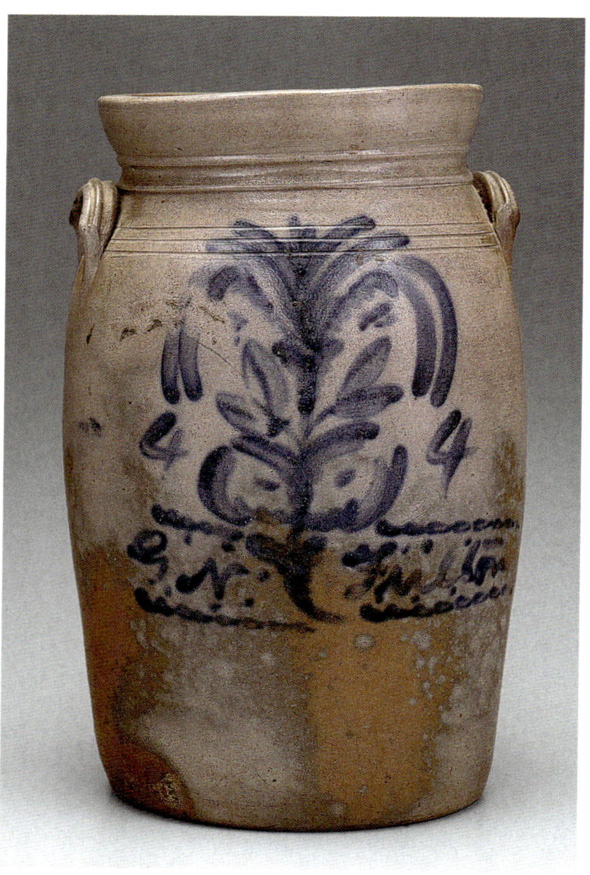

Figure 8 Churn, Fulton Pottery, Alleghany County, Virginia, 1867–1885. Salt-glazed stoneware. H. 16". (Kurt Russ Collection; photo, Gavin Ashworth.) This four-gallon churn is decorated with a brushed blue-cobalt floral design and includes a centrally placed "palm" tree and signature.

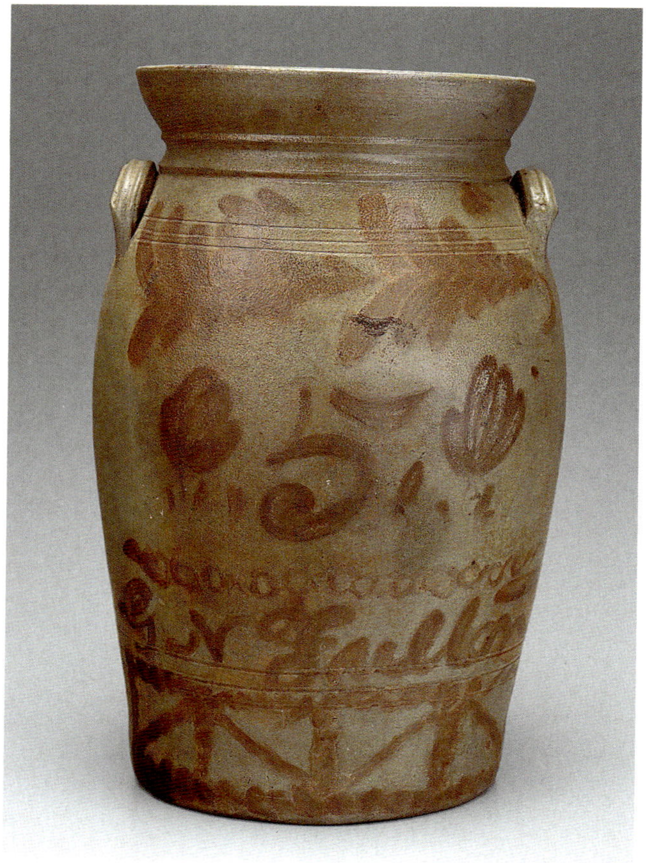

Figure 9 Churn, Fulton Pottery, Alleghany County, Virginia, 1867–1885. Salt-glazed stoneware. H. $17\frac{1}{8}$". (Kurt Russ Collection; photo, Gavin Ashworth.) A five-gallon churn with a flaring rim, a well-defined collar, and applied crescent-shaped extruded handles exhibiting elaborate brushed manganese-dioxide decoration, including horizontally and vertically oriented floral motifs, a centrally placed "5" indicating vessel capacity, and the signature "G. N. Fulton" enclosed by horizontal wavy lines.

brushwork on the Keesee & Parr workshop jar illustrated in figure 1 can be firmly attributed to Fulton, based on his Unionist views and his location in Richmond at the onset of the Civil War.[18]

It is worth noting that the Stephen B. Sweeney family, proprietors of the only other documented stoneware pottery in the Richmond area at the time, was more visibly dedicated to slavery and the Confederate cause than were the Parrs (fig. 10). Sweeney's pottery was part of his larger farm operation; in the 1850 and 1860 census he is listed as a farmer and his son, Stephen Sweeney Jr., is noted as a farm manager in the 1860 census. Sweeney enslaved twenty-six people in 1850 and twenty-three people in 1860. While most probably labored on the farm, it is possible that some individuals labored in the pottery. Other individuals within Sweeney's household are listed in these censuses as potters: the aforementioned Watt Green, as well as white potters Edward J. Clarke in 1850 and Patrick Murphy and another of Sweeney's sons, Charles, in 1860.[19] Both Stephen Sweeney Jr. and Charles H. Sweeney served in the Confederate Army.[20] Because of its proximity to Bailey and Fourmile Creeks along the James River, the pottery was caught in the middle of several Union attempts to overtake Confederate troops and seize Richmond during the war.[21]

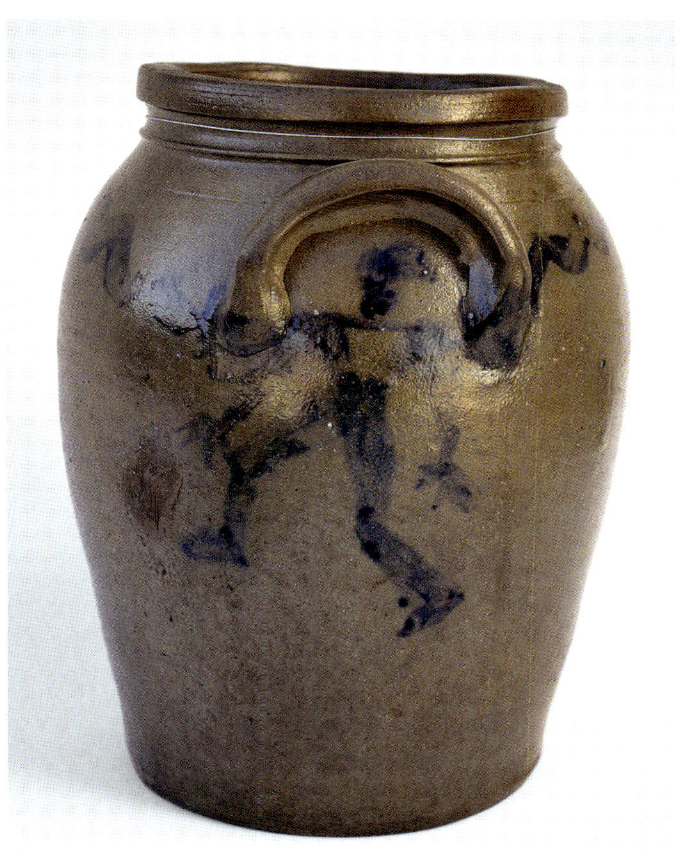

Figure 10 Storage jar, attributed to Stephen B. Sweeney, Henrico County, Virginia, 1838–1863. Salt-glazed stoneware. H. 9½". (Private collection; photo, Kurt Russ.) The decorative motif on this one-gallon jar is a brushed-cobalt dancing man beneath one of the handles.

Reading the Jar

Any number of visual sources could have inspired the decorator's imagery. The sardonic nature of the hanged figures correlates with the tone of contemporary political cartoons, which had become more abundant in the United States in the mid-nineteenth century. The popularity of *Frank Leslie's Illustrated Newspaper*, first published in 1855, accelerated regular publication of political cartoons in widely circulating media. *Harper's Weekly* and *Vanity Fair* followed, in 1857.[22] The South added its own publication, *Southern Punch*, in 1860.[23]

Other popular prints, such as those by Currier & Ives, added to this plethora of visual culture and iconographic permutations in the years leading up to and during the Civil War. Hanging Jefferson Davis was a common theme in political cartoons from the beginning of the war. In a Currier & Ives print from 1861, Davis is draped in the "Stars and Bars," standing on a platform at the gallows (fig. 11). Union soldiers sang about hanging Jefferson Davis from the old sour-apple tree from the beginning of the war, and this became another popular treatment of the Confederate

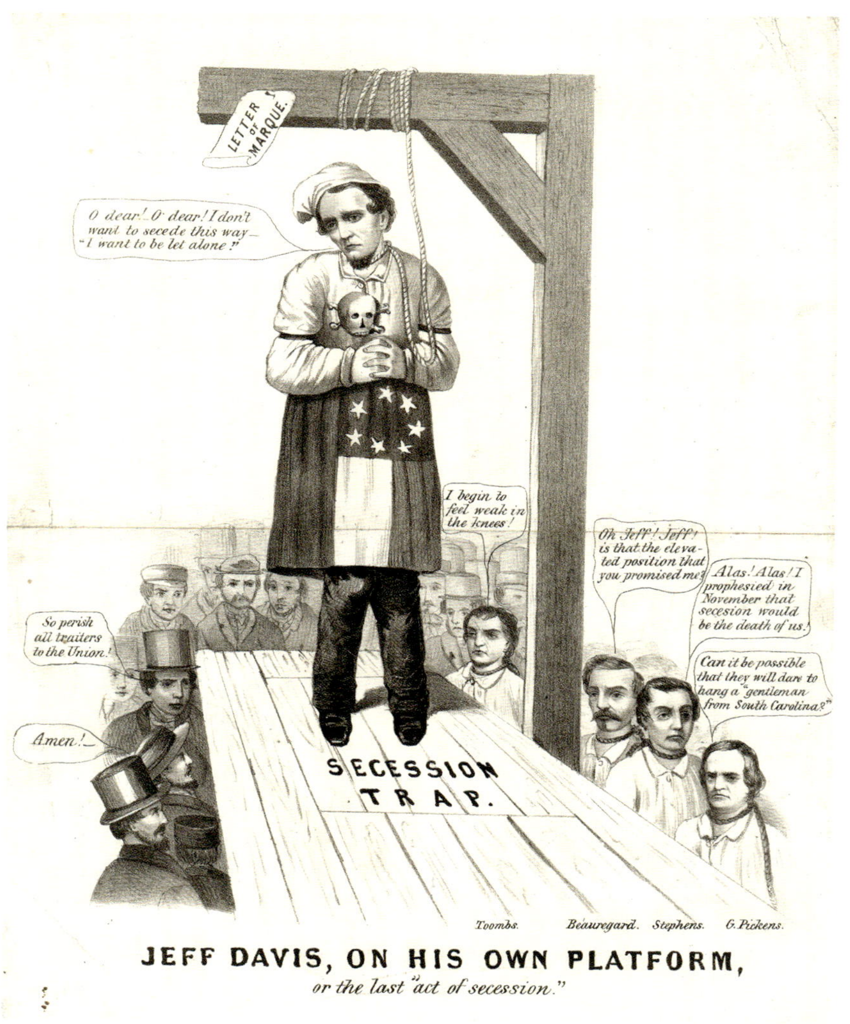

Figure 11 "JJEFF DAVIS, ON HIS OWN PLATFORM, or the last '*act of secession*.'" Currier & Ives, New York, ca. 1861. Lithograph on wove paper. 12 13/16 x 11". (Library of Congress.)

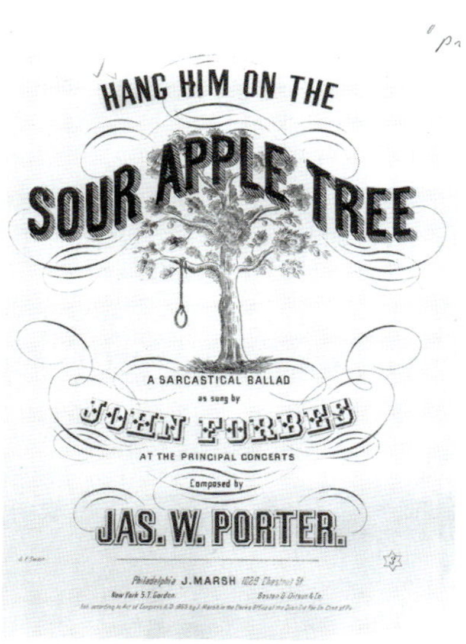

Figure 12 James W. Porter, *Hang Him on the Sour Apple Tree*, J. Marsh, Philadelphia, 1865. Notated music. (Library of Congress.) https://www.loc.gov/item/ihas.200001255/.

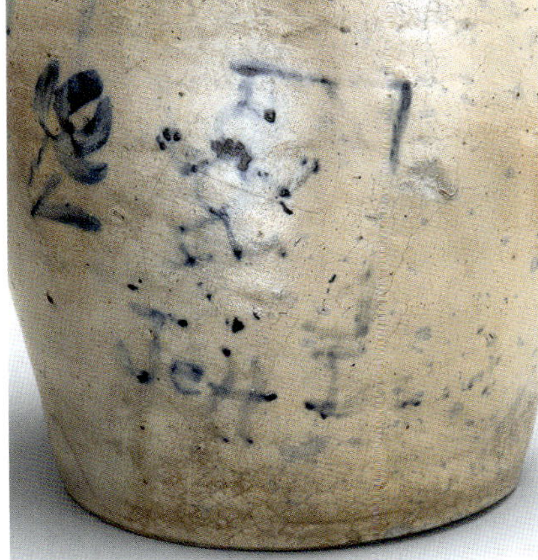

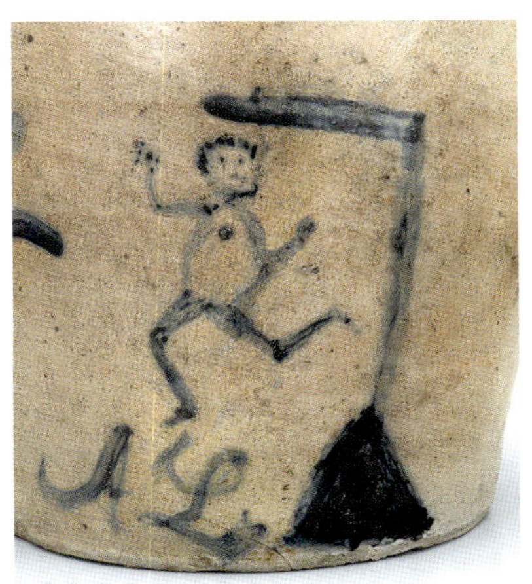

Figure 13 Detail of the jar illustrated in fig. 4.

Figure 14 Detail of the jar illustrated in fig. 2. Inscribed: "A L." Note how the script of the letters is similar to those used on the signed Keesee & Parr jar illustrated in fig. 7.

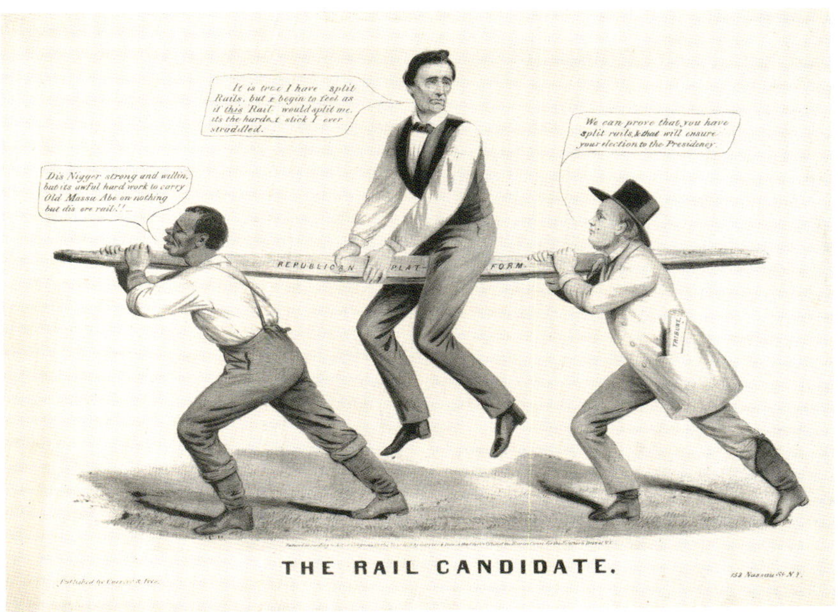

Figure 15 "The Rail Candidate," Currier & Ives, New York, 1860. Lithograph. 10⅝ x 14⅛". (Library of Congress.)

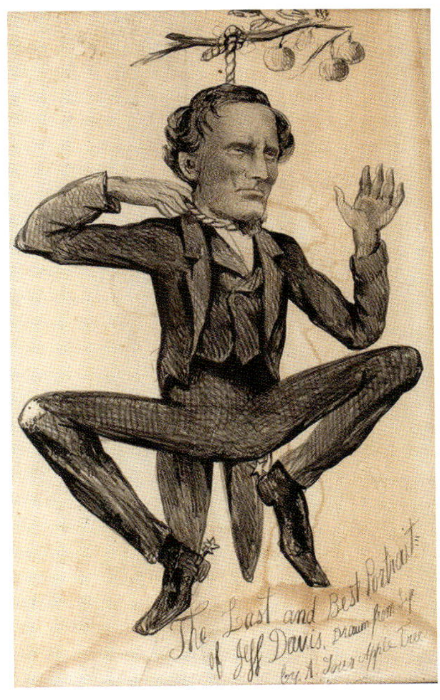

Figure 16 Jefferson Davis, undated. Drawing on paper. 10¼ x 16½". Handwritten inscription in lower right: "The Last and Best Portrait of Jeff Davis. Drawn from Life by A Sour Apple Tree." (Heritage Auctions.) The drawing shows the president of the Confederate States struggling as he hangs from an apple tree.

president in contemporary media (fig. 12). In response, Confederate troops adapted the song with their own lyrics: "We'll hang Abe Lincoln up a sower apple tree."[24]

The depiction of Jefferson Davis on the jar is somewhat indistinct, perhaps due to firing or a tentative initial application (fig. 13), but Abraham Lincoln is easily recognized by his chin whiskers, even without the initials (fig. 14). Contemporary caricatures of Lincoln, including those that portray him in a positive light, exaggerate the tall statesman's long legs. Likewise, the figure's on the jar's odd, splayed legs frequently were depicted in a similar manner in political cartoons. Further emphasizing his physique, the arrangement of his body echoes the numerous depictions of Lincoln riding a split rail that proliferated during his presidential candidacy (fig. 15). The hanging position of both presidents evokes dancing, with their arms and legs bent rather than limp, suggesting that the images are intended to be sarcastic and humorous (fig. 16).

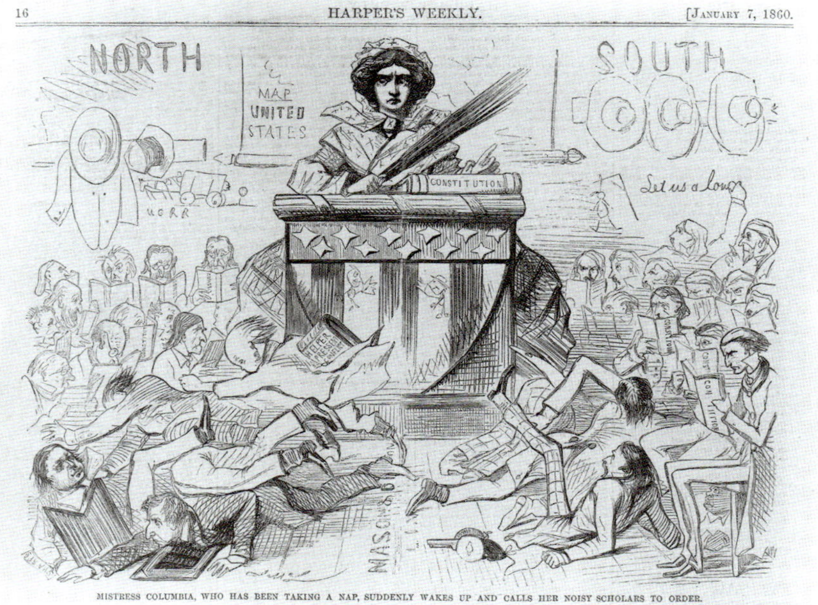

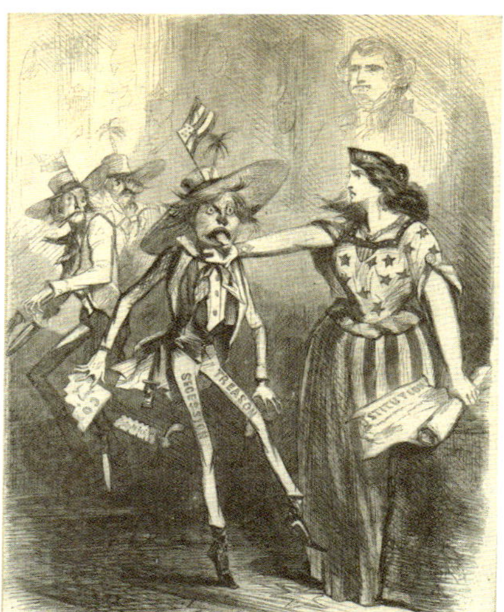

Figure 17 "Mistress Columbia," *Harper's Weekly* 4, no. 158 (January 7, 1860): 16. (Library of Congress.)

Figure 18 "Columbia Awake at Last," *Harper's Weekly* (June 8, 1861): 368. (Wikimedia Commons.)

The expression on the face painted under the jar's handle is also found in contemporary political cartoons, especially those that depict "Miss Columbia," a personification of the United States. In one, published in *Harper's Weekly* in 1860, Miss Columbia is fashioned as a schoolteacher presiding over a rowdy classroom of misbehaving congressmen/students. Her large eyes are narrowed and angular, registering her frustration with representatives from the North and South alike (fig. 17). In another cartoon from *Harper's Weekly*, published in 1861, Columbia has awoken and grasps a ghoulish figure, likely Jefferson Davis, by his neckerchief. Her face is arranged in the same firm-lipped, angered expression as before, but this time she stands in front of a portrait, likely of a founding father (fig. 18). Rather than mimicking Columbia, the decorator of the jar appears to have applied to a caricature of George Washington the typical conventions used

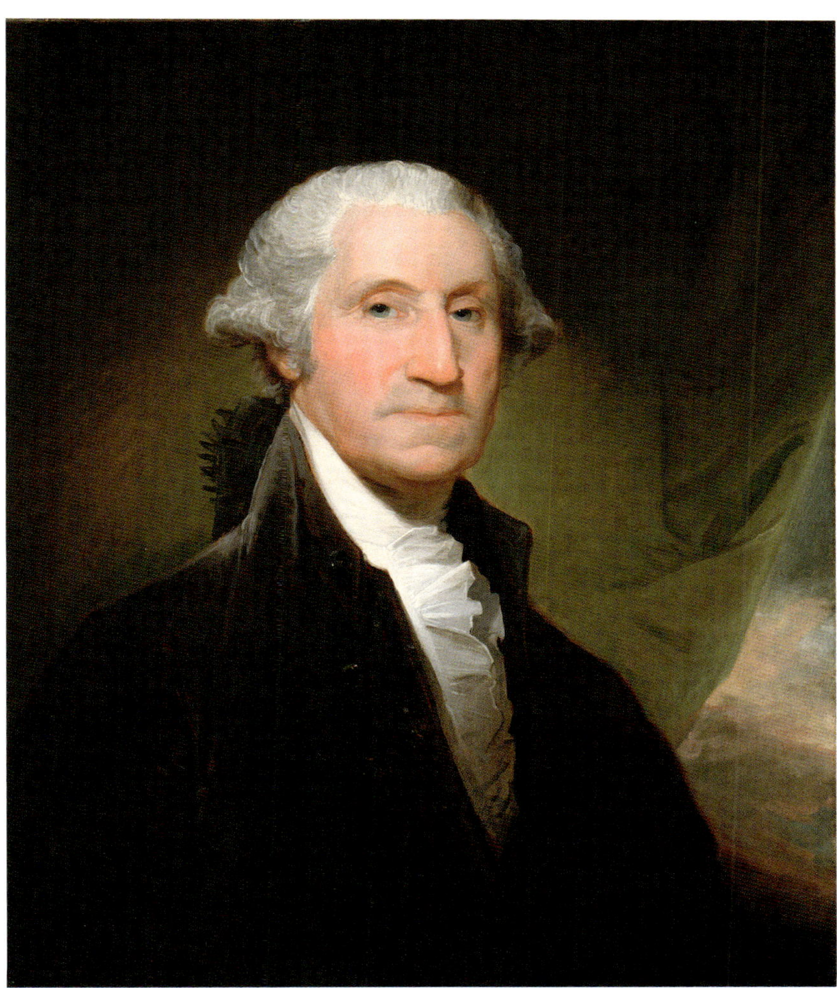

Figure 19 Gilbert Stuart (1755–1828), *George Washington*, begun 1795. Oil on canvas. 30¼ x 25¼". (Metropolitan Museum of Art.)

to convey frustration and anger. The cobalt sweep over the handle terminates in slightly curved ends (see fig. 5), much like the curls of a powdered wig around a face (see figs. 4 and 19). The face's toothy grimace implies clenched jaws, and references one of Washington's most infamous features unseen in his portraits. He sees what is happening to the United States and is not pleased.

As much as this face alludes to George Washington's anger at the state of his legacy, it also likely reflects the artist's emotional state. Admittedly, without knowing precisely who the decorator or potter is or having any documentation of their attitude, or whether the piece was executed for a specific client, assigning a particular perspective or emotion to an artist is risky. However, no matter how humorous, the treatment assigned to Lincoln and Davis, as well as the conflicted nature of representing symbols of both sides in the Civil War, speaks to considerable frustration. If representative of the views of the decorator, George Washington becomes a proxy for the self. The Washington/decorator's face therefore serves as a marker of bearing witness, of watching the country deteriorate into chaos and being unable to stop it.

Summary

As historian Michael E. Woods argues, Americans' understanding of emotions leading up to and during the Civil War played a critical role in their comprehension of political events and decision-making processes. In many instances, emotions were cited as the common, bonding force for the country's disparate groups. "Good feelings," or "maintaining good feelings," rather than political or national ties, allowed the states to remain joined together harmoniously. Disruptions to those good feelings, sparked by abolitionists in the North or fanned by secessionists in the South, would, in this framing, naturally dissolve those bonds.[25] Woods contends that various political groups played on the idea that emotional bonds could form communities and in turn encourage the creation of separate, sectional identities, essentially utilizing the discourse of emotion to amplify the key political and economic issues of the period.[26] Similarly, Kyle Osborn asserts that the kind of righteous anger and hatred of "the Yankee" encouraged by secessionists served as a unifying element for Southerners, who in actuality did not have much more of a singular "national" identity than did the rest of the United States.[27] Thus, the anger and frustration on display on the sides of the Richmond jar can be seen as twofold: partly at the leaders or groups that the decorator perceived as leading the country into war and chaos, and partly at the loss of an emotional community.

This stoneware storage jar, therefore, illuminates one of the forgotten paths that many Americans trod in the early stages of the Civil War: that of the unwilling participant. It offers an important reminder that, no matter our contemporary perspective and/or predominant tropes, the individuals who lived through major historical events often experienced them with much greater confusion than our hindsight affords. Rather than the black-and-white clarity of historians' texts, the actual moment was, for many, a hopeless blur of blue and gray.

1. Kurt C. Russ, Robert Hunter, Oliver Mueller-Heubach, and Marshall Goodman, "The Remarkable 19th-Century Stoneware of Virginia's Lower James River Valley," in *Ceramics in America*, edited by Robert Hunter (Hanover, N.H.: University Press of New England for the Chipstone Foundation, 2013), 200–258; Elizabeth J. Monroe, David W. Lewes, and Joe B. Jonas, "Preliminary Archaeological Assessment of a Waster Pit Associated with the Parr Pottery Works (44He0806), City of Richmond, Virginia" (Richmond: Virginia Department of Historic Resources, 2010).

2. Ex collection of Rex Stark, who purchased it from the Earl Rogers Jr. Collection at Skinner's "Americana Auction," March 24, 1983, lot 95; acquired for the William C. and Susan S. Mariner Private Foundation. The jar was the subject of study for the senior author and discussed at the MESDA Summer Institute Final Presentations, July 16, 2021, sponsored by a William C. and Susan S. Mariner Southern Ceramics Fellowship.

3. Wms. C. Wickham, "The State Convention," *Richmond Dispatch*, Thursday, January 17, 1861, p. 2.

4. "House of Delegates, Thursday, January 27," *Richmond Dispatch*, January 28, 1860, p. 1.

5. Michael E. Woods, "Secession and Disunion," in *The Cambridge History of the American Civil War*, edited by Aaron Sheehan-Dean, 3 vols. (Cambridge: Cambridge University Press, 2019), 2:44–45, 56, 59–61.

6. United States Census of Manufactures, Virginia State Table, 1860, https://www.census.gov/library/publications/1865/dec/1860c.html (accessed July 2, 2021); "Stephen B. Sweeney" and "Keesee & Parr," United States Census of Manufactures, 1860, Eastern District, Henrico,

Virginia, https://www.ancestry.com/imageviewer/collections/1276/images/T1132_8-00510?ssrc=&backlabel=Return&pId=3060096 (accessed July 12, 2021).

7. Oliver Mueller-Heubach, "From Kaolin to Claymount: Landscapes of the 19th-Century James River Stoneware Industry," Ph.D. diss., College of William & Mary, 2013, pp. 244, 248–50.

8. Russ et al., "Remarkable 19th-Century Stoneware of Virginia's Lower James River Valley," p. 233.

9. Richmond City Directory, 1869, U.S. City Directories, 1822–1995, https://www.ancestry.com/discoveryui-content/view/690102648:2469?tid=&pid=&queryId=8649be444c1116924f90d74ff7d32d91&_phsrc=iDw2&_phstart=successSource.

10. Advertisement, *Richmond Dispatch*, April 27, 1852, p. 2.

11. Advertisement, *Richmond Dispatch*, October 10, 1862, p. 4; Mueller-Heubach, "From Kaolin to Claymount," pp. 112–13.

12. Advertisement, *Richmond Dispatch*, July 1, 1857, p. 2; advertisement, *Richmond Times*, November 13, 1866, p. 3; "Notes," *Richmond Times*, April 11, 1867, p. 4. On the history of the Methodist Episcopal Church in Rocketts, "Notes" credits David Parr as the first superintendent of the Rocketts Sunday School.

13. Advertisement, *Richmond Dispatch*, September 12, 1853, p. 3.

14. Advertisement, *Richmond Enquirer*, September 13, 1864, p. 3.

15. Russ et al., "Remarkable 19th-Century Stoneware of Virginia's Lower James River Valley," p. 212.

16. "Joseph B. Ramey," Historical Data Systems, Duxbury, Mass., American Civil War Research Database, https://www.ancestry.com/discoveryui-content/view/321599:1555?tid=&pid=&queryId=71bc28726b9e5d8aa740e46d4609db0a&_phsrc=zKE6&_phstart=successSource (accessed July 12, 2021).

17. https://en.wikipedia.org/wiki/George_N._Fulton.

18. Kurt C. Russ, "The Remarkable Stoneware of George N. Fulton, circa 1856–1894," in *Ceramics in America*, edited by Robert Hunter (Hanover, N.H.: University Press of New England for the Chipstone Foundation, 2004), pp. 158, 162–73.

19. United States Federal Census, 1850, Henrico, Virginia, https://www.ancestry.com/imageviewer/collections/8054/images/4206372_00527?usePUB=true&_phsrc=loA2&_phstart=successSource&usePUBJs=true&pId=15152057 (accessed July 12, 2021); United States Federal Census, 1860, Eastern Division, Henrico, Virginia, https://www.ancestry.com/discoveryui-content/view/34299168:7667?tid=&pid=&queryId=e647649feb2377019b8c3d81fa8d01b5&_phsrc=eJx1&_phstart=successSource (accessed July 12, 2021).

20. "Charles H. Sweeney," National Park Service, United States, Civil War Soldiers, 1861–1865, https://www.ancestry.com/discoveryui-content/view/5329831:1138?tid=&pid=&queryId=a091244d0430c44a68074bfc3615adf6&_phsrc=qrt3&_phstart=successSource (accessed July 12, 2021); "Stephen B. Sweeney," Historical Data Systems, Inc., Duxbury, Mass., American Civil War Research Database, https://www.ancestry.com/discoveryui-content/view/2371885:1555?tid=&pid=&queryId=f64cb8061f92017e21d8801db5bc3b54&_phsrc=qrt6&_phstart=successSource (accessed July 12, 2021).

21. Mueller-Heubach, "From Kaolin to Claymount," pp. 108–9.

22. J. G. Lewin and P. J. Huff, *Lines of Contention: Political Cartoons of the Civil War* (New York: Collins, 2007), p. x.

23. Kristen M. Smith, ed., *The Lines Are Drawn: Political Cartoons of the Civil War* (Athens, Ga.: Hill Street Press, 1999), p. xv.

24. See Heritage Auctions, "Civil War-Era Manuscripts, Poems, and Letters," December 12, 2015, lot 47213. A version of the song is included in Marty Duncan's *A Civil War Romance* (Pittsburgh, Pa.: Red Lead Press, 2011), p. 49.

25. Michael E. Woods, *Emotional and Sectional Conflict in the Antebellum United States* (New York: Cambridge University Press, 2014), pp. 25–28.

26. Ibid., pp. 29–31.

27. Kyle N. Osborn, "An Emotional Rebellion: Wrecking the Old South's Emotional Community," in *Southern Communities: Identity, Conflict, and Memory in the American South*, edited by Steven E. Nash and Bruce E. Stewart (Athens: University of Georgia Press, 2019), p. 82.

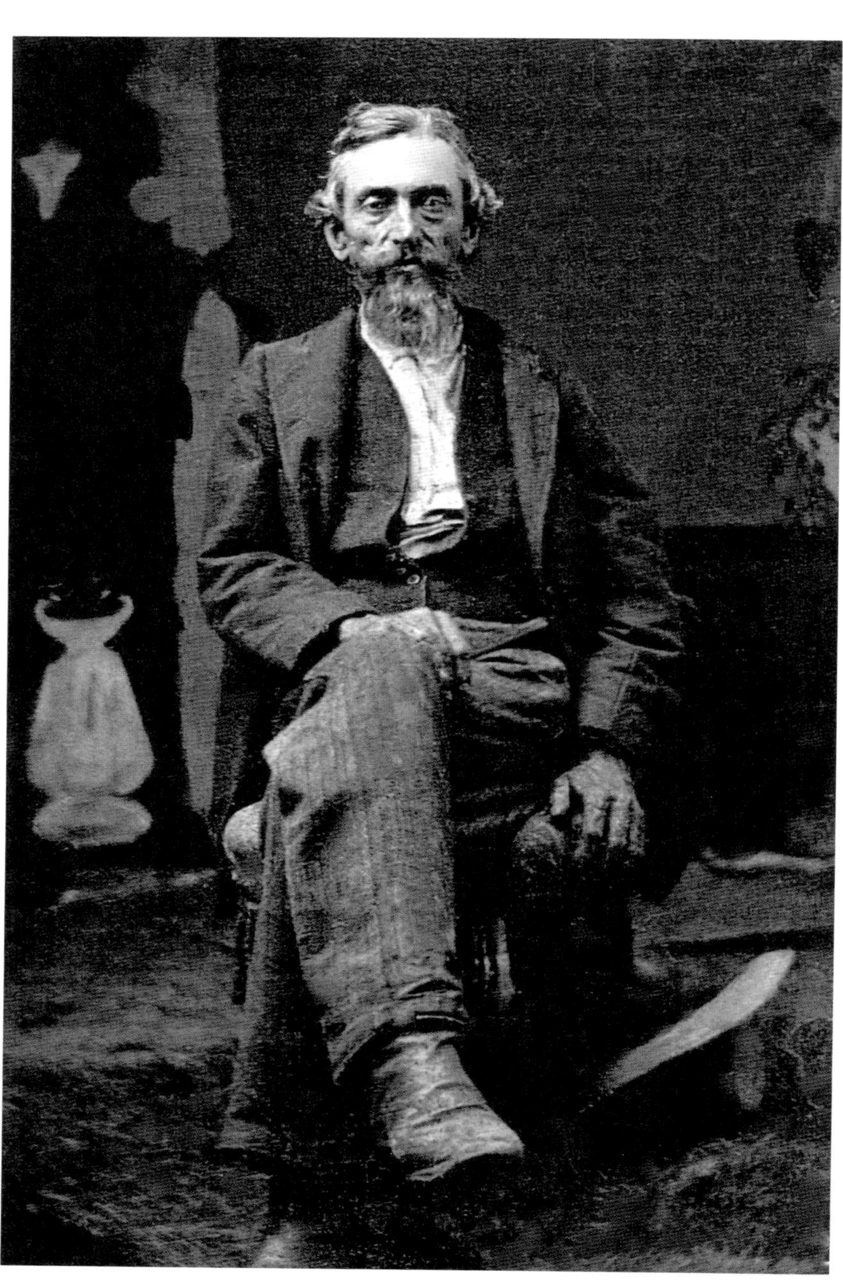

Figure 1 Photograph of John Wesley Carpenter (1842–1913), ca. 1880–1885. (Courtesy of the Carpenter family.)

Stephen C. Compton

John Wesley Carpenter (1842–1913): Tradition, Innovation, and Adaptation in the Post–Civil War South

▼ THIS ACCOUNT IS ABOUT the eighteenth-century migration of German-speaking farmers and artisans from Pennsylvania to North Carolina's backcountry, and focuses on one of the families that was affected in immeasurable ways by a nation and state divided by revolution and civil war. It is also the tale of how a member of that family, an entrepreneurial artisan named John Wesley Carpenter, brought new hope and a degree of prosperity to his beleaguered and war-weary family when he journeyed with them from North Carolina to Pipers Gap, Virginia, where he operated a pottery shop, planted orchards, made peach and apple brandy, and peddled herbal medications (fig. 1).[1]

The Carpenters in the Catawba Valley

A scarcity of available tillable land in Pennsylvania led many settlers to migrate to North Carolina during the second half of the eighteenth and the early nineteenth centuries. Perhaps hearing of the Moravians' successes in North Carolina and the fertile land available there, other German-speaking farmers and artisans moved into the area's western Piedmont Region to the Catawba Valley section.[2] The Catawba Valley region mainly encompasses Lincoln and Catawba counties, where family names like Crouse, Heafner, Huffman, and Reinhardt remain prominent. Moreover, the Catawba Valley is known among pottery collectors for its uniquely Southern alkaline-glazed stoneware tradition.

One eighteenth-century pioneer who relocated from Pennsylvania to the South Fork of the Catawba River was Hans Zimmerman (ca. 1702–1794). A friend of Moravian bishop August Gottlieb Spangenberg (1704–1792), Zimmerman might have been called John Carpenter in North Carolina, as early American Zimmermans frequently adopted the anglicized name Carpenter to accommodate naturalization.[3] Carpenter family histories suggest that Hans Zimmerman, who was probably Swiss by birth, and his wife, Salome, were John Wesley Carpenter's earliest North Carolina ancestors.[4]

Hans Zimmerman's son, Christian "CZ" (a.k.a. Christopher) Carpenter (ca. 1720/22–1800), was active in community affairs, and in 1775 was one of forty-eight Tryon County citizens who signed a document establishing the Tryon Association. Lincoln County was formed in 1779 from a portion of now-defunct Tryon County. The signers of the Tryon Resolves did so in protest of British actions taken earlier in Boston.[5] According to Lincoln County historian William L. Sherrill, CZ Carpenter was among those who strongly advocated American independence.[6] However, the cause of liberty often divided families, and some Carpenters apparently sided with the Tories. Christian Carpenter's son, John, a British Loyalist, moved to Nova Scotia and later Prince Edward Island after being wounded as a Tory at Ramsour's Mill.[7] Like his brother John (1742–1816), Christopher (also called Christian and Christy) Carpenter (ca. 1745/50–after 1810) abruptly fled North Carolina sometime after 1779, suggesting that he, too, was a Tory.[8] Christopher Carpenter is John Wesley Carpenter's great-grandfather through CZ Carpenter and Hans Zimmerman.

About 1830, John Wesley Carpenter's grandfather "Cumberland" John Carpenter (ca. 1775–after 1850), John Wesley's apparent namesake and the son of Christopher Carpenter, moved from Lincoln County, North Carolina, to Bedford (later Marshall) County, Tennessee. Before his departure, John's son Elias (1812–1881) was born in North Carolina. Elias may have been the first in the Carpenter family to make pottery.

In addition to John Wesley, at least three more of Elias's sons and a grandson made pottery. In 1860 Elias's household included a twenty-one-year-old "crocker" named Alexander Stamey (1821–1893). Potter John Alrand (b. 1834) lived next door.[9] All of this together supposes Elias's involvement in the trade. Both Stamey and Alrand came to Lincoln County from neighboring Burke County, North Carolina, though little more is known about Alrand. Stamey's brother, John (ca. 1798–1885), is referred to as "Potter Stamey" in a Clay County, North Carolina, estate-settlement document, suggesting that more than one family member made pottery.[10]

German-speaking neighbors surrounded the Carpenters. Almost everyone farmed, and some were also artisans who provided essential services and products to community residents. Potters were among the first to arrive in the region, among them Christopher Culp, John Dietz, David Hartzog, John Hefner, David Mauney, Henry Miller, John Pope, Peter Reese, Daniel (and perhaps his father, Adam) Seagle, Moses Seitz, Jacob Weaver, and Andrew Yount.[11]

Elias Carpenter married Sarah "Sally" Salina Johnson (1811–1880), whose brother, Amon Locke Johnson (1816–1893), was a potter, as were his sons, Harvey Make (1846–1931), Joseph Daniel (1848–1948), and Wade Dixon Cooper (1850–1931).

Amon Johnson's nephew, Eli (1836–1917), the son of storekeeper William Burgin Johnson (1808–1866) and Elizabeth Carpenter (ca. 1804–after 1880), was a potter, too. William Burgin Johnson married Elias Carpenter's sister, Elizabeth, in 1834.[12] While serving in the Confederate Army, Eli Johnson received a leg wound from a gunshot in 1864.[13] In 1870 Eli resided in Bandys Township, Catawba County, North Carolina. His cousins Joseph and Harvey Johnson lived with him and his wife, Mary (Martha A.) Lawrence Johnson. Each man was called a "mechanic," describing his role as an artisan.[14] In 1880 Eli Johnson worked in the Jacobs Fork Township as a Catawba County potter.[15] Eli's brother John Johnson says that Eli "moved his pottery to Virginia after the Civil War and there continued in the same work for many years."[16] By 1900, Eli

Johnson lived in the Pine Creek Magisterial District of Carroll County, Virginia, putting his residence to the northeast of, but not far from, his Carroll County Carpenter relatives.[17]

Amon Johnson operated a pottery shop in Lincoln County (later Catawba County) in an area called Jugtown.[18] He also served as Jugtown's postmaster, as did his son, Wade D. C. Johnson.[19] During the Civil War, Amon served in Company C, 4th Regiment, North Carolina Senior Reserves. When he enlisted, in 1864, he was forty-seven years old.[20] After the war, his son Wade remained in North Carolina and made pottery alongside his father for the rest of his life (figs. 2, 3). Amon Johnson's sons, Harvey Make (after whom John Wesley Carpenter named his first son) and Joseph Daniel Johnson, moved to South Carolina, married Lanford sisters there, and set up a pottery shop near Lanford Station in Laurens County.[21]

In 1840 Amon Johnson lived only a few households away from notable potters Daniel Seagle (ca. 1805–1867), David Hartzog (1808–1883), and

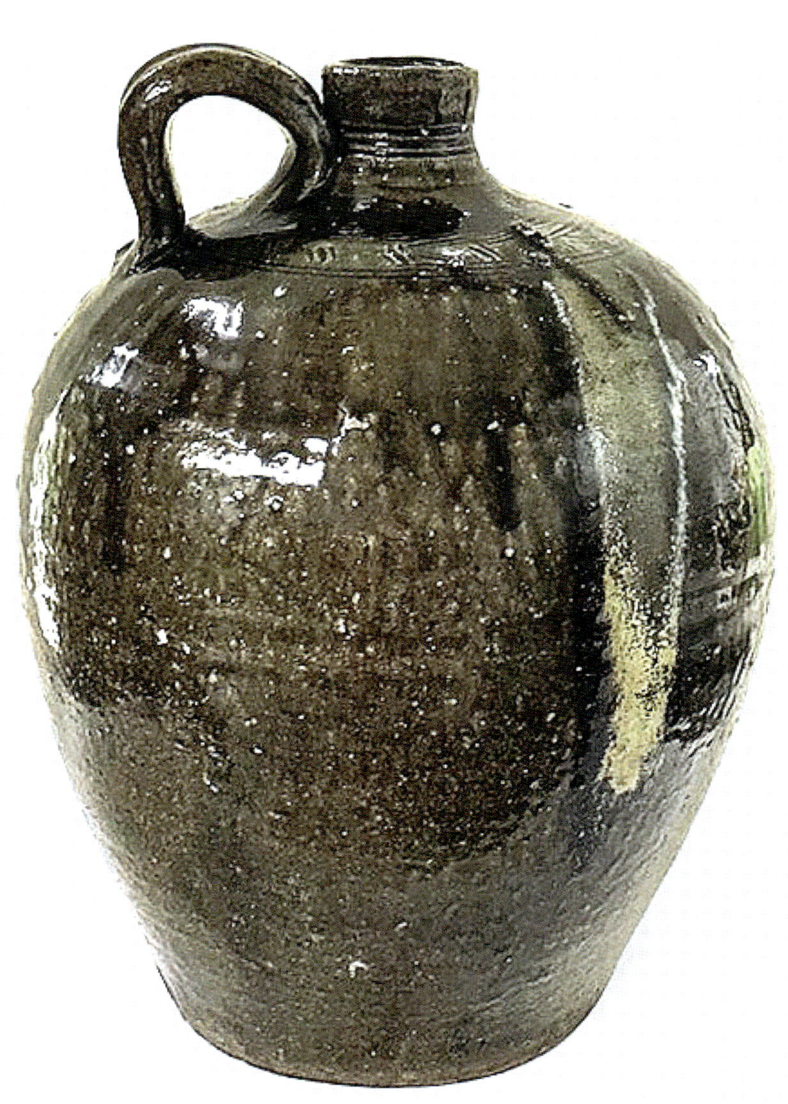

Figure 2 Jug, attributed to Wade D. C. Johnson (1850–1931), Catawba County, North Carolina, ca. 1880–1900. Alkaline-glazed stoneware. H. 13¼". Mark: incised "W J" four times. (Courtesy, Southern Folk Pottery Collectors Society.)

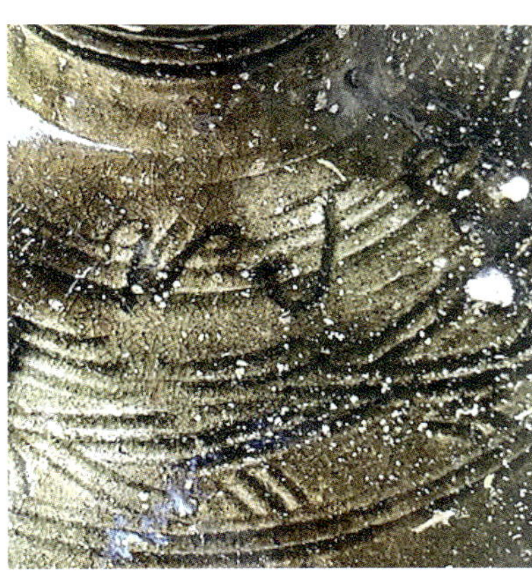

Figure 3 Detail of the jug illustrated in fig. 2.

Daniel Holly (1811–1899).[22] Holly was apprenticed to Seagle in 1828. As their contemporary, it stands to reason that he learned pottery-making from one of them or a potter associated with them. Perhaps Amon Johnson and Elias Carpenter were trained together, leading to Carpenter's introduction to Johnson's sister, Sarah Salina, whom he married in 1832.[23]

The Johnson family had close ties to the pottery-making Ritchie (Rüetschi) family. Wares made by Johnson and Carpenter potters are noted for traits similar to those seen on Ritchie-made pottery, so it is likely that training, or a working relationship, connected these families. Wade D. C. Johnson married Sarah Lavina Wyont Ritchie (1854–1915), the widow of potter Joseph Walter Ritchie (1854–1883).[24] Joseph's father was potter Thomas Ritchie (1825–1909). Amon Johnson's daughter, Sarah Ann (1843–1923), widow of Alfred A. Heavner (Havnaer; Havner), married Thomas Ritchie's brother, Henry (b. 1822).[25] The Heavners' sons, Royal Pinkney (1868–1929) and Harvey Hightower (1874–1961), made pottery in Catawba County.[26] They may have learned the trade from their stepfather, Henry, or another Ritchie potter. Susannah "Susan" Johnson (1850–1922), the daughter of William Burgin and Elizabeth Carpenter Johnson, and niece of Amon Johnson and Elias Carpenter, lived with and worked as a servant/housekeeper for Thomas Ritchie and, later, for his sons Robert and Luther Seth Ritchie.[27]

Thomas and Henry Ritchie were sons of potter Moses Ritchie (b. ca. 1793). Moses Ritchie's first cousin, Paul Ritchie (b. 1810), also was a potter.[28] Born in Cabarrus County, North Carolina, Moses Ritchie may have been trained there by an earthenware potter before moving to Surry County (later Yadkin County), North Carolina, where he lived near Huntsville (est. 1792). Silas Vestal (b. 1799) operated a pottery shop there before moving to Greene County, Tennessee, and Ritchie may have worked there as a journeyman.[29] Three of Ritchie's sons—Henry (b. 1822), Thomas (b. 1825), and Joseph (b. ca. 1829), all born in Surry County—made pottery. Moses Ritchie could have received his training through apprenticeship to one of several potters who worked in the vicinity of Cabarrus County, including Henry (Johann Heinrich) Wenzel (1734–1797), Benedict Mull (Moll) (1777–1857), or Thomas Pasinger (b. 1765), who was apprenticed under Moravian potter Henry (Johann Heinrich) Barroth (d. 1799) in Salisbury, Rowan County, North Carolina.[30] On the other hand, he could have learned the trade in the Catawba Valley from someone among the Seagle-Hartzog school of potters.[31]

Elias and Sarah Salina Johnson Carpenter had four daughters and six sons.[32] Their eldest son, William Franklin "Frank" Carpenter (1833–1873), called himself a carriage maker in 1860.[33] Alkaline-glazed stoneware marked "WFC" suggests that he was also a potter (fig. 4). John Johnson, whose brother was potter Eli Johnson, confirmed in a letter written in 1928 that "Franklin Carpenter was a potter until his death about 65 years ago."[34]

Having more than one trade at the time was not unusual. Potters often called themselves farmers even when it was known that they made pottery; similarly, others who called themselves blacksmiths, teachers, or ministers also were known to practice the trade of potter. Decorative incised-line patterns added to WFC-marked pieces further connect Frank Carpenter to other family members' pottery making and traits associated with Seagle, Hartzog, and especially Ritchie family potters.

Frank Carpenter's leg was wounded at the Battle of Gettysburg on July 1, 1863.[35] During the war, he suffered numerous bouts of illness and spent much of the time in hospitals, at home on sick leave, and as a prisoner of war.[36] In 1870 he called himself a Lincoln County farmer.[37] Three years later, on April 10, 1873, he died from an unknown cause. By then, three of his brothers were living in Carroll County, Virginia, where they made pottery. In 1880 his widow, Mary Hoffman Carpenter, resided near Lincoln County potters James F. Seagle (1829–1892), son of Daniel, and John Goodman (1822–1907), who married Daniel Seagle's daughter, Barbara.[38] Goodman's brothers, Michael (b. 1824) and Jacob Tobias (b. 1828), from Cabarrus County (like Moses Ritchie), were potters. In 1850 Michael Goodman's neighbor was potter Alexander Hill (b. ca. 1813), a Surry County native and an acquaintance of Moses Ritchie.[39] According to family historian Robert C. Carpenter, "The family of William Franklin Carpenter tell (*sic*) the story that all of his relatives left Lincoln Co. They returned once and found his widow Mary E. and family in severe poverty. They left some items for the family."[40] Edith Carpenter Riggins (1931–2021) claimed that family members moved from Lincoln County to Carroll County, Virginia, due to an overabundance of potters and impoverishment.[41]

Figure 4 Details of the jugs illustrated in fig. 8, both inscribed "WFC" and "2".

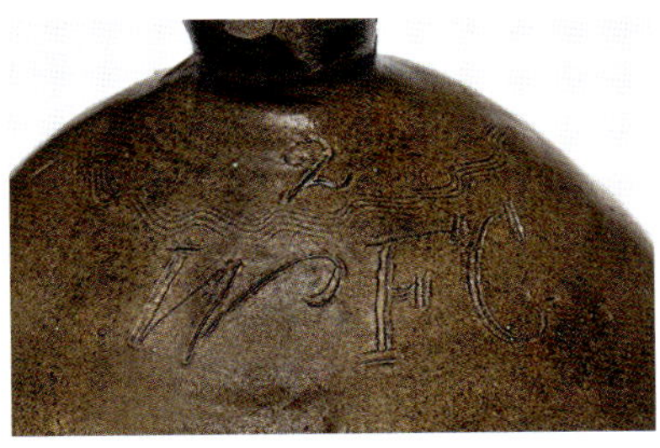

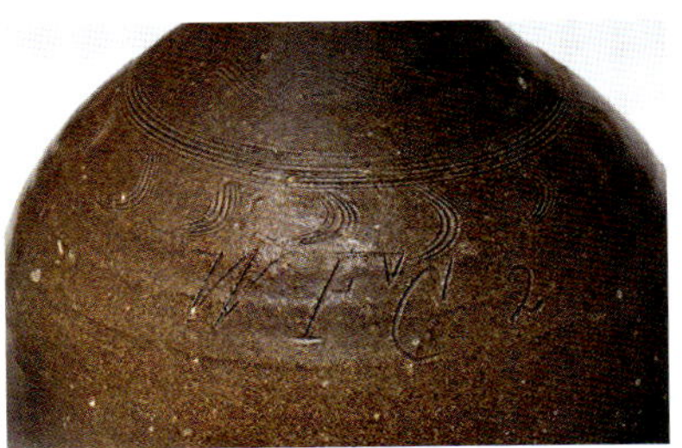

The second son of Elias and Sarah Salina Carpenter, Jacob Carpenter (1837–1862), called himself a blacksmith when enlisting to serve the Confederacy on August 8, 1861. Six months later, on February 13, 1862, he died at home while on furlough due to an unidentified sickness.[42] Given that three of his brothers, and perhaps his father, Elias, made pottery, it is likely that he was trained as a potter, too.

Days after Jacob's death, on February 22, 1862, Private John C. Speagle (b. ca. 1839), who married Elias and Sarah Salina Carpenter's daughter, Martha M. Carpenter (1840–1918), died from acute meningitis at Camp Fisher, Virginia.[43] In 1870 his widow and his son Andrew Franklin "Frank" Speagle (b. ca. 1858) lived with Elias and Sally Carpenter.[44] Frank Speagle may have worked as a potter with Wythe County, Virginia, potter Ephraim Buck around 1880 when he lived about three houses away.[45] Following his first wife's death, Frank Speagle married Carroll County, Virginia, native Malinda Jones on December 14, 1880.[46]

Elias's son, Michael "Mike" Rufus Carpenter (1844–1917), was wounded in Virginia on October 14, 1863, at the Battle of Bristoe Station. He received a Minié ball shot to his left leg, just below his knee, injuring his tibia. Afterward, as his recovery allowed, he worked as an ambulance driver and drove a cooking utensil wagon as a regimental teamster. Captured by Union forces near Petersburg on March 27, 1865, he was released after the war on June 26, 1865.[47] His disability troubled him for the remainder of his life, though he farmed and worked in John Wesley Carpenter's Pipers Gap, Virginia, pottery shop to the best of his ability. On September 1, 1917, Mike Carpenter died from injuries received from a fall, no doubt related to failing strength in his leg. His spinal cord was broken, causing complete paralysis of his lower body.[48]

When Elias's son Adolphus Lafayette Carpenter (1846–1933) enlisted with the Confederacy at age seventeen, he united with Company B, 8th Battalion, North Carolina Junior Reserves. As with so many others, dysentery (attributed to colitis) placed him in a military hospital and furloughed him for home recovery.[49] Though he called himself a farmer when he enlisted, in 1870 and 1880 he told the Carroll County, Virginia's census taker that he was a potter.[50] By 1880 Elias, Sarah Salina, and their daughter, Barbara, resided in Carroll County, next to Adolphus and his wife, Mary Lingafelt (Lingerfelt) Carpenter.[51] Around 1884, Adolphus moved his family to Sni-A-Bar township, Jackson County, Missouri, where he lived for the remainder of his life. It is not known if he made pottery there.[52]

Figure 5 Genealogical chart showing the interrelationship between several pottery-making families, among them Carpenters, Johnsons, and Ritchies.

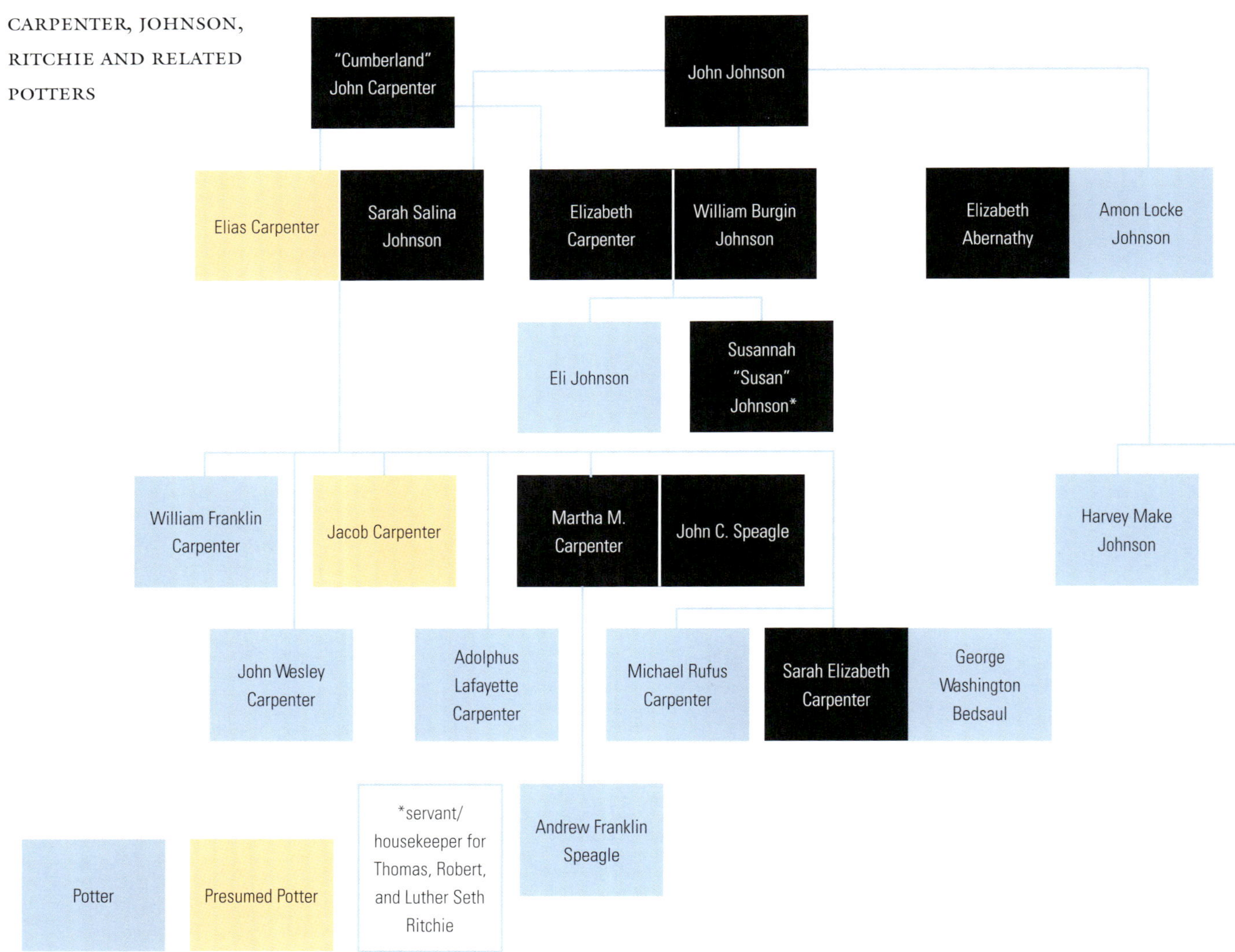

According to granddaughter Edith Carpenter Riggins, one of John Wesley Carpenter's legs was shorter than the other, likely preventing his enlistment as an infantry soldier during the Civil War.[53] A pension application filed by his wife, Emily, suggests that he enrolled in Company E, 9th Regiment, North Carolina Reserves.[54] Records for this unit are scarce, and the range of his military activity is unclear.

Following the war, when John Wesley Carpenter, still a single man, departed from Lincoln County to make a new start in Pipers Gap, Carroll County, Virginia, he and his brothers, Adolphus and Michael, carried with them the memories of war, sickness, death, and disruption of a promising future. Their grief was compounded when, not long after the war's end, their brother Frank died, too.

The Carpenters' woeful memories surely extended to the Johnson family. According to potter Harvey Make Johnson's daughter, "Papa was a poor little foot soldier who joined the 11th North Carolina Regiment, in the Confederate Army, when he was 16. He was captured in his first battle

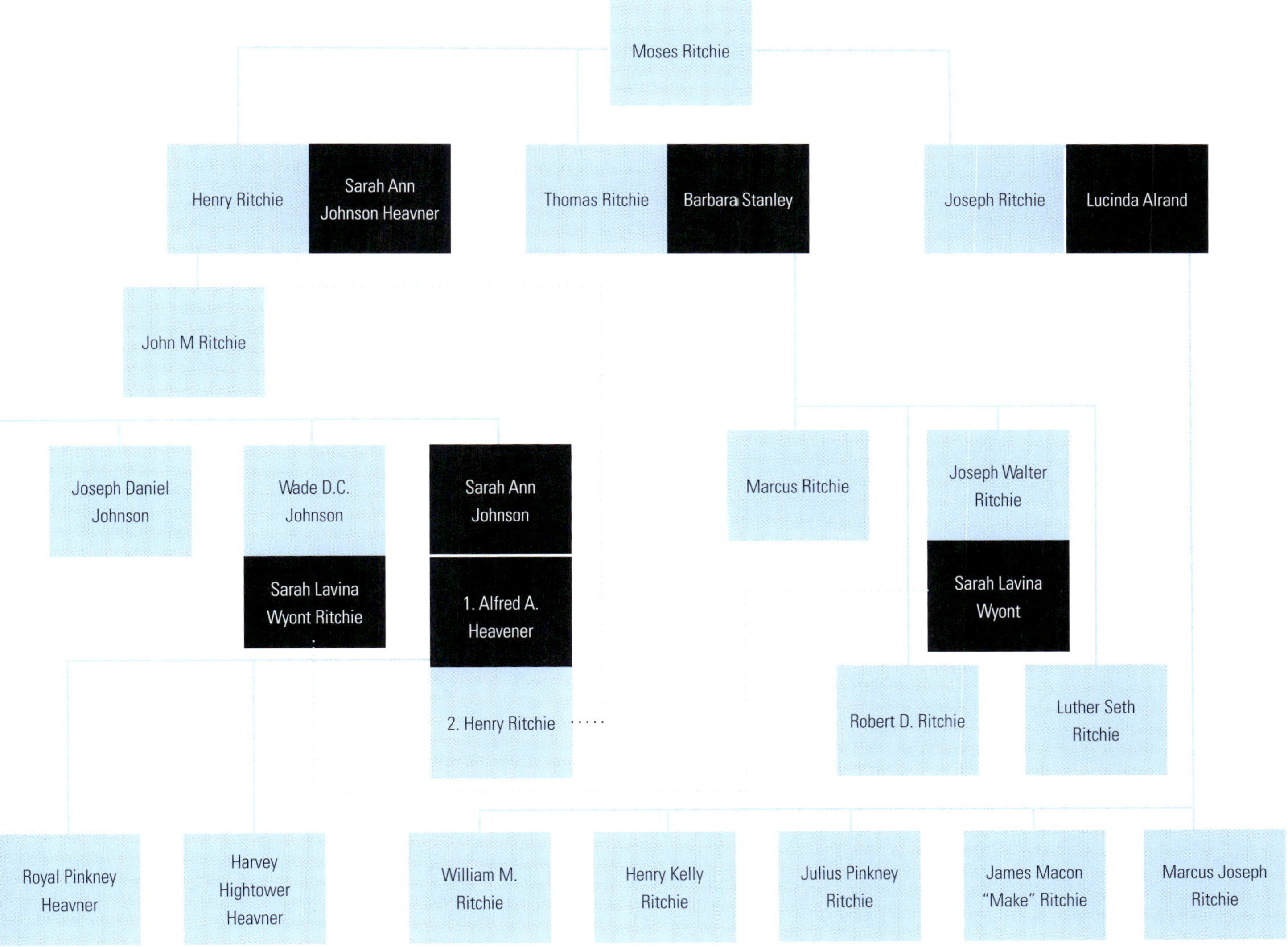

and not paroled until the war ended. We'd ask him about how the war was and he'd say, 'Horrible. Horrible.'"[55]

John Wesley Carpenter, who was neither the eldest nor the youngest of his male siblings, took on the task of guiding his surviving family members beyond their postwar miseries toward a new, more hopeful future. His own war experience may not have been as traumatic as that of his brothers and brother-in-law, but the pain of their loss and suffering indeed weighed heavily upon the Carpenter family. Their move away from Lincoln County to Pipers Gap, Virginia, initiated their restoration of prewar dreams. The Carpenters did not go to Pipers Gap without a purpose or essential skills required for their success. They were potters before they arrived there, and pottery-making was their best hope for finding their way forward (fig. 5).

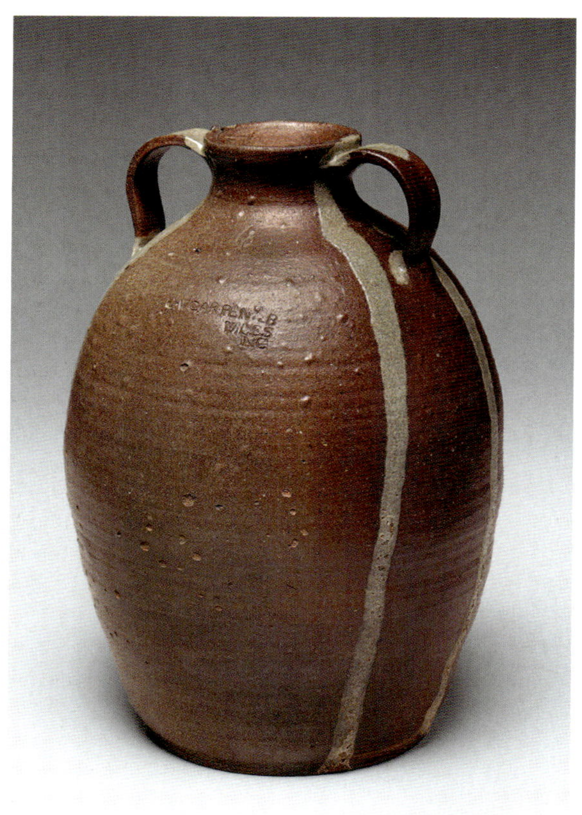

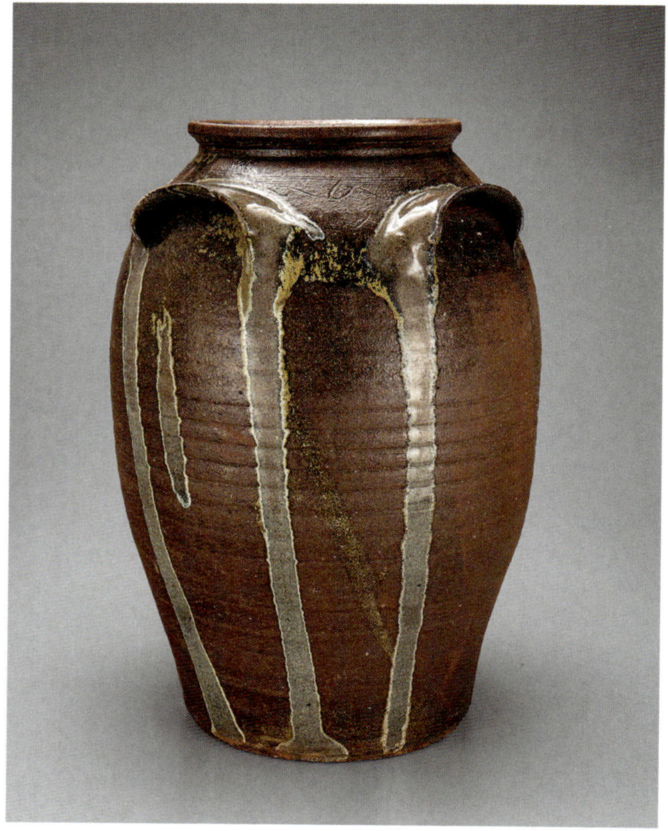

Figure 6 Six-gallon jug, J. W. Carpenter Pottery, Wiles, Wilkes County, North Carolina, ca. 1890. Salt-glazed stoneware with glass runs. H. 17⅜". Mark: "J.W. CARPEN[TE]R /WILES/NC" (Courtesy, Wilkes Heritage Museum, Kenneth Johnson Collection; photo, Tim Barnwell Photography.) Long presumed to be associated with John Wesley Carpenter, this late-nineteenth-century pottery shop was owned and operated by James Welborn Carpenter. No family relationship between the two potters is known.

Figure 7 Six-gallon jar with four lug handles, attributed to J. W. Carpenter Pottery, Wiles, Wilkes County, North Carolina, ca. 1890. Salt-glazed stoneware with glass runs. H. 16½". Mark: "6" (William C. and Susan S. Mariner Collection; photo, Robert Hunter.)

The Catawba Valley Wares

It has long been supposed that alkaline-glazed stoneware marked "JWC" and "JC" and attributed to John Wesley Carpenter was made in association with the J. W. Carpenter pottery, located in Wiles, Wilkes County, North Carolina (figs. 6, 7). However, that shop belonged to James Welborn Carpenter, not John Wesley Carpenter, and no evidence of their association has been found. An 1892 Wilkes County deed made out by J. W. and Elizabeth Carpenter to the State of North Carolina in order to secure a fine due from a convicted man named R. F. Baldwin, describes the thirty-five-acre tract as "where on we live and on which is located J. W. Carpenter's jug factory."[56] Additional documents identify this man as James Welborn Carpenter. Philip Carpenter (ca. 1835–1918), originally of Wake County, North Carolina, was Welborn Carpenter's father. No record of kinship to John Wesley Carpenter has been discovered.[57]

With that long-held misunderstanding resolved, it is now believed that John Wesley Carpenter and his family members made alkaline-glazed stoneware in Lincoln County before moving to Virginia, with some of it marked "JWC" (for John Wesley Carpenter) and "WFC" (for William Franklin Carpenter).

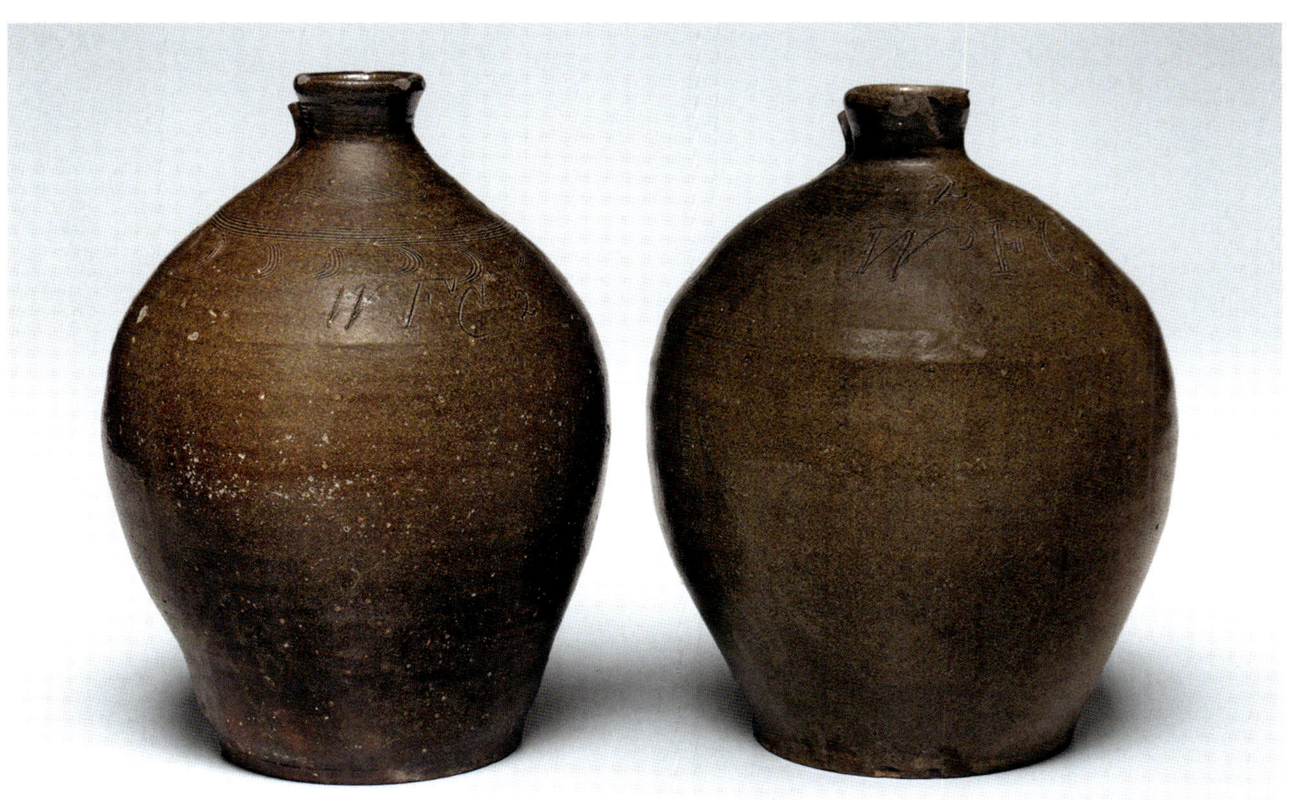

Figure 8 Two-gallon jugs, attributed to William Franklin Carpenter, Lincoln County, North Carolina, ca. 1865–1873. Alkaline-glazed stoneware. *Left*: H. 13". Marks: incised "WFC" and "2" (Southern Folk Pottery Collectors Society Collection.) *Right*: H. 12½". Marks: incised "WFC" and "2" (Author's collection; photo, Tim Barnwell Photography.)

Both of the alkaline-glazed jugs shown in figure 8 bear the initials "WFC" (see figure 4) and incised, combed lines of decoration. The "2" on each one indicates two-gallon capacity. Close examination reveals fine lines (reeding) encircling the spout neck of the jug on the left in the image. Based on Frank Carpenter's age, these jugs were probably made between 1850 and 1862, or after the Civil War to the time of his death, from 1865 to 1873.

More examples signed "JWC" are known. In addition to its glass runs, the bulbous, two-handle jug shown in figure 9 shows a tapered, reeded spout neck made up of a series of finely cut lines and a band of incised-line decoration around its middle. The jug shown in figure 10 has a similar spout neck and simple parallel lines of incised decoration. Spout necks styled like these are also seen on jugs made in Thomas Ritchie's shop, such as the one shown in figure 11. The jug signed "JWC" that is shown in figure 12

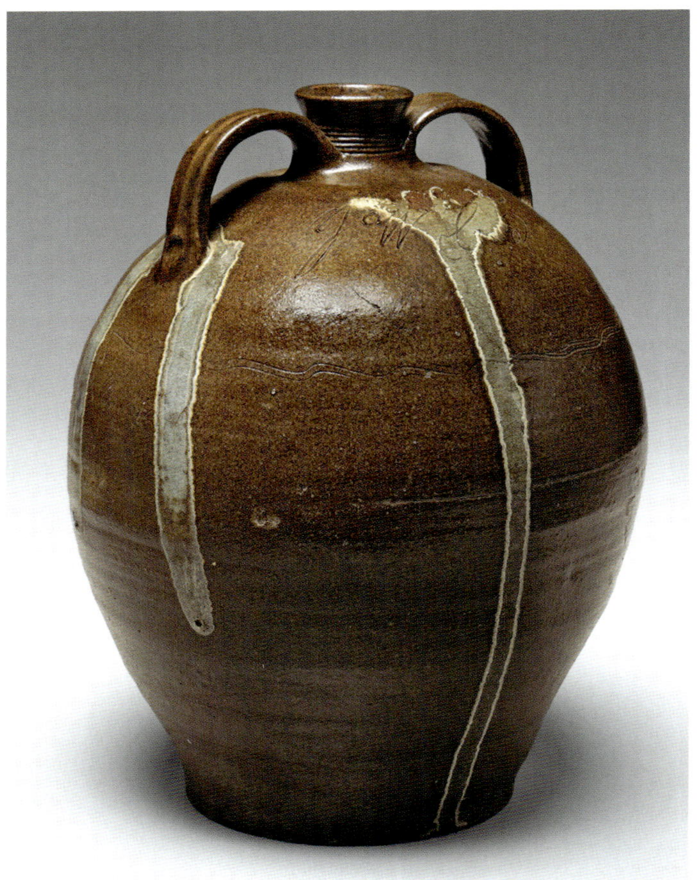

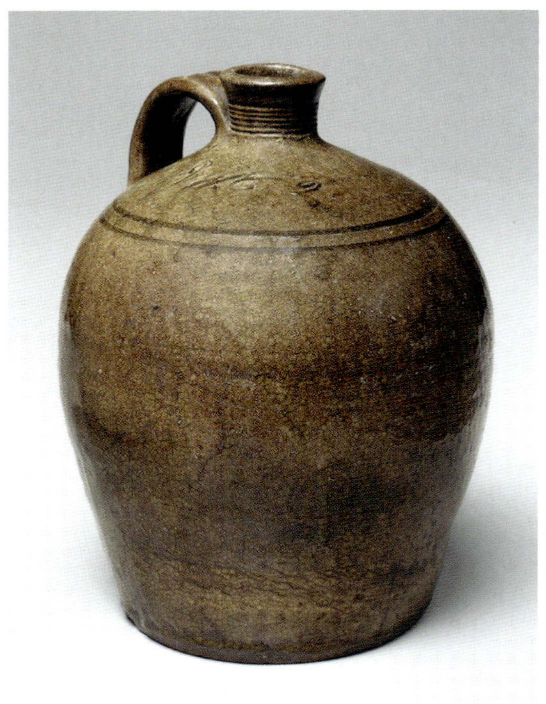

Figure 9 Five-gallon jug, attributed to John Wesley Carpenter, Lincoln County, North Carolina, ca. 1865–1870. Alkaline-glazed stoneware with glass runs. H. 16½". Mark: incised "JWC 5" (Courtesy, Wilkes Heritage Museum, Kenneth Johnson Collection; photo, Tim Barnwell Photography.) Opposite the signature are inscribed additional indecipherable letters/numerals. This jug, and other wares signed "JWC" in script, were probably made by Carpenter in Lincoln County, North Carolina, prior to his relocation to Pipers Gap, Virginia.

Figure 10 Two-gallon jug, attributed to John Wesley Carpenter, Lincoln County, North Carolina, ca. 1865–1870. Alkaline-glazed stoneware. H. 12½". Mark: incised "JWC 2" (Courtesy, Wilkes Heritage Museum, Kenneth Johnson Collection; photo, Tim Barnwell Photography.)

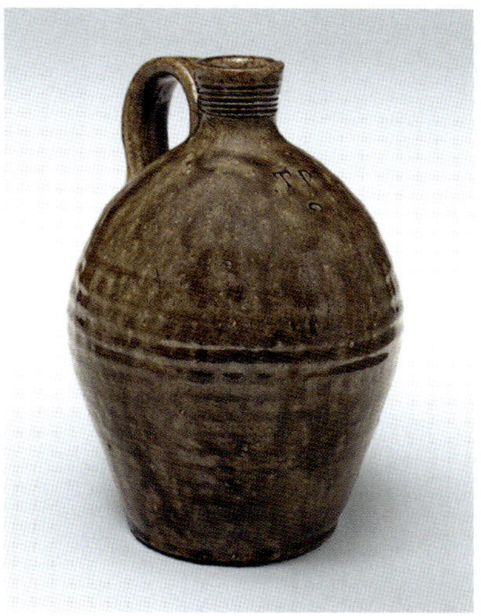

Figure 11 Half-gallon jug, Thomas Ritchie Pottery, Lincoln or Catawba County, North Carolina, second half of the nineteenth century. Alkaline-glazed stoneware. H. 8½". Mark: "TR 2" (J. M. Cline Collection; photo, Tim Barnwell Photography.) This jug's resemblance to the one attributed to John Wesley Carpenter in fig. 10—especially its tapered, fine-line reeded spout neck—suggests that Carpenter made it while working for Ritchie.

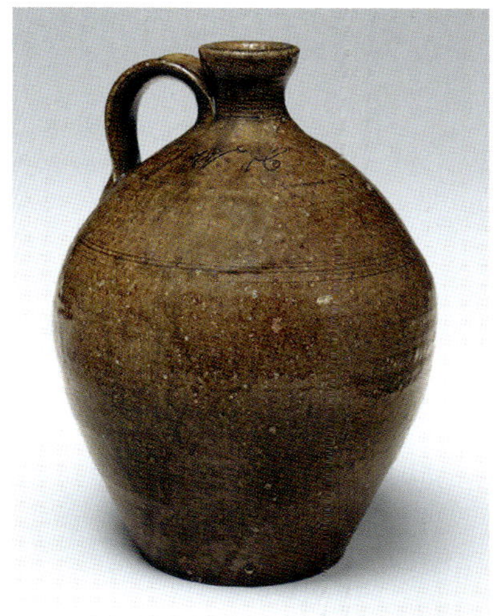

Figure 12 One-gallon jug, attributed to the John Wesley Carpenter pottery shop, Lincoln County, North Carolina, ca. 1865–1870. Alkaline-glazed stoneware. H. 11¼". Mark: incised "JWC 1" (numeral formed by a vertical series of dots). (Courtesy, Wilkes Heritage Museum, Kenneth Johnson Collection; photo, Tim Barnwell Photography.) This jug's form differs enough from the one in fig. 10 to suggest that a different potter was engaged in its production for John Wesley Carpenter's shop.

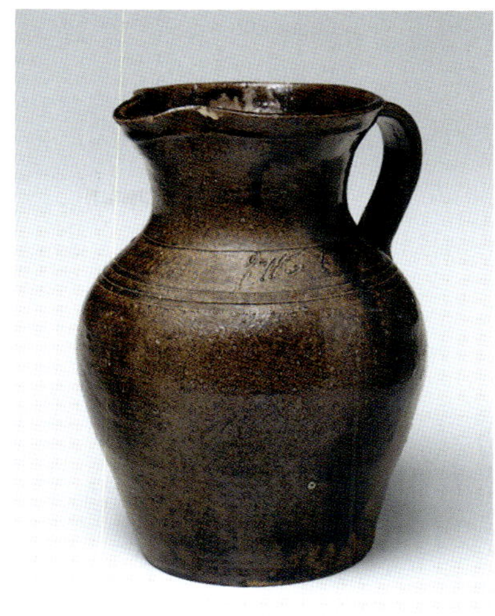

Figure 13 One-gallon pitcher, attributed to John Wesley Carpenter, Lincoln County, North Carolina, ca. 1865–1870. Alkaline-glazed stoneware. H. 9¾". Mark: incised "JWC 1" (Kenneth Johnson Collection; photo, Tim Barnwell Photography.) The handle has been restored.

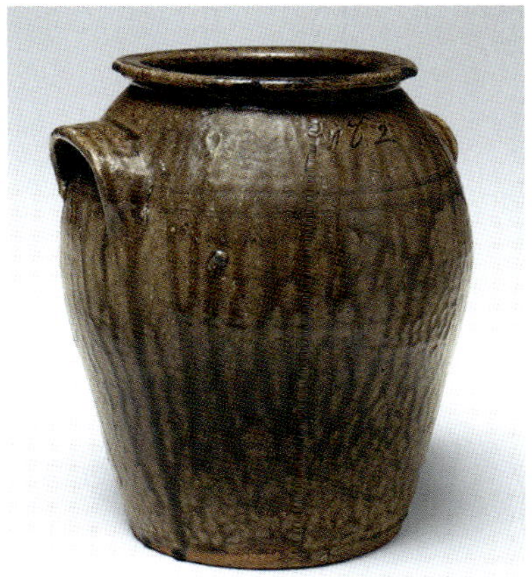

Figure 14 Two-gallon storage jar, attributed to John Wesley Carpenter, Lincoln County, North Carolina, ca. 1865–1870. Alkaline-glazed stoneware. H. 10¼". Mark: incised "JWC 2" (John Haynes Collection; photo, Tim Barnwell Photography.)

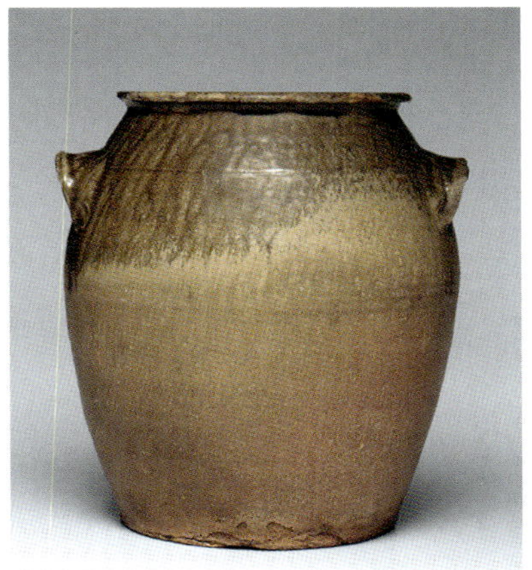

Figure 15 Four-gallon storage jar, attributed to John Wesley Carpenter, Pipers Gap, Virginia, last quarter of the nineteenth century. Alkaline-glazed stoneware. H. 13". (Carpenter Family Collection; photo, Tim Barnwell Photography.) This jar was recovered from an abandoned cellar situated below a chicken coop on the John Wesley and Emily Carpenter farm. The Carpenter pottery shop in Pipers Gap made salt-glazed and alkaline-glazed stoneware.

differs enough from the one shown in figure 10 to suggest that someone else working alongside John Wesley Carpenter made it. Lines of decoration surround the body of the pitcher shown in figure 13. The ovoid jar marked "JWC" in figure 14 is reminiscent of an unsigned alkaline-glazed example discovered in an abandoned chicken coop located at the home of John Wesley and Emily Carpenter in Piper's Gap, Virginia (fig. 15).

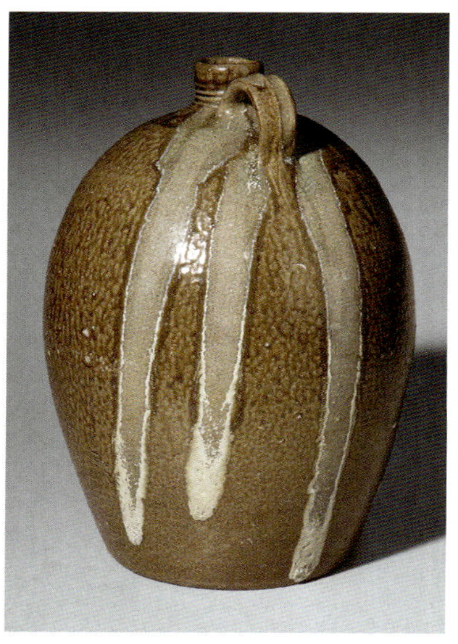

Figure 16 Four-gallon jug, Daniel Seagle, Lincoln County, North Carolina, ca. 1850. Alkaline-glazed stoneware with reeded spout neck and glass runs. H. 16". (Ackland Fund, Ackland Art Museum, The University of North Carolina at Chapel Hill, 82.19.2; photo, Jason Dowdle Photography.)

Figure 17 Jug, David Hartzog, Lincoln County, North Carolina, ca. 1830–1840. Alkaline-glazed stoneware with glass and iron slip runs. H. 12⅞". Mark: stamped "DAVIDHARTZOGHISMAKE" (The Museum of Early Southern Decorative Arts [MESDA] at Old Salem, 5812.)

Figures 18 Reverse view of the jug illustrated in fig. 17, showing the glass run from the handle.

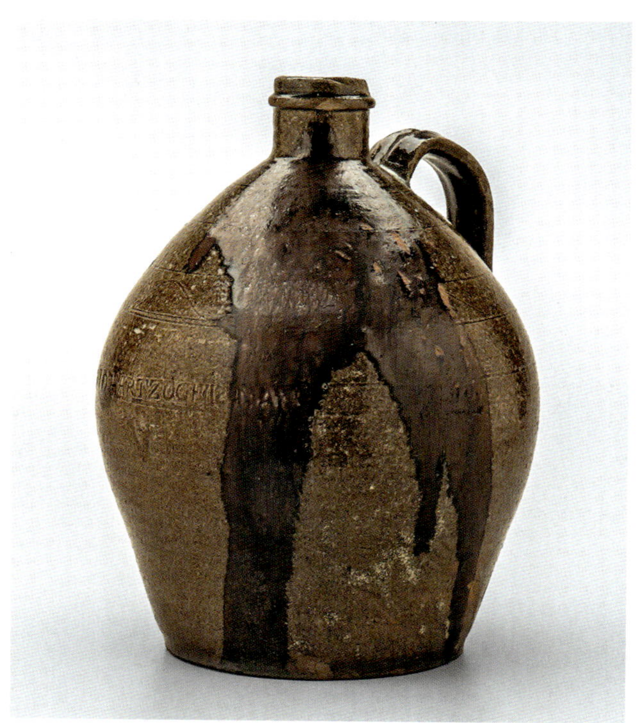

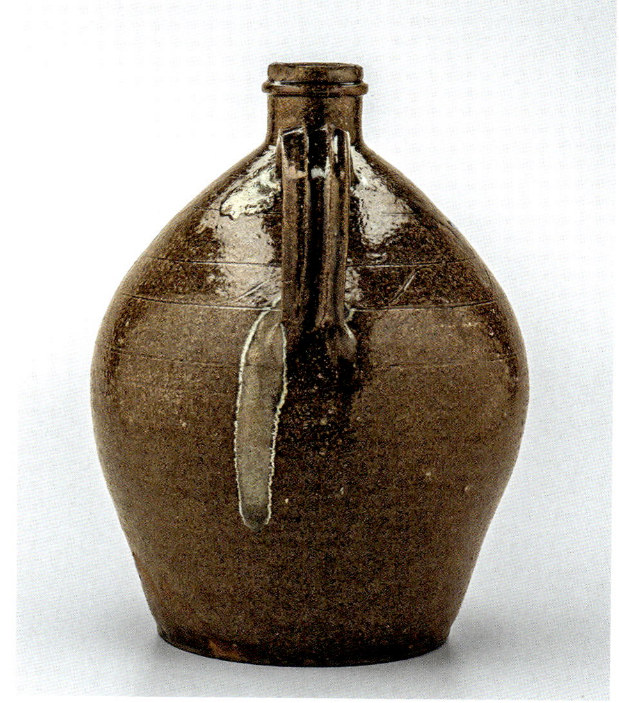

Undoubtedly, the Carpenter potters and their Johnson kin are connected through training. For example, the jug shown in figure 2—signed "WJ" (for Wade Johnson), like the Frank and John Wesley Carpenter examples—displays a reeded spout neck, straight and wavy lines of incised decoration, and a glass run. Those stylistic traits have long been associated with early Catawba Valley stoneware makers Daniel Seagle and David Hartzog. Wares made by Ritchie family potters share the characteristics, as likely do those made by others who learned the trade from someone in the Seagle-Hartzog school of potters.

The striking Daniel Seagle jug shown in figure 16 has a reeded spout neck and glass runs streaming through its alkaline glaze. Though it lacks a reeded spout neck, a David Hartzog jug has a glass run (and another that may contain iron) and a band of incised-line decoration (figs. 17, 18). Within the decorative band, Hartzog inscribed his mark: DAVIDHARTZOGHIƧMAKE.

The first Carpenter potter (presumably Elias Carpenter) and Johnson potter (Amon Johnson) surely learned the trade from one of the Catawba Valley's earliest stoneware makers. Given their age, those two men could have learned pottery-making ca. 1826–1837. If their sons did not learn the trade from them, then someone in the Ritchie family might have taught

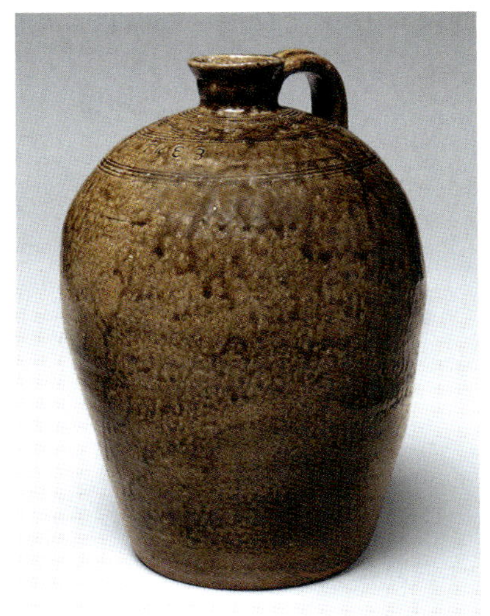

Figure 19 Three-gallon jug, Thomas Ritchie Pottery, Lincoln or Catawba County, North Carolina, second half of the nineteenth century. Alkaline-glazed stoneware. H. 14⅝". Mark: "TR Ɛ 3" (Robert and Beverly Simpson Collection; photo, Tim Barnwell Photography.) The jug has incised bands of decorative straight and wavy lines similar to those seen on numerous Carpenter pottery wares.

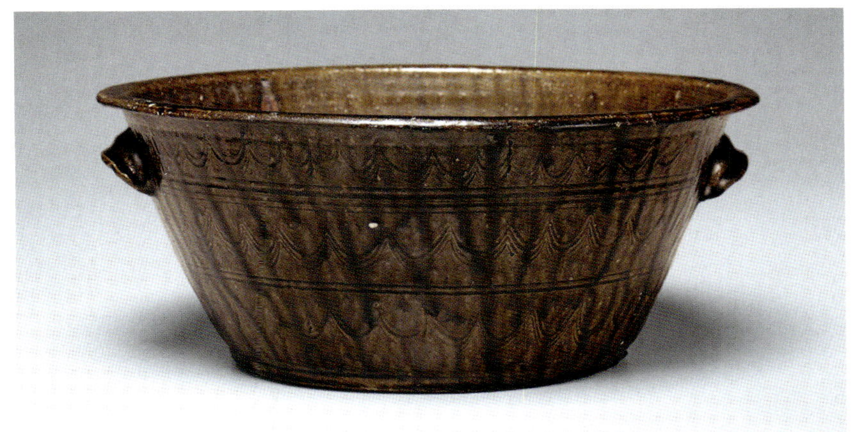

Figure 20 Pan, attributed to Thomas Ritchie Pottery, Lincoln or Catawba County, North Carolina, third quarter of the nineteenth century. Alkaline-glazed stoneware, H. 7", D. of rim 16". (Author's collection; photo, Tim Barnwell Photography.) This pan was ostensibly used by a Catawba Valley church for a Christian foot-washing ritual. Its form (especially its rim and handles) and decorative style suggest that John Wesley Carpenter was its maker, at his own or at Ritchie's Catawba Valley shop.

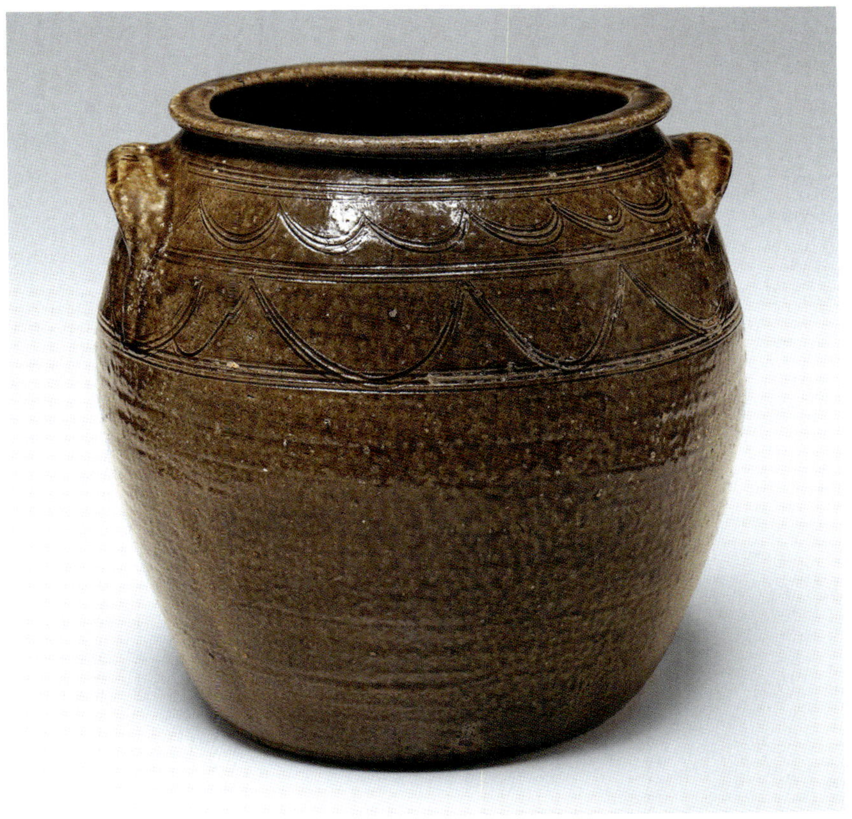

Figure 21 Four-gallon storage jar, attributed to Thomas Ritchie Pottery, Lincoln or Catawba County, North Carolina, second half of the nineteenth century. Alkaline-glazed stoneware. H. 12". Multiple marks, on handles: "4" (Robin and Kem Roberts Collection; photo, Tim Barnwell Photography.) A stamped four-gallon mark used by John Wesley Carpenter is similar. The horizontal rim form, handle shape, and decoration are similar to what is observed on some John Wesley Carpenter wares.

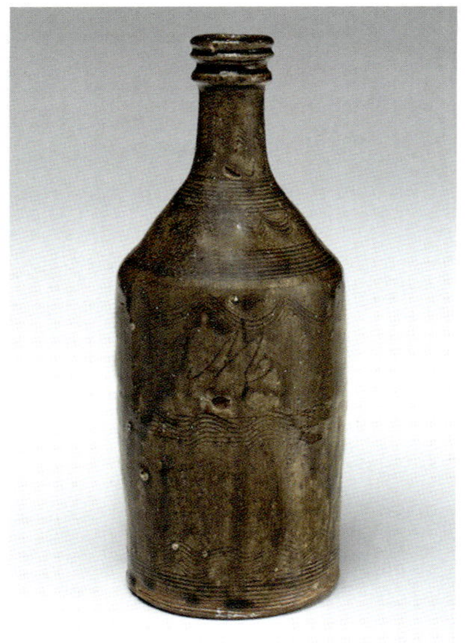

Figure 22 Bottle, attributed to Marcus Ritchie (ca. 1851–1883), Catawba County, North Carolina, ca. 1880. Alkaline-glazed stoneware. H. 10$\frac{13}{16}$". Mark: inscribed "M" (Danny Richard Collection; photo, Tim Barnwell Photography.) The style of the letter *M* matches an "MR" signature inscribed on a line-decorated storage jar dated 1882 (not shown). Marcus was the son of Thomas Ritchie (1825–1909).

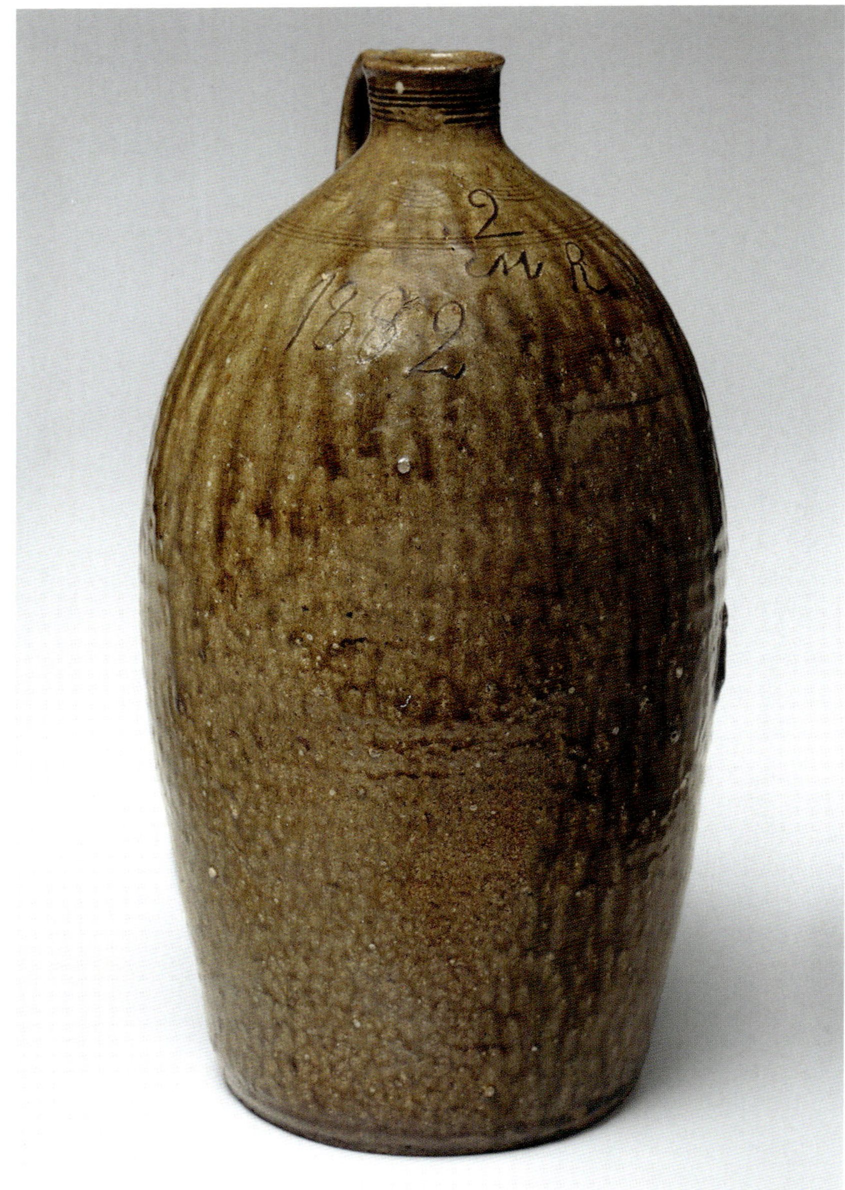

Figure 23 Two-gallon jug, attributed to Marcus Ritchie, Catawba County, North Carolina, dated 1882. Alkaline-glazed stoneware. H. 16". Marks: inscribed "MR / 2" and "1882" (David Parker Collection; photo, Tim Barnwell Photography.)

them. A prime candidate is Thomas Ritchie, son of potter Moses Ritchie. The decorative patterns seen on the "TR"-marked jug in figure 19 are similar to those found on numerous Carpenter-shop wares.

The pan shown in figure 20 and the ovoid jar shown in figure 21 are thought to have originated in Thomas Ritchie's shop. Each exhibits incised-line decoration remarkably similar to that applied by the Carpenters and associated potters to Pipers Gap, Virginia, wares. Many Thomas Ritchie jugs marked "TR" have reeded spout necks, and Ritchie sometimes added glass runs to his alkaline-glazed wares.

Comparing their decorated wares further advances a Ritchie connection to the Carpenters, including some made by Thomas Ritchie's son, Marcus, such as the bottle and jug shown in figures 22 and 23. Adolphus Carpenter and Marcus Ritchie were about the same age, and generationally, the sons of Thomas Ritchie, Elias Carpenter, and Amon Johnson were contemporaries. The similarity between the atypical jug spout seen on the Thomas Ritchie shop's jug and the one seen on the Carpenter Pottery's Pipers Gap jug (fig. 24) further suggests that one of the Carpenters was a trainee or worker at the Ritchie pottery.[58]

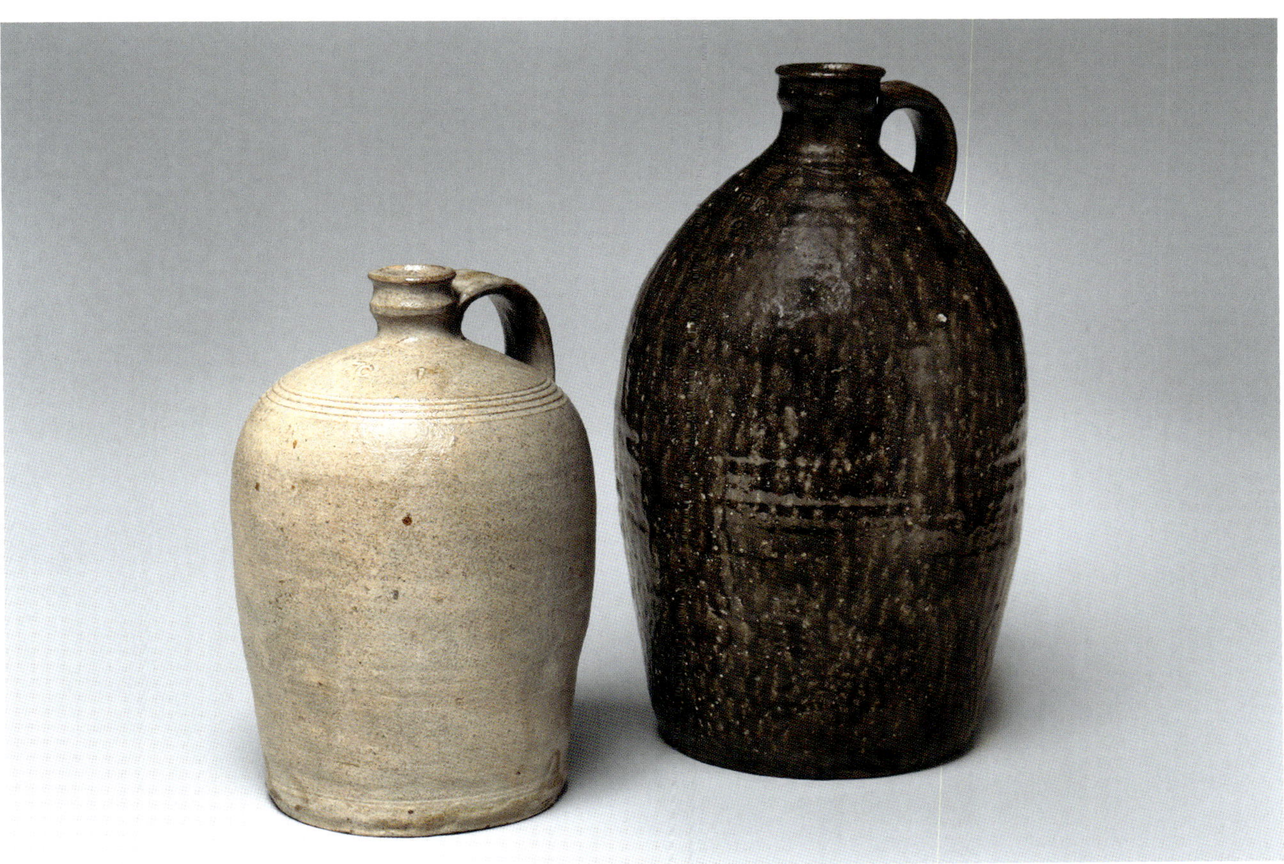

Figure 24 *Left*: Jug, Carpenter Pottery, Pipers Gap, Carroll County, Virginia, last quarter of the nineteenth century. Salt-glazed stoneware over kaolin slip. H. 10⅞". Mark: "JC 1" (L. A. and Suzan Rhyne Collection.) *Right*: Thomas Ritchie Pottery, Lincoln or Catawba County, North Carolina, second half of the nineteenth century. Alkaline-glazed stoneware with multi-line band of incised decoration below neck. H. 14¾". Mark: "TR 2" (Southern Folk Pottery Collectors Society Collection; photo, Tim Barnwell Photography.)

The Carpenters in Pipers Gap

Regardless of the miseries he and others endured during the Civil War, John Wesley Carpenter must have struck out from the Catawba Valley for Virginia with a sense of hope (fig. 25). He possessed the skills of a potter and farmer. An entrepreneurial spirit and dreams bolstered those skills for a better future for himself and his extended family.

The amount of Virginia land he eventually possessed suggests that he farmed, which probably included cultivating fruit trees for brandy production.

Figure 25 Map showing a conjectured route traveled by Carpenter family members from their Catawba Valley home to Virginia. The route shown was well traveled in the 1860–1870 period. Its path ran east of the mountains and passed through or nearby the town of Huntsville, where Moses Ritchie once resided and probably made pottery, before climbing in its last miles up the Blue Ridge escarpment to Pipers Gap.

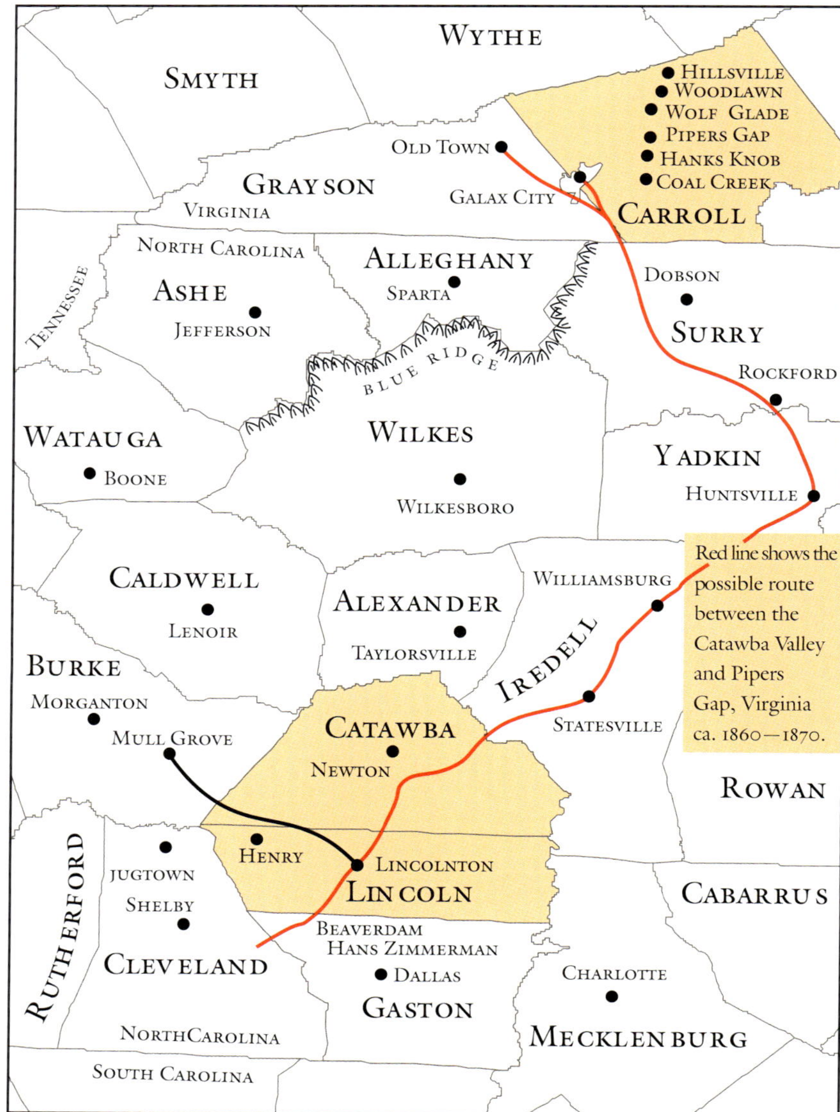

A 1910 letter to him from The Great American Herb Company of Washington, D.C., shows that he, as their agent, sold the enterprise's Indian Herbs products (figs. 26, 27). The company's assistant manager made plain their expectations of Carpenter: "We want your undivided interest in the work this year, and we are sure if you will work to get your people interested in their physical condition and in INDIAN HERBS as the safest and simplest remedy for them, you will not want to do anything else and will not need to."[59] The letter encouraged Carpenter to make a strong appeal to his prospective customers, that Indian Herbs was a remedy for numerous ailments: "Tell the sick people around you what we have told you, then make them understand that INDIAN HERBS is simple and harmless, but acts directly on the blood and liver, starting right and doing the work of rebuilding right from the foundation, so that the cure is sure and lasting when it is accomplished, and the patient can stay cured."[60]

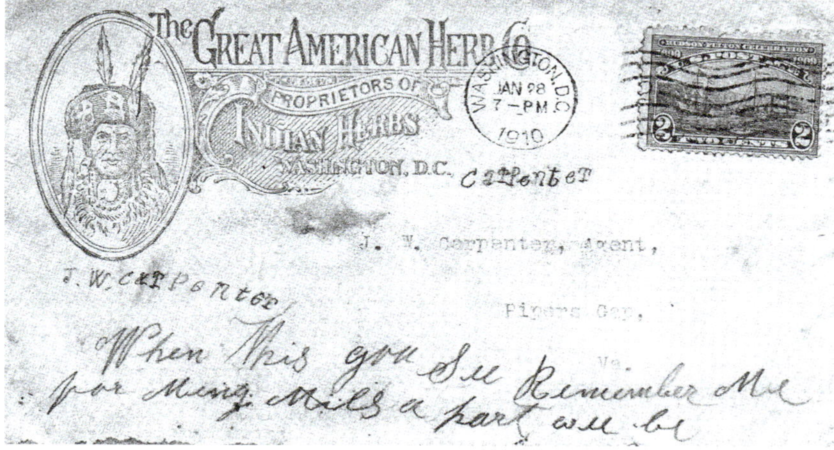

Figure 26 Postal envelope addressed to "J. W. Carpenter, Agent," from the Great American Herb Company, Washington, D.C., dated January 28, 1910. (John Carpenter Collection.)

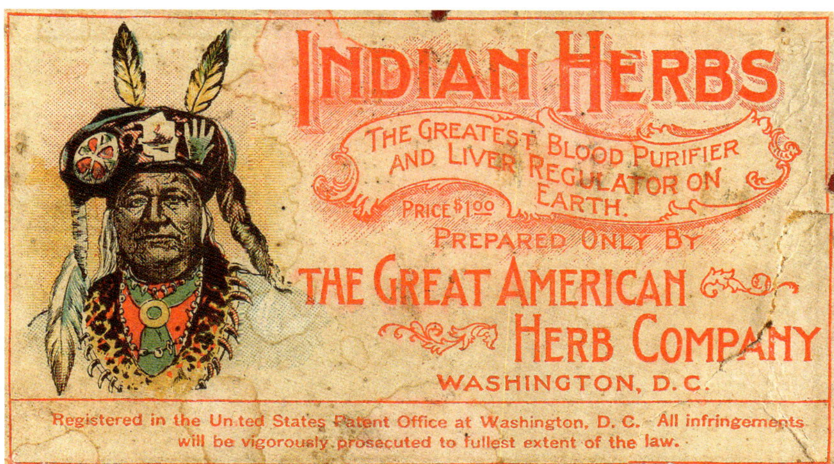

Figure 27 Box lid for Indian Herbs of the Great American Herb Company, Washington, D.C., ca. 1910. (John Carpenter Collection.)

Unfortunately, according to one family member's account, John Wesley Carpenter's belief in herbal medicine may have contributed to his death. After the removal with a pocket knife of a splinter lodged beneath his thumbnail led to blood poisoning, he died while relying on herbal treatment to cure his sickness.[61]

John Wesley and his brothers made many gains in Virginia. About 1868, brothers Michael Rufus and Adolphus Lafayette Carpenter left Lincoln County and settled just above the North Carolina state line near Pipers Gap in Carroll County, Virginia.[62] According to family lore, the Carpenters chose their new home because suitable clay for making pottery was available there, and their post–Civil War Lincoln County community was overrun by potters, which made making a living at their trade difficult.[63]

Both brothers called themselves potters when the 1870 U.S. Census taker visited in August of that year.[64] Michael, not yet married to Jane Bedsaul, resided with his brother Adolphus's family. Their brother, John Wesley Carpenter, lived in Carroll County before February 6, 1873, when he married Surphina Bedsaul.[65] His location when the 1870 census was made is not known. Since the ownership of the Pipers Gap pottery is most often associated with John Wesley (and most wares made there bear the initials JC or JWC), then it is possible that he arrived at about the same time as his brothers but was overlooked by the census taker. He called himself a potter when the next count was made, in 1880.[66] By then, the three Carpenter brothers had been joined in Pipers Gap by their parents, Elias and Sarah Salina, and their sister, Barbara. Elias's family residence is listed between those of potters Adolphus Carpenter and George [Washington] Bedsaul (1857–1889). John Wesley and Michael Carpenter lived a few miles away.

A search of land records suggests that the Carpenters did not immediately purchase land after moving to Virginia. All Carroll County land acquisitions appear to have been made jointly in the names of John Wesley and Michael Rufus Carpenter. Between 1875 and 1892, they purchased at least 263 acres. In 1897 John Wesley paid Michael and his wife, Jane Carpenter, $250 for 166 acres. On that same date, John Wesley, Emily (his second wife), and Michael Carpenter conveyed 133½ acres to Jane Carpenter for the sum of $250.[67]

The Carpenters may have been lured to Pipers Gap by Carroll County resident William R. Bedsaul. Since land deeds do not indicate that any one of the three brothers acquired property before 1875, some eight years after arriving in the county, it is possible that they first worked in partnership with him. Perhaps they were tenants on his land until they had enough capital of their own to purchase property and to take charge of their business affairs independently. F. Clyde Bedsaul (1900–1987) says that his grandfather, William R. Bedsaul, and John Wesley Carpenter were partners, lending credence to this idea.[68]

Adolphus Carpenter may have set up a pottery in the Coal Creek section of Carroll County apart from the one operated by his brothers, John and Michael. His brother-in-law, potter George W. Bedsaul, lived nearby. On the other hand, Bedsaul may have run a shop there.[69] Neighbor David Campbell (ca. 1854–1925), whose father was potter William Campbell (ca. 1814–1899) of Lincoln and Catawba Counties, North Carolina, purchased land from Adolphus Carpenter near the time when Adolphus's family (and George W. Bedsaul) moved to Missouri.[70] After leaving North Carolina, William Campbell worked as a potter in Wythe and Smyth counties, Virginia.[71] In 1880 David Campbell's Pipers Gap household included his brother, potter William Dess Campbell (ca. 1852–1912). Two more of David Campbell's brothers, Lindsey (ca. 1849–1883) and Hosea (ca. 1855–after 1920), were potters in Tennessee and southwest Virginia, so David Campbell might have been a potter, too.[72] Lindsey Campbell's pottery in Johnson County, Tennessee, produced alkaline-glazed stoneware in a groundhog-styled kiln measuring about 19 feet by 11.7 feet, comparable in size to those used by North Carolina's Catawba Valley potters.[73]

In 1880, potter Charles Cole (1827–1929) and his son, Wiley Cole (1857–1930), lived and worked in Pipers Gap township.[74] Born in Grayson County to Hawk Cole, Charles Cole moved to Carroll County between 1866 and 1868. In 1870 he called himself a saddler, and in 1900 he was a harness maker. Wiley Cole worked as a farm laborer in 1870. Perhaps the

Coles set up a pottery to compete with the Carpenters. However, it seems more likely that they worked with the Carpenters after being trained by them.[75]

Michael Carpenter's son, James Emmett Carpenter (1872–1964), supplied substantial evidence about John Wesley Carpenter's pottery shop in Pipers Gap when he was interviewed in 1959 by F. Clyde Bedsaul. Additional information came from other longtime Carroll County residents. As stated above, Bedsaul claimed that his grandfather William R. Bedsaul (1833–1909) and John Wesley Carpenter were business partners. Bedsaul recounts that "Three Carpenter brothers, John C. [W.], Mike and Adolphus, accompanied by William R. Bedsaul, went to Lincolnton, N.C., to learn the pottery trade."[76]

In fact, the opposite is true. The Carpenters came to Virginia from Lincoln County fully prepared for pottery making. William R. Bedsaul's involvement in the trade is less certain. As a prominent farmer and justice of the peace, Bedsaul might have traveled to Lincoln County to recruit the Carpenters to come to Pipers Gap. Bedsaul's son, George, may have gone to the Catawba Valley as a potter's apprentice (perhaps for Thomas Ritchie), leading to his and his father's acquaintance with the Carpenters. Thereafter they might have been enticed to relocate to Pipers Gap to set up a pottery shop with the elder Bedsaul as a partner.

Undoubtedly, the Carpenter-Bedsaul relationship was strong. William R. Bedsaul's daughter, Surphina Jane (1854–1880), was the first wife of John Wesley Carpenter and the mother of their two children, Mollie (1873–1894) and Harvey Make Carpenter (1877–1960). Bedsaul's son, George Washington Bedsaul, was a potter who undoubtedly worked with

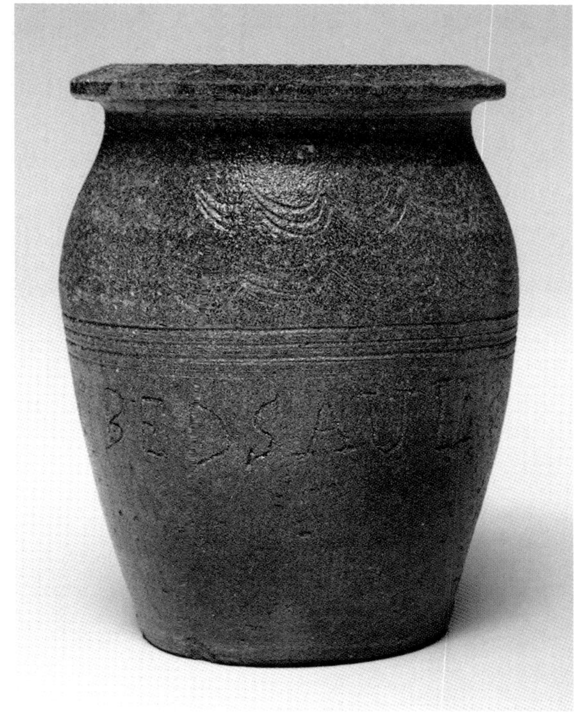

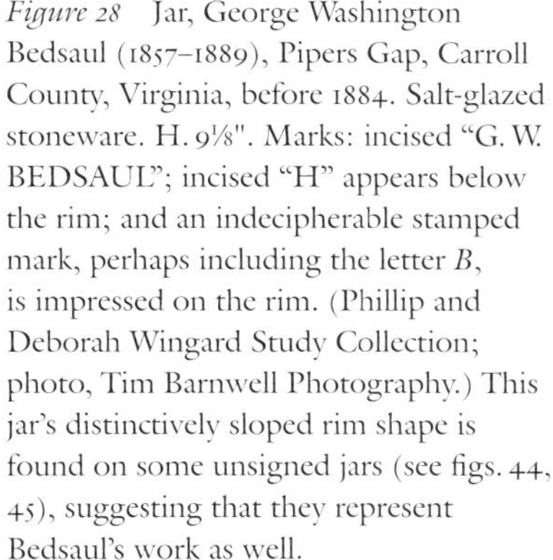

Figure 28 Jar, George Washington Bedsaul (1857–1889), Pipers Gap, Carroll County, Virginia, before 1884. Salt-glazed stoneware. H. 9⅛". Marks: incised "G. W. BEDSAUL"; incised "H" appears below the rim; and an indecipherable stamped mark, perhaps including the letter *B*, is impressed on the rim. (Phillip and Deborah Wingard Study Collection; photo, Tim Barnwell Photography.) This jar's distinctively sloped rim shape is found on some unsigned jars (see figs. 44, 45), suggesting that they represent Bedsaul's work as well.

his Carpenter brothers-in-law. He married Sarah Elizabeth Carpenter (1853–1933), the daughter of Elias and Sarah Salina Johnson Carpenter.[77] Michael Carpenter married Jane Bedsaul. A jar bearing the name G. W. Bedsaul, with incised decoration like that applied to many Carpenter-made wares, has been identified (fig. 28). In 1881 George W. and Sarah E. Bedsaul purchased from Martin and Jane Hanks 15½ acres lying adjacent to the lands of Adolphus Carpenter. On July 7, 1883, the deed was delivered to William R. Bedsaul for the grantee.[78] Like Adolphus Carpenter, George W. Bedsaul moved from Carroll County to Missouri sometime around 1884. Family accounts say that he died in Oak Grove, Missouri, on July 17, 1889. In 1910 his widow, Sarah E. Carpenter Bedsaul, was in Oak Grove, near Adolphus and Mary Carpenter.

Figure 29 *Left*: One-gallon jug, attributed to John Wesley Carpenter, Pipers Gap, Carroll County, Virginia, last quarter of the nineteenth century. Salt-glazed stoneware. H. 11". Mark: "JC 1" (Wesley Hall Collection.) *Right*: 1½-gallon cream riser, attributed to John Wesley Carpenter, Pipers Gap, Carroll County, Virginia, last quarter of the nineteenth century. Salt-glazed stoneware. H. 7½". Mark, on rim: "JC 1½". (Courtesy, Wilkes Heritage Museum, Kenneth Johnson Collection; photo, Tim Barnwell Photography.) Some Carpenter salt-glazed stoneware is dark in color, perhaps due to the use of iron-laden clay. Some collectors mistakenly believe it was made in Wilkes County, North Carolina, where salt-glazed stoneware often looks the same. The dark coloration may have led John Wesley Carpenter to add white kaolin slip to greenware before firing it, to lighten its appearance.

The Clay

In 1959 Emmett Carpenter recalled as a boy hauling ox-driven wagon-loads of white clay to the John Wesley Carpenter pottery. The shop's clay was dug at two sites, and it took half a day to transport it about five miles on winding, unpaved roads. Some of it came from Philip Kinzer's bottomland near Wolf Glade, and the rest came from Tom Jones's farm at Woodlawn.[79] His mention of white clay is significant because most of the Carpenters' salt-glazed ware was slip-coated with white clay before being placed in the kiln. This unique trait makes the shop's pottery immediately recognizable, with or without the presence of John Wesley Carpenter's

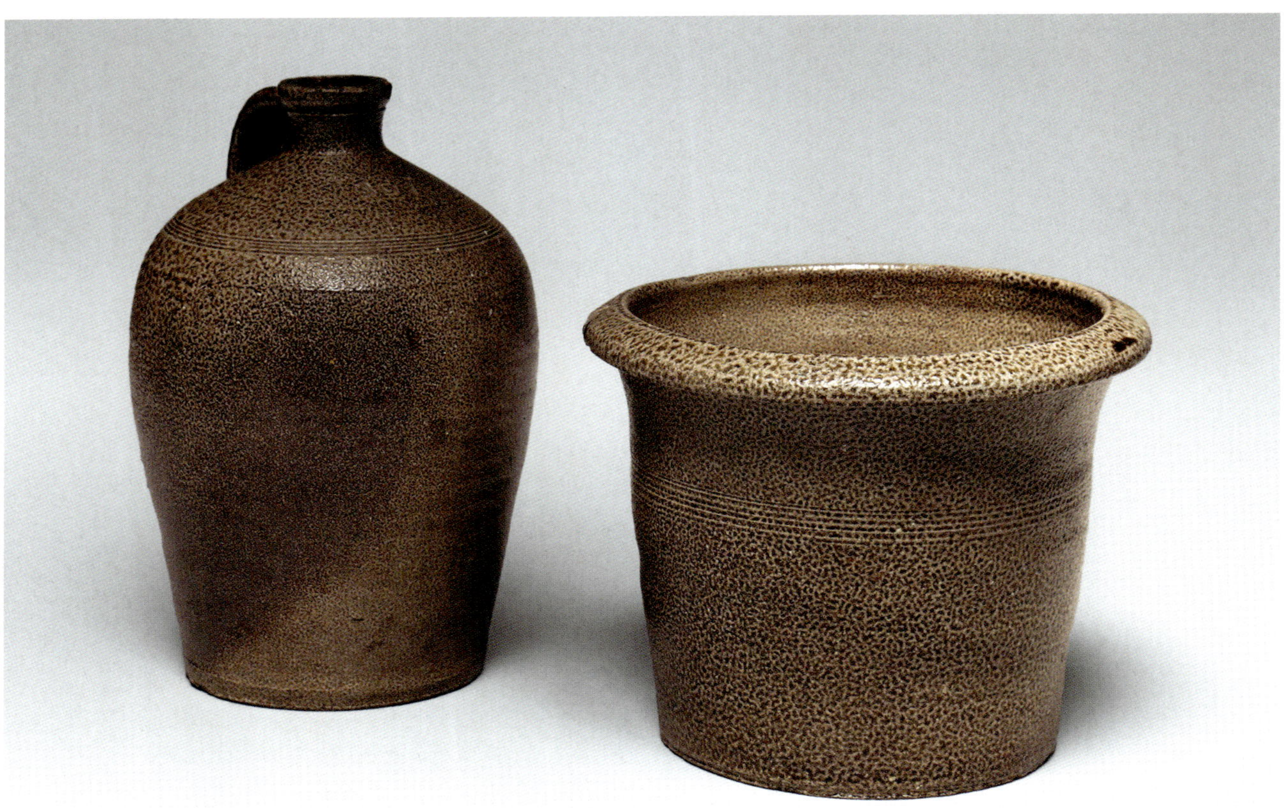

abundant "JC" and capacity marks. A Virginia geological survey suggests that pink feldspar, weathered from arkosic beds (sandstone > 25% feldspar), was the white kaolin's source.[80]

The same survey says that the persistence of limonite in the area's residual clay "indicates that these hydrous iron oxides were derived from the solution of disseminated iron-bearing minerals in the rocks . . . during weathering" and were subsequently "concentrated by deposition in the residual clays."[81] If the clay found by the Carpenters was like this, then its iron content might have generated an undesirably dark salt-glazed body. Some (perhaps early) examples of their Carroll County output, like those shown in figures 29 and 30, are dark-colored, causing them occasionally to be confused with Wilkes County, North Carolina, wares, which likewise were created using clay high in iron content. The Carpenters' problem was resolved when the choice was made to coat each piece of pottery with a

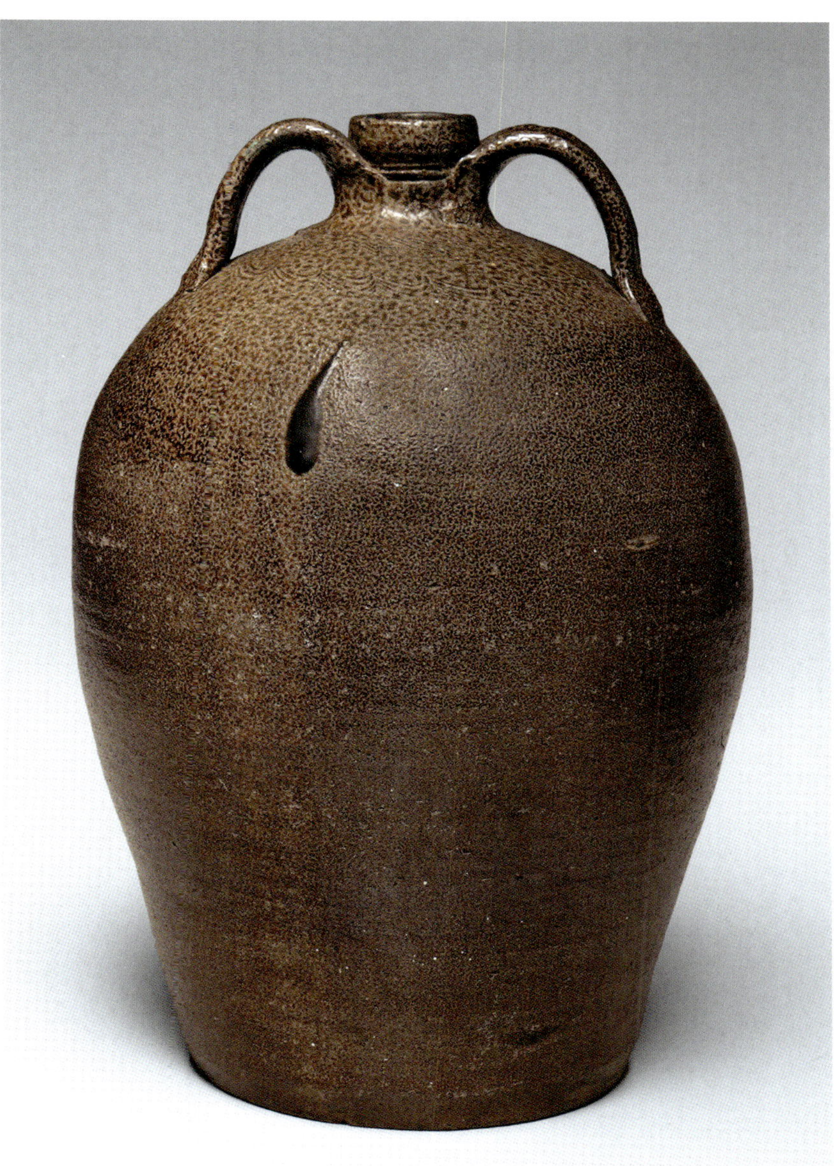

Figure 30 Five-gallon jug, attributed to John Wesley Carpenter, Pipers Gap, Carroll County, Virginia, last quarter of the nineteenth century. Salt-glazed stoneware. H. 17⅝". (Author's collection; photo, Tim Barnwell Photography.)

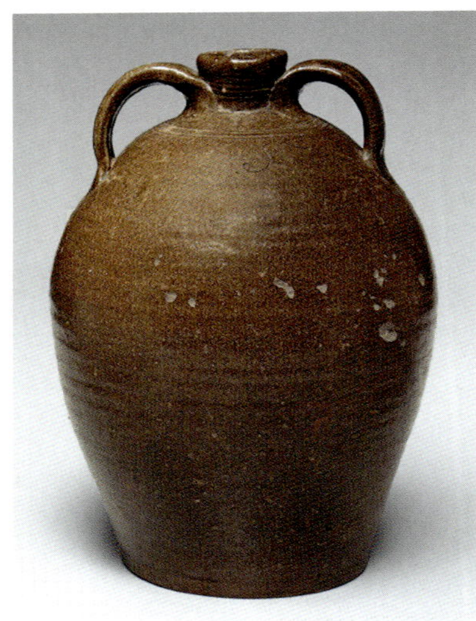

Figure 31 Five-gallon jug, attributed to John Wesley Carpenter, Lincoln County, North Carolina, ca. 1865–1870. Alkaline-glazed stoneware. H. 17½". Mark: "5" (gallons). (Brian Treverrow Collection; photo, Tim Barnwell Photography.) A similarly inscribed "5" is found on the signed "JWC" jug illustrated in fig. 9.

kaolin-derived slip before salt-glazing. As a near twin to the jug shown in figure 30, the alkaline-glazed example shown in figure 31 exhibits the contrast between the Carpenters' salt- and alkaline-glaze treatments.

Emmett Carpenter described how the clay was processed and prepared for kiln-firing. Bedsaul relays what Carpenter told him about it:

> The "mud mill" was crude and consisted of a vertical beam of wood, armed with four or five metal knives, which turned in a square box. This upright shaft was pegged to a sweep and rotated slowly when pulled by a plodding farm horse. It operated much like the old-fashioned cane mill. Raw clay was cut and mixed as water was added to form the desired consistency. It took three or four hours to finish this first process. Then the prepared clay was dipped out of the box with bare hands, shaped into large balls, stored in pits and covered with wet cloths.[82]

Once formed into jugs, crocks, and other shapes, unfired vessels were set aside to dry on shelves in a shed where they sat for four or five days. Then, an unusual step was added to the process: "They were returned to the wheel where a thin layer of very white clay solution was 'glazed' or rubbed on. After two more days of drying they were carefully carried into the furnace."[83]

Sometimes potters substituted Albany slip or Bristol glaze for alkaline glaze or salt glaze. What makes the Carpenters' Virginia pottery unusual, perhaps unique, is the addition of a white kaolin slip before salt-glazing.

Turning the Clay

Emmett Carpenter describes how the shop's wheel that was used to turn clay was like those typically found in traditional North Carolina potteries.[84] Each one's heavy flywheel was pushed into a turning motion by way of a foot-powered treadle. Bedsaul, in his account, refers to the treadle as a foot pedal.[85] A ball of clay, placed on a twelve-inch lathe head connected to the flywheel by a vertical iron crankshaft, was transformed into a useful vessel when the turner's wetted hands brought out its profile from the shapeless lump of clay. Once satisfied with the shape, the potter used a wire pulled between his two hands to cut away the still-pliable jug, churn, crock, pitcher, or chamber pot from the lathe head.

Many of the region's potters stood on one leg at the wheel while pushing the treadle with the other. The potter's wheel described by Bedsaul from Emmett Carpenter's memory allowed the turner to sit astride a saddle-like seat while working. A photograph taken circa 1931 shows Lincoln County–born potter Albert Fulbright (1867–1950) straddling a treadle wheel's plank seat, confirming its use in western North Carolina (fig. 32).[86] The saddle-like arrangement may have been helpful in the Carpenter shop, given Michael Carpenter's battle-derived disability that at times required him to use crutches while standing and John Wesley Carpenter's reported uneven leg length.

The Kiln

The Carpenters' Pipers Gap pottery kiln, once used to fire salt-glazed stoneware and some alkaline-glazed ware, was dismantled around 1912.[87] The large soapstone blocks that had been employed when constructing the

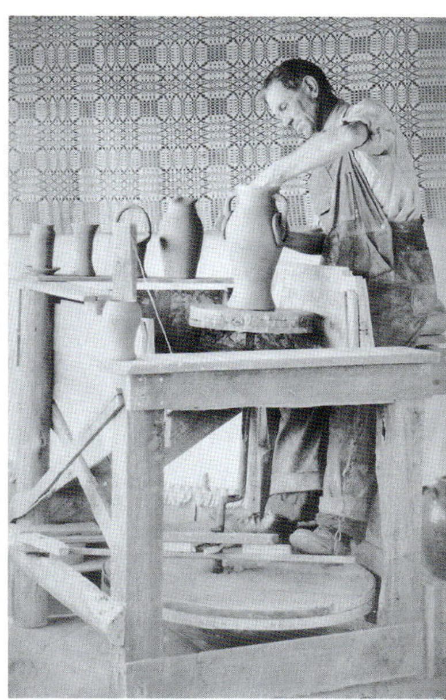

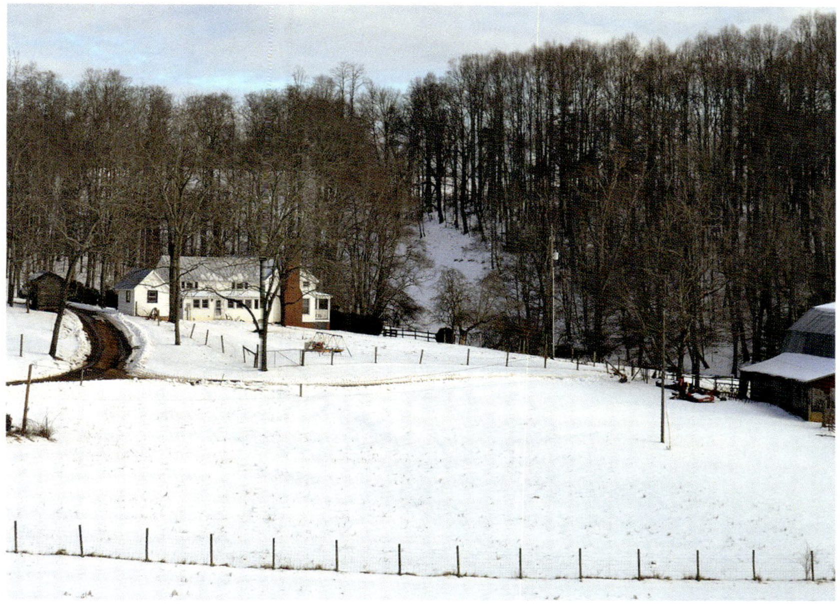

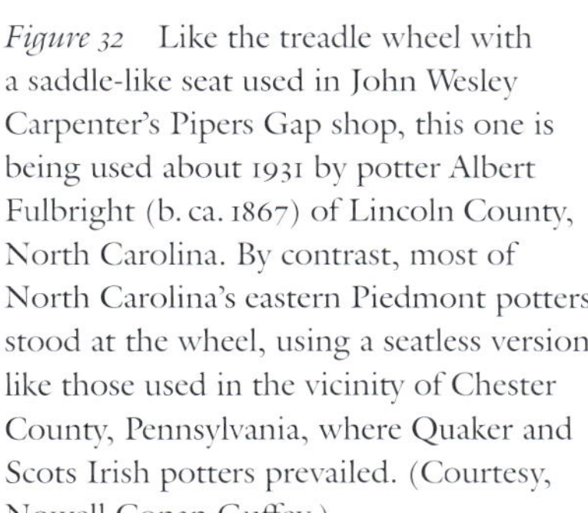

Figure 32 Like the treadle wheel with a saddle-like seat used in John Wesley Carpenter's Pipers Gap shop, this one is being used about 1931 by potter Albert Fulbright (b. ca. 1867) of Lincoln County, North Carolina. By contrast, most of North Carolina's eastern Piedmont potters stood at the wheel, using a seatless version like those used in the vicinity of Chester County, Pennsylvania, where Quaker and Scots Irish potters prevailed. (Courtesy, Nowell Conan Guffey.)

Figure 33 The ca. 1912–1913 home of John Wesley and Emily Hanks Carpenter, Pipers Gap, Virginia, 2022. (Photo, Stephen C. Compton.) The Carpenter pottery was located nearby, over the hill beyond the house.

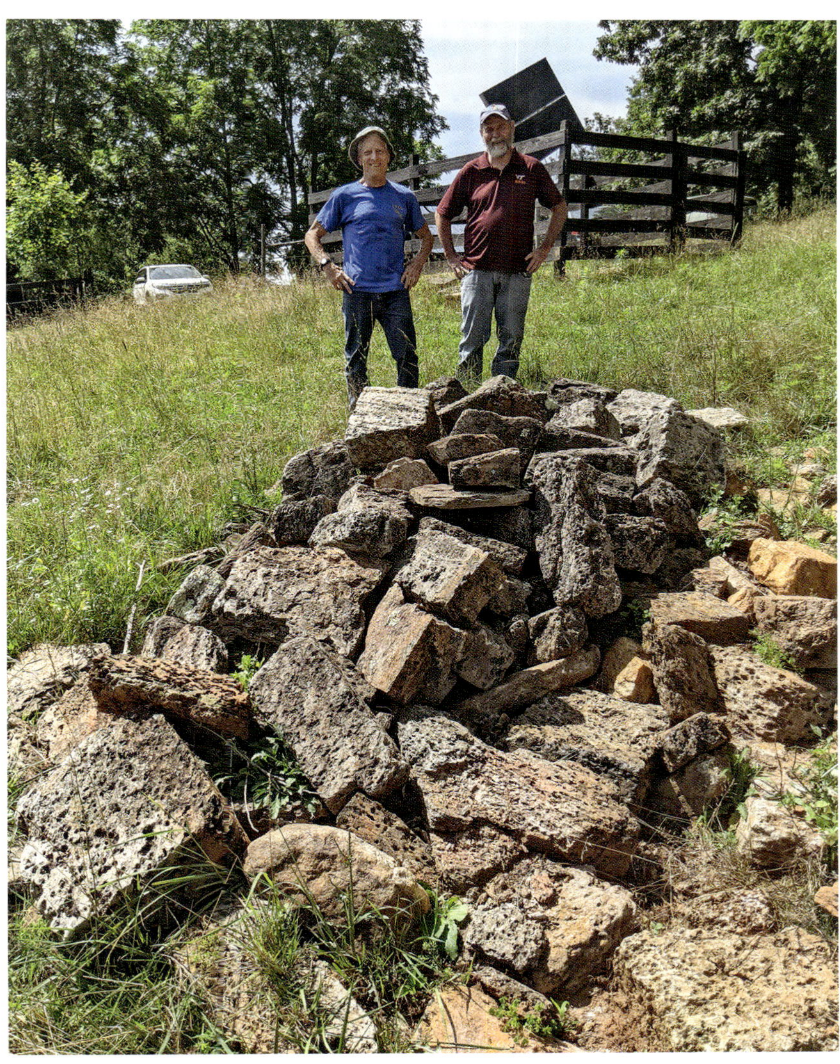

Figure 34 Robert Riggins (at left) and his cousin John Wesley Carpenter, great-grandsons of potter John Wesley Carpenter, stand above a pile of soapstone blocks cut by hand a mile away on Hanks Knob. (Photo, Stephen C. Compton.) First used in the construction of a kiln near John Wesley's original home, they were used to build a chimney for his and his wife's new house, illustrated in fig. 33. In 1989 remnants of Hurricane Hugo damaged the chimney, which led to its dismantling. The remaining kiln blocks have been stored nearby.

kiln's walls were used to build a chimney for a house constructed by John Wesley Carpenter for himself and his wife, Emily (fig. 33). The chimney was damaged in 1989 by winds from the tropical remnant of Hurricane Hugo, and subsequently was taken down. The soapstone blocks were piled nearby, where they are preserved (fig. 34).

The kiln's hand-cut soapstone blocks were quarried about a mile from the pottery shop, near Hanks Knob. From the arch of a geologic fold near Hanks Knob, hornblende gneiss passes southwesterly into a source

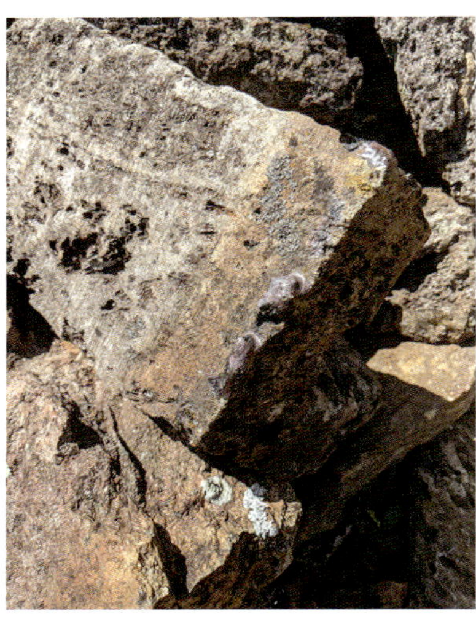

Figure 35 Detail of soapstone blocks once used in the Carpenter kiln. (Photo, Stephen C. Compton.) Close examination reveals evidence of thermal alteration, including deep discoloration, as seen here in a darkened band of stone. Melted kiln arch material has adhered to the edge of the soapstone block. Except for the inclusion of salting ports in its arch, the Pipers Gap kiln was identical to ones used in North Carolina's Catawba Valley for making alkaline-glazed stoneware.

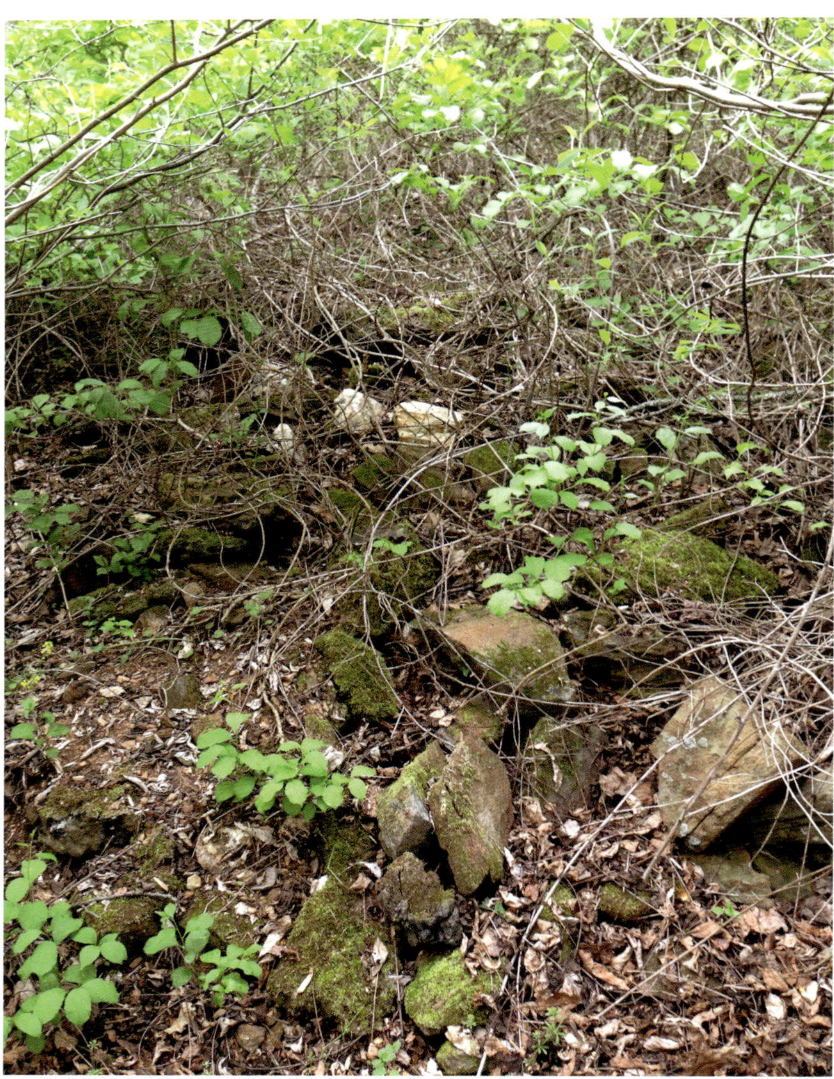

Figure 36 The Carpenter kiln site as it appeared in 2015. (Photo, January Costa.) A remnant of the large Catawba Valley-styled groundhog kiln extends into the hillside. Rocks, including some soapstone blocks, and bricks, are scattered about in the underbrush. John Wesley Carpenter removed most of the defunct kiln's soapstone blocks around 1912 when constructing his new home's chimney.

of soapstone. The geologic survey referenced earlier states that soapstone found in the area tends to be "pale-greenish gray, saws readily, and breaks into slabs along the schistosity." Much of it is heavily pitted, and some holes are filled with limonite.[88] The Carpenter pottery's soapstone kiln blocks are likewise heavily pitted (fig. 35).

In the spring of 2014, John Wesley Carpenter's granddaughter, Edith Carpenter Riggins, revealed the kiln's location to Marc King. King's research identified John Wesley Carpenter as the potter long known to collectors who frequently marked his pots with the letters JC—a fact confirmed by Edith Riggins. He described the site as overgrown with a few scattered rocks remaining from the kiln's prior construction. A portion of the kiln extended into the base of a hill that was bordered by two small spring-fed streams. In 2016, archaeologist January Costa, along with others representing North Carolina's Lincoln County Historical Association, visited the site where she photographed its remains and measured its dimensions (fig. 36).

Bedsaul's retelling of Carpenter's memories of the site provides an illustrative description of the kiln and its use:

> The furnace and all equipment was home-made—built by their own hands. Soapstone blocks were cut in a quarry on the Creed Hanks Knob and hauled for nearly a mile.
>
> The furnace was an arched structure extending 24 feet into a hillside, 13 feet wide and about five high. Three doorways or flues, 27 inches wide and three or four feet high, were equally spaced across the front.
>
> A broad chimney of home-burned bricks extended eight feet above the back end. The floor had two levels. A fire pit of about one-fourth the length was first. The remaining space, extending on back to the chimney, was two feet higher. Crocks were burned upon this upper level. The soapstone arch over this area was pierced by numerous holes or small windows. These were stoppered with earthenware plugs which bore chines on their outer ends.
>
> This made it possible to lift them out, hot, by use of forked sticks when it was time to pour glazing material upon the white-hot vessels below. Wooden catwalks extended across the furnace to protect the workers from the heated arch during the glazing operations. The whole furnace was sheltered by a board-covered shed.[89]

Anyone familiar with kilns utilized in North Carolina's Catawba Valley region will recognize this kiln's similarity to those used there in the production of alkaline-glazed stoneware. These kilns have long been compared to German Cassel kilns, exhibiting similar design and functionality. Daniel Seagle was one of the Catawba Valley's earliest potters. His kiln, excavated by Linda Carnes-McNaughton in 1987, was remarkably similar in size (23' by 10') to the Carpenter kiln (24' by 13'). Two more Catawba Valley kilns, built by brothers Enoch and Harvey Reinhardt, are nearly identical, each measuring approximately 24' 11" by 11' 6". Both Reinhardt kilns had three fireports, like the ones described by Emmett Carpenter, spaced out across their front walls and opening into a fire pit.[90]

Cassel kilns typically had an interior bag (flash) wall to separate the fire pit from the setting floor, where wares were arranged for firing. However, Catawba Valley kilns used for alkaline glazing appear to lack this feature. The purpose of a bag wall is to prevent wares from being directly impacted by wood thrown into the fire pit or by stirred-up wood ashes. Since Emmett Carpenter's kiln description fails to mention a bag wall, perhaps his memory was faulty or the Carpenter kiln lacked that component. Also, Catawba Valley potters loaded and unloaded their kilns through an opening at the base of the furnace's chimney, and even though Emmett Carpenter might not have mentioned this fact, the kiln's overall design suggests it was true there.

The addition of ports with removable earthenware plugs in the Carpenter kiln's arch is the most significant modification to an otherwise typical Catawba Valley–styled furnace. Further, they burned dry chestnut wood, not pine; it was, according to Charles G. Zug III, "the only wood used in the Catawba Valley."[91] These openings made glazing the pots possible by pouring salt into the kiln while the wares were white-hot.[92] Emmett Carpenter told Clyde Bedsaul that workers crossed over the arch on wooden catwalks to disperse seventy-five pounds of salt into the kiln. Afterward, heavy sheets of metal sealed off the kiln's three openings. Over two days, the wares inside cooled enough to be removed.

So, except for the addition of salting ports, the Carpenter kiln was like the North Carolina alkaline-glazing stoneware kilns used in the Catawba Valley region, primarily by potters of German descent. In both cases, the type is fundamentally a modified Cassel kiln.

Unlike the Catawba Valley kilns, the ones used by North Carolina's salt-glazed stoneware production in the state's eastern Piedmont Region were smaller in size, typically had one opening leading to the firebox, were loaded and unloaded through this opening rather than through the chimney, and had a taller, narrower chimney.

The Carpenters' use of a Catawba Valley–styled kiln, primarily used by them for creating salt-glazed stoneware, might be a unique adaptation among Southern potters and potteries. It is unknown why they decided to produce salt-glazed stoneware in Virginia instead of the alkaline-glazed ware they had made in North Carolina. The choice of a kiln like theirs to make salt-glazed stoneware suggests that it was an idea of their own, not one taught them by a salt-glazer. Had that been the case, they might have been persuaded to use another, smaller, kiln design altogether. In any event, the Carpenters could well be the only Southern potters successfully to produce alkaline-glazed and salt-glazed stoneware at the same site—perhaps in the same kiln.

The Pipers Gap Wares

The Carpenters undoubtedly were skilled at alkaline-glazed stoneware production, so one must wonder what led them to switch to salt-glazed stoneware after moving to Virginia. When they arrived in Carroll County, potters to their northeast in Richmond, Petersburg, and Alexandria made significant quantities of cobalt-decorated salt-glazed stoneware. Increasingly, in the state's Shenandoah Valley potteries, especially in Shenandoah and Rockingham counties, earthenware was being supplanted by salt-glazed stoneware. According to H. E. Comstock, beginning around 1870 through the end of the century, seventy-five percent of the total production of Shenandoah Valley ceramics consisted of stoneware. The demand for salt-glazed stoneware, in some instances, called for the construction of new kilns for this purpose.[93] Perhaps the Carpenters learned early on in their Pipers Gap venture that Virginia buyers preferred the appearance of salt-glazed over alkaline-glazed pottery and thus adapted their operation to accommodate the market's demands.

Salt was in short supply during the Civil War, but after it there was an increasingly plentiful supply. In Virginia's Smyth and Washington counties, the Saltville Salt Works, located not far from Carroll County, could have amply supplied the Carpenters' needs for glazing with salt. The Carpenter kiln, groundhog in design, probably performed well from the beginning when so utilized. Salt vapors, which wreak havoc on kilns' brick walls and arches over time, were not likely problematic since the kilns' burning chamber walls were made of soapstone.

Salt-glazing is a more straightforward yet no less challenging process than alkaline-glazing. Alkaline glazing requires a mixture of finely ground glass (or another source of silica), some clay for binding, water, and a flux (typically wood ashes). Once formulated, this glaze was placed on ware surfaces before kiln-firing, requiring considerable labor. With salt glaze, no such "glaze" is needed. Instead, unglazed pots, when exposed to the gaseous vapors created when common salt is introduced into a kiln at very high temperature, "leak" out native silica from their clay, creating a glassy, often "orange peel" textured surface.

At first, John Wesley and his brothers may have pursued the simplest form of salt-glazing, as previously described, without the addition of kaolin slip. The glazing on these examples seems adequate, but the dark clay color, when burned, might not have been deemed satisfactory by John Carpenter or his earliest buyers. Perhaps the region's iron- and manganese-stained clays prevented the creation of lighter-colored wares. The Carpenters' solution—one that added back work not typically required when salt glazing—was to coat each pot with a kaolin-based slip before salt glazing. Apparently it was John Carpenter's good fortune to discover a white clay that sufficiently adhered to and matched the shrinkage of his pots' underlying clay without diminishing the desired effect of salt glazing.

Sometimes, earthenware potters covered red or dark-burning clays with a lighter-colored engobe to create a brighter surface to which slip-trailed decoration could be added. The overall surface was then coated with a clear lead glaze. Applying a similar two-step process for stoneware production, like that achieved by the Carpenters, is rare, perhaps unique, among Southern potters. The examples shown in figures 37–41 exhibit the Carpenter pottery's distinctive light- to medium-gray color achieved by the slip-coating and salt-glazing process described above.

John Wesley Carpenter never abandoned the skills for making alkaline-glazed stoneware that he learned as a Catawba Valley potter. F. Clyde Bedsaul, drawing on his conversation with Emmett Carpenter in 1959, makes that clear when describing the shop's method for grinding glass for glazing:

> Another odd piece of equipment was a mill for grinding glass. It consisted of one stationary "mill rock" and a smaller, revolving one on top. One edge of this upper stone was supported by a small wooden beam,

swinging from a tripod. This eccentric connection made it possible for a man to turn it by hand.

The "walloping" and sliding of one rock upon another ground the broken glass into powder which was used instead of salt for glazing special wares.[94]

Some alkaline-glazed wares marked with capacity numbers and the initials JC are known. They seem to represent John Wesley Carpenter's "special

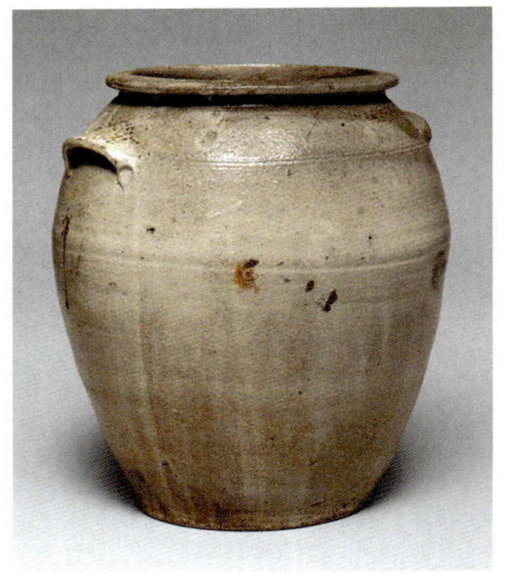

Figure 37 Storage jar with two lug handles, Carpenter Pottery, Pipers Gap, Carroll County, Virginia, ca. 1868–1912. Stoneware with salt glaze over kaolin slip. H. 16". (Kenneth Johnson Collection; photo, Tim Barnwell Photography.)

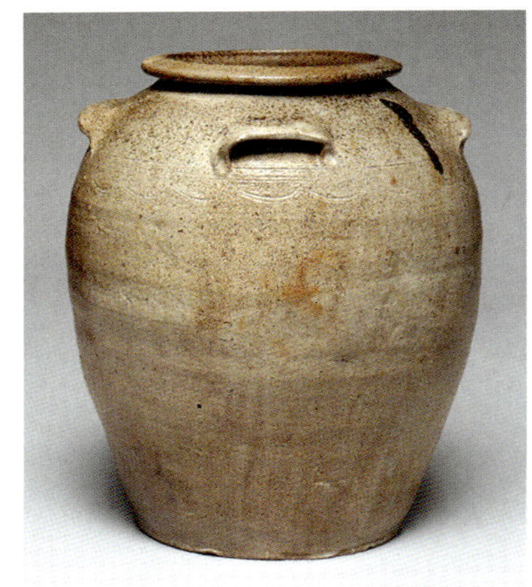

Figure 38 Storage jar with four lug handles, Carpenter Pottery, Pipers Gap, Carroll County, Virginia, last quarter of the nineteenth century. Salt-glazed stoneware glaze over kaolin slip. H. 17". (Kenneth Johnson Collection; photo, Tim Barnwell Photography.)

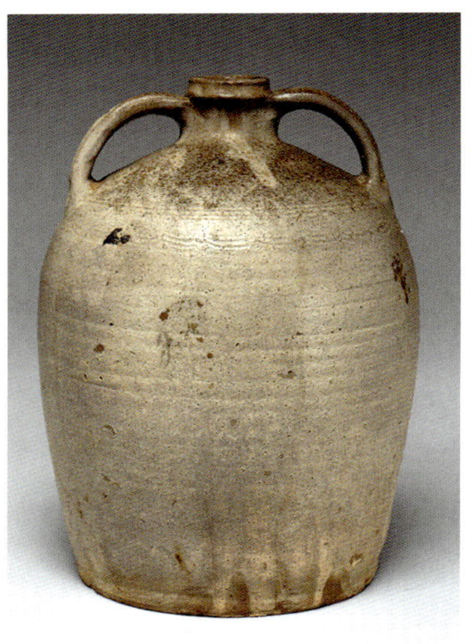

Figure 39 Four-gallon jug, Carpenter Pottery, Pipers Gap, Carroll County, Virginia, last quarter of the nineteenth century. Salt-glazed stoneware glaze over kaolin slip. H. 15¾". Mark: "JC 4" (John Carpenter Collection; photo, Tim Barnwell Photography.)

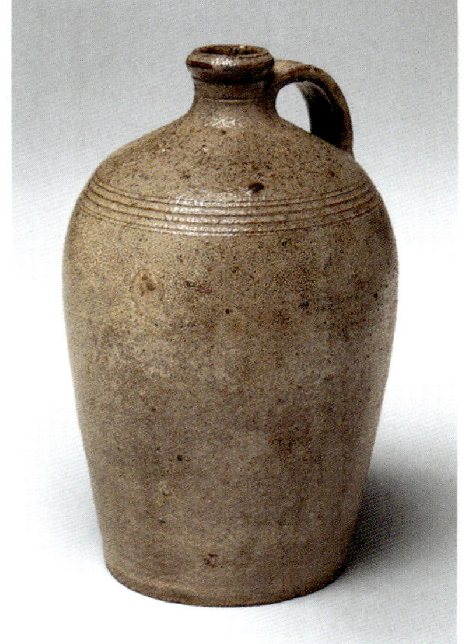

Figure 40 One-gallon jug, Carpenter Pottery, Pipers Gap, Carroll County, Virginia, last quarter of the nineteenth century. Salt-glazed stoneware over kaolin slip. H. 11¼". Mark: "JC 1" (Author's collection; photo, Tim Barnwell Photography.)

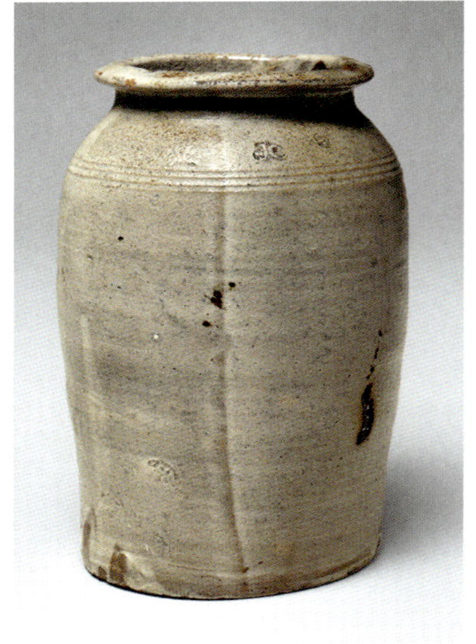

Figure 41 Two-gallon storage jar, Carpenter Pottery, Pipers Gap, Carroll County, Virginia, last quarter of the nineteenth century. Salt-glazed stoneware over kaolin slip. H. 11⅞". Mark: "JC 2" (Author's collection; photo, Tim Barnwell Photography.) The vertical line dividing the jar's slip coating suggests that the jar was dipped horizontally into a larger container filled with a slurry of kaolin slip.

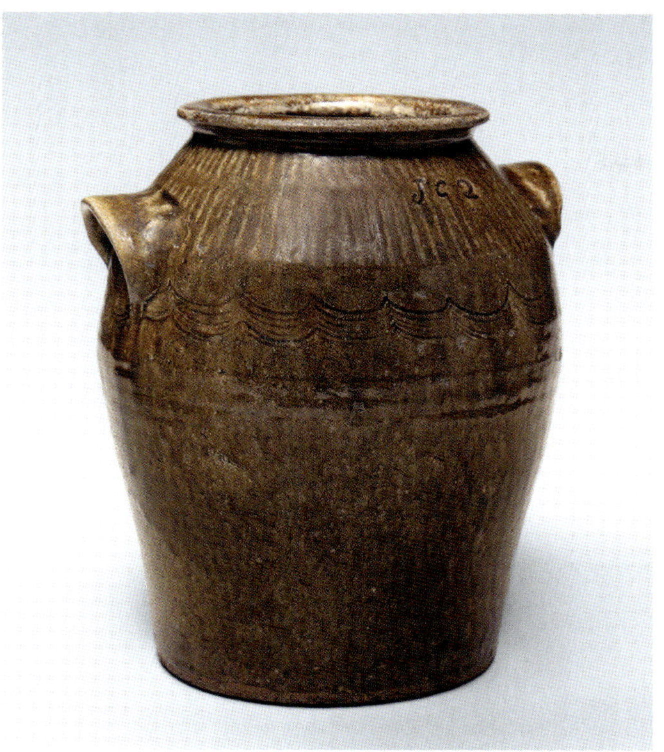

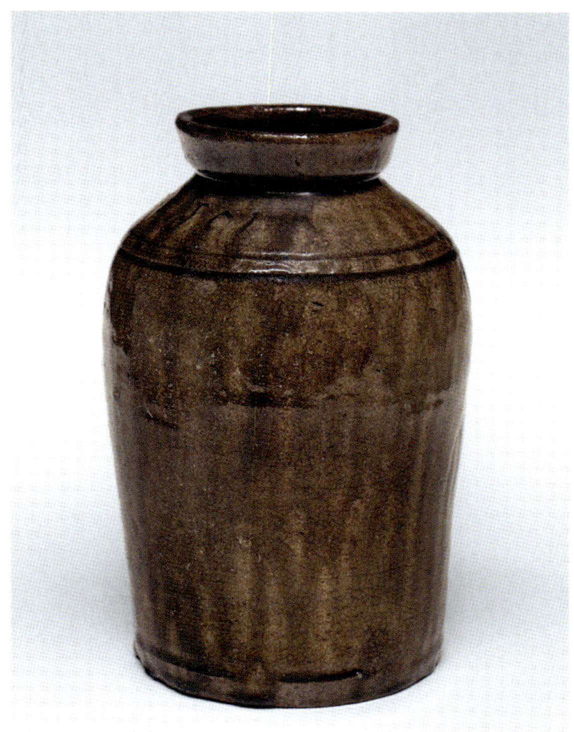

Figure 42 Two-gallon storage jar, attributed to John Wesley Carpenter, Pipers Gap, Carroll County, Virginia, last quarter of the nineteenth century. Alkaline-glazed stoneware. H. 11⅛". Mark: "JC 2" (Author's collection; photo, Tim Barnwell Photography.) In addition to salt-glazed stoneware, on special occasions John Wesley Carpenter produced alkaline-glazed stoneware like he once made in North Carolina. That he made both kinds at the same site, and perhaps using the same kiln, likely makes his operation unique among Southern and, more broadly, American potteries.

Figure 43 One-gallon storage jar, attributed to John Wesley Carpenter, Pipers Gap, Carroll County, Virginia, ca. 1868–1912. Alkaline-glazed stoneware. H. 10⅛". Mark: "JC 1" (L. A. and Suzan Rhyne Collection; photo, Tim Barnwell Photography.)

wares" made the Catawba Valley way. The example shown in figure 42, marked "JC 2" (for two gallons) and coated with a brown-green alkaline glaze, bears a wavy band of incised, combed decoration like that observed on many of the pottery's salt-glazed pots. The one-gallon storage jar illustrated in figure 43 is marked "JC 1" (one gallon).

Though unsigned, the alkaline-glazed jar in figure 44, twice dated 1884 on its rim, is attributed to the Pipers Gap pottery. Its sloping, angled rim is similar to that on the signed G. W. Bedsaul jar in figure 28. The significance of the year is unclear, although it might be when both Adolphus Carpenter and George Bedsaul departed Pipers Gap for Missouri.

The outstanding alkaline-glazed example in figure 45 is not signed, but its form, glaze, and decoration (including glass runs) strongly suggest its association with the Carpenter pottery. It displays both of the commonly applied decorations used there, for example combed bands of horizontal and wavy lines. Although its expert creation suggests a John Wesley Carpenter product, its rim is similar to one on the jar in figure 28 signed "G. W. BEDSAUL" and the large crock in figure 44 dated 1884. Its decorative lines, as executed, resemble the ones applied to the signed Bedsaul jar. If it is Bedsaul's work, he learned the trade well and created a masterpiece pot.

The most unusual of the Carpenters' creations are examples like those in figures 47 and 48. Other similarly decorated specimens are known, including pitchers, a lidded jar, and a mug dated 1881. The jug (see fig. 47) bears John Wesley Carpenter's initials, J.W.C., the date 1881, a series of crosses, a pine tree, and the figure of a man; the pitcher (see fig. 48) is signed "E. M.

Figure 44 Storage jar, attributed to George Washington Bedsaul, Carpenter Pottery, Pipers Gap, Carroll County, Virginia, 1884. Alkaline-glazed stoneware. H. 9½". Mark: "1884" twice on rim. (Colonial Williamsburg Art Museums; photo, Robert Hunter.)

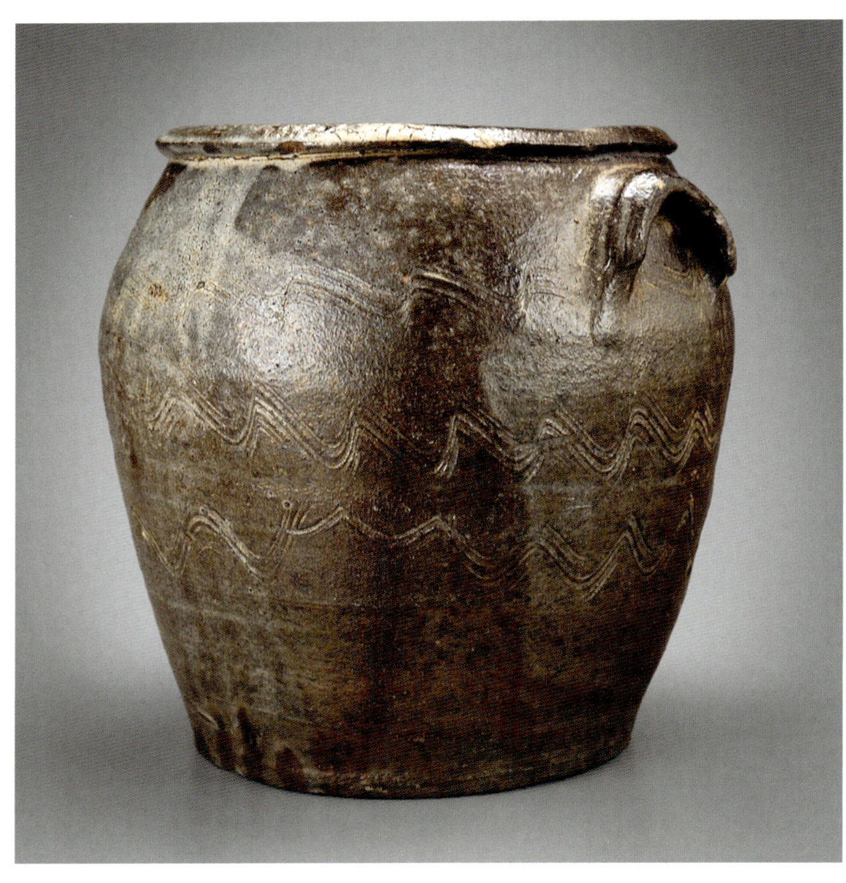

Figure 45 Storage jar, attributed to George Washington Bedsaul, Carpenter Pottery, Pipers Gap, Carroll County, Virginia, ca. 1880. Alkaline-glazed stoneware with glass runs. H. 9¾". (William C. and Susan S. Mariner Foundation; photo, Robert Hunter.) The use of glass fragments for decoration is to some extent a common practice among North Carolina's Catawba Valley alkaline-glaze stoneware makers.

Figure 46 Detail of the storage jar illustrated in fig. 45, showing glass decoration as it was applied to the handles.

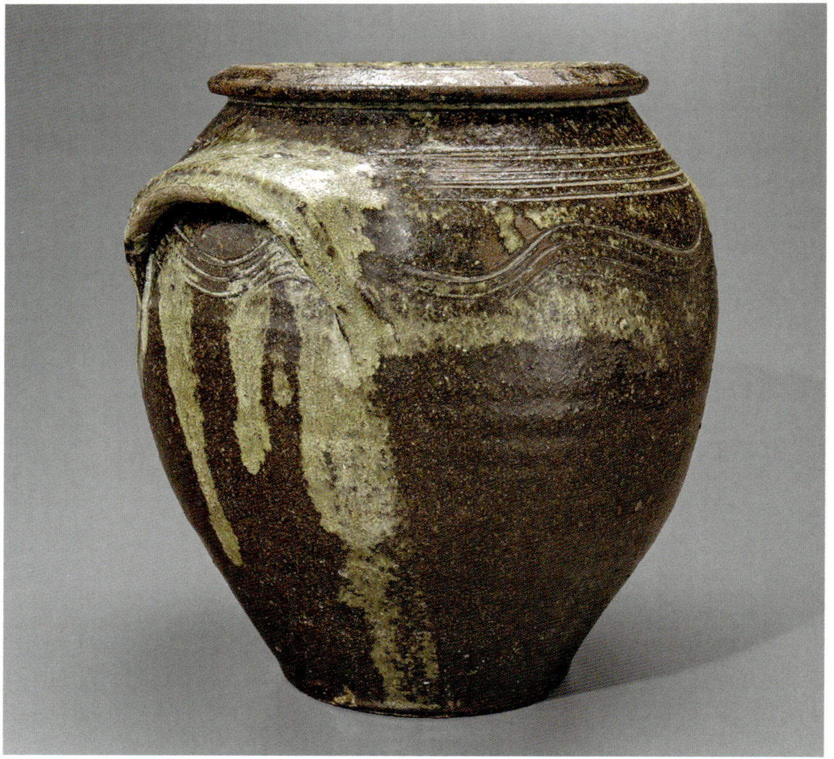

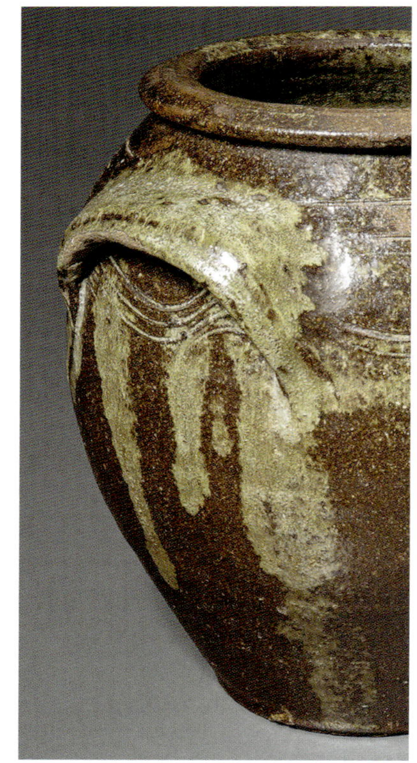

Carpenter." Members of the Carpenter family possess both vessels. John Wesley Carpenter married Emily Hanks on December 16, 1880. Although some records have her name as Emily Amanda, U.S. Census records have her listed as Emily M. Carpenter on more than one occasion. The pitcher has two kinds of crosses, a pine tree and a symbol shaped like a whirligig.

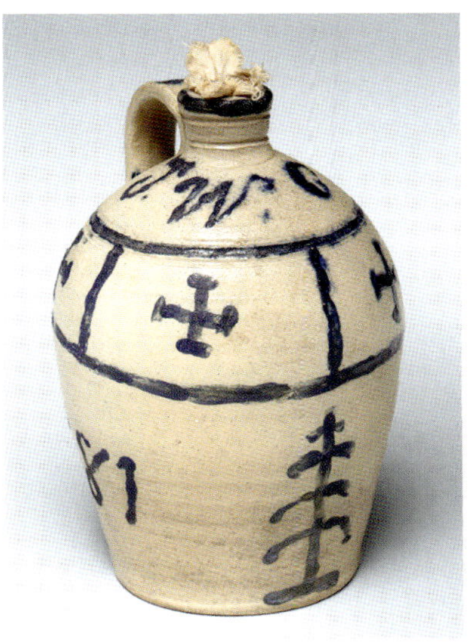

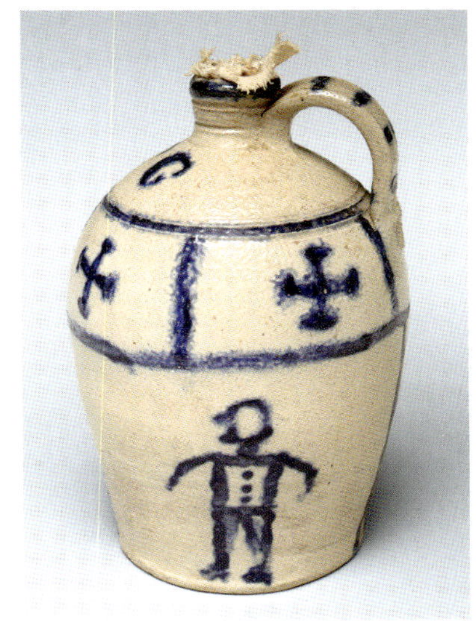

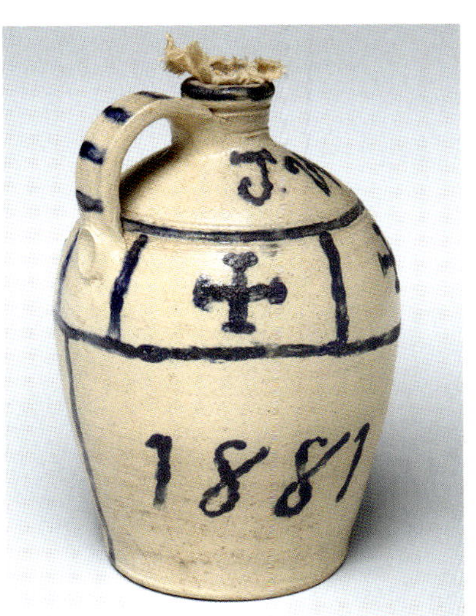

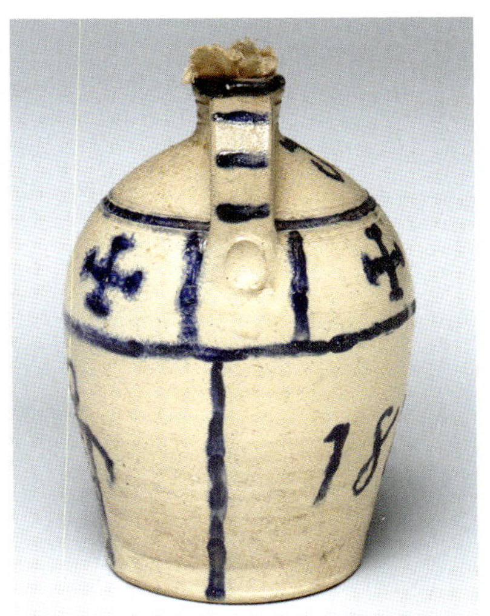

Figure 47 Jug, John Wesley Carpenter, Pipers Gap, Carroll County, Virginia, dated 1881. Stoneware with salt glaze over kaolin slip. H. 8". Marks: inscribed "J.W.C." and "1881" (Carpenter Family Collection; photo, Tim Barnwell Photography.) Several objects decorated in this fashion are known. In addition to John Wesley Carpenter's initials and the date, this example includes stylized crosses, a pine tree, and a male figure.

Another similarly decorated pitcher, associated with the Bedsaul family in Missouri, is known (fig. 49). It includes a whirligig, a cross, and pine tree motifs. A note found inside the pitcher when it was purchased, written by Frances E. Bedsaul in 1984, states that her grandfather, Peter Bedsaul (1845–1932) of Missouri, acquired the pitcher in Carroll County, Virginia, while visiting family members there.[95]

Cobalt smalt on Carpenter wares has not otherwise been observed, except when applying stenciled numerals and the initials J.C. and J.W.C. on some presumably late wares (fig. 50). Carpenter sometimes combined his more typical stamped "JC" mark and capacity marks with stenciled

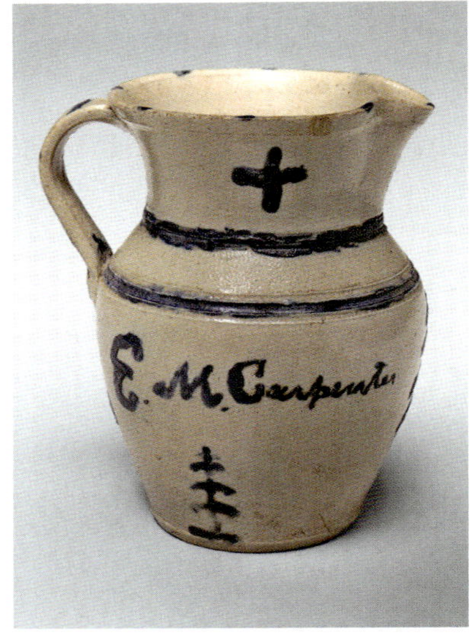

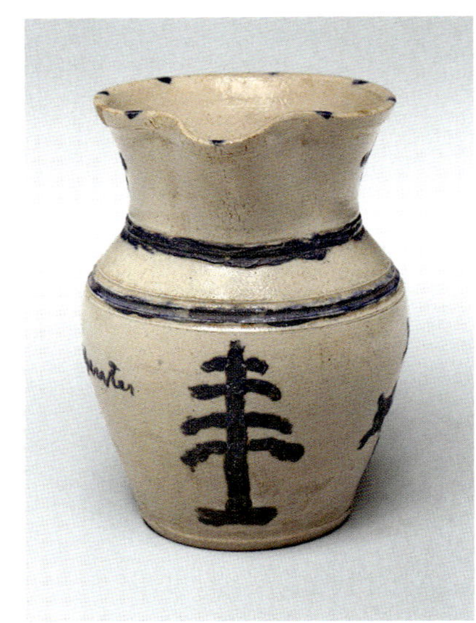

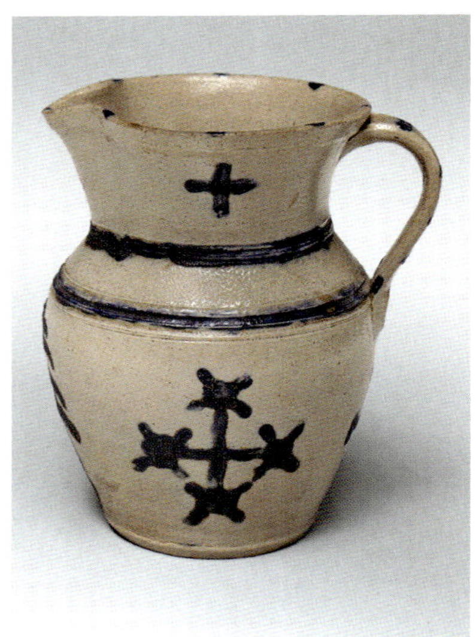

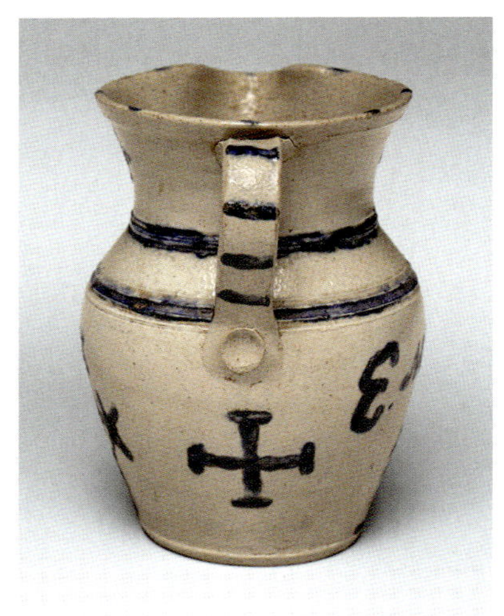

Figure 48 Pitcher, attributed to John Wesley Carpenter, Pipers Gap, Carroll County, Virginia, ca. 1881. Salt-glazed stoneware over kaolin slip. H. 7¼". Mark: "E. M. Carpenter" (Carpenter Family Collection; photo, Tim Barnwell Photography.) John Wesley and Emily Hanks Carpenter were married in 1880. This piece displays crosses, pine trees, and a whirligig-type figure. The decorator is unknown.

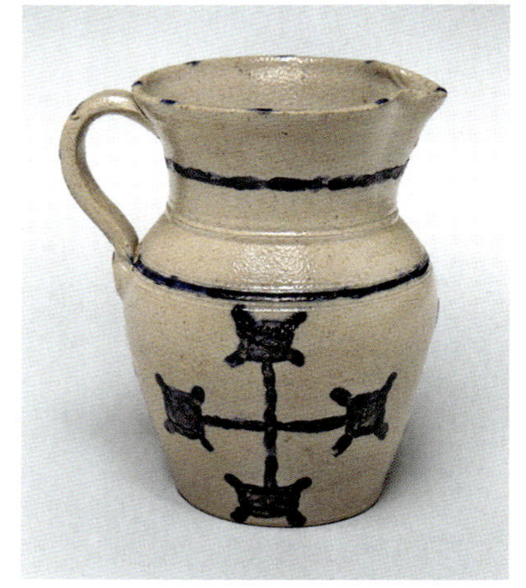

Figure 49 Pitcher, attributed to John Wesley Carpenter, Pipers Gap, Carroll County, Virginia, ca. 1881. Salt-glazed stoneware over kaolin slip. H. 6⅞". (Wesley Hall Collection; photo, Tim Barnwell Photography.) This piece displays crosses, a pine tree, and a whirligig-type figure like the one seen on the pitcher illustrated in fig. 48.

Figure 50 Three-gallon storage jar, Carpenter Pottery, Pipers Gap, Carroll County, Virginia, late nineteenth to early twentieth century. Salt-glazed stoneware over kaolin slip. H. 11". Mark: stenciled "J.W. C. 3" with cobalt smalt. (Carpenter Family Collection; photo, Tim Barnwell Photography.)

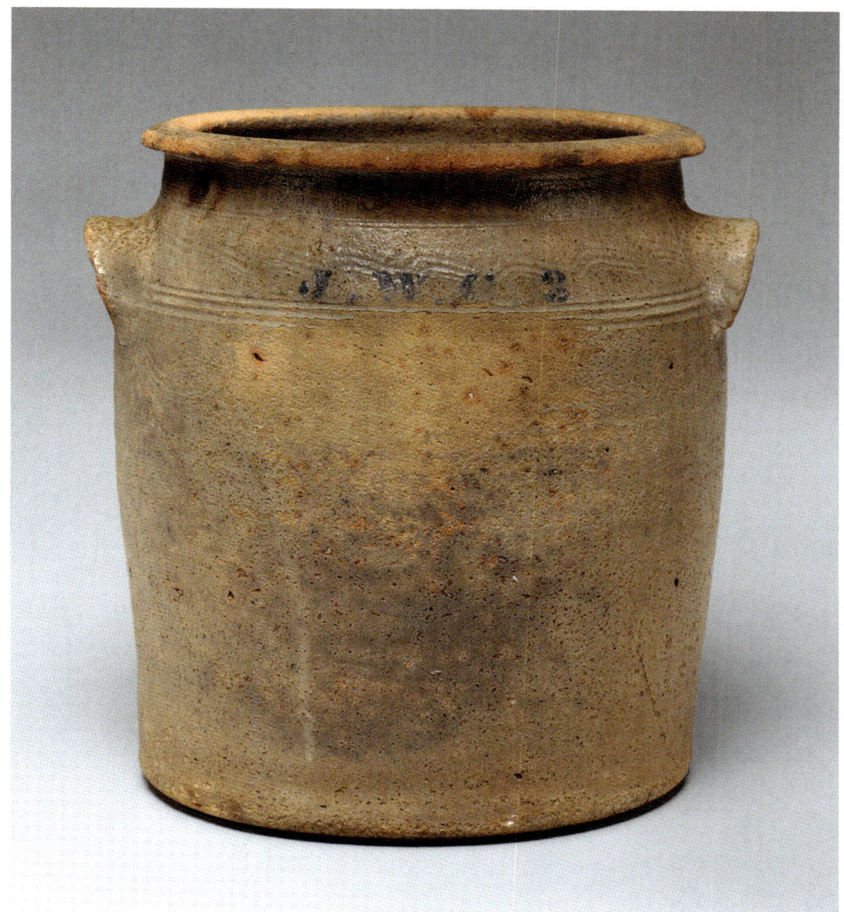

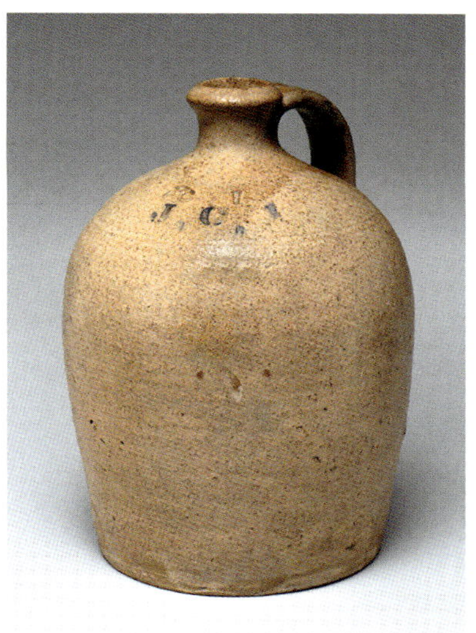

Figure 51 One-gallon jug, Carpenter Pottery, Pipers Gap, Carroll County, Virginia, late nineteenth to early twentieth century. Salt-glazed stoneware over kaolin slip. H. 10¼". Marks: stamp-impressed "JC 1"; stenciled "J.C. 1" (Wesley Hall Collection; photo, Tim Barnwell Photography.)

Figure 52 Gravestone fragment, Carpenter Pottery, Pipers Gap, Carroll County, Virginia, late nineteenth to early twentieth century. Salt-glazed stoneware over kaolin slip. 6 x 4¾ x $2\frac{3}{16}$". Mark: stenciled "J • C." with cobalt smalt. (Carpenter Family Collection; photo, Tim Barnwell Photography.)

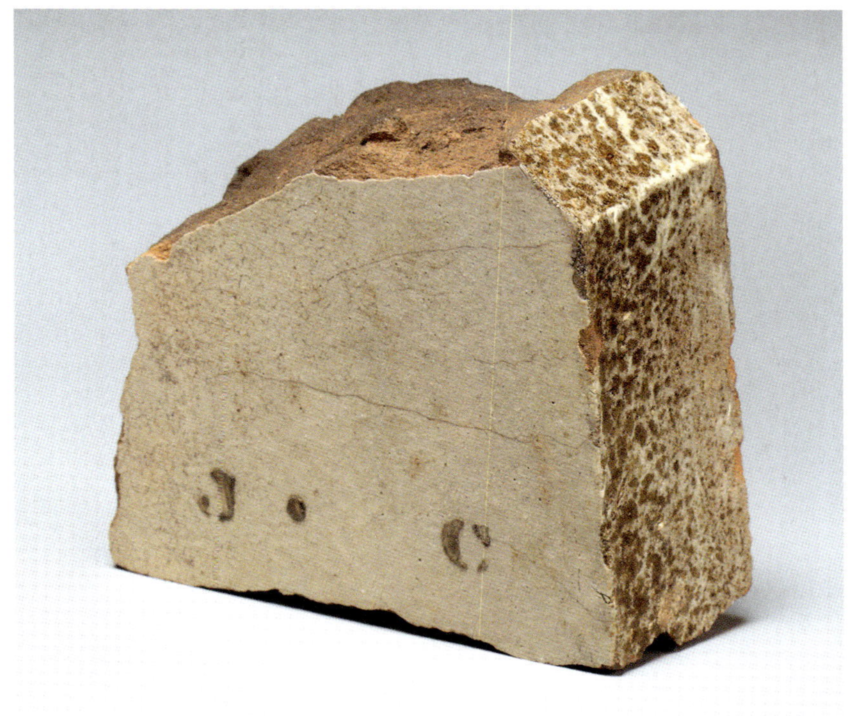

versions (fig. 51). For example, his cobalt stenciled application is found on the remnant of a prototype headstone made by John Wesley Carpenter and bearing his initials (fig. 52). According to family members, this later venture failed because the thick slabs were prone to cracking due to insufficient drying.

Decoration

Many of the Carpenter shop's jugs, crocks, pitchers, and other forms are decorated with incised, combed bands of parallel lines. Some bands encompass a series of thin, horizontal lines; some, using the same multiline combing technique, are made up of undulating waves of lines (fig. 53). Other potters used similar motifs. The Fox family, potters of German descent who resided in Chatham County, North Carolina, made salt-glazed stoneware and sometimes executed similar decorations, including combed bands of horizontal and wavy lines. Lincoln (now Catawba) County earthenware potter, Jacob Weaver (1774–ca. 1846), slip-trailed similar bands of straight and wavy lines inside earthenware bowls and pans. Early Catawba

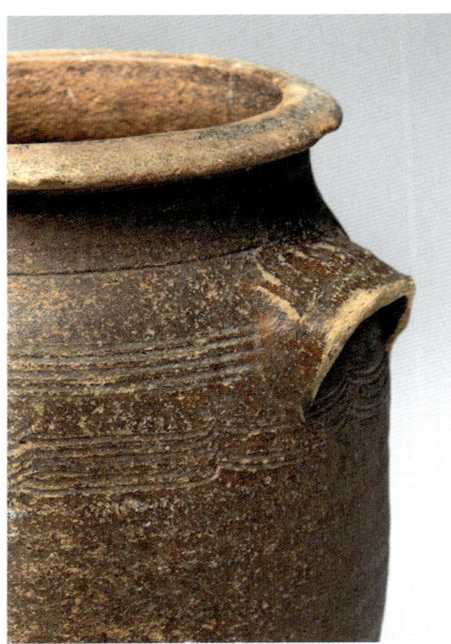

Figure 53 Detail of a four-gallon jar, Carpenter Pottery, Pipers Gap, Carroll County, Virginia, last quarter of the nineteenth century. H. 15". Mark: stamped "JC 4" on rim. (Author's collection; photo, Tim Barnwell Photography.) Harking back to decorations added to Catawba Valley–made alkaline-glazed wares, especially those associated with Thomas Ritchie's pottery, the Carpenter shop potters often added these combined straight- and wavy-line incised patterns to their pottery. Absent a "JC" or "JWC" mark, such embellishments often reliably substitute for a Carpenter shop signature.

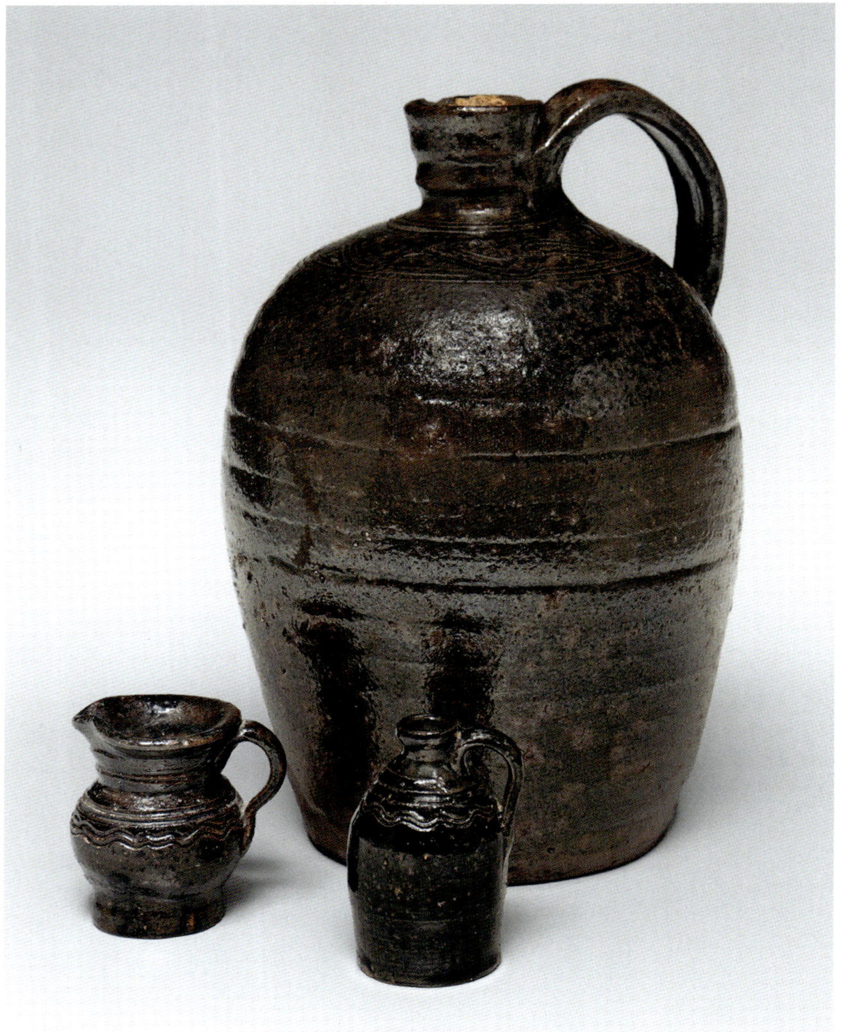

Figure 54 Vessels, attributed to Poley Carp Hartsoe (1876–1960), Catawba County, North Carolina, first half of the twentieth century. Albany slip and alkaline-glazed stoneware. H. of tall jug 11", h. of small jug 3¼", h. of pitcher 2⅞". (Author's collection; photo, Tim Barnwell Photography.) Even into the early years of the twentieth century, North Carolina's Catawba Valley potters applied incised line decoration to their vessels' surfaces. The practice is common among potters associated with the Seagle, Hartzog, and Ritchie family potteries, including members of the Carpenter and Johnson families. Poley Carp Hartsoe was the son of potter Sylvanus Leander Hartsoe (1850–1926) and grandson of potter David Hartzog (1808–1883).

Valley stoneware potters, like David Hartzog, Daniel Seagle, and members of the Ritchie family, all of Germanic descent like the Foxes and Weaver, often included incised line decoration when turning out their pots. A grandson of David Hartzog, Poley Carp Hartsoe (1876–1960), applied similar incised decorations to his ware well into the twentieth century (fig. 54). As noted earlier, wares attributed to William Franklin Carpenter, John Wesley Carpenter, and Johnson family potters that were associated with them are decorated in this manner. From this tradition, the Carpenters most likely derived their style using a combing implement, perhaps the same type used by John Wesley Carpenter when tooling finely reeded necks on his Catawba Valley–made jug spouts.

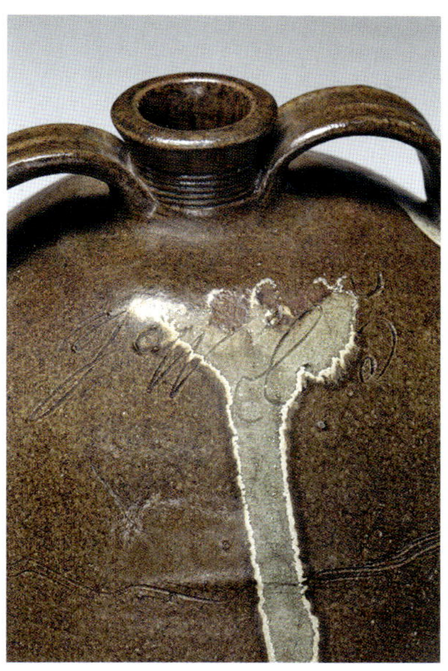

Figure 55 Detail of the jug illustrated in fig. 9. John Wesley Carpenter knew how adding bits of glass to glazed ware before firing could produce dramatic decorative highlights like this one, seen here in a detail from a masterpiece jug signed with his initials, as if to declare with pride, "I made this." It seems that he mostly abandoned the practice after moving to Virginia.

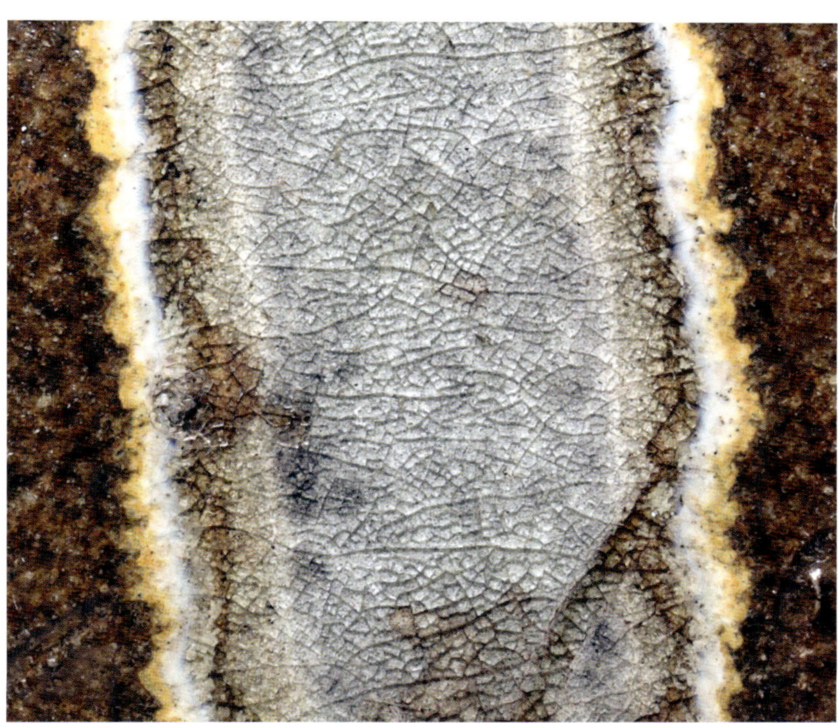

Figure 56 Detail of the glass run illustrated in figs. 9 and 55.

A technique less used by the Carpenters in Carroll County than in Lincoln County is the addition of glass fragments to rims, handles, and spouts, which creates attractive drips and runs through vessels' primary glaze. Glass runs show up plainly against alkaline glaze, as is evident when applied to the jar illustrated in figure 9. If added to the Carpenters' kaolin slip-coated and salt-glazed surfaces, they would be less dramatic in appearance, which could explain the apparent absence of glass runs used by them in Virginia (figs. 55, 56).

Conclusion

Charles G. Zug III, folklorist and author of *Turners and Burners: The Folk Potters of North Carolina*, lists a single Carpenter potter in his index of North Carolina potters—Franklin Carpenter of Lincoln County—but says nothing more about him. Howard A. Smith's *Index of Southern Potters* has no potter named Carpenter. Christopher England's *England's Quick Reference to North Carolina Makers* includes J. W. Carpenter of Wiles, North Carolina, who, as explained above, is unrelated to Lincoln County's Carpenter potters. The MESDA Craftsman Database, maintained by the Museum of Early Southern Decorative Arts (Winston-Salem, N.C.), does not refer to potters named Carpenter.

As this article has demonstrated, however, Franklin Carpenter's brothers John Wesley, Michael Rufus, and Adolphus made pottery, as did their nephew, Andrew F. Speagle. Their father, Elias, might have been a potter. Their pottery-making connects them to numerous potters, among them Bedsaul, Campbell, Cole, Johnson, Ritchie, Stamey, and perhaps other turners, including the Goodmans, Hartzogs, and Seagles. Pottery-making may have been the key to their adaptation to life in the post–Civil War South.

Building on the value of their craft, John Wesley Carpenter appears to be the one who led his family to make some life-altering decisions. The Carpenters first worked in North Carolina but left behind generations of family and community ties when they moved to Pipers Gap, Virginia, seeking freedom from impoverishment. There they produced both alkaline-glazed and salt-glazed stoneware, a fact setting them apart from other Southern potters. A thin slip of kaolin added to their turned wares' surfaces before salt glazing made their work unique. Their Virginia wares' decorative motifs unquestionably tied them to their makers' Catawba Valley, North Carolina, heritage, making it both functional and, at times, quite beautiful. Those were purposeful choices.

While a potter might acknowledge the artistry of his work, Zug's seminal work describing the history of North Carolina's folk potters makes clear that a traditional potter's craft was principally a business to him. As Zug put it, "In purely human terms, the folk pottery provided the extra income that could raise the quality of life for an ambitious man and his family."[96] Both aspects of his trade were familiar to John Wesley Carpenter. Moreover, he sensed how his family's emergence from personal tragedy and a war-ravaged Southern economy depended on their ability to produce pottery in a new way for a new market. Consequently, he charted a course as potter, farmer, brandy maker, and herbal remedy salesman, but mostly as a family leader. Although no one in the Carpenter family makes pottery today, his legacy as an artisan persists through his great-grandson and namesake, John Wesley Carpenter, who is a Pipers Gap, Carroll County, Virginia, schoolteacher, songwriter, and woodworker, a talent befitting the Carpenter family name.

1. I appreciate the assistance of Carpenter family members John Wesley Carpenter, Edith Carpenter Riggins, Robert Riggins, Ken Riggins, Cindy Quesenberry Akers, and Kathy Showalter Dalton.

2. Robert W. Ramsey, *Carolina Cradle: Settlement of the Northwest Carolina Frontier, 1747–1762* (Chapel Hill: University of North Carolina Press, 1964), p. 150.

3. Mark Smith, *Lifting High the Cross for 200 Years: St. John's Lutheran Church* (Baltimore, Md.: Gateway Press, 1998), p. 26.

4. In his book *Carpenters A Plenty* ([1982; reprint, Baltimore, Md.: Gateway Press, 1993], pp. 1–14), Robert C. Carpenter makes a strong case for this assertion. One source claims that

Hans Zimmerman, upon his arrival in North Carolina, was the high priest for a religious group referred to as New Lights or New Mooners. See Smith, *Lifting High the Cross for 200 Years*, p. 26.

5. William L. Sherrill, *The Annals of Lincoln County North Carolina* (1937; reprint, Baltimore, Md.: Regional, 1967), p. 21.

6. Ibid., p. 36.

7. Carpenter, *Carpenters A Plenty*, p. 33.

8. Ibid., p. 36.

9. U.S. Federal Census, 1860, Lincoln County, North Carolina.

10. "Potter Stamey" (John Stamey), Clay County, North Carolina, U.S., Wills and Probate Records, 1665–1998.

11. The names of some of these potters were first brought to the author's attention by Scott W. Smith in an article titled "Documenting Early Catawba Valley 'Potters,'" in *Traditions in Clay*, no. 13 (Raleigh: North Carolina Pottery Collectors' Guild, 2006), pp. 2–7, and a chapter by the same author titled "The Earliest Catawba Valley Potters," in *Valley Ablaze: Pottery Tradition in the Catawba Valley* (Conover, N.C.: Lincoln County Historical Association, 2012), pp. 1–4.

12. Carpenter, *Carpenters A Plenty*, p. 38.

13. "Eli Johnson," ancestry.com, U.S., Civil War Soldier Records and Profiles, 1861–1865.

14. U.S. Federal Census, 1870, Lincoln County, North Carolina.

15. U.S. Federal Census, 1880, Lincoln County, North Carolina.

16. Sherrill, *Annals of Lincoln County North Carolina*, p. 444.

17. U.S. Federal Census, 1900, Carroll County, Virginia.

18. Bethia Caffery, "Mr. Johnson's Daughters," *St. Petersburg* (Fla.) *Independent*, February 24, 1976, p. 2-B.

19. "Amon L. Johnson," appointment as Postmaster, Jugtown, Catawba County, North Carolina, August 6, 1875, ancestry.com. U.S. Appointments of U.S. Postmasters, 1832–1971.

20. "A. L. Johnson," Confederate service record, www.fold3.com

21. Caffery, "Mr. Johnson's Daughters," p. 2-B.

22. U.S. Federal Census, 1840, Lincoln County, North Carolina.

23. Elias Carpenter and Sally S. Johnson, license for a marriage, Lincoln County, North Carolina, September 26, 1832, ancestry.com, North Carolina, U.S., Marriage Records, 1741–2011.

24. Wade D. C. Johnson and Sarah L. Ritchie, certificate of marriage, March 14, 1885, Catawba County, North Carolina, ancestry.com, North Carolina, U.S., Marriage Records, 1741–2011.

25. Henry Ritchie and Sarah Heavner, certificate of marriage, September 26, 1885, Catawba County, North Carolina, ancestry.com, North Carolina, U.S., Marriage Records, 1741–2011.

26. Charles G. Zug III, *Turners and Burners: The Folk Potters of North Carolina* (Chapel Hill: University of North Carolina Press, 1986), p. 440.

27. U.S. Federal Census, 1880, Bandys Township, Catawba County, North Carolina; U.S. Federal Census, 1900, Jacobs Fork Township, Catawba County, North Carolina; U.S. Federal Census, 1920, Jacobs Fork Township, Catawba County, North Carolina. Susan Johnston (*sic*) is called a "lodger." See also North Carolina Standard Certificate of Death for Susan Johnson, Jacobs Fork, Catawba County, North Carolina, filed March 20, 1922, where it is stated that she "Made home with L. S. Ritckey [*sic*]."

28. U.S. Federal Census, 1850, Lincoln County, North Carolina.

29. The 1820 U.S. Federal Census for Surry County, North Carolina, shows that four people in Silas Vestal's household were "engaged in manufactures." In the 1820s Silas Vestal moved to Greene County, Tennessee, and operated a pottery there. According to a Russell family historian, Greene County resident Benjamin Allen Russell was an apprentice to Silas Vestal around 1825 before working as a potter for Peter Harmon.

30. See Stephen C. Compton, "Research Note: The Eighteenth-Century Potters of Salisbury and Rowan County, North Carolina," *Journal of Early Southern Decorative Arts* 39 (2018): 143–56.

31. The similarity of some Ritchie (and Johnson, Carpenter, and Bedsaul) wares to Seagle wares leaves open the possibility that Moses Ritchie learned the trade from Adam Seagle before passing along Seagle family traits to his sons, including Thomas Ritchie. After working in Huntsville, North Carolina, Moses Ritchie moved to the Catawba Valley, where he made pottery.

32. William Franklin, Mary A., Jacob, Martha M., John Wesley, Michael Rufus, Adolphus Lafayette, Christopher Sylvanus, Sarah Elizabeth, and Barbara Frances.

33. U.S. Federal Census, 1860, Lincoln County, North Carolina.

34. Sherrill, *Annals of Lincoln County North Carolina*, p. 445.

35. John W Busey and Travis W. Busey, "William Frank Carpenter," *Confederate Casualties at Gettysburg: A Comprehensive Record*, vol. 2 (Jefferson, N.C.: McFarland & Co., 2017), p. 892.

36. "William Frank Carpenter," Confederate service record, www.fold3.com.

37. U.S. Federal Census, 1870, Lincoln County, North Carolina.

38. U.S. Federal Census, 1880, Lincoln County, North Carolina.

39. Brothers John, Michael, and Jacob Tobias Goodman were sons of Daniel and Margaret Kluttz Goodman of Cabarrus County, North Carolina. Michael and Tobias are first identified as potters in the 1850 U.S. Federal Census.

40. Carpenter, *Carpenters A Plenty*, p. 52.

41. Marc King, "Mysterious JC, Potter, Identified," *Voices* 20 (2016): 2.

42. "Jacob Carpenter," Confederate service record, www.fold3.com.

43. "Jno Speagle," Confederate service record, www.fold3.com.

44. U.S. Federal Census, 1870, Lincoln County, North Carolina.

45. U.S. Federal Census, 1880, Wythe County, Virginia; J. Roderick Moore, *Index of Great Road Potters*, "Earthenware Potters Along the Great Road in Virginia and Tennessee" (Ferrum, Va.: Blue Ridge Institute and Museum, 1983).

46. "A. F. Speagle and Melinda J. Jones," marriage certificate, Surry County, North Carolina, December 14, 1880. North Carolina, U.S., Marriage Records, 1741–2011.

47. "Michael Carpenter," Confederate service record, www.fold3.com.

48. "Michael Rufus Carpenter," certificate of death, September 1, 1917, Carroll County, Virginia, U.S., Death Records, 1912–2014.

49. "Adolphus Carpenter," Confederate service record, www.fold3.com.

50. U.S. Federal Census, 1870, 1880, Carroll County, Virginia.

51. U.S. Federal Census, 1880, Carroll County, Virginia.

52. A J.C.-marked jug has been collected in Missouri, and a cobalt-decorated pitcher attributed to the Carpenter pottery shop and associated with the Bedsaul family has been observed. Both appear to be Virginia-made Carpenter products. Like Adolphus Carpenter, potter George Washington Bedsaul moved ca. 1884 from Carroll County, Virginia, to Missouri.

53. King, "Mysterious JC, Potter, Identified," p. 3.

54. "Emily B. Carpenter," application of a widow for a Confederate pension, 1914, Alabama, Texas, and Virginia, U.S. Confederate Pensions, 1884–1958.

55. Caffery, "Mr. Johnson's Daughters," p. 2-B.

56. J. W. Carpenter and wife, Elizabeth, to the State of North Carolina, deed, Wilkes County, North Carolina, March 26, 1892, DB 15:49, Wilkes County Register of Deeds, Wilkesboro, North Carolina.

57. Carpenter, *Carpenters A Plenty*, p. 1007.

58. Potter Eli Johnson's brother, John Johnson, recalled in 1928, at age eighty-seven, that Moses Ritchie ran a "jug factory" about "75 or 80 years ago," and that "he had three sons, Thomas, Henry, and Joseph, who engaged in pottery after their father died." Sherrill, *Annals of Lincoln County North Carolina*, p. 444.

59. Letter to J. W. Carpenter from M. E. Stevens, The Great American Herb Co., Washington, D.C., January 27, 1910, *Carroll County Chronicles* 27, no. 1 (Spring 2008): 27.

60. Ibid.

61. King, "Mysterious JC, Potter, Identified," p. 2.

62. Adolphus and Mary Carpenter's daughter, Martha Maybelle, was born in Lincoln County, North Carolina, on March 22, 1867. Their son, William Pinkney, was born in Carroll County, Virginia, on July 8, 1869.

63. King, "Mysterious JC, Potter, Identified," p. 2.

64. U.S. Federal Census, 1870, Pipers Gap, Carroll County, Virginia.

65. "John W. Carpenter," Virginia, U.S., Select Marriages, 1785–1940.

66. U.S. Federal Census, 1880, Pipers Gap, Carroll County, Virginia.

67. DB 13:402–403, DB 16:92–93, DB 17:295, DB 20:446, DB 22:508–509, DB 22:519–520, Carroll County, North Carolina, Register of Deeds Office, Hillsville, Virginia.

68. F. Clyde Bedsaul, "Pottery Industry Once Flourished in Carroll," *The Roanoke* (Va.) *Times*, July 19, 1959, p. B-8.

69. A salt-glazed storage jar (see fig. 28), clearly marked with the incised name "G. W. BEDSAUL," bears what appears to be a stamped numeral or letter followed by what seems to be a letter *B* on its rim. Many of John Wesley Carpenter pottery vessels are similarly marked on their rims with the letters *JC*. Catawba Valley pottery-shop owners also marked their wares in this manner, including those made by turners employed by them.

70. Deed, Adolphus and Mary Carpenter to David Campbell, December 11, 1880, Carroll County, Virginia, DB 14:423–424; Deed, C. C. and Elizabeth Snow to Adolphus Carpenter, June 14, 1879, delivered to David Campbell on February 18, 1884, Carroll County, Virginia, DB 14:18–19.

71. U.S. Federal Census, 1870, Wytheville, Wythe County, Virginia; U.S. Federal Census, 1880, Rich Valley, Smyth County, Virginia. According to John Johnson, William Campbell worked as a potter in North Carolina "for several years" but "moved to Virginia after the Civil War and there continued the same work." Sherrill, *Annals of Lincoln County North Carolina*, p. 444.

72. See Samuel D. Smith and Stephen T. Rogers, *Tennessee Potteries, Pots, and Potters: 1790s to 1950*, Research Series 18 (Nashville: Tennessee Department of Environment and Conservation, Division of Archaeology, 2011), 2:599–603.

73. Ibid., 1:188.

74. U.S. Federal Census, 1880, Pipers Gap, Carroll County, Virginia.

75. In his novel *Spring Valley* (Radford, Va.: Commonwealth Press, 1975), F. Clyde Bedsaul substitutes the surname Cole for Carpenter when describing John Wesley Carpenter's pottery operation.

76. Bedsaul, "Pottery Industry Once Flourished in Carroll," p. B-8.

77. "George Bedsaul and Eliza Carpenter," North Carolina, U.S. Marriage Index, 1741–2004.

78. Deed, Martin and Jane Hanks to George W. and Sarah E. Bedsaul, September 10, 1881, Carroll County, Virginia, DB 15:8.

79. Bedsaul, "Pottery Industry Once Flourished in Carroll," p. B-8.

80. Anna J. Stose and George W. Stose, *Geology and Mineral Resources of the Gossan Lead District and Adjacent Areas in Virginia* (Charlottesville, Va.: Dept. of Conservation and Development, Virginia Division of Mineral Resources, 1957), p. 91.

81. Ibid., p. 211.

82. Bedsaul, "Pottery Industry Once Flourished in Carroll," p. B-8.

83. Ibid.

84. Ibid.

85. Ibid.

86. Appreciation to Nowell Conan Guffey for this information.

87. A second, undocumented kiln for alkaline-glazing may have been used for this purpose. Since Carpenter's manufacture of alkaline-glazed ware was limited, the expense of building and maintaining a second kiln might have led him to use the same furnace for making it and salt-glazed stoneware.

88. Stose and Stose, *Geology and Mineral Resources of the Gossan Lead District and Adjacent Areas in Virginia*, p. 214.

89. Bedsaul, "Pottery Industry Once Flourished in Carroll," p. B-8.

90. Linda F. Carnes-McNaughton, "Transitions and Continuity: Earthenware and Stoneware Pottery Production in Nineteenth Century North Carolina," Ph.D. diss., University of North Carolina–Chapel Hill (1997), pp. 142, 152.

91. Zug, *Turners and Burners*, p. 205.

92. In his novel *Spring Valley*, F. Clyde Bedsaul describes the removable salt port covers as "many little crocklike lids with rounded knobs for handles" (Radford, Va.: Commonwealth Press, 1975), p. 41.

93. H. E. Comstock, *The Pottery of the Shenandoah Valley Region* (Winston-Salem, N.C.: Museum of Early Southern Decorative Arts, 1994), pp. 16–17.

94. Bedsaul, "Pottery Industry Once Flourished in Carroll," p. B-8.

95. Peter Bedsaul lived in Oak Grove, Missouri, in the vicinity of potters Adolphus Carpenter and George Washington Bedsaul. The note describing the circumstances of his acquisition of the decorated pitcher was brought to my attention by its current owner, Wesley Hall.

96. Zug, *Turners and Burners*, p. 284.

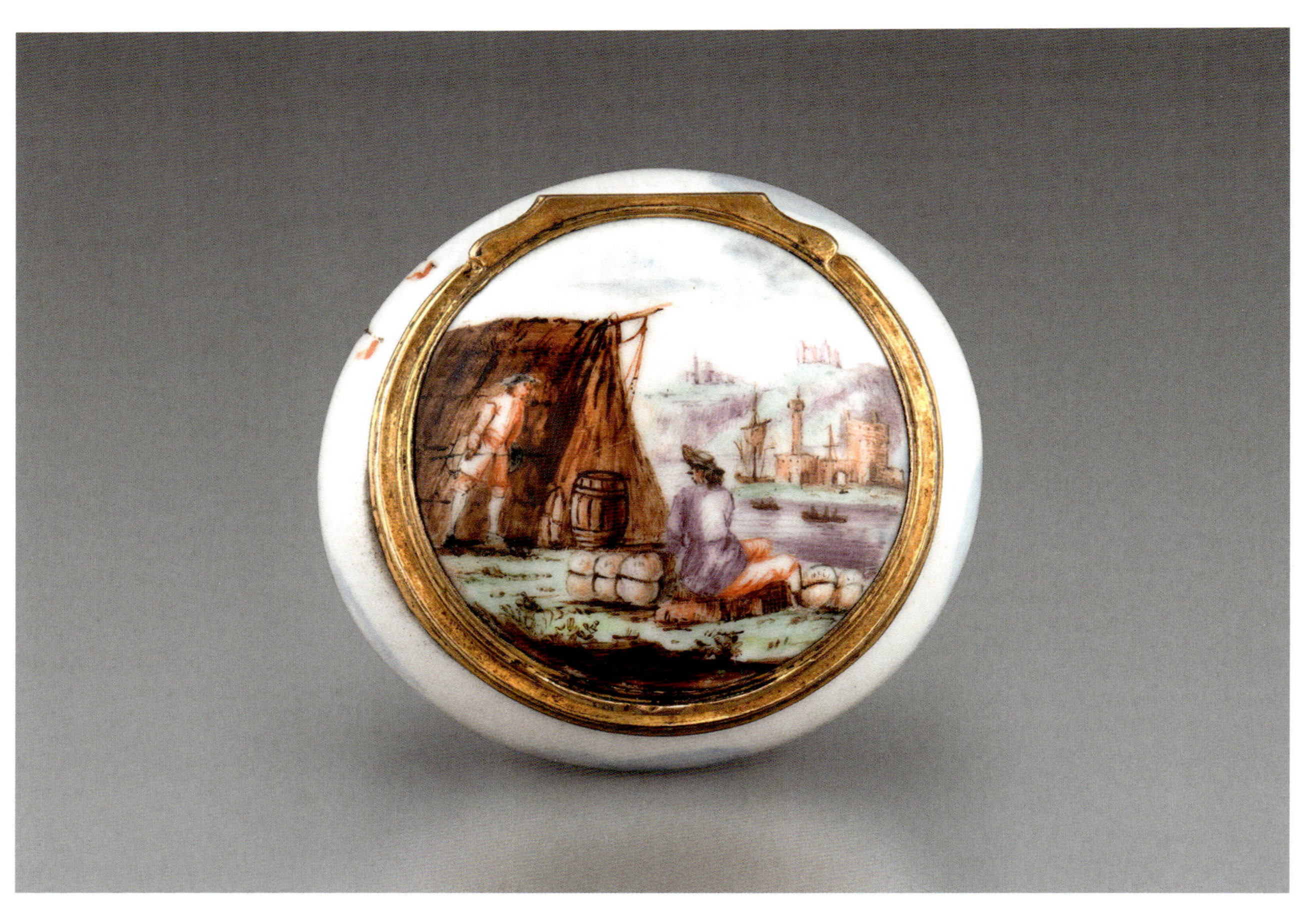

Figure 1 Detail of the lid of the snuff box illustrated in fig. 2. (Chipstone Foundation; photo, Gavin Ashworth.)

W. Ross Ramsay, Howell G. M. Edwards, Errol Manners, and Ashley Howkins

Geochemical Investigation of a Ceramic Snuff Box—A-Marked English Porcelain Attribution Confirmed

▼ AN EIGHTEENTH-CENTURY porcelain ceramic snuff box came up for sale at a leading auction house in London in 2012. This box had been previously attributed to the Italian factory of Doccia, but at this sale, based on the shape of the box and a scan of the glaze acquired using a handheld X-ray fluorescence (XRF) analyzer, the item was reattributed to the small group of A-marked porcelains now attributed to the 1744 patent of Edward Heylyn and Thomas Frye and, by implication, to the Bow porcelain manufactory. A feature of this scan was the prominent peaks in the spectra for lead, an element not associated with the A-marked group. The body, glaze, and on-glaze enamels for this snuff box have now been nondestructively reanalyzed using JEOL JSM-IT200 scanning electron microscope (SEM) and quantitative Energy Dispersive X-ray Spectroscopy (EDX) system and the data are presented and discussed. The lead previously reported in the glaze is shown to be surface glaze contamination. Based on body and glaze compositions the conclusion is that this box conforms to the 1744 patent specification and hence is attributable to the high-fired A-marked group of English porcelains.

Background of the A-marked Porcelains Group

A small group of porcelains known as the A-marked porcelains or 1744 patent porcelains was first recognized on December 14, 1937, at the Albemarle Club, London, when four items were discussed at a meeting.[1] No agreement was reached as to the group's attribution, however. Subsequently, Arthur Lane assembled seven objects from this group and conferred on them the name "A-marked."[2] Lane noted that the porcelain body was much harder than typical English soft-paste porcelains and he proposed that their bodies were of a "hybrid" type containing some kaolin clay. This hardness of the body once led some to suggest a continental origin but a paper by Robert J. Charleston and John V. G. Mallet established that this group was British in origin.[3] Subsequent research has confirmed that these porcelains conform to the 1744 patent specification of Edward Heylyn and Thomas Frye, and that the key ingredient of that specification was the so-called Cherokee clay imported from the Carolinas of America. The 1744 patent specified the use of a clay, "an earth, the produce of the Chirokee nation in America, called by the natives unaker."[4]

Ruthie Dibble and Joseph Zordan have recently emphasized the importance of this white clay to the Cherokee people having aesthetic, spiritual, and relational values and they claim the clay to have an inalienable kinship with the Cherokees.[5] A summary of this group of porcelains now comprising some forty members and made from this white clay, has been just published in 2022.[6] This latest account provides an outline of the history of these A-marked porcelains, their various attributions proposed over time, and a summary of all published analyses of this group—both body and glaze. These authors concluded that the A-marked porcelain group can now be regarded as arguably the first fully commercial 'hard-paste' porcelain wares to have been produced in mid-eighteenth-century England and, quoting a commentator, they noted that as a corollary there needs to be a reassessment of the assumed premier position of the Chelsea Porcelain Works.

Initial Examination of the Snuff Box

The snuff box with a gilt-metal mount is illustrated in figures 1–5 and measures 1⅞ x 2½ x 2⅜ inches. A detail of the bottom, illustrated in figure 6, shows use-wear to the enameled decoration as might be expected. Initially assumed to be unmarked, when examined by co-author Manners, an indistinct incised "A" mark in the interior of the bottom was observed. This mark had been overlooked or unrecorded. When subsequently photographed in raking light using a polarizing filter on the camera to minimize glare, the incised "A" becomes much more apparent (fig. 7). In this present account the body, glaze, and on-glaze enamels of the porcelain snuff box are examined nondestructively—and a firm attribution to the A-marked group of porcelains is made.

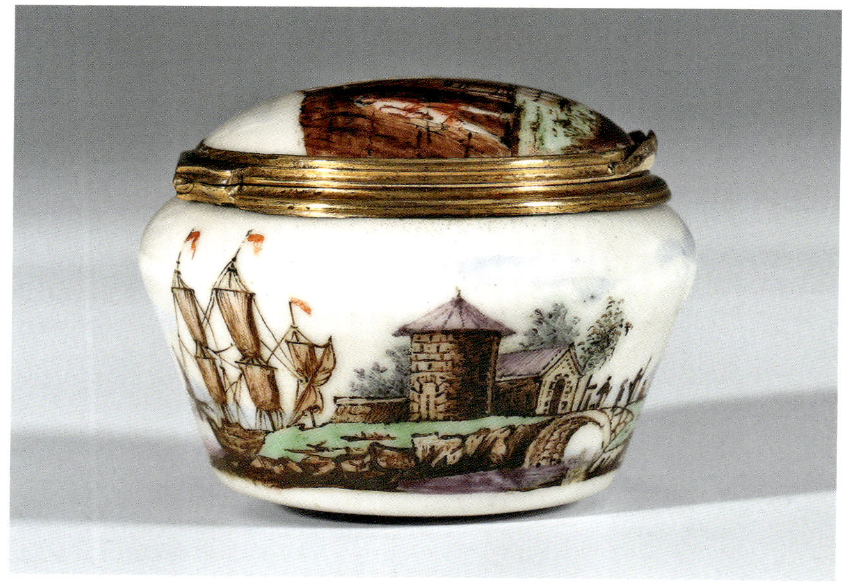

Figure 2 Snuff box, attributed to the A-marked group, east London, England, ca. 1744–1745. Hard-paste porcelain with enamels. D. 2⅜". (Chipstone Foundation; photo, courtesy Errol Manners.)

Figure 3 View of the snuff box illustrated in fig. 2 with the lid open showing its gilded copper collar. (Chipstone Foundation; photo, courtesy Errol Manners.)

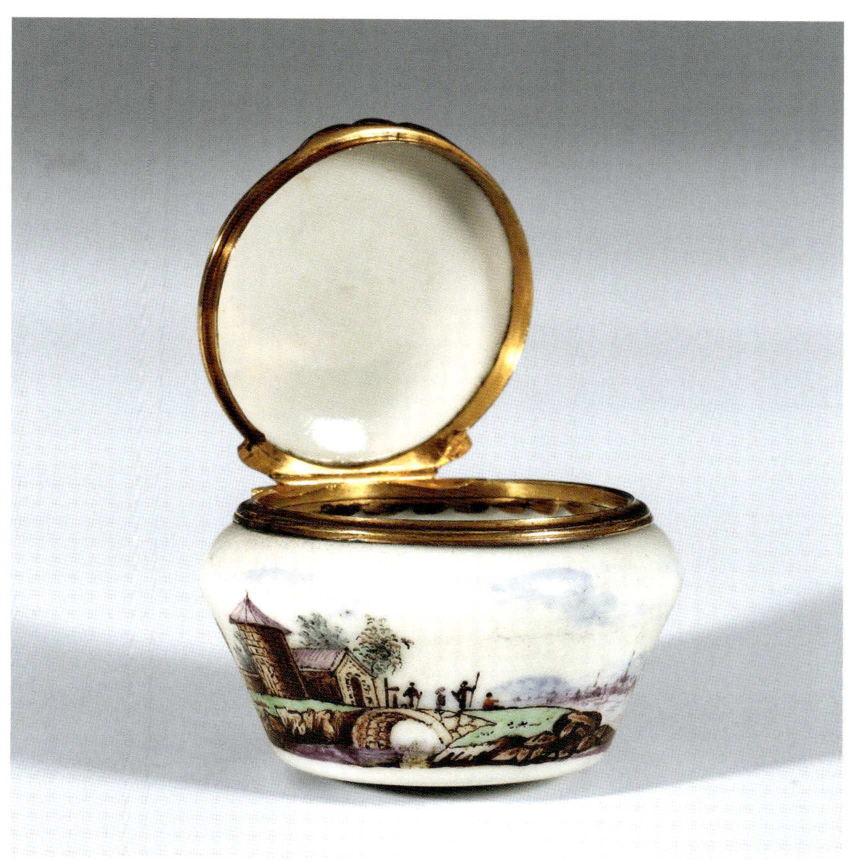

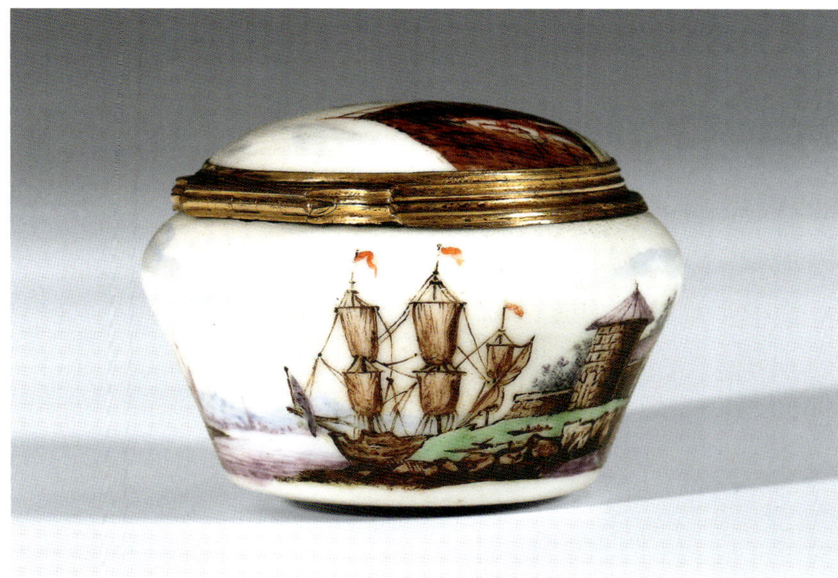

Figure 4 Side view of the snuff box illustrated in fig. 2 with sailing vessel and castle (Chipstone Foundation; photo, courtesy Errol Manners.)

Figure 5 Side view of the snuff box illustrated in fig. 2 with castle and bridge. (Chipstone Foundation; photo, courtesy Errol Manners.)

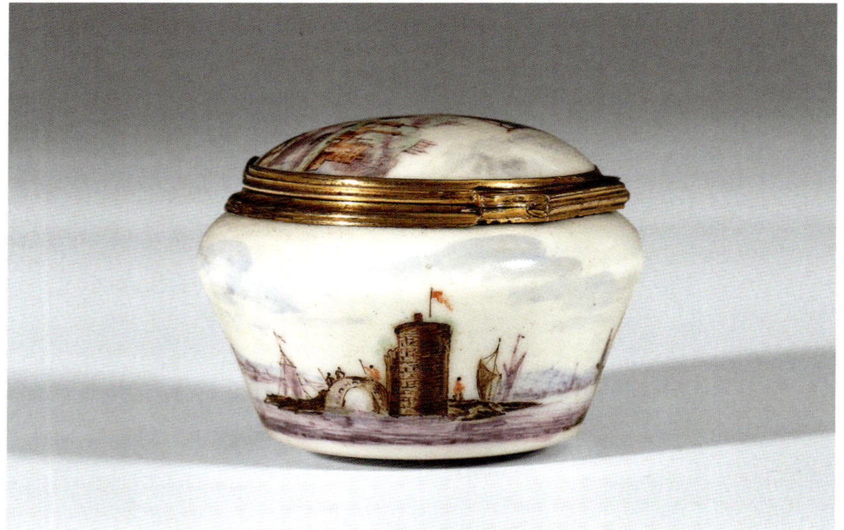

Figure 6 View of the bottom of the snuff box illustrated in fig. 2. (Chipstone Foundation; photo, Gavin Ashworth.)

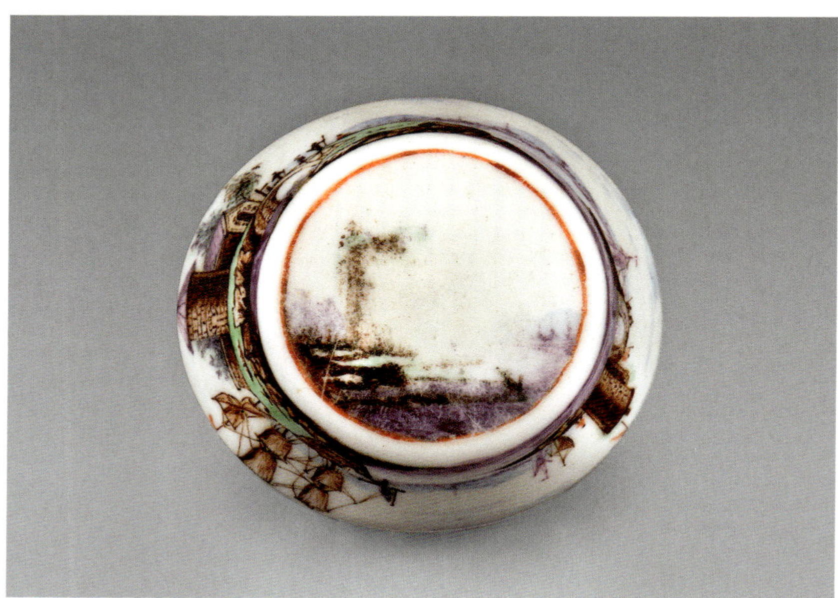

The snuff box is one of three that can be attributed to the A-marked group, which has long intrigued ceramic scholars. All three are of near identical form and size and have the same gilt-copper hinged mounts, but each is decorated differently. The box under discussion is painted with merchants and ships in harbor scenes in the Meissen "Kauffahrtei" style. Similar decoration of castellated towers, casks, and barrels by the same hand is also found on the cover of a box in the National Museum of Wales, Cardiff (fig. 8). A third box, sold by Stockspring Antiques in 2012 and now in the Peter and Mary White collection, is painted with a butterfly and fruit (fig. 9). All three boxes use the same basic palette of brown, green, purple, blue, yellow, and iron-red to different effect.

The Cardiff snuff box also has an indistinct incised mark that has been read as an *A*. Likewise, elements of the decoration, notably the iron-red

Figure 7 View of the interior bottom of the snuff box illustrated in fig. 2 revealing a faintly incised "A" mark. (Chipstone Foundation; photo, Gavin Ashworth.)

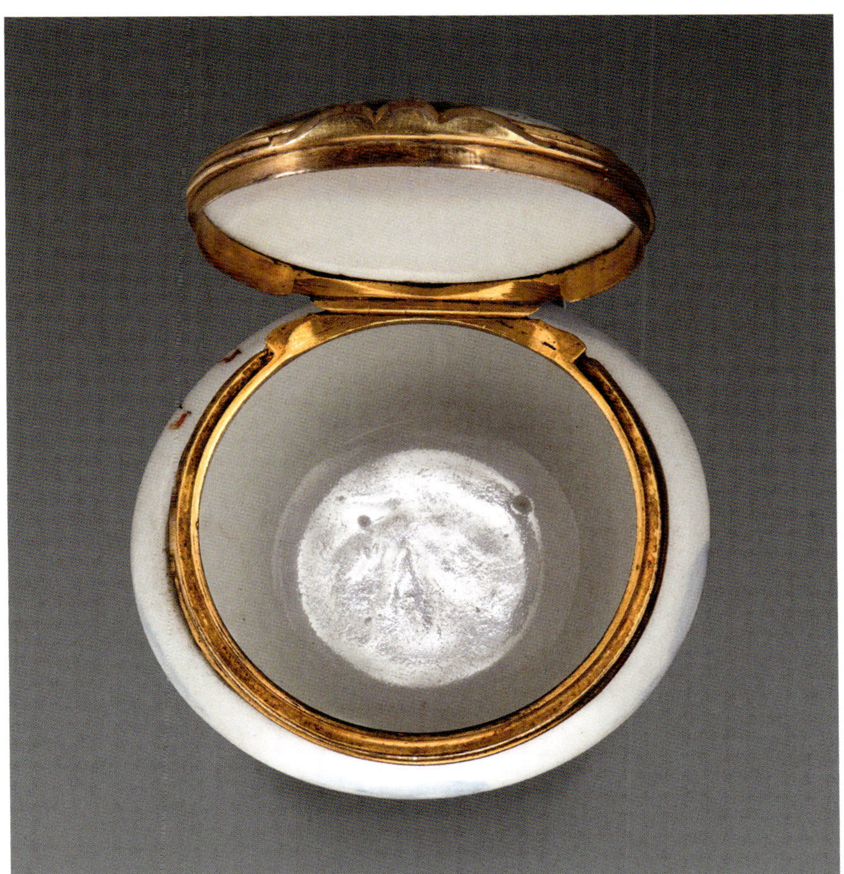

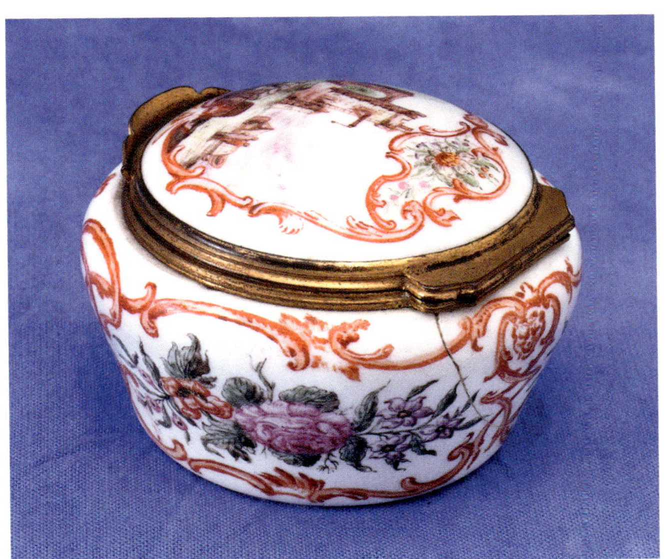

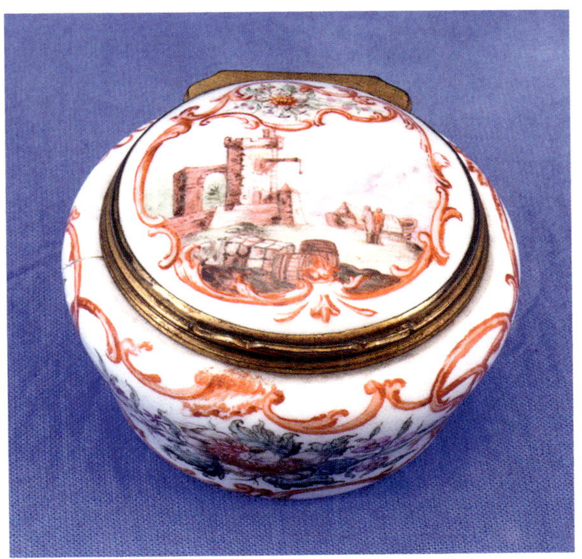

Figure 8 Snuff box, attributed to the A-marked group, east London, England, ca. 1744–1745. Hard-paste porcelain with enamels. Diam. 2⅜". (National Museum of Wales, Cardiff, De Winton Collection of Continental Porcelain, acc. no. D.W. 552). Enameled with an "A" or "V" incised. The body of the box is decorated with various flowers and leaves within panels of intertwined scrolls. A scene set within a scrolled cartouche comprising a castellated building and barrels is depicted on the lid.

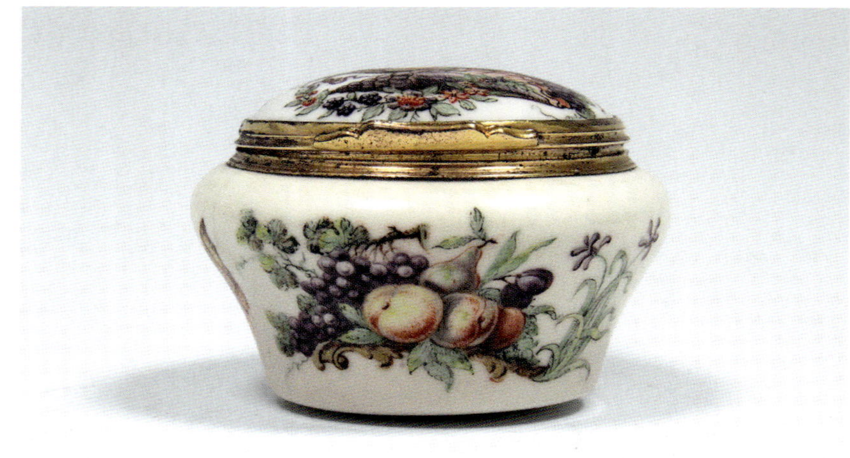

Figure 9 Snuff box, attributed to the A-marked group, east London, England, ca. 1744–1745. Hard-paste porcelain with enamels. Diam. 2⅜". (Private collection.) The body and lid are enameled with a butterfly, fruit, flowers, and leaves.

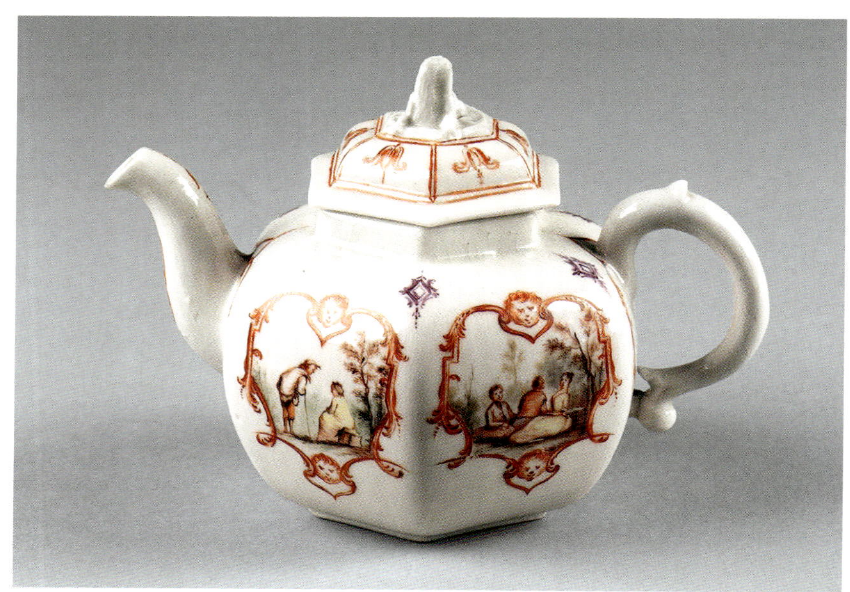

Figure 10 Hexagonal teapot, attributed to the A-marked group, east London, England, ca. 1744–1745. Hard-paste porcelain with enamels. H. 4¼." (V&A Museum collections, C.207-1937.) Underglaze blue "A" under base and inside lid. The iron-red cartouche and the mascarons link this teapot to the Cardiff snuff box illustrated in fig. 8.

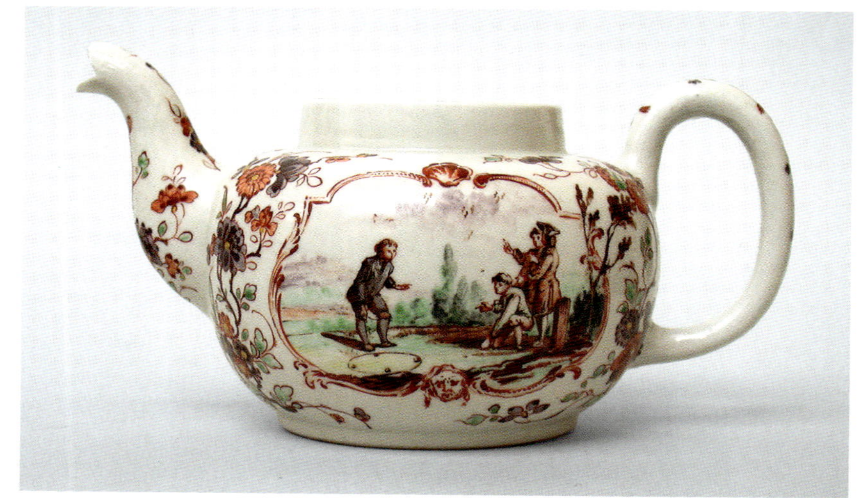

Figure 11 Teapot, attributed to the A-marked group, east London, England, ca. 1744–1745. Hard-paste porcelain with enamels. H. 3⁷⁄₁₆". Underglaze "A" on base. (V&A Museum collections, C.1-1991.) This teapot, formerly in the Geoffrey Godden Collection, uses scenes from a series of youthful diversions designed by Gravelot and published by Cole on October 24, 1740. The two scenes depicted are titled *Bow and Arrows* and *Playing with Marbles*. The pot is also linked to the Cardiff snuff box by way of an iron-red cartouche and mascarons.

scroll work of the Cardiff box and the fruit garlands of the Stockspring/White example link them to marked High Style teawares of the A-marked group. The term *High Style* was introduced by Charleston and Mallet to differentiate the more painterly wares of the A-marked group from the simpler stock patterns.[7]

The treatment of the iron-red rococo scrolls and lion head mascarons on the Cardiff box can be matched to the cartouche scrolls on two A-marked teapots in the Victoria and Albert Museum and are most likely by the same hand (figs. 10, 11). The scrolls and mascarons follow closely the borders in the engraving by Jacques Bachelet after Hubert-François Gravelot of *Le Jeu de la Crosse* and in the engraved sheet, "The Second part of Youthful Diversions, published according to Act of Parliament 7th May 1739," which is the source for decoration on other members of the A-marked wares.[8] The bunches of fruit on the box in the private collection (see fig. 9) match the fruit falling from the cornucopia on the unique cane handle located by Elizabeth Adams and now in the Victoria and Albert collections (fig. 12). The iron-red shell and small figures on the cane handle can, in turn, be closely linked to the two teapots.

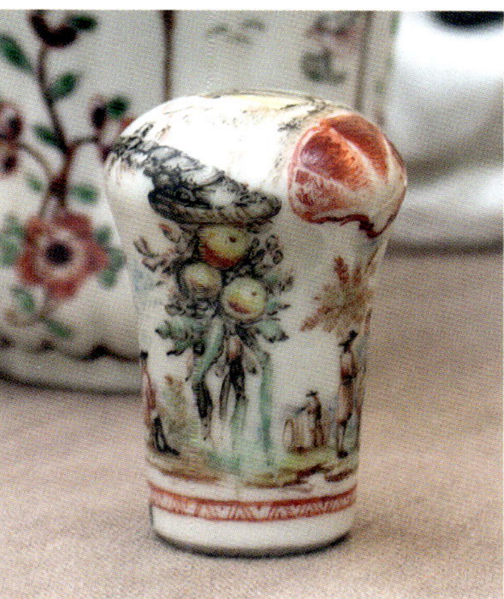

Figure 12 Cane handle, attributed to the A-marked group, east London, England, ca. 1744–1745. Hard-paste porcelain with enamels. H. 1¾". Unmarked. (V&A Museum collections, C.148-1993.) Three flanking scenes supposedly in the Meissen manner with a prominent shell in iron red. Elizabeth Adams, "'Birmingham' Porcelain," *Antique Dealer and Collectors Guide* (November 1992): 22–27.

The box illustrated in figure 2 was once in an Italian collection acquired through the Rome dealers Lukacs-Donath in 1966, who often bought in London.[9] It was then mistakenly published as Doccia, as the paste does bear some similarity. It was correctly identified by Nette Megens of Bonhams, London, in 2011, as belonging to the A-marked group because of its close similarities in shape with the Cardiff box. Tests carried out by Kelly Domoney and Prof. Andrew Shortland of Cranfield University with a SEA6000VX mapping XRF confirmed that the glaze matched the Cardiff box and differed from Doccia.[10] However, in a discussion on these glaze spectra Ramsay and Ramsay questioned the high lead levels reported, and argued that such glaze compositions are not in accord with the 1744 patent specification of Heylyn and Frye.[11] Consequently, it was decided to reanalyze this snuff box—body, glaze, and enamels—at Brunel University on March 14, 2022, through the courtesy of Dr. Ashley Howkins.

Analytical and Technical Background to Analyses at Brunel University

SEM imaging was carried out using a JEOL JSM-IT200 SEM, and quantitative EDX analysis was carried out using an Oxford Xplore 15mm² EDX detector with accompanying Aztec software (fig. 13). The SEM was oper-

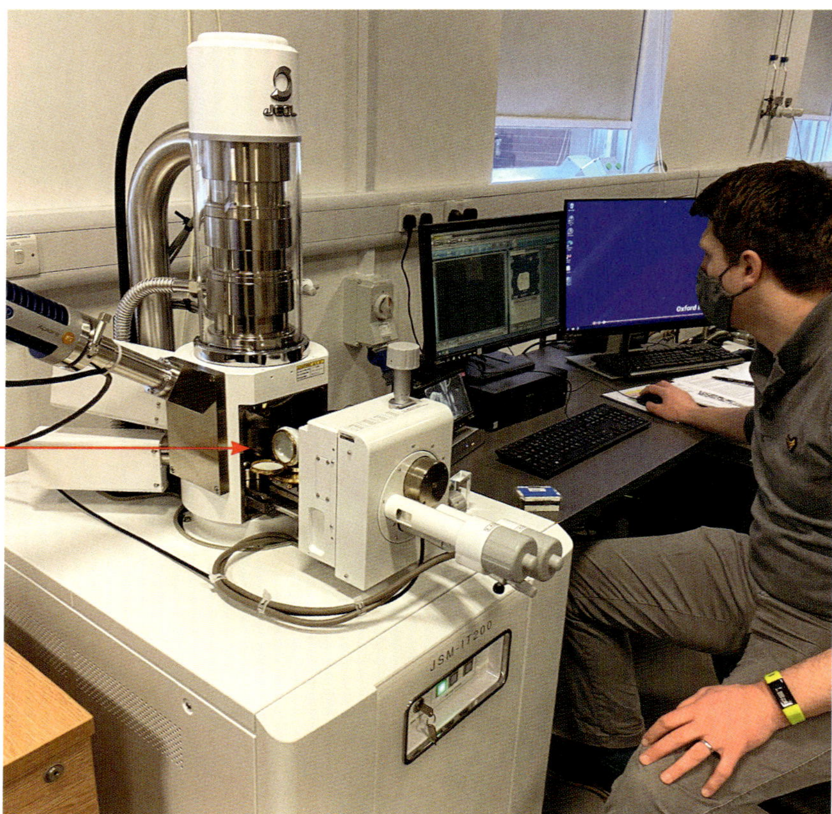

Figure 13 The JEOL JSM-IT200 SEM coupled with an Oxford Xplore 15mm² EDX detector, Brunel University, London, operated by Dr. Ashley Howkins. The snuff box can be seen on its side with its lid open prior to being inserted into the SEM chamber (red arrow)

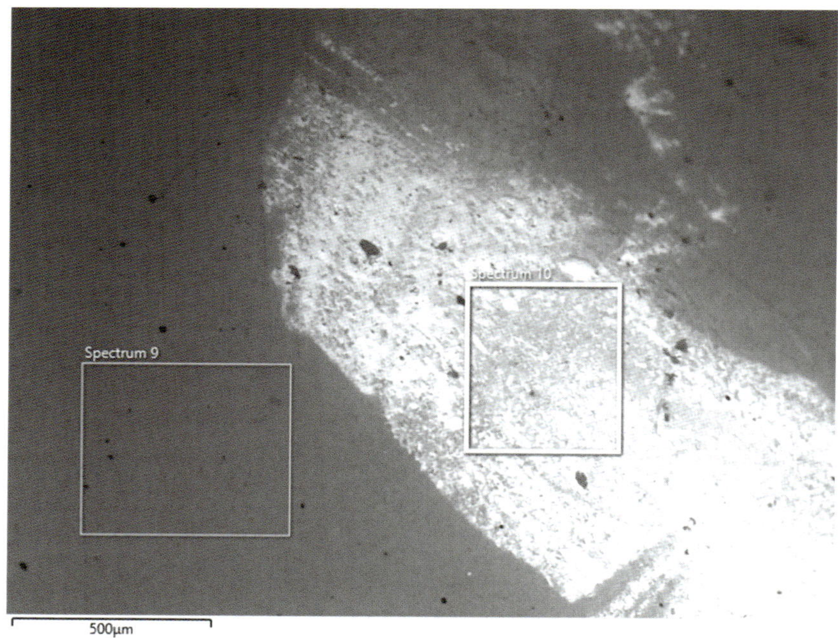

Figure 14 Compositional back-scattered electron SEM micrograph acquired from the area of the red flag enamel design on the main body of the porcelain snuff box illustrated in fig. 2. The high-contrast region (brighter) is from the pigmentation of the red enamel, whereas the gray regions are from the background white glaze of the porcelain. Boxes demonstrate small area EDX analyses carried out within areas of interest.

ated under low vacuum conditions, 30-60Pa, with an accelerating voltage of 20kV, which enables charge-free imaging. EDX analysis was done with a minimum count rate of 1,000 counts per second and 30–100s live-time acquisition.

Back-scattered electron images were acquired in compositional and shadowing modes, which enable identification of regions of elemental difference and topography, respectively. Operating the SEM in such imaging

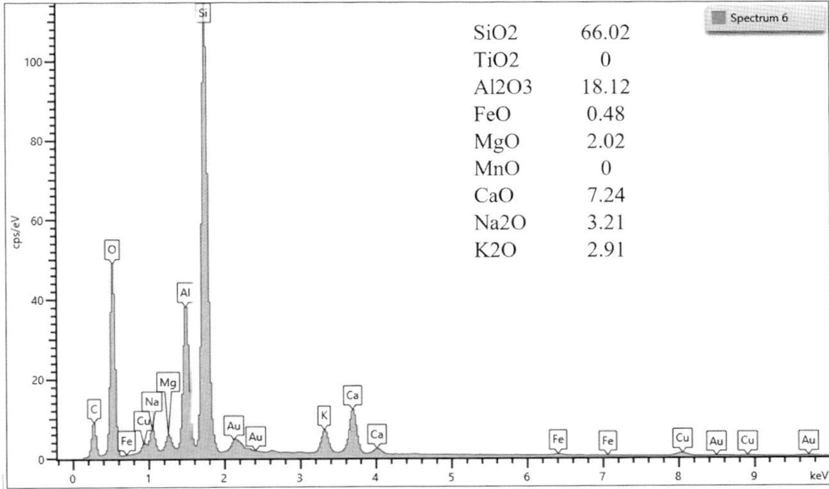

Figure 15 Spectrum 6 of the porcelain body on the rim to the snuff box adjacent to gold-copper collar, free of glaze. The calculated analysis shown in the right in the figure has had both gold (3.36 wt% Au_2O_3) and copper (1.95 wt% CuO) removed.

modes enabled differentiation of areas of enamel from the glaze, and areas where the glaze had worn away as a result of a rubbing action from the metal rim revealing the underlying porcelain (fig. 14).

Discussion on the Snuff Box Porcelain Body

Fourteen scans of the snuff box—body, glaze, and on-glaze enamels—were undertaken at Brunel University. The box is fully glaze-covered but a glaze-denuded area adjacent to the gold-copper metal collar revealed the underlying porcelain body (Spectrum No. 6). This spectrum is presented in figure 15. Contamination by gold, copper, and/or lead was experienced and in the case of Spectrum 6 gold and copper oxides comprise 5.3 wt% of the analysis (Table 1). Both oxides are regarded as contaminants from the copper-gilt mounts and have been removed with the resultant total being recast to 100%.

Currently there are nine A-marked porcelain body analyses in the literature as summarized in Edwards et al. The body analysis of this snuff box as provided here raises the total to ten.[12] A feature often overlooked in some previous A-marked studies is that there is a wide range of A-marked body compositions. The 1744 patent specification stated that porcelain compositions produced could range from 50 wt% Cherokee clay: 50 wt% lime-alkali bottle glass through to 80:20 wt%. Analyses to date have identified examples of this porcelain group ranging from 50:50 through to 70:30 wt%, but a composition of 80:20 wt% has yet to be identified.[13] The body composition of this snuff box falls within the 50:50 wt% group and two other examples of this type present themselves, namely the two cups investigated by Edwards et al (fig. 16).[14] Comparative analyses of all three are given in Table 1 below.

Table 1 Porcelain body analyses. Initial analysis of the snuff box taken from Spectrum 6 with 3.36 wt% Au_2O_3 and 1.95 wt% CuO contamination. Also shown is the analysis recalculated free of both gold and copper compared with similar body analysis taken from two A-marked cups, Cup 1 and Cup 2. Edwards, Jay, and Ramsay, "High-Fired Early English Porcelains of the 'A'-Marked Group, East London (c. 1744)."

	1	2	3	4
SiO_2	62.22	66.02	63.8	60.9
TiO_2			0.3	0.1
Al_2O_3	17.38	18.12	17.9	20.1
FeO	0.45	0.48	0.5	0.4
MgO	1.95	2.02	0.7	0.7
MnO				0.1
CaO	6.84	7.24	9.7	10.4
Na_2O	3.09	3.21	1.9	1.6
K_2O	2.76	2.91	4.2	4.1
P_2O_5			0.3	0.2
PbO			0.5	0.2
Au_2O_3	3.36			
CuO	1.95			
SnO_2				1.1
	100	100	99.8	99.9

1. Analysis of snuff box porcelain body Spectrum 6, with gold and copper surface impurities
2. Analysis of snuff box porcelain body with gold and copper surface impurities removed
3. Analysis of porcelain body in Cup 1
4. Analysis of porcelain body in Cup 2

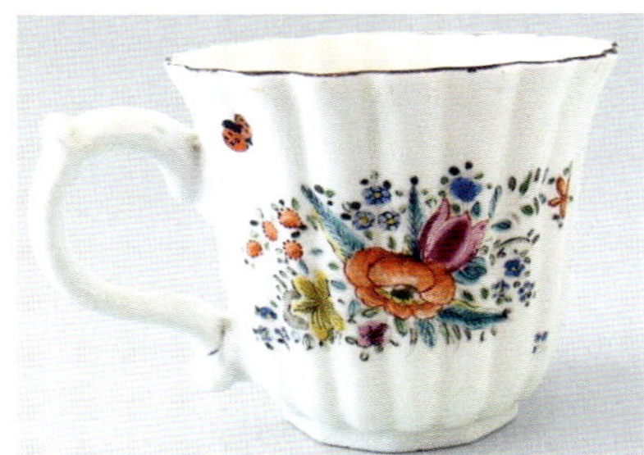

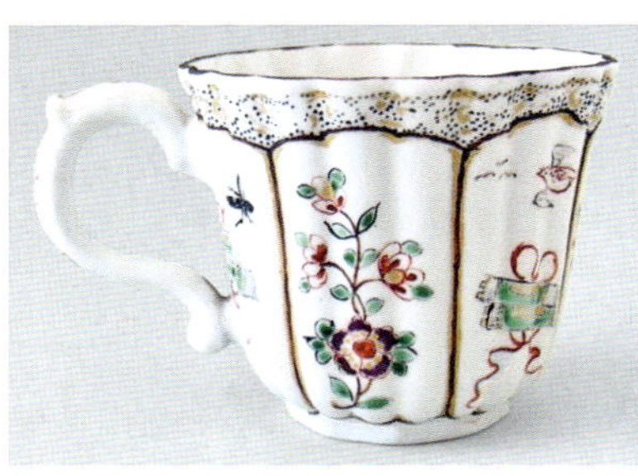

Figure 16 Two coffee cups, attributed to the A-marked group, east London, England, ca. 1744–1745. Hard-paste porcelain with enamels. H. of top cup 2⅜", H. of bottom cup 2¼". (Private collections; courtesy of John Wiley & Sons, Ltd.) Both are slip-cast with decagonal foot rims. The cup on the top is decorated with European-style flower sprays; the cup on the bottom has six alternating vertical panels with flowers, scrolls, and a bird.

The results from Spectrum 6 demonstrate that the body of the snuff box was produced according to the specifications of the 1744 Heylyn and Frye patent. Key chemical features of this spectrum that support this conclusion are:

- High Al_2O_3 at 18.1 wt% indicative of a refractory body.[15]
- Prominent alkali and alkali earth oxide fluxes with CaO > K_2O + Na_2O.
- Absence or very low levels of the colorant oxides MnO, FeO, and TiO_2 whose low levels indicate the apparent use of a primary clay in the porcelain body rather than a secondary clay.[16]
- The level of MgO (2.02 wt%) is higher in this snuff box than recorded for the two cups and this is assumed to reflect higher MgO in the lime-alkali glass cullet used for the box.

- Virtual absence or very low levels of P_2O_5 and PbO. This absence of lead or very low levels in both body and glaze is a characteristic feature of the A-marked group.[17] This feature suggests that the proprietors bought in 'job lots' of lime-alkali glass cullet contaminated with minor amounts of flint glass.
- Cup 2 recorded the presence of cassiterite (SnO_2) in the body (Table 1).[18] This was not recorded in the snuff box.[19]

Discussion on the Snuff-Box Glaze

For the purposes of this discussion on the glaze composition of the snuff box, the following spectra captured by Brunel University, 13, 19, and 20 (figs. 17–20) are used. In addition, the glaze compositions obtained for A-marked Cups 1 and 2 are reproduced, along with the calculated theoretical glaze composition based on a porcelain body with 50 wt% Cherokee clay and 50 wt% lime-alkali bottle glass as derived from the 1744 Heylyn and Frye patent specification.[20]

A feature of all three Brunel University glaze scans, coupled with a fourth (Spectrum 7, Table 2), is that they have been contaminated to varying degrees with Au, Cu and/or Pb. In each case this contamination has been subtracted and the analysis recast to total 100 wt%. These recast analyses are shown in Table 2 to the right of each initial Brunel analysis. It should be noted that the glaze compositions for Cups 1 and 2 do have very low PbO levels, thought to reflect the contamination by small amounts of flint glass. For this discussion, the lead values recorded—together with those for copper and gold in the three Brunel University spectra—have been removed.

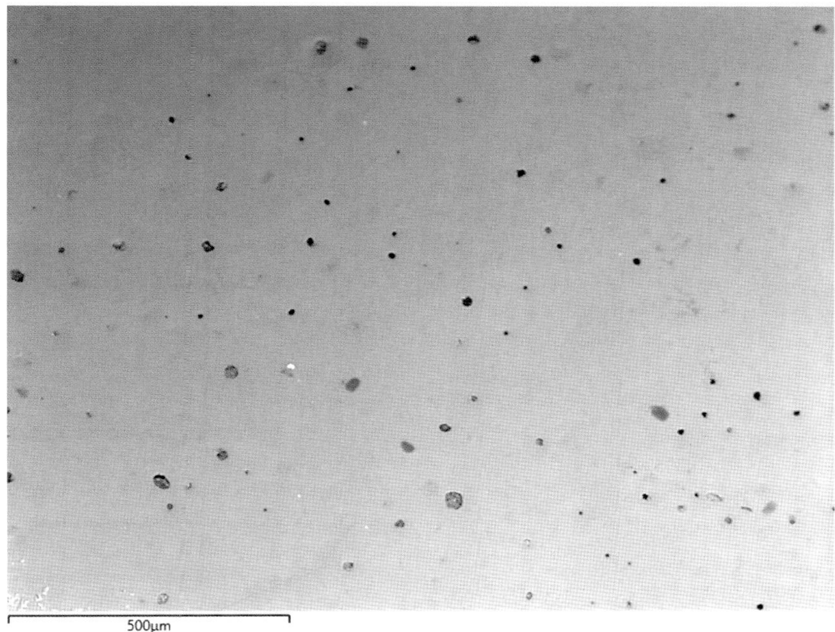

Figure 17 Image of glaze surface analyzed for Spectrum 13 on the snuff box.

Figure 18 Analysis for the glazed surface illustrated in fig. 17 with analysis (wt%) provided in top right. Gold (0.82 wt% Au_2O_3), copper (0.34 wt% CuO), and lead (0.53 wt% PbO)—regarded as contaminants—have been removed and the resultant analysis summed to 100%.

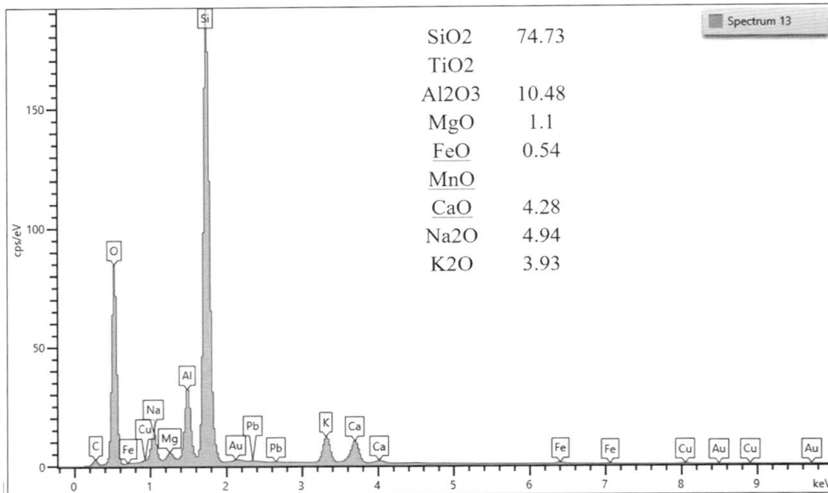

Figure 19 Image of the glaze surface on the base of the snuff box analyzed for Spectra 19 and 20.

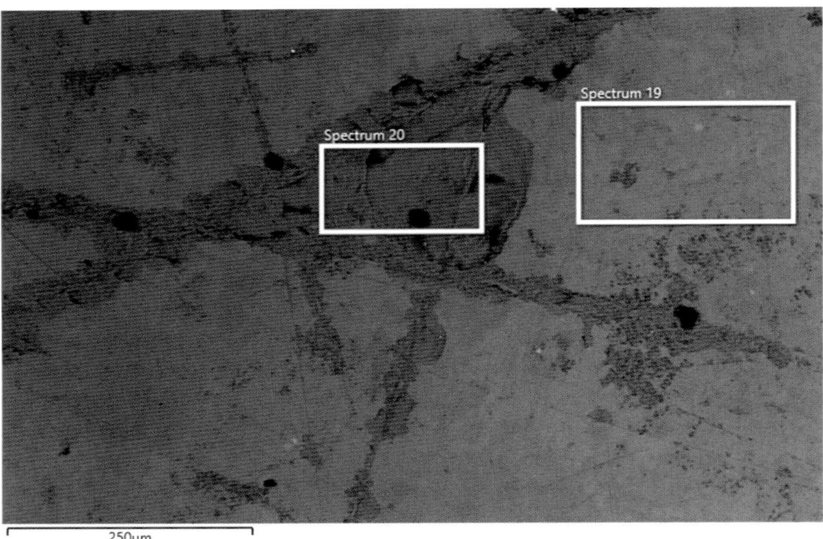

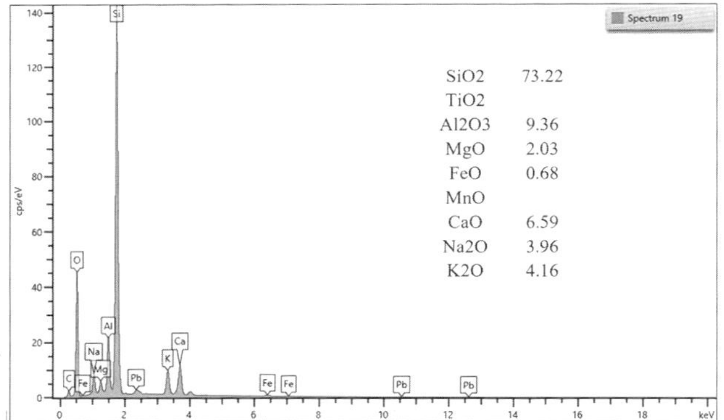

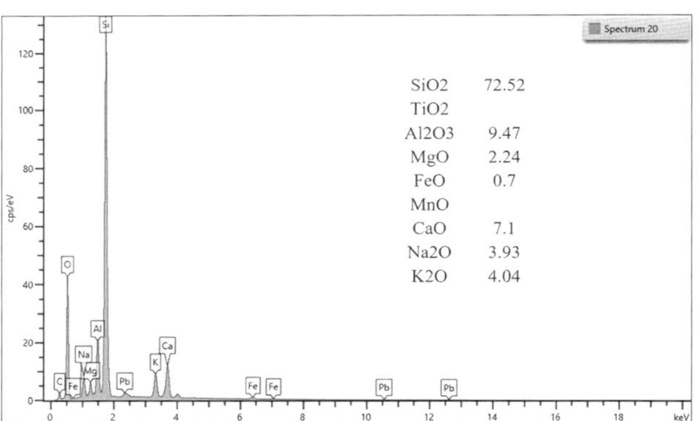

Figures 20a, b Spectra 19 and 20 generated from the glazed base of the snuff box. For both analyses lead was regarded as a contaminant and removed. The resultant analyses were then summed to 100 wt% and the values reproduced in the top right of both figures in wt%.

Key features of the Brunel University glaze scans are:

- The distinctly aluminous composition of the glazes in all four scans with Al_2O_3 varying from 9.36–11.57 wt%.
- The high levels of the alkali and alkali earth oxides with typically CaO ~ K_2O + Na_2O, with the exception of Spectrum 13 where CaO = 4.28 and K_2O + Na_2O = 8.87 wt%.
- Total alkali and alkali earth oxides (K_2O + Na_2O + MgO + CaO) are high ranging from 14.25–17.31 wt%.
- Absence of significant lead (PbO) from the glaze analyses.

Those features are likewise reflected in the theoretical glaze composition and in the analyses of two A-marked cups (see Table 2). The conclusion reached is that the glaze composition found on this snuff box is of the high-fired Si-Al-Ca glaze type, first developed in Britain apparently by John Dwight in the 1670s and brought to perfection in the 1744 patent

Table 2 Glaze Analyses. Glaze composition for the snuff box compared with glaze compositions for Cups 1 and 2 (Edwards, Jay, and Ramsay, "High-Fired Early English Porcelains of the 'A'-Marked Group, East London [c. 1744]") and the theoretical glaze composition as calculated by Ramsay et al. (Ramsay, Gabszewicz, and Ramsay, "Chemistry of 'A'-Marked Porcelain and Its Relation to the Heylyn and Frye Patent of 1744").

	1	2	3	4	5	6	7	8	9	10	11
SiO_2	70.37	72.64	73.47	74.73	71.8	73.22	71.32	72.52	68.3	68.9	68.6
TiO_2										0.1	0.1
Al_2O_3	11.21	11.57	10.3	10.48	9.18	9.36	9.31	9.47	12.2	11	13.1
MgO	1.75	1.81	1.08	1.1	1.99	2.03	2.2	2.24	1.8	0.1	2.1
FeO	0.54	0.56	0.53	0.54	0.67	0.68	0.69	0.7		0.7	0.4
MnO											0.1
CaO	6.36	6.56	4.21	4.28	6.46	6.59	6.98	7.1	7.5	12.2	10.2
Na_2O	3.21	3.31	4.86	4.94	3.88	3.96	3.87	3.93	6	1.1	2.8
K_2O	3.44	3.55	3.86	3.93	4.08	4.16	3.98	4.04	3.6	4.7	2.3
P_2O_5										0.2	0.3
PbO			0.53		1.94		1.64		0.4	0.9	0.05
SnO_2										0.05	0.05
Au_2O_3	1.9		0.82								
CuO	1.22		0.34								
	100	100	100	100	100	100	99.99	100	99.8	99.95	100.1

1. Spectrum 7 glaze analysis, Brunel University
2. Spectrum 7 analysis, Brunel University with gold and copper removed
3. Spectrum 13 glaze analysis, Brunel University
4. Spectrum 13 analysis, Brunel University with lead, gold, and copper removed
5. Spectrum 19 glaze analysis, Brunel University
6. Spectrum 19 analysis, Brunel University with lead removed
7. Spectrum 20 glaze analysis, Brunel University
8. Spectrum 20 analysis, Brunel University with lead removed
9. Theoretical glaze composition based on a 50:50 clay:flux body[21]
10. Glaze analysis, Cup 1[22]
11. Glaze analysis, Cup 2[23]

specification of Heylyn and Frye.[24] These results lend further support to the claim that this snuff box conforms to the specification contained in the 1744 patent.

Discussion of the On-Glaze Enamels

A range of pigmented sites were analyzed on the lid and side of the snuff box: these comprised red, brown/black, purple and green regions. There was no evidence of a blue, orange, or yellow pigment usage on the snuff box. The most characteristic general feature of the pigments analyzed here was the presence of significant signals for lead and silica in all. The former did not appear in the glaze or body of the specimen, which strongly indicates that a lead-rich powdered glass, predominantly chemically a lead silicate, $PbSiO_3$, was used to compound the pigment prior to its application. It is noteworthy that the surrounding glaze and body substrate are both very low in lead signals. The four pigmented areas studies will now be considered individually with their major elemental oxide components:

RED

Two areas were sampled, one was the red flag borne by the ship (see fig. 2) and the other a red area at the rim base (see fig. 6). The former region, the red flag represented by Spectrum 10 (not illustrated), shows an elemental composition of lead 31%, silica 47%, and iron 11%. This clearly can be assigned to haematite, Fe_2O_3. A minor trace of copper at 0.4% present could possibly signify the inclusion of a small amount of cuprous oxide, Cu_2O, which being brown in color would give a more subdued tone to the red pigment used at this site.

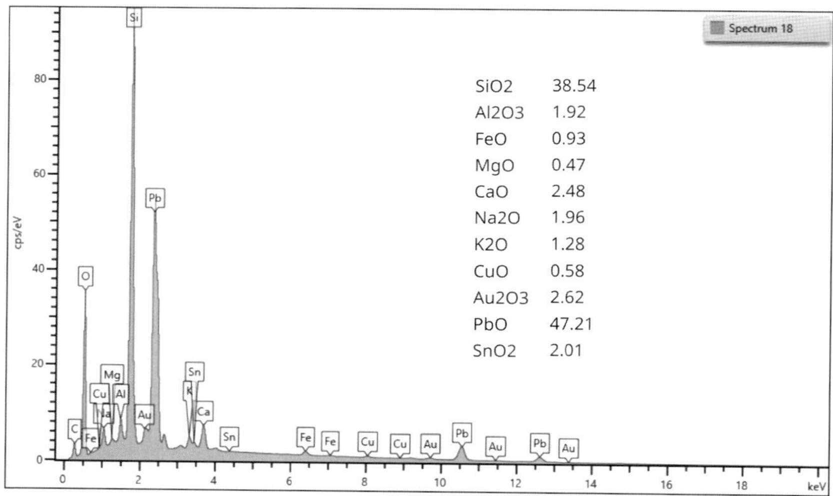

Figure 21 Spectrum 22 of red enamel at the edge of the snuff box rim showing a high lead (48.9 wt% PbO) and silica (34.3 wt% SiO_2) and prominent iron (10.6 wt% FeO).

The second red area at the edge of the basal rim, represented by Spectrum 22 (fig. 21), again shows a lead-rich composition at 48.9% and silica at 34.3%, and with a similar iron content at 10.6%. There is no trace of a copper signal found in this area. The assignment to haematite for this pigment is also proposed.

PURPLE

Located on the seated gentleman's purple coat on the lid (see fig. 1), Spectrum 18 (fig. 22), with high lead at 47.2% and silica at 38.5%, the other significant elemental percentages are gold at 2.6%, tin at 2% and iron at 1 wt%. The combination of gold and tin together is indicative of the use of a purple of Cassius pigment, which is basically a colloidal gold precipitated onto tin oxide particles. Named after Andreas Cassius of Hamburg, who discovered the pigment in 1666, its preparation involved the reduction of chloroauric acid (formed from the dissolution of gold in aqua regia) by stannous chloride (tin II)—the atomic gold particles being colloidally dispersed onto the oxidized stannic oxide particles (tin IV). The depth of color produced is dependent on the amount of gold present; here, the pale purple color would reflect a smaller amount of gold perhaps being used in the pigment preparation. The presence of iron at around 1% could be a contamination from the pigment preparation itself or perhaps indicative of the use of the purple iron pigment, caput mortuum, as a diluent to achieve a particular tonal shade of purple. Caput mortuum, a purple nodular form of haematite mineral with the chemical formula Fe_2O_3, was sourced since Roman times in Britain at the Clearwell Caves in the Forest of Dean and was much admired for its purple color.

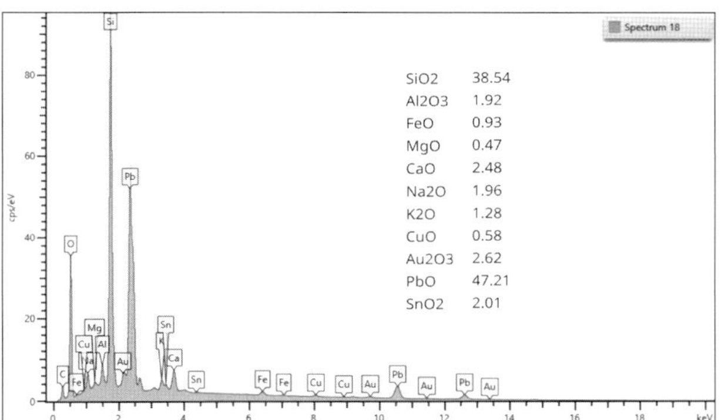

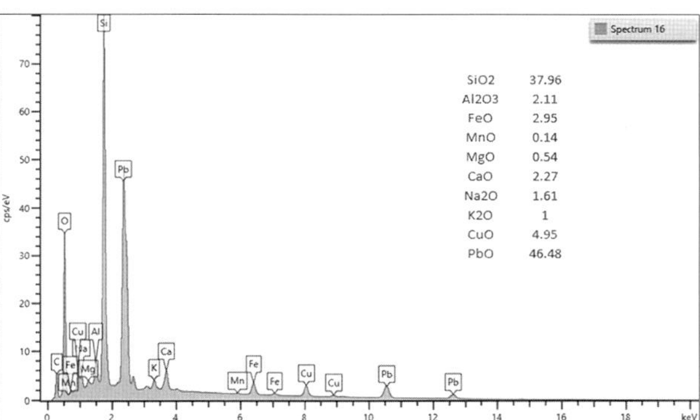

Figure 22 Spectrum 18 of the purple coat on the lid of the snuff box illustrated in fig. 1. This enamel is characterized by high lead (47.2 wt% PbO) and a small amount of gold (1.92 wt% Au_2O_3) and tin (2 wt% SnO_2), indicative of the presence of purple of Cassius.

Figure 23 Spectrum 16 of the green area on the lid of the snuff box. Notice the high lead content (46.48 wt% PbO) and the presence of prominent copper (4.95 wt% CuO).

GREEN

The large area of green on the lid and side of the specimen, represented by Spectrum 16 (fig. 23), with lead at 46.5%, silica at 38%, and copper at 5% and iron at 3%, is indicative of the use of verdigris, basic copper acetate $Cu(OH)_2 \cdot Cu(CH_3CO_2)_2$ and terre verte, a green earth of complex formulation represented chemically by $K(AlFe^{3+})(Fe^{2+}Mg)AlSi_7O_{10}(OH)_2$. The former was prepared by the immersion of thin copper sheets in stale wine (vinegar), whereas the latter originated from the minerals celadonite and glauconite: the most desirable but expensive and pure form of celadonite green earth pigment was sourced in Monte Baldo, Lake Garda, Italy. The presence of the copper and iron elemental signatures in the green pigment on the snuff box indicates that potentially a mixture of green earth and verdigris was used.

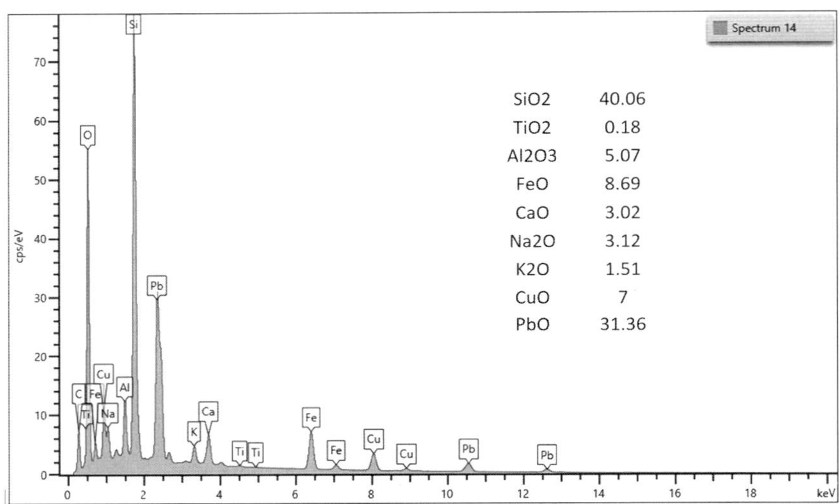

Figure 24 Spectrum 14 of the black mast on the lid containing high lead (31.36 wt% PbO), iron (8.69 wt% FeO), and copper (7 wt% CuO).

BLACK

The black area, represented by the ship's mast in Spectrum 14 (fig. 24), is described visually as having a brownish-black tone, again with a high lead content at 31.4%, silica at 40%, and with iron at 8.7% and copper at 7%. The combination of copper and iron indicates a mixed pigment composition based on black magnetite, Fe_3O_4, and black cupric oxide (tenorite) CuO, which are both available as minerals geologically. Magnetite (Mars black) was a popular black pigment used as an alternative to carbon black and ivory black, which were absent here in the specimen being studied. The hint of a brown color could have been achieved by the incorporation of brown cuprous oxide, Cu_2O, or possibly the brown-colored mineral plattnerite PbO_2, whose presence would be masked by the high lead signal from the background lead silicate.

The absence of synthetic pigments that are associated chronologically with later periods of decoration and porcelain manufacture is to be noted and this indicates that the snuff box has not been retouched or restored using these in modern times. In particular, the use of the strong pigments favored in the nineteenth century for the colors—such as cadmium sulfide red, pyrolusite manganese black, viridian chrome green, and synthetic ultramarine blue in admixture with iron Mars red for purple—are noteworthy for their absence.

Doccia Porcelain Factory

In 1737 marchese Carlo Ginori established the Ginori porcelain factory in Doccia, near Florence where Ginori apparently experimented with a variety of clays.[25] The snuff box under discussion first appeared in a publication by Barbara Beaucamp-Markowsky in which the box is illustrated and attributed to Doccia.[26] In its catalog for the sale of the snuff box, Bonhams recorded this entry by Beaucamp-Markowsky and noted that it was attributed to Doccia by that author.[27] Aniko Bezur and Francesca Casadio recently carried out two analyses of Doccia porcelains, which appear to be refractory judging by their aluminous bodies (Table 3).[28]

Table 3 Doccia Porcelain Body. Analyses of Doccia porcelains after Bezur and Casadio, "Du Paquier Porcelain: Artistic Expression and Technological Mastery, a Scientific Evaluation of the Materials," in *Fired by Passion: Vienna Baroque Porcelain of Claudius Innocentius Du Paquier*, edited by Meredith Chilton, 3 vols. (Stuttgart: Arnoldsche, 2009), 3:1165–1211.

	1988.269	SG.DO. 11.mug
SiO_2	77.4	73.5
TiO_2	0.3	0.2
Al_2O_3	15	22.7
Fe_2O_3	0.8	0.5
CaO	1	0.4
K_2O	5.5	2.8
	100	100.1

Although the use of a handheld XRF prevented the recognition of both Na_2O and MgO in the Doccia porcelains, the plotting of K_2O vs CaO (fig. 25) does allow the separation of this snuff box from Doccia porcelains, which are characterized by a potassic flux. The high level of CaO in the snuff box shown in the shaded blue area allows for its inclusion within the field of A-marked porcelains.

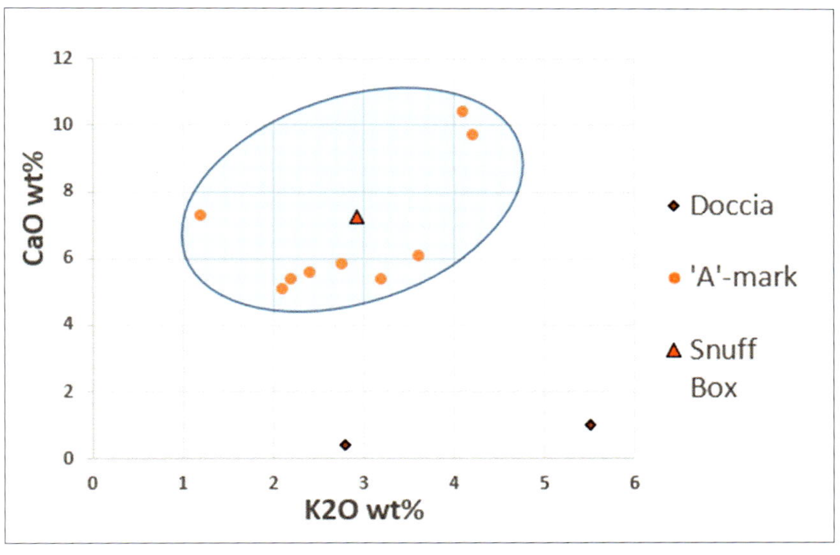

Figure 25 Plot of K_2O vs CaO (wt%) for published analyses of Doccia porcelain bodies (Bezur and Casadio, "Du Paquier Porcelain," 3:1165–1211) and A-marked porcelains (Edwards, Jay, and Ramsay, "High-Fired Early English Porcelains of the 'A'-Marked Group, East London (c. 1744)." Also shown is the composition of the snuff box, the subject of this study. Note that the snuff box falls in the A-marked porcelain field.

The Use and Abuse of Nondestructive Analyses of Porcelains

Although the necessity of the provision and inclusion of chemical analytical data in the attribution of porcelains to factory sources is deemed essential for the holistic forensic assessment to be carried out, it is clear that this approach must be undertaken with the proper protocols and an appreciation of the pitfalls that can entrap the unwary. In the related field of oil paintings, it is now established practice that important works of art are accompanied by the appropriate scientific analytical data to assist in their assignment to specific artists and to chronological periods, along with historical provenance, previous ownership reference, documentation, and connoisseurship. The latter refers particularly to the opinion of established experts who have spent many years studying the artistic style and palette of the artists, their techniques, and their usage of pigments and materials in the creation of their artworks. The holistic approach that has seen the adoption of chemical and physical analysis as a *de rigueur* requirement for attribution of oil paintings has revealed the significance of potential errors that have been made historically where connoisseurship alone has been found sadly wanting: in a recent publication that accompanied the exhibition "Close Examination: Fakes, Mistakes and Discoveries," Marjorie Wieseman cited seven paintings from sixteen studied, apparently all genuine on the basis of connoisseurship opinion alone, which had to be downgraded to copies and fakes when scientific analytical data were incorporated, representing a significant 44% of misattributions.[29]

A similar situation could certainly exist for the attribution of porcelain specimens from unknown factory sources unless the incorporation of analytical scientific data is recognized for the holistic assignment of ceramic works of art. The major difference between the analytical studies that are undertaken for oil paintings and those for porcelains is that the former can be undertaken on small specimens of pigment that can be excised prior to restoration and conservation of a painting. In contrast, the removal of small specimens of glaze, pigment, or body from a ceramic specimen is normally strongly disfavored, which means that nondestructive analytical techniques are necessary, as used in this study.

The nondestructive chemical analytical techniques that usually are applied to ceramics are SEM/EDAXS, spectroscopy, and XRF spectroscopy (for the elemental composition) and Raman or FTIR spectroscopy for the molecular composition. The elemental composition as undertaken by SEM/EDAXS involves the acquisition of data from micro-regions with a footprint of some hundreds of nanometers and multiple replicate sampling is usually undertaken to account for specimen inhomogeneity.

The limitation of the SEM/EDAXS technique is the finite size of the sample chamber of the instrument used, which requires evacuation or low-vacuum to avoid applications of a coating of carbon or gold on the sampling region. Therefore, large ceramic items are not usually accessed in this way; the technique of choice becomes portable XRF spectroscopy, which uses miniaturized instrumentation to access the specimen. A particular disadvantage of XRF spectroscopy (or handheld XRF) is that the intensity of the analytical signal is dependent on the atomic number of the element concerned so that lighter elements with low atomic numbers, such as carbon, boron, oxygen, sodium, and magnesium, are often not detectable. It is commonly found that the limit of detection by portable XRF spectroscopy is shown to be at the limit of sodium (atomic number 11) and magnesium (atomic number 12). Both techniques are qualitative and quantitative in the analytical data that are obtained.

Raman and FTIR spectroscopy are surface techniques and need access to appropriate regions of the specimen for analysis to be performed, which usually can be undertaken using remote probes and offset image acquisition devices. Rarely is it desirable or necessary to remove a sample from an undamaged porcelain artifact to undertake analysis unless this can be achieved without detriment to the object concerned—and indeed most collectors and museum curators would not entertain this except in the most critical of cases for which the analytical data would be expected to provide definitive results. It is a rather different scenario, of course, with damaged ceramics for which the removal of a sample would not be viewed as compromising the integrity of the artifact, and for sherds that have been recovered from the archaeological excavation of porcelain manufactory waste pits.

The criteria operating for the chemical analysis of porcelains, therefore, should be enumerated as follows:

- Has the correct analytical technique and associated procedure been adopted to determine the appropriate data and parameters? For instance, if the determination of sodium oxide (Na_2O) and magnesium oxide (MgO) are adjudged to be critical and XRF has been the analytical technique used, it is unlikely that the analytical data detection limits will be acceptable.
- If the important data set refers to the detection of elements derived from raw material impurities or from minor additives that have been noted in the formulations and recipes of porcelain manufactories then the detection limit(s) of the techniques adopted are vitally important. It is pointless using handheld XRF to determine the presence of boron that has been derived from the addition of borax to the body paste formulation because it is too light an element (atomic number 5) to be detected. It is equally important that the presence of minor heavy metals or elements such as titanium, sulphur, and cobalt are recognized and not ignored since they can be extremely useful in determining the geographical source of raw materials or whether minor additions of gypsum, alum, or smalt have been made to the porcelain paste formulation. In particular, the presence of certain elements in pigments, for example, can be related to the chronological usage of specific pigments by the manufactory concerned. This can be invaluable for the chronological placement of the enameling decoration on a porcelain artifact; it is especially important for the analytical detection of fakes and later additions to the decoration. Certain pigments were used historically by manufactories over narrow periods of production timelines, and that information can be useful for the correct placement of a piece chronologically. In the snuff box under discussion, the absence of such compounds as cadmium sulfide red, pyrolusite manganese black, viridian chrome green, and synthetic ultramarine blue in admixture with iron Mars red for purple indicate that the enamels used predate the nineteenth century.
- The nondestructive spatial interrogation of a ceramic specimen must be accomplished with reference to the primary objective that is being sought in that particular scenario: is the experiment designed to analyze

the pigment composition, the glaze, or the body paste? This calls upon the analyst to select the proper sites for the analytical determination to be accomplished, so that the results obtained are meaningful. For example, it is not acceptable to attempt to analyze the body paste through the glaze unless one is certain that the glaze compositional data are also not being interrogated simultaneously in the process, which would then compromise the data set. It is clear that, for example, a lead-rich glaze being interrogated along with ostensibly a body paste determination could lead to the erroneous conclusion that the body paste itself also comprised a significant contribution from a lead additive, such as flint-glass cullet or various oxides of lead.

- Replicate data sets are necessary to assist the interpretation of inhomogeneous specimens, which most ceramics are in microscale; there could be regions that are rich in particular elemental composition which do not reflect the bulk material as a whole.
- The most significant aspect of an analytical determination, however, is the interpretation of the elemental or molecular data sets obtained in the light of existing documentation relating to the manufactory procedures and usage of raw materials. Unfortunately, much historical information of this kind has been lost or was simply never recorded in the first place. Equally important is the realization that manufactory proprietors were generally empirical experimentalists, and in the few cases where their notes have survived, it is very revealing to experience their attempts to improve the perceived deficiencies in their porcelain output with impromptu changes made to their body paste or glaze formulations to achieve a better compatibility of product.

What is clear is that all components of the holistic appraisal of porcelain for attribution purposes must be verified; otherwise, one or more might be accredited falsely as being of importance when in fact it is suspect in its origins. As regards analytical data, this means that the determinations have been carried out effectively and reliably so that the compositional data can assuredly and uncompromisingly be related to the body paste, the glaze, or the enamel pigments from which evidential interpretation can then be forthcoming. The same criteria must also apply to the reliability of provenancing documentation and its matching to the art work under study, including notes and information relating to the formulations and recipes used at the manufactory. In addition, connoisseurship opinion based on stylistic considerations, is invariably reliant on access to standard exemplars purportedly originating from the manufactory for comparative assessment. In this case the specification contained in the 1744 patent of Heylyn and Frye has been critical in recognizing the source and attribution of the A-marked porcelain group. Above all, as in the case of oil paintings, it would be facile to dismiss the analytical data as irrelevant or weak solely because they do not conform to established opinion about an art work that has evolved historically, often with little other evidentiary support.

ACKNOWLEDGMENTS We acknowledge the Victoria and Albert Museum for permission to publish the images of two A-marked teapots in their collection and the cane handle. We also thank the National Museum of Wales for two images of their A-marked snuff box, and Peter and Mary White for permission to publish an image of their snuff box.

1. Mrs. L. Wilson, "A Miscellany of Pieces: Report of a Meeting Held at the Albemarle Club on December 14th, 1937," *English Ceramic Circle Transactions* 2, no. 7 (1939): 83.

2. Arthur Lane, "Unidentified Italian or English Porcelains: The A Marked Group," *Mitteilungsblatt (Keramik Freunde der Schweiz)*, no. 43 (1958): 15–18.

3. Robert J. Charleston and John V. G. Mallet, "A Problematical Group of Eighteenth-Century Porcelains," *English Ceramic Circle Transactions* 8, no. 1 (1971): 80–121.

4. Her Majesty's Stationery Office, *A.D. 1744: Manufacture of Earthenware, Heylyn and Frye's Specification, Patent No. 610* (London: HMSO, 1856), pp. 1–3; Ian C. Freestone, "'A'-Marked Porcelain: Some Recent Scientific Work," *English Ceramic Circle Transactions* 16, no. 1 (1996): 76–84; W.R.H. Ramsay, Anton Gabszewicz, and E. Gael Ramsay, "*Unaker* or Cherokee Clay and Its Relationship to the 'Bow' Porcelain Manufactory," *English Ceramic Circle Transactions* 17, no. 3 (2001): 473–99; W.R.H. Ramsay, Anton Gabszewicz, and E. Gael Ramsay, "The Chemistry of 'A'-Marked Porcelain and Its Relation to the Heylyn and Frye Patent of 1744," *English Ceramic Circle Transactions* 18, no. 2 (2003): 264–83; W.R.H. Ramsay, Judith A. Hansen, and E. Gael Ramsay, "An 'A-Marked' Covered Porcelain Bowl, Cherokee Clay, and Colonial America's Contribution to the English Porcelain Industry," in *Ceramics in America*, edited by Robert Hunter (Hanover, N.H.: University Press of New England for the Chipstone Foundation, 2004), pp. 60–77; W.R.H. Ramsay, Frank A. Davenport, and E. G. Ramsay, "The 1744 Ceramic Patent of Heylyn and Frye: 'Unworkable *Unaker* Formula' or Landmark Document in the History of English Ceramics?," *Proceedings of the Royal Society of Victoria* 118, no. 1 (2006): 11–34; W.R.H. Ramsay and E. G. Ramsay, "A Classification of Bow Porcelain from First Patent to Closure: c. 1743–1774," *Proceedings of the Royal Society of Victoria* 119, no. 1 (2007): 1–68; Pat Daniels, *The Origin & Development of Bow Porcelain, 1730–1747: Including the Participation of the Royal Society, Andrew Duchè and the American Contribution* (Oxon, U.K.: Resurgat, 2007).

5. R. Ruthie Dibble and Joseph Mizhakii Zordan, "Cherokee Unaker, British Ceramics, and Productions of Whiteness in Eighteenth-Century Atlantic Worlds," *British Art Studies* 21 (2021): https://doi.org/10.17658/issn.2058-5462/issue-21/dibblezordan.

6. Howell G. M. Edwards, William H. Jay, and W. Ross H. Ramsay, "High-Fired Early English Porcelains of the 'A'-Marked Group, East London (c. 1744): A Raman Spectroscopy and Electron Microscopy Compositional Study," *Journal Raman Spectroscopy* 53, no. 4 (2022): 785–809.

7. Charleston and Mallet, "Problematical Group of Eighteenth-Century Porcelains."

8. Ibid.; Daniels, *Origin & Development of Bow Porcelain, 1730–1747*.

9. Collezione Procida Mirabelli di Lauro, Naples, no. 67. Acquired from Lukacs-Donath in 1966, Bonhams, April 18, 2012, lot 168.

10. Bonhams, *Fine British Pottery, Porcelain & Enamels*, sale cat., April 18, 2012 (London: Bonhams, 2012), lot 168.

11. W.R.H. Ramsay and E. Gael Ramsay, *The Evolution and Compositional Development of English Porcelains from the 16th C to Lund's Bristol c. 1750 and Worcester c. 1752—The Golden Chain* (Invercargill, N.Z.: [Ross Ramsay], 2017), Appendix 3.

12. Edwards, Jay, and Ramsay, "High-Fired Early English Porcelains of the 'A'-Marked Group, East London (c. 1744)."

13. Ibid.

14. Ibid.

15. W.R.H. Ramsay, G. R. Hill, and E. Gael Ramsay, "Re-creation of the 1744 Heylyn and Frye Ceramic Patent Wares using Cherokee Clay: Implications for Raw Materials, Kiln Conditions, and the Earliest English Porcelain Production," *Geoarchaeology* 19, no. 7 (2004): 635–55.

16. Freestone, "'A'-Marked Porcelain"; Ramsay, Gabszewicz, and Ramsay, "Chemistry of 'A'-Marked Porcelain."

17. Freestone, "'A'-Marked Porcelain"; Ramsay, Gabszewicz, and Ramsay, "Chemistry of 'A'-Marked Porcelain"; Ramsay, Hansen, and Ramsay, "An 'A-Marked' Covered Porcelain

Bowl"; Ramsay, Hill, and Ramsay, "Re-creation of the 1744 Heylyn and Frye Ceramic Patent Wares using Cherokee Clay"; Ramsay, Davenport, and Ramsay, "1744 Ceramic Patent of Heylyn and Frye."

18. Edwards, Jay, and Ramsay, "High-Fired Early English Porcelains of the 'A'-Marked Group, East London (c. 1744)."

19. However, see Freestone, "'A'-Marked Porcelain."

20. Edwards, Jay, and Ramsay, "High-Fired Early English Porcelains of the 'A'-Marked Group, East London (c. 1744)"; Ramsay, Gabszewicz, and Ramsay, "Chemistry of 'A'-Marked Porcelain."

21. Ramsay, Gabszewicz, and Ramsay, "Chemistry of 'A'-Marked Porcelain."

22. Edwards, Jay, and Ramsay, "High-Fired Early English Porcelains of the 'A'-Marked Group, East London (c. 1744)."

23. Ibid.

24. Ramsay and Gael Ramsay, *Evolution and Compositional Development of English Porcelains*.

25. Andreina d'Agliano, "The Ginori Porcelain Factory in Doccia," in *Fascination of Fragility: Masterpieces of European Porcelain*, edited by Ulrich Pietsch and Theresa Witting (Dresden: Staatliche Kunstsammlungen Dresden, 2010), pp. 78–87.

26. Barbara Beaucamp-Markowsky, *Porzellandosen des 18. Jahrhunderts* (Munich: Klinkhardt & Biermann, 1985), no. 476, p. 518.

27. Bonhams, *Fine British Pottery, Porcelain & Enamels*, sale cat., April 18, 2012 (London: Bonhams, 2012), lot 168.

28. Aniko Bezur and Francesca Casadio, "Du Paquier Porcelain: Artistic Expression and Technological Mastery, a Scientific Evaluation of the Materials," in *Fired by Passion: Vienna Baroque Porcelain of Claudius Innocentius Du Paquier*, edited by Meredith Chilton, 3 vols. (Stuttgart: Arnoldsche, 2009), 3:1165–1211.

29. Marjorie E. Wieseman, *A Closer Look: Deceptions and Discoveries* (London: National Gallery, 2010).

Daniel S. Sousa

"From Death to Life": Slavery and Emancipation in the British West Indies as Revealed on a Child's Plate

▼ IN AUGUST 1838, Epaphras Hoyt (1765–1850) of Deerfield, Massachusetts, recorded in his diary the momentous events unfolding in the British West Indies some 1,700 miles to the south:[1]

> This morning early, our people were roused from their slumbers by the brisk ringing of our village bells. Some not knowing the cause, ran to their doors expecting to hear the cry of fire! Not so! The news soon circulated of the fact of the total emancipation of slavery in the British West India Islands, on the 1st of August 1838. What a glorious event in the annals of Great Britain! That Nation under an hereditary monarchy, has nobly stepped forward and emancipated half a million of their fellow beings, from the chains and lashes of their assumed masters![2]

The town of Deerfield's more ardent anti-slavery activists, as noted in the writings of the Rev. Samuel Willard (1775–1859), also marked the occasion with hymns and speeches. Willard privately contemplated emancipation's transformative effects, noting how the formerly enslaved were raised "from death to life" and elevated from "things" to "human beings":

> When in 1838 the slaves in the British West Indies were on the first of August set free, nearly all the family either sat up till midnight, or rose at that hour, and sang a hymn prepared for the occasion; and, if I ever felt devout, I believe it was then, filled as I was with the thought, that in that hour more than seven hundred thousand men arose from death to life,—were transformed from things into human beings. . . . At my instance that day was solemnized in Deerfield by a meeting of those who were interested in the occasion, and appropriate speeches were made.[3]

Notwithstanding the enthusiastic optimism of Willard, Hoyt, and others who celebrated Britain's Emancipation Act, emancipation did not immediately cease the struggles of the formerly enslaved in the British West Indies. A transfer-printed plate, a recent addition to Historic Deerfield's British ceramics collection and the subject of recent research, documents that reality as well as the experiences of the formerly enslaved living in the British West Indies in the aftermath of emancipation (fig. 1).

When Historic Deerfield acquired the plate in 2020, the plate's connection to post-emancipation life in the British West Indies was unknown. Indeed, very little was understood about the plate itself. Its size and subject matter suggest it had been made for a child or young person, but an older audience is possible.[4]

The plate's transfer-printed scene, titled "SUGAR / How it Grows & How it's made. / CANE MILL," appears to show a group of enslaved individuals processing sugar cane. Because the plate depicts only one step in

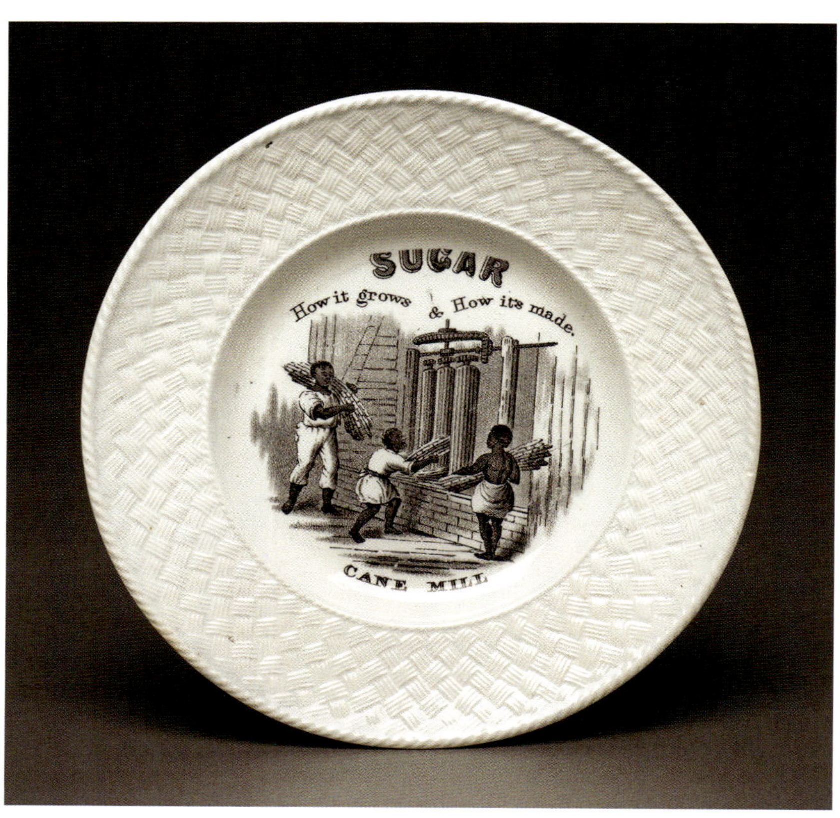

Figure 1 Plate, possibly John Carr & Son(s), North Shields, Northumberland, England, ca. 1854–1861. Lead-glazed white earthenware, black enamel. D. 7⅛". Marks: on the obverse, "SUGAR / How it grows & How it's made. / CANE MILL"; printed "G" on the reverse. (Historic Deerfield, Museum Collections Fund, 2020.3.1; photo, Penny Leveritt.)

the process of refining sugar—running sugar cane through a cane mill—it was believed to have been part of a set illustrating the sugar-refining process as a whole. The scene had likely been copied directly from an engraving in a book or other printed publication, as was common for many transfer-printed designs of this period, but the design source had not been identified. Although the plate was marked with a printed "G" on its reverse, its maker was also unknown (fig. 2). However, the plate's design and subject matter indicated it had been produced in England circa 1850, just over ten years following emancipation in the British West Indies.

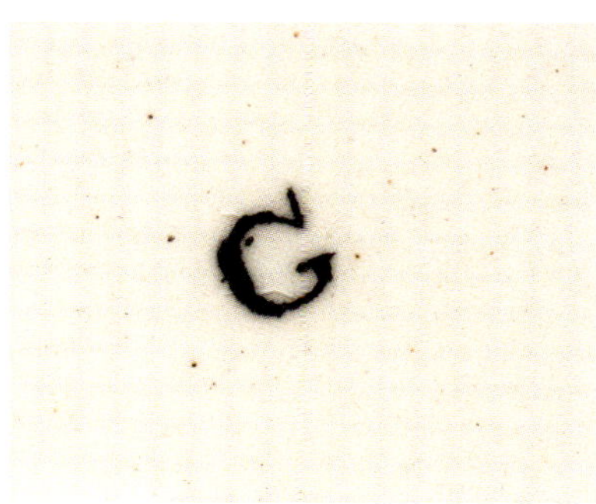

Figure 2 Detail of the printed "G" mark on the reverse of the plate illustrated in fig. 1

The printed scene was initially understood to convey an anti-slavery message. Potteries might have created the plate's message with that in mind, or perhaps purchasers imbued it with that meaning. The subject of sugar and sugar production was closely connected with the anti-slavery movement in Britain. As a product produced by enslaved persons, West Indian sugar was boycotted by some anti-slavery activists as early as 1791.[5] Activists' refusal to buy these products led them to seek out substitutes, such as those marked "East India Sugar Not Made by Slaves" or "East India Sugar. The produce of Free Labour"—phrases inscribed on several English ceramic and glass sugar bowls made 1820–1830.[6] In this context, the plate's scene might have been designed, or interpreted by some, to highlight or denounce the dangerous work that enslaved persons of various age groups were forced to endure while working on sugar plantations.[7]

On the center of the plate, several persons of color, an adult and possibly two children, are shown feeding stalks of sugar cane into a three-roller grinding mill. These mills crushed the freshly cut stalks in order to extract the plant's juices. Accidents were not uncommon, including the loss of limbs, as workers were forced to work quickly and for long periods so that the juices did not spoil.[8] In this view, one of the child's hands is extended precariously close to one of the rollers. The danger conveyed in the scene may have encouraged some to relinquish sugar entirely, or at least to seek out an alternative.

The treatment of enslaved men and women on sugar plantations was addressed in British anti-slavery publications as well. For example, a scene similar to the one depicted on this plate (see fig. 1) was employed in an earlier anti-slavery pamphlet written by Amelia Opie titled *The Black Man's Lament: Or, How to Make Sugar* (1826). The book recounts, in poetic verses, the sad tale of the capture of Africans in their native homeland, and their transport to the West Indies to labor on sugar plantations. One of the book's engravings depicts enslaved persons feeding cane into a grinding mill. Drawing attention to the plight of the enslaved, Opie explains how workers are forced to constantly toil and feed the mill:

> That mill, our labour, every hour,
> Must with fresh loads of canes supply;
> And if we faint, the cart-whip's power,
> Gives force which *nature's* powers *deny*.[9]

For laborers, work on a sugar plantation was usually fast-paced, dangerous, and physically exhausting, and plates of this nature might have been used to teach young people about that grim reality.

The plate's production some ten or more years following emancipation in the British West Indies does not rule out the possibility that it was made by British pottery makers, or that buyers interpreted the plate's scene with anti-slavery notions in mind. Indeed, in the aftermath of emancipation, many in England continued to fight for the end of slavery abroad, and British potteries continued to cater to that market by producing ceramics with explicit anti-slavery scenes and messages.[10] For example, the British and Foreign Anti-Slavery Society, established in 1839, worked for "the universal extinction of Slavery and the Slave-trade."[11] In order to accomplish that goal, they sought, among other things, "to open a correspondence with Abolitionists in America, France, and other countries, and to encourage them in the prosecution of their objects by all methods consistent with the principles of this Society."[12] In addition to illustrating the hardships of slavery, then, the plate might have signified the work that still needed to be done in the international fight against slavery.

The American abolitionists whom the British and Foreign Anti-Slavery Society sought to aid may have interpreted the plate's scene in a similar light. Although it is unknown whether these plates were available in America, American abolitionists—some of whom also boycotted sugar produced by enslaved persons—may have also interpreted the plate's scene as a criticism of enslaved labor.[13] Those activists might have been reminded of enslaved persons laboring on sugar plantations in the South, including in the state of Louisiana. Louisiana sugar plantations utilized equipment similar to the mill depicted on this plate, and discussions and images of this equipment—and the sugar production process more generally—found its way into popular publications.[14] Similarly, the plate's scene may have also reminded American anti-slavery activists of information they had encountered in abolitionist literature. For example, Solomon Northup (b. 1807/8), a free Black who was captured, enslaved, and then later released, described in his book *Twelve Years a Slave* (1853) not only his experience working on a sugar plantation as an enslaved person, but also the equipment that was used to process the sugar, including the "two great iron rollers" used for crushing the cane.[15] Therefore, as owners or purchasers encountered the scenes on these types of plates, they may have recalled scenes of slavery they had seen or read about elsewhere. In doing so, they possibly assigned meanings to these objects that supported their anti-slavery beliefs or efforts, and used them either as domestic ornaments or tools to educate young people about sugar making and the horrors of slavery.[16]

The recent discovery of the plate's design source, however, served to greatly expand the plate's interpretation. The transfer-printed scene was copied from an engraving, "Cane Mill," in the book *Sugar: How It Grows, and How It Is Made: A Pleasing Account for Young People* by "J.L.S." (identity unknown) (fig. 3).[17] Published in London about 1845 by Darton & Clark, the book can be classified under a type of literary genre that historian

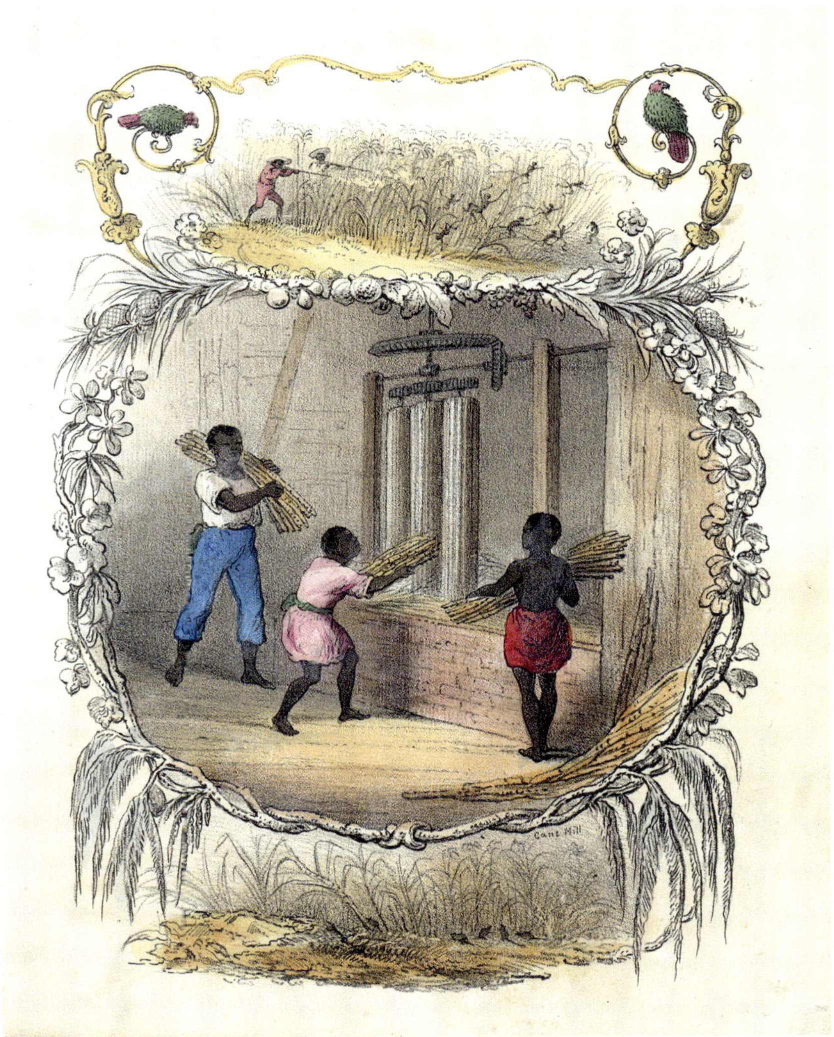

Figure 3 "Cane Mill," from J.L.S., *Sugar: How It Grows, and How It Is Made: A Pleasing Account for Young People* (London: Darton and Clark, ca. 1845). (Courtesy, Lilly Library, Indiana University, Bloomington.) This engraving served as the design source for the transfer-printed scene on the plate illustrated in fig. 1.

Elizabeth Massa Hoiem describes as the "production story."[18] A product of the late eighteenth century, these stories provided young people with illustrations and information—oftentimes quite detailed and technical—concerning the production of a variety of goods and materials.[19] However, the book's possible inclusion in the collection of the Mercantile Library of Baltimore in 1851 suggests that the market extended to an adult audience.[20] In the book, the author provides readers with detailed descriptions of the

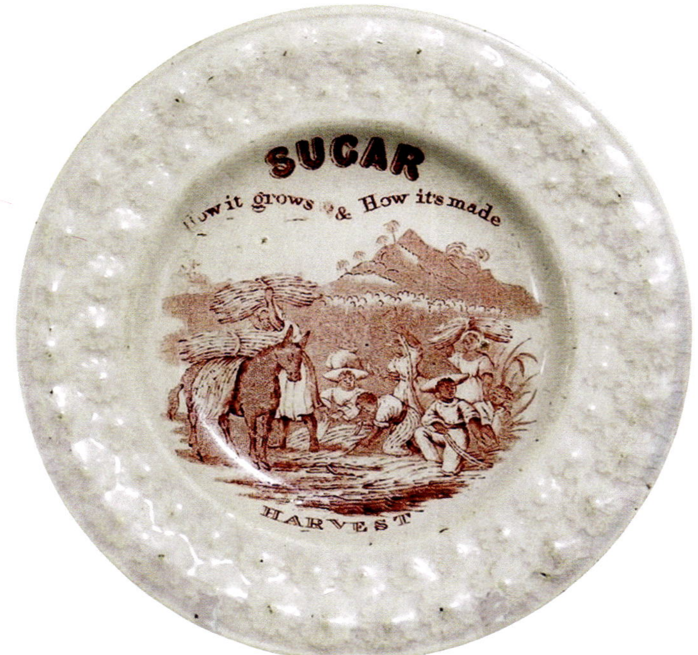

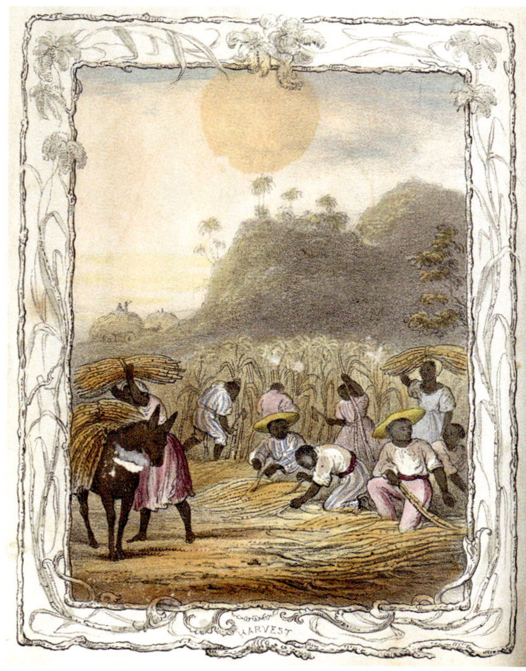

Figure 4 Plate, John Carr & Sons, North Shields, Northumberland, England, ca. 1861. Lead-glazed white earthenware, red enamel. D. 8¼". Marks: on obverse, "SUGAR / How it grows & How it's made / HARVEST"; impressed on reverse, "JOHN CARR & SONS" with anchor and stag's head. (Courtesy, Transferware Collectors Club Database of Patterns and Sources.)

Figure 5 "Harvest," from J.L.S., *Sugar: How It Grows, and How It Is Made: A Pleasing Account for Young People* (London: Darton and Clark, ca. 1845). (Courtesy, Lilly Library, Indiana University, Bloomington, Indiana.) This engraving served as the design source for the transfer-printed scene on the plate illustrated in fig. 4.

sugar cultivation process, particularly on the island of Jamaica, as well as the processes for producing refined sugar. The book's eight hand-colored engravings supplement the text by illustrating various stages of the production process.

Two other transfer-printed plates are known whose design source was prints copied from *Sugar*, including one titled "Harvest" and the other "Open Pan Boiling," suggesting that these plates formed sets (figs. 4–7).[21] Plates with the "Cane Mill" scene, however, survive in greater numbers with different molded borders, suggesting that it was the most popular.[22] The "Harvest" and "Open Pan Boiling" examples are larger in size (approximately 8¼" in diameter) than the current example of "Cane Mill," and are different in decoration. The "Harvest" plate is transfer-printed in red, and features a molded "daisy" border; the "Open Pan Boiling" plate is transfer-printed in black, and features a molded border with polychrome painted roses. Both plates seem to be by the same maker: the "Harvest" plate bears the mark of John Carr & Sons of North Shields, Northumberland, England; and the "Open Pan Boiling" plate reportedly is also marked "J. Carr & Co." The John Carr & Sons mark began to be used in 1861, whereas the John Carr & Co. mark is first found around 1850.[23] Whether Carr exported his wares to the United States is currently unknown, but, in addition to making wares for the domestic market, he appears to have carried on a large export business with markets in the Middle East (including Iran), the Mediterranean, and Bombay, India.[24] Based on these marked examples, John Carr's pottery might have produced Historic Deerfield's plate as well.[25]

Sugar is decidedly anti-slavery in its outlook, and seems to celebrate emancipation by drawing readers' attention to the "happy" life of the

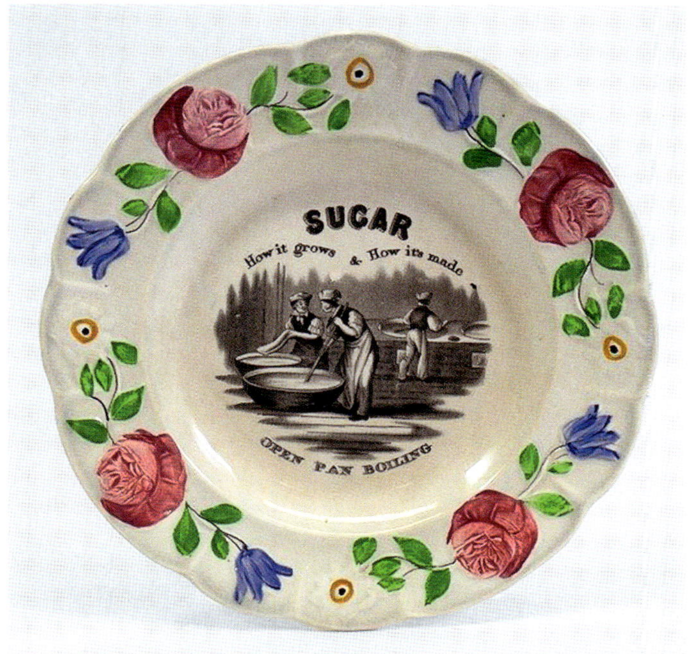

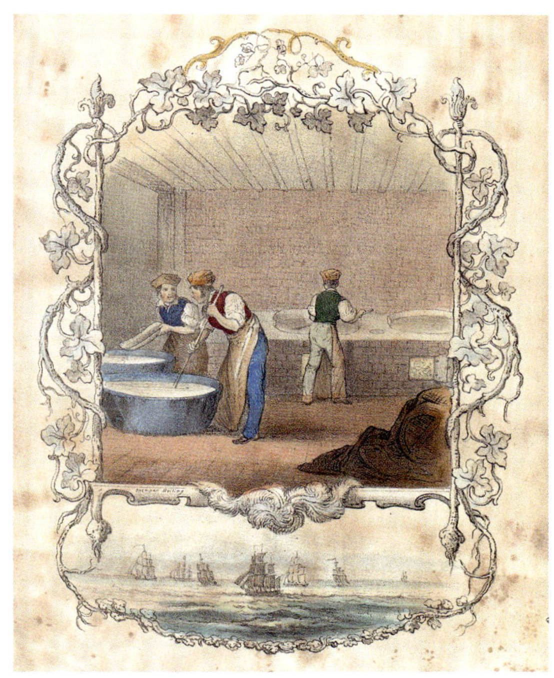

Figure 6 Plate, John Carr & Co., North Shields, Northumberland, England, ca. 1850. Pearlware, polychrome enamels. D. 8¼". Marks: on obverse, "SUGAR / How it grows & How it's made / OPEN PAN BOILING"; reportedly impressed on reverse, "J. CARR & Co" (Courtesy, Kinghams Auctioneers.)

Figure 7 "Open Pan Boiling," from J.L.S., *Sugar: How It Grows, and How It Is Made: A Pleasing Account for Young People* (London: Darton and Clark, ca. 1845). (Courtesy, Lilly Library, Indiana University, Bloomington, Indiana.) This engraving served as the design source for the transfer-printed scene on the plate illustrated in fig. 6.

newly emancipated in the British West Indies—presumably those living in Jamaica—and by pointing to their changed condition of life. At the outset of the book the author notes how these individuals "used to be slaves, and were hardly treated, but they are now all free, and work for their masters at fair wages. They are now better used, and are taught in schools, and are as happy as hard working men can be."[26] This positive view is also reflected in several of the book's engravings. In these scenes, Black laborers—including the ones depicted on this plate—work without physical strain or duress and appear content. For example, the book's second engraving, which immediately precedes the title page, depicts two Black women and two Black children seated on the ground in front of two wooden barrels. Their postures are relaxed, and three of the four sitters appear to be smiling. The uncritical reader is left with the impression that life has improved for the formerly enslaved population, shown to be comfortable and satisfied with their new lives. Indeed, the book's language and imagery, as the title suggests, seems to offer readers a "pleasing account" of Black life in post-emancipation Jamaica. A nineteenth-century reader of the book or owner of this plate similarly might have taken comfort in the notion that emancipation had done much to improve the lives of the formerly enslaved.

While painting a "pleasing" picture of Black life in post-emancipation Jamaica, the book as a whole provides very little evidence that much had changed for the formerly enslaved population of the island. The scene on this plate, for an example, is virtually indistinguishable from (or could be easily confused with) other scenes of plantation life before emancipation. As the engravings in the book demonstrate, all of the labor-intensive tasks involved with making sugar—such as harvesting the cane and running it through the cane mill—continued to be done by members of the Black community. Since all of those tasks are accomplished in the early stages of sugar production, nearly all of the engravings in the first half of the book depict Black laborers. The Black laborers are also drawn in a very similar manner, with round heads, short hair, and obscured facial details, which, when compared with the book's more detailed and varied portrayals of White people, detracts from their individuality as human beings.[27] It is only when the raw sugar leaves the West Indies and travels to Europe to be refined that White laborers enter the picture (see fig. 7). Accordingly, all of the laborers depicted in the engravings in the second half of the book are White.[28] The language employed in the book, in fact, attempts to rationalize or justify the racially divided labor force. As the author explains, "The negroes only are employed in all the hard work, for white men could not do it, not being used to hot climates. The negro labourers are black men from Africa, which is a very hot country. . . ."[29] A nineteenth-century owner of a plate like this might have perceived the scene as simply representing the racial status quo, where Black workers carried out tasks that White laborers purportedly could not accomplish.[30] Overall, the book's engravings and language suggest that a strict racial divide persisted in the actual labor force involved in the sugar-making process, revealing that emancipation and pro-emancipation literature did little to change or challenge the racial biases and stereotypes of the White population.

The historical record also supports the book's visual and textual evidence. Indeed, despite the impression that *Sugar* might convey, post-emancipation life in Jamaica was not easy for the formerly enslaved. Although the book states that free workers received fair wages, low wages were a reality for some as well as a common complaint among the laboring poor of Jamaica in the decades following emancipation.[31] Additionally, as many authors have observed, emancipation did not mean equality:

> While the lives of some black people improved after emancipation, freedom did not result in the transformation that had been expected. The gross inequity between the lives of the poor and the elite barely changed; unemployment was rife, and basic facilities such as medical care, which had sometimes been available on the plantations, were virtually nonexistent. The Jamaica Assembly, still dominated by planters, enacted harsh legislation that curtailed many aspects of life for the poor.[32]

Many White West Indians continued to hold onto ideas of White superiority, and adopted the mindset that the formerly enslaved needed to be "civilized" (i.e., adopt White religious and cultural traditions) in order to be good and productive citizens in British society.[33] Those realities support Hoiem's argument "that production stories" like *Sugar* "reveal surprising details about technical processes for making things, but conceal the human cost of production" and the experiences of laborers.[34] With its long technical explanations of the methods used in cultivating and refining sugar, *Sugar* ignores the human aspect of the production story.[35] The book's text and engravings, including the one printed on this plate, present a very sanitized version of plantation life in Jamaica that hide the true experiences of the formerly enslaved.

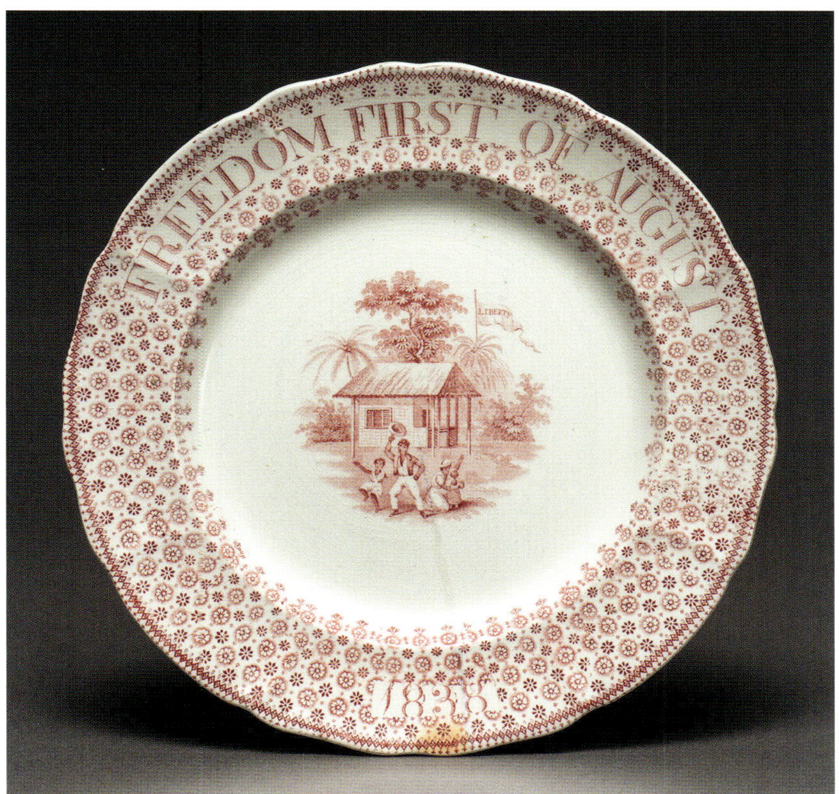

Figure 8 Plate, probably Staffordshire, England, ca. 1838. Lead-glazed earthenware. D. 10½". Marks: on rim, "FREEDOM FIRST OF AUGUST / 1838"; on flag, "LIBERTY" (Historic Deerfield, Museum Collections Fund, 2020.28; photo, Penny Leveritt.) The emancipation of the enslaved in the British West Indies on August 1, 1838, was commemorated on a number of British ceramics, such as this plate. Although a cause for celebration, emancipation did not immediately end the struggles of the formerly enslaved in the British West Indies.

In this light, the plate assumed entirely new meaning and significance. While the plate may very well have been understood to communicate an anti-slavery message, it also became symbolic of a society in a state of social and ideological transition—from a society in which slavery was legal to one in which it was illegal. On the one hand, while serious legal changes had been enacted with the end of slavery in the British West Indies on August 1, 1838, the experiences of the formerly enslaved and individuals' perceptions regarding race had changed very little in the ensuing decades (fig. 8). Freedom codified in law did not automatically translate into conditions of freedom or equality in reality. Willard's fervent expectation that emancipation would confer the status of "human being" upon the formerly enslaved was not borne out in the eyes of society. Racial equality proved to be an elusive goal in Jamaica in the years following emancipation, foreshadowing in many respects the discrimination Blacks would continue to experience in the United States following their emancipation in 1865. The seemingly simple scene on this plate helps to document this complex and troubling reality, and illustrates that slavery's legacy in the British West Indies persisted long after emancipation.

ACKNOWLEDGMENTS The author thanks Amanda E. Lange and Barbara A. Mathews for their generous help and assistance preparing this article.

1. According to *Merriam-Webster's Geographical Dictionary*, 3rd ed. (Springfield, Mass.: Merriam-Webster, 2001), the "West Indies" comprise the "islands, enclosing the Caribbean Sea, lying bet. [between] SE [south eastern] North America and N [northern] South America."

2. Epaphras Hoyt, "Sketch-book No. 11" (1838, pp. 63–64). Epaphras Hoyt Sketch-book Collection, Historic Deerfield Library, Deerfield, Mass.

3. Mary Willard, ed., *The Life of Rev. Samuel Willard, D.D., A.A.S. of Deerfield Mass.* (Boston: Geo. H. Ellis, 1892), p. 181.

4. Speaking of children's ceramics, Noël Riley writes, "While it would be reasonable to suggest that plates with moulded alphabet borders, transfer prints from children's book illustrations or mugs and plates with individual names inscribed on them were made especially for children, many more may have been aimed at a wider market that embraced both children and adults." See Noël Riley, *Gifts for Good Children: The History of Children's China, Part I, 1790–1890* (Ilminster, Somerset, Eng.: Richard Dennis, 1991), p. 8.

5. Sam Margolin, "'And Freedom to the Slave': Antislavery Ceramics, 1787–1865," *Ceramics in America*, edited by Robert Hunter (Hanover, N.H.: University Press of New England for the Chipstone Foundation, 2002), pp. 88–89.

6. Examples can be found in the collections of the Colonial Williamsburg Foundation (1998-37), the Chipstone Foundation (1999.22.a–b), the National Museums Liverpool (MMM.1994.111), and the British Museum (2002,0904.1).

7. Daniel Sousa, "Anti-Slavery Ceramics at Historic Deerfield," *Magazine of the Decorative Arts Trust* 7, no. 1 (Summer 2020): p. 14.

8. Linda Gail France, "Sugar Manufacturing in the West Indies: A Study of Innovation and Variation" (master's thesis, The College of William and Mary, 1984), pp. 40–41, 62–63.

9. Amelia Opie, *The Black Man's Lament: Or, How to Make Sugar* (London: Printed for Harvey and Darton, Gracechurch-Street, 1826), p. 17.

10. Two examples include a ca. 1840 English whiteware child's mug depicting European slavers capturing Africans in their native homeland, and a ca. 1850 English porcelain mug inscribed "Health to the Sick / Honour to the Brave / Success to the Lover / And Freedom to the Slave." See Margolin, "'And Freedom to the Slave,'" pp. 86–87, figs. 12 and 17.

11. "Constitution and Objects of the British and Foreign Anti-Slavery Society," *British and Foreign Anti-Slavery Reporter* 1, no. 1 (January 15, 1840): 1.

12. Ibid.

13. One American, David Lee Child (1794–1874), husband of Lydia Maria Child (1802–1880), worked to boycott sugar produced by enslaved persons by establishing a farm in Northampton, Massachusetts, in the late 1830s to grow beets for the production of beet sugar. See Carol Faulkner, "The Root of the Evil: Free Produce and Racial Antislavery, 1820–1860," *Journal of the Early Republic* 27, no. 3 (2007): 388–89; and David Lee Child, *The Culture of the Beet, and Manufacture of Beet Sugar* (Boston: Weeks, Jordan, and Co.; Northampton, Mass.: J. H. Butler, 1840), pp. 3–4.

14. T. B. Thorpe, "Sugar and the Sugar Region of Louisiana," *Harper's New Monthly Magazine* 7, no. 42 (November 1853): 746–67.

15. Solomon Northup, *Twelve Years a Slave* (Auburn, N.Y.: Derby and Miller, 1853), p. 211. See also Khalil Gibran Muhammad, "The Barbaric History of Sugar in America," *New York Times Magazine*, August 18, 2019.

16. Riley, *Gifts for Good Children*, pp. 7–9.

17. J.L.S., *Sugar: How It Grows, and How It Is Made: A Pleasing Account for Young People* (London: Darton and Clark, ca. 1845).

18. Elizabeth Massa Hoiem, "The Progress of Sugar: Consumption as Complicity in Children's Books about Slavery and Manufacturing, 1790–2015," *Children's Literature in Education* 52 (2021): 163. John Maw Darton (1809–1881) and Samuel Clark (1810–1875) formed their publishing partnership in 1836. John was the son of William Darton Jr. (1781–1854) and the grandson of William Darton Sr. (1755–1819), both of whom worked as publishers and published several anti-slavery books for children, including William Cowper's *The Negro's Complaint: A Poem. To Which Is Added, Pity for Poor Africans* (1826). See Linda David, "Children's Books Published by William Darton and His Sons: A Catalogue of an Exhibition at the Lilly Library, Indiana University, April–June, 1992," Lilly Library, Indiana University, Bloomington. https://collections.libraries.indiana.edu/lilly/exhibitions_legacy/etexts/darton/index.shtml.

19. Hoiem, "Progress of Sugar," pp. 162–63, 166.

20. *Catalogue of the Mercantile Library of Baltimore 1851* (Baltimore: John W. Woods, Printer, 1851), p. 105, 236. The catalog lists the book as "Sugar, how it Grows, and how it is Made."

21. For "Harvest," see Transferware Collectors Club Database of Patterns and Sources, Pattern Number: 16524, https://www.transferwarecollectorsclub.org/members/database. For "Open Pan Boiling," see Kinghams Auctioneers, Moreton-in-Marsh, Gloucestershire, England, May 3, 2019, lot 1041.

22. Email from Martyn Edgell to author, June 9, 2022. Two different plates with the "Cane Mill" scene and molded "daisy" borders sold at auction in 2021. One sold at Hansons Auctioneers, Bishton Hall, Staffordshire, England, April 9, 2021, lot 178, and the other at The Canterbury Auction Galleries, Canterbury, Kent, England, April 12, 2021, lot 1329.

23. "John Carr (& Co) (& Son)," A–Z of Stoke-on-Trent Potters, http://www.thepotteries.org/allpotters/217a.htm.

24. Jaap Otte and Willem Floor, "English Ceramics in Iran, 1810–1910," *Northern Ceramic Society Journal* 36 (2020): 110.

25. For additional information on John Carr's pottery, see R. C. Bell, *Tyneside Pottery* (London: Studio Vista, 1971), pp. 133–34, 139.

26. J.L.S., *Sugar*, p. 6.

27. The portrayal of persons of color in this manner was common not only among pro-slavery advocates, but abolitionists as well. See Hoiem, "Progress of Sugar," pp. 170–71; Kenneth DiMaggio, "Uncle Tom's Ceramics: How a Popular Antislavery Novel Became Popular Postslavery Knick-Knacks," *International Journal of the Image* 9, no. 1 (2018): 1–10; Margolin, "'And Freedom to the Slave,'" p. 106.

28. This division of labor is indistinguishable from what persisted prior to emancipation. Referring to products produced by enslaved persons, Hoiem writes, "Commodities eaten or worn on the body, like sugar, cotton, and diamonds, began with enslaved persons working in one part of the globe, before raw materials were shipped to manufactories in other countries, where free workers refined, spun, packaged, and sold the products." See Hoiem, "Progress of Sugar," p. 167.

29. J.L.S., *Sugar*, p. 6.

30. Hoiem argues that some production stories encourage children to "accept the status quo [relating especially to labor conditions] in exchange for material plenty." See Hoiem, "Progress of Sugar," p. 169.

31. Gad Heuman, "Victorian Jamaica: The View from the Colonial Office," in *Victorian Jamaica*, edited by Tim Barringer and Wayne Modest (Durham, N.C.: Duke University Press, 2018), p. 150; Tim Barringer, "Land, Labor, Landscape: Views of the Plantation in Victorian Jamaica," in *Victorian Jamaica*, pp. 304–5.

32. Barringer and Modest, introduction to *Victorian Jamaica*, p. 9.

33. Ibid., p. 5.

34. Hoiem, "Progress of Sugar," p. 162.

35. As Hoiem ultimately argues, this is a common theme found in production stories. See Hoiem, "Progress of Sugar," pp. 162–65.

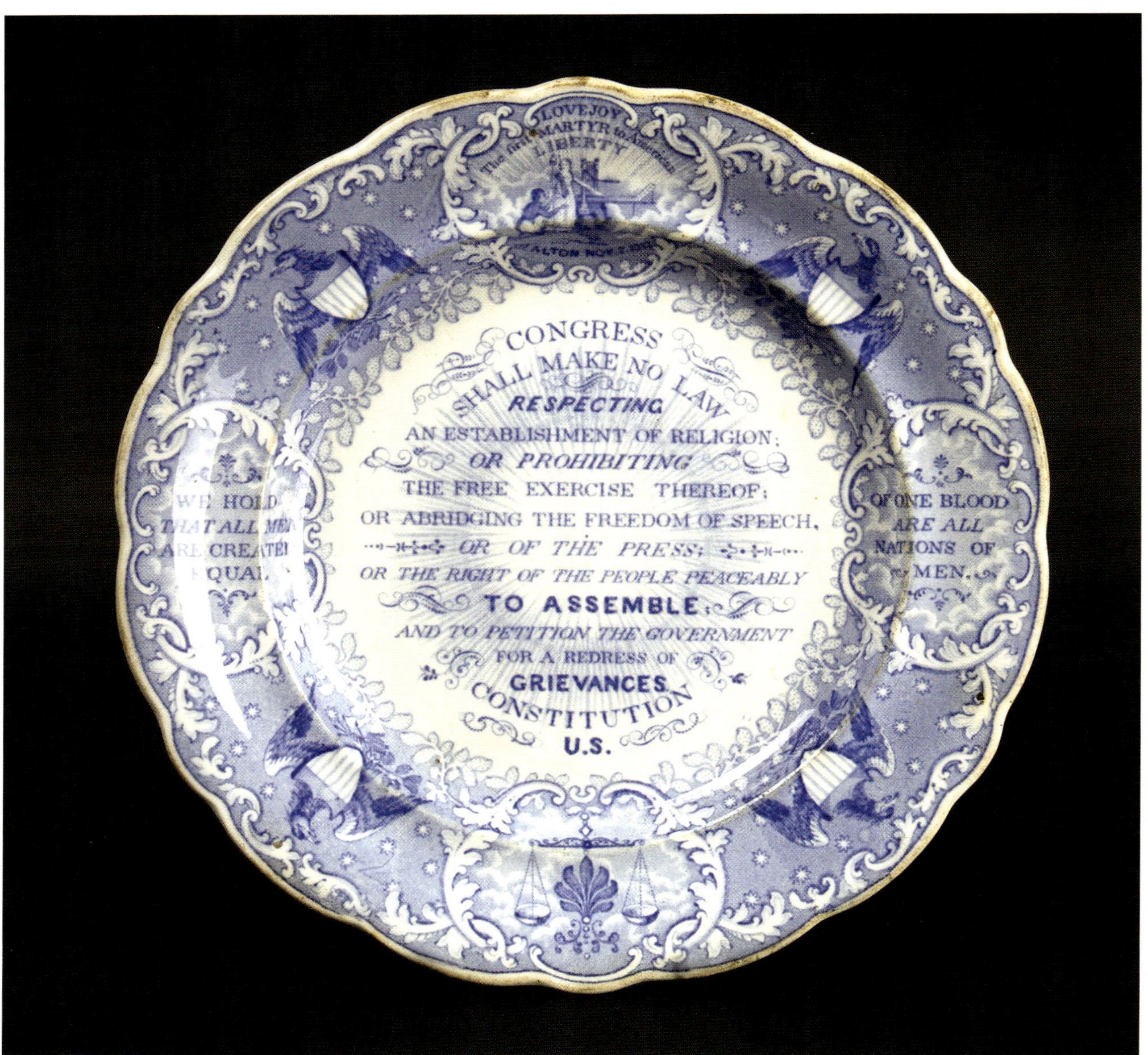

Figure 1 Plate, Staffordshire, England, ca. 1838. Lead-glazed earthenware. D. 7¾". (Private collection; photo, Neil Ewins.)

Neil Ewins

Hidden Histories: The Case of Elijah Lovejoy and the Production of Anti-slavery Ceramics

▼ ONE OF THE ATTRACTIONS OF ceramic history is the possibility of finding new information that questions previous views and assumptions. A case in point is the production of ceramics commemorating the death of the Reverend Elijah Lovejoy (1802–1837), the proprietor of an abolitionist newspaper in Alton, Illinois, who was murdered by a pro-slavery mob on November 7, 1837 (figs. 1–3). This article examines how the design originally was interpreted as derived from a careful examination of advertising and other press accounts.

The Tragic Act

The murder of Elijah Lovejoy was widely reported in the contemporary press and galvanized anti-slavery activists. One of Lovejoy's friends, the Reverend Edward Beecher (1803–1895), even wrote *Narrative of Riots at Alton*, first published in 1838. The reverend's sister, Harriet Beecher Stowe (1811–1896), later published *Uncle Tom's Cabin*, indicating how firmly various members of the Beecher family were committed to the abolitionist cause.

At a glance, the facts seem straightforward. Lovejoy moved to Alton where he attempted to run his abolitionist newspaper. He was met with

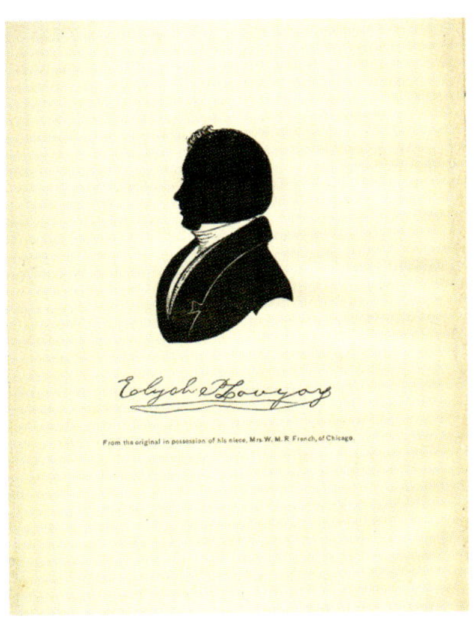

Figure 2 "Elijah P. Lovejoy," from Henry Tanner, *The Martyrdom of Lovejoy* (1881), unpaginated. (Special Collections and College Archives, Musselman Library, Gettysburg College.)

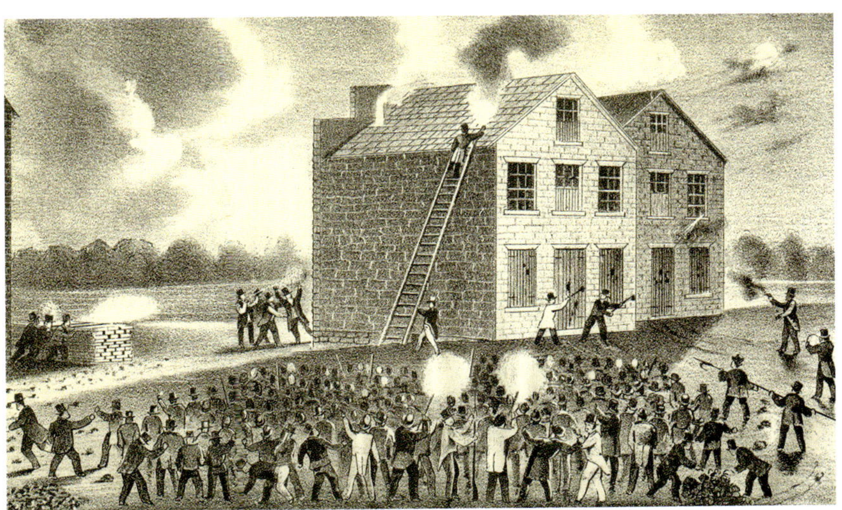

Figure 3 "The mob attacking the warehouse of Godfrey Gilman & Co., Alton, Ill., on the night of the 7th of November, 1837, at the time Lovejoy was murdered and his press destroyed," from Henry Tanner, *The Martyrdom of Lovejoy* (1881), unpaginated. (Special Collections and College Archives, Musselman Library, Gettysburg College.)

local resistance by pro-slavery activists. There was a riot, and in the ensuing chaos Lovejoy was shot and killed. As a form of protest, transfer-printed designs were manufactured, which came to be known as "Constitutional" or "Anti-slavery" wares.

The Myth

Interest in so-called historical Staffordshire wares (that is, ceramics manufactured for the American market and decorated with American scenes) by ceramic historians and collectors developed rapidly in the second half of the nineteenth century. Early-American ceramic historians developed various theories as to why certain designs were produced, and the Lovejoy design received a fair amount of attention. For instance, Alice Morse Earle stated in *China Collecting in America* (1892): "It is asserted that the pieces bearing this design were the gift of the English Anti-Slavery Society to the American Abolitionists, shortly after the death of Lovejoy; that they were sold at auction in New York, and the proceeds devoted to the objects of the Society of Abolitionists. If this account is true, these plates are certainly among the most interesting relics of those interesting days."[1]

In 1903, N. Hudson Moore (another Early American ceramics historian) suggested that this ceramic design was a gift from English anti-slavery supporters to the American abolitionists, and even indicated that these plates had been targeted for forgery.[2] Ellouise Baker Larsen (the author who produced the most comprehensive survey of printed wares destined for the American market) believed that the design was certainly manufactured in Staffordshire, and was used to raise money for freeing enslaved people in the United States.[3]

Gradually the interpretations shifted from speculative to opinions more engrained into the fabric of ceramic history.[4] Sam Margolin's 2002 article "'And Freedom to the Slave': Antislavery Ceramics, 1787–1865" repeated the idea that the wares were donated by British abolitionists to raise money for the anti-slavery cause, and that the design was faked in the late nineteenth century. He suggests that in a wave of indignation the "Staffordshire potters memorialized" Lovejoy in their wares.[5] This view fits more easily into a typical notion of ceramic history, whereby the manufacturer produces merchandise skillfully adapted to appeal to consumer demand. Any contribution that intermediaries may have had in this process has often been neglected.

JOINT STOCK SLAVE BANK LAWS IN THE TERRITORIES OF THE UNITED STATES TO BE REPEALED.—The subscriber, at 87 Water street, has just received and for sale, Blue Printed Earthenware, made expressly to his order, of a new pattern, containing suitable devices, with the following article from the Constitution of the United States: "Congress shall make no law respecting an establishment of religion or prohibiting the free exercise thereof, or abridging the freedom of speech, or of the press, or the right of the people peaceably to assemble, and to petition the government for a redress of grievances."

THOMAS F. FIELD.

New York, 2d October, 1838 2m.

Figure 4 Advertisement, *The Emancipator* (New York), November 8, 1838, p. 101. (Courtesy, NewsBank / Readex.)

The Reality

On closer analysis, the relation between the manufacturer and importers and dealers was more complex. In 1838 Thomas F. Field, a crockery dealer in New York, claimed that a printed design (matching a description of the Lovejoy wares) was "made expressly to his order, of a new pattern" (fig. 4). It is interesting how advertisements for these Lovejoy wares and for Edward Beecher's *Narrative of Riots at Alton* appeared in the same column of *The Emancipator* in October 1838. The advertisement quotes the phrase "Congress shall make no law . . . ," which is also what appears on the printed

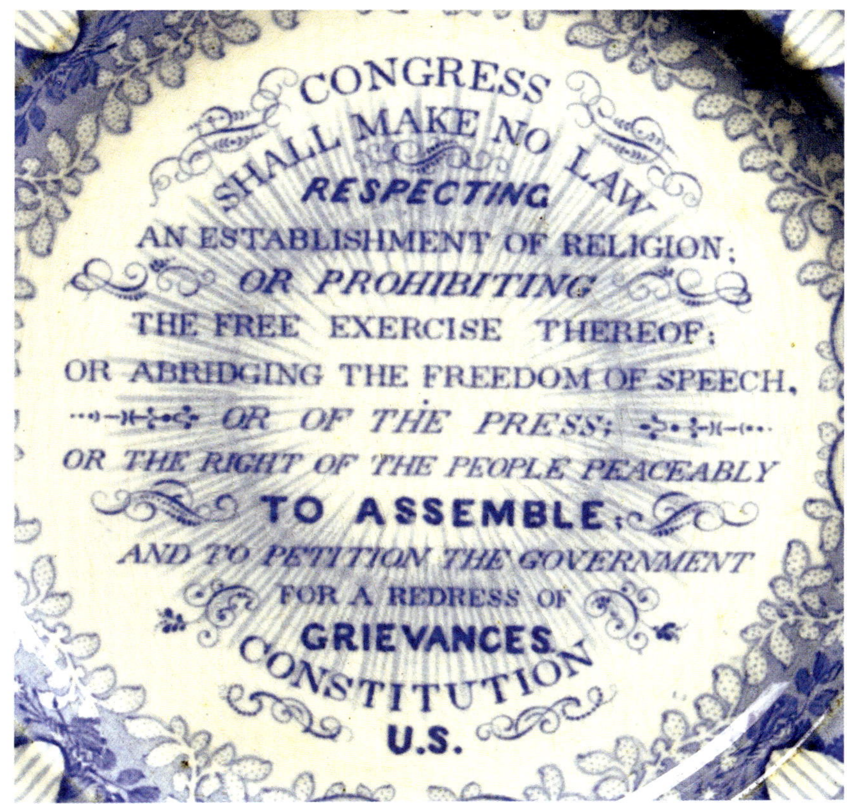

Figure 5 Detail of the plate illustrated in fig. 1 showing the First Amendment of the United States Constitution.

CONSTITUTIONAL WARE.—We have seen a specimen of the ware advertised by Mr. Field, and can attest to its quality and value. On the rim are three inscriptions. The first is embellished with a device representing a slave kneeling in supplication to Liberty, who points to the Printing Press, while over it you read, "LOVEJOY, the first MARTYR TO AMERICAN LIBERTY, at Alton, Nov. 7, 1837." On the right is, "OF ONE BLOOD ARE ALL NATIONS OF MEN." On the left, "WE HOLD THAT ALL MEN ARE CREATED EQUAL." In the centre, amidst a blaze of effulgence, we trace the redeeming clause of the American Constitution:

CONGRESS
SHALL MAKE NO LAW
RESPECTING
AN ESTABLISHMENT OF RELIGION;
OR PROHIBITING
THE FREE EXERCISE THEREOF:
OR ABRIDGING THE FREEDOM OF SPEECH
OR OF THE PRESS;
Or the Right of the People Peaceably
TO ASSEMBLE;
AND TO PETITION THE GOVERNMENT
FOR A REDRESS OF
GRIEVANCES.

—*Constitution of U. S.*—

Mr. Adams' Speech is at length received at the office, for sale. The (to us) unaccountable delay has deprived many of our friends, we fear, of their opportunity to procure it, but the speech itself has lost neither interest nor importance.

☞ Price, 25 cents.

Figure 6 Advertisement, *The Emancipator* (New York), October 11, 1838, p. 97. (Courtesy, NewsBank / Readex.)

wares commemorating the death of the Rev. Elijah Lovejoy (fig. 5). *The Emancipator* included a more detailed description of so-called Constitutional Ware, and poignantly mentions how the design incorporated an enslaved man kneeling at the figure of Liberty pointing to a printing press (figs. 6, 7). Silk ribbons were printed with the same image, and it was either

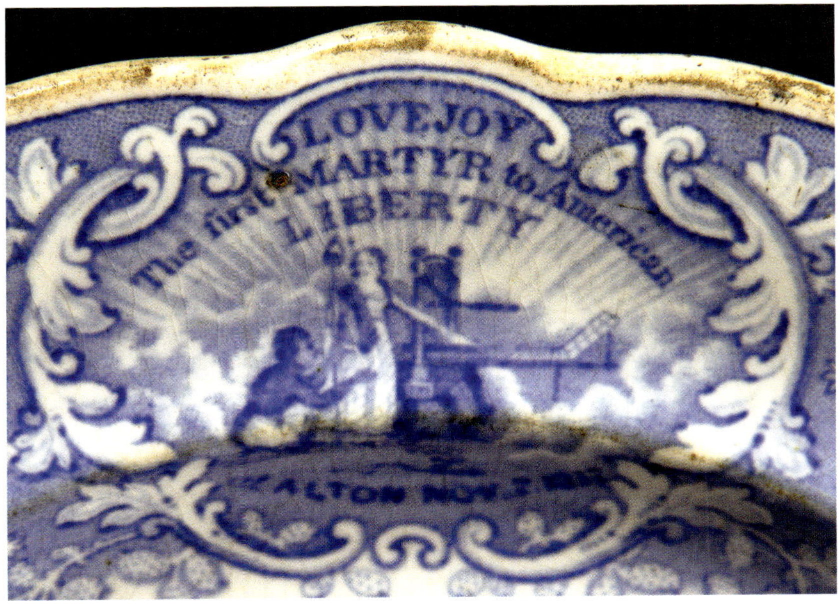

Figure 7 Detail of the plate illustrated in fig. 1 depicting a printing press and an enslaved person. Inscribed: LOVEJOY / The first MARTYR to American / LIBERTY / ALTON NOV. 7. 1837. (Private collection; photo, Neil Ewins.)

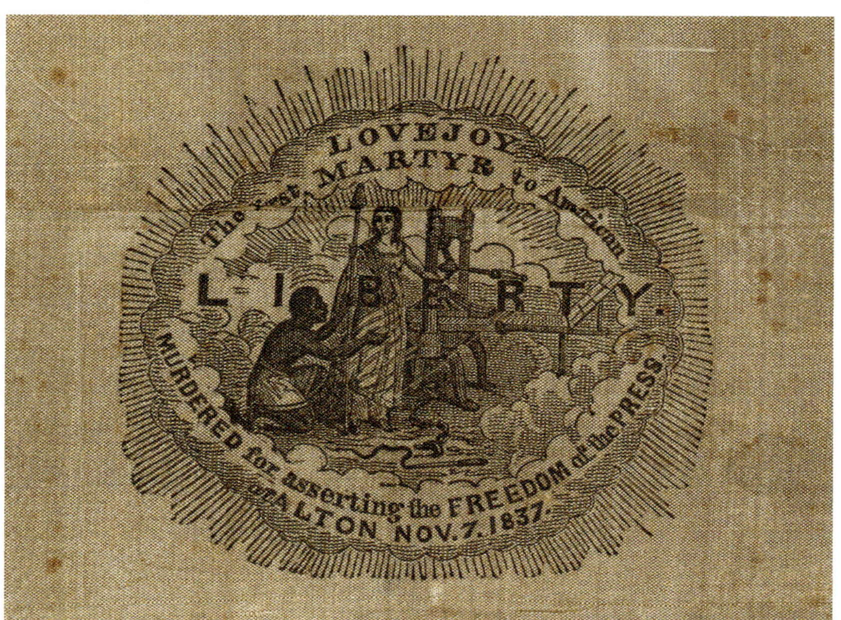

Figure 8 Printed ribbon, United States, 1837–1840. Silk. L. 4¼". (Colonial Williamsburg Foundation.)

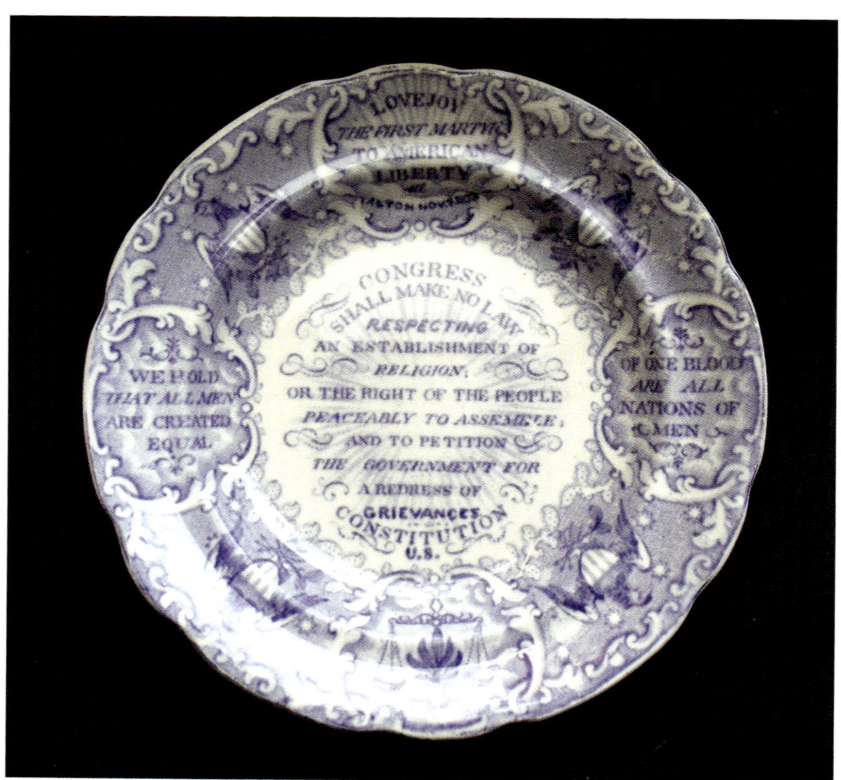

Figure 9 Cup plate, Staffordshire, England, ca. 1838. Lead-glazed earthenware. D. 4". (Private collection; photo, Neil Ewins.)

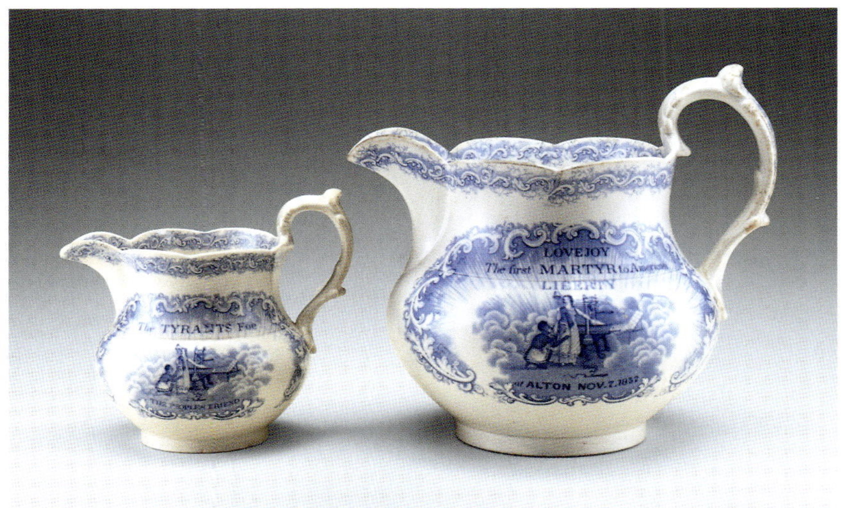

Figure 10 Jugs, Staffordshire, England, ca. 1838. Lead-glazed earthenware. H. of tallest 6¼". (Collection of Rex Stark; photo, Gavin Ashworth.)

them or a broadside or book that Field used as the design source (fig. 8).[6] In addition to plates, cup plates and jugs are known (figs. 9, 10).

From about 1822, Thomas F. Field was located in Utica, a city in upstate New York that was a center of abolitionist activity, and was described as being in a partnership with one Theodore Clark from 1824 until 1829.[7] By 1833 Field was in New York City running a china store.[8] Transfer-printed ceramics exist with the impressed mark of "Field & Clark, Importers of Earthenware, Utica", that were manufactured by Enoch Wood of Burslem. Given that these marked pieces show a direct connection between Enoch Wood and Field & Clark, it is possible that the Elijah Lovejoy commemorative design was manufactured by Enoch Wood & Sons. However, no marked pieces have been identified that would prove this attribution.

On April 7, 1823, Thomas F. Field, a "merchant of Utica," married "Miss Mary Ann, eldest daughter of David Roberts of this city," at a ceremony officiated by the Rev. John Williams of the Baptist Church on Oliver Street in New York City.[9] At a meeting held on February 18, 1828, at the Methodist Chapel in Utica, Thomas Field was appointed as one of the commissioners resolved to prevent violation of the Sabbath.[10] Field became president of the Baptist Central Tract Society of Utica, founded in April 1828, and secretary of the Oneida Bible Society of New York.[11] The Baptist Central Tract Society claimed to have distributed 150,000 tracts in 1830, and Field was still active as the president in 1831.[12] Clearly Field had strong religious convictions, and it is apparent that his Baptist values affected his behavior. In 1841 he was described as president of the Baptist Anti-Slavery Society of New York, emphasizing how his sociopolitical and religious views mirrored what he promoted.[13]

In an article in *The Friend of Man*, Utica's abolitionist newspaper, it was reported that specimens of Field's plates had been discovered in October 1838 at the Anti-Slavery Office in New York City. The author of the newspaper article explained how he had proceeded to Field's New York store at 87 Water Street to purchase a dozen plates for his personal use. The writer also believed that "[t]he pattern was made to his [Thomas Field's] own order, and, so far as we know, he is the only man in his business who has dared to put his finger upon the 'peculiar institution.'"[14] A comment that appeared under the heading "Scraps" in a Hartford, Connecticut, newspaper mentions how Messrs. Field & Co. was advertising "anti-slavery earthenware," but then asked, "What sort of an animal is that?"[15]

Based on these comments, it is uncertain there was sufficient demand for the design to generate enough profits to benefit enslaved individuals, as several authors have suggested. Thus, it is important to recognize how the design was, at that time, considered to be touching on an issue of acute sociopolitical tension rather than an example of Field (or the Staffordshire manufacturer) identifying some marketing opportunity. As indicated above, Field's own position on abolitionism was made clear when he became president of the Baptist Anti-Slavery Society in 1841. The contemporaneous interpretation, pieced together from newspaper notices and advertisements, is rather different from the opinions expressed by nineteenth-century collectors and writers.

There is nothing in Field's advertisements to indicate that any profits were used to support anti-slavery activities, nor is there evidence to support the theory that it was a gift (as Alice Morse Earle suggested) from the English Anti-Slavery Society to be sold at auction. Although the anti-slavery plate might not have been in high demand, the importance to contemporaries was, according to *The Friend of Man*, that dining tables were furnished with this crockery, and the plates could at least "silently preach abolitionism" to guests and children "on sound principles."[16] Clearly, it was envisaged that the Lovejoy design was for use and not merely for display, and Field continued to advertise his "Anti-Slavery Earthenware" plates and pitchers in the New York *Spectator* from March until June 1839.[17]

The Unpalatable Truth

A positive result of this article would have been for it to convey a new interpretation of the Lovejoy design, infinitely more desirable than the historical myth. Alas, this was not to be the case. Jeffrey B. Snyder wrote in *Historical Staffordshire: American Patriots and Views* (1995) that the Lovejoy plate "was popular with the Abolitionist's movement in the Northern states of the United States,"[18] but on closer analysis it is doubtful that Thomas F. Field was responding to American demand. Field had his views, and it was observed in a Boston newspaper of 1834 that he had courageously marketed his New York business as an "Abolition China Store" long before the death of the Rev. Elijah Lovejoy in 1837. A notice in the *Liberator* in August 1834 as to what the mob might do to Field's crockery store is a poignant reminder of how the views of merchants were not necessarily in unison with attitudes of the consumers. The actual notice read: "Thomas F. Field, of New-York, 'offers for sale an amalgamation of colors and qualities of French, English, and India China Tea and Dining Seats [*sic*],' and styles his store an 'Abolition China Store.' If the mob scent out this amalgamation, there may be shocking work among the crockery."[19]

The example of the Lovejoy design rather reinforces how importers could have multidimensional personalities, as well as being involved in their mercantile trade. In fact, Thomas F. Field's obituary indicates that apart from being described as the "oldest crockery merchant or dealer in this State," he "was at one time prominent in municipal politics, first as a Whig, then as an Abolitionist, and finally, as a Republican."[20] When Field stood as an Abolition candidate for mayor of New York in 1842, he received only 136 votes, whereas the Democrat candidate received more than 20,000 and the Whig more than 18,000.[21]

Conclusion

Although the early publications concerning historical Staffordshire ceramics appeared to have jumped to an incorrect conclusion as to why the Lovejoy design was produced, the pioneering research by connoisseurs still has significance. These publications already began to recognize how some designs were rarer than others, impacting on their collectible status. N. Hudson Moore's *The Old China Book* (1903) pointed out: "A year or two ago I wrote that 'historic cup-plates were worth their weight in gold,' and some of my correspondents took exception to my statement [see fig. 9]. Within a few weeks I have heard of two four-inch Lovejoy cup-plates which have come upon the market. . . . The first was sold at public auction in New York City, and brought twenty-three dollars."[22]

While it is now appreciated that ceramic patterns could be commissioned by a single importer, the implications of this are that the number manufactured, sold, and distributed was probably limited. Hence, we begin to have an explanation as to why some ceramic designs associated with the American market were seemingly rare. In 1903 Moore pointed out that "[i]t is unfortunate that this fine old piece was selected for forgery. Any person who is used to handling this old ware gets to detect the differences by mere touch that would escape the casual observer. Not only were the forged plates heavier, but they were thicker, and colder to the hand."[23]

Two versions of the plates are known and seem to support Moore's fear that there were later versions; there are surviving plates printed in a lighter tone, of a slightly larger size, which are thicker and more in ivory color than the originals (figs. 1 and 11).[24] That suggests that these larger plates are later, either as honest copies made to celebrate another occasion, or as dishonest forgeries meant to fulfill a demand for the rare originals.

While there has been growing recognition of how ceramic importers and dealers could influence production, this is normally on the basis that intermediaries—being closer to the consumer—had a better understanding of demand. For example, Regina Blaszczyk's *Imagining Consumers: Design and Innovation from Wedgwood to Corning* (2000) argues that merchants were in touch with the consumer and, therefore, "harvested meaningful data about tastes and purchasing habits."[25] In actuality, the comments of contemporaries infer that the Lovejoy subject was a controversial one, and when it is appreciated that this ceramic design was actually orchestrated by an importer who was originally from England, it is perhaps more akin to an

Figure 11 Plate, Staffordshire, England, late nineteenth century. Lead-glazed earthenware. D. 9¼". (Reeves Museum of Ceramics, Washington and Lee University; photo, Robert Hunter.)

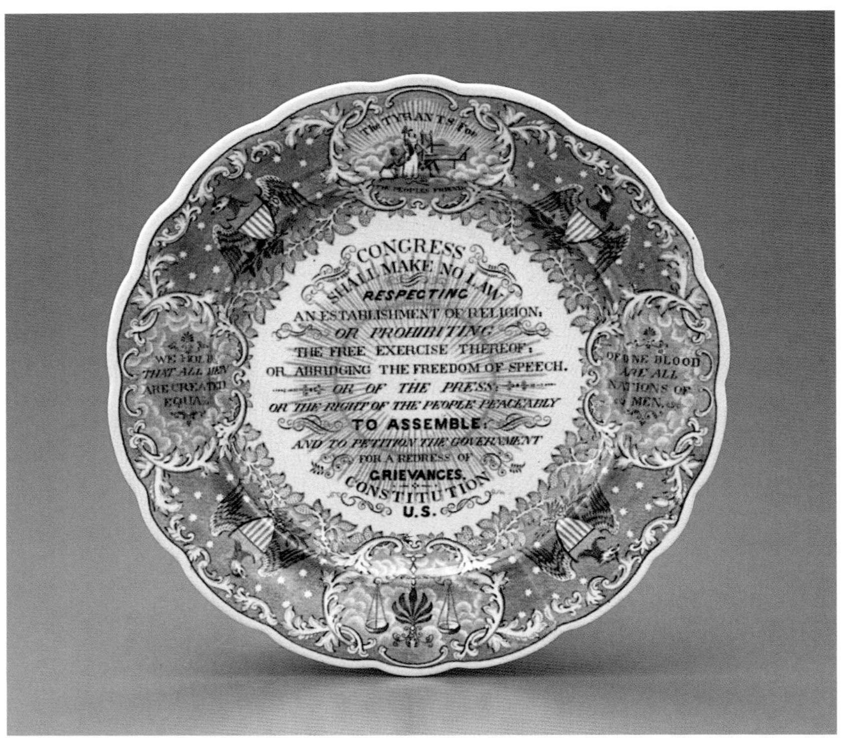

outsider making a comment about slavery in the United States.[26] In certain instances, what was marketed by importers and dealers could reflect their own, individual concerns.

For ceramic historians today, it remains important to reexamine previous interpretations of what certain ceramic objects might signify. Even from a twenty-first-century perspective, David Fischer has interpreted the Lovejoy ceramic design (now shown to be commissioned by Thomas F. Field) as one example of the "outpouring" of imagery concerned with abolition and civil liberties after the Reverend Lovejoy's murder in 1837—assuming that the production of the physical object was a logical reflection of prevailing attitudes.[27] As this article has demonstrated, the importance of examining the origins, backgrounds, and identities of crockery importers and dealers grows in significance, since what was advertised did not simply emanate from the Staffordshire manufacturer or was a response to the perceived demands of the consumer.

1. Alice M. Earle, *China Collecting in America* (New York: Charles Scribner's Sons, 1892), p. 333.

2. N. Hudson Moore, *The Old China Book, including Staffordshire, Wedgwood, Lustre, and Other English Pottery and Porcelain* (New York: Frederick A. Stokes Co., 1903), p. 79.

3. Ellouise Larsen, *American Historical Views on Staffordshire China*, rev. ed. (1939; New York: Doubleday, 1950), p. 242.

4. Marian Klamkin, *American Patriotic and Political China* (New York: Charles Scribner's Sons, 1973), pp. 102–4; Bridget T. Heneghan, *Whitewashing America: Material Culture and Race in the Antebellum Imagination* (Jackson: University Press of Mississippi, 2003), p. 14.

5. Sam Margolin, "'And Freedom to the Slave': Antislavery Ceramics, 1787–1865," in *Ceramics in America*, edited by Robert Hunter (Hanover, N.H.: University Press of New England for the Chipstone Foundation, 2002), pp. 95–97.

6. Ribbons like these were designed to be worn around the arm as a sign of mourning.

7. Robert H. McCauley, "American Importers of Staffordshire," *Antiques* (June 1944): 295–97, indicates that Field opened a crockery store at Utica in 1822; advertisement, "Utica, May 25, *First arrival from Liverpool*—Messrs Field and Clark . . . 50 packages [of] elegant crockery ware," *Watch-Tower* (Cooperstown, N.Y.), May 31, 1824, p. 3; "Dissolution" notice, *Christian Journal* (Utica, N.Y.), October 16, 1829, p. 4.

8. *Longworth's American Almanac, New-York Register and City Directory* (New York: Thomas Longworth, 1833), p. 258.

9. "Married," *National Advocate* (New York, N.Y.), April 9, 1823, p. 2.

10. "Meeting at Utica," *Connecticut Observer* (Hartford), March 3, 1828, p. 1.

11. Notice, *New-York Baptist Register* (Utica), November 28, 1828, p. 3; "Oneida Bible Society, N.Y.," *Philadelphian*, May 23, 1829, p. 1.

12. "Religious Compendium," *Christian Watchman* (Boston), February 12, 1830, p. 3; "Utica Central Baptist Tract Society," *New-England Baptist Register* (Boston), February 9, 1831, p. 3.

13. "Baptist A. S. Soc. of N.Y. City and Vicinity," *Christian Reflector* (Worcester, Mass.), June 16, 1841, p. 3.

14. "Anti-Slavery Earthen Ware," *Friend of Man* (Utica, N.Y.), October 17, 1838, p. 279.

15. "Scraps," *Times* (Hartford, Conn.), September 21, 1839, p. 1.

16. "Anti-Slavery Earthen Ware," *Friend of Man* (Utica, N.Y.), October 17, 1838, p. 279.

17. The advertisement reads: "ANTI-SLAVERY EARTHENWARE - Plates and pitchers, and a general assortment of China, glass and earthenware of the latest and best patterns for sale. Country merchants who regard the quality of ware will find it to their interest to call and examine my stock at 87 Water Street. Thomas F. Field." *Spectator* (New York), March 18, 1839, p. 3.

18. Jeffrey B. Snyder, *Historical Staffordshire: American Patriots and Views* (Atglen, Pa.: Schiffer Publishing, 1995), p. 108.

19. "Notice," *Liberator* (Boston), August 30, 1834, p. 139.

20. "Obituary," *New York Tribune*, September 15, 1877, p. 5.

21. "The Vote for Mayor," *Albany Argus* (Albany, N.Y.), April 22, 1842, p. 3.

22. Moore, *The Old China Book*, p. 46.

23. Ibid. pp. 79–80.

24. I am extremely grateful to Ron Fuchs II and Robert Hunter for undertaking an analysis of the Lovejoy plates in the collection of the Reeves Museum of Ceramics, Washington and Lee University.

25. Regina Blaszczyk, *Imagining Consumers: Design and Innovation from Wedgwood to Corning* (Baltimore, Md.: Johns Hopkins University Press, 2000), pp. 32–33.

26. Certificate of Death, Thomas F. Field, September 15, 1877, Brooklyn, New York. New York City Municipal Archives. The certificate indicates that Thomas Field arrived in the United States in circa 1815; 1870 Census, Brooklyn, New York.

27. David H. Fischer, *Liberty and Freedom: A Visual History of America's Founding Ideas* (Oxford: Oxford University Press, 2005), p. 280.

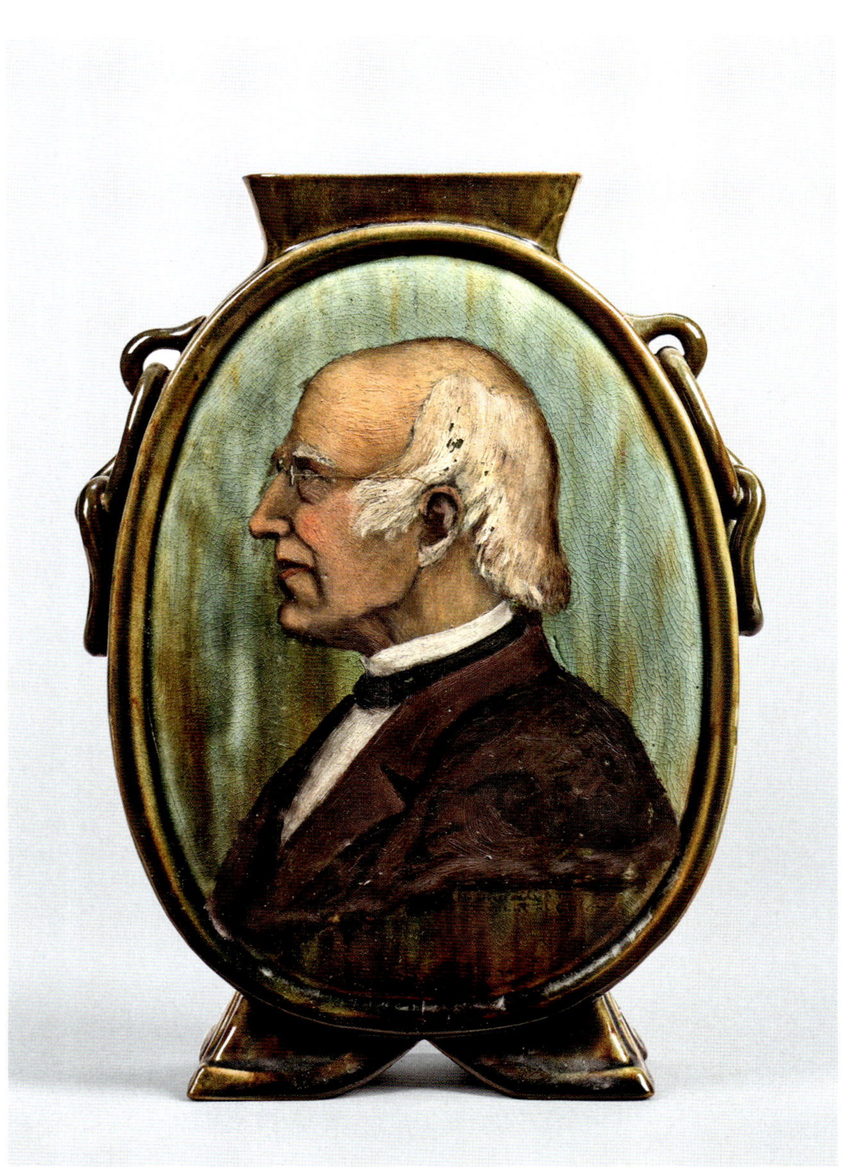

Figure 1 Vase, Chelsea Keramic Art Works, Chelsea, Massachusetts, ca. 1879. Lead-glazed earthenware. H. 12½". (Private collection; photo, Jeff Antkowiak.)

James D. Kaufman

A Chelsea Keramic Art Works Vase with a Portrait of William Lloyd Garrison

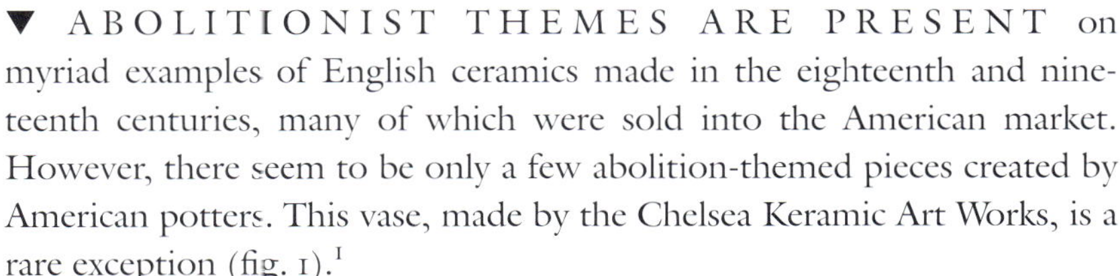

▼ ABOLITIONIST THEMES ARE PRESENT on myriad examples of English ceramics made in the eighteenth and nineteenth centuries, many of which were sold into the American market. However, there seem to be only a few abolition-themed pieces created by American potters. This vase, made by the Chelsea Keramic Art Works, is a rare exception (fig. 1).[1]

The green-glazed, flat-sided oval vase features a portrait of the prominent American abolitionist William Lloyd Garrison (1805–1879) and handles in the form of broken chains (fig. 2). Painted or inscribed faintly under the glaze and beneath the portrait is a quote that seems to read "No distinction on account of color" followed by "Garrison" (fig. 3).

William Lloyd Garrison was perhaps the most prominent white abolitionist of the nineteenth century. He was an eloquent and prolific speaker and writer, and one of the founders of the American Anti-Slavery Society. *The Liberator*, the newspaper he published in Boston from 1831 until the end of slavery in the United States in 1865, was one of the nation's leading anti-slavery publications.

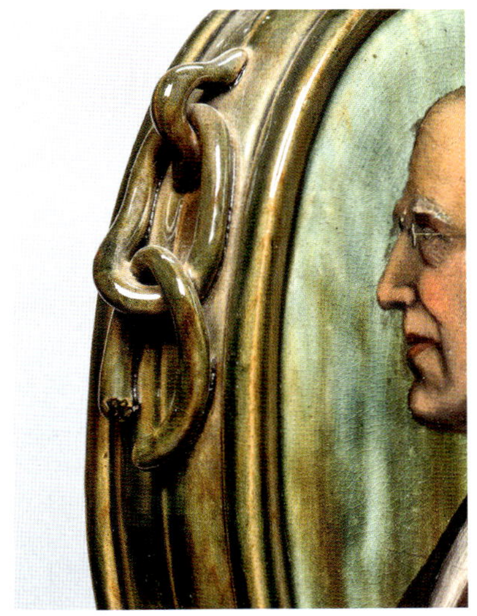

Figure 2 Detail of the handles of the vase illustrated in fig. 1.

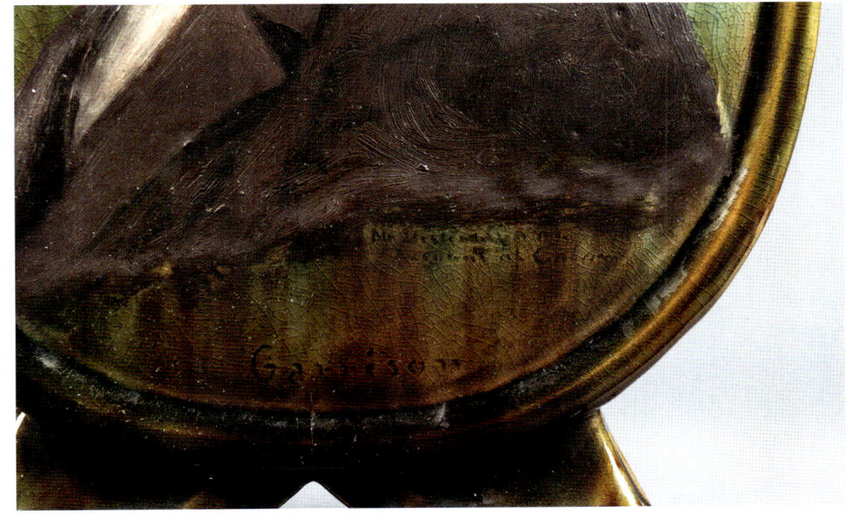

Figure 3 Detail of the inscription "Garrison" and "No distinction on account of color" on the vase illustrated in fig. 1.

Garrison died in 1879, and this piece was probably made shortly thereafter as a memorial tribute. It is not wholly surprising that an abolitionist theme would appear on a piece of ceramics made in Massachusetts, which had a large and active community of anti-slavery activists and where slavery was outlawed in 1783, seventy-seven years before the Civil War.

The Chelsea Keramic Art Works, Robertson & Sons was the first pottery to identify itself as an "art pottery" in the United States. It was founded in 1866 by Alexander Robertson (1840–1925) in Chelsea, Massachusetts, just north of Boston. His younger brother, Hugh Robertson (1845–1908) joined him in 1868. By 1872 their father, James (1810–1880), and brother George (1835–1914) had also joined the family enterprise, which became known as the Chelsea Keramic Art Works. Throughout the next two decades they produced a wide variety of decorative vessels, some imitating the shapes and decoration of ancient Greek pottery and others capturing the distinct influence of Chinese and Japanese ceramics.[2]

Figure 4 Vase, Chelsea Keramic Art Works, Chelsea, Massachusetts, 1870–1880. Lead-glazed earthenware. H. 12½". (Private collection; photo, Jeff Antkowiak.)

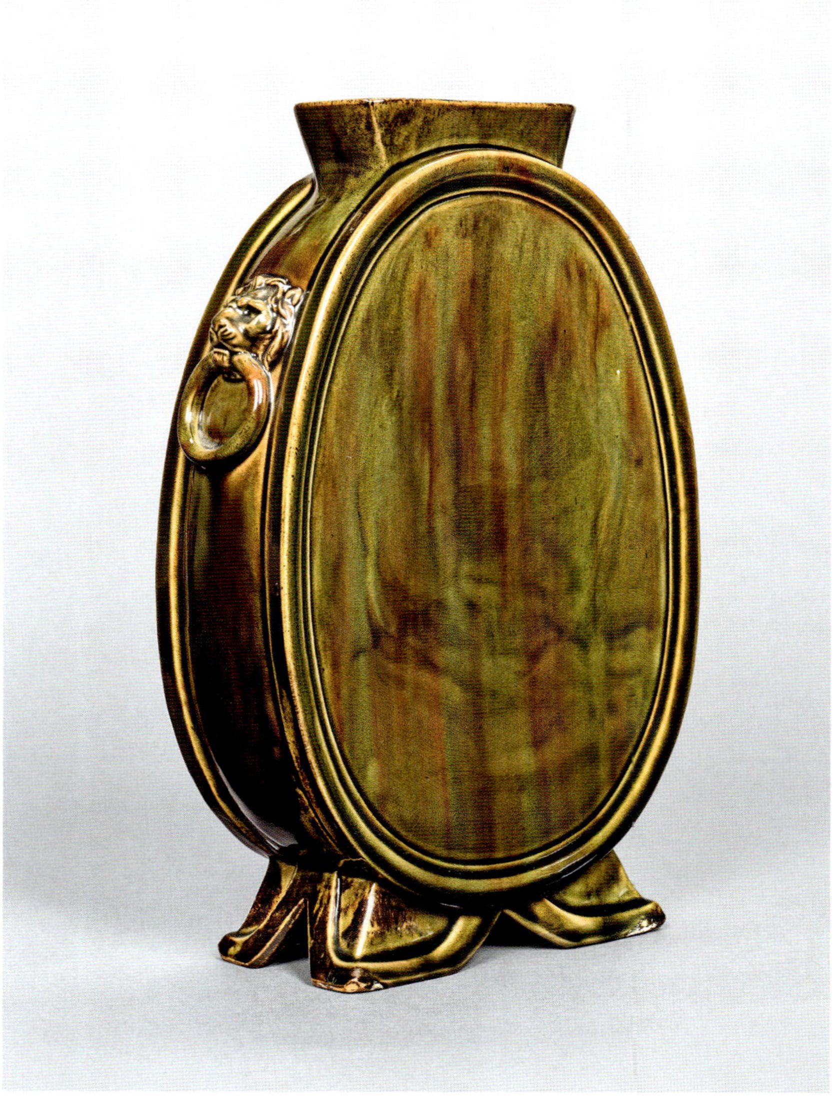

Chelsea Keramic quickly received attention and praise for its wares. In 1878 Jennie J. Young, the author of *The Ceramic Art*, wrote:

> The artists and collectors of Boston soon discovered certain qualities in the Chelsea potters and their works deserving recognition. They may possibly have reached the conviction that Chelsea is to be numbered among the places where artists value their work solely according to its truth, excellence, and beauty. Without affecting to disregard commercial considerations, they succeed in giving their art the precedence. It is not, therefore, a matter of surprise either that they should have convinced a section of the public that Chelsea can do noble service in the cause of American art, or that many excellent works should bear its mark.[3]

Much of Chelsea Keramic's products were modeled by Hugh Robertson, who possessed notable talent as a sculptor in clay. The pottery's wares were made of either red or buff earthenware, and except for the imitations of Greek pieces, were routinely covered by a thin, glossy glaze. During the late 1870s and early 1880s, Chelsea Keramic's lead glazes were predominantly olive greens, muted blues, shades of yellow, and browns.

The footed pillow-form vase was a common form made there. It is found most frequently with no decoration on either of its two oval flat sides, but some examples have either molded images or cold-painted designs (fig. 4).[4] Typically, these vases are found with handles in the form of lion heads, but in this example the handles are formed of broken chains, almost certainly a reference to the abolition of slavery in the United States (figs. 4 and 2). This is the only known example of a Chelsea Keramic piece with that decorative device, confirming that the overall piece was intended to carry an abolitionist theme and to be an explicit tribute to William Lloyd Garrison. Solidifying that conclusion is the inscribed or painted motto "No distinction on account of color" and "Garrison" under the portrait.

It is not entirely clear why the quote "no distinction on account of color" was used, as it does not seem to have been originated with Garrison. The phrase was used by other anti-slavery activists, most prominently by the African-American activist Frederick Douglass (1817/1818– 1895), who in a letter to Garrison that he published in *The Liberator* in 1846, wrote of his time in London,

> My visit to this city has been exceedingly gratifying, on account of the freedom I have enjoyed in visiting such places of instruction and amusement as those from which I have been carefully excluded by the inveterate prejudice against color in the United States. Botanic and Zoological gardens, Museums and Panoramas, Halls of Statuary and Galleries of Paintings, are as free to the black as the white man in London. There is no distinction on account of color. The white man gains nothing by being white, and the black man loses nothing by being black.[5]

Given the forethought of the specific abolitionist reference of the handles and the quote, it is surprising that the Garrison portrait was cold-painted and not molded. Perhaps cold-painting allowed a broader range of natural colors than what would have been available for underglaze decoration?

While the vase carries the standard impressed "Chelsea Keramic Art Works Robertson & Sons" mark on the underside, neither the modeler nor the painter seems to have inscribed either personal initials or a rebus. Perhaps it was Hugh Robertson, as he was responsible for many of Chelsea Keramik's models, and painted or sculpted several other portraits on Chelsea Keramic vases; in fact, there are no other portraits signed by anyone other than Hugh Robertson known at this time.[6] Hugh Robertson was also somewhat of a social progressive for his era, lauding the "free thinker" Horace Seaver with a poem for Seaver's funeral and honoring him with a sculpted bust. It is easy to imagine him commemorating Garrison with a vase.

In his eulogy for Garrison, Frederick Douglass asked that Americans "guard his memory as precious inheritance, let us teach our children the story of his life, let us try to imitate his virtues, and endeavor as he did to leave the world freer, nobler, and better than we found it."[7] The potter who made this vase may have been motivated by the same sentiments to create this memorial.

1. The vase surfaced at a sale at Rago Arts and Auctions, Lambertville, New Jersey, August 21, 2020.

2. Paul Evans, *Art Pottery of the United States: An Encyclopedia of Producers and Their Marks* (New York: Charles Scribner's Sons, 1974), pp. 46–51; Doreen Burke, et al., *In Pursuit of Beauty: Americans and the Aesthetic Movement* (New York: Metropolitan Museum of Art, 1986), pp. 212–16; Lloyd E. Hawes, *The Dedham Pottery and the Earlier Robertson's Chelsea Potteries* (Dedham, Mass.: Dedham Historical Society, 1968), p. 11.

3. Jennie Young, *The Ceramic Art: A Compendium of the History and Manufacture of Pottery and Porcelain* (New York: Harper & Brothers, 1878), p. 469.

4. Cold-painting is the paint decoration of ceramics after the final firing of the piece. The decoration is not fused into the glaze.

5. Letter from Frederick Douglass to William Lloyd Garrison, London (England), May 23, 1846, *Life and Writings of Frederick Douglass* edited by Philip Foner, 5 vols. (New York: International, 1950), 1:165.

6. Other portraits by Hugh C. Robertson that are known on Chelsea Keramic vases, tiles, and plaques include: the poets Henry Wadsworth Longfellow and Robert Burns; Wilkins Micawber, a character from Charles Dickens's *David Copperfield*; Presidents James Garfield and Ulysses S. Grant; and Hugh's father, James Robertson. All of those portraits are molded.

7. Frederick Douglass, Speech on the Death of William Lloyd Garrison, June 2, 1879, Frederick Douglass Papers: Speech, Article, and Book File, 1846–1894; Library of Congress, http://hdl.loc.gov/loc.mss/ms000009.mss11879.00426.

David Mack

Earth, Fire, and the Abolitionist: The Emancipation of Clay for Social Change

▼ BORN AND RAISED in Baltimore, Maryland, I was a functional potter early in my ceramics career (fig. 1). From 1962 to 1964, I attended the Norfolk Division of Virginia State College, Norfolk, Virginia, currently known as Norfolk State University, and was taught by master potter Howard Johnson. Professor Johnson was the first professional potter I saw demonstrate live. He elevated my rough approach of throwing on the wheel and allowed my hands to be ONE with the clay. My second most influential art teacher was professor and sculptor James Lewis of Morgan State College, which I attended 1964–66 and then from 1969 to 1971 (in 1966 I was drafted into the US Army, where I served one year as an enlisted soldier, then attended Officers Candidate School, graduating as a 2nd Lieutenant; twenty-eight years later I retired at the rank of Lieutenant Colonel). Although I never took a ceramic class at Morgan State, Professor Lewis's drawing class helped me to understand how the 2D linear visual process complements the 3D clay process and to pay attention to details. Johnson, in his late 80s, is still exhibiting and working in clay. Both of these great African-American artists and HBCU teachers were important mentors to my professional clay career.

From 1971 to 1975, I studied at the Maryland Institute College of Art under the tutelage of Professor Doug Baldwin (1939–2018). There I witnessed demonstrations by such legendary clay luminaries as Peter Voulkos (1924–2002), Daniel Rhodes (1911–1989), Toshiko Takaezu (1922–2011), and Rudy Autio (1926–2007).

Growing up, my life was intertwined with Marylanders who were connected to slavery and abolition, including Roger Brooke Taney (1777–1864), Chief Justice of the Supreme Court who wrote the majority opinion in the Dred Scott case; Thurgood Marshall (1908–1993), civil rights activist and the first African-American justice on the Supreme Court; and the abolitionist Frederick Douglass (1817/1818–1895). Taney was from Calvert County, Maryland, the same county as my great-great-great grandmother Henrietta Johnson, who was born a slave. I attended Frederick Douglass High School in Baltimore, Maryland, where Douglass had given the commencement address in 1894, one year before his death. Thurgood Marshall was also a graduate of Douglass High School.

After graduating, I taught art/ceramics K–12 in two school districts—Baltimore City and Clark County, Nevada—and I was an adjunct associate professor of ceramics at two colleges, Essex Community College in Maryland, and the Clearwater Campus of St. Petersburg College in Florida. In other

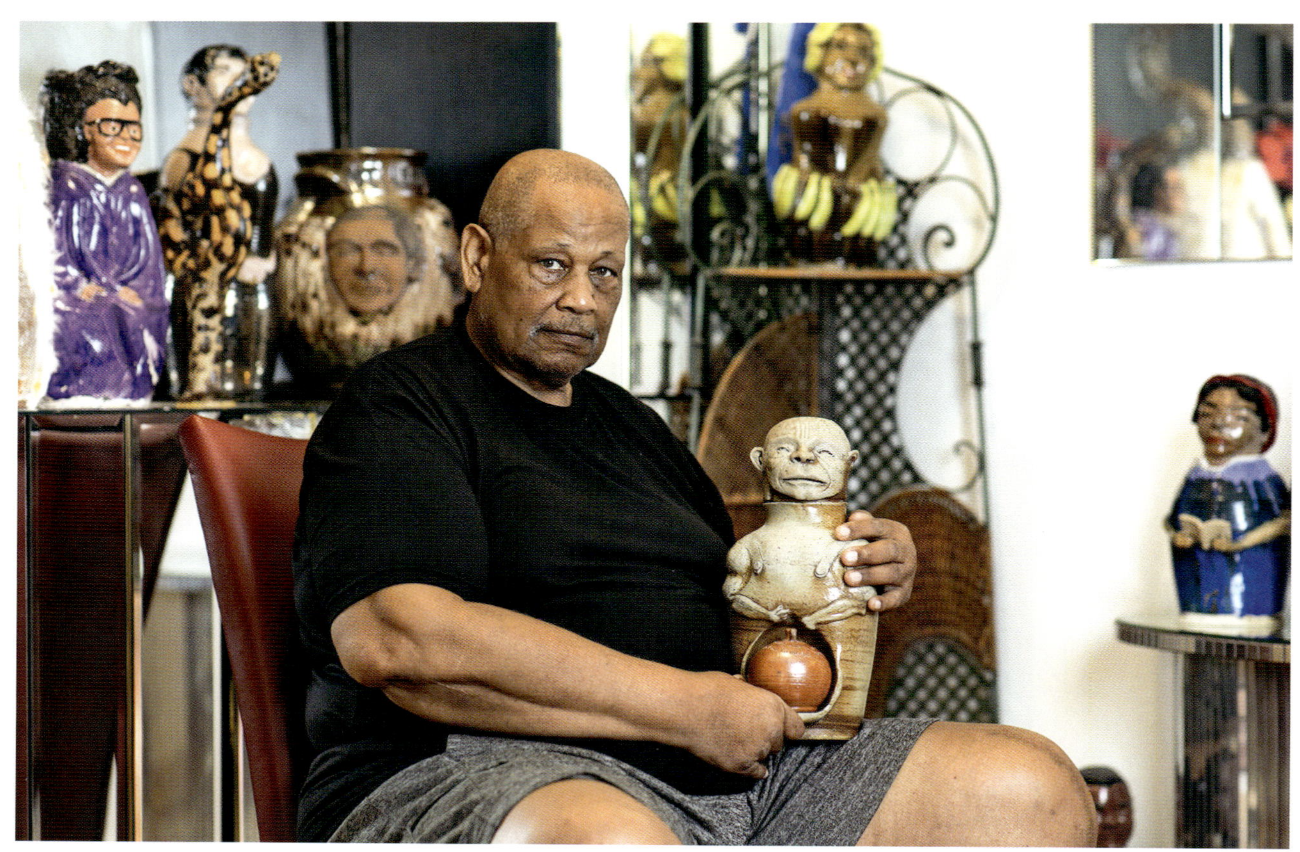

Figure 1 David Mack, Spring Hill, Florida, 2022. (Photo, Carver Mostardi.)

words, I was a proficient potter, but while I felt comfortable in my skin and at the wheel, deep inside I felt something was missing. Because I was an art teacher, I did not have to rely on pottery to pay the bills. However, occasionally I would test my skills in the marketplace by participating in weekend outdoor art shows. My functional work was equal to that of my peers, but I soon recognized there was another element of concern—race. Most of my peers didn't look like me, and that affected my sales.

The Emancipation of Clay

In 2004 I began to investigate that intangible, hidden element. I started to throw large vessels with sculptured faces of distinguished "people of color." Suddenly, not only was I a minority potter but a minority innovator. Moreover, I felt proud, inspired, empowered, and connected to a lost Black cultural generation of heroes and sheroes (fig. 2).

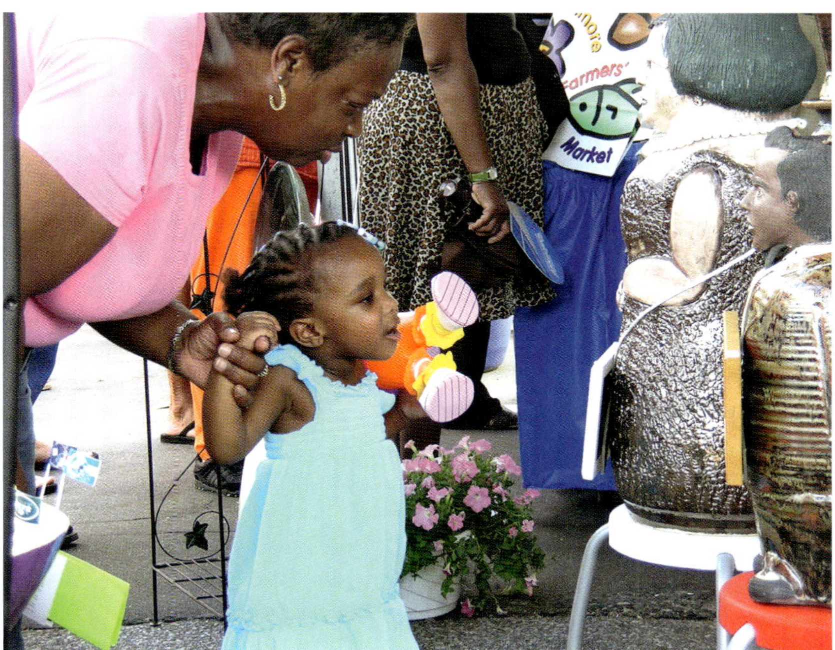

Figure 2 The power of pottery: a grandmother educates her grandchild about the legacy of Madame C. J. Walker at Baltimore's Artscape Festival, Baltimore, Maryland, 2006. (Photo, David Mack.)

Before discussing my connection to the history and spirit of the Abolitionist movement, let me first dig deeper into world history and investigate the reason for abolitionism—slavery. Many people believe slavery began with the transatlantic slave trade that brought men, women, and children from the West Coast of Africa to the Americas. However, the Indian Ocean slave trade, also known as the East African slave trade or the Arab slave trade, occurred as early as 3500 BCE with ancient Babylonians, Egyptians, Greeks, and Persians.

The Indian slave trade persecuted people based on their religion, whereas the transatlantic slave trade persecuted people by the color of their skin, their race. The Indian slave trade consisted of concubines, sex slaves, and soldiers who could be manumitted. In contrast, the transatlantic slaves were abducted and sent to the Americas as a labor force, with no options for freedom. This deplorable condition, to control a human's life, mind, and soul as expendable property, gave rise to some of the most daring revolts in history, such as the siege of Port-au-Prince during the Haitian Revolution (1793), the Armistead Revolt (1839), the commandeering of a Confederate ship by Robert Smalls (1862), and Harriet Tubman's raid on Combahee Ferry (1863).

My Practice

I believe the most important part of working with clay is the first stage of wedging and kneading. Without connecting with the clay as "one," the process is incomplete. Even my limited knowledge of Native American and Japanese pottery helps me to focus on the spiritual aspect of this magical raw material, and to remember to respect the process at all times. I started throwing thirty–forty pounds of clay on the wheel to make a single, rectangular human form. These ultimately became the beginnings of my series Heritage Face Vessels.

After completing pots depicting the inventor *Elijah McCoy* (fig. 3), entrepreneur, philanthropist, and activist *Madam C. J. Walker*, (fig. 4), and some other large pots, I realized the pieces were too heavy to transport for display at outdoor exhibition spaces. To make them more convenient

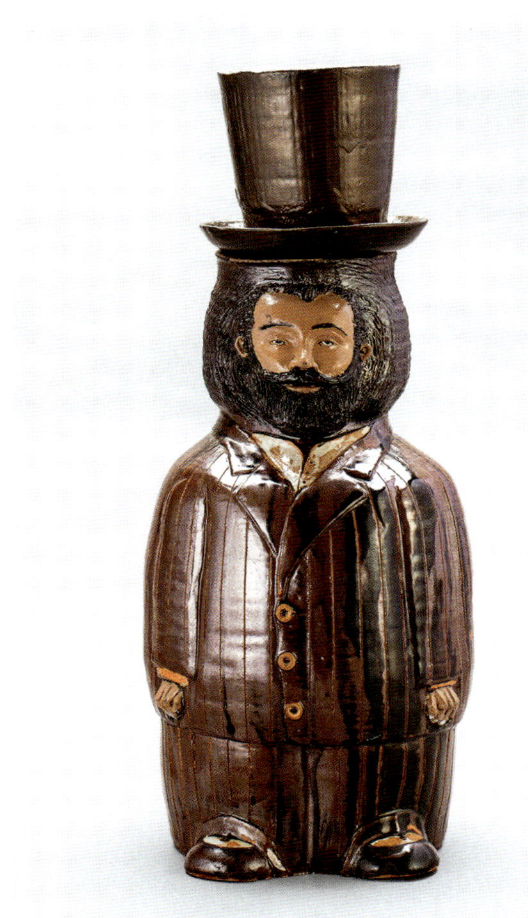

Figure 3 *Elijah McCoy*, face pot, David Mack, Spring Hill, Florida, 2006. Stoneware. H. 24". (Photo, Carver Mostardi.)

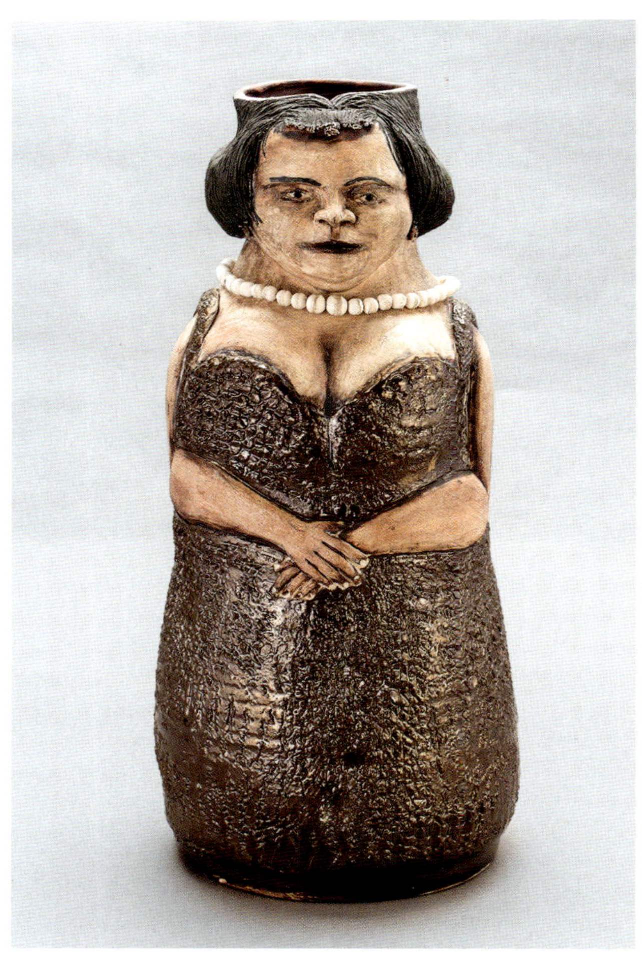

Figure 4 *Madam C. J. Walker*, face pot, David Mack, Spring Hill, Florida, 2010. Stoneware. H. 25". (Photo, Carver Mostardi.)

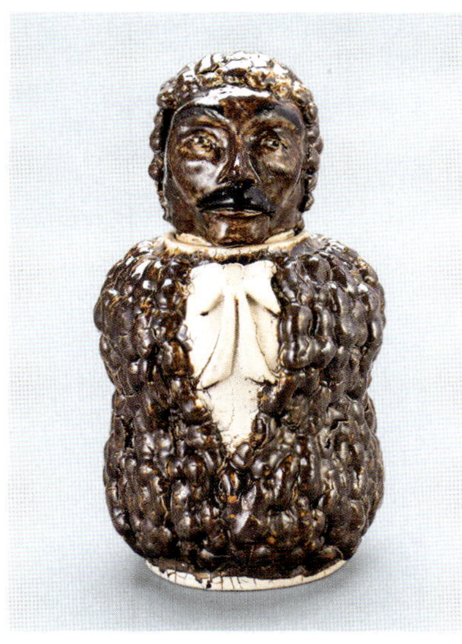

Figure 5 *George Washington Carver*, face pot, David Mack, Spring Hill, Florida, 2012. Porcelain. H. 13½". (Photo, Carver Mostardi.)

and affordable, I decided to throw ten pounds instead. Most of my work is stoneware clay that was electric-fired at cone 5, glazed or treated with underglaze decoration before bisque firing, and then glazed and fired again.

The *George Washington Carver* (1864–1943) vessel celebrating the agricultural scientist is my most ambitious project (fig. 5). I used natural peanut shells dipped in porcelain slip, bisque, and glazed fired. The real shells burned off, resulting in perfect porcelain ones.

Despite some visual similarities, I was not influenced by nineteenth-century American face vessels. I woke up one day with the vision to make this a more inclusive, diverse world by creating clay vessels depicting distinguished and forgotten people of color. The first face pot I created was *The Three Faces of Martin Luther King Jr.* (fig. 6). Martin Luther King Jr. (1929–1968) had a profound impact on the Black community, the civil rights movement, and specifically my generation of baby boomers.

I selected my earliest pre-revolutionary vessel to be of *Crispus Attucks* (fig. 7). Not much is known about Attucks (1723–1770) except that he was the first American shot during the Boston Tea Party in 1773, a martyr of the American Revolution. *Crispus Attucks* won top ceramic honors at the 2020 Star Spangle Art Show, sponsored by the Military Officers Association of America, Tampa Chapter, The James A. Haley Veterans' Hospital,

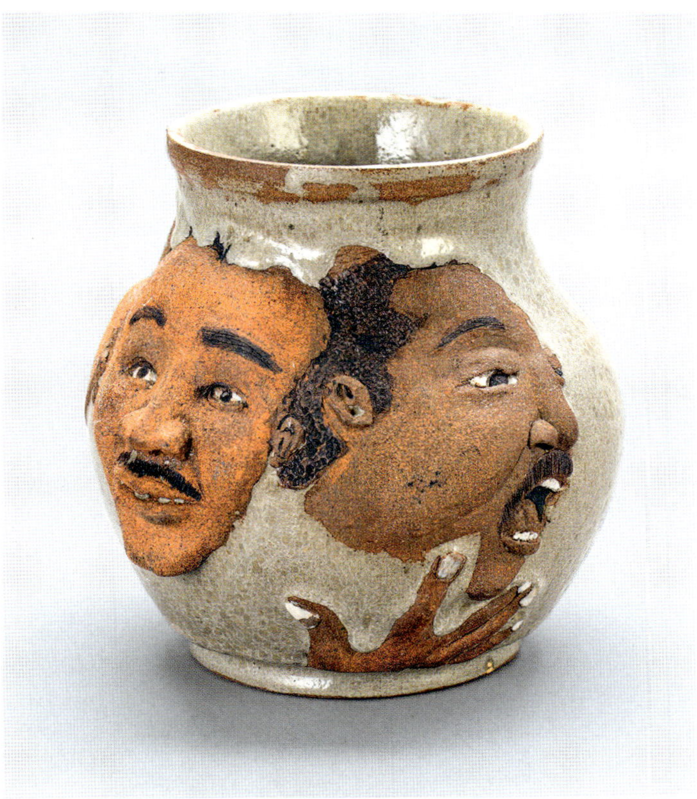

Figure 6 *The Three Faces of Martin Luther King Jr.*, face pot, David Mack, Henderson, Nevada, 2004. Stoneware. H. 9 15/16". (Photo, Carver Mostardi.)

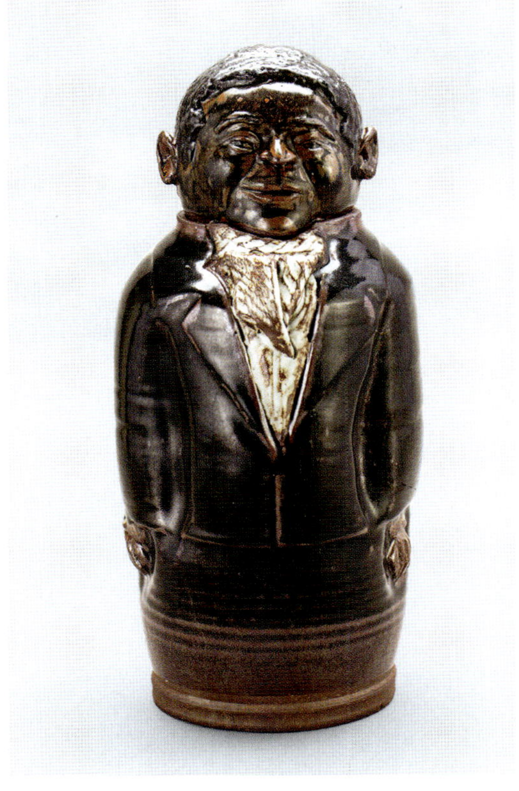

Figure 7 *Crispus Attucks*, face pot, David Mack, Spring Hill, Florida, 2010. Stoneware. H. 13". (Photo, Carver Mostardi.)

Figure 8 *Harriet Tubman*, face pot, David Mack, Spring Hill, Florida, 2006. Stoneware. H. 17". (Photo, courtesy of the author.)

Figure 9 *Sojourner Truth*, face pot, David Mack, Spring Hill, Florida, 2011. Stoneware. H. 14". (Photo, Carver Mostardi.)

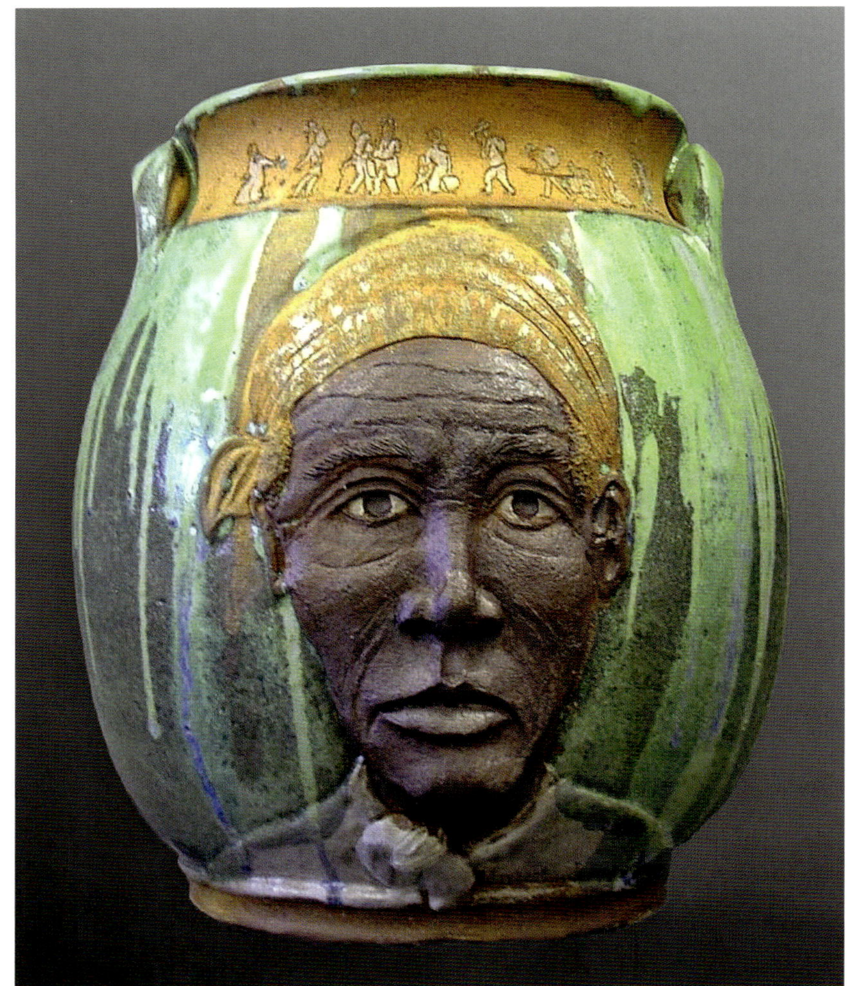

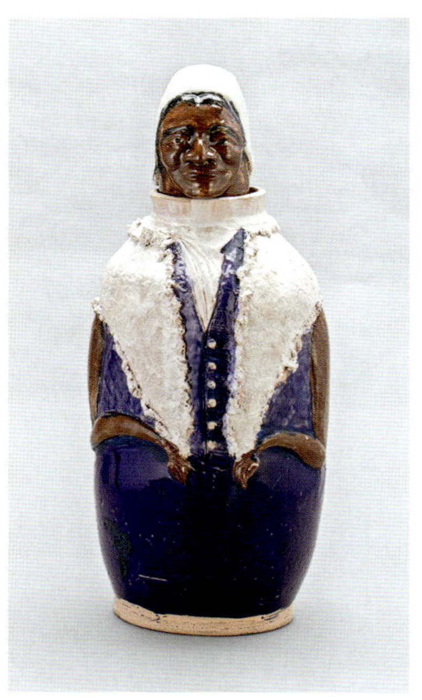

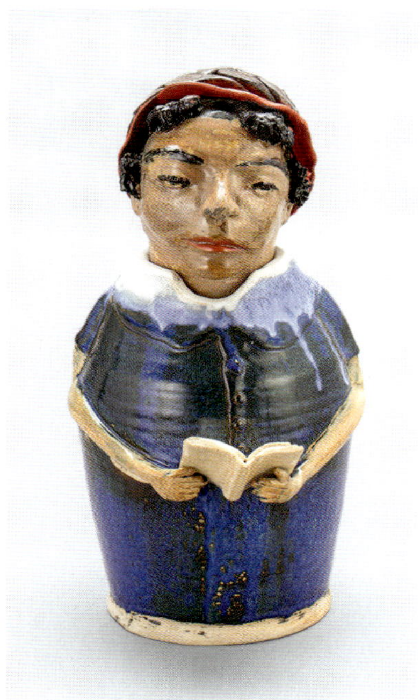

and Leepa-Rattner Museum of Art at the Tarpon Springs Campus of St. Petersburg College.

Harriet Tubman (ca. 1822–1913), the abolitionist who escaped slavery and then led thirteen missions via the Underground Railroad to rescue others, and Sojourner Truth (ca. 1797–1883), the abolitionist and woman's rights activist, were etched into my brain at an early age and became subjects of two of my pots (figs. 8, 9).[1]

In addition to celebrating activists, I also focused on African-American cultural, scientific, business, and military leaders. Phillis Wheatley (ca. 1753–1784), born a slave and educated in Boston, was the first African-American woman to publish a book of poems, many of which spoke out against slavery (fig. 10). Tragically, she died at age thirty-one. When folks talk about "The Real McCoy," it is not Hatfield vs. McCoy but Elijah, the Real

Figure 10 *Phillis Wheatley*, face pot, David Mack, Spring Hill, Florida, 2012. Stoneware. H. 14". (Photo, Carver Mostardi.)

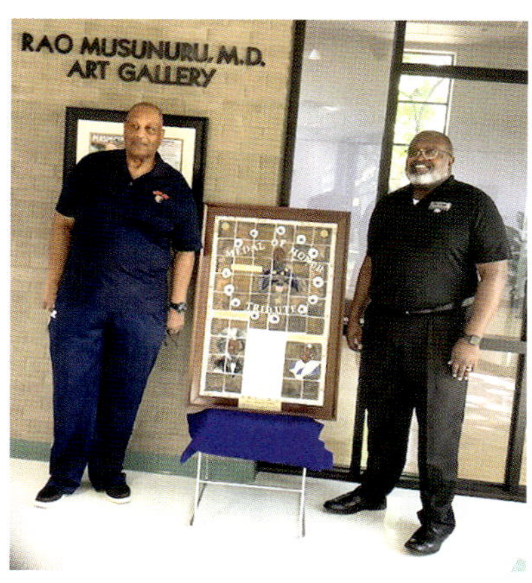

Figure 11 David Mack and Luther T. Buie, Associate Dean, Pasco-Hernando State College, *Sargent William Carney with Frederick Douglass and Harriet Tubman*, tile panel, David Mack, Tampa, Florida, 2019. Stoneware. 24 x 48".

McCoy (1844–1929) (see fig. 3), who invented an automatic lubrication machine that would allow steam engines to continue operations without shutting down. Although Madame C. J. Walker (1867–1919) did not invent the straightening comb, her hair products and cosmetics were distributed globally (see fig. 4). She became a self-made millionaire, and her products are still popular today.

So dear to my military heart are the heroics of Sargent William Carney (1840–1908), from the famed 54th Massachusetts Infantry Regiment, who would not allow the American flag to touch the ground during the Civil War battle of Fort Sumter, South Carolina (fig. 11). Wounded several times, Carney became the first African-American to receive the Medal of Honor, the nation's highest military award.

The great Frederick Douglass (1818–1895) was always a man I admired and felt connected to (fig. 12). Many folks are unaware that Douglass met with Abraham Lincoln to promote Black soldiers' participation in the Civil War. Douglass helped to mobilize the 54th Massachusetts All Black Infantry Division, of which his sons were members. Douglass thought that he would become the first Black Brigadier General, although that did not happen. I wrote a military dissertation on Douglass, and I continue to search my roots to confirm the stories told to me by my beloved mother, Ethel Mack, that I am a descendant.

In addition to portraying people of color on my pots, I also began to advocate for recognition of the potters of color who have gone before us. In 2020 I published "Enslaved and Freed African American Potters" in *Ceramic Monthly*, which presented an argument for the return of artifacts made by enslaved artists to their rightful descendants.[2] A year later, a congressional act was born, the Stolen Bones Act of 1619 (SBA), and as I write this in the spring of 2022, efforts to amend SBA with HR 3005, a bill directing the replacement of a bust of Roger Brooke Taney in the old Supreme Court Chamber of the U.S. Capitol with one of Thurgood Marshall, is a real possibility.

David Drake

The last vessel from my collection illustrated here is of the talented, rebellious David Drake (ca. 1801–after 1870), slave, poet, and potter who lost three wives, and eight children (figs. 13, 14).[3] Drake defied South Carolina law by writing and signing his pots.[4] His work is now rightly celebrated, featured prominently in museums and selling for vast amounts; one of his pots sold in 2021 for $1.56 million, the highest price yet paid for a piece of American pottery, although his descendants received no compensation.[5]

As we move forward, it is important to recognize the differences between "enslaved" and "freed" Black potters. We should never forget that one operated within a lifetime of bondage and the other as a free man. Museums sometimes forget to consider those complexities, emphasizing only the aesthetic qualities of the artwork. To combine an exhibition of the works of enslaved potter David Drake with freed potter Thomas Commeraw is surely disrespectful, discourteous, and insulting.

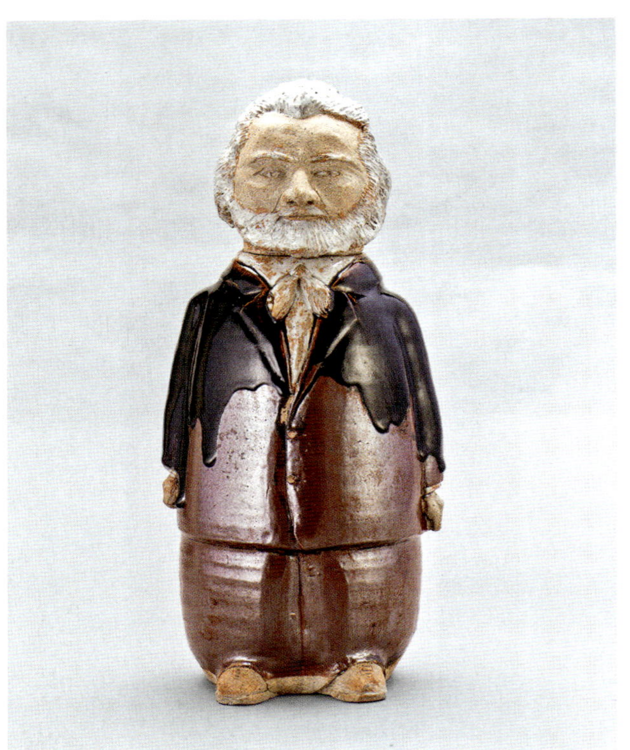

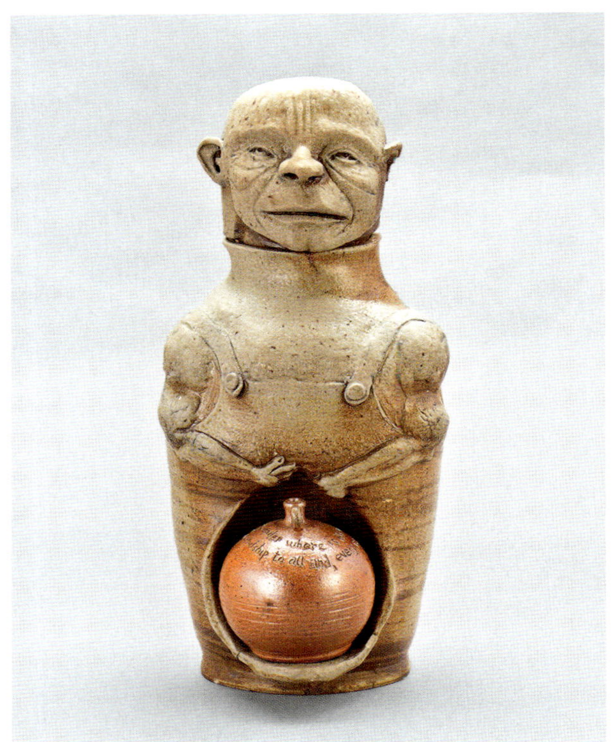

Figure 12 *Frederick Douglass*, face pot, David Mack, Spring Hill, Florida, 2008. Stoneware. H. 15". (Photo, Carver Mostardi.)

Figure 13 *Dave "The Slave Potter" Drake*, face pot, third edition, David Mack, Spring Hill, Florida, 2014. Stoneware. H. 15". (Photo, Carver Mostardi.)

Figure 14 Detail of the pot illustrated in fig. 13 (Photo, Carver Mostardi.) Inscribed on the pot: "I wonder where is all my relations / friendship to all – and every nation"

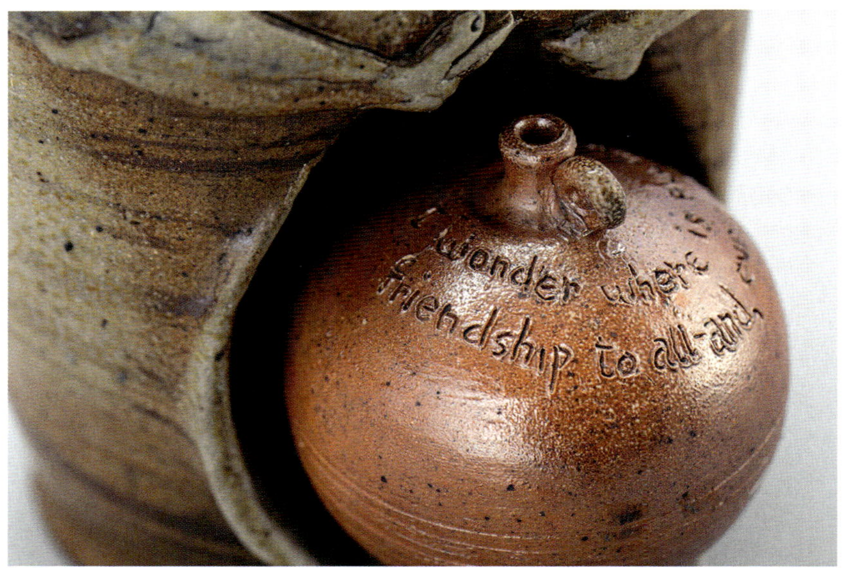

When writing or talking about enslaved potters, you must show the good, the bad, and the ugly. Be holistic and tell the whole story... the toxic nature of mixing and firing clays, the danger of lead-glaze formulation, the unsanitary factory conditions, dawn-to-dusk work hours, family separations, physical and sexual abuse, and theft of birth. Museums must get this right, or we will continue to perpetuate the old myth that all slaves were happy and beloved property, that one could lose a limb only by a speeding train: the David Drake saga.

Some have said that David Drake's leg was cut off by a train when he got drunk one night and fell across a train track. I and other historians believe that story is nonsense! I believe his leg was amputated by his master for writing on his pots, and possibly teaching other slaves to read and write. Between 1843 and 1848, immediately after the leg incident, Dave went through a silent period where he did not write on a pot for five years. Coincidence? I don't think so.

A Baltimore Connection to Edgefield

Thomas Chandler (1810–1854), born in Virginia and trained in the potteries of Baltimore, became one of the more prolific potters working in the Edgefield District of South Carolina and was linked to David Drake and the white potters who owned him.[6] As a native Baltimorean, I was

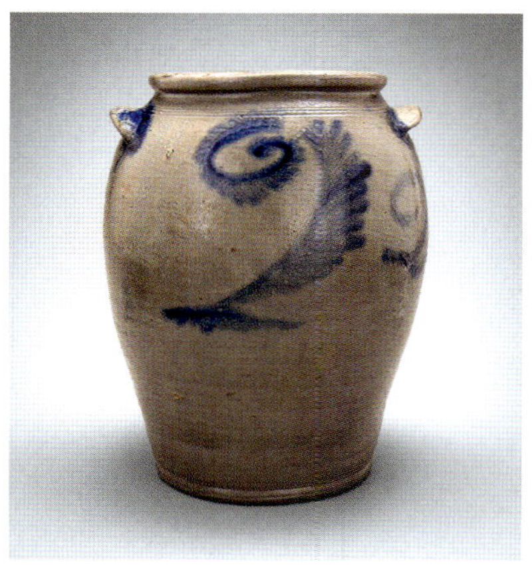

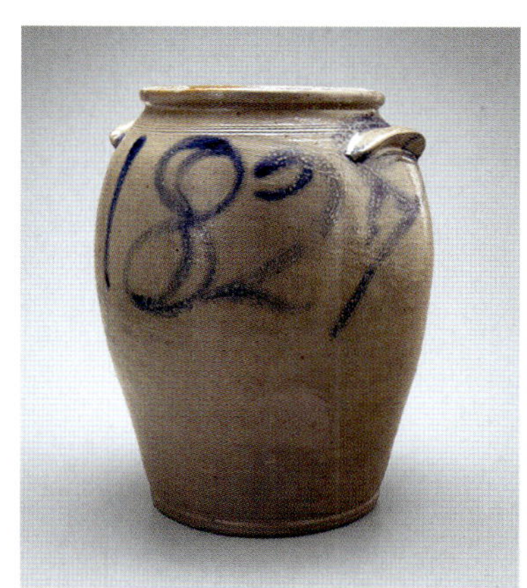

Figure 15 Jar, attributed to Thomas Chandler, Baltimore, Maryland, 1827. Salt-glazed stoneware. H. 12½". (William C. and Susan S. Mariner Private Foundation; photo, Robert Hunter.)

intrigued by Thomas Chandler's connection to Baltimore, Edgefield, and Guadalupe, Texas. In the nineteenth century Baltimore was the epicenter of pottery manufacturing due to its rich deposits of raw clay, the transatlantic slave trade, and shipping infrastructure. It is of little wonder that Chandler landed in Baltimore to complete his ceramic apprenticeship (fig. 15). However, I weep with sorrow when reading Chandler's Deed of Trust that listed his estate: wagon, mules, horse, furniture, and—on the same page with no distinction—four slaves: Simon, Ned, Easter, and John. To list one's personal property along with a "Godly Created Human Being" is beyond comprehension, but that was the culture of slavery. However, when you enlist in the military to defend and serve your country, as Chandler did, then go AWOL on three occasions, being a slave owner would not necessarily be out of character. America, do you understand why Black Americans hate and despise the Confederate flag and all icons/statues that represent the cause of the Civil War and slavery?!

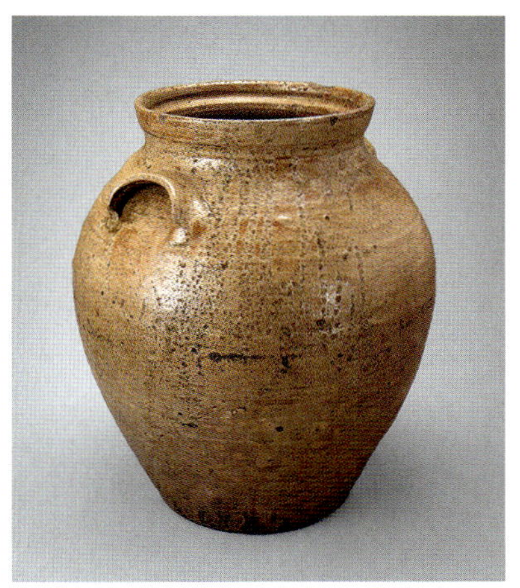

Figure 16 Jar, attributed to Marion Durham/Edgefield District, South Carolina, ca. 1840. Alkaline-glazed stoneware. H. 16½". (Private collection; photo, Robert Hunter.)

As we continue to connect the dots, Chandler's slave John eventually attained freedom and migrated to Guadalupe, Texas, with a white potter, Marion Durham, to work for a slave-labored pottery factory owned by the Rev. John M. Wilson. Some believe they brought with them the Edgefield alkaline-glaze formula (fig. 16). The Durham and Chandler pottery partnership was a rare interracial relationship during the Antebellum era. The Rev. Wilson's slave-labored pottery factory would also develop and produce the Wilson Brothers Pottery, the first Black entrepreneurs to operate and own a business in the state of Texas. After Emancipation, the founder Hiram, with brothers James and Wallace, opened a factory in Capote, Texas, and manufactured clay pots from 1869 until Hiram died in 1884. Distribution of their pottery reached as far as California. Their business was so successful they built a school, church, and a cemetery for their community. Along with the three brothers, the pottery staff included potters Andrew Wilson and George Wilson, who had also worked at the Guadalupe pottery.

The Ongoing Journey

I continue to work toward the broader recognition of the accomplishments of Black ceramic artists to keep hope alive. Museums, universities, and other organizations that exhibit, publish, or study ceramics must educate the next generation about the contributions of the Black artists of the past, such as Augusta Savage (1892–1962), Thomas Commeraw, Edmonia Lewis (1844–1907), Richmond Barthe (1901–1989), and Selma Burke (1900–1995), as well as those of the present, among them Larry Allen, Jim McDowell, David MacDonald, Winnie Owens, Howard Johnson, Dudley Vaccianna, and James Watkins, to mention just a few. Kudos to the up-and-coming clay activists Roberto Lugo, Kelly and Kyle Phelps, Niki Savva, PJ Anderson, and Osa Atoe for taking up the baton and standing on the shoulders of our great Black clay ancestors. I also continue to make pots for my Heritage Face Vessels series, the most recent celebrating Vice President Kamala Harris and Associate Justice of the Supreme Court Ketanji Brown Jackson (fig. 17).

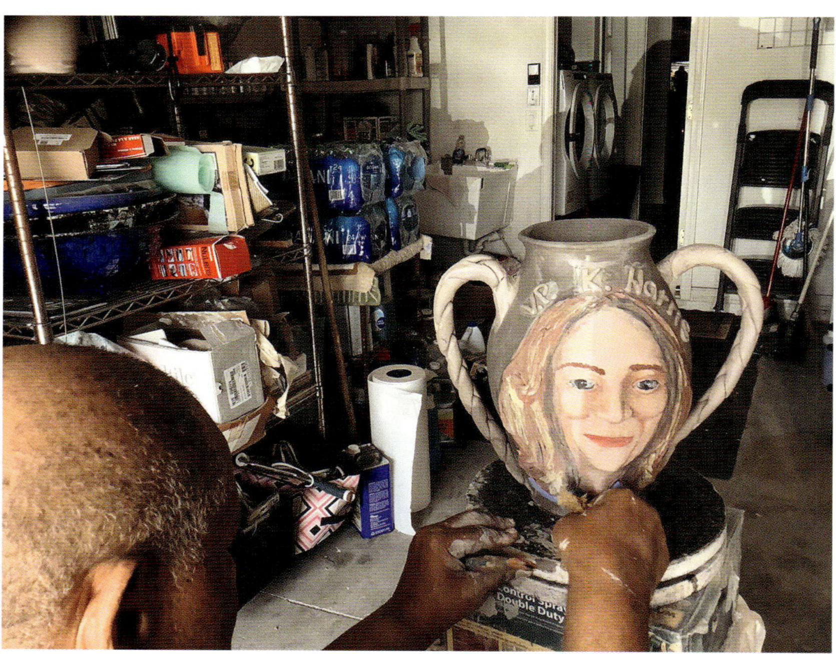

Figure 17 Making *Vice President Kamala Harris and Associate Justice of the Supreme Court Ketanji Brown Jackson*, face pot, David Mack, Spring Hill, Florida, 2022. Stoneware. H. 12". (Photo, Linda Mack.)

Institutions, organizations, and publications need to educate their readers about Black ceramic artists and provide minority residency, workshops, and programming that are diverse and inclusive. Black students must see a ceramic artist that looks like them, and believe it is attainable to have a successful career in clay as a minority artist. Congratulations to Penland, Arrowmont, *Ceramic Monthly*, the National Council on Education for the Ceramic Arts (NCECA), *Ceramics in America*, and others for adopting inclusive minority transparency.

ACKNOWLEDGMENTS For the readers who were unaware of the accomplishments of my Heritage Face Vessels, thank you for allowing me to educate you. For those who were already privileged to this information, please share it with your friends. My thanks to Rob Hunter, Ron Fuchs, and the Chipstone Foundation for the opportunity to showcase my abolitionist monuments and share a part of my fifty-year ceramic experience with readers of *Ceramics in America*.

1. I attended Morgan State College, one of the nation's historically Black colleges and universities, in Baltimore, Maryland, where two female dormitories were named Truth Hall and Tubman Hall.

2. David F. Mack, "Enslaved and Freed African-American Potters," *Ceramics Monthly* (September 2020), available online at https://ceramicartsnetwork.org/ceramics-monthly/ceramics-monthly-article/Enslaved-and-Freed-African-American-Potters# (accessed June 8, 2022).

3. April Hynes, "Where Is All My Relation . . ." blog post, *The Wanderer Project*, July 12, 2016, available online at https://thewandererproject.wordpress.com/2016/07/12/where-is-all-my-relation/ (accessed August 18, 2022).

4. There are numerous publications on the life and work of David Drake, including Jill Beute Koverman, *I made this jar: The Life and Works of the Enslaved African-American Potter, Dave* (Columbia, S.C.: McKissick Museum, 1998); Arthur Goldberg and James Witkowski, "Beneath His Magic Touch: The Dated Vessels of the African-American Slave Potter Dave," in *Ceramics in America*, edited by Robert Hunter (Hanover, N.H.: University Press of New England for the Chipstone Foundation, 2006), pp. 58–92; Leonard Todd, *Carolina Clay: The Life and Legend of the Slave Potter Dave* (New York: W.W. Norton, 2008); Lisa Farrington, *African-American Art: A Visual and Cultural History* (New York: Oxford University Press, 2017); Michael Chaney, ed., *Where Is All My Relation? The Poetics of Dave the Potter* (New York: Oxford University Press, 2018).

5. "Crocker Farm Smashes American Pottery Record with $1.56 Million Dave Jar," *Antiques and the Arts Weekly*, August 7, 2021, available online at https://www.antiquesandthearts.com/crocker-farm-smashes-american-pottery-record-with-1-56-million-dave-jar/ (accessed June 12, 2022).

6. Philip Wingard, "From Baltimore to the South Carolina Backcountry: Thomas Chandler's Influence on 19th-Century Stoneware," in *Ceramics in America*, edited by Robert Hunter (Hanover, N.H.: University Press of New England for the Chipstone Foundation, 2013), pp. 38–76.

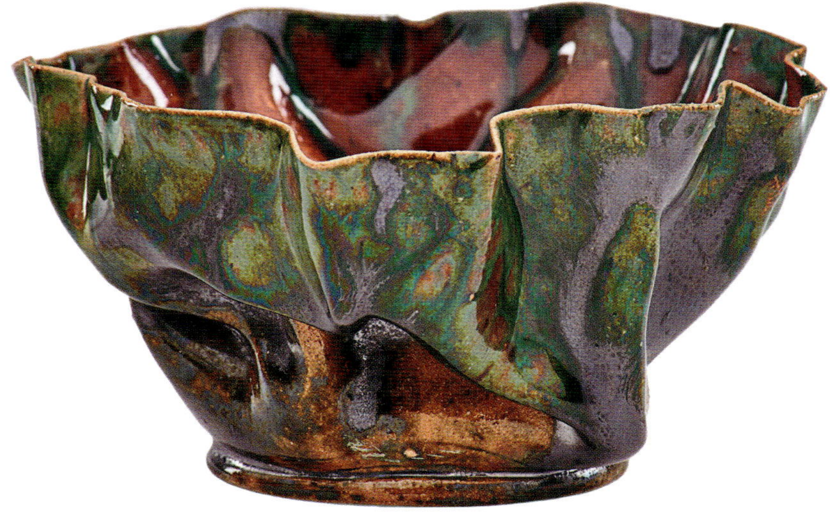

Figure 1 George Ohr (1856–1917), crumpled vessel, Biloxi, Mississippi, ca. 1895–96. Lead-glazed earthenware. H. 2½". (Courtesy, Rago Auctions, ragoarts.com.)

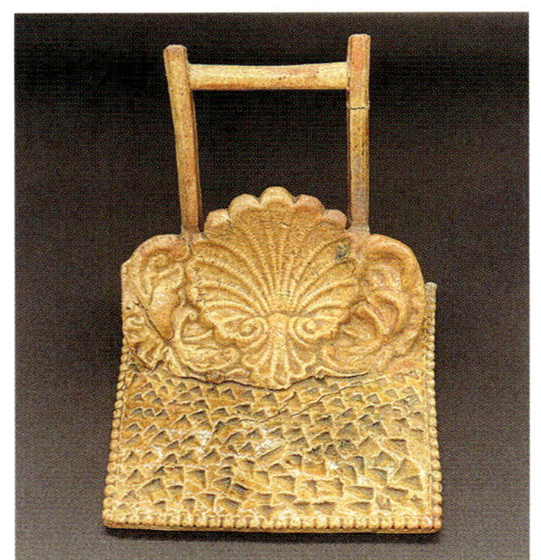

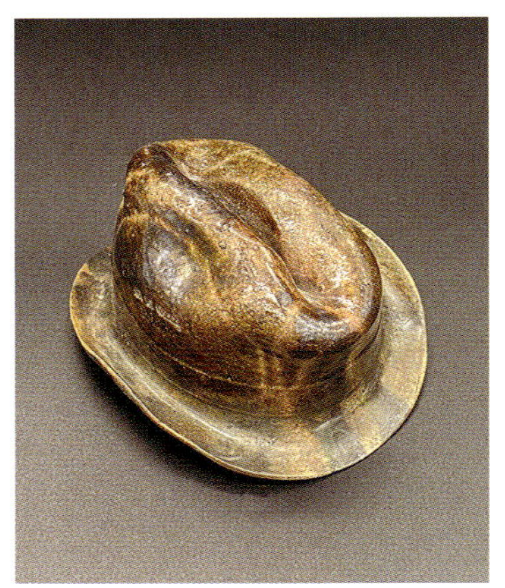

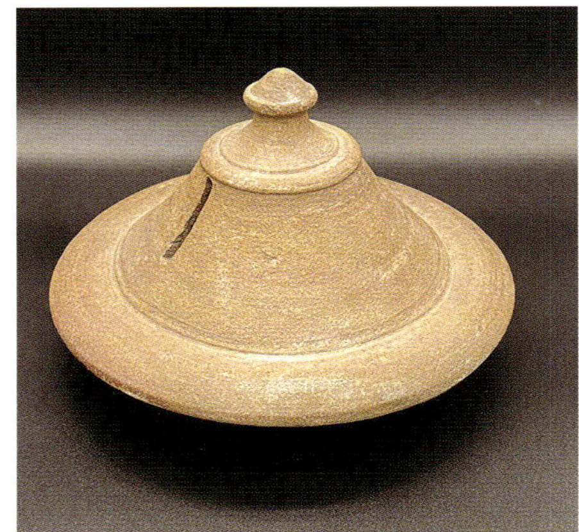

Figure 2 George Ohr, cardholder, sculpted hat, and Bank, Biloxi, Mississippi, ca. 1885–1900. Lead-glazed earthenware. Cardholder, 4¼ x 4¼ x 3¾"; sculpted hat, 2¼ x 3 x 4¼"; bank, 4¼ x 5 x 5". (Unless otherwise noted, all photos courtesy of the author.)

Ellen J. Lippert

Souvenirs of Fantasy: George Ohr's Clay Tokens

▼ WITHIN THE POTTER George Ohr's oeuvre of nearly ten thousand ceramic objects, consisting mostly of vibrantly colored and extremely manipulated hand-thrown pots (fig. 1), are six clay tokens. Though trinkets and baubles such as banks, cardholders, and paperweights (fig. 2) are also mixed in, the tokens are in a category of their own. They bear no glaze, no severe manipulations, and no maker's mark. They are made from molds, whereas the rest of the collection is hand-thrown or a built one-of-a-kind creation. Ohr, who prided himself on the exceptional singularity of most of his objects, makes no mention of the molds in extant documents (fig. 3). Perhaps most striking are the obscene sexual messages they bear, formed using combinations of letters, numbers, and images.

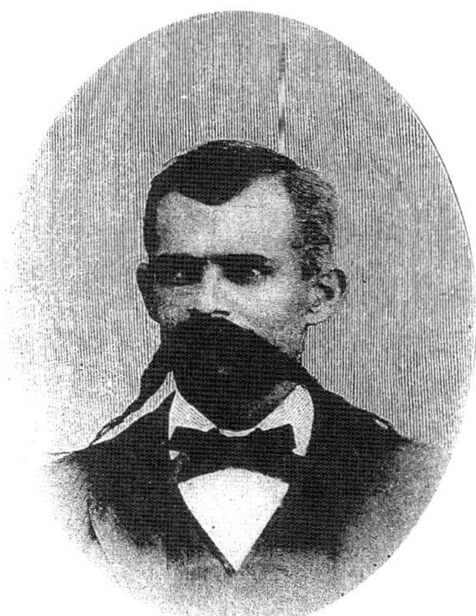

Figure 3 Portrait of George Ohr. From George Ohr, "Some Facts in the History of a Unique Personality," *Crockery and Glass Journal* 54 (1901).

The tokens have largely been overlooked by critics in favor of the more conspicuous vessels forms. It it is not known when they were made, if/where they were sold, what they cost, how popular they were, or who bought them. Perhaps they have also been overlooked because they are so anomalous to the remainder of the oeuvre. Taken by themselves they are easily written off as commonplace trinkets, but their brazen messages are anything but commonplace and, unlike the unremarkable bank card or cardholder, they express a sentiment not applicable to most moments or places in one's daily life. They could not be kept on one's desk nor handed out at the corner store. One might be reluctant even to carry one in one's pocket on most occasions. However, put within their proper context these tokens emerge as souvenirs of prominent sites of fantasy in the last quarter of America's nineteenth century.

This article will offer suggestions as to the tokens' proper function within their intended context. In order to better understand them, it is necessary to know something about their creator and the time in which he existed.

George Ohr (1856–1917) and the Gilded Age

In the 1960s, antiques dealer James Carpenter discovered thousands of dust-covered pots stacked in the attic of the garage of George Ohr's sons in Biloxi, Mississippi. The pots, created by George Ohr, Biloxi's famed "Mad Potter," had been stored there for over a half century, ever since the potter's retirement and subsequent death. Carpenter's discovery thrust Ohr's odd clay creations onto the stage of the 1960s' art world.[1]

Ohr's contorted, abused forms, which he often coated in vibrant, blistered glazes, have become highly prized, routinely fetching multiple thousands of dollars at auction, and have been collected by such famed artists as Andy Warhol and Jasper Johns. Art critics and collectors of the 1960s and later were taken by Ohr's strange, unconventional style. Most American art pottery of the nineteenth century was pure and serene in design, often borrowing its shape from Chinese or Greek vases. Ohr's collapsing shapes and bleeding glazes appeared to both emulate and mock the popular styles of the day, and came to be seen as ahead of their time, akin to the totemic symbolism of the abstract expressionists.[2]

Before all his posthumous fame, however, George Ohr was a spirited, eccentric potter and self-promoter living and working in the period that has come to be known as the Gilded Age, a tumultuous and formative time in the nation's history.

As gilding is a thin covering masking a baser material, so too did the increased wealth and material well-being of the Gilded Age mask underlying socioeconomic and spiritual turmoil. It saw the emergence of large-scale corporations and mass production, as well as the advent of modern mass culture—new forms of advertising and commercial display as well as a proliferation of newspapers, magazines, and books. Conversely, various threads of individualism combated the increased mechanization of society, and socialism fought the unequal distribution of wealth. Darwinism undermined traditional religious beliefs while a more general spiritualism developed. The country was torn between progress and tradition, wealth and despairing poverty, American ambition and citizens' rights.

As a Southern craftsman, independent businessman, shrewd self-promoter, and sympathizer to socialist causes, Ohr was enmeshed in the zeitgeist of his time. Little primary documentation exists about him, but we do know that he learned to throw pots from a family friend living in New Orleans, and that as soon as he knew how to "boss a little piece of clay into a gallon jug" he took off on a two-year, sixteen-state sojourn to learn all he could about the process and business of pottery, and "never missed a show window, illustration or literary dab on ceramics since that time, 1881."[3]

When he returned home, around 1883, Ohr started his own studio and set out to become the "World's Greatest Art Potter." Like all good businessmen, he recognized the importance of having a gimmick, and his long handlebar mustache and eccentric writing style became his trademarks. This observer's description is typical of the impression Ohr made:

> Entering the house that Ohr built, you find, bending over his wheel or patting into shape—more probably out of it—his latest creation, the potter himself. His eyes hold you first—wonderful eyes, big, bright, brown, wild like those of a startled animal. And then your gaze gets tangled in the meshes of his mustache and so lost for awhile. For it is impossible to tear your fascinated eyes away until they have followed all the twists and turn of that hirsute ornament and discovered its ends as they curl for the third time about his ears.[4]

Samples of Ohr's writing, which can be found in contemporary journals and newspapers across the country as well as etched into his own pottery, are just as telling of his eccentricity:

> Now then, my Dear, Good Readers, and all the rest of yease . . . let me radiate & while U R reading, don't think between D lines, 'Smart Aleck, damphool potter,' etc. A duck doesn't knead his brains 2 float as he is built 2 hold water, B in it & stay dry & I don't need any 2 mash mud or push a pencil, Because I'm built that way. . . .[5]

Ohr's writings are often confusing and take some time to comprehend. Here, he deliberately confuses the appearance of the passage: he used "damphool" for "damn fool" and "knead" for "need," even though neither misspelling actually changes the pronunciation of the word. In fact, he spelled "need" correctly later in the same sentence. Further, the only function his consistent use of numbers and letters for words—as in 2 B for "to be," U R for "you are," and "D" for "the"—served was to confuse and dramatize the paragraph visually, not to aid in pronunciation. Ohr's inimitable phrases, such as "mash mud" (make pottery) or "push a pencil" (write) were not reflective of his regional dialect, only of his distinctive way of writing or talking. Clearly he was trying to make an impression on the public by consciously emphasizing his peculiarities. It is important to note that there is a tradition among Southern characters to phonetically manipulate their words in order to emphasize the "dumb" Southern persona that readers and audiences of the North had come to expect. A good example is Sut Lovingood, a caricature of a stereotypical farmer of rural Southern Appalachia created by the American humorist George Washington Harris (1814–1869).[6]

Given that Ohr was able to support himself and his family as a potter he was a success, but his life and career were marked with ups and downs. He and his wife suffered the loss of five of their ten children. In 1893 his first studio burned to the ground, along with many pots. Nevertheless, he achieved recognition from critics across the country, was included in Edwin Atlee Barber's *Pottery and Porcelain of the United States*, and was even the inspiration for the main character of a novel.[7]

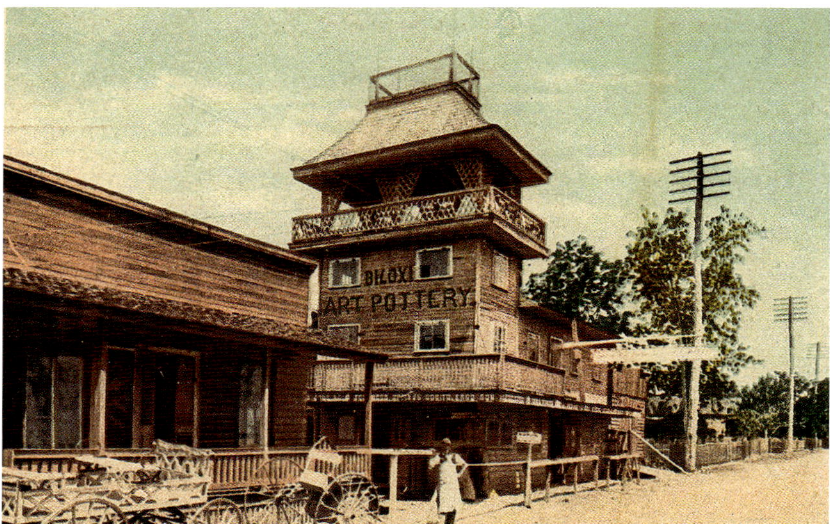

Figure 4 Postcard, The Biloxi Pottery, Biloxi, Mississipi, Detroit Photographing Company, 1901. (Collection of the author.) This postcard features a photograph of Ohr's second studio, which was built ca. 1895.

Despite those accolades, Ohr never felt he got the recognition he deserved. To him, each pot was a one-of-a-kind masterpiece worthy of museum collections and critical acclaim. Twice he sent unsolicited samples of his wares to museums and both times museum officials chose a few pieces and returned the rest. Ohr had not intended for the samples to be broken up, saying "To distribute what I have is like distributing a poets work—by giving hundreds of lines too [*sic*] hundreds of creatures—hundreds of miles apart." This continued rejection, perceived or real, wore on Ohr and in 1908 he quit making pottery, boxed his wares up, and tucked them away in the attic of his sons' car garage, to be discovered almost fifty years after his death by James Carpenter.[8]

As is often the case, one's impact is often recognized in retrospect. After Carpenter found Ohr's pots, Ohr was celebrated for his cutting-edge ceramic forms despite his relative isolation in Biloxi, Mississippi, and he was characterized as "the most prescient prophet in Western ceramic art."[9]

Ohr was not isolated, unaware, or unaffected by his time period, however. He knew enough about the shifting consumer culture to create a distinct and noticeable persona for himself, one that played to his specific consumer base and Northern expectations of Southern craftsmen. He built an eccentric pagoda-shaped studio (fig. 4), which towered over the other buildings in Biloxi and advertised his own over-the-top products. He was a socialist in a time when capitalism ruled the American economy.[10] And then, of course, there is his pottery. Just as eccentric and deliberate as the rest of the man, his pots were disfigured, functional forms rendered unusable, and coated in grotesque colors and textures.

Given his response to the world around him, it is difficult to think of his tokens as mere trinkets or gags, unrelated to events surrounding him.

Ohr's Tokens

The entirety of Ohr's token collection consists of six double-sided clay coins bearing pictures, words, and numbers combined to form twelve messages, all crudely sexual. Five of the six known designs are illustrated in figures 5–9. The design and message of the tokens differ very little; some have ridged perimeters and some are smooth, indicating at least two different casts. The least offensive message reads:

> Good for one screw
> I love you dear
> Give me some
> A Screwing Match
> Let's go to bed

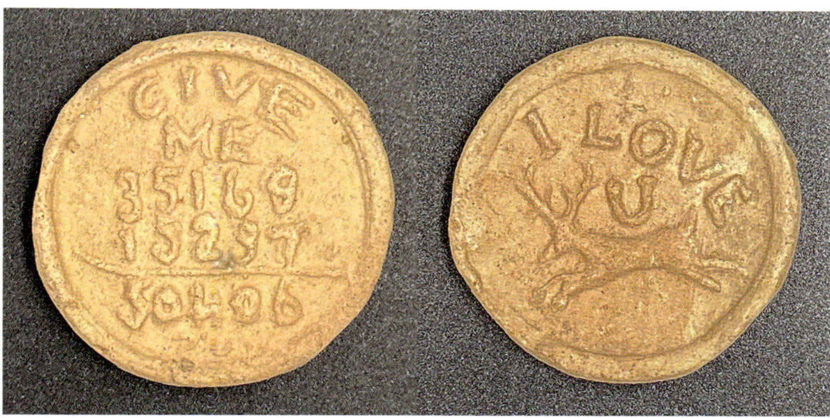

Figure 5 George Ohr, token, Biloxi, Mississippi, ca. 1885–1900. Unglazed earthenware. D. 1¼". (Collection of the author.)

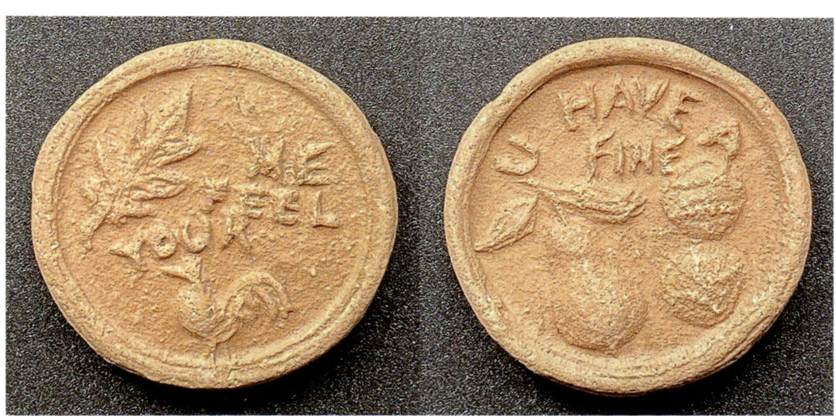

Figure 6 George Ohr, token, Biloxi, Mississippi, ca. 1885–1900. Unglazed earthenware. D. 1¼". (Collection of the author.)

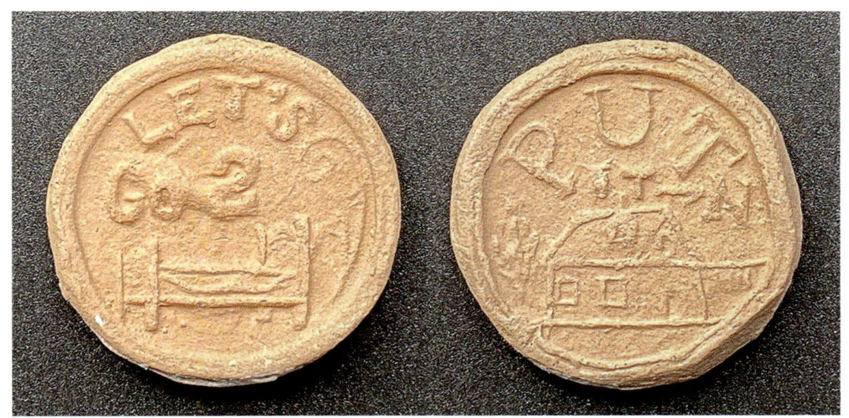

Figure 7 George Ohr, token, Biloxi, Mississippi, ca. 1885–1900. Unglazed earthenware. D. 1¼". (Collection of the author.)

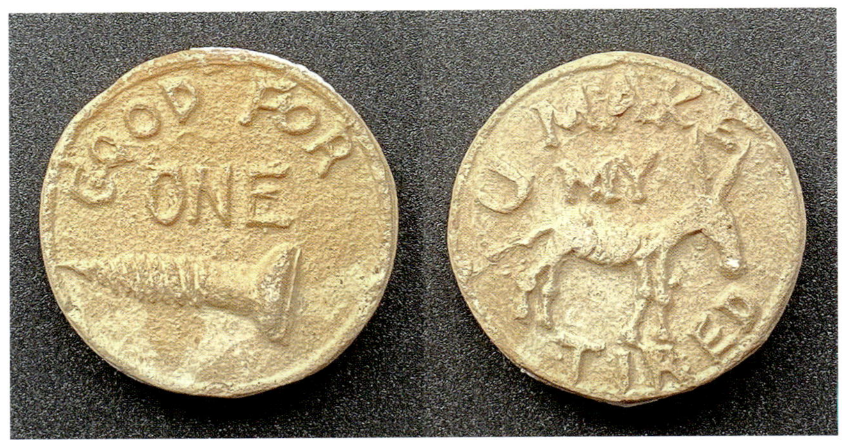

Figure 8 George Ohr, token, Biloxi, Mississippi, ca. 1885–1900. Unglazed earthenware. D. 1¼". (Collection of the author.)

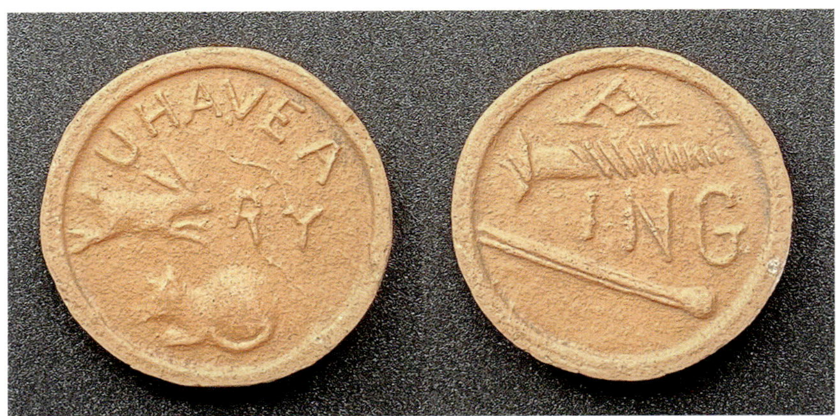

Figure 9 George Ohr, token, Biloxi, Mississippi, ca. 1885–1900. Unglazed earthenware. D. 1¼". (Collection of the author.)

Because of the nature of the pictographs on them, these coins are sometimes referred to as "brothel tokens," although there is no evidence they were ever used as such. They certainly carried no currency in actual brothel houses nor did they name specific businesses or locations. Ohr did not sign or date them, nor did he write about them as he did his other pots. Critics have considered Ohr's tokens to be trinkets or "novelties," not of the same significance as his other pots. The terms *novelties*, *trinkets*, and *gags* suggest that Ohr's tokens were playful—even clever—but ultimately meaningless. They are still collected even though they do not fetch anywhere near what his art pots would. To this day their purpose remains unknown, but two important events of this time period seem likely sources of inspiration: the phenomena of world's fairs, and Storyville in New Orleans.[11]

Ohr at World's Fairs

Ohr attended numerous world's fairs, including the World's Industrial and Cotton Centennial Exposition in New Orleans (1884–1885), the World's

Columbian Exposition in Chicago (1893), the Cotton States and International Exposition in Atlanta (1895), the Pan-American Exposition in Buffalo (1901), and the Louisiana Purchase Exposition in Saint Louis (1904).

World's fairs were a chance for countries and regions across the world to showcase their latest technological, scientific, and cultural advancements. Fairs hosted by American cities were typically organized to celebrate American bravery or achievement. For example, the New Orleans' World's Industrial and Cotton Centennial Exposition celebrated the 100th anniversary of the cotton industry; the World's Columbian Exposition in Chicago (1893) was organized around the 400th anniversary of Columbus's "discovery" of the New World; and the Louisiana Purchase Exposition (1904) commemorated perhaps the greatest land bargain in U.S. history.

While research has shown that world's fairs held in the United States during this period overwhelmingly emphasized the accomplishments of white people, they nevertheless celebrated human achievement and drew enormous crowds from across the country, resulting in significant cultural influence across all classes of society.[12]

Crowds flocked to buildings designated for fine arts, mines and metallurgy, machinery, agriculture, forestry, and the like, but another big draw was the "midway section," a standard feature of every major show. Although the name of the area might have been termed something different from fair to fair, the content was the same: a carnivalesque atmosphere that trafficked in spectacle and vendors not suitable for the mainstream program, which purported to be more educational. Not surprisingly, it was in the midway section, not fine arts, that Ohr could be found.

In its pamphlet, the Louisiana Purchase Exposition in Saint Louis (1904) termed its midway section "the Pike":

> What was the Pike? The Pike was whatever the fantasy of the beholder wished to make it. It was the carnival and sideshow aspect of the fair. So famous were its attractions, that for all time in the future, listless without-a-care personas would be called Pikers. It was an adventure for those who seldom dared the risque, and a fertile area for those who dealt in such vices which skirted the acceptability of the law. It was a child's fantasy of allure and adventure.[13]

The Pike contained such exhibitions as the U.S. Navy, the Galveston Flood, the South Sea Islands, the Curious Cliff Dwellers, the Esquimaux, a Chinese and Japanese Village, streets of Paris and Cairo, and more. Although those places actually existed and therefore were not places of fantasy, their geographic, social, and ideological differences were distant enough from the norms of American life that they were described and promoted as such.

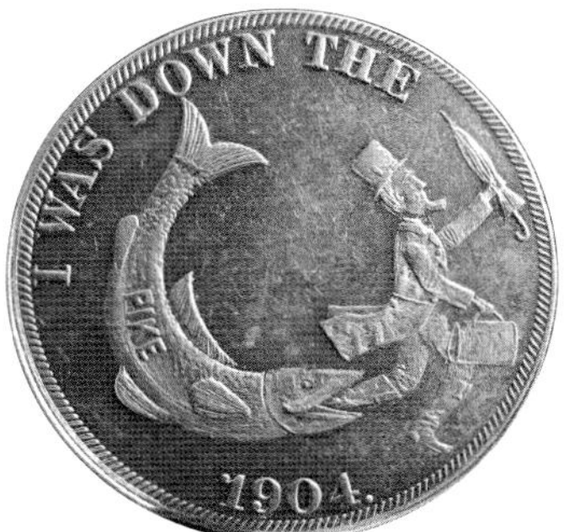

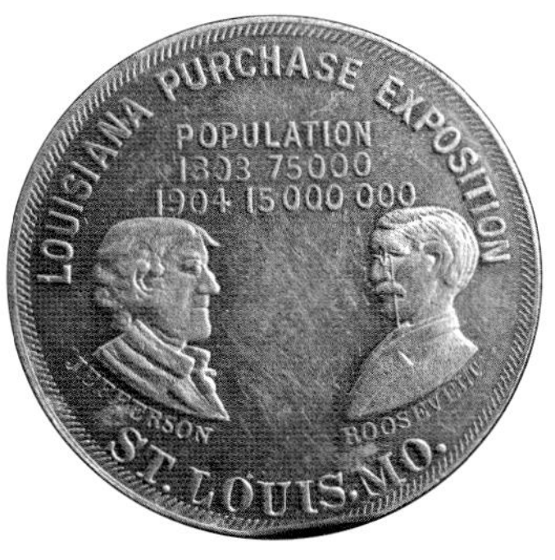

Figure 10 Louisiana Purchase Exposition commemorative medal, St. Louis, Missouri, 1904. Aluminum. 1½". (Photo, courtesy of Jeff Shevlin, So-CalledDollar .com.)

Various medals existed to promote the fair and the Pike. Of particular interest to this discussion is one that features a well-dressed man holding a closed umbrella being eaten by a large fish labeled "PIKE" (fig. 10). Along the top left edge are the words "I WAS DOWN THE" and below it the fish biting the man's leg, with the date "1904" on the bottom. The image of a well-to-do man being consumed by the lowbrow curiosities offered by the Pike section of the exposition is a captivating subtext.

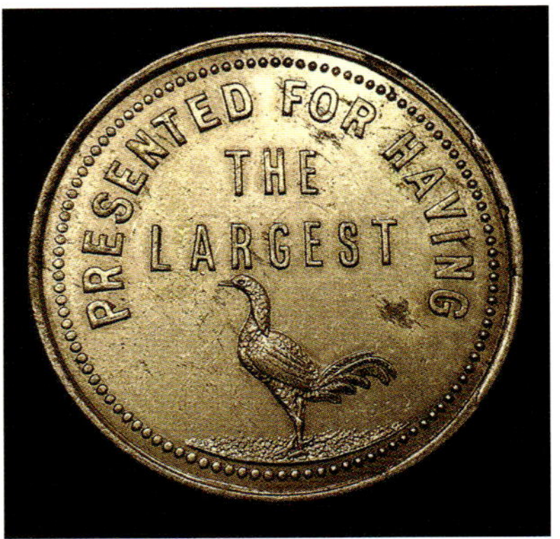

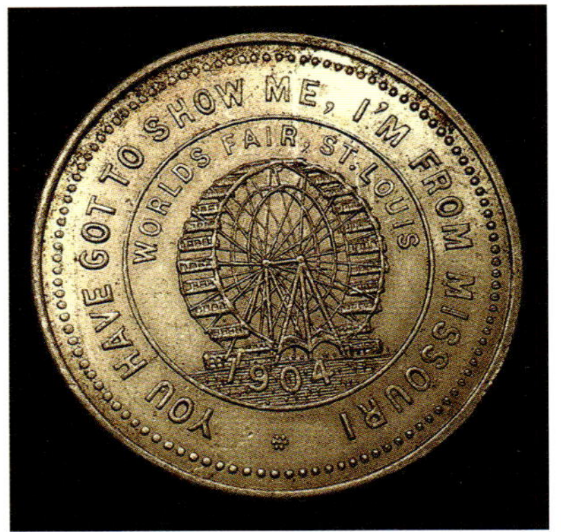

Figure 11 Louisiana Purchase Exposition commemorative medal, St. Louis, Missouri, 1904. Aluminum. D. 1⅜". (Photo, courtesy of Jeff Shevlin, So-CalledDollar.com.)

Another coin features the Ferris wheel (fig. 11). While not in the Pike area, the Ferris wheel was a notable component of the Louisiana Purchase Exposition. The exposition's wheel had been invented by George Washington Ferris and was built for the World's Columbian Exposition in Chicago (1893). Despite its success in Chicago, Ferris declared bankruptcy after the fair closed and died of typhoid fever a couple years later. A wrecking company bought the wheel and sold it to the Louisiana Purchase Exposition. Clearly, the Ferris wheel was a destination in and of itself by the time it reached Louisiana.[14] The Louisiana Purchase coin featuring the Ferris wheel pictures the wheel surrounded by the words "You Have Got to Show Me, I'm From Missouri" and "World's Fair St. Louis 1904." The reverse of the coin is especially interesting. It reads "Presented for Having the Largest" accompanied by an image of a rooster, or cock.

The double meaning of the cock is surprisingly close to Ohr's own use of the word, especially given that this particular pictograph had not yet proven to be very common. While it is premature to say that Ohr was influenced by the Louisiana Exposition or any other exposition, it is fair to assume that he would have encountered souvenir tokens like these. This coin is visual confirmation of two important suppositions regarding meaning and purpose behind Ohr's clay tokens: that obscene image and wordplay were part of the culture of world's fairs; and that monetary value need not be attached to such coins. They could have acted as souvenirs or promotional items handed out free of charge.

The midway area of world's fairs was promoted as a realm of fantasy. An opportunity to safely walk on the wild side and experience the thrills and spectacle far beyond one's own backyard. It was no matter that these sites of fantasy were based on geographically real places. The spectacle surrounding them heightened the drama and encouraged the fantasy. This particular world's-fair space was a controlled free fall.

Ohr and Storyville

Another popular site of fantasy, Storyville, also emerged during this time. Storyville was not the first but probably the nation's best-known experiment with legalized prostitution. Begun on January 1, 1898, Storyville lasted for almost nineteen years, until the United States entered World War I. At that time the federal government passed a law prohibiting prostitution within a five-mile radius of any military installation, thus forcing Storyville to close.[15]

Storyville was a socioeconomic experiment that will be forever remembered in both regional and national history. New Orleans, always a thriving and busy port city, was home to prostitutes and brothels at least since its acquisition by the U.S. in 1803, and undoubtedly before. While prostitution was not actively discouraged, numerous ordinances were passed to control and limit the areas of New Orleans in which prostitutes could ply their trade. Storyville came to be when Alderman Sidney Story introduced legislation denying housing for immoral purposes outside a designated area. Said area, just north of the French Quarter, soon came to be known as Storyville, to Mr. Story's disgust. By confining the highly lucrative profession of prostitution to a single area, officials hoped to manage the illicit practice while taxing the businesses and systematically and legally reaping its benefits for the greater good.[16]

Ohr frequented New Orleans in the years prior to Storyville's beginnings: during the first half of the 1880s he was a student of Joseph Meyer's in New Orleans; from 1885 to 1890 he worked at the New Orleans Art Pottery; and in 1889 he lived at 249 Baronne Street, just three blocks south of Basin Street, a main thoroughfare in Storyville. Though these dates are several years prior to Storyville's beginnings, it isn't hard to accept that Ohr would have continued to travel there, especially given the business opportunity that Storyville presented.[17]

Ohr's coins were not used as currency, but other tokens did function that way in Storyville's houses. According to Louis Crawford and Glyn Farber, authors of *Louisiana Trade Tokens*, the only book to index and research the various trade coins used in Louisiana, "[t]okens were . . . used in houses of ill repute, primarily in the famed 'Storyville' district of New Orleans. . . . The customer would buy the token from a contact (often the bartender) and after services were rendered, he would give the girl the token plus whatever tip he deemed sufficient. In this way, the Madam was assured of getting her cut while the girl was able to keep all her tips."[18]

The authors further note that "[s]everal tokens are known from businesses that have been documented to be connected with brothels, but since most indicate a numerical redemptive value they may have been simply bar checks rather than 'house' tokens."[19] A coin for the Arlington Saloon reading "Good for 5¢ in Trade" is a good example. Exactly which "trade" the coin holds value for is undefined.

Ohr's coins do not resemble the tokens used in Storyville, which were largely about identifying worth and trade-for-service value. Indeed, none of his coins denotes any financial value with one exception, which reads "Good for one Screw." Ohr's tokens are so different in design and meaning because he was not attempting to sell a service. Instead, he was offering a souvenir, a memory and reminder of the wild times and fantasy of Storyville.

Brothel tokens, whether exchanged for value or not, are not real currency. Abstractions of value from an already abstracted system of value, they have worth only in a very specific place for a very specific thing. They cannot be carried down the street and used to purchase a candy bar. Likewise, the face value of a coin is not accurate—that is, the amount of money needed to purchase a single "screw" is far more than the value of a coin reading "Good for One Screw." While some brothel coins could be redeemed for actual service, particularly in Storyville, they largely dealt in the realm of fantasy.[20] Ohr's tokens drop the currency pretense completely, and exploit the crude and authentic fantasy around which Storyville was built. In this light the vulgarity of his coins not only make sense, but are well suited to the atmosphere:

> Leave me feel your cock
> Give me some
> Let's go to bed
> Put it inside
> Can I screw you

Ohr's Tokens and Gilded Age Fantasy

The Gilded Age was a tumultuous time, as described above, but also a time of increased fantasy. Amusement parks, dime museums, burlesque shows, and vaudeville shows, enabled by increased disposable income and free time, flourished. Such sites of fantasy were also a response to the tectonic shifts in social roles and identity that the modernizing force of mechanization instituted. Mechanization shifted the social meaning of strength and fitness from the physical to the financial. For many, a workday in the Gilded Age often meant sitting in an office or managing workers, not working one's own land or performing physical labor. Long-established traditional roles of men and women within society were changing, too. If the traditionally male-dominated workforce no longer required physical strength, then how was masculinity measured? And why could women not hold those positions? Newly arising amusements were designed to emphasize fantasy that would help audiences escape the realities and stress of a culture in flux.

Within this context our understanding of Ohr's tokens gains mass. While perhaps still mere trinkets or souvenirs, like all souvenirs they are physical manifestations of memory, made significant because of personal experience. His coins were designed to recall lowered inhibitions and libidinous freedom. A memento of a controlled free fall, like the experiences viewers and participants would have had at Storyville and the midways of various world's fairs. In this way Ohr's tokens are also cultural artifacts of the Gilded Age, a time of shifting American ideals and ways of life.

1. The moniker "Mad Potter" has been used by various authors to describe Ohr, most notably in *The Mad Potter of Biloxi: The Art and Life of George E. Ohr* by Garth Clark, Eugene Hecht, and Robert Ellison (New York: Abbeville Press, 1989).

2. Garth Clark, "George E. Ohr: Avant-Garde Volumes," *Studio Potter* 12 (1983): 10–19.

3. Only about twenty-three articles about Ohr exist that were written during his lifetime. They include autobiographical sources, such as his own three-page autobiography "Some Facts in the History of a Unique Personality," *Crockery and Glass Journal* 54 (1901), from which the quote is drawn.

4. William King, "The Pallisy of Biloxi," *Illustrated BuValo Express*, March 12, 1899, quoting an unidentified observer.

5. George Ohr, "Letter & Answer No. 2", 1903. From loose pages of an unidentified journal found at the Biloxi Public Library.

6. See Carol Boykin, "Sut's Speech: The Dialect of a 'Nat'ral Borned' Mountaineer," in *The Lovingood Papers*, edited by Ben Harris McClary (Knoxville: University of Tennessee Press, 1965).

7. Buffalo art critic William King wrote about Ohr in "The Palissy of Biloxi," *Illustrated Buffalo Express*, March 12, 1899, 4. Edwin Atlee Barber was a noted authority on pottery and author of the seminal *Pottery and Porcelain of the United States*, 2nd ed. rev. and enl. (New York: G. P. Putnam's Sons, 1902). The character fashioned after Ohr is Giacomo Barse in Mary Trace Earle's *The Wonderful Wheel* (New York: Century Co., 1896).

8. Ohr sent samples to both the Smithsonian Institute in Washington, D.C., and the Delgado Museum of Art, now the New Orleans Museum of Art. George Ohr, "Biloxi Heard From: Geo. E. Ohr Thinks He Is the 'Missing Lynx,'" *Crockery and Glass Journal* 53 (1901), quoting *Times-Picayune*, October 1894.

9. Clark, "George E. Ohr," p. 19.

10. Ohr was affiliated with the Mississippi Socialist Party of America and contributed to *The Appeal to Reason*, a prominent socialist newspaper published from 1895 until 1922.

11. Eugene Hecht and Robert Blasberg repeatedly use the terms *novelties*, *trinkets*, and *gags* when describing and categorizing Ohr's wares in their books *After the Fire: George Ohr, an American Genius* (Lambertville, N.J.: Arts and Crafts Quarterly Press, 1994), and *George Ohr and His Biloxi Pottery* (New York: J. W. Carpenter, 1973), respectively. Garth Clark in *The Mad Potter of Biloxi* (New York: Abbeville Press, 1989), p. 124, notes that in Ohr's coins "[t]here were neither ironies nor transformations . . . to make them anything more than novelties."

12. See Robert W. Rydell, *All the World's a Fair: Visions of Empire at American International Expositions, 1876–1916* (Chicago: University of Chicago Press, 1984). Nearly 100 million people visited the expositions held at Atlanta, Buffalo, Chicago, Nashville, New Orleans, Omaha, Philadelphia, Portland, Saint Louis, San Diego, San Francisco, and Seattle.

13. This account was written by Clifford Mishler, a publisher at Krause Publications, as part of the foreword to the Saint Louis Exposition pamphlet. The pamphlet is published in its entirety in Kurt R. Krueger, *Meet Me in St. Louie: The Exonumia of the 1904 World's Fair* ([Iola, Wis.]: Krause Publications, 1979), p. 6.

14. Information on George Washington Ferris and the fate of his wheel can be found at https://www.smithsonianmag.com/history/history-ferris-wheel-180955300/.

15. Pamela D. Arceneaux, *Guidebooks to Sin: The Blue Books of Storyville, New Orleans* (New Orleans, La.: The Historic New Orleans Collection, 2017), p. 29. It was in Virginia City, Nevada, that prostitutes were assigned to a geographically prescribed area for the first time. Arceneaux also notes that Omaha, Nebraska, and Waco and San Antonio, Texas, implemented similar legislation in the late 1880s.

16. Various versions of the so-called Lorette ordinance, passed in 1857 and 1865, did not outlaw prostitution but instead tried to restrict it to certain areas. See Arceneaux, *Guidebooks to Sin*, p. 28. An entertaining outline of Storyville's beginnings is offered in Al Rose, *Storyville, New Orleans* (Tuscaloosa: University of Alabama Press, 1974).

17. The facts of Ohr's life come largely from his autobiography "Some Facts in the History of a Unique Personality." *Crockery and Glass Journal* 54 (1901): 123–25. For information about his association with the New Orleans Art Pottery, see Jessie Poesch, *Newcomb Pottery: An Enterprise for Southern Women, 1895–1940* (Exton, Pa.: Schiffer, 1984). Eugene Hecht (*After the Fire*, p. 14) notes that the New Orleans city directory for 1889 carries the entry: "Ohr George E Potter, r. 249 Baronne," so we know he was in residence there for at least that year. Hecht confirms that Ohr split his time between Biloxi and New Orleans because his wife, Josie, still in Biloxi, became pregnant with their second son, Leo Ernest, during this time.

18. Louis Crawford and Glyn Farber, *Louisiana Trade Tokens: A Listing and History of the Known Trade Tokens Used in the State of Louisiana*, 2nd ed. (Lake Mary, Fla.: Token and Medal Society, 1996), p. 11.

19. Ibid.

20. Carly A. Kocurek, "'Good for One Screw': A History of Brothel Tokens," *The Atlantic*, https://www.theatlantic.com/business/archive/2014/02/good-for-one-screw-a-history-of-brothel-tokens/283915/.

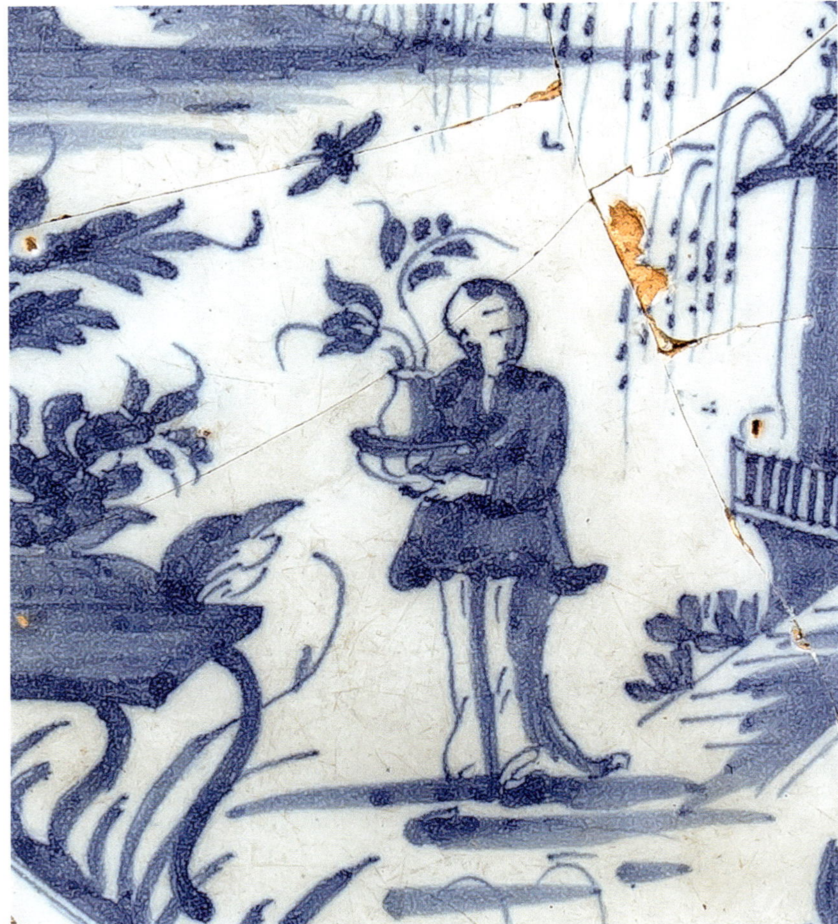

Figure 1 Detail of the plate illustrated in fig. 6.

Elizabeth Donison, Ned Rose, and Angelika Kuettner

English Delft for Colonial Tavern Tables in King William County and Williamsburg, Virginia

▼ A RECENT ARCHAEOLOGICAL survey and test excavation by DATA Investigations LLC at King William County Courthouse produced a large quantity and wide range of eighteenth-century artifacts related to a colonial-era tavern (fig. 1). The small project was commissioned by the King William County Historical Society as part of a research and public outreach initiative, with plans to curate an exhibit on taverns using local archaeological material. One of the recovered objects was a nearly complete English delft dish that has important parallels with similar plates excavated in Williamsburg, Virginia.

The King William Courthouse and the surrounding area are highly significant sites on Virginia's Middle Peninsula. The courthouse itself was built about 1725 and is a prime example of Virginia's rural judicial and social system that revolved around courthouse activities (fig. 2).[1] Because of their proceedings, these courthouses depended on taverns (sometimes referred to as ordinaries) and those who kept such places in business.

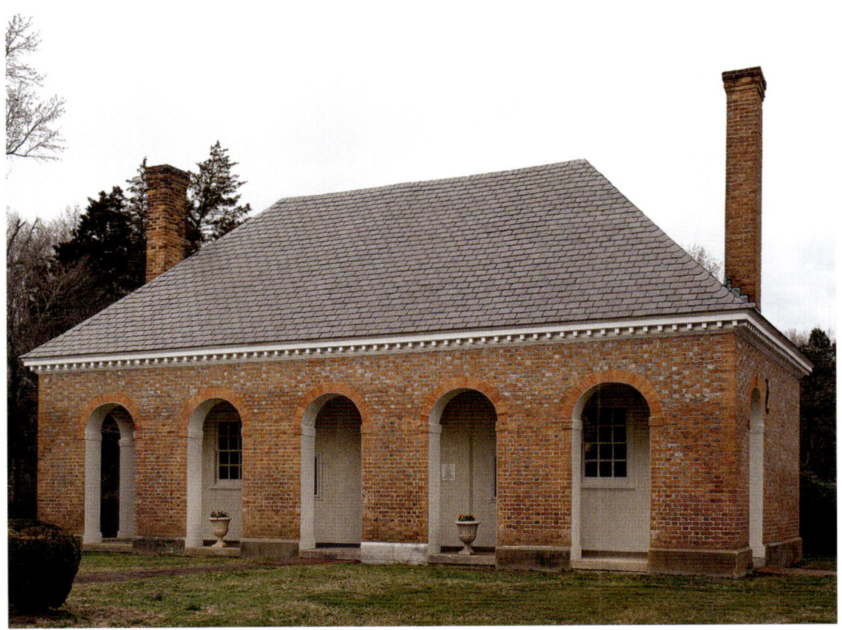

Figure 2 King William Courthouse, King William County, Virginia, ca. 1725–1726. (Photo, Robert Hunter.) The building, which faces south, is a one-story structure of red-colored brick laid in Flemish bond. The courthouse is the oldest courthouse still in use in the United States.

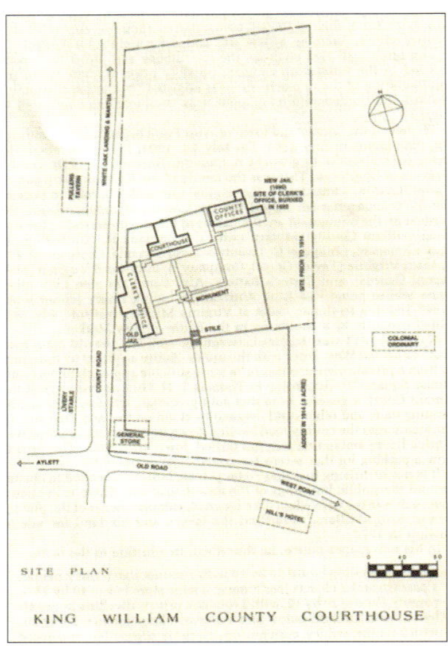

Figure 3 A plan of the King William County Courthouse property showing the conjectural locations of historic buildings, including the eighteenth-century "Colonial Ordinary" to the east. The plan was made by the architect Graham Evans and is published in Alonzo Thomas Dill, *King William County Courthouse: A Memorial to Virginia Self-Government* (King William, Va.: King William County Board of Supervisors, 1984), p. 10.

Little information exists about an early tavern near the courthouse except for a map from 1983 that outlines a projected location (fig. 3).[2] There are records of a John (also spelled Jon) Doncastle operating a tavern there by 1746.[3] Doncastle appears to have left approximately six years later to manage tavern keeper Henry Wetherburn's establishment in Williamsburg (fig. 4).[4] Advertisements placed in the *Virginia Gazette* published in Williamsburg confirm the tavern continued to operate at least until 1780, and catered to high-ranking military officials and wealthy landowners.[5] The tavern had notable frequent visitors such as George Washington, and one could presume its archaeological material would reflect an innkeeper's typical attempts to keep up with the latest hostelry trends in colonial Virginia.[6]

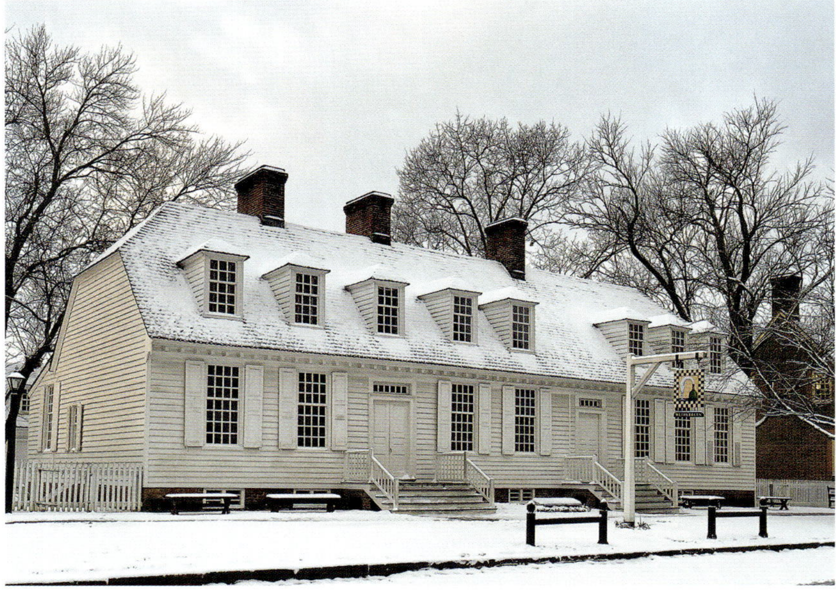

Figure 4 Wetherburn's Tavern, Williamsburg, 2022. (Photo, Robert Hunter.) Now a Colonial Williamsburg exhibition building, this tavern was built ca. 1742 and operated throughout most of the eighteenth century.

To find the tavern's location, DATA Investigations conducted an archaeological survey east of the main courthouse area, and eventually came across a single, brick-wide foundation (fig. 5). One test unit further exposed this foundation, along with two trash-filled features, two post holes, and an extensive amount of cultural material. One of the features was a large, circular depression filled with a dense concentration of wine-bottle glass, a broken case bottle, and a wide array of ceramics including a broken delft plate (fig. 6). The plate was broken in several places but, based on its relatively flat deposition in the ground, it appears that it was nearly intact before someone discarded it. The overall quantity, quality, and diversity of drinking and dining vessels recovered from this small area is consistent with assemblages excavated at other colonial taverns across Virginia.[7]

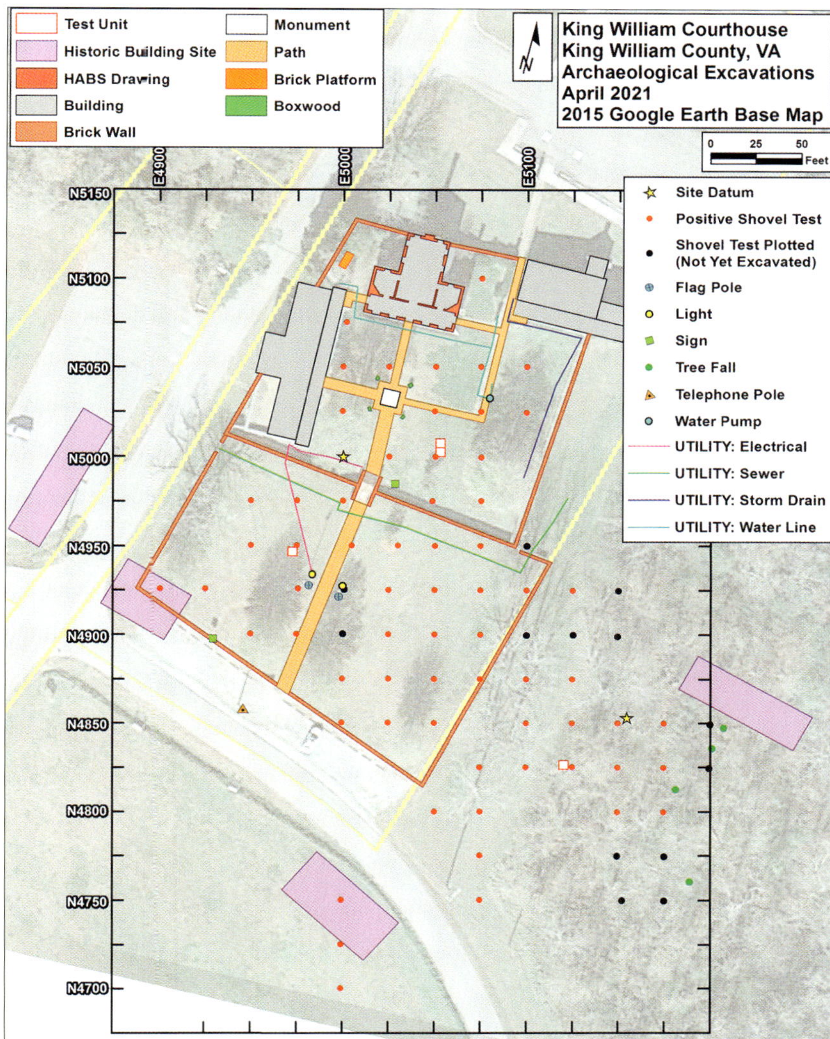

Figure 5 Plan of the King William Courthouse Archaeological Excavations, King William Country, Virginia, 2021. (Courtesy, DATA Investigations.)

Figure 6 Plate, Liverpool, England, ca. 1740–1745. Tin-glazed earthenware. D. 9". (King William Historical Society; photo, Robert Hunter.)

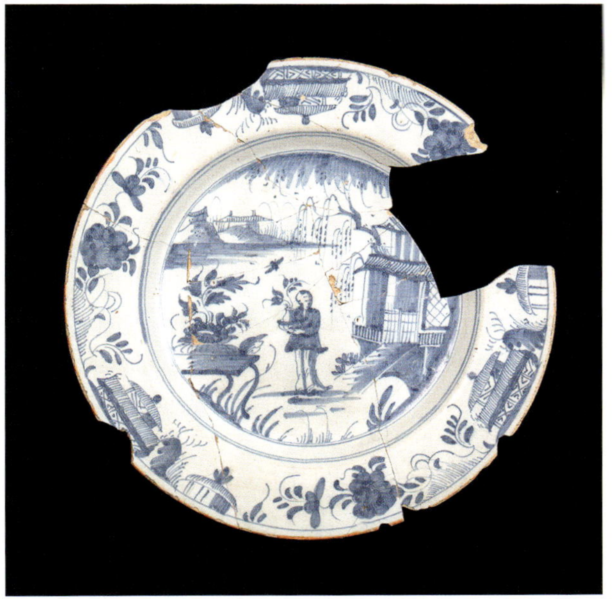

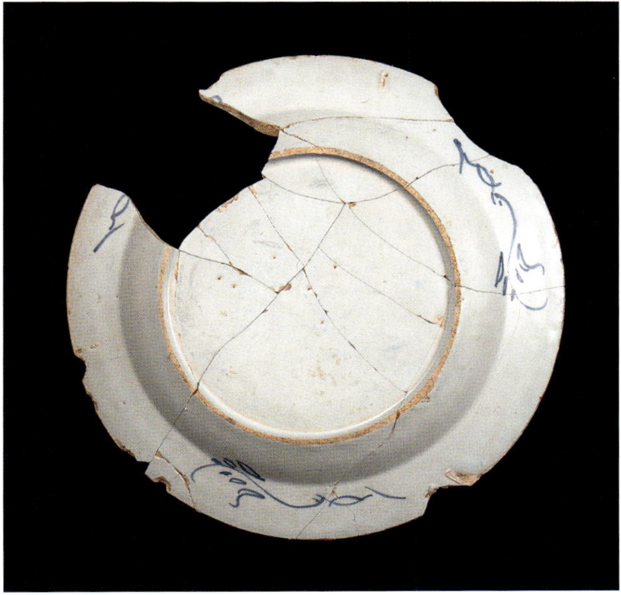

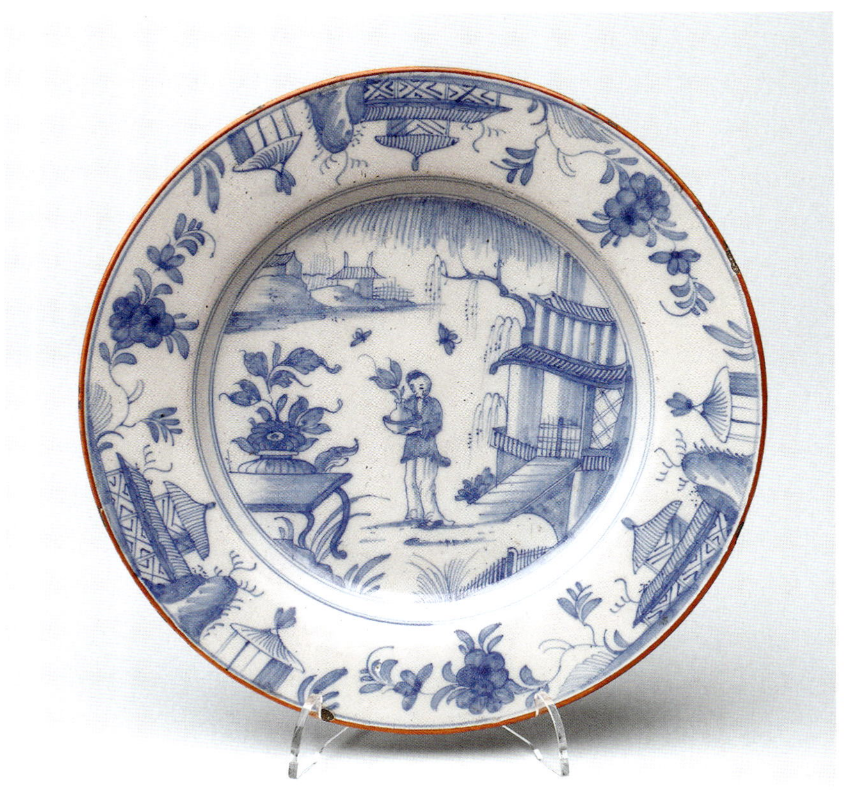

Figure 7 Plate, Liverpool, England, 1744. Tin-glazed earthenware. D. 8¾". Marks: inscribed on underside, R⋮/• I • E • / 1744 (National Museums of Liverpool.)

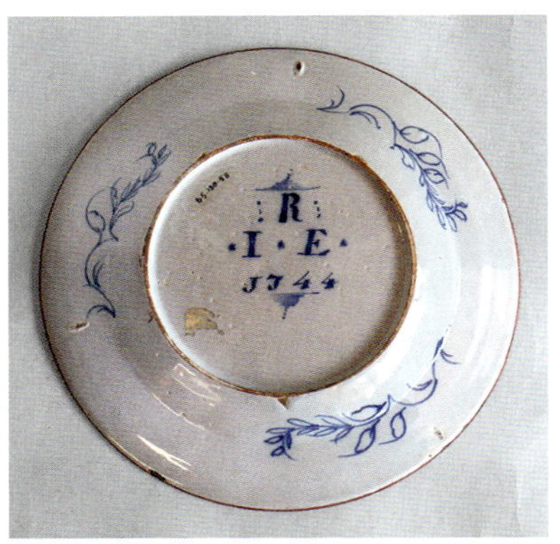

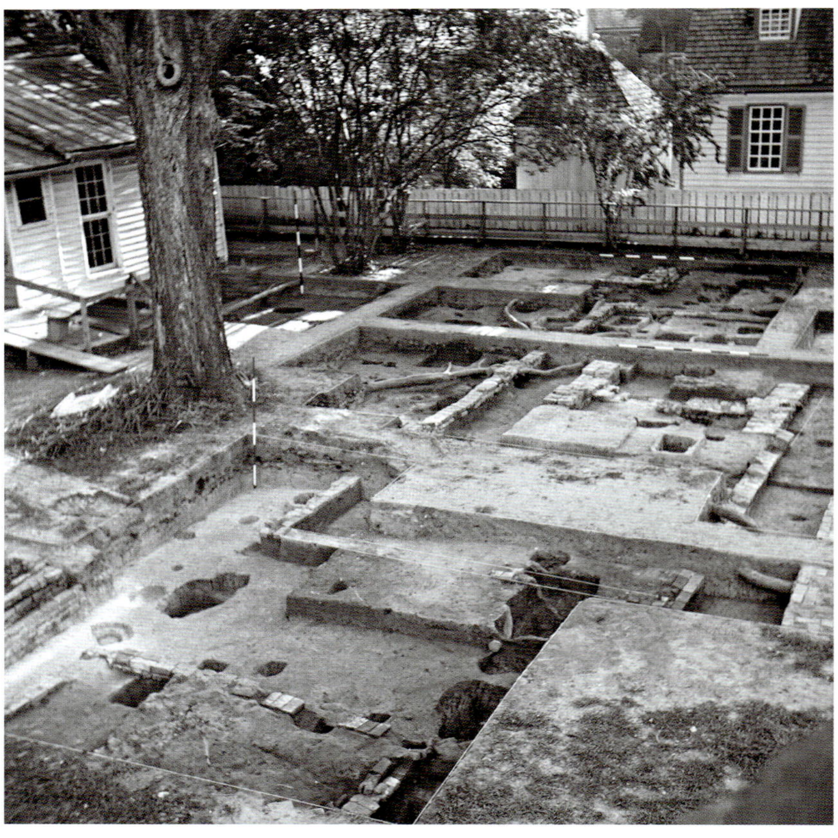

Figure 8 Archaeological excavations at Wetherburn's Tavern, Williamsburg, Virginia, ca. 1966. (Photo, Colonial Williamsburg Foundation.)

Cleaning and mending the fragments revealed the central decoration featuring a Chinese figure standing with a vase and bowl between a large Chinese pavilion shaded by a weeping willow tree and a table containing a floral arrangement. In the background is an island with two additional buildings; the broad rim of the plate is painted with a border of alternating buildings and floral sprays. As we pieced together the fragments, we discovered even more minute details, such as an insect flying over the figure's head. This elaborate design is suggestive of the wealthier clientele who reportedly dined at the King William tavern. Two delft plates dated 1744 from the British ceramics collections of the National Museums Liverpool in England match the border and central decoration found on the King William tavern fragments (fig. 7).[8]

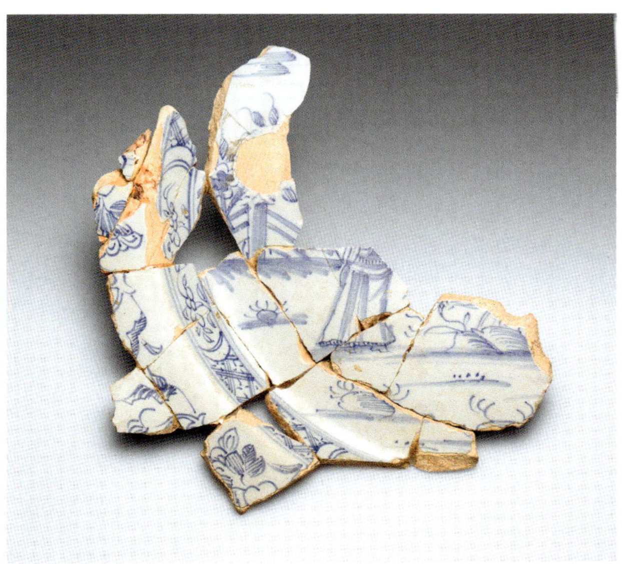

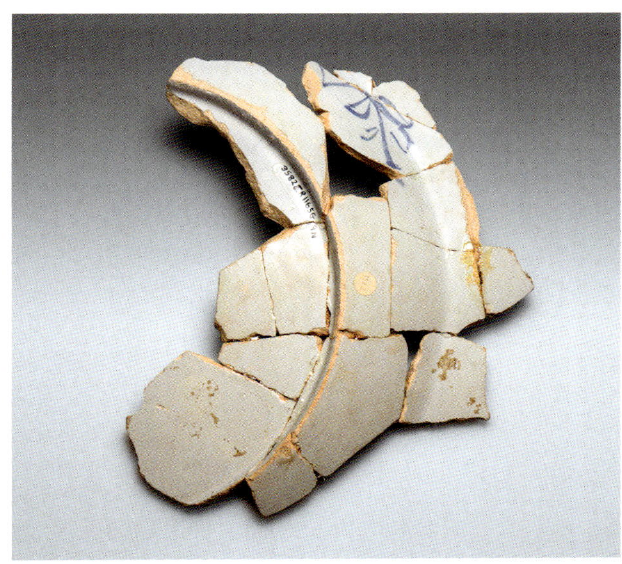

Figure 9 Plate fragments, Liverpool, England, ca. 1740. Tin-glazed earthenware. D. approx. 9". (Colonial Williamsburg Foundation Archaeological Collections.) Cross-mended plate fragments recovered from the site of Henry Wetherburn's Tavern (OBJ-09NA-07379), Williamsburg, Virginia.

The discovery of the plate was just the beginning of a more layered story. During the 1965–1966 excavations of the site of Henry Wetherburn's Tavern in Williamsburg, Virginia, archaeologist Ivor Noël Hume recovered fragments of several British tin-glazed earthenware plates with a stylistically similar chinoiserie pattern (figs. 8, 9).[9] Analysis of the fragments revealed at least seven of these decorated plates in three sizes.[10] Mere miles from the King William tavern, this seemingly circumstantial coincidence gives rise to a more tangible connection when examining John Doncastle's career as extrapolated from newspapers and other documentary sources.

The *Virginia Gazette* reveals Doncastle's tenure as manager of a tavern in Fredericksburg in the early 1740s, and by 1746 records him as being in King William Courthouse.[11] According to the *Gazette*, by 1752 he was in Williamsburg renting from local resident Henry Wetherburn beginning March 1 that year; by the late 1750s he had relocated to the King William tavern. But it is clear from the newspapers and other accounts that his time managing the King William tavern or ordinary overlapped with his time at Henry Wetherburn's Tavern.[12]

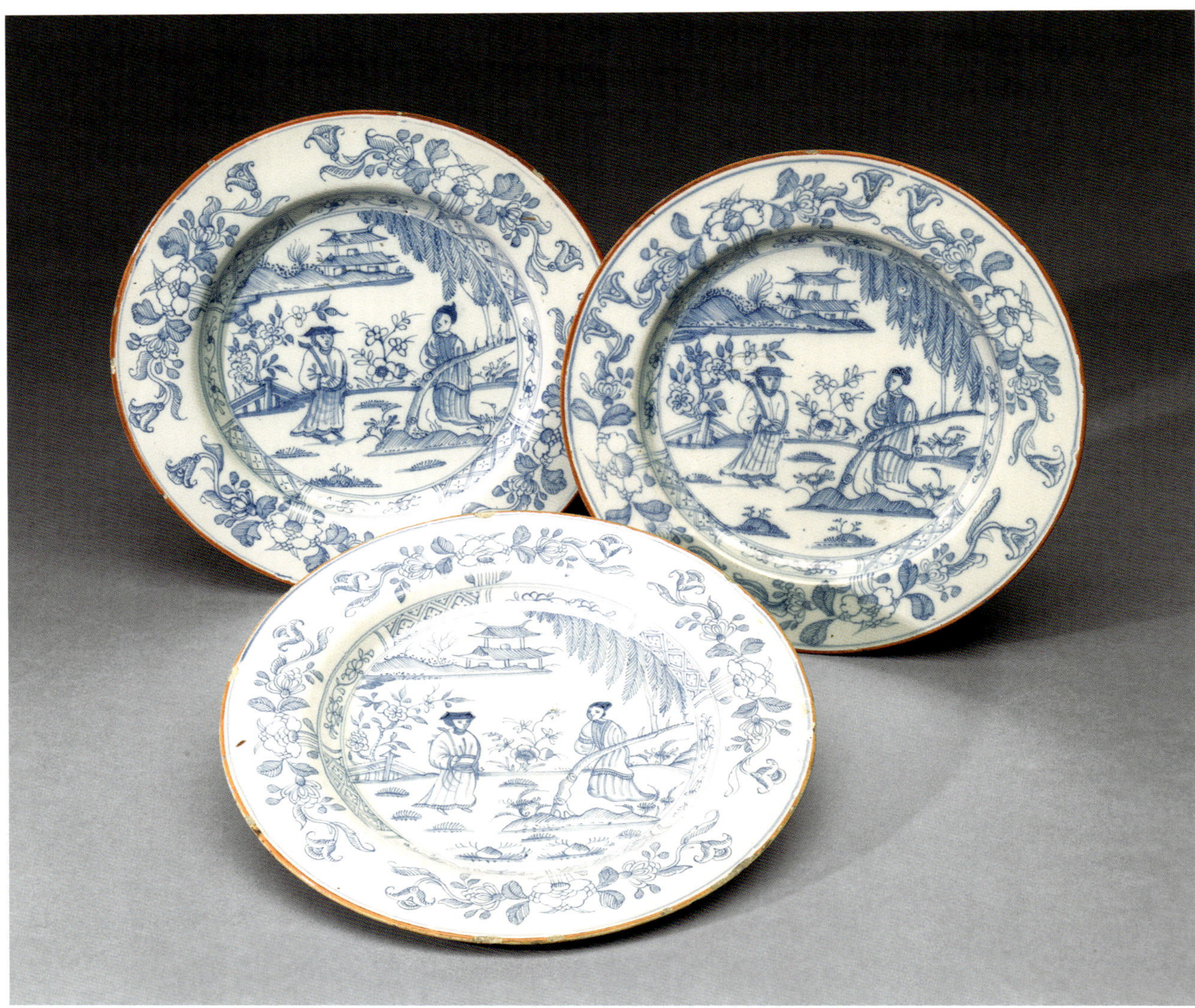

Figure 10 Three plates, Liverpool, England, ca. 1742. Tin-glazed earthenware. D. 8¾". (Colonial Williamsburg Foundation Collections. Museum purchase and gift funds from Mr. & Mrs. Davis W. Moore.)

The plate fragments recovered from the site of Henry Wetherburn's Tavern are clearly similar to those recovered at the King William ordinary. The tin-glazed earthenware fragments from both sites include Chinese-influenced decoration with central figures and pagoda-like structures amid stylized landscapes with weeping willow trees and prunus branches, and brown or reddish-brown rims, all closely copying highly prized Chinese porcelain of the same period. The fragments from Wetherburn's tavern are also similar to intact tin-glazed earthenware examples in the collections of the Colonial Williamsburg Foundation (fig. 10). One of the three plates bears the date 1742, revealing a close parallel with the 1744 dated example in the collections of the National Museums Liverpool.

Based on the dated plates of the National Museums Liverpool and the Colonial Williamsburg Foundation, and John Doncastle's association with the taverns in King William and Williamsburg, it is intriguing to think that he might have played a part in selecting the plates and other dishes that outfitted the respective taverns. The King William tavern plate has an important story to reveal about its journey from England to King William County—who served meals on it, who ate from it, who washed it, and who eventually broke and discarded it. It also underscores the popularity of chinoiserie decoration in the mid-eighteenth-century decorative landscape of American colonists. Furthermore, this link helps substantiate the claim that archaeologists are close to uncovering the site of the King William tavern. The foundation uncovered might not be the tavern itself, but could represent an outbuilding near which tavern employees deposited trash. Future excavations are planned to better delineate the location of the tavern and understand its central role in life at the eighteenth-century King William Courthouse.

1. Alonzo Thomas Dill, *King William County Courthouse: A Memorial to Virginia Self-Government* (King William, Va.: King William County Board of Supervisors, 1984), p. 10.

2. Ibid., p. 31.

3. *Virginia Gazette*, July 3, 1746, p. 4.

4. *Virginia Gazette*, November 3, 1752, p. 2.

5. *Virginia Gazette*, February 4, 1768, p. 4; *Virginia Gazette*, February 4, 1768, p. 3.

6. George Washington, *The Diaries of George Washington*, edited by Donald Jackson and Dorothy Twohig, 6 vols. (Charlottesville: University of Virginia Press, 1979), 2:108–238; ibid., 3:40–269; *Virginia Gazette*, April 19, 1770, p. 3.

7. Robert Hunter, "English Delft from Williamsburg's Archaeological Contexts," in *British Delft at Williamsburg* by John C. Austin (Williamsburg, Va.: Colonial Williamsburg Foundation in association with Jonathan Horne Publications, 1992), pp. 26–27.

8. Louis L. Lipski, *Dated English Delftware: Tin-glazed Earthenware, 1600–1800* (London: Sotheby Publications, 1984), p. 311, fig. 490.

9. Audrey Noël Hume, *The Wetherburn Site, Block 9, Area N, Colonial Lots 20 and 21: Report on the Archaeological Excavations of 1965–1966. Volume II, Part 2—Ceramics: Delftware and White Saltglaze*, Colonial Williamsburg Foundation Library Research Report Series RR-1180 (Williamsburg, Va.: Colonial Williamsburg Foundation, 1970).

10. John C. Austin, *British Delft at Williamsburg* (London: Jonathan Horne, 1992), p. 158; Hunter, "English Delft from Williamsburg's Archaeological Contexts" in ibid., p. 27.

11. *Virginia Gazette*, September 12, 1745, p. 4.

12. *Virginia Gazette*, November 3, 1752, p. 2; Raymond R. Townsend, *Wetherburn's Tavern Historical Report: Block 9, Building 31, Lot 20 & 21*, Colonial Williamsburg Foundation Library Research Report Series 1171 (1966; Alexandria, Va.: Chadwyck-Healey, 1990), pp. 11–13.

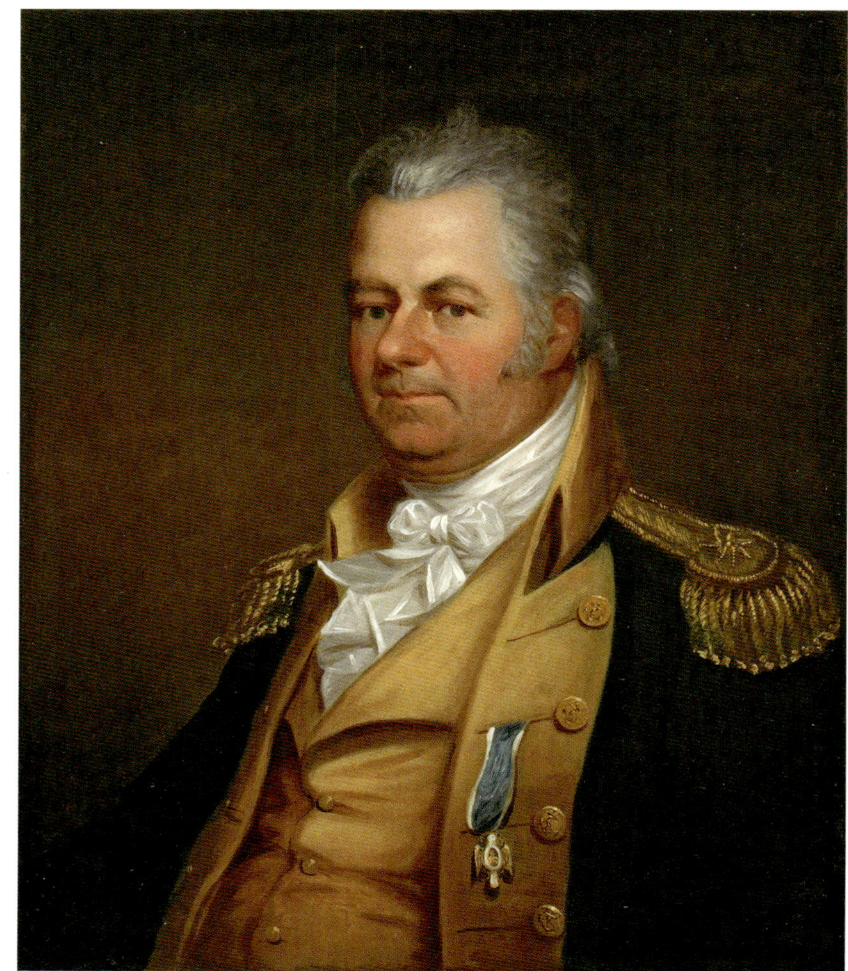

Figure 1 Bass Otis, *Commodore Thomas Truxtun*, ca. 1817. Oil on canvas. 30 x 25". (Courtesy, Brooklyn Public Library, Center for Brooklyn History, 1974.118.)

Amanda Creekman
Isaac and
Captain Charles T. Creekman

A Tale of Two Chinese Porcelain Punch Bowls

▼ INTRODUCTION In the spring of 1799, wine and punch flowed freely to the toast of "Brave Truxtun!" among ardent Federalists and patriots throughout the United States. Captain Thomas Truxtun (1755–1822) of the American frigate *Constellation*, "the Vanguard of Columbia's Naval Glory," had captured the French frigate *L'Insurgente* in a hard-fought action on February 9, 1799, that proved the promise and prowess of the infant U.S. Navy in the opening stages of the Quasi-War with revolutionary France.[1] Truxtun's victories over *L'Insurgente* and then, a year later, over the French frigate *La Vengeance*, quickly elevated him to the status of a hero in the early American popular pantheon (fig. 1).[2] His name and fame became a selling point for a host of consumer goods, from English transfer-printed earthenware and enameled porcelain cloak pins to tricorn hats and patriotic ribbons (fig. 2).[3]

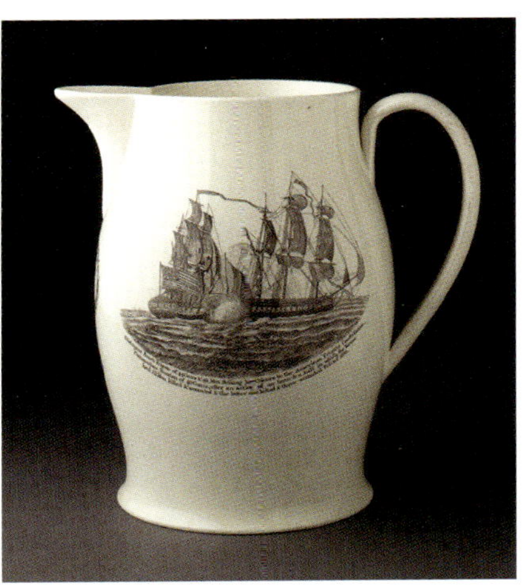

Figure 2 Jug showing battle between *Constellation* and *L'Insurgente*, Herculaneum Factory, Liverpool, England, ca. 1799–1810. Earthenware and lead glaze. H. 9⅞". (Courtesy, Winterthur Museum, Gift of S. Robert Teitelman, Roy T. Lefkoe, and Sydney Ann Lefkoe in memory of S. Robert Teitelman, 2009.0023.012.)

Navel historians consider Truxtun to be one of the founders of the U.S. Navy for his exemplary actions, writings on naval organization and architecture, and training of officers, which brought much-needed discipline and organization in the early days of the service. The fickle winds of politics, though, removed Truxtun from the national stage and his exploits remain little remembered today outside the navy. As a result, his connection to two distinctive Chinese export porcelain punch bowls has not been fully explored (fig. 3).

The two bowls began life together in a shop in Guangzhou, China (known to Americans at the time as Canton), but were launched on separate

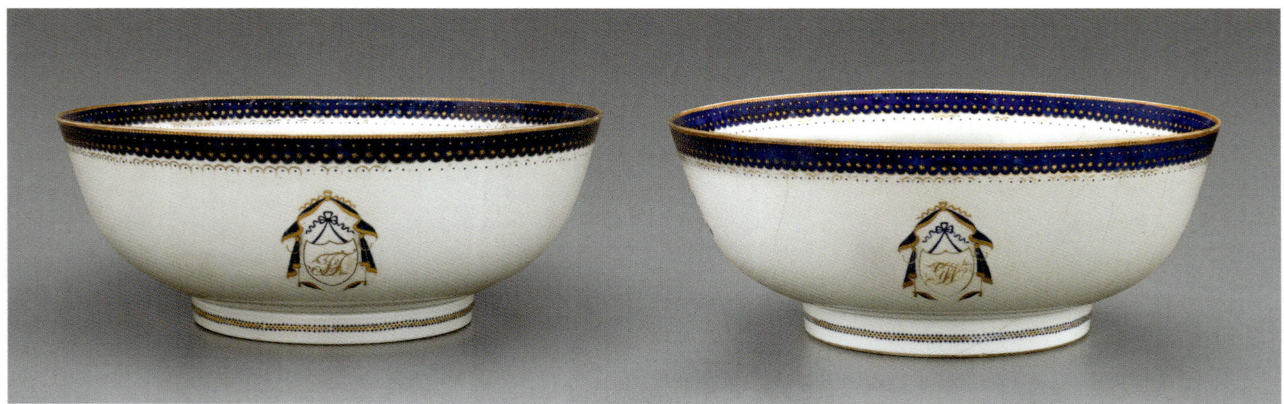

Figure 3 Punch bowls, Jingdezhen, decorated in Guangzhou, China, ca. 1795–1799. Hard-paste porcelain. D. of TT bowl (*left*) 15¾", D. of GW bowl (*right*) 15⅞". (Naval Historical Foundation, 1949.0036.001, and Mount Vernon Ladies' Association, W-2662; photo, Gavin Ashworth.)

paths soon after their arrival in the U.S. They now reside in the collections of the Mount Vernon Ladies' Association and the Naval Historical Foundation, both in the greater Washington, D.C. area. Large but not enormous, each bowl is between 15¾ and 15⅞ inches in diameter. On two sides of each is a pseudo-armorial, composed of an ermine-lined blue drapery with gold fringe and tassels surrounding a shield with the gold initials of the original owners: "GW" for President George Washington and "TT" for Commodore Thomas Truxtun.[4] (Hereafter, each bowl will be referred to by its initials.) Loose sprigs of roses combined with carnations and other flowers, in blue enamel highlighted with gold, enliven the other sides. Red, blue, and gold borders decorate the rim (figs. 4, 5).

Figure 4 Side of the TT bowl illustrated in fig. 3, left. (Courtesy, Naval Historical Foundation, 1949.0036.001; photo, Gavin Ashworth.)

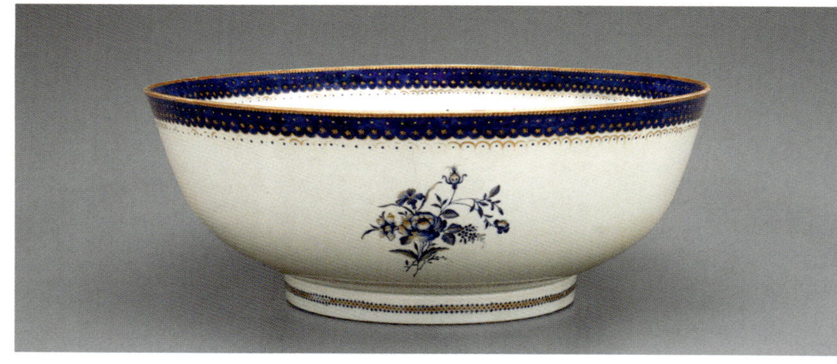

Figure 5 Detail of the border of the GW bowl illustrated in fig. 3, right. (Courtesy, Mount Vernon Ladies' Association, W-2662; photo, Gavin Ashworth.)

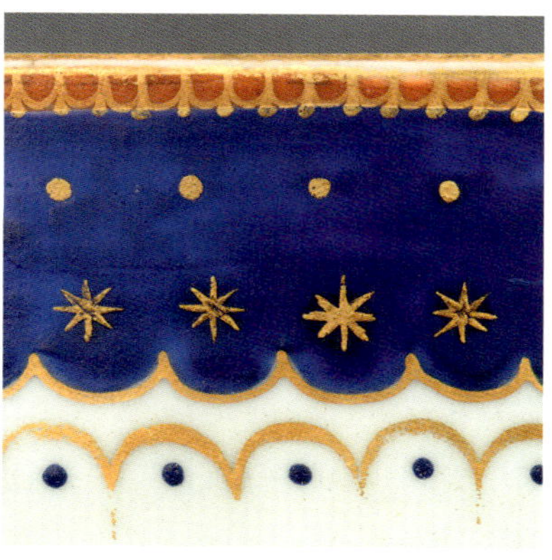

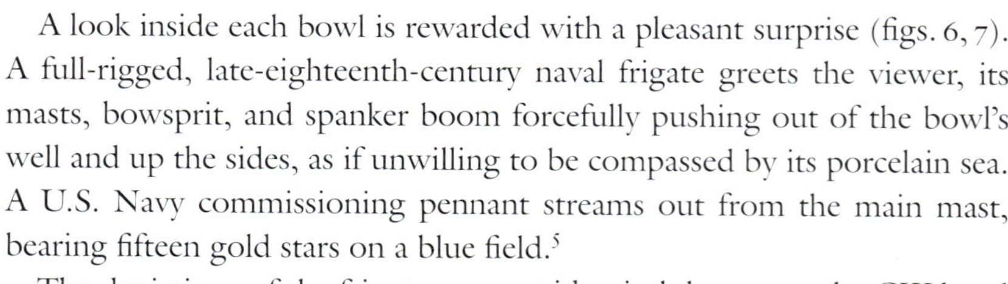

A look inside each bowl is rewarded with a pleasant surprise (figs. 6, 7). A full-rigged, late-eighteenth-century naval frigate greets the viewer, its masts, bowsprit, and spanker boom forcefully pushing out of the bowl's well and up the sides, as if unwilling to be compassed by its porcelain sea. A U.S. Navy commissioning pennant streams out from the main mast, bearing fifteen gold stars on a blue field.[5]

The depictions of the frigates are not identical, however; the GW bowl has "DEFENDER" in black block letters below the ship; the TT bowl has no name. The enormous size of the ship design relative to the bowl makes these bowls extraordinary among the genre of ship-decorated punch bowls and porcelains, and provokes the question: What inspired their creation?[6]

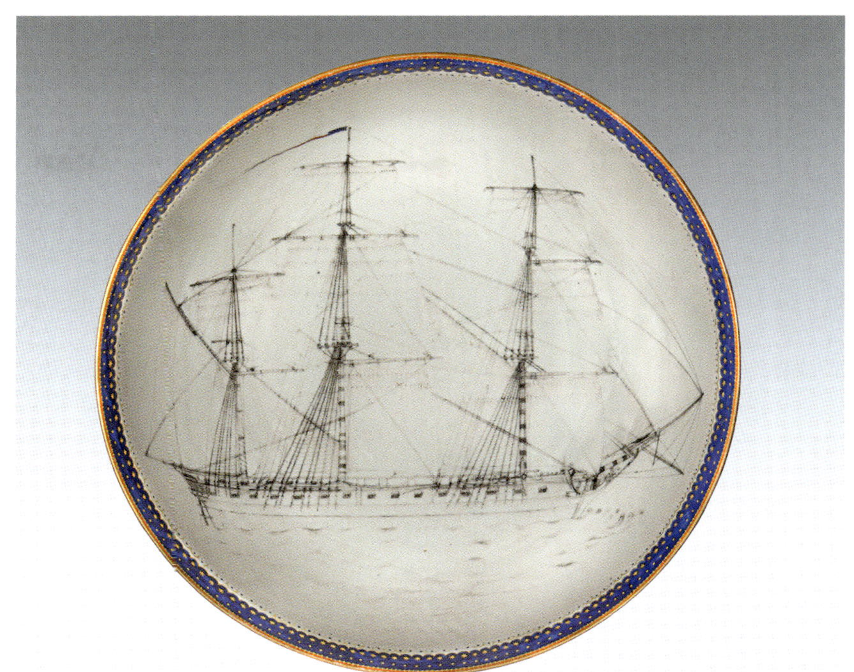

Figure 6 Interior of the TT bowl illustrated in fig. 3, left. (Courtesy, Naval Historical Foundation, 1949.0036.001; photo, Gavin Ashworth.)

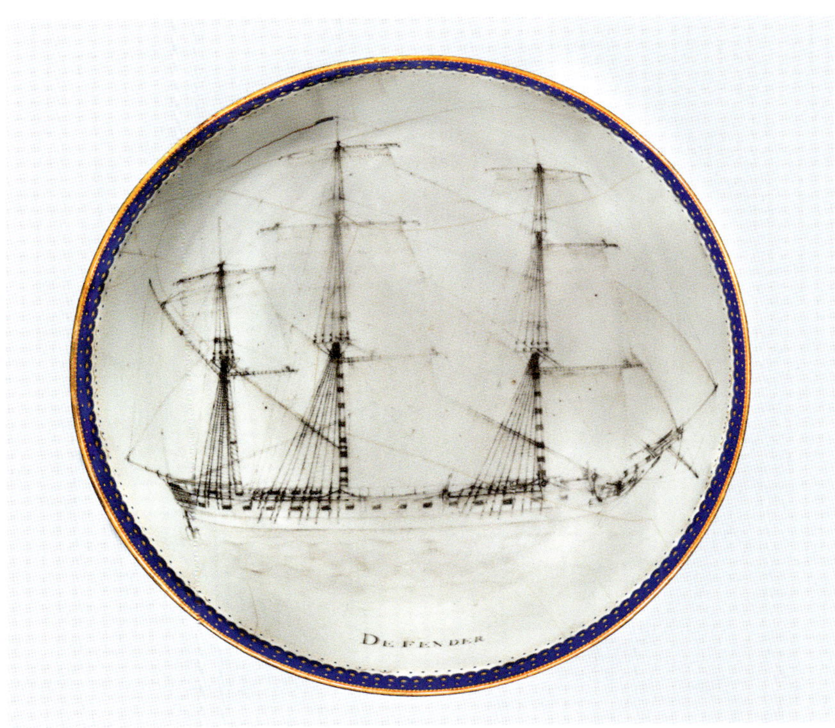

Figure 7 Interior of the GW bowl illustrated in fig. 3, right. (Courtesy, Mount Vernon Ladies' Association, W-2662; photo, Gavin Ashworth.)

In 1981, upon the first reunion of the bowls since they were made, Mount Vernon curator Christine Meadows and Naval Historical Foundation executive director, retired navy Captain David Long, researched the ship design and identified it as a copy of an engraving in Thomas Truxtun's *Remarks, Instructions, and Examples Relating to the Latitude and Longitude etc. etc. etc.* published in late 1794 or early 1795 (fig. 8).[7] They surmised Truxtun as the likely commissioner of both bowls, and Meadows identified the first known documentary reference to the bowl in Martha Washington's will, drafted in September 1800, where she specifically bequeathed "the bowl that has a ship in it" to her grandson. These two facts established a

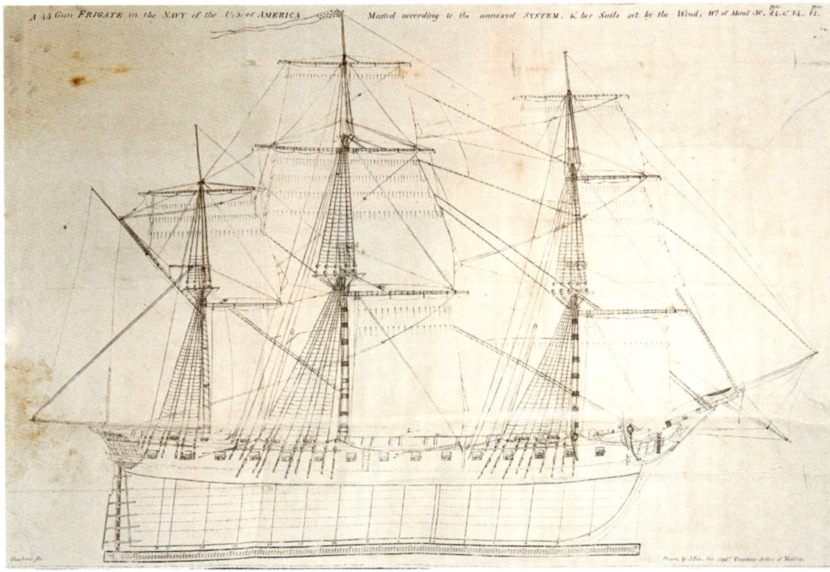

Figure 8 Josiah Fox, "A 44 Gun Frigate in the Navy of the U. S. of America Masted according to the present System," plate 2 from *Remarks, Instructions and Examples Relating to the Latitude and Longitude; Also the Variation of the Compass, etc. etc. etc.* (Philadelphia: T. Dobson, 1794). (Courtesy, Navy Department Library, Naval History and Heritage Command; photo, Sierra Medellin.)

relatively narrow, window, 1795–1800, in which the bowls were ordered, created in China, and shipped back to the United States.[8] Left unanswered was the question of what motivated Truxtun to have the bowls made. Were they souvenirs of a voyage, gifts to friends or supporters, celebrations of a particular event or milestone, or a means of currying favor? This essay explores the historical context surrounding the bowls' creation, and argues that they were no mere decorative accents for a Federal parlor, but rather products of an ambitious and far-reaching vision for personal and national advancement.

Commodore Thomas Truxtun

Victory for the colonists and their French allies in the American Revolution was the culmination of a prolonged, determined campaign. While the land battles are better remembered, maritime power was a major factor in the war. Just weeks after British General Cornwallis's October 1781 surrender at Yorktown, Virginia, due in no small measure to France's army and navy, General George Washington wrote to his friend and protégé the Marquis de Lafayette: "It follows then as certain as that night succeeds the day, that with out a Decisive Naval force we can do nothing definitive, and with it, every thing honourable and glorious."[9]

At the time of the American Revolution, the French navy had the only ships capable of challenging the British navy in line-of-battle combat where two opposing fleets sailing in a column or line were able to fire their broadside guns at each other without endangering friendly ships. The sacrifice of maneuverability for firepower led to ships of the line typically mounting at least seventy cannon. A ship of that size had never been built in the American colonies, and the Americans had no hope of obtaining or building enough of them to be able to meet the British fleets on an equal footing. Accordingly, the Americans turned to commerce raiding rather than direct engagement with British naval power whenever possible. Undaunted by the odds, the fledging Continental Navy, together with government-chartered privateers (private individuals authorized by Congress to seek out and capture British vessels) carried out sustained operations against British commerce throughout the conflict. This sufficiently exasperated British leaders and made eventual settlement of the conflict more pressing to that global empire. Among the intrepid privateers was a young captain from Hempstead, New York, named Thomas Truxtun.

Orphaned at age ten, Truxtun was apprenticed in 1767 to the captain of a British merchant vessel, beginning a three-and-a-half-decade career at sea. Impressed into the Royal Navy in 1771, as Britain was dealing with its first crisis over the sovereignty of the South Atlantic Falkland Islands, Truxtun was able to return to the merchant fleet soon thereafter when the diplomatic standoff was settled short of war with Spain. His brief exposure to Royal Navy organization, customs, and traditions had a lasting influence on his thoughts about shipboard routine, training, and discipline.[10]

By 1775, all of twenty years old, Truxtun married and was the master of his own vessel, the *Charming Polly*, in New York. With the colonies already in a state of rebellion against British authority, and on just his third trading voyage in that ship, Truxtun was captured in the Caribbean by a Royal Navy sloop-of-war. With his vessel and cargo condemned and sold as a prize of war, Truxtun made his way to Philadelphia where he successfully joined the crew of the newly fitted-out privateer *Congress* for her first voyage in early 1776. Nearly two years later, after successful cruises in that ship and two subsequent vessels he commanded, he shifted back to the merchant fleet to meet the pressing need for war supplies for the struggling new nation. That duty was equally dangerous, and by the close of the war he had distinguished himself at sea and gained a reputation as a knowledgeable seaman and excellent leader.

On March 17, 1782, with the war's end in sight, Truxtun attended a public dinner in Philadelphia for General George Washington. As Truxtun himself later recalled, Washington reportedly acknowledged Truxtun's valuable contributions to American victory by declaring him to have "been as a regiment to the United States," in effect saying Truxtun's actions, in diverting British ships and curtailing the delivery of war materiel to the British, were equivalent to the advantage gained by a regiment of more than four hundred soldiers opposing the enemy.[11] Over the years, Truxtun and Washington appear to have forged an amicable professional relationship, born of a sense of common cause in their country's revolutionary beginnings and shared Federalist political views, with a strong commitment to national defense.

Peace brought a postwar military drawdown and sell-off of Continental Navy ships, as well as a surge in American commercial voyages worldwide,

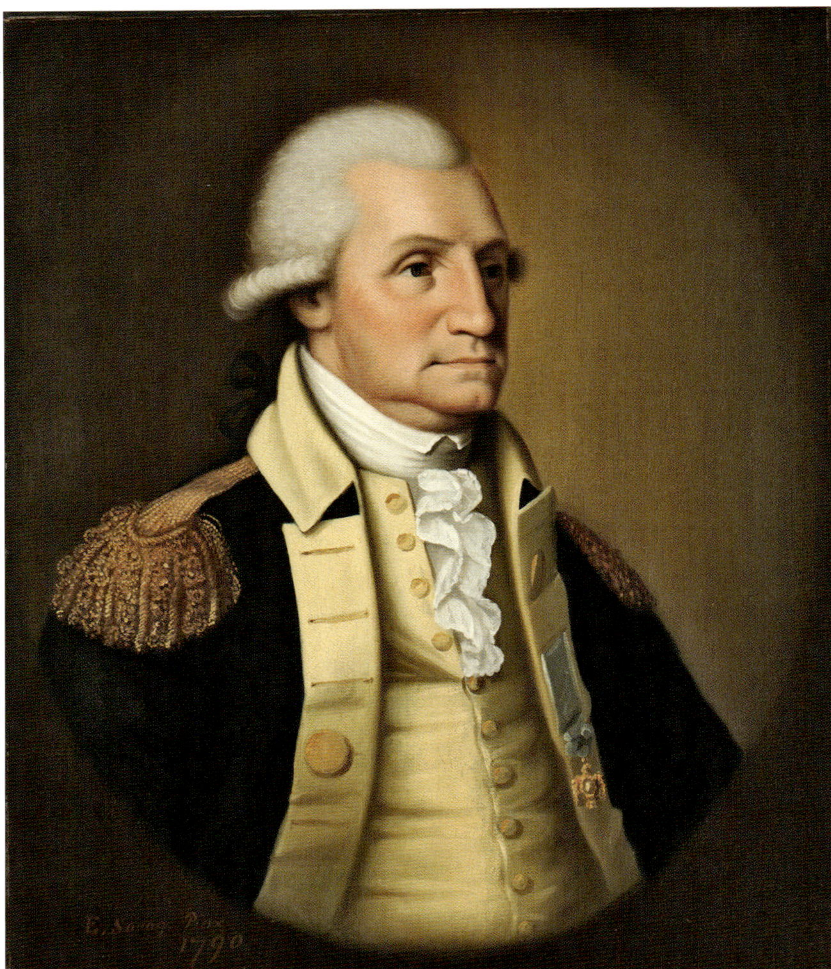

Figure 9 Edward Savage, *George Washington* (1732–1799), 1790. Oil on canvas, 30⅗16 x 25⅜". (Harvard University Portrait Collection, Gift of Edward Savage to Harvard College, 1791; photo, © President and Fellows of Harvard College, H49.)

unfettered by British trade constraints but unprotected by British naval power. Truxtun was heavily involved in that trade expansion, and over the next decade he captained several ships, including the appropriately named *Canton*, which in late 1785 embarked on one of the earliest American voyages to China. His series of successful cruises—to China (1785–1787 and 1787–1789) and India (1789–1791 and 1791–1793)—brought back valuable cargoes of tea, cotton, and porcelain to eager consumers, and solidified his reputation for reliability among the international merchant community.[12] Being in London in the spring of 1794 placed him in position to do a favor for President George Washington: to bring home a gold watch and chain ordered for Mrs. Washington.[13]

1794 proved to be a pivotal year for Truxtun and the as-yet-unborn U.S. Navy. The new nation's expanding maritime commerce had been under attack for several years in the Mediterranean Sea by Barbary Coast corsairs (state-sponsored privateers from Algiers and Tripoli). Belatedly recognizing the need to protect its merchant shipping, and with the Continental Navy ships long gone, in March 1794 Congress passed "An Act to provide a Naval Armament," authorizing six frigates to be built.[14] Six maritime ports along the eastern seaboard, from Maine to Virginia, were selected as shipbuilding sites—in recognition of both the need for broad political support for such an expensive national undertaking, as well as the reality of limited manpower and ship construction timber and other resources in any one port.[15]

By June 1794 President Washington had appointed the commanding officers for the six frigates, intending that each supervise the building of his own ship (fig. 9). Truxtun, the most junior and the only one of the six who had not served in the Revolutionary War as a Continental Navy officer, was assigned to the 36-gun ship to be built in Baltimore, Maryland.

Naval architect Joshua Humphreys was responsible for the excellent hull designs for the frigates. However, the placement and height of their three masts and the location and length of the yards that held the sails (collectively known as spars) was openly debated by Humphreys and the captains of the six ships from June 1794 to January 1796. At issue was whether the United States could design a ship to compete with the British (and potentially the French) navy. Calculating that any American warship could only hope to be victorious in a single-ship engagement with another frigate, Humphreys designed his American frigates to exceed the size and hull strength of a typical British or French frigate, and to possess the sailing capabilities and speed to evade a heavier gunned ship or any group of enemy ships his frigates might encounter.[16] Wind-powered sails being the only feasible means of motive power in the late eighteenth century for open ocean voyages, designating the size and location of the masts and the size of the yards and their positions on those masts was paramount. Truxtun forcefully expressed his views on the subject to his five fellow frigate captains, the Secretary of War, and the President. He soon met with stiff opposition from Joshua Humphreys who, having reviewed Truxtun's system, summarily dismissed it as "erroneous."[17]

Despite his lower naval rank, Truxtun had more than twenty years of at-sea experience and an undiminished ambition. He was determined to share his organizational and navigational knowledge broadly in order to shape the structure of the new navy—specifically the design of those first six ships. To this end, he sent a brief but pointed letter to Secretary of War Henry Knox (the secretary of the navy position would not be established until 1798) in which he stressed his opinion that the new frigates should have masts and their associated yards sized and placed according to his calculations. At the same time, he was also compiling a manuscript to broadcast his knowledge of sailing and his views on ship design, titled "Remarks, Instructions, and Examples relating to the Latitude and Longitude etc etc etc."[18] To illustrate his masting system, Truxtun commissioned Josiah Fox (who was already working as Humphreys's assistant) to produce a diagram that he intended to publish together with a printed copy of his letter to Knox in the book. "Let me have it as soon as possible, and attend to the dimensions here enclosed of all the spars," wrote Truxtun to Fox in November 1794, promising "When you have done, I will make you a present of a handsome piece of India cloth for your wife."[19] For Truxtun, the use of commodities as payment or payback was familiar, and it seems likely this was neither the first nor last time he would leverage his access to desirable Asian exports. Little did Fox realize that his side-view image of a notional 44-gun frigate hull incorporating Truxtun's masting design was destined to live long after the men involved had passed from the scene.

In 1795 Timothy Pickering, Knox's successor as secretary of war, had a brief, one-year tour in that position but played several key parts in the frigate saga. First, he distributed copies of Truxtun's book with its masting image to the other five frigate commanding officers.[20] Washington also received a copy of Truxtun's work, possibly from Pickering though it may have been a gift directly from Truxtun.[21] Second, Pickering presented to President Washington a selection of ten possible names for the six frigates (fig. 10). Washington's response to this naming opportunity has not been found, but five of those initial names would in fact be bestowed on the ships—*President*, *Congress*, *United States*, *Constellation*, and *Constitution*.[22] Among those not used was *Defender*.[23]

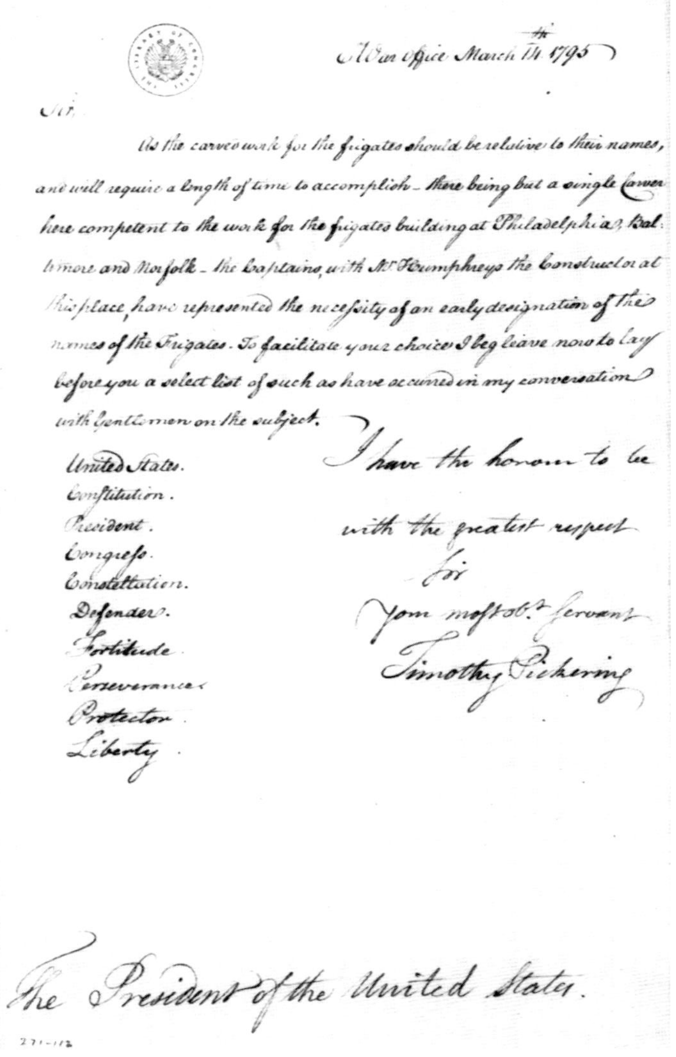

War Office March 4th 1795

Sir,

As the carved work for the frigates should be relative to their names, and will require a length of time to accomplish – there being but a single Carver here competent to the work for the frigates building at Philadelphia, Baltimore and Norfolk – the Captains, with Mr Humphreys the Constructor at this place, have represented the necessity of an early designation of the names of the Frigates. To facilitate your choice I beg leave now to lay before you a select list of such as have occurred in my conversation with Gentlemen on the subject.

United States.
Constitution.
President.
Congress.
Constellation.
Defender.
Fortitude.
Perseverance.
Protector.
Liberty.

I have the honour to be
with the greatest respect
Sir
Your most obt servant
Timothy Pickering

The President of the United States.

Figure 10 Letter from Timothy Pickering to George Washington, March 4, 1795, listing proposed names for the first frigates. (Library of Congress.)

Pickering optimistically asked Humphreys and Captains Truxtun, Barry, and Talbot to "consult together" and prepare a unified opinion on the masting and sparring of the ships, but that never materialized. When Pickering's successor as secretary of war, James McHenry, took office in early 1796, a circular from his office ended the debate by simply announcing that the six sets of captains and shipbuilders "shall have liberty to Mast and Spar their own Ship."[24]

1796 brought unexpected disruption to the frigate-building plans. A peace accord with Algiers triggered a provision of the original naval act that threatened to halt all ship construction, since the perceived foreign naval threat would be diminished. Truxtun realized that his low seniority could derail his career should a likely compromise with Congress result in only a few of the six ships being completed. Turning to President Washington, Truxtun wrote an impassioned plea to be able to both complete and command his Baltimore-built frigate: "I shall take a particular pleasure, in exerting my utmost abilities, to have her speedily compleated, and in a way that will do honor to the United States."[25]

Washington was indeed able to convince Congress to complete construction of three of the six frigates with an April 1796 act authorizing that work. Furthermore, he confirmed that the captains for the three ships being built in Boston, Philadelphia, and Baltimore would remain as originally assigned, Truxtun among them (fig. 11).

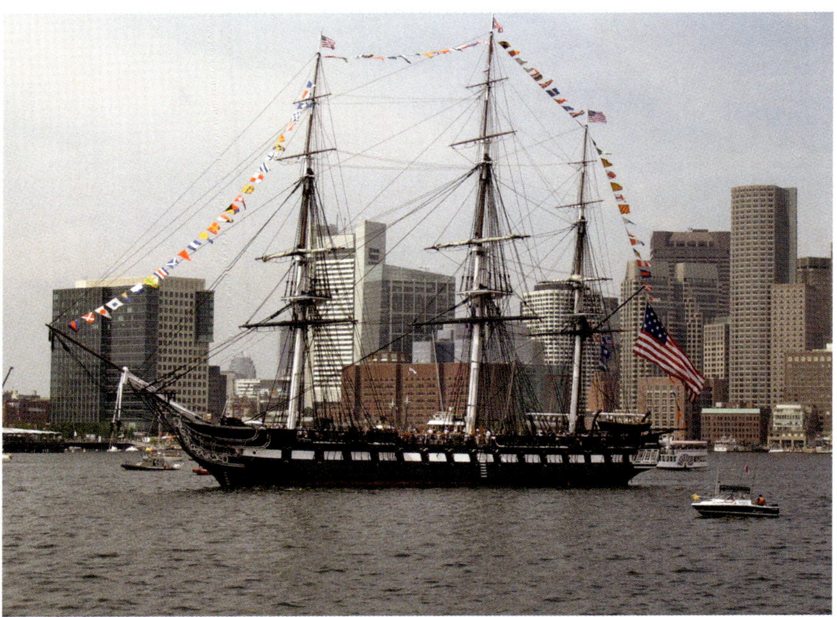

Figure 11 USS *Constitution*, the oldest commissioned warship afloat, shown on its yearly turnaround cruise in Boston Harbor, July 4, 2011. (Photo, Charles T. Creekman.) This frigate is one of the original six of the U.S. Navy.

As work progressed on his 36-gun frigate, Truxtun remained in Baltimore but continued to think beyond that busy shipyard scene and contemplate the naval operations to come. He had already included in his earlier book his recommendations for the general duties of each officer aboard a warship, based on his years at sea and his familiarity with Royal Navy routine. Now he turned to the complex challenge of communicating between ships with flags in that pre-electronic era. Once again considering himself to be the standard-setter for this young navy, he published a signal book in 1797.[26]

Truxtun successfully completed *Constellation* (to the specifications of his masting system, of course) and launched the frigate in September 1797.[27] By June 1798, he proudly reported that she "goes through the Water with great Swiftness."[28] Cruising in the Caribbean to protect American shipping, Truxtun and his well-trained crew on *Constellation* fought and captured French frigate *L'Insurgente* (fig. 12). President John Adams exclaimed, "I wish all the other officers had as much zeal as Truxton."[29]

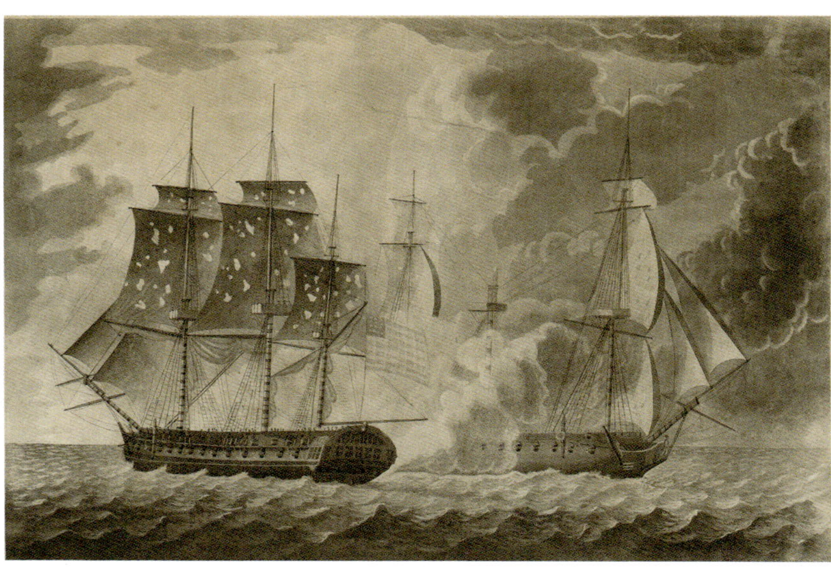

Figure 12 Edward Savage, *Action between the Constellation and L'Insurgent on the 9th February 1799*, published May 20, 1799. Aquatint; ink on paper. 15¾ x 21¹⁵⁄₁₆". (Courtesy, Mount Vernon Ladies' Association, M-5855.)

The Merchants and Underwriters at Lloyd's Coffeehouse of London presented Truxtun with an elegant silver urn in thanks for his efforts in preserving merchant shipping from harassment by the French. At Mount Vernon, Washington received tangible reminders of Truxtun's victory from artist Edward Savage, a pair of prints depicting the chase and engagement.[30] Although retired from the presidency, Washington had returned to the military stage as commander in chief of the Provisional Army, authorized by President Adams over concern of open war with France.

The Point of Crisis

The years in which the bowls must have been ordered and created (1795–1800) were tumultuous, to say the least, for both Truxtun and the nation. When set against this context, it seems most likely that Truxtun commissioned the pair of bowls when the future of his career and the navy were hanging in the balance (1795–1797), and when he most needed President Washington's support and backing.

Punch Bowls as Gifts

By the 1790s, the custom of giving punch bowls as gifts was already well established, particularly among hard-drinking mariners who welcomed the opportunity to imbibe punch and toast the success of their ventures. As centerpieces of the convivial table, punch bowls offered a welcome means of celebration and refreshment, particularly in the male environs of the captain's quarters, officers' mess, or the gentlemen's club, fostering social and business relationships around the shared drink. By the mid-18th century, Liverpool potteries catered to their merchant and maritime clientele, offering tin-glazed earthenware and later creamware punch bowls custom-decorated with ships, some of which were gifts for masters and owners.[31]

By virtue of their relative rarity and the skill of Chinese painters, punch bowls of Chinese export porcelain developed a reputation as desirable gifts. A 1779 report by officers of the Vereenigde Oostindische Compagnie (Dutch East India Company) stated that punch bowls "with the factory . . . which are now and then brought in by private individuals must be considered as rarities, which one makes a present of to friends in one or twos . . . ."[32] John Green, captain of the *Empress of China*, the first American ship to travel to China, brought back "1 tubb containing 4 factory painted bowles" which were probably intended as gifts to family, friends, or business associates.[33]

Custom-decorated bowls could be tailored to particular occasions or messages. A punch bowl decorated with a stock image of a ship labeled *Grand Turk* was reportedly given to Captain West of the *Grand Turk*, by Pinqua, a Chinese porcelain dealer who had risen to become a hong merchant, one of the select group authorized to secure and manage trade with foreigners.[34] The bowl gift may have been an apt means of fostering the new business relationship with the U.S. traders. A later punch bowl commissioned by General Jacob Morton of New York left no doubt as to its purpose. The inscription around the exterior described the occasion and recipient: "Presented by General Jacob Morton, to the Corporation of the City of New York, July 4th, 1812." On the interior, together with a view of New York Harbor, is the exhortation, "Drink deep. You will preserve the City and encourage Canals." At the time, Morton was serving as the clerk to the city council. His gift, a lasting memorial of his political interests, was reportedly used for many years by city officials at public banquets.[35]

Truxtun's bowl for President Washington lacked an inscription, but it seems to have had a similar purpose as a lobbying gift. Its decoration speaks volumes. The full-size design on the interior showcased the proposed 44-gun frigate, the new class of ships that would be the projected glory of the United States, and offered a convenient prompt to raise a toast to its future. More specifically, it advertised Truxtun's theories and contributions to the force.

The name given to the ship is also telling. "Defender" was one of the proposed names for the six frigates, and Truxtun intended it as a clear compliment to Washington. In the years following the Revolution, individuals and groups regularly applied the title "Defender" to Washington, alluding to his role both as a warrior and a statesman. In 1789 the ladies of Trenton proclaimed that Washington, the "Defender of the Mothers will also Protect their Daughters," on an archway under which he traveled on the way to the inauguration.[36] The people of Boston saluted President Washington as the "*Defender* of their *Freedom* and *Independence*" during his northern tour, and the officials of Charleston, South Carolina, addressed the "Defender of the liberties of America" during his southern tour.[37] After his appointment as commander in chief in 1798, friends and associates congratulated him and addressed him again as "Defender of your Country."[38]

Launching the Bowls

Truxtun, heavily engaged with the fitting out and launching of his frigate, *Constellation*, did not make a voyage to China between 1795 and 1800, but instead presumably entrusted his instructions and a copy of the engraving to a friend or associate sailing for Guangzhou during that time. Typically arriving with the summer monsoon winds between June and September, a ship and her crew had 3–6 months in port before making the return voyage in the winter months. Following customary practice, the order would have been placed with a Chinese merchant soon after arrival in the hope that the order would be completed by the time the ship was ready to sail. If not, it would have to wait for a ship returning the next season.[39]

In Guangzhou, Truxtun's agent probably would have gone to a merchant who specialized in porcelain to commission the bowls, someone like Yam Shinqua, "CHINA-WARE MERCHANT at Canton," who advertised in the *Providence Gazette* in 1804 that he "BEGS Leave respectfully to inform the American Merchants, Supercargoes, and Captains, that he procures to be manufactured, in the best Manner, all Sorts of CHINA-WARE, with Arms, Cyphers, and other Decorations (if required) painted in a very superior Style, and on the most reasonable Terms. All Orders carefully and promptly attended to."[40]

Many of the porcelain merchants and others who catered to foreign traders were located on Jingyuan Jie ("Profoundly Tranquil Street"), known to foreigners as Porcelain Street, China Street, New Street, or New China Street. It ran perpendicular to the river and the quay in front of the hongs, or factories, the large buildings in which European, American, and other foreign merchants lived, worked, and stored their goods.[41]

In the porcelain shop, Truxtun's agent would have provided the Chinese merchant with the engraving of the ship and the text for the inscriptions, chosen a border pattern, and discussed the size and overall design of the bowls, the price, and the date of completion. The discussion would have taken place through a Chinese interpreter or in a pidgin English that likely would have included some Chinese vocabulary and phrases.

Once agreed upon, the Chinese merchant would pass the designs and instructions on to a painter, who either worked on the premises or in a nearby workshop. He would paint the designs in overglaze enamels onto porcelain blanks, and then fire them in a muffle kiln, which melted and fixed the enamel decoration onto the surface of the bowls.

The Chinese artist meticulously copied the engraving, capturing all the details of Truxtun's masting and sparring system. The detailed care with which the artist painted is also seen in the figurehead, a figure of Liberty wearing a winged cap and holding a liberty cap on a pole (fig. 13). In place of the dotted scale lines that appear below the waterline in the original engraving, the artist painted rolling waves.

Notably, the painter rendered the ship at the same scale as the engraving instead of reducing it to fit in the center of the well, as was more common on ship-decorated bowls (fig. 14). Comparison of the measurements of the painted designs on both bowls with that of the original engraving shows that the painted version varies by only 5⁄16" at most. This visual hyperbole, where the design nearly overwhelms the surface of the bowl, might have been the choice of the painter, who thus avoided having to change the scale of the engraving. It is possible, though, that it was intentional, directed by Truxtun at the outset to ensure that the ship and the ideas it represented could not be missed.

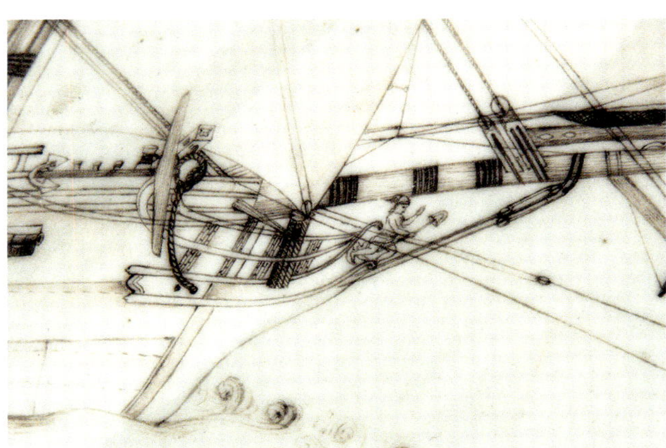

Figure 13 Detail of the figurehead of the ship on the TT bowl illustrated in fig. 3, left. (Courtesy, Naval Historical Foundation, 1949.0036.001; photo, Gavin Ashworth.)

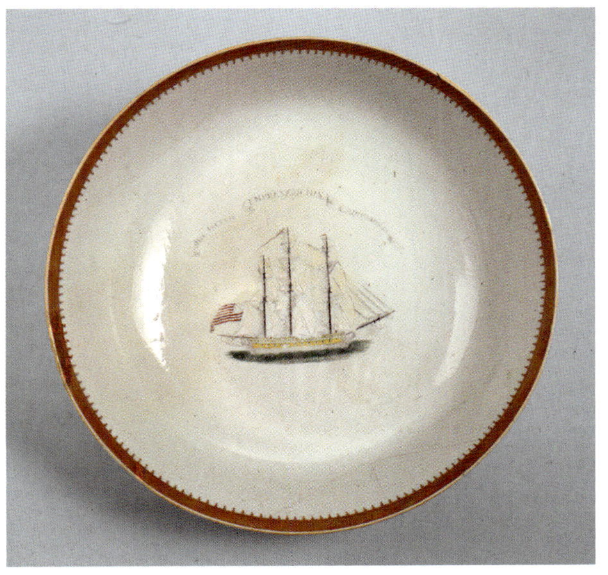

Figure 14 Punch bowl, Jingdezhen, decorated in Guangzhou, China, ca. 1784. Hard-paste porcelain. D. 15¼". (Courtesy, New Jersey State Museum, CH1969.244 a, Gift of Mr. Richard V. Lindabury.) Ships decorating the wells of punch bowls were typically more modest, as is this one, in a bowl acquired by Capt. John Green of the *Empress of China*. The ship design was adapted from the frontispiece of a quarto-sized book, *A Treatise of Practical Seamanship*, by William Hutchinson (Liverpool, 1777).

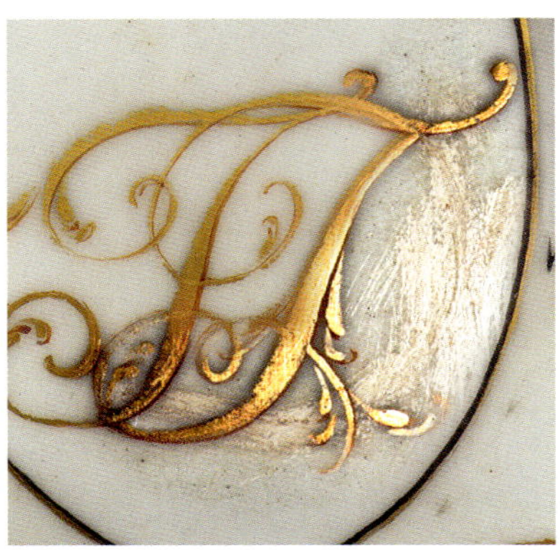

Figure 15 Detail of "TT" with abraded area on the pseudo-armorial of the TT bowl illustrated in fig. 3, left. (Courtesy, Naval Historical Foundation, 1949.0036.001; photo, Gavin Ashworth.)

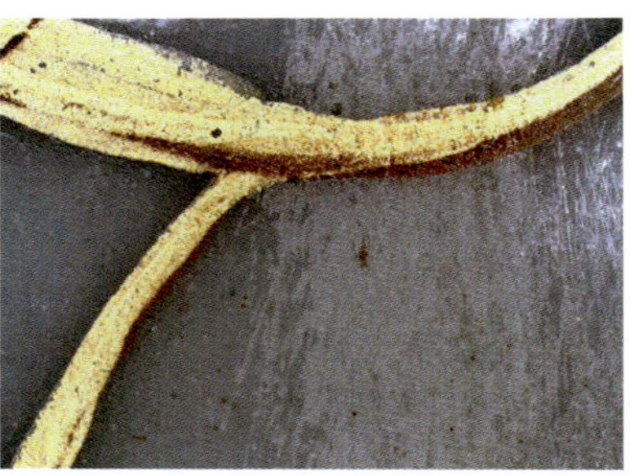

Figure 16 Microscopic detail of the top serif of the second "T" of the cypher on the TT bowl illustrated in fig. 3, left, showing the area of erasure and the gilt over top. (Courtesy, Naval Historical Foundation, 1949.0036.001; photo, Amanda Isaac and Linda Landry.)

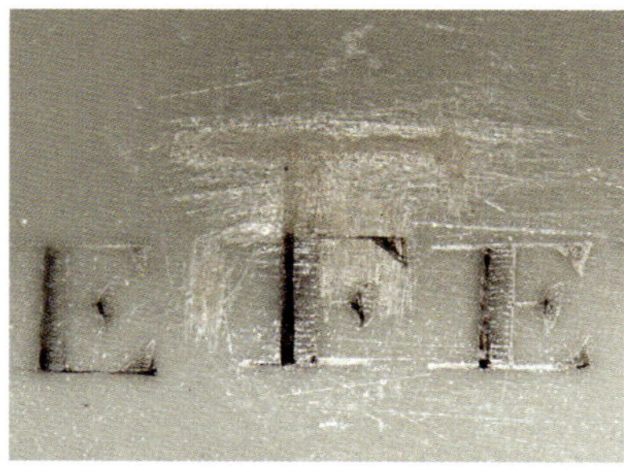

Figure 17 Detail showing the altered "F" of the GW bowl illustrated in fig. 3, right. (Courtesy, Mount Vernon Ladies' Association, W-2662; photo, Gavin Ashworth.)

Truxtun's Surprise, or a Hasty Reversal

Depending on the ship's schedule, the time between the ordering of the bowls and their delivery would have been 1–2 years. Excited as Truxtun must have been to receive the bowls, it appears he had a shock when he unpacked them.

Visual examination of the TT bowl shows a notable difference in the finish color around the initials on each shield (fig. 15). Microscopic examination confirmed the reason: a series of abrasions made with a sharp-edged tool had removed areas of gilding and red enamel, and cut through the glazed surface to reveal the porcelain body (fig. 16). Examination of the GW bowl revealed a change had been made in like fashion to the "F" in "Defender" (fig. 17).

It appears that Truxtun's agent failed to accurately convey some important details of the bowl's design. Trusting instructions to an intermediary is a risky business, especially considering the distance, the number of people involved, and the linguistic and cultural differences, all of which provide ample opportunities for misunderstandings and mistakes. In this case, evidently the bowl had originally been painted with the initials "TD" (fig. 18). After scraping off the unwanted loop, the repairer then added additional gold to extend the top serif of the T and added additional flourishes. On the GW bowl, the repairer scraped off the top of an "F," indicating that the original title had been lettered like a French word, "De Fender." The repairer then extended the original middle stroke, to create the top serif, and added a new middle stroke.

To date, no other example of this type of alteration has been identified on Chinese export porcelain of this period. The crudeness and apparent hastiness of the alteration suggests the changes took place in the United States, after receipt of the bowls, rather than at the workshop in Guangzhou.[42] If that is the case, it would suggest that Truxtun, after discovering the mistakes, took the bowls to a china painter in Philadelphia, New York, or Baltimore to make the corrections. In the case of the GW bowl, the fact that an otherwise small lettering error was altered further indicates the significance of the bowl as a presentation piece. The correction ensured that Truxtun's intended compliment to Washington was received. In the case of the TT bowl, it seems reasonable to suppose that Truxtun would not have wished to retain a bowl with the wrong initials in his home. The change raises the question of whether someone other than Truxtun was the original intended recipient. While the possibility is intriguing, it seems unlikely, as no one has been identified who had a "TD" monogram and was associated with the American voyages to Canton of that period.

A Punch Bowl for the President

Truxtun likely presented the corrected bowl to Washington sometime between 1796, while Washington was still president, and the fall of 1799, by the time of Truxtun's final dinner with Washington on September 12.[43]

Whether the bowl arrived, was corrected, and presented in the midst of the crisis over the establishment of the navy or afterward, the GW bowl

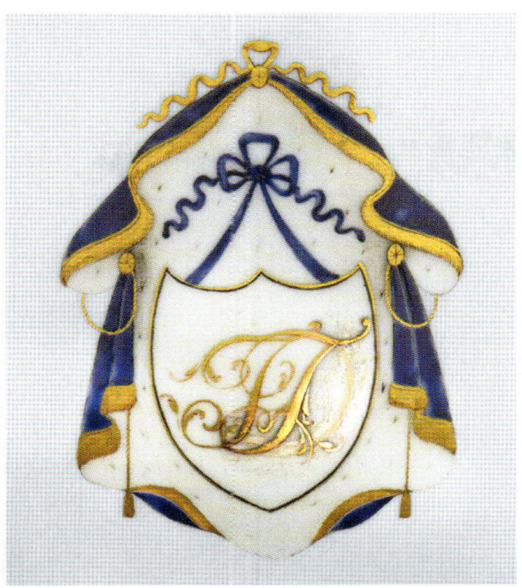

Figure 18 Speculative rendering of the pseudo-armorial of the TT bowl illustrated in fig. 3, left. (Courtesy, Naval Historical Foundation, 1949.0036.001), digitally overlaid with a gilt "D" from a teabowl from another Chinese export porcelain service of ca. 1795. (Detroit Institute of Art, 1930.0307.011; digital photo, Gavin Ashworth.)

effectively kept Truxtun's name, achievements, and availability for command ever visible to the commander in chief, a strategy Truxtun may have considered necessary since he did not yet have any brilliant naval victories to his name. In this he followed the pattern of numerous authors, artists, and artisans who gave gifts to Washington to advertise their abilities and services. If so, Truxtun's choice was akin to the comte de Custine's 1782 gift of a porcelain service to Mrs. Washington, decorated with the laurel-crowned cypher of Washington. It honored the victorious general, but it also reflected glory back on the giver of the gift: with Custine's service, the different patterns on each of the pieces attested to the quality and virtuosity of wares from his Niderviller porcelain factory, advertising his goods to an American market that had been newly opened to France after the colonies' break with England.[44]

Glass entrepreneur and German immigrant John Frederick Amelung used a similar tactic after establishing a glass factory in New Bremen, Maryland. In March 1789 he personally traveled to Mount Vernon and presented "two capacious goblets of double flint glass, exhibiting the General's coat of arms, &c." Even before the presentation, Washington seems to have heard of Amelung's efforts and was promoting him as a "capitol artist" whose industry would benefit from Washington's own pet project, the establishment of the Potomac canal to connect eastern manufacturers with western markets. Four months after the visit, Washington approved a ten percent duty on glass imports, to protect infant industries like Amelung's glass factory.[45]

Washington scrupulously avoided a system of official patronage, but by virtue of his position and reputation, his endorsement, albeit unofficial, was golden, and his table and home were necessarily public stages, showcasing objects, their makers, and givers worthy of emulation and support. While the precise moment and nature of the gift to Washington remains elusive, in themselves, the two punch bowls defined the essence of the message Truxtun sent. By twinning, he materially linked the two households, the commodore's and the president's, and linked his own fortunes to those of his perceived patron.

The GW bowl would have had plenty of opportunities for use after its presentation, both in the president's residence and in retirement at Mount Vernon. As was customary, the Washingtons served punch both as a refreshment to guests arriving in between meals or during times of celebration.[46] In the executive residence, hired steward Frederick Kitt would have overseen the service of punch. At Mount Vernon, the enslaved butler Frank Lee directed the preparation of rum punch and the filling of the bowl for the constant stream of visitors in those years, including extended family, friends, political and business connections, and admirers from around the world.

The bowl's chance to display Truxtun's merits as a seaman and philosopher did not last long. With Washington's death on December 14, 1799, Truxtun lost his strongest political ally. Within a few years, the bowl transformed from a politically energized centerpiece to a relic of an American legend.

Truxtun's Exit

Returning to the United States as a hero in March 1799 following his victory over *L'Insurgente*, Truxtun became embroiled in a debate on his seniority in relation to the other navy captains, and resigned on August 1st. After some months, and the dinner with Washington, he resolved his differences and returned to command of the *Constellation*. Underway the day before Christmas 1799 and headed to the Caribbean once again, Truxtun's most significant naval exploit lay just ahead. Engaging the more heavily armed French frigate *La Vengeance* in early February 1800 during a bloody battle that lasted long after sunset, Truxtun claimed victory when his badly damaged opponent limped away under cover of darkness. Once again the nation extolled Truxtun's accomplishments. Congress voted him a gold medal—the first such Congressional award since the Revolutionary War.[47]

The years following Truxtun's last meeting with Washington were stormy. Now a national hero for his at-sea exploits, Truxtun was in line to command a forward-deployed squadron of U.S. Navy ships in the Mediterranean Sea when, in early 1802, his pugnacious personality reasserted itself in an unfortunate manner. Threatening to "quit the service" again if navy leadership would not acquiesce to his request to have a flagship captain appointed to the ship in which he would cruise, Secretary of the Navy Robert Smith called his bluff and accepted his resignation.[48] In the years that followed, Truxtun returned time and again in letter and publication to his perceived poor treatment by the navy and the nation, but was not returned to active service. "Were Washington now alive," he railed in 1806, "what must have been his astonishment at the alacrity with which the present administration embraces a poor pretext to throw out of office, a man, who, thirty-nine years since, came into naval life."[49]

Later Travels of the TT Bowl

The deaths of George Washington in 1799 and Martha in 1802 launched the two punch bowls on separate but equally fascinating voyages of their own through the 225 years since their creation.

Truxtun lived in retirement in New Jersey and later in Pennsylvania. He never returned to sea and therefore missed participating in the War of 1812 with Great Britain—a conflict that saw the six frigates in action and many Truxtun-trained officers winning victories at sea. Truxtun, in his final public service, was elected sheriff of Philadelphia County from 1816 to 1819. Meanwhile, the TT bowl settled down in Truxtun's home among a large collection of trophies, such as the silver urn presented by Lloyd's, and luxuries brought back from China and India, described by one visitor as his "Eastern Magnificence."[50] It might have taken center stage on visits from old friends like John Barry or celebratory occasions, such as the weddings of his daughters.

Truxtun died in 1822 and was buried in Philadelphia. His legacy of training, organization, and valor at sea remains alive in a series of six U.S. Navy warships named *Truxtun*, whose active service has spanned 180 years of our nation's history. The current namesake, a guided missile destroyer DDG-103, was commissioned in 2009.

The TT bowl descended to Truxtun's eldest daughter, Sarah Truxtun Benbridge. Her descendants' relocation to Indiana took the TT bowl out of sight for nearly eighty years, during which period the connection of the bowl's image with Truxtun's book was forgotten. His descendants came to believe it depicted his China Trade vessel *Canton*. In 1949 Truxtun's great-great-grandson Richard Wetherill Benbridge donated the bowl to the Naval Historical Foundation in Washington, D.C.[51]

"down to the hull"

Upon her death in 1802, Mrs. Washington bequeathed "the bowl that has a ship in it" to her only grandson and male heir, George Washington Parke Custis (1781–1857), together with all the family silver, portraits, and the Society of Cincinnati and States china.[52] The punch bowl's inclusion among these dynastic objects suggests Mrs. Washington saw it as part of the conveyance of family identity, wealth, and status. Washington had no children of his own, but had adopted George Washington Parke Custis, the son of John Parke Custis, Martha Washington's son from her first marriage, and the boy had grown up in the presidential households and at Mount Vernon. As a teenager he had witnessed the construction of the frigate *United States* in Philadelphia with Washington, and likely would have been familiar with, if not present at, the presentation of the bowl by Truxtun.[53] Washington, who had worked hard to assist his ward in finding a profession, secured Custis an officer's commission in the Provisional Army.[54]

In the years to come, Custis touted his filial relationship to Washington and used his collection of Washington relics, the "Washington treasury," at his home, Arlington, to undergird and boost his own social and political status. Presenting himself as a gatekeeper and mediary of Washington's values, he brought out artifacts as showpieces at his entertainments.[55] The GW bowl appears to have been one of the relics that saw regular use on those occasions. Col. John N. Macomb Jr. (1811–1889) recalled how Custis used the bowl to close the nightly merriment surrounding the wedding festivities of Sydney Smith Lee in 1834. Eleanor Harris, the enslaved housekeeper at the time, likely oversaw the use of the bowl, the preparation of the punch, and its safekeeping during this time.[56] As Macomb later told it, "Every night before the party retired punch was bounteously dispensed from a punch-bowl which had belonged to General Washington. In the bottom of the bowl was a painting of a ship, the hull resting in the bottom, the mast projecting to the rim. The rule was to drink down to the hull—a rule strictly observed."[57] The ship's purpose had initially promoted one man's reputation and vision for a faster, stronger navy, but a generation after its presentation, all that was forgotten. Instead, the ship in the bowl now served as a convenient excuse to imbibe even more.

Later Travels of the GW Bowl

Custis's frequent use of the bowl made it familiar to Arlington guests and intimates of the family. Historian Benson Lossing brought the bowl to the attention of a national audience, first by spotlighting it in an article in Harper's *New Monthly Magazine* in 1853, and then in his book *Mount Vernon and Its Associations* in 1859 (fig. 19). The illustration enlarged the bowl, visually exaggerating its importance and making it appear to be half the size of the standard Pembroke table with which it was paired. Lossing's description clearly identified all of the essential elements of decoration: "It is pure white porcelain, with a deep blue border at the rim, ornamented with gilt stars and dots. In the bottom is a picture of a frigate, and on the side are the initials G. W. in gilt, upon a shield with ornamental surroundings."[58] Its fame established, thereafter the bowl could not easily pass as anything other than what it was, Washington's own punch bowl.

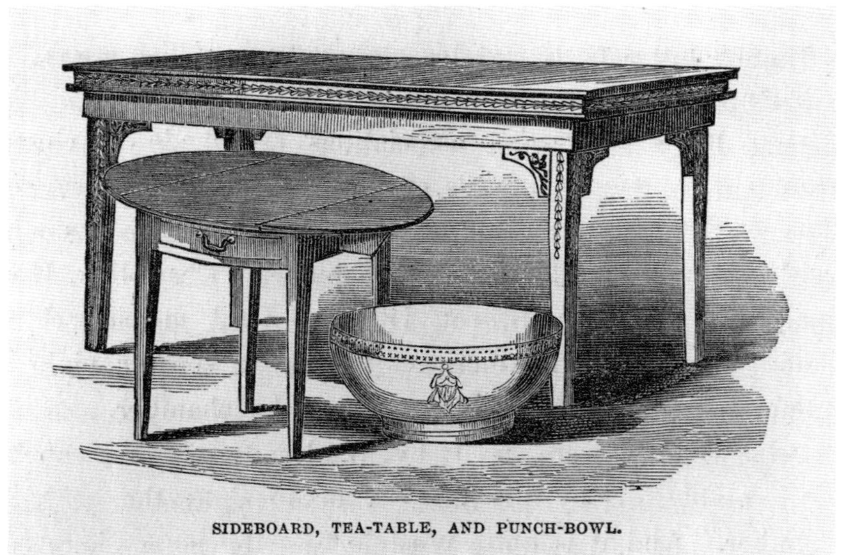

Figure 19 Sideboard, Pembroke tea table, and GW punch bowl. From Benson Lossing, *Mount Vernon and Its Associations: Descriptive, Historical, and Pictorial* (New York: W. A. Townsend & Co., 1859), p. 303. (Courtesy, Mount Vernon Ladies' Association.)

Following Custis's death in 1857, his daughter, Mary Custis Lee (1807–1873), inherited and cared for the bowl until 1861. After her husband, Robert E. Lee (1807–1870), decided to join the Confederacy that spring,

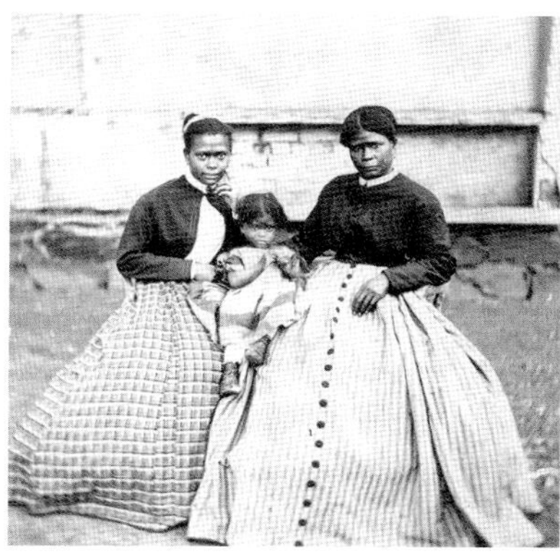

Figure 20 "General Lee's Slaves, Arlington House," believed to be Selina Gray at far right with two of her daughters, ca. 1860s. Stereograph. 3⁵⁄₃₂ x 6¹¹⁄₁₆". (Courtesy, Arlington House, The Robert E. Lee Memorial, National Park Service, ARHO 15585.)

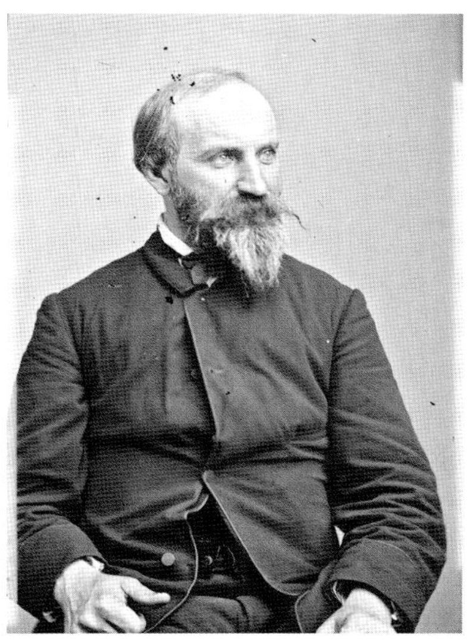

Figure 21 Caleb Lyon, ca. 1855–1865. (Brady-Handy Collection, Library of Congress.)

the United States army planned to occupy Arlington. In addition to being considered the property of a rebel, the plantation occupied a strategic position overlooking Washington, D.C. Forewarned by her husband and preparing for departure, Mary Lee had important Washington and Custis family artifacts, including the furniture, paintings, and silver, packed and sent to family and friends for safekeeping. Optimistically thinking she would return, she left behind numerous other pieces of the "Washington treasury," including the Society of the Cincinnati porcelain purchased by Washington, the States porcelain service given to Mrs. Washington, and the Defender punch bowl. She locked them in the cellar and entrusted their care to Selina Gray (1823–1907), her enslaved housekeeper (fig. 20).[59]

At some point in the seven months between the initial Union occupation of Arlington on May 28, 1861, and January 7, 1862, both the cellar and the attic were breached and the contents began to be dispersed. Selina Gray reported the burglary to General Irvin McDowell, who first officially reported to headquarters on the status of the Washington relics in his letter of January 7, 1862. McDowell explained that "last week the Hon. Caleb Lyons [*sic*], being here on a visit and learning of these facts [the burglary], expressed a wish to see this china, as having frequently been a guest of Mr. Custis he was well acquainted with everything in his possession which had belonged to General Washington."[60] A poet and acclaimed lecturer, Lyon (1822–1875) had parlayed his rhetorical talents and social connections into occasional stints of public service, serving, among other short posts, a term in the U.S. Congress from 1853 to 1855 (fig. 21). Lyon also avidly collected historical curiosities, contemporary paintings, and porcelain, and had an eye for the main chance.

McDowell reported the results of Lyon's inspection, describing the Washington relics and, for corroboration, referencing Lossing's descriptions and illustrations. As for the punch bowl: "General Washington's punch bowl, with the picture of a ship in it, . . . was here but a short time before (as I am informed by those who saw it in the cellar,) but has been stolen." It was almost certainly Gray's testimony as well as that of the other enslaved men and women still at Arlington that corroborated the initial presence of the bowl. McDowell, noting the national importance artifacts and their endangerment in the unsecured house, particularly with the "crowd of curiosity seekers constantly coming here," advocated for the transfer of the remaining relics to the Patent Office or Smithsonian.[61] The news was widely reported, highlighting Lyon's role in the discovery of the "priceless prize."[62] Lyon was asked to superintend the transfer of the objects, and on January 28, the *National Republican* reported that the relics had been "artistically arranged by Caleb Lyon" at the Patent Office.[63] While this select group of objects had been secured for the Union and posterity, a significant number of artifacts had effectively been looted, including the punch bowl, and made their way into private hands.[64] The hunt was on for those knowing enough to obtain a piece of Washington history.

Twenty years later, the bowl reappeared in the 1882 catalog of the auction of Lyon's estate, described as "Punch bowl belonging to Geo. Washington, has been carefully repaired; ornamented with his initials on the side."[65] Circumstantial evidence suggests that Lyon may have stolen the bowl outright in 1862, having had both motive and opportunity—he had been at Arlington and had been in charge of the relics around the time the bowl and several other pieces went missing, and he was an "antiquarian, vigorous and insatiable."[66] To be fair, it is also possible that the bowl had been taken prior to Lyon's arrival and inventory, and that he later hunted it down, and had no compunction about acquiring it as his own rather than returning it to the U.S. government.

Lyon's embezzlement of government funds while governor of Idaho (1864–1866), among other controversies, finally forced his retirement from public life, but along the way he had amassed a respected collection of historical bric-a-brac and porcelain. The sales of his collection, in 1876 and 1882, drew the attention of the leading Americana and porcelain collectors of the time.[67] Even though broken and repaired, Washington's punch bowl took top dollar at the 1882 auction, selling for $320 to an unnamed buyer, bested only by the paintings.[68]

Thereafter, the bowl rested in private hands, enjoying a relatively quiet existence after the tumultuous war years.[69] In the early twentieth century, the bowl descended to Major Carlos de Zafra (1882–1967), a naval architect and engineer, who could well appreciate the finely drawn rendering of the frigate. He served briefly as the curator of shipbuilding and navigation at the Museum of Science and Industry in Chicago, caring for exhibits on the development of navigation and the collection of ship models.[70] If he recognized the design of the ship in the bowl, he unfortunately left no record of it. His son, Robert de Zafra, inherited the bowl, and in a 1973 letter of inquiry to the Association shared his observations of it with then curator Christine Meadows, noting that the ship was "carefully drawn in profile, rather like a naval architect's rendering," and correctly dating the bowl based on the fifteen-star pennant.[71] Meadows confirmed the bowl's Washington history, and de Zafra generously loaned it to the Mount Vernon Ladies' Association in 1975.

The bowl's public display in Mount Vernon's museum proved fortuitous. In 1981 Evan Randolph IV, a descendant of Thomas Truxtun, visited Mount Vernon and recognized the Washington bowl as the pair to one that had descended in his family and was on display at the National Museum of the United States Navy.[72] Through Randolph's efforts, the two bowls were reunited and studied. Working together, Meadows and Captain David Long, the first executive director of the Naval Historical Foundation, rediscovered the source of the ship design in Truxtun's book. The next year, Susan Detweiler published the story of the two bowls in her seminal work, *George Washington's Chinaware*, placing it in the context of Washington's relationship with ceramics, his consumer choices, and the gifts he received.[73] In 2018 the late Robert de Zafra and his wife, Dr. Julia M. P. Quagliata de Zafra, gave the bowl to Mount Vernon in furtherance of their abiding interest in preserving the history of the United States. As a result, their gift enabled further study of the bowl and this article.

Conclusion

Now that it is properly situated against the backdrop of Truxtun's own career and the historical context of the late 1790s, the Washington bowl can be seen more clearly as a calculated political gift, not just a neutral decorative object. The twin bowls were created at a time of great uncertainty, for Truxtun personally and for the nation as a whole, when the concept of a standing navy was controversial and yet to be decided. In commissioning the bowls and giving one to the president and commander in chief, Truxtun seems to have been using every means he could to sway or solidify Washington's opinion, to gain support for his own career and the establishment of the U.S. Navy. With the death of Washington and the removal of the bowl from its prominence on Washington's table, Truxtun's gift lost its original influence, and instead became an artifact of a fascinating period of American history. The ship in the bowls—the result of Truxtun's concept, Fox's drawing, and a Chinese porcelain painter's skill—ultimately outlived Truxtun's short-term personal goals and endowed both bowls with a timeless patriotic appeal that transcended the political maneuvering of the early republic.

ACKNOWLEDGMENTS This article would not have been possible without the joint support of the Naval Historical Foundation (NHF) and the Mount Vernon Ladies' Association (MVLA). At the NHF, Rear Admiral Edward Masso and Dr. David Winkler enthusiastically encouraged the reunion and analysis of the bowls at Mount Vernon. Mark Weber and Wesley Schwenk of the National Museum of the United States Navy assisted with our research and ensured that the TT bowl was transported with special care, while Christian Higgins and Megan Casey of the Navy Department Library enabled us to examine copies of Truxtun's book and provided measurements of the original engraving. At Mount Vernon, Dr. Susan Schoelwer, Adam Erby, and Mary Thompson shared their own research and provided important feedback and critiques. Samantha Snyder filled countless interlibrary loans and tracked down obscure sources, and Dawn Bonner searched for and scanned images. Lori Trusheim conserved the GW bowl, and Linda Landry captured clear microscope views of the alterations on both bowls. Dr. Erich Uffelmann of Washington and Lee University generously donated his time and expertise to perform XRF analysis on the bowls' enamels. Finally, we are deeply grateful to Ron Fuchs for encouraging the writing of this article, and to him, Hannah Boettcher, and Dr. Cassandra Good for sharing their extensive research and knowledge.

1. Eugene S. Ferguson, *Truxtun of the* Constellation*: The Life of Commodore Thomas Truxtun, U.S. Navy, 1755–1822* (1956; reprint, Baltimore, Md.: Johns Hopkins University Press, 2000), p. 171.

2. The most demonstrative example of this is Truxtun's inclusion in the gallery of portraits of distinguished Americans organized by Joseph Delaplaine in Philadelphia. *Brooklyn before the Bridge: American Paintings from the Long Island Historical Society* (New York: Brooklyn Museum, 1982), p. 86. Bass Otis's portrait of Truxtun shows him wearing the badge of the Society of the Cincinnati, to which Truxtun was admitted as an honorary member in New York on July 4, 1800, following his naval victories. John Schuyler, *The Institution of the Society of the Cincinnati* (New York: Douglas Taylor, 1886), p. 85.

3. In the collection of Winterthur Museum, among others, are examples of the Liverpool jugs and mugs (2009.023.012, 2009.023.009, 1968.0083), the Staffordshire blue transferware American Naval Heroes series (1958.1842), and cloak pins (labeled Truxtun but bearing the image of Lord Nelson (1965.2407.002). For the hats and ribbons, see the advertisement of Benjamin S. Judah & Brothers, *Commercial Advertiser*, New York, January 6, 1800, p. 1, and Ferguson, *Truxtun of the* Constellation, p. 171.

4. By naval tradition, the title "commodore" is assumed by an officer assigned to command more than one ship. Although an officer's rank for pay purposes might be captain, commanding a squadron of ships, as Truxtun did during the Quasi-War, entitled him to be addressed as commodore while in command and after relinquishing command as an honorary title.

5. A commissioning pennant is a long streamer in some version of the national colors of the navy that flies it, which serves as the distinguishing mark of a commissioned vessel in many navies. The pennant is flown at all times as long as a ship is in commissioned status, except when a flag officer or civilian official is embarked and flies his personal flag in its place.

6. David Sanctuary Howard, "The Sailing Ship on Chinese Porcelain: A Brief Survey, 1700–1850," *Catalogue of the Ellis Memorial Antiques Show* (Boston: Ellis Memorial Antiques Show, November 1977), pp. 45–54; Ron Fuchs II, "Ahoy! Ship Bowls in Pottery and Porcelain," paper presented at Winterthur Ceramics Conference, April 16, 2010.

7. Thomas Truxtun, *Remarks, Instructions and Examples Relating to the Latitude and Longitude; etc. etc. etc.* (Philadelphia: T. Dobson, 1794).

8. "Reunion at Mount Vernon," *Mount Vernon Ladies' Association Annual Report* (1975), pp. 18–23; "Family Reunions," *Pull Together: Naval Historical Foundation Newsletter* 21, no. 2 (Fall 1981): 1.

9. George Washington to the Marquis de Lafayette, 15 November 1781, *The Writings of George Washington from the Original Manuscript Sources 1745–1799, 39* vols. (Washington, D.C.: U.S. GPO, 1937), 23:341. See also "From George Washington to Marie-Joseph-Paul-Yves-Roch-Gilbert du Motier, Marquis de Lafayette, 15 November 1781," Founders Online, National Archives, https://founders.archives.gov/documents/Washington/99-01-02-07408.

10. The details of Truxtun's life and career are taken from Ferguson, *Truxtun of the* Constellation, the seminal biography on Truxton.

11. Thomas Truxtun, *Reply of Commodore Truxtun to an Attack Made on Him in the National Intelligencer in June, 1806* (Philadelphia, 1806), p. 25.

12. Ferguson, *Truxtun of the* Constellation, pp. 60–99; Jean Gordon Lee, *Philadelphians and the China Trade 1784–1844* (Philadelphia: Philadelphia Museum of Art, 1984), pp. 21, 28; Jean McClure Mudge, *Chinese Export Porcelain for the American Trade: 1785–1835* (Wilmington: University of Delaware Press, 1962), pp. 98–100. Numerous newspaper advertisements attest to the variety of cargoes he brought back for merchants. See, e.g., advertisement for Mordecai Lewis & Co., *Independent Gazetteer*, Philadelphia, May 23, 1787, p. 3, and advertisement for Meeker, Cochran & Co., *Dunlap's American Daily Advertiser*, Philadelphia, April 23, 1794, p. 2.

13. Tobias Lear to George Washington, 12 February 1794, *The Papers of George Washington Digital Edition*, 13 February 1794 entry, Tobias Lear account, 4R, Ledger C, George Washington Ledger of Accounts, Lloyd W. Smith Collection, Morristown National Historical Park.

14. Dudley W. Knox, ed., *Naval Documents Relating to the United States Wars with the Barbary Powers.* Vol. 1: *Naval Operations, Including Diplomatic Background from 1785 through 1801* (Washington, D.C.: GPO, 1939), pp. 69–70.

15. The construction of the frigates is ably described at length in Ian Toll, *Six Frigates: The Epic Founding of the U.S. Navy* (New York: W. W. Norton & Co., 2006).

16. Joshua Humphreys to Robert Morris, 6 January 1793, Joshua Humphreys Papers: Letter Book 1793–1797, Historical Society of Philadelphia.

17. Joshua Humphreys to Thomas Truxtun, n.d. [late 1794–early 1795], p. 69, Joshua Humphreys Papers: Letter Book 1793–1797, Historical Society of Philadelphia.

18. Truxtun, *Remarks, Instructions and Examples*, Appendix, pp. i–ix and accompanying plate.

19. Thomas Truxtun to Josiah Fox, 21 November 1794, Josiah Fox Papers, Manuscript Collection MH-11, Phillips Library, Peabody-Essex Museum, Salem, Mass.

20. National Archives and Records Administration, Record Group 45, Naval Records Collection of the Office of Naval Records and Library, Records of the War Department, 1790–1831, Letters Sent Concerning Naval Matters, October 1790–June 1798, entry 374 (M739).

21. George Washington's copy of Truxtun's book, signed by Washington on the flyleaf, is currently in the collection of the Boston Athenaeum.

22. Timothy Pickering to George Washington, 14 March 1795, *The Papers of George Washington Digital Edition*. Those first five names described the new republic's unique attributes, with "Constellation" referring to the Continental Congress's Flag Act of 1777: "Resolved, That the flag of the thirteen United States be thirteen stripes, alternate red and white; that the union be thirteen stars, white in a blue field, representing a new constellation." Worthington Chauncey Ford, ed., *Journals of the Continental Congress 1774–1789*, 34 vols. (Washington, D.C.: GPO, 1904–1937), 8:464.

23. The U.S. Navy did not commission a ship with the name *Defender* for nearly 200 years, until September 1989, when mine countermeasures ship MCM-2 joined the fleet.

24. Knox, *Naval Documents Related to the United States Wars with the Barbary Powers*, 1:128.

25. Thomas Truxtun to George Washington, 4 February 1796, *The Papers of George Washington Digital Edition*.

26. Thomas Truxtun, *Instructions, Signals, and Explanations, offered for the United States Fleet* (Baltimore, Md.: John Hayes, 1797). The only known extant copy, Truxtun's personal copy, is in the Navy Department Library.

27. While the historic ship currently on display in Baltimore's Inner Harbor is indeed the former USS *Constellation*, it is not the 1797 frigate commanded by Truxtun but rather the 1854 sloop-of-war with a proud history of its own in antislavery patrols and Civil War service. For a full history, see Dana M. Wegner, *Fouled Anchors: The* Constellation *Question Answered*, Technical and Administrative Services Department Research and Development Report (Bethesda, Md.: David Taylor Research Center, September 1991); available online at https://www.navsea.navy.mil/Portals/103/Documents/NSWC_Carderock/fouled_anchors-1.pdf.

28. Knox, *Naval Documents Relating to the United States Wars with the Barbary Powers*, 1:133.

29. "From John Adams to Benjamin Stoddert, 22 April 1799," Founders Online, National Archives, https://founders.archives.gov/documents/Adams/99-02-02-3453.

30. Edward Savage to George Washington, 17 June 1799, *The Papers of George Washington Digital Edition*.

31. Rina Prentice, *A Celebration of the Sea: The Decorative Art Collection of the National Maritime Museum* (London: The Stationary Office, 1994), pp. 8–10; Bernard Watney and Caroline Roberts, "Liverpool Porcelain Ship Bowls in Blue and White," *Transactions of the English Ceramic Circle* 15, pt. 1 (1993): 1–23.

32. Quoted in Christiaan Jörg, *Porcelain and the Dutch China Trade* (The Hague: Martinus Nijhoff, 1982), p. 128.

33. Philip Chadwick Foster Smith, *The Empress of China* (Philadelphia: Philadelphia Maritime Museum, 1984), p. 294.

34. William Sargent, *Treasures of Chinese Export Ceramics from the Peabody Essex Museum* (New Haven, Conn.: Yale University Press, 2012), pp. 401–2; Robert E. Peabody, *The Log of the Grand Turks* (Cambridge, Mass.: Riverside Press, 1926), 94. On Pinqua's career, see Paul A. Van Dyke, "Yang Pinqua, Merchant of Canton and Macao, 1747–1795," *Revista de Culture* (2020): 62–89.

35. David Sanctuary Howard, *New York and the China Trade* (New York: New-York Historical Society, 1984), pp. 114–15; Mary E. Nealy, "A Remarkable Old Punch Bowl," *Clay Worker* 31, no. 5 (May 1899): 429.

36. "From George Washington to the Ladies of Trenton, 21 April 1789," Founders Online, National Archives, https://founders.archives.gov/documents/Washington/05-02-02-0095.

37. *Boston Gazette*, 26 October 1789, cited in Timothy H. Breen, *George Washington's Journey* (New York: Simon & Schuster, 2016), p. 130; "From George Washington to the Officials of Charleston, 3 May 1791," Founders Online, National Archives, https://founders.archives.gov/documents/Washington/05-08-02-0117.

38. "To George Washington from William Heth, 13 July 1798," Founders Online, National Archives, https://founders.archives.gov/documents/Washington/06-02-02-0316; "To George Washington from John Trumbull, 18 September 1798," Founders Online, National Archives, https://founders.archives.gov/documents/Washington/06-03-02-0006.

39. Ronald W. Fuchs II with David S. Howard, *Made in China: Export Porcelain from the Leo and Doris Hodroff Collection at Winterthur* (Winterthur, Del.: Henry Francis du Pont Winterthur Museum, 2005), p. 31.

40. "Advertisement." *Providence* (R.I.) *Gazette* 41, no. 2106, May 12, 1804: [3]. *Readex: America's Historical Newspapers*. https://infoweb-newsbank-com.ezproxy.wlu.edu/apps/readex/doc?p=EANX&docref=image/v2%3A10380B58EB4A4298%40EANX-1056B5A3F0ACE334%402380089-1056B5A430002EEE%402-1056B5A4E6F5C343%40Advertisement.

41. Paul van Dyke and Maria Kar-wing Mok, *Images of the Canton Factories 1760–1822: Reading History in Art* (Hong Kong: Hong Kong University Press, 2015), p. xvii.

42. I am indebted to William Sargent, Dr. Christiann Jörg, Angela Howard, and Ron Fuchs for their expert review and opinion on this case. XRF analysis of the areas on each bowl that had been repainted, conducted by Dr. Erich Uffelman of Washington and Lee University, confirmed that there was no significant difference in the composition of the gilding used on the lettering of the TT bowl or on the enamel of the GW bowl in those areas.

43. While the exact date of the presentation cannot be determined, it seems most likely to have occurred prior to the September 1799 dinner. Truxtun could not have anticipated that final meeting with enough time to order the bowl for the occasion. The first documentary mention of the bowl is Martha Washington's September 1800 draft of her will.

44. Susan Gray Detweiler, *George Washington's Chinaware* (New York: Harry N. Abrams, 1982), pp. 67–76.

45. The goblets remain unlocated. Dwight P. Lanmon et al., *John Frederick Amelung: Early American Glassmaker* (Corning, N.Y.: Corning Museum of Glass, 1990), p. 30; "Extract of a letter from a gentleman in Alexandria, to the edition hereof, dated March 28, 1789," *Pennsylvania Packet*, 10 April 1789; "From George Washington to Thomas Jefferson, 13 February 1789," Founders Online, National Archives, https://founders.archives.gov/documents/Washington/05-01-02-0219.

46. Contemporary accounts indicated that President Washington typically had punch served on significant holidays during his presidency. Abigail Adams referenced the Washingtons serving punch to a large number of guests on July 4 during the presidency, while Senator William Maclay mentioned a bowl of punch as part of the New Year's Day refreshments. "Abigail Adams to Mary Smith Cranch, 23 June 1797," Founders Online, National Archives, https://founders.archives.gov/documents/Adams/04-12-02-0103. Senator William Maclay, as quoted in William Spohn Baker, *Washington after the Revolution, 1784–1799* (Philadelphia, Pa.: J. B. Lippincott, 1898), p. 204. I am indebted for these references to Mary Thompson and her research on holidays and foodways in the Washington household.

47. Chris Neuzil, Lenny Vaccaro, and Todd Creekman, "Captain Truxtun's Congressional Medal," *Numismatist* 120, no. 2 (February 2007): 32–41.

48. Ferguson, *Truxtun of the* Constellation, p. 224.

49. Truxtun, *Reply of Commodore Truxtun to an Attack Made on Him*, p. 26.

50. As quoted in Katherine M. Beekman, "A Colonial Capital: Perth Amboy, and its Church Warden, James Parker," *Proceedings of the New Jersey Historical Society* n.s., 1/III (1918):14.

51. The TT bowl was exhibited at the Naval Historical Foundation's Truxtun-Decatur Museum at historic Decatur House near the White House in downtown Washington, D.C., and later was placed on loan to the Navy in the National Museum of the U.S. Navy at the Washington Navy Yard in southeast D.C., where it remains displayed today. Naval Historical Foundation Accession Card # 49-36-1. Chinese porcelain bowl with "TT" monogram for Thomas Truxtun, donated 28 November 1949 from Mr. "Weatherow Bendridge." [actually Mr. Richard Wetherill Benbridge]; Information on Thomas Truxtun's porcelain bowl provided by Mr. Richard Benbridge Wetherill of Lafayette, Indiana, on 23 January 1940. Naval History and Heritage Command's (NHHC) ZB file in Navy Department Library; Maria S. B. Chance, *A Chronicle of the Family of Edward F. Beale of Philadelphia* (Haverford, Pa.: 1943), p. 78.

52. John C. Fitzpatrick, ed., *The Last Will and Testament of George Washington . . . the Last Will and Testament of Martha Washington* (Mount Vernon, Va.: Mount Vernon Ladies' Association, 1992), p. 56.

53. George Washington Parke Custis recalled visiting the Philadelphia Navy Yard in an 1844 letter to a descendant of naval architect Joshua Humphreys. George Washington's diary mentions visiting the yard on at least one occasion, January 2, 1796. See Henry Humphreys et al., "Who Built the First American Navy?," *Pennsylvania Magazine of History and Biography* 40, no. 4 (1916): 390–91; Diary entry: 2 January 1796, *The Papers of George Washington Digital Edition*. https://rotunda.upress.virginia.edu/founders/GEWN-01-06-02-0005-0001-0002.

54. "From George Washington to James McHenry, 14 December 1798," Founders Online, National Archives, https://founders.archives.gov/documents/Washington/06-03-02-0181.

55. For a cogent analysis of George Washington Parke Custis's use of social and cultural capital, and his conscious crafting of the Washington legacy as well as his own identity as a child of Mount Vernon, see Cassandra Good, "Washington Family Fortune: Lineage and

Capital in Nineteenth-Century America," *Early American Studies* (Winter 2020): 90–133; and Seth Bruggeman, "'More than Ordinary Patriotism': Living History in the Memory Work of George Washington Parke Custis," in *Remembering the Revolution: Memory, History, and Nation Making from Independence to the Civil War*, edited by Michael A. McDonnell et al. (Amherst: University of Massachusetts Press, 2013), pp. 127–43.

56. Email correspondence with Cassandra Good, 25 January 2022; and Mary Grassick, "Historic Furnishings Report: Arlington House" (Washington, D.C.: National Park Service: 2016), pp. 41–42.

57. A. L. Long, *The Memoirs of Robert E. Lee* (New York: J. M. Stoddart & Co., 1886), p. 38.

58. Benson Lossing, *Harper's New Monthly Magazine* 40, no. 8 (September 1853): 440. The bowl is also mentioned in an obituary for Custis: "The Late G. W. P. Custis," *Harper's Weekly* (October 24, 1857): 68.

59. Grassick, "Historic Furnishings Report: Arlington House," p. 33.

60. "Mount Vernon Relics," Report, House of Representatives, 41st Congress, 2d Session, Report #36, p. 2.

61. "Mount Vernon Relics," Report, House of Representatives, 41st Congress, 2d Session, Report #36, pp. 1–2.

62. "Relics of the Washington Family," *The Press*, Philadelphia, January 14, 1862.

63. "The Washington Relics," *National Republican*, Washington, D.C., January 28, 1862.

64. These included a Custis family Bible, a Martha Washington dress, and numerous pieces of Society of Cincinnati porcelain. Ruth Preston Lee, "Mrs. General Lee's Attempts to Regain Her Possessions after the Civil War," *Arlington Historical Society Magazine* 6 (1978): 28–35; T. Michael Miller, "The Mystery Surrounding G. W. P. Custis' Painting of George Washington at Yorktown," *Alexandria Chronicle* 6, no. 4 (Fall 1998): 1–11.

65. George A. Leavitt & Co., *Catalogue of porcelains, and various objects of art, furniture, etc. . . . the whole belonging to the estate of the late Governor Caleb Lyon . . .* (New York: George A. Leavitt & Co., 1882), lot 17, p. 12 (Washington Library, Mount Vernon, Virginia).

66. "Relics of the Washington Family," *The Press*, Philadelphia, January 14, 1862.

67. Alice Morse Earle cited the selling prices at the Lyon sales as the benchmark for china prices in the late nineteenth century. See Alice Morse Earle, *China Collecting in America* (New York: Charles Scribner's Sons, 1892), pp. 124, 203, 239, 254, 346; and James Grant Wilson, "About Bric-à-Brac," *Art Journal* n.s., 4 (1878): 314.

68. "Art Objects at Auction: Sale of the Caleb Lyon Collection of Porcelains, Bric-a-Brac, and Paintings," *New York Times*, January 26, 1882.

69. A Mary Hathaway of New Bedford, Massachusetts, owned the bowl in 1899. This was likely Mary B Hathaway (1841–1916), daughter of William H. Hathaway Jr. (1798–1885). Upon her death, the bowl passed to her friend Emma de Zafra Roderick (d. 1930), and thence to her son, Major Carlos de Zafra. In 1934 antique dealer Charles Woolsey Lyon (no direct relation to Caleb), acting as agent for the owner, offered to sell the bowl to the Mount Vernon Ladies' Association for $1,200. Operating with limited funds due to the Depression, the MVLA declined. See Memorandum of C. W. Lyon, 15 February 1934; Letter of C. W. Lyon to Miss Annie B. Jennings, 15 February 1934; Robert de Zafra to Christine Meadows, 28 April 1973; Meadows to de Zafra, 20 May 1973, and de Zafra to Meadows, 15 June 1973, Curatorial File for W-2662. I am indebted to Dr. Susan Schoelwer for her genealogical research identifying Mary Hathaway.

70. S. M. O'Connor, "Who was Major Carlos de Zafra?," In the Garden City blog, https://inthegardencity.com/2018/04/24/who-was-major-carlos-de-zafra-by-s-m-oconnor/#_ftn2.

71. Robert de Zafra to Christine Meadows, 28 April 1973, Mount Vernon Curatorial File for W-2662.

72. "Family Reunions," *Pull Together: Naval Historical Foundation Newsletter* 21, no. 2 (Fall 1981): 1.

73. Detweiler, *George Washington's Chinaware*, pp. 149–53.

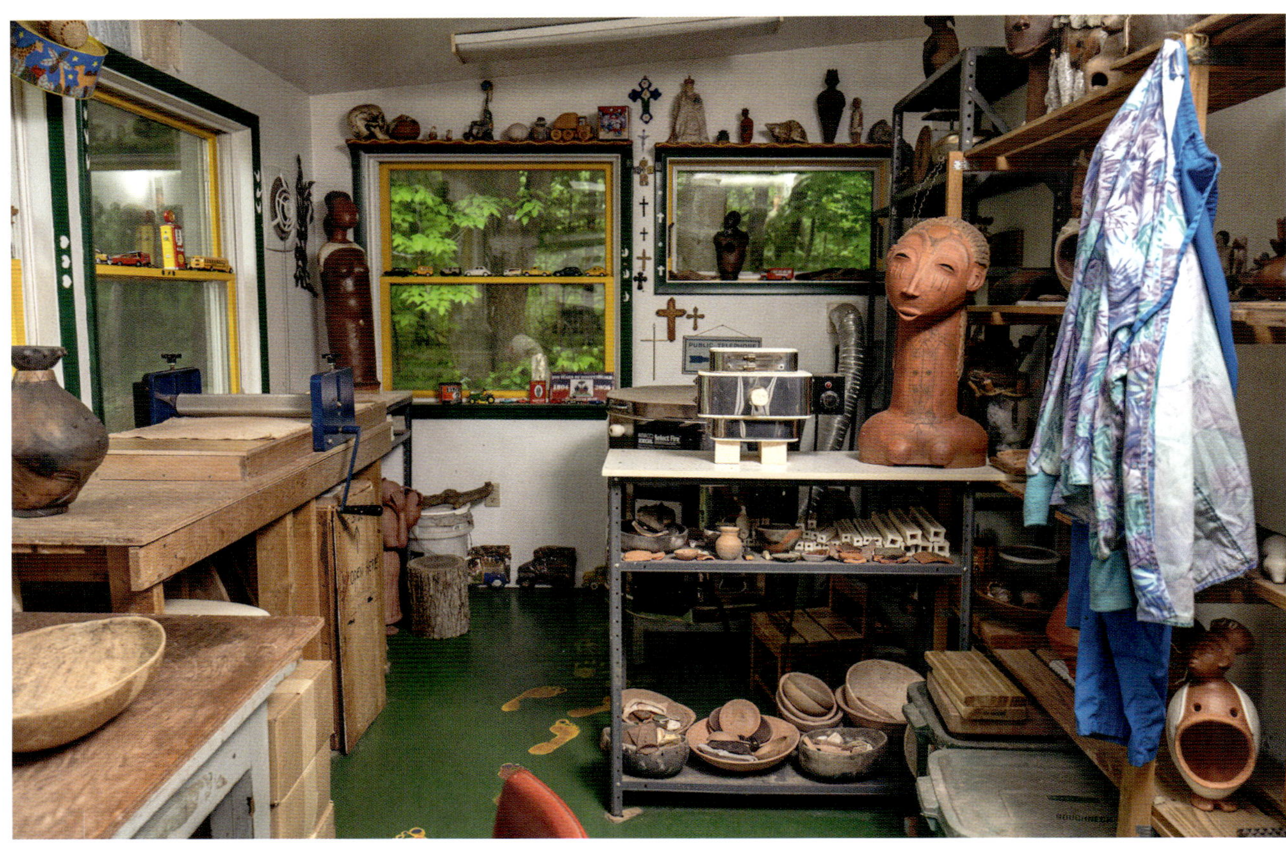

Figure 1 Studio of Babette Wainwright, Madison, Wisconsin, 2022. (Unless otherwise noted, all photography by Dakota Mace.)

R. Ruthie Dibble

Family Reunion: The Clay Sculptures of Babette Wainwright

▼ FOR MANY ARTISTS, the studio is a revealing accretion of lifelong inspirations, experimental processes, and future trajectories. This biographical quality is especially true for the artist Babette Wainwright (b. 1952), whose studio at her home in Madison, Wisconsin, is richly layered with memorabilia, artworks, tools, and materials from a decades-long process of exploring her Haitian identity through the medium of clay.

The space is anchored by a wall of handbuilt wooden shelves holding many of Wainwright's most personally meaningful work. Each earthenware sculpture is intimate and meditative, combining the warm earthenware materiality of utilitarian pots from her childhood in Haiti, the aesthetics of Taíno pottery, and female figures embodying Haitian culture and spirituality (fig. 1). Handmade tools and molds, as well as clay ready to be used, are carefully stacked and arranged around her workbench; large windows lined with keepsakes from her travels back to Haiti and elsewhere frame views of her kiln and garden (fig. 2).

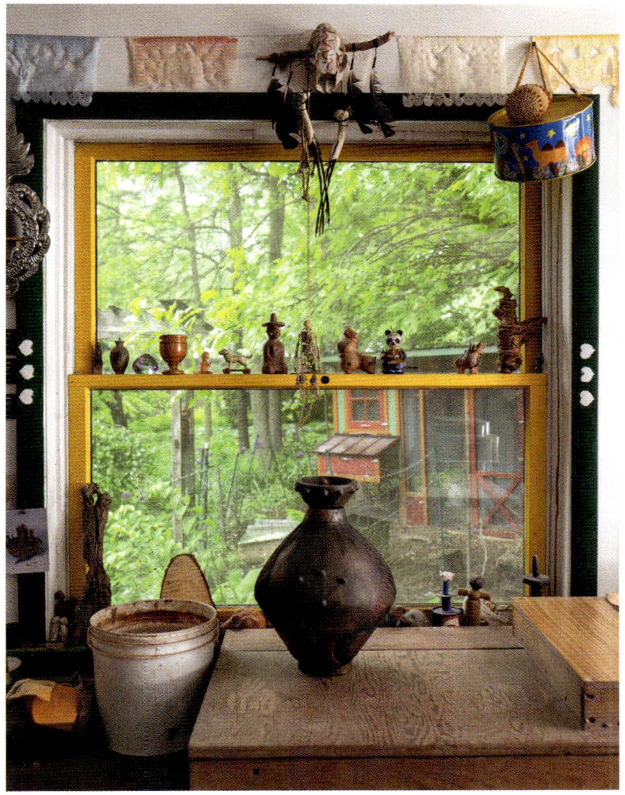

Figure 2 Studio of Babette Wainwright, Madison, Wisconsin, 2022.

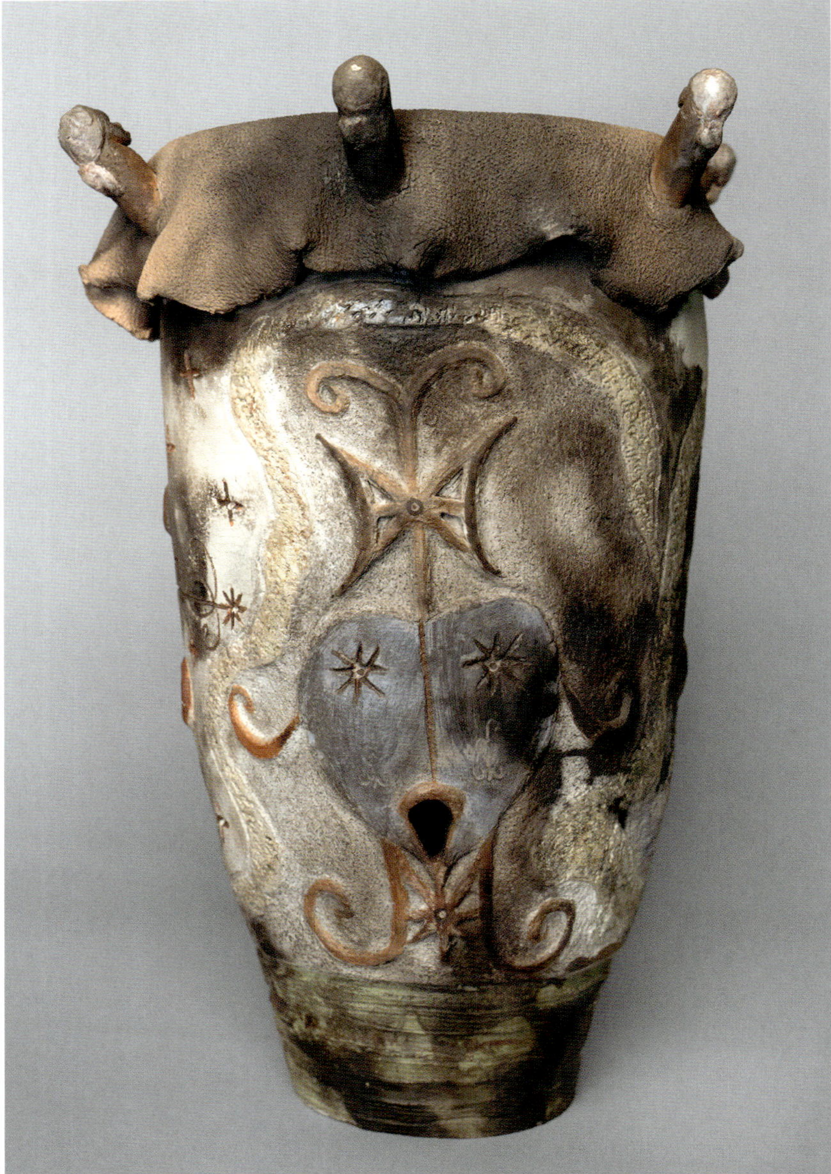

Figure 3 Babette Wainwright, *Night Whispers*, Madison, Wisconsin, 1999. Commercial clay and pigments. H. 19".

This neat, spare space reflects the values Wainwright absorbed in her childhood from her mother, who would remind the budding artist that the *tres cher* art supplies imported to Port-au-Prince from France required great care. Wainwright's studio is still marked by conscientious caretaking of the physical environment, which extends into each artwork she makes and the African diasporic experiences they embody. This maternal ethos is fitting, because Wainwright has always believed that her work in clay is "a family reunion," a creative calling to conjure familial beings and belonging into the often lonely and uprooted spaces of her diasporic experience. In April 2022 I joined Wainwright in her studio, to explore why clay is her chosen medium, and how the milestone works that live in her studio illuminate her deeply personal and innovative ceramic practice.

The Journey

Wainwright will never sell *Night Whispers* (fig. 3), a coil-built clay vessel in the tapering shape of a Boula, the smallest of the Rada drums, that sits on a shelf behind her workbench. In its materials, *Night Whispers* is an outlier dating to the very beginning of Wainwright's ceramic career when she was an MFA student in ceramics at the University of Wisconsin—it is the last work she made with commercial clay. And yet, because it sets forth the spiritual landscape of the artist's life, *Night Whispers* is a "self portrait." The title nestles us within her intergenerational memory of Haiti and conveys her intentions for the work. As Wainwright explains, "Night whispers is the time in Haiti when the work is done and you gather together on the terrace and you tell stories . . . ghost stories, stories with a moral, and any Haitian, any diaspora person, who carries on the culture, is telling sacred stories of your people, your sense of morality, your sense of history, of your history."[1] For Wainwright, these stories are "about the passage, leaving one for the other; journeys across geographies and through the changes of life."

On *Night Whispers*, the pegs of the Boula take on the form of *manbo* (Vodou priestesses), identifiable by the white handkerchiefs on their heads.

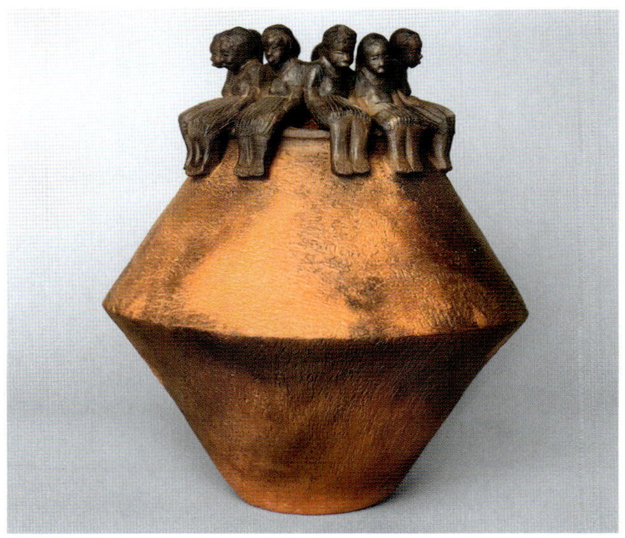

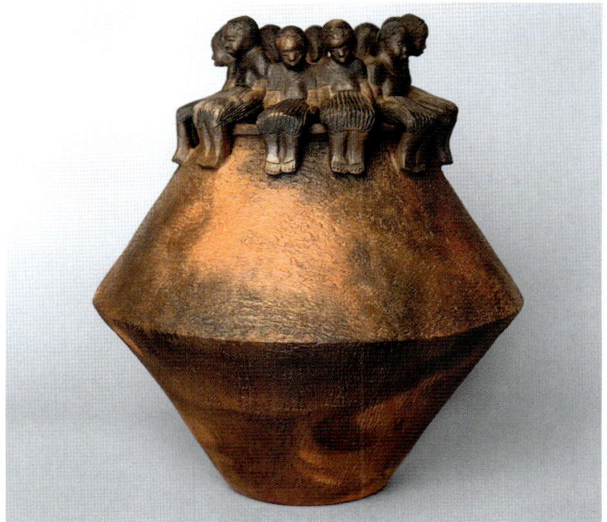

Figure 4 Babette Wainwright, *Prayer Circle*, Madison, Wisconsin, 2021. Low-fired earthenware and pigments. H. 12".

The gathering of *manbo* figures remains an ongoing theme in Wainwright's work. In her vessel *Prayer Circle* (fig. 4), the *manbo* Rada-drumming calls on ancestral spirits—*lwa*—for their aid, instruction, and special powers; in Wainwright's words, "the drum is the storyteller" in Haitian culture. Rada drums are often carved and painted with the vèvè, or religious symbols that also call forth the *lwa* (fig. 5).[2] On the surface of Wainwright's drum are the vèvè of the *lwa* who have shaped her life, most fundamentally Erzulie, embodiment of love and women, an overwhelmingly creative force who often claims gay and queer artists.[3] Wainwright's Erzulie vèvè is rubbed with blue and red pigments and contains the only opening in *Night Whispers*. That hole evokes the boundlessness of this *lwa's* maternal love: "She's a heart and she bleeds; she bleeds love, she bleeds sadness, she is the ulti-

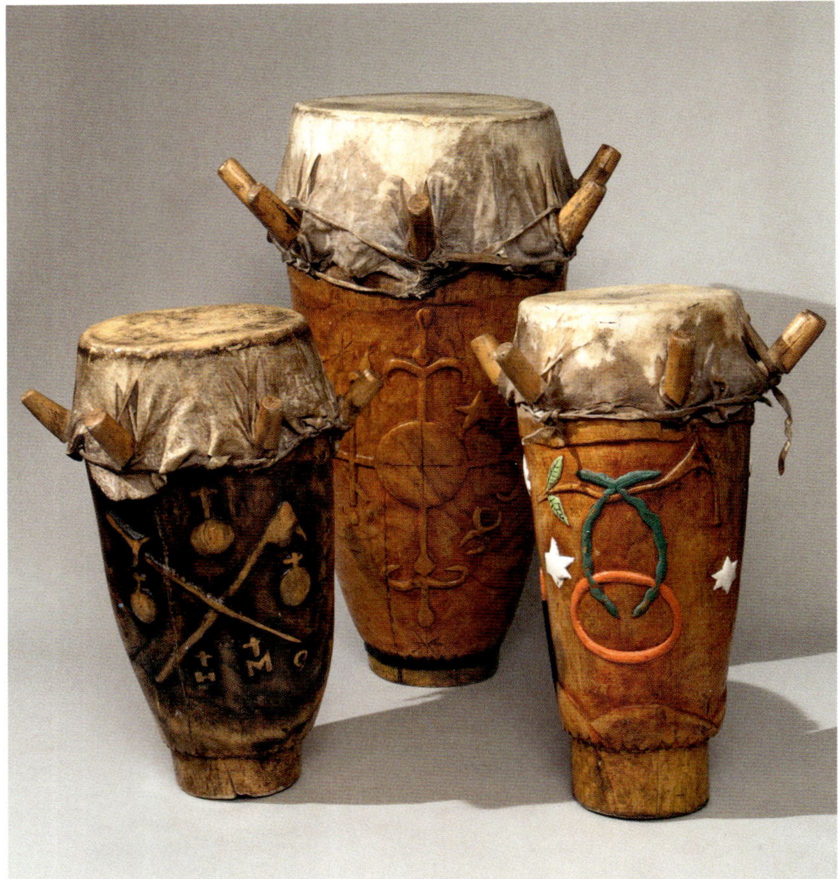

Figure 5 Unidentified Haitian artist, Maman, Segon, and Boula (Vodou drum set) with *vèvè*, circa 1960. Haitian hardwoods and cowhide. H. of tallest 31½". (Courtesy of Duke University, Sacred Arts of the Black Atlantic.) Dr. J. Lorand Matory, Lawrence Richardson Distinguished Professor of Cultural Anthropology at Duke University, purchased this drum set from a Voudouizan in Boston in 2008.

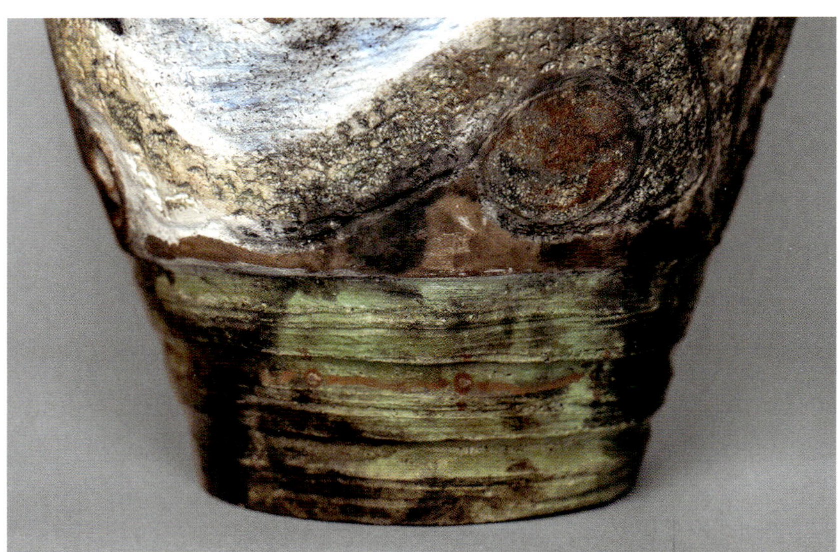

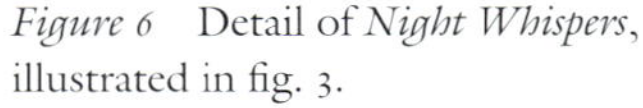

Figure 6 Detail of *Night Whispers*, illustrated in fig. 3.

mate mother." Through her paternal grandfather, Alexandre Wainwright, a lawyer and *Vodouisant* (practitioner of Vodou) who was also her godfather, Wainwright became an initiate of Erzulie minutes after she was baptized in the Catholic faith, when he carried her straight from the church to the *ounfò* (Vodou temple).

On *Night Whispers*, the sailboat *vèvè* of Agwé, the *lwa* who rules over the sea, and the mast *vèvè* of Badé, the *lwa* of wind and "keeper of the four directions," emerge from a matte background carved in shallow relief and burnished and pigmented. They are enwrapped by the scaly bodies of Ayida and Dumballa, the water serpents that represent life and death, man and woman, and that have followed and protected Wainwright and her ancestors across many journeys. The *vèvè* float over a green, mountainous landscape that wraps around the base of *Night Whispers* (fig. 6). The iconography of *Night Whispers* looks back at the culture and spirituality that shaped Wainwright, her journey into the social and psychological space of becoming a Haitian refugee, and her awakening to ceramics as her chosen medium. This flux in time runs through Wainwright and into her work. As sociologist Sarah Daynes has observed, "Events that produce meaning, in particular when they have not been 'resolved,' never stop 'surviving'; in the case of the African diaspora, the past of slavery still makes sense today, as if the slave ships were still crossing the Atlantic each day, over and over again. Indeed, memory is not a linear phenomenon."[4] Likewise, Wainwright's artistic exploration of African diasporic experiences are nonlinear narratives, *Night Whispers* included: "This whole thing is me, she has stories to tell, she's telling you stories, all you have to do is listen."

Beginnings

Babette Wainwright's explorations of her personal history with clay begins with a small, lidded vessel she made, easily overlooked among her larger sculptural work (fig. 7). Resting on the sunny yellow muntin of the window above her workbench, the object is a miniature *kanari*, the traditional,

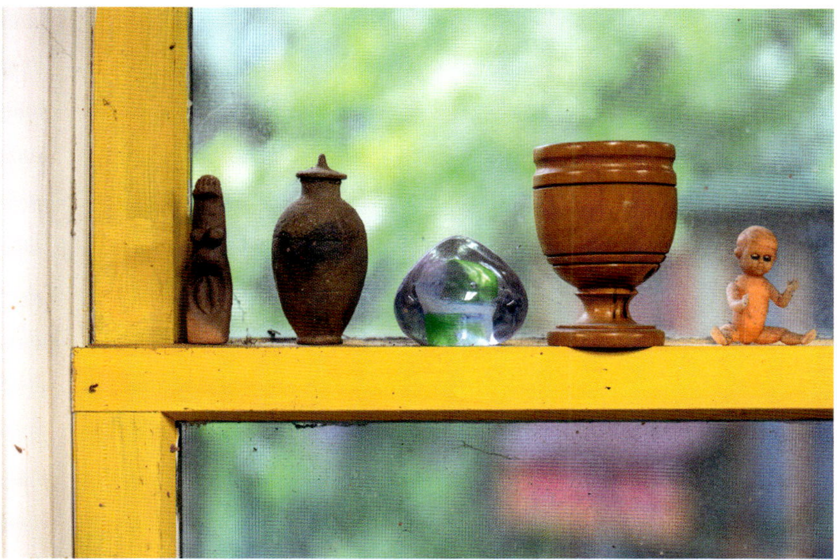

Figure 7 Detail of Babette Wainwright's studio window with miniature *kanari*, 2022.

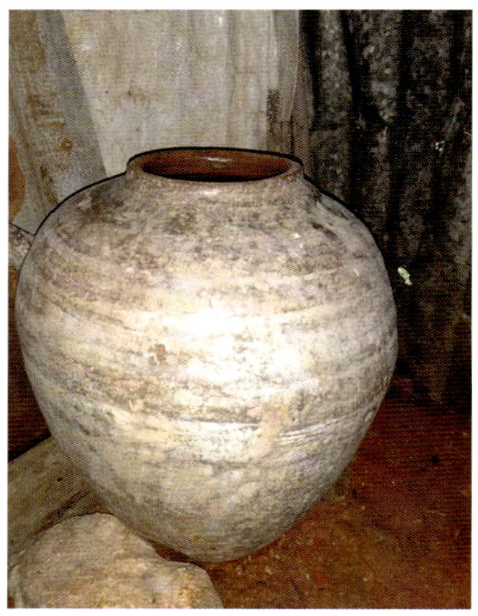

Figure 8 *Kanari* in the kitchen of the Paul Family Home, 2023, Désormeau neighborhood, Dame-Marie, Haiti. Digital photograph. (Courtesy of Culcoit Paul.)

coil-built earthenware urns made in Haiti to hold water (fig. 8). If, as the literary theorist Susan Stewart has observed, "the miniature is a world of arrested time," this small work makes ever present the time of Babette's childhood in Haiti in the 1950–60s, when earthenware *kanari* were ubiquitous and a necessary part of Haitian foodways and spirituality.[5] Wainwright and her family lived in a "cute little house in a tamarind grove," where the kitchen, in keeping with Haitian domestic architecture, was a small, separate structure at the back of the house. There, the family stored their *kanari*, which was kept full of cool, clear water by the family's cook. To the young Wainwright, the large storage vessel was enchanting. It "felt ancient and magical because the water that was kept in it was always cool, and you could talk into it and hear your voice echoing back." Even then, Wainwright sensed a connection between clay vessels and the women of Haiti. The fulsome, echoing vessel felt "like a big woman."

Wainwright would also encounter *kanari* and other island-made vessels in Haiti's Vodou religion. She has noted that in Haiti ceramics are "ritual objects; I didn't grow up seeing things like that as artwork." Indeed, as the scholar Roberto Strongman has observed, "Unlike the Western idea of the body as the enclosure of the soul, in Haiti Vodou, the soul is an open vessel that finds metaphoric and aesthetic expression in seemingly utilitarian vessels," not only the *kanari* but also the *kwi* (calbash bowl) and *govi* (a ceremonial jar or bottle made of red clay).[6] Indeed, the *badji* in any *ounfò*, or altar in any Vodou temple, holds a "profusion of pottery" organized in tiers and clusters, and ceramic vessels are often at the heart of Vodou ceremonies, including offerings to Marassa Jumeaux, the divine twins of Vodou, who are offered *manje marassa*, or twins' food, from conjoined coiled pots symbolizing their twinned identities (fig. 9).[7] This crucial metaphor for the soul binds the Haitian diaspora to their Dahomean ancestors in West Africa, a history explored in relation to Wainwright's work by Kyrah Malika Daniels, who has rightly identified the artist as "a creator with deep spiritual knowledge about the power of mystic pots."[8]

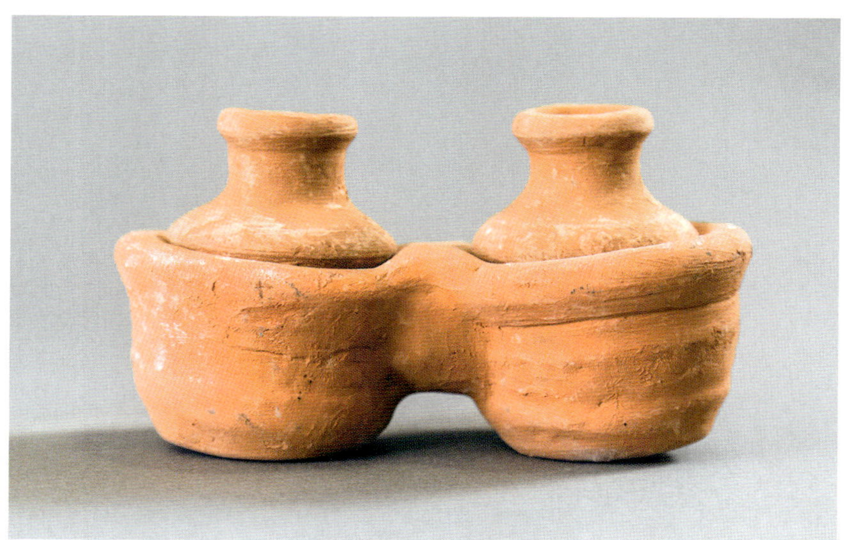

Figure 9 Unidentified Haitian artist, double pot and drink vessels for the Marassa Spirits, 2017. Low-fired earthenware. W. 8". (Courtesy of Duke University, Sacred Arts of the Black Atlantic.) Dr. Matory purchased these Marassa pots at Marché Hippolyte in Port-au-Prince, Haiti.

Although Haitian-made earthenware was everywhere in the foodways and spirituality of Wainwright's childhood, and she played at shaping earth into vessels as a small child, it was excluded from the dominantly francophone arts education. Instead, art instruction was dominated by drawing and painting, and Wainwright excelled in them. As she recalls, "I have never not made art," and some of her earliest memories come from developing and colorizing portraits for her father in his photography studio in Port-au-Prince. Her family, and especially her mother, supported her artistic talents. She was enrolled in formal art classes, where her teachers promulgated the aesthetics and subject matter of the Haitian "Renaissance" that began in the 1940s with the arrival of the American artist and English teacher Dewitt Peters, the founding of the Centre d'Art in 1944, and the popularization of Haitian artists such as Hector Hyppolite and Philomé Obin in the ensuing years.[9] Wainwright has vivid memories of secluding herself with paints and canvas in the refined silence of *le salon*—the formal parlor—in her family home: "surrounded by wooden floors, and glass all around, I would paint and listen to music and read and draw." In the cosmopolitan art scene of Haiti's capital, Wainwright achieved significant success and exhibited at the prestigious Centre d'Art when she was still a teenager.

At the same time, Wainwright strained against the colonialist dynamics endemic to mid-twentieth-century Haitian art. Her teachers, she remembers, "would give me an art book and I would flip through and look at the masters; I wanted enough with masters! I had enough with those white men telling me what's the best way to put your brush. Dewitt Peters had introduced canvas and tubes and European things that no one can afford, and the few that could afford to be artists only knew to become painters." Through the worldview promulgated by her teachers, ceramics was not an art form worthy of study.

The forces shaping Wainwright's artistic practice were the same that prevented Haitians from learning and speaking Creole at school, challenging francophone culture, or protesting the increasingly authoritarian government of François Duvalier, who served as president of Haiti from 1957 to 1971 and whose regime had become rapidly autocratic and despotic after a military coup d'etat in 1958. Knowing that her strong-willed daughter would become another casualty of Duvalier's death squad, Wainwright's mother sent her to live with her father in Brooklyn in 1968, when she was seventeen years old. Wainwright became one of the thousands of Haitian refugees of the Duvalier regime to experience the alienation of being doubly diasporic. "Haitian people, we know we're from the big continent of Africa, but we don't know where we're *from*," Wainwright has said. In Brooklyn, she was uprooted from the homeland that was already a diaspora to another also haunted by the multigenerational violence of slavery and colonialism. In the United States, Wainwright turned to writing instead of visual arts and pursued a career as a psychotherapist, a choice spurred on by her instinct to care for those hurt by the intergenerational traumas that shaped her life and her homeland.

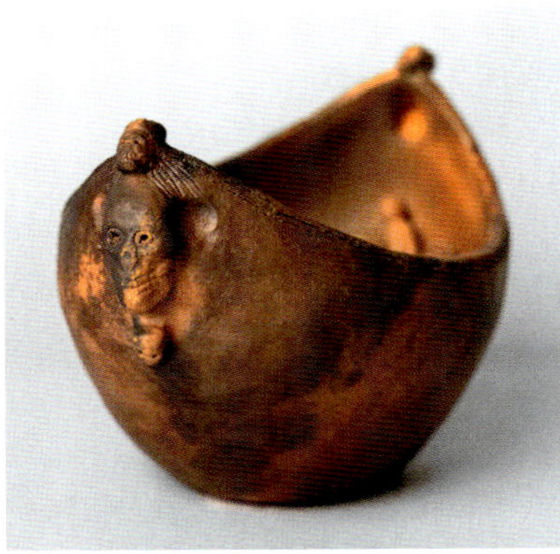

Figure 10 Babette Wainwright, *Taíno Vessel*, Madison, Wisconsin, 2021. Low-fired earthenware. H. 7".

Finding Her Materia Prima

On a shelf in Wainwright's studio is an earthenware bowl, its unglazed, warm surface mottled with black swirls of smoke (fig. 10). Oblong in form and pointed at each end like the hull of a small boat, the rim is encircled by incised lines and the ends punctuated by a trio of smoothly sculpted human skulls looking out like goulish figureheads. Wainwright made this bowl as an homage to the ceramic artistry of the Taíno peoples, the diverse societies that inhabited the Antilles archipelago before European contact, whose forms of cultural expression include distinctive ceramics, petroglyphs, and stone and wooden sculpture. Murdered, (The Taíno language is also the source of the word *Haiti*, or Ay-ti, meaning "land of mountains.") enslaved, and infected with disease by European explorers and settlers beginning with Christopher Columbus's landing on the island of Hispaniola in 1492, the Taíno peoples nonetheless remain present not only through their rich and complex artistic legacy, but also in present-day Caribbean music, language, religion, and people, many of whom—Haitians included—are descended from Taíno as well as African and European peoples. Of all Wainwright's oeuvre, her Taíno-inspired bowls are the only ones that reproduce a traditional form, marking a personal and professional turning point—the seed of her work with low-fired earthenware.

On a return trip to Haiti in 1985, Wainwright found herself at the newly founded Musée du Panthéon National Haïtien. There she encountered a museum freighted with the aftereffects of colonialism. An armed guard followed her and her girlfriend through the museum, and the fragmentary collection bespoke centuries of colonialist predation, not only of Haitian works of art but also of Haitian capital.[10] In this museum, however, Wainwright saw for the first time Taíno art, including ceramics recovered from archaeological contexts, among them an earthenware bowl in Taíno people's distinctive boat-like form, with anthropomorphic handles and an incised geometric pattern around the rim made between the thirteenth and

Figure 11 Unidentified Taíno artist, Bowl, thirteenth–fifteenth century. Low-fired earthenware. W. 9". (Metropolitan Museum of Art, Gift of Vincent and Margaret Fay, 1993, 1993.523.2.)

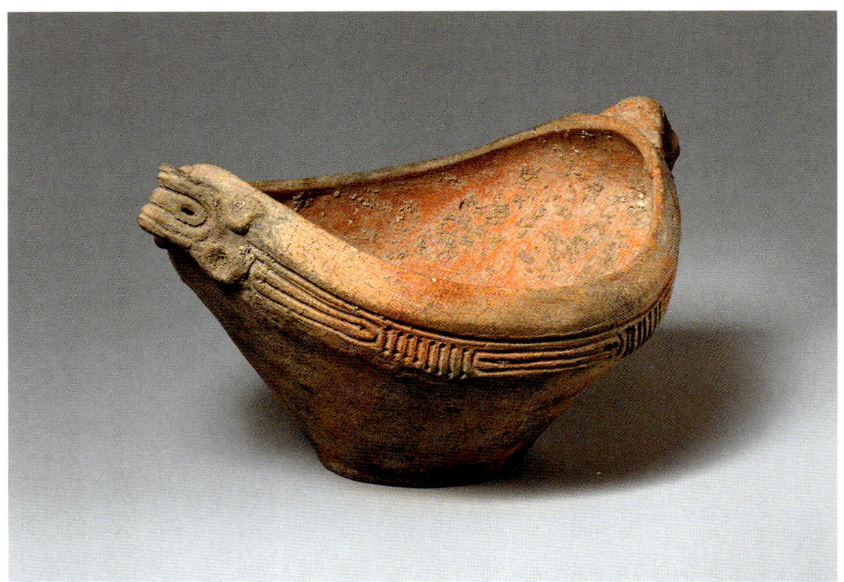

fifteenth centuries (fig. 11). These vessels were used by spiritual leaders in Taíno religious ceremonies.[11] For Wainwright, learning of this suppressed history of Haitian art opened a world beyond painting and canvas, of Indigenous explorations of clay, abstraction, and ritual, with sacred purpose.

In Wainwright's studio, her Taíno-inspired bowl holds several miniature pots and clay figures of Black women and children (fig. 12). She models

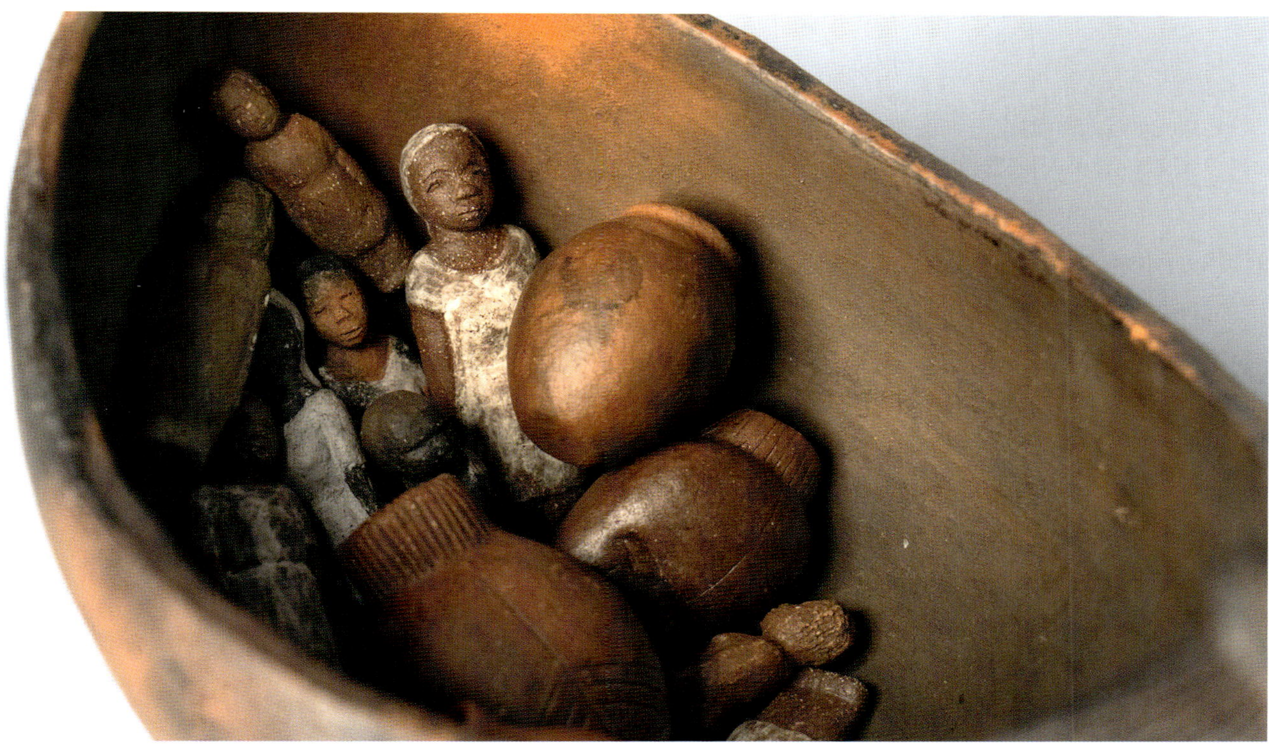

Figure 12 Detail of *Taíno Vessel* illustrated in fig. 10.

each figure with individuated face and clothes, highlighting dresses and headwraps with pigment rubbed into the surface of the clay. Like many details of Wainwright's work, the presence of these small sculptures in her Taíno bowl is both incidental and meaningful. She has made dozens of these figures throughout her career, often sculpting them as a way to pass time during the firing process, and they migrate from one vessel to the next as work moves through her studio. Placed for the time being in her Taíno bowl, they remind the viewer that this work is a vessel whose fundamental meaning emerges from the potentiality of its purpose to hold the sacred. Specifically, they call attention to the work's hull-like shape, evoking the traumatic Middle Passage of human trafficking that brought Wainwright's ancestors to Haiti. Each small figure embodies Wainwright's awareness that during the Middle Passage, "ancestors' energies pack in with us, follow us; their descendants are accompanied by them."

In the Musée du Panthéon National Haïtien, understanding that there was an artistic tradition indigenous to Haiti that worked with the island's earth rather than with imported colonial supplies was epiphanic. As Wainwright recalls,

> The museum got me angry, sad, and proud: angry that we were raped, that the French and the then government took everything from us; sad that we have beauty beyond what we knew from the painting movement, proud because I could dig my own damn mud, it's my and my ancestors' materia prima. I don't have to go to an expensive store and buy it, I don't have to go to Europe.

Wainwright realized that clay could allow her to articulate a longing for home and address a profound and shared sense of uprootedness. "I imagine the people that I don't know, I imagine them working in clay, so by doing it I'm connecting back to people from where I was born, I just imagine they've touched the material, they've put their emotion in this material the same way." The Taíno ceramics led Wainwright to begin a new artistic path, an M.F.A. in ceramics at the University of Wisconsin–Madison, which she completed in 2000. She was mentored there by the Ho-Chunk sculptor and installation artist Truman Lowe, Bruce Howdle—a ceramic artist known for his large-scale ceramic murals—and the textile and social-practice artist Sonya Clark.

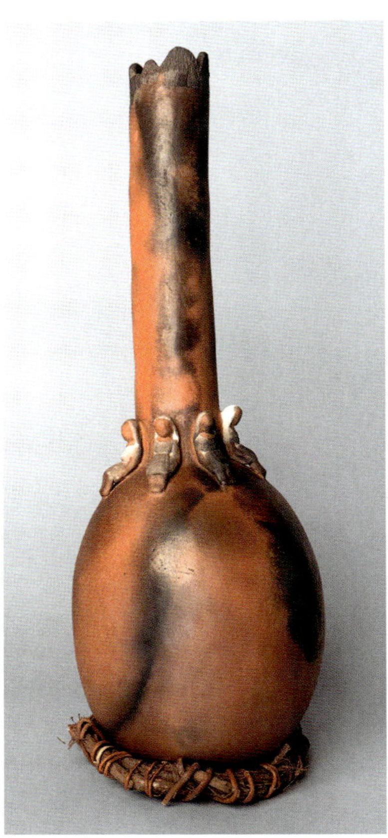

Figure 13 Babette Wainwright, *Dreaming of Rising*, Madison, Wisconsin, 2006. Low-fired earthenware. H. 22".

At UW, Wainwright was introduced to different types of commercial clays and found them "nice but not speaking my language." Seeking a clay body that "my people might have worked with," Wainwright settled on an earthenware clay that is a combination of Paoli clay and clays dug from her backyard in Madison that she processes herself, tempered with grog and sometimes sawdust. For Wainwright, this warm earthenware "is my color, the color I grew up seeing, the color of things in the market" in Port-au-Prince. The fragility of low-fired earthenware is meaningful. Some of Wainwright's work "you could almost crush," and yet it endures, like the Taíno archaeological remnants that "have survived eons, it can break and yet it's so strong. I like that because it's like life. It doesn't last forever."

Process

Wainwright observed that throughout her twenty-year career as a ceramic artist, her process has been characterized by an exploration of how the "malleability of clay can give form to my deepest thoughts and emotions." "Making art to put your stamp on the world is a white male thing, I don't see it like that at all, I see it as something that is born and needs to come up." With inventiveness and technical skill, Wainwright moves among coiling, molding, modeling, and carving to shape the meaning and appearance of her work. "If I like a design I mold it, somethings I coil, somethings I model; I model whatever I want, and I carve, so I don't do one thing." Working without a set product in mind, she instead attends to her relationship with the clay and her inner subconscious: "when I'm sitting here, I'm really connecting; there is a communing that happens; and maybe I even conjure because sometimes something pops up and I say, who are you?"

One technique meaningfully absent from Wainwright's practice is wheel-throwing. While completing her M.F.A., Wainwright studied with Pueblo potters at Ghost Ranch in Abiquiu, New Mexico, and with traditional potters in Otumba, Mexico, learning coiling, pit firing, and bur-

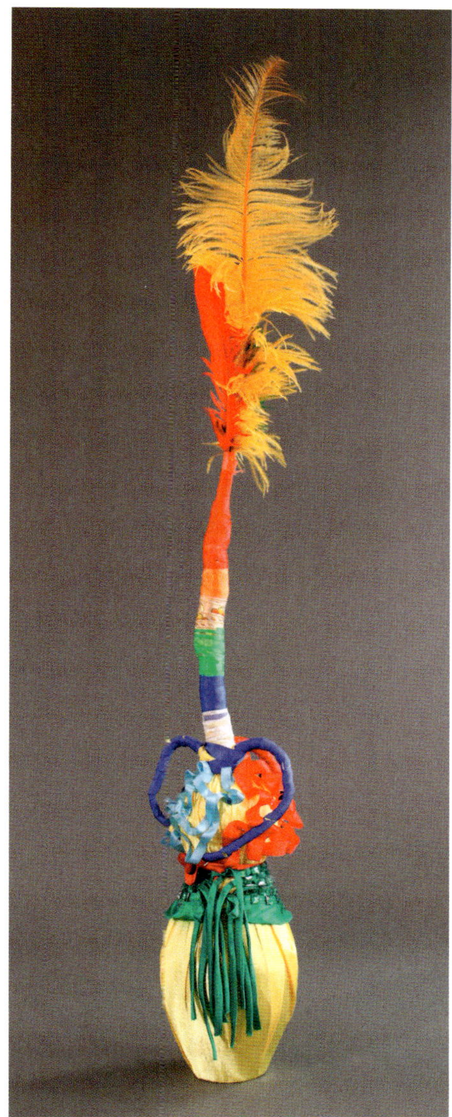

Figure 14 Unidentified Haitian artist, *Pakèt Kongo for Papa Loko*, 2018, feathers, satin ribbon, and mixed media, 26" x 6". (Photo courtesy of Duke University, Sacred Arts of the Black Atlantic.) Manmi Maude and the other priests of the Sosyete Nago Temple in Jacmel, Haiti, prepared this pakèt kongo for Dr. Matory in a series of ceremonies in 2018.

nishing. The subtle asymmetries of coiling breathes life into her vessels, like *Dreaming of Rising*, a sculptural vessel with a strikingly elongated form echoing the stem-on-globe construction of certain *pakèt kongo*, Haitian vodou objects that creolize Kongo *nkisi* forms (figs. 13, 14). The verticality of this work captures the landscape of aspiration in Haiti: "in Haiti, the hill is the well to do; the lower, hoping and praying that they can move higher." On the shoulders of the vessel sit small figures representing a prayer circle of *manbo* priestesses. At the rim, Wainwright has inscribed, carved, and rubbed with pigment a cluster of thatch-roof mud houses that represent home to the artist "because that's where we came from before slavery." Punctuating vessels with visually and formally surprising elements around the rim is a particular strength of Wainwright's designs. Just as *pakèt kongo* are made to guard households against harm, *Dreaming of Rising* also is a kind of charm, embodying the hope that Haiti will overcome its oppressors.

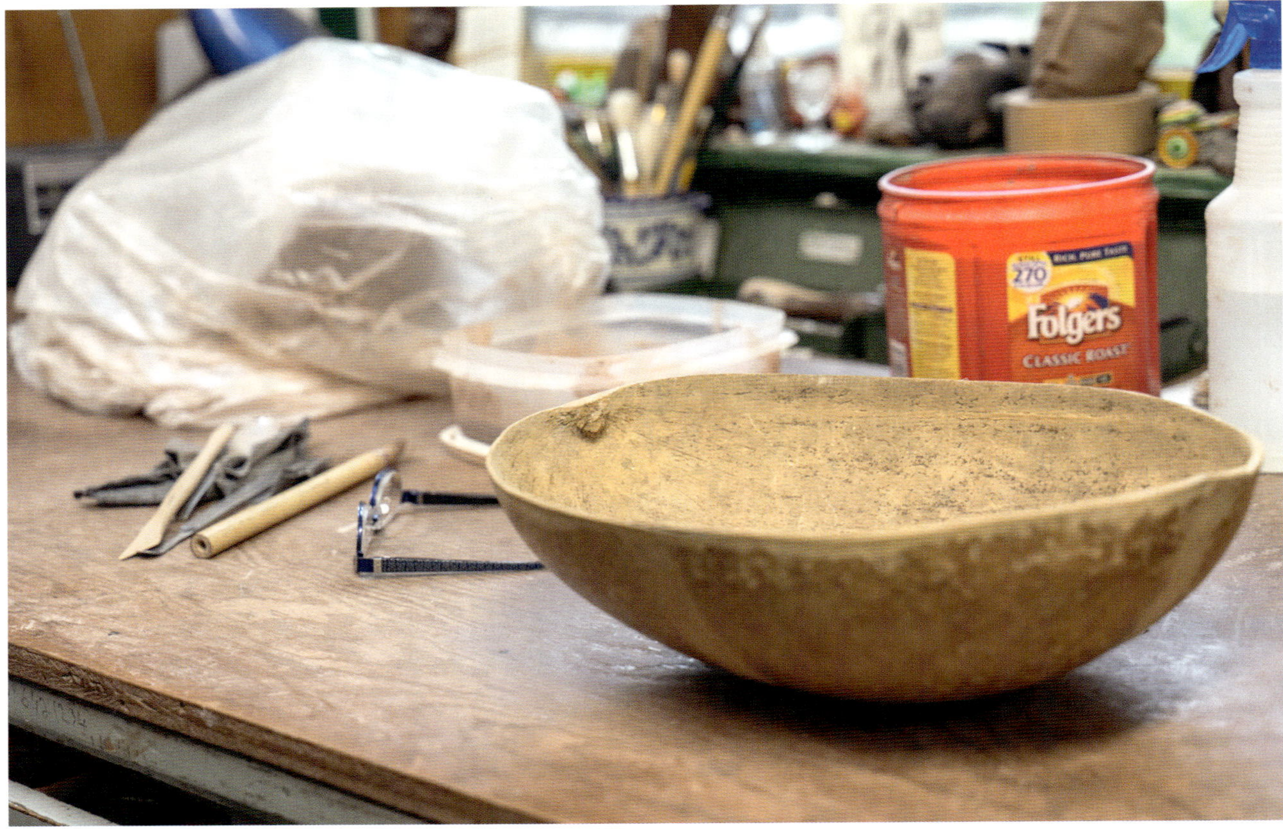

Figure 15 *Kalbas*, Babette Wainwright's Studio, Madison, Wisconsin, 2022.

While the stem of *Dreaming of Rising* is hand-coiled, Wainwright formed the base using molds she makes using the hull of a Haitian *kalbas* (calabash) gourd (fig. 15). Like the ceramic *kanari*, the *kalbas* has a deep practical and spiritual purpose in Haiti, as well as in Wainwright's work. "It's ubiquitous," she says, "You cook in it, eat in it, carry water in it; you do vodou in it; everybody in the countryside has one or two." In Wainwright's practice, the *kalbas* hull form and abundant potential embodies Haitian womanhood. "I love it because it has this soft, rounded shape like a baby or a woman's stomach, that feels magical to me." Shaped in clay, the *kalbas* form, Wainwright explains, allows her to "use forms that define beauty in terms of who I am, a woman of the African diaspora."

In Wainwright's studio, the imposing figure of *Water Bearer* also grew from the *kalbas* form, which she used to mold the shoulders and back (fig. 16). *Water Bearer* wears her tresses threaded into a crown resembling Nigerian women's tall house hair sculpture, a symbol for Wainwright of the figure's queenly status. Her oval face with downcast eyes, scarification patterns, and elongated nose echoes the finely carved form of Senufo and other West African face masks (fig. 17). A cluster of circles impressed into her forehead as if she possesses a third eye further signals her powerful spirituality. On the skirt, Wainwright inscribed an abstract landscape of thatch-roofed houses nestled in the Haitian mountains. Between them, meandering rivers flow down and across the front of the skirt to *Water*

Bearer's feet, which stand firmly planted, braced to carry a pot balanced on her back. Lines from the Barbadian poet Sandra Sealy's poem "Haitian Water Bearer" seemingly brings Wainwright's sculpture to life:

> She rises—
> hips rippling
> to a silent merengue
> bearing sloshing vessels homeward,
> a little water breaking the relief
> of dust on her feet-[12]

Wainwright's *Water Bearer* also carries out a homecoming; she returns from the source, whether that is Africa or the river—and she is the source—bringing spiritual sustenance as crucial as water to ancestors preserving

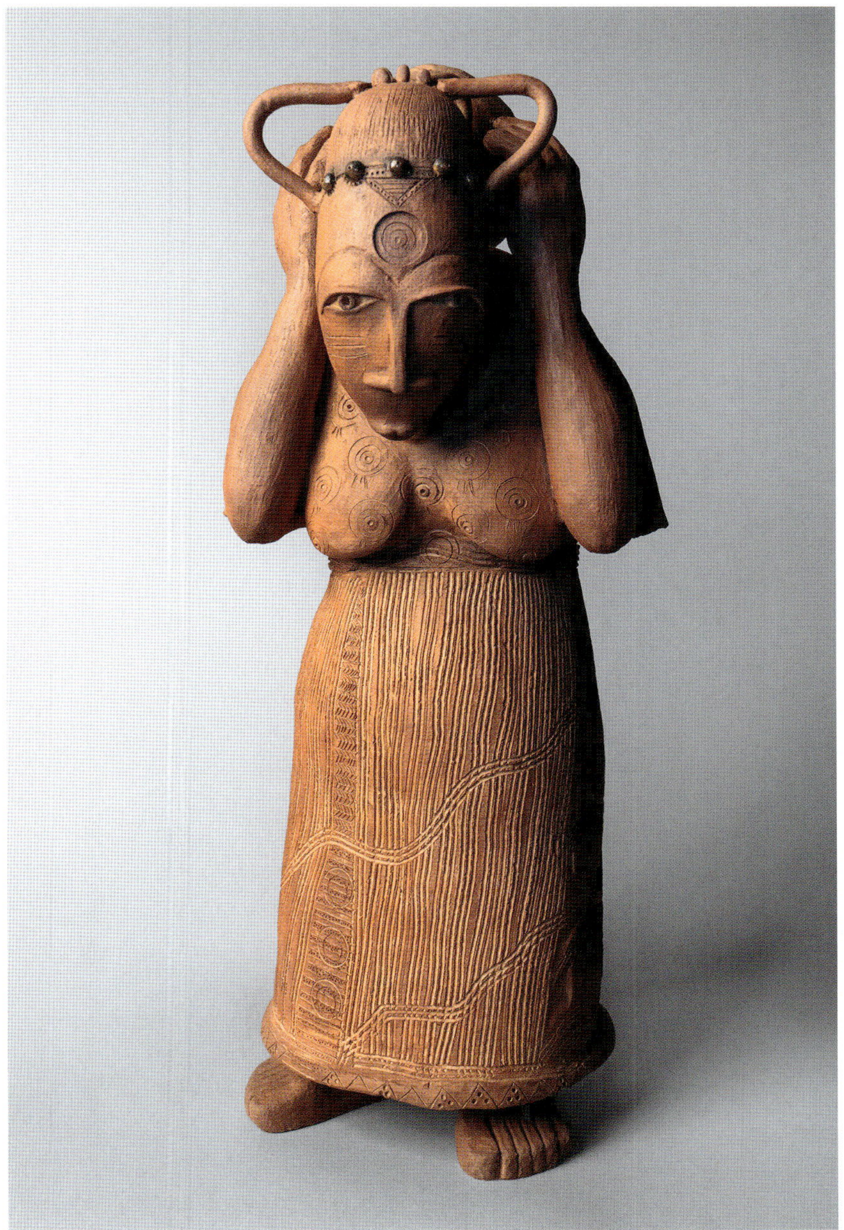

Figure 16 Babette Wainwright, *Water Bearer*, Madison, Wisconsin, 2008. Low-fired earthenware. H. 24".

Figure 17 Detail of *Water Bearer*, illustrated in fig. 16.

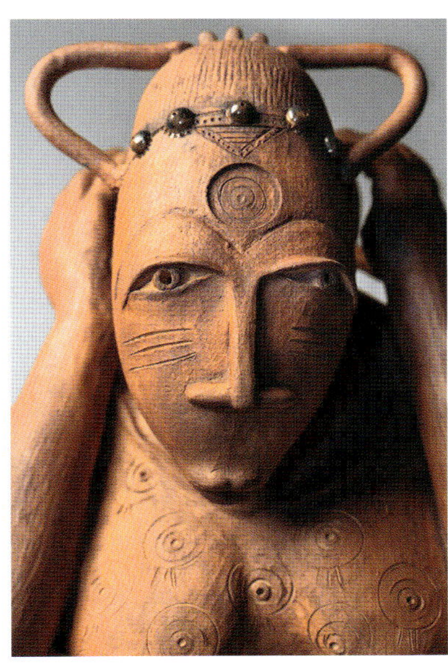

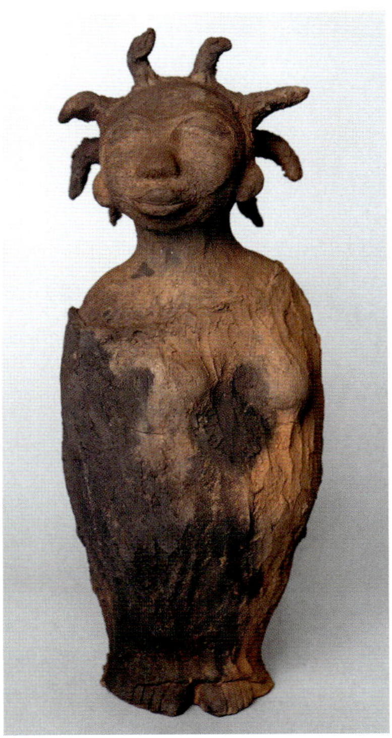

Figure 18 Babette Wainwright, *Kiln Watcher*, Madison, Wisconsin, 2000. Low-fired earthenware. H. 14".

religious and cultural traditions in Haiti. As Wainwright says, "everything sprouts from woman, she can be the earth, everything's her."

When Wainwright first began firing her work, beginning with her thesis show in 2000, she used a traditional pit fire but experienced high losses, particularly as she began sculpting with complex figural forms beyond the self-contained vessel shapes ideal for pit firing. *Kiln Watcher* (2000) is a work from that experimental time (fig. 18). Presiding over Wainwright's studio and the kiln from a top shelf, the sculpture is both figural and vasiform, a female figure whose body follows the silhouette of a tall vase—foot is feet, shoulder is shoulders, neck is neck—with a beatific smile, smooth, high cheekbones, and rounded brow capped by hair threaded into a sunburst. This sculpture became Wainwright's "kiln goddess" after all eight of the threaded locks defied the odds and survived a pit fire. Seeking a firing technique that would allow her to further explore figural clay sculpture, in the early 2000s Wainwright conferred with the ceramic artist and scholar of traditional Caribbean pottery-making Patricia Fey, now professor of art at Florida Gulf Coast University. Fey shared with Wainwright her research on women potters of St. Lucia, who use low bisque fires to reduce breakage.[13] Back in Madison, Wainwright adapted that technique to her practice, bisque-firing in an electric kiln between 900 and 1800 degrees Fahrenheit, then using an aboveground pit fire she built in her backyard (the soil in Wisconsin is too damp for a true pit) and nesting her pieces in sawdust with the flammable on top. When the sawdust catches fire, she covers it and lets it smoke, as she says, "like I'm smoking a ham." In this way she successfully fires complex forms like *Water Bearer* and achieves smoke effects that are organic and serendipitous.

"Stains" of pigment suspended in engobe, rubbed into the clay before firing, creates subtle and earthy tonalities to Wainwright's work, reflecting her academic training as a painter. Like the smoke effects that characterize much of her work, she appreciates the accidental in this process: "I like it because when you put it in the pit, it does things," particularly darkening the pigment and creating a weathered aesthetic. *Sel Lakay Ki Kraze* (2010), an earthenware sculpture whose Kreyòl (Haitian Creole) title means "only the houses are broken," showcases Wainwright's command of surface effects (fig. 19). Wainwright made the sculpture as a testament to the resilience of the Haitian people after the catastrophic earthquake that struck the nation on January 12, 2010, killing between 100,000 and 160,000 Haitians and destroying 250,000 homes. A female figure looks upward toward a vision unseen. She is joined by other women modeled in miniature—one balanced on her head, one on her belly, and others arranged around her skirt—who stand looking outward from the front doors of relief-carved, thatch-roofed mud houses that withstood the earthquake when modern cement buildings collapsed (fig. 20). As they often are in Haiti, each house is painted with the protective *vèvè* of a *lwa*—including Grand Bois (the *lwa* associated with growing plants and trees) and Bosou (the *lwa* of action). Over many textures—the glowing burnished skin of the figure, the rough mud and thatch of the houses, and the striated textile—a color composi-

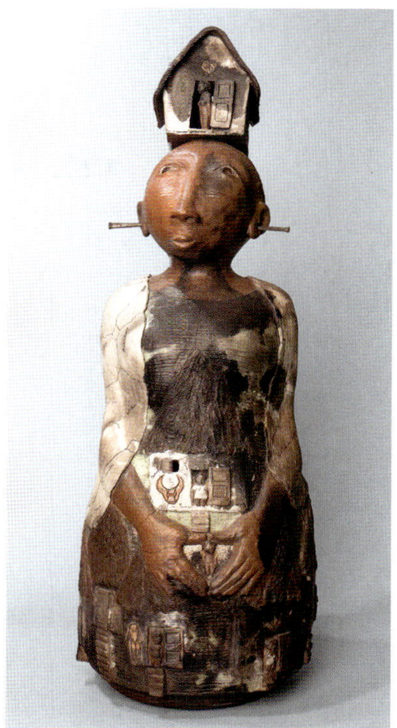

Figure 19 Babette Wainwright, *Sel Lakay Ki Kraze*, Madison, Wisconsin, 2010. Low-fired earthenware and pigments. H. 28½".

Figure 20 Detail of *Sel Lakay Ki Kraze*, illustrated in fig. 19.

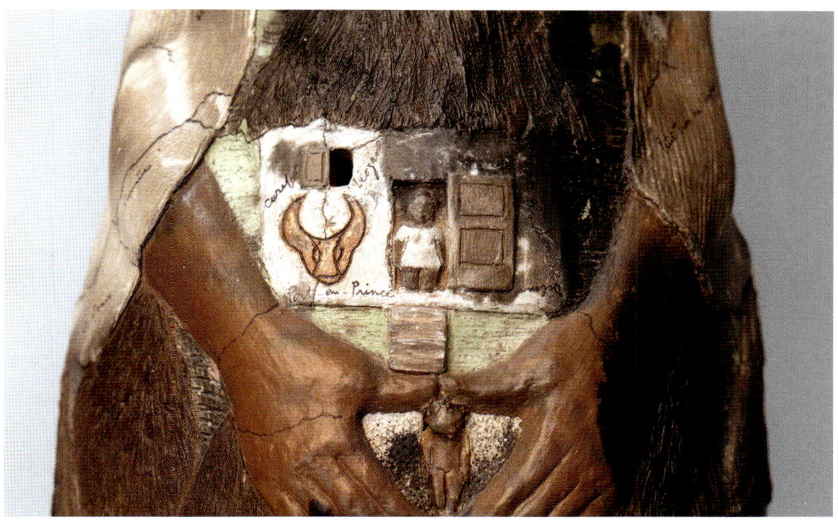

tion of black, white, and brown is augmented with a gentle green. Mapped over the entire figure are the names of Haitian towns and arrondissements, with borders delineated by black lines that appear like cracks—in clay and earth. At the center of the sculpture is a baby, a new beginning for Haiti. To Wainwright, "she is the seed."

Conclusion: Art with a Purpose

Like many works in Babette's studio, the six-foot-tall sculpture *Potomitan* has a purpose (fig. 21). The work is named for and modeled after the central wooden post that is an essential structural feature of the *ounfò* in Haitian vodou, through which the *lwa* descend to earth to inhabit, for a time, the bodies of the faithful through spirit possession. *Potomitan* are themselves works of art, often carved and painted to enhance their powers and articulate their purpose and power. Wainwright re-creates and expands on the spiritual landscape in her work and her studio:

> I am an artist who is focused on practice and self-expression; my ancestors made with a purpose, to assuage, to call rain, working with a purpose, it's not art for the sake of art, it's art with a purpose.

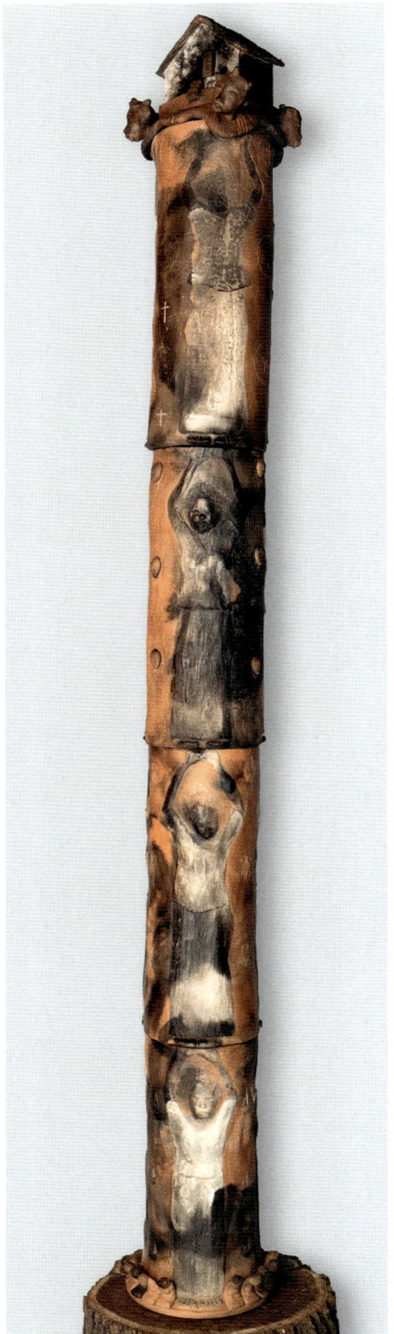

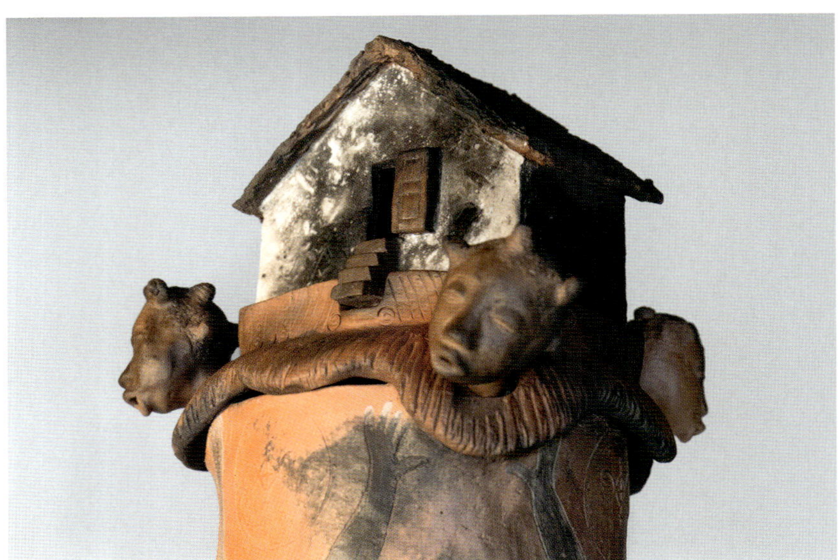

Figure 21 Babette Wainwright, *Potomitan*, Madison, Wisconsin, 2002. Low-fired earthenware. H. 75".

Figure 22 Detail of *Potomitan*, illustrated in fig. 21.

Potomitan has a personal purpose for Babette, but it is also about the spiritual purposefulness of Haitian art and womanhood. Around the column, *manbo* stand in their white robes with arms raised. The sculpture has a restrained but rich color scheme of warm terracotta color of earthenware, white robes of the *manbo*, and black smoke that dances across the surface of figures and background, heightening each figures' sense of movement and fluidity. Each of the four tiers of figures seems to hold up the next, and their forms emerge from the column with three-dimensional modeling, so that they seem to exist between the sculptural and the pictorial, the real and the unreal. At the top, women's heads are finely sculpted with mouths open, as if *Potomitan* is speaking (fig. 22).

Potomitan are an essential metaphor for Haitian womanhood. As it is said in Kreyòl, "*fanm se poto mitan*" (women are the pillars of society).[14] As Wainwright describes the matrifocal nature of Haitian society: "Haitian women are not on a pedestal, they are the central pillar, to be gathered around to seek strength, knowledge, wisdom, protection, and nurture;

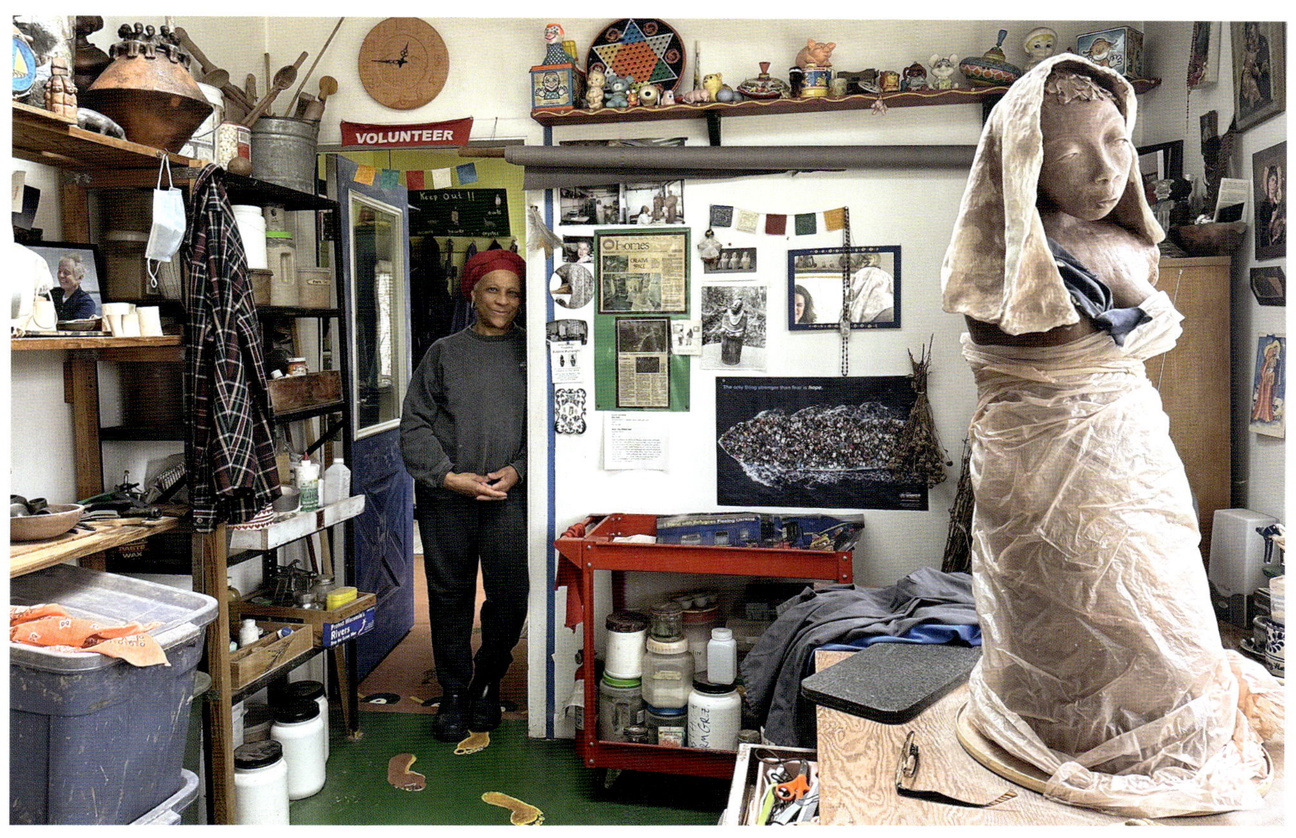

Figure 23 Babette Wainwright in her studio, Madison, Wisconsin, 2022. (Photo, R. Ruthie Dibble.)

she's the source that you go to for water and without it you can't survive; through her life comes everything, and in return she is nourished through gifts and gathering."

The metaphor of *Potomitan* animates not only Wainwright's artistic practice but also her relationship with her studio. Around her she has carefully gathered objects and works that she cares for and of which she is the source. In turn they nourish her, her memories, and her emotions, which she channels into each work. Surrounded by clay, she is the ultimate vessel (fig. 23).

1. Interview of Babette Wainwright by R. Ruthie Dibble at the artist's studio in Madison, Wisconsin, April 2020. Throughout the article, all quotations of Wainwright are from that interview. I thank Ms. Wainwright for so generously sharing her powerful art and life stories; Dr. Kyrah Malika Daniels for her soul-stirring scholarship on Haitian spirituality in Ms. Wainwright's artistic practice; and Dr. J. Lorand Matory for making available crucial information about his groundbreaking digital humanities project Sacred Arts of the Black Atlantic at Duke University.

2. Lois Wilcken and Frisner Augustin, *The Drums of Vodou* (Tempe, Ariz.: White Cliffs Media, 1992), p. 37.

3. Omis'eke Natasha Tinsley, *Ezili's Mirrors: Imagining Black Queer Genders* (Durham, N.C.: Duke University Press, 2018), pp. 3–28.

4. Sarah Daynes, *Time and Memory in Reggae Music: The Politics of Hope* (Manchester, U.K.: Manchester University Press, 2010), pp. 85–104.

5. Susan Stewart, *On Longing: Narratives of the Miniature, the Gigantic, the Souvenir, the Collection* (Durham, N.C.: Duke University Press, 1992), p. 44.

6. For further discussion of Haitian conceptions of the soul, see Roberto Strongman, "The Afro-Diasporic Body in Haitian Vodou and the Transcending of Gendered Cartesian Corporeality," *Kunapipi* 30, no. 2 (2008): 11–29.

7. Robert Ferris Thompson, *Flash of the Spirit: African and Afro-American Art & Philosophy* (New York: Vintage Books, 1984), pp. 182–83.

8. Kyrah Malika Daniels, "Vodou Harmonizes the Head-Pot, or, Haiti's Multi-Soul Complex," *Religion* 52, no. 3 (2021): 359–583; and "Soul Pots & Mortuary Vessels: Sacred Arts in Haitian Vodou's Private & Public Sectors," In *Africana Religion and Public Life*, ed. Jacob K. Olúpọ̀nà (forthcoming 2024).

9. Michel-Rolph Trouillot and Daniel Simidor, et al., "Haitian Art Before and After 1944 and Dewit Peters," available online at http://faculty.webster.edu/corbetre/haiti/art/pre-1944.htm.

10. As recently as 2020, the United States returned 470 examples of historical and cultural antiquities to Haiti. "CATF Members Support Repatriation to Haiti," Bureau of Education and Cultural Affairs, April 27, 2020, available online at https://eca.state.gov/highlight/catf-members-support-repatriation-haiti. Catherine Porter and Constant Méheut, et al., "The Root of Haiti's Misery: Reparations to Enslavers," *New York Times*, May 20, 2022, available online at https://www.nytimes.com/2022/05/20/world/americas/haiti-history-colonized-france.html.

11. The English naturalist Hans Sloane recorded that in Jamaica in the 1680s, a planter discovered a cave with Taíno burials, where ancestors' bones were held in earthenware bowls. Joanna Ostapkowicz and Jonathan A. Hanna, et al., *Real, Recent, or Replica: Precolumbian Caribbean Heritage as Art, Commodity, and Inspiration* (Tuscaloosa, Ala.: University of Alabama Press, 2021), p. 111.

12. Sandra Sealy, "Haitian Water Bearer," in *WomenSpeak, a Journal of Writing and Art by Caribbean Women* 7 (2013): 81.

13. Patricia Fay, *Creole Clay: Heritage Ceramics in the Contemporary Caribbean* (Gainesville: University Press of Florida, 2017).

14. Marie-José N'Zengou-Tayo, "Fanm Se Poto Mitan: Haitian Woman, the Pillar of Society," *Feminist Review* 59, no. 1 (June 1998): 118–42.

Index

Adams, Abigail, 194*n*46
Adams, Elizabeth, 97(&fig.)
Adams, John, 180
African diaspora, Wainwright and, 198, 201, 208
Agwé *vèvè*, 201
Albany slip, 72
Albemarle Club (London), 91
Algiers, 176, 179
Alleghany County (Virginia), 42–43(&figs. 8 & 9)
Allen, Larry, 148
Alrand, John, 52
Alton (Illinois), 125–26
A-marked porcelains, 91–97(&figs.)
Amelung, John Frederick, 185
American Anti-Slavery Society, 135
American Civil War, 37, 39, 41, 44–48, 53, 55–56, 57, 77, 145
American Revolution, 143, 174–75
Anderson, Jeffrey, 29
Anderson, PJ, 148
"And Freedom to the Slave" (Margolin), 126
Angelica archangelica (Archangelica officinalis), 20(&fig. 32)
The Appeal to Reason (newspaper), 161*n*10
Arlington (house), 187, 188, 189, 190
Arlington Saloon, 159
Armistead Revolt, 142
Arrowmont School of Arts and Crafts, 149
Artscape Festival (Baltimore), 141(fig.)
Atkinson, Thomas, 41
Atoe, Osa, 148
Attucks, Crispus, 143–44(&fig. 7)
Autio, Rudy, 139
Ayida, 201
Aztec software, 98–99

Bade *vèvè*, 201
Badji, 202
Baldwin, Doug, 139
Baltimore (Maryland), 139, 141(fig.), 147, 177, 179–80, 184
Baltimore City, 139
Bandys Township (Catawba County, North Carolina), 52
Baptist Anti-Slavery Society, 129, 130
Baptist Central Tract Society, 129
Barbary Coast, 176
Barber, Edwin Atlee, 153, 161*n*7
Barnard College, 8
Barroth, Henry (Johann Heinrich), 54
Barry, John, 179, 187
Barthe, Richmond, 148
Bartmann or Bellarmine bottle, 17(&fig.), 18(fig. 26)
Battle of Bristoe Station, 55
Battle of Gettysburg, 55
Beaucamp-Markowsky, Barbara, 106
Bedford County (Tennessee), 52
Bedsaul, F. Clyde, 68, 69, 72, 75, 76, 77–78, 89*n*71
Bedsaul, Frances E., 81
Bedsaul, George Washington, 68, 69–70(&fig. 28), 79, 80(figs. 44–46), 88*n*52, 89*n*95
Bedsaul, Jane, 67, 68, 70
Bedsaul, Peter, 81, 89*n*95
Bedsaul, Sarah E., 70
Bedsaul, Surphina Jane, 67, 69
Bedsaul, William R., 68, 69
Bedsaul family, 86
Beecher, Edward, 125, 126–27
Belladonnas, 27
Benbridge, Richard Wetherill, 187
Benbridge, Sarah Truxtun, 187
Bennington (Vermont), 20
Benoit, Pierre Jacques, 5(fig. 3)
Berendt, John, 29
Bezur, Aniko, 106–7
Bibb, Henry Walton, 6
Bible (King James Version), 20–21(&figs. 35 & 36), 34*n*75
Biloxi (Mississippi), 150(figs.), 152
Biloxi Pottery, 154(fig.)
Bird's Eye View of the City of Columbia, South Carolina (Drie), 13(fig. 17)
"Black Dust Blues" (Ma Rainey), 26(fig.)
The Black Man's Lament: Or, How to Make Sugar (Opie), 115–16
"The Blackville Gallery" (photogravure), 24(fig. 40)
Blassingame, John, 6
Blaszczyk, Regina, 131
Bonhams, 97
Bosou *vèvè*, 210
Boston (Massachusetts), 179, 182
Boston Athenaeum, 192*n*21
Boston Harbor, 179(fig.)
Boston Tea Party, 143
Boula, 200(fig. 5)
Bourbon Street (New Orleans), 29
Bow and Arrow (scene), 96(fig. 11)
Bow porcelain manufactory, 91
Brauche/Braucherei, 6

Bristol glaze, 72
British and Foreign Anti-Slavery Society, 116
British Museum, 122*n*6
Brooklyn (New York), Wainwright and, 203
Brown, Bessie, 3
Brown, William Wells, 6–7
Brunel University, 97–104
Brunson, C. P., 16
Buck, Ephraim, 55
Buie, Luther T., 145(fig.)
Burchfield, Rick Meech, 20
Burke, Selma, 148
Burke County (North Carolina), 52
Burns, Robert, 138*n*6
Burslem (England), 129

Cabarrus County (North Carolina), 54, 55
Calvert County (Maryland), 139
Camden Chronicle (newspaper), 16
Campbell, David, 68
Campbell, Hosea, 68
Campbell, Lindsey, 68
Campbell, William, 68, 89*n*71
Campbell, William Dess, 68
Campbell family potters, 86
"Cane Mill" print, 117(&fig.), 118
Canton (ship), 176, 187
Capote (Texas), 148
Cardholder (Ohr), 150(fig. 2)
Carnes-McNaughton, Linda, 75
Carney, William, 145
Carpenter, Adolphus Lafayette, 56, 57, 65, 67–68, 69, 70, 79, 86, 88*n*32, 88*n*52, 88*n*62, 89*n*95
Carpenter, Barbara, 56, 67, 88*n*32
Carpenter, Christian "CZ," 51–52
Carpenter, Christopher, 52, 88n32
Carpenter, "Cumberland" John, 52
Carpenter, Elias, 52, 54, 55, 56, 63, 65, 67, 70, 86
Carpenter, Elizabeth, 52, 88*n*56
Carpenter, Emily Hanks, 57, 61, 68, 73(fig. 33), 74, 81, 82(fig. 48)
Carpenter, Emmett, 70, 72, 75–76, 77
Carpenter, Frank, 57, 60, 85
Carpenter, Franklin, 86
Carpenter, Harvey Make, 69
Carpenter, Jacob, 55, 88*n*32
Carpenter, James, 152, 154
Carpenter, James Emmett, 69
Carpenter, James Welborn, 58(figs.), 59
Carpenter, Jane Bedsaul, 67, 68, 70
Carpenter, John, 52, 77
Carpenter, John Wesley, 52, 53, 55–56, 57, 88*n*32; Catawba Valley wares, 59–65(&figs. 9, 10, 12–15), 84–85, 86; clay, 70–72; kiln, 72–76(&figs. 35 & 36); photo of, 50(fig.); in Pipers Gap, 51, 58, 65–71(&figs. 25–27, 29–30), 73(figs.), 77–84(&figs. 42–43, 47–49), 86
Carpenter, John Wesley (grandson), 73(fig. 34)
Carpenter, J. W., 86, 88*n*56
Carpenter, Martha Maybelle, 55, 88*n*32, 88*n*62
Carpenter, Mary, 70, 88*n*62
Carpenter, Mary A., 88*n*32
Carpenter, Mary E., 55
Carpenter, Mary Hoffman, 55
Carpenter, Mary Lingafelt (Lingerfelt), 56
Carpenter, Michael "Mike" Rufus, 55–56, 57, 67–68, 69, 70, 72, 86, 88*n*32
Carpenter, Mollie, 69
Carpenter, Robert C., 55, 86*n*4
Carpenter, Sarah Elizabeth, 70, 88*n*32
Carpenter, Sarah Salina, 54, 55, 56, 67, 70
Carpenter, William Franklin, 55, 59–60(&fig.), 62, 85, 88*n*32
Carpenter, William Franklin "Frank," 54–55
Carpenter, William Pinkney, 88*n*62
Carpenter family potters, 51–58(&fig. 5), 85–86, 86*n*1
Carpenter Pottery (Pipers Gap, Virginia), 65(fig.), 76–84(&figs. 37–53)
Carroll County (Virginia), 55, 56, 68, 88*n*52. *See also* Pipers Gap (Virginia)
Carver, George Washington, 143(&fig. 5)
Casadio, Francesca, 106–7
Cassel kiln, 75, 76
Cassius, Andreas, 105
Cassius pigment, 105(&fig. 22)
Catawba County (North Carolina), 51, 53(fig.), 63(figs.), 64(figs.), 84–85(&fig. 54), 86
Catawba Valley (North Carolina): kilns, 75–76; potters, 51–58; wares, 59–65(&figs.)
Centre d'Art (Haiti), 203
The Ceramic Art (Young), 137
Ceramic Monthly (journal), 145, 149
Chandler, Thomas, 147–48
Charleston (South Carolina), 182
Charleston, Robert J., 91, 97
Charleston Museum, 10
Charlotte News (newspaper), 16–17(&fig. 24)
Charming Polly (ship), 175
Chatham County (North Carolina), 84
Chelsea (Massachusetts), 134(fig.), 136(&fig.)
Chelsea Keramic Art Works, 134(fig.), 135–38(&figs.)
Chelsea Porcelain Works, 92
Cherokee clay, 91–92, 99–100, 101
Cherokee people, 91–92
Child, David Lee, 122*n*13
Child, Lydia Maria, 122*n*13
China Collecting in America (Earle), 126
Chinese export porcelain, 171–74 (&figs. 2–7), 181–86(&figs. 13–18)
Chipstone Foundation, 10(&fig. 10), 122*n*6
Clark, Samuel, 122*n*18
Clark, Sonya, 206
Clark, Theodore, 129
Clark County (Nevada), 139
Clarke, Edward J., 43
Clay County (North Carolina), 52
Clearwell Caves, 105
Cleveland Public Library, 8, 24
"Close Examination: Fakes, Mistakes and Discoveries" (Wieseman), 108
Cole (publisher), 96(fig. 11)
Cole, Charles, 68–69
Cole, Hawk, 68
Cole, Wiley, 68–69
Cole family potters, 86
Colonial Williamsburg, 26(fig.), 122*n*6, 164(fig. 4), 168
Colored Asylum Cemetery (South Carolina State Hospital Cemetery for African Americans), 17
Columbia (South Carolina): Edward and Robert Stork Pottery, 2(fig.), 4–5(&fig. 2), 10–12(&figs. 11–13)
"Columbia Awake at Last" (cartoon), 46(fig. 18)
Columbia University, 8
Columbus, Christopher, 204
Combahee Ferry, 142
Commeraw, Thomas, 145, 148
Commodore Thomas Truxtun (Otis), 170(fig.)
Comstock, H. E., 76

Confederacy (Confederate States of America), 37, 39, 41, 43, 55, 56, 188
Confederate Army, 43, 57–58
Congress, 175, 176, 186, 189
Congress (privateer), 175
Constellation (frigate), 171(&fig.), 180(&fig.), 182
Constellation (ship), 186, 192*n*27
Constitutional wares, 124(fig.), 126–32(&figs.)
Continental Navy, 175, 176
Cooper, Wade Dixon, 52
Cornwallis, Charles, 174
Costa, January, 75
Cotton States and International Exposition, 157
"Court Case Spell," 28(fig.)
Court Case Spell Kit, 29(fig.)
Cowper, William, 122*n*18
Cranfield University, 97
Crawford, Louis, 159
Creole, 203
Crispus Attucks (Mack), 143–44(&fig. 7)
Crockery and Glass Journal, 151(fig.), 160*n*3
Crumpled Vessel (Ohr), 150(fig. 1)
Culp, Christopher, 52
Curious Cliff Dwellers, 157
Currier & Ives, 44(&fig. 11), 45(fig. 15)
Custis, George Washington Parke, 187–88, 194*n*53, 194*n*55, 195*n*58
Custis, John Parke, 187
Cypro-Geometric III-Cypro-Archaic I, 10(fig. 8)

Daemonologie (James I), 3
Dahomeans, 202
Daniel, Joseph, 52
Daniels, Kyrah Malika, 202
Darton, John Maw, 122*n*18
Darton, William, Jr., 122*n*18
Darton, William, Sr., 122*n*18
Darton & Clark, 117
Darwinism, 152
DATA Investigations LLC, 163, 164
Dave "The Slave Potter" Drake (Mack), 146(fig. 13)
David Copperfield (Dickens), 138*n*6
Davis, Jane, 12
Davis, Jefferson, 37, 39, 44–45 (&figs. 12, 16), 46, 47
Davis, Peter: hoodoo and, 5, 28–29; imagined rendering of, 23, 24–26(&fig. 43); life of, 12–17 (& figs. 18–20); re-creation of medical bag, 26–28(&fig. 46); ring bottle, 4(&fig.), 11(&fig. 13), 30
Daynes, Sarah, 201
de Custine, Adam, 185
Deerfield (Massachusetts), 113
Defender (ship), 178, 192*n*23
"Defender" punch bowl, 172, 173(fig. 7), 182, 184, 184(&fig. 17), 189–90
Delaplaine, Joseph, 191*n*2
Delaware County (Pennsylvania), 18
Delgado Museum, 161n8
Dentsville (South Carolina), 11
Detweiler, Susan, 190
DeVeaux, Mamie Wade Avant, 24 (fig. 42), 34*n*65
de Zafra, Carlos, 190, 195*n*69
de Zafra, Julia M. P. Quagliata, 190
de Zafra, Robert, 190
Dibble, R. Ruthie, 91–92
Dickens, Charles, 138*n*6
Dietz, John, 52
Dill, Alonzo Thomas, 164(fig. 3)
Doccia Porcelain Factory, 91, 97, 106–7
Domoney, Kelly, 97
Doncastle, John (Jon), 164, 167, 168
Dorchester County (Maryland), 18–19(&fig. 27)
Douglass, Frederick, 7, 137, 138, 139, 145, 146(fig. 12)
Drake, David, 145–47(&fig. 13)
Dreaming of Rising (Wainwright), 206(fig.), 207–8
Dred Scott case, 139
Drie, C. N., 13(fig. 17)
Dumballa, 201
Durham, Marion, 147–48(&fig. 16)
Durkin, John, 6(fig.)
Dutch Folk area (Columbia, South Carolina), 28
Duvalier, François, 203
Dwight, John, 103

Earle, Alice Morse, 126, 130, 195*n*67
Earle, Mary Trace, 161*n*7
Eatonville (Florida), 8
Edgefield District potters, 147–48(&fig. 16)
Edgefield face vessels, 4, 19–20(&figs. 28–30), 34*n*65
Edward and Robert Stork Pottery, 2(fig.), 11–12(&fig. 13)
Edwards, Howell G. M., 99–100
Elijah McCoy (Mack), 142(&fig. 3)
Emancipation Act (British), 113
The Emancipator (newspaper), 126–27(&figs. 4, 6)
Empress of China (ship), 181, 183(fig. 14)
Energy Dispersive X-ray Spectroscopy (EDX) system, 91, 98–99
England, Christopher, 86
England's Quick Reference to North Carolina Makers (England), 86
English Anti-Slavery Society, 126, 130
"Enslaved and Freed African American Potters" (Mack), 145
Erzulie *vèvè*, 199–200
Esquimaux, 157
Essex Community College (Maryland), 139
Evans, Graham, 164(fig. 3)

The Faces of Martin Luther King Jr. (Mack), 143(&fig. 6)
Falkland Islands, 175
Farber, Glyn, 159
Federal Census (1880), 13(figs. 15 & 16)
Ferris, George Washington, 158, 161*n*14
Ferris Wheel, 158(&fig.)
Fett, Sharla M., 7
Fey, Patricia, 210
Field, Mary Ann Roberts, 129
Field, Thomas F., 126, 129–30, 131, 132
Field & Clark, 129–30
54th Massachusetts All Black Infantry Division, 145
54th Massachusetts Infantry Regiment, 145
1st West Virginia Veteran Volunteer Infantry Regiment, 42
First Amendment, 124(fig.), 127(fig. 5), 128(fig. 9), 132(fig. 11)
Fischer, David, 132
Flag Act (1777), 193*n*22
Folk Beliefs of the Southern Negro (Puckett), 8
"Folk-Tales and Conjure" (*Southern Workman*), 30(&fig.)
Forest of Dean, 105
Fort Sumter, 39–40, 145
Fox, Josiah, 174(fig.), 177–78, 191
Fox family potters, 84
France, 171, 180
Frank Leslie's Illustrated Newspaper, 44
Frechen (Germany), 17(fig.)
Frederick Douglass (Mack), 146(fig. 12)
Frederick Douglass High School (Baltimore), 139
Freedmen's Bureau, 7
"Freedom First of August," 121(fig.)

The Friend of Man (newspaper), 129, 130
Front Royal (Virginia), 41
Frye, Thomas, 91, 97, 100, 101, 104, 110
Fuchs, Ron, II, 133*n*24
Fulbright, Albert, 72, 73(fig. 32)
Fulton, George Newman, 41–43(&fig. 9)
Fulton, James, 41
Fultonham (Ohio), 41
Fulton Pottery, 42–43(&figs. 8 & 9)

Galveston Flood, 157
Garfield, James, 138n6
Garrison, William Lloyd, 134(fig.), 135–36, 137, 138
"General Lee's Slaves, Arlington House," 189(fig. 20)
Geoffrey Godden Collection, 96(fig. 11)
George Washington Carver (Mack), 143(&fig. 5)
George Washington's Chinaware (Detweiler), 190
Ghost Ranch (Abiquiu, New Mexico), 206
Gilded Age, 152–54, 160
Ginori, Carlo, 106
Glanvill, Joseph, 17
Glave, E. J., 20
Godfrey Gilman & Co., 125(fig. 3)
Goodman, Daniel and Margaret Kluttz, 88*n*39
Goodman, Jacob Tobias, 55, 88*n*39
Goodman, John, 55, 88*n*39
Goodman, Michael, 55, 88*n*39
Goodman family potters, 86
Govi, 202
Grand Bois *vèvè*, 210
Grand Turk (ship), 181
Grant, Ulysses S., 138*n*6
Gravelot, Hubert-François, 96 (fig. 11), 97
Gray, Selina, 189(&fig. 20)
Great American Herb Company, 66, 67(figs.)
Green, John, 181, 183(fig. 13)
Green, Watt, 40, 43
Greene County (Tennessee), 54
Guangzhou (China), 171, 172(figs.), 182, 183(fig. 14)

Haiti, 5, 142, 214*n*10; Wainwright and, 197–214
Haitian diaspora, 201, 202, 203
Haitian "Renaissance," 203
Haitian Revolution, 142
"Haitian Water Bearer" (Sealy), 209
Haiti Vodou, 202, 211–12
Hall, Wesley, 89*n*95
Hampton Institute, 8
Hang Him on the Sour Apple Tree (Porter), 44(fig.)
Hanks, Emily, 81, 82(fig. 48)
Hanks Knob (Virginia), 73(fig. 34), 74, 75
Harmon, Peter, 87*n*29
Harper's Weekly (periodical), 6(fig.), 44, 46(&figs.)
Harriet Tubman (Mack), 144(&fig. 8)
Harris, Eleanor, 188
Harris, George Washington, 153
Harris, Kamala, 148(&fig.)
Hartsoe, Poley Carp, 84(fig. 54), 85
Hartsoe, Sylvanus Leander, 84(fig. 54)
Hartzog, David, 52, 53–54, 62(&fig. 17), 63, 84(fig. 54), 85
Hartzog family potters, 55, 84(fig. 54), 86
"Harvest" print, 118(&figs.)
Hathaway, Mary B., 195*n*69
Hathaway, William H., Jr., 195*n*69
Hazzard-Donald, Katrina, 7
Heavner, Harvey Hightower, 54
Heavner, Royal Pinkney, 54
Heavner (Havnaer; Havner), Alfred A., 54
Hefner, John, 52
Hempstead (New York), 175
Henderson (Nevada), 143(fig. 6)
Henrico County (Virginia), 43(fig.)
Herculaneum Factory (Liverpool), 171(fig.)
Heritage Face Vessels (Mack), 142–47(&figs. 3–14), 148(&fig.)
Heylyn, Edward, 91, 97, 100, 101, 104, 110
High John the Conqueror, 27, 30(&fig.)
High Style teawares, 97
Hill, Alexander, 55
Hispaniola, 204
Historical Staffordshire (Snyder), 130
Historic Deerfield, 113–14, 118
Ho-Chunk, 206
Hoiem, Elizabeth Massa, 117, 123*n*28, 123*n*30
Holly, Daniel, 54
Holmes, Billy, 41
Holuv (Hulob, Hublov, Hohler), Adolph (Adolphus), 14–17, 27(fig.), 28
"Hoodoo Blues" (Brown), 3
Hoodoo–Conjuration–Witchcraft–Rootwork (Hyatt), 9(&fig.)
"Hoodoo in America" (Hurston), 8–9
"Hoodoo Man" song, 29
Hopkins, Andrew, 24–26(&figs. 43 & 44)
Howdle, Bruce, 206
Howkins, Ashley, 97, 98(fig. 13)
Hoyt, Epaphras, 113
Hume, Ivor Noël, 167
Humphreys, Joshua, 177, 178, 194*n*53
Hunter, Robert, 133*n*24
Huntsville (North Carolina), 54
Hurricane Hugo, 74
Hurston, Zora Neale, 8–9, 26
Hutchinson, William, 183(fig. 14)
Hyatt, Harry Middleton, 9(&fig.), 21, 34*n*75
Hynes, April, 14
Hyppolite, Hector, 203

Illustrated Buffalo Express (periodical), 161*n*7
Imagining Consumers (Blaszczyk), 131
Imamagine del manoscritto Zorvaster Clavis Artis, 22(fig. 38)
Index of Southern Potters (Smith), 85–86
Indian Herbs, 66, 67(figs.)
Inner Harbor (Baltimore), 192*n*27
L'Insurgente (ship), 180(&fig.), 186

Jackson, Ketanji Brown, 148(&fig.)
Jacobs Fork Township (Catawba County, North Carolina), 52
Jamaica, 118, 119–21
The James A. Haley Veterans' Hospital, 143
James I, 3
James River (Virginia), 40, 43
James River Valley (Virginia), 37
Jay, William H., 99–100
JEOL JSM-IT200 scanning electron microscope (SEM), 91, 98–99(&fig. 13)
Le Jeu de la Crosse, 97
Jingdenzhen (China), 172(figs.), 183(fig. 13)
John Carr & Sons, 118(&fig. 4), 119(fig. 6)
John Carr & Son(s), 114(fig.)
Johns, Jasper, 152
Johnson, Amon Locke, 52, 53–54, 63, 65
Johnson, Eli, 52–53, 54, 88*n*58

Johnson, Elizabeth Carpenter, 54
Johnson, Harvey Make, 52, 53, 57–58
Johnson, Henrietta, 139
Johnson, Howard, 139, 148
Johnson, John, 52, 54, 88*n*58, 89*n*71
Johnson, Joseph Daniel, 52, 53
Johnson, Mary (Martha A.) Lawrence, 52
Johnson, Sarah Ann, 54
Johnson, Sarah "Sally" Salina, 52, 54
Johnson, Susannah "Susan," 54, 87*n*27
Johnson, Wade D. C., 53(&fig.), 54, 62
Johnson, William Burgin, 52, 54
Johnson County (Tennessee), 68
Johnson family potters, 56(fig. 5), 84(fig. 54), 85, 86
John Stork Pottery (Columbia, South Carolina), 11(&figs. 11 & 12)
Jones, Malinda, 55
Jones, Tom, 70
Jugtown (Catawba County, North Carolina), 53
Jung, Carl, 23
J. W. Carpenter Pottery, 58(figs.), 59

Kalbas, 208(&fig.)
Kanari, 201–2(&figs. 7 & 8), 208
Keesee, Thomas, 41
Keesee & Parr Pottery, 36(figs.), 37, 38(figs.), 40–41(&fig. 6), 41(&fig.), 43
Kiln Watcher (Wainwright), 210(&fig.)
King, Marc, 74–75
King, Martin Luther, Jr., 143(&fig. 6)
King, William, 161*n*7
King Alex, 23(&fig.)
King of the Voodoos (engraving), 22(fig. 37)
King William County Courthouse, 163–69(&figs. 2–3, 5)
King William County Courthouse (Dill), 164(fig. 3)
King William County Historical Society, 163
Kinzer, Philip, 70
Kitchen of the Paul Family Home (Haiti), 202(fig. 8)
Kitt, Frederick, 186
Knox, Henry, 177
Kongo *nkisi* forms, 207
Kreyòl, 210, 212
Kwi, 202

Lafayette, Marquis de, 174
Landrum, Abner, 10–11
Landrum, Linneaus, 10
Lane, Arthur, 91
Lanford Station (North Carolina), 53
Larsen, Ellouise Baker, 126
Laurens Advertiser (newspaper), 15(&fig. 22)
Laveau, Marie, 8, 24, 25–26(&fig. 44), 29
Lear, Tobias, 192*n*13
Leder, Stephen, 20
Lee, Frank, 186
Lee, Mary Custis, 188–89
Lee, Robert E., 188–89
Lee, Sydney Smith, 188
Leepa-Rattner Museum of Art, 144
Leslie's Weekly (magazine), 24(&fig. 40)
Lewis, Edmonia, 148
Lewis, James, 139
The Liberator (newspaper), 130, 135, 137
"Liberty" image, 121(fig.)
Lincoln, Abraham, 37, 39, 45(&fig 15), 47, 145
Lincoln County (North Carolina), 51, 52, 55, 60–63(figs. 9–14, 16–21), 65(fig.), 72(fig.), 84, 85, 86
Lincoln County Historical Association, 75
Lincolnton (North Carolina), 69
Linneaus Landrum Pottery (Richland County, South Carolina), 10(&fig. 10)
L'Insurgente, 171(&fig.)
"List of Licensed Physicians and Surgeons of the State" (Richland County, South Carolina), 14(fig. 20)
Liverpool (England), 165(fig. 6), 166(fig. 7), 167–68(figs.), 171(fig.)
Lloyd's (insurer), 180, 187
London (east), 90(fig.), 92–97(figs.)
Long, David, 173, 190
Longfellow, Henry Wadsworth, 138*n*6
Lorette ordinance, 161*n*16
Lossing, Benson, 188(&fig.), 189
Loudoun County (Virginia), 41
Louisiana, 116. *See also* New Orleans
Louisiana Purchase Exposition, 157–58(&figs.)
Louisiana Trade Tokens (Crawford & Farber), 159
Lovejoy, Elijah, 125–26(&fig. 2)
Lovejoy design, 124(fig.), 126–32(&figs. 5, 7–11)

Lowe, Truman, 206
Lowndes County (Mississippi), 8
Lucky Mojo Curio Company, 10, 29(fig.)
Lugo, Roberto, 148
Lukacs-Doonath, 97
Lwa, 199, 201, 210, 212
Lyon, Caleb, 189–90(&fig. 21)
Lyon, Charles Woolsey, 195*n*69

Macbeth (Shakespeare), 3
MacDonald, David, 148
Mack, David, 139–45(&figs. 1, 3–14), 148–49(&fig.)
Mack, Ethel, 145
Maclay, William, 194*n*46
Macomb, John N., Jr., 187–88
Madame C. J. Walker (Mack), 142(&fig. 4)
Madison (Wisconsin). *See* Wainwright, Babette
Madou, Jean-Baptiste, 5(fig. 3)
"Mad Potter" (George Ohr), 152, 160*n*1
Make, Harvey, 52
Mallet, John V. G., 91, 97
Maman, 200(fig. 5)
La Mama-snekle…faisant ses conjurations (Madou & Benoit), 5(fig. 3)
Manners, Errol, 92
"Map of Folklore Field Work" (Hyatt), 9(fig.)
Marassa Jumeaux, 202
Marassa Spirits pots, 202(fig. 9)
Marché Hippolyte (Haiti), 202(fig. 9)
Margolin, Sam, 126
Mars black, 106
Marshall, Thurgood, 139, 145
The Martydrom of Lovejoy (Tanner), 125(figs.)
Maryland Institute College of Art, 139
Maude, Manmi, 207(fig.)
Mauney, David, 52
McCoy, Elijah, 142(&fig. 3), 144–45
McDowell, Irvin, 189
McDowell, Jim, 148
McHenry, James, 179
Meadows, Christine, 173–74, 190
Medal of Honor, 145
Mediterranean Sea, 176, 186
Megens, Nette, 97
Meissen "Kauffahrtei" style, 94
Memphis Daily Appeal (newspaper), 7–8
Mercantile Library of Baltimore, 117
MESDA Craftsman Database, 86

Methodist Episcopal Church (Rocketts, Virginia), 41
Meyer, Joseph, 159
Micawber, Wilkins, 138*n*6
Middle Passage, 205
Middle Peninsula (Virginia), 163
Midnight in the Garden of Good and Evil (Berendt), 20
Military Officers Association of America, 143
Miller, Henry, 52
Minerva (root doctor), 20
Mishler, Clifford, 161*n*13
"Mississippi Hoodoo Doctor" (photograph), 24(fig. 41)
Mississippi Socialist Party of America, 161*n*10
Missouri, 8, 56, 68, 70, 88*n*52, 89*n*95
"Mistress Columbia" (cartoon), 46(&fig. 17)
Monte Baldo (Italy), 105
Montgomery, Jack, 23, 28
Montgomery County (Kentucky), 6
Moore, N. Hudson, 126, 131
Moravians, 51
Morgan State College, 139, 149*n*1
Morton, Jacob, 181
Mount Vernon, 173
Mount Vernon (house), 180, 185–86, 187, 190, 194*n*53
Mount Vernon and Its Associations (Lossing), 188(&fig.)
Mount Vernon Ladies' Association, 172, 190, 195*n*69
Mules and Men (Hurston), 9, 26
Mull (Moll), Benedict, 54
Murphy, Patrick, 43
Musée du Panthéon National Haïtien, 204, 205–6
Museum of Early Southern Decorative Arts (MESDA), 86
Museum of Science and Industry, 190

Narrative of Riots at Alton (Beecher), 125, 126–27
National Council on Education for the Ceramic Arts (NCECA), 149
National Museum of the United States Navy, 190, 194n51
National Museum of Wales, 94
National Museums Liverpool, 122*n*6, 167, 168
National Republican (newspaper), 189
Naval Historical Foundation, 172, 173, 187, 190, 194*n*51
The Negro's Complaint (Cowper), 122*n*18
New Lights (New Mooners), 87*n*4
New Monthly Magazine, 188
New Orleans, 5–6, 29, 152, 156, 158–60
New Orleans Art Pottery, 159, 161*n*17
New Orleans Museum of Art, 161*n*8
New York (New York), ring bottle, 10(fig. 9)
New York Harbor, 181
New York Times (newspaper), 14(&fig. 18)
Niderviller porcelain factory, 185
Night Whispers (Wainwright), 198(fig.), 199, 200–1(&fig. 6)
9th West Virginia Volunteer Infantry Regiment, 42
Norfolk State University, 139
North Carolina Junior Reserves, Company B, 8th Battalion, 56
North Carolina Reserves, Company E, 9th Regiment, 57
North Carolina Senior Reserves, Company C, 4th Regiment, 53
North Shields (England), 114(fig.), 118(&fig. 4), 119(fig. 6)
Northup, Solomon, 116
Notasulga (Alabama), 8
Nova Scotia, 52

Oak Grove (Missouri), 70, 89*n*95
Obeah, 5
Obeah Man (painting), 5(fig. 4)
Obi, 7
Obin, Philomé, 203
Officers Candidate School, 139
Ohr, George, 150(figs.), 151–52(&fig.); Gilded Age and, 152–54, 160; Storyville and, 158–60; tokens, 151, 154–56(&figs. 5–9); World's Fairs and, 156–58
Ohr, Josie, 161*n*17
The Old China Book (Moore), 131
Old Rabbit, the Voodoo, and Other Sorcerers (Owen), 8(&fig.), 23(&fig.)
Oneida Bible Society, 129
"Open Pan Boiling" print, 118, 119(figs.)
Opie, Amelia, 115–16
Orange (Georgia), 12(fig.)
Orangeburg Court of General Sessions, 17
Orangeburg Enterprise (newspaper), 16
Osborn, Kyle, 48
Otis, Bass, 170(fig.), 191*n*2
Otumba (Mexico), 206
Owen, Juliette A., 8(fig.)
Owen, Mary Alicia, 8(&fig.), 23
Owens, Winnie, 148
Oxford Xplore 15mm^2 EDX, 98–99(&fig. 13)

Pakèt Kongo for Papa Loko, 207(fig.)
"The Palissy of Biloxi" (King), 161*n*7
Pan-American Exposition, 157
Paoli clay, 206
Parr, David, Jr., 41
Parr, David, Sr., 40–41, 42
Parr, James, 41
Parr, John L., 41
Pasinger, Thomas, 54
Patent Office, 189
Piedmont Region (North Carolina), 76
Penland School of Crafts, 149
Pennsylvania, 51, 175
Perine, David Maulden, 40–41
Peter and Mary White collection, 94
Peters, Dewitt, 203
Phelps, Kelly and Kyle, 148
Philadelphia (Pennsylvania), 175, 179, 184
Phillis Wheatley (Mack), 144(&fig. 10)
Pickering, Timothy, 178–79(&fig. 10)
Pike (Louisiana Purchase Exposition), 157
Pinqua, 181
Pipers Gap (Virginia): John Wesley Carpenter and, 51, 56–58, 61(&fig. 15), 65(fig.), 70–76(&figs.), 77–85(&figs. 42, 43, 47–49, 55), 86; Carpenter family in, 65–70; wares, 69(fig.), 76–84(&figs. 37–53)
Pitt Rivers Museum, 17(fig.)
Playing with Marbles (scene), 96(fig. 11)
Pope, John, 52
Porcelain Street (Guangzhou), 182
Port-au-Prince (Haiti), 142, 198, 202(fig. 9), 203, 206
Porter, James W., 44(fig.)
Potomitan (Wainwright), 211–12&figs. 21 & 22), 214
Pottery and Porcelain of the United States (Barber), 153, 161*n*7
Powwow, 6
Prayer Circle (Wainwright), 199–200(&fig. 4)
Prince Edward Island, 52
Providence Gazette (newspaper), 182
Provisional Army, 180

Puckett, Newbell Niles, 8, 23, 24
Puckett Collection, 24(fig. 41)

Quasi-War, 171, 192*n*4

Rada drums, 199, 202
"The Rail Candidate" (Currier & Ives), 45(fig. 15)
Rainey, Ma, 26(fig.)
Raman or FTIR spectroscopy, 108, 109
Ramey, Joseph B., 41
Ramsay, E. Gael, 97
Ramsay, Ross H., 99–100
Ramsay, W. Ross, 97
Ramsour's Mill, 52
Randolph, Evan, IV, 190
Reese, Peter, 52
Reeves Museum of Ceramics, 133*n*24
Reinhardt, Enoch and Harvey, 75
Remarks, Instructions, and Examples Relating to the Latitude and Longitude etc. etc. etc. (Truxtun), 173–74(&fig. 8)
Revolutionary War, 177
Rhodes, Daniel, 139
Rice, Curtis, 20
Richland County (South Carolina), 10(&fig. 10)
Richmond (Virginia), 36(figs, 37, 38(figs.), 40–43(&fig. 6)
Riggins, Edith Carpenter, 55, 57, 74–75
Riggins, Robert, 73(fig. 34)
Riley, Noël, 122*n*4
Ritchie, Henry, 54, 88*n*58
Ritchie, Joseph, 54, 88*n*58
Ritchie, Joseph Walter, 54
Ritchie, Marcus, 64(figs.), 65
Ritchie, Moses, 54, 55, 64, 66(fig.), 87*n*31, 88*n*58
Ritchie, Paul, 54
Ritchie, Robert and Luther Seth, 54
Ritchie, Sarah Lavina Wyont, 54
Ritchie, Thomas, 54, 60, 61(fig. 11), 63(figs.), 64–65, 69, 84(fig. 53), 87*n*31, 88*n*58
Ritchie (Rüetschi) family potters, 54, 55, 57(fig. 5), 62, 63–64, 84(fig. 54), 85, 86
Ritual Supplies Mail Order Source Occult Supplies, 28(fig.)
Roberts, David, 129
Robertson, Alexander, 136
Robertson, George, 136
Robertson, Hugh, 136, 137, 138, 138*n*6
Robertson, James, 136, 138*n*6
Robertson & Sons, 136–38
Rockingham County (Virginia), 76
Roderick, Emma de Zafra, 195*n*69
Rose Marie Spiritual Gifted Reader & Advisor, 27
Rosewell, Harry Herman, 35*n*84
Royal Navy, 175
Russell, Benjamin Allen, 87*n*29

Sacred Arts of the Black Atlantic (Duke University), 214*n*1
Saducismus Triumphatus (Glanvill), 17
St. Francis Catholic Shop, 27
St. Joseph (Missouri), 8
St. Lucia, 210
St. Petersburg College, 139, 144
Salisbury (North Carolina), 54
Saltville Salt Works, 77
Savage, Augusta, 148
Savage, Edward, 176(fig.), 180(&fig.)
Savva, Niki, 148
Sculpted Hat (Ohr), 150(fig. 2)
SEA6000VX mapping XRF, 97
Seagle, Adam, 52, 87*n*31
Seagle, Barbara, 55
Seagle, Daniel, 52, 53–54, 55, 62(&fig. 16), 63, 75, 85
Seagle, James F., 55
Seagle family potters, 55, 84(fig. 54), 86
Seagle-Hartzog school, 62
Sealy, Sandra, 209
Seaver, Horace, 138
"The Second Part of Youthful Diversions...Act of Parliament 7th May 1739," 97
Segon, 200(fig. 5)
Seitz, Moses, 52
Sel Lakay Ki Kraze (Wainwright), 210–11(&figs. 19 & 20)
SEM/EDAXS, 108
Senufo, 208
Seven Rays Book Store, 27
Shakespeare, William, 3, 28
Shenandoah Valley potteries, 76–77
Sherrill, William L., 51–52
Shortland, Andrew, 97
Sloane, Hans, 214*n*11
Smalls, Robert, 142
Smith, Howard A., 85–86
Smith, Robert, 186
Smithsonian Institute, 161*n*8, 189
Smyth County (Virginia), 68, 77
Sni-A-Bar Township (Missouri), 56
Snyder, Jeffrey B., 130
Society of Cincinnati, 191n2
Society of Cincinnati porcelain, 187, 189, 195n64
Sojourner Truth (Mack), 144(&fig. 9)
Solomon's Temple, 27
"Some Facts in the History of a Unique Personality" (Ohr), 151(fig.), 160*n*3
Sosyete Nago Temple (Jacmel, Haiti), 207(fig.)
Southern Punch (periodical), 44
Southern Workman and Hampton School Record (journal), 8, 30(&fig.)
South Sea Islands, 157
Spangenberg, Gottlieb, 51
Speagle, Andrew Franklin "Frank," 55, 86
Speagle, John C., 55
Spectator (newspaper), 130, 133*n*17
Sphinx Paw, 27
Spring Hill (Florida), 142–44(figs. 3–5, 7–10), 146(figs. 12 & 13), 148(fig.)
Spring Valley (Bedsaul), 89*n*75
Staffordshire (England), 121(fig.), 124(fig.), 126, 128(fig. 9), 129(fig.), 132(&fig.)
Stamey, Alexander, 52
Stamey, John, 52
Stamey family potters, 86
Star Spangle Art Show, 143–44
The State (newspaper), 16(&fig. 23)
State Hospital for the Mentally Ill (South Carolina), 17
States porcelain, 187, 189
Stewart, Susan, 202
Stockspring Antiques, 94
Stolen Bones Act of 1619 (SBA), 145
Stork, Edward Leslie, 2(fig.), 11–12(&fig. 13)
Stork, John J., 11(&figs. 11 & 12)
Stork, Robert Manning, 11
Story, Sidney, 159
Storyville (New Orleans), 156, 158–60
Stowe, Harriet Beecher, 125
Strongman, Roberto, 202
Stuart, Gilbert, 47(fig.)
Sugar: How It Grows, and How It Is Made (J. L. S.), 117–20(&figs. 3, 5, 7)
Supreme Court, 139, 145
Surry County (North Carolina), 54
Sweeney, Charles H., 43
Sweeney, Stephen, Jr., 43
Sweeney, Stephen B., 40(&fig.), 43(&fig.)

Taíno art, 204–5(&fig. 11)
Taíno burials, 214*n*11
Taíno pottery, 197, 204, 205–6
Taíno Vessel (Wainwright), 204(fig. 10), 205(&fig.)
Takaezu, Toshiko, 139
Talbot, Silas, 179
Taney, Roger Brooke, 139, 145
Tanner, Henry, 125(figs.)
Thomas Ritchie Pottery, 61(fig. 11), 63(figs.), 64–65
Three Witches, 3, 28
Times and Democrat (newspaper), 15(&fig. 21)
Tories, 52
Toussaint, Corbett, 4
A Treatise of Practical Seamanship (Hutchinson), 183(fig. 14)
Trenton (New Jersey), 182
Truth, Sojourner, 144(&fig. 9)
Truxton (ship), 187
Truxton, Thomas, 170–71, 173–80, 190, 191*n*2; GW punch-bowl gift and, 172(figs. 3, 5), 180–86(&fig. 17), 191; punch bowl and, 183(fig. 13), 184(&figs. 15 & 16), 185(fig.), 187, 194*n*51; TT punch bowl and, 172–74(&figs. 3, 4, 6)
Truxton-Decatur Museum, 194*n*51
Tryon County (North Carolina), 51
Tryon Resolves, 51
Tubman, Harriet, 142, 144(&fig. 8)
Turners and Burners (Zug), 85
Twelve Years a Slave (Northup), 116

Uffelman, Erich, 194*n*42
Uncle Tom's Cabin (Stowe), 125
Underground Railroad, 144
Union Army, 41, 42, 43
United States (frigate), 187
U.S. Army, 139
U.S. Capitol, 145
U.S. Census, 67, 81
U.S. Manufacturers' Census, 40
U.S. Navy, 157, 171, 172, 176–80, 186, 190, 191, 193*n*23
USS *Constitution* (frigate), 179(fig.)
University of Wisconsin, 199, 206

Vaccianna, Dudley, 148
Valley of Virginia, 20
Vanity Fair (periodical), 44
La Vengeance (ship), 171, 186
Vereennigde Oostindische Compagnie (Dutch East India Company), 181
Vestal, Silas, 54, 87*n*29
Vestal, Tilighman, 41
Vèvè. See Agwé, Bade, Bosou, Erzulie, and Grand Bois
Vice President Kamala Harris and Associate Justice of the Supreme Court Ketanji Brown Jackson (Mack), 148(&fig.)
Victoria and Albert Museum, 97
Virginia Gazette (newspaper), 164, 167
Virginia State College, 139
Vlach, John, 20, 34*n*67
Vodouisant, 200
Vodou/voodoo, 5–6, 7–8; Haitian, 202, 211–12
"A Voodoo Dance" (Durkin), 6(fig.)
Voulkos, Peter, 139
Wain, Louis, 8(fig.), 23(fig.)
Wainwright, Alexandre, 200
Wainwright, Babette, 196–214; *Dreaming of Rising,* 206(fig.), 207–8; *Kalbas,* 208(&fig.); *Kiln Watcher,* 210(&fig.); *Night Whispers,* 198(fig.), 199, 200–1(&fig. 6); photo of, 213(fig.); *Potomitan,* 211–12(&figs. 21 & 22), 214; *Prayer Circle,* 199–200(&fig. 4); process, 206–11; *Sel Lakay Ki Kraze,* 210–11(&figs. 19 & 20); studio, 196(fig.), 197(&fig.); *Taíno Vessel,* 204(fig. 10), 205(&fig.); *Water Bearer,* 208–10(&figs. 16 & 17)
Walker, Madame C. J., 141(fig.), 142(&fig. 4), 145
Warhol, Andy, 152
War of 1812, 187
Warren, Edward, 17(fig.)
Washington, George, 46–47(&fig. 19), 164, 174, 176(fig.), 177, 192*n*13, 194*n*46; GW punch bowl, 172–74 (&figs. 3, 5, 7), 184–86(&fig. 17), 188–91(fig. 19); Pickering and, 178–79(&fig. 10); Truxton and, 175, 176, 179, 180, 181–82, 185–86, 192*n*21
Washington, Martha, 174, 176, 185, 186, 187, 189, 194*n*43
Washington County (Virginia), 77
Water Bearer (Wainwright), 208–10(&figs. 16 & 17)
Watkins, James, 148
Weaver, Jacob, 52, 84
Wenzel, Henry (Johann Heinrich), 54
West African face masks, 208
West Indies (British), 5, 7, 113–21, 122*n*1
Wetherburn, Henry, 164, 167
Wetherburn's Tavern (Williamsburg, Virginia), 164(&fig. 4), 166(fig. 8), 167–69(&fig. 9)
Wetherill, Richard Benbridge, 194*n*51
Wheatley, Phillis, 144(&fig. 10)
White Oak Site (Dorchester County, Maryland), 18(fig. 27)
White Sulfur Springs (West Virginia), 42
Wieseman, Marjorie, 108
Wiles (North Carolina), 58(figs.), 59, 86
Wilkes County (North Carolina), 70(fig.), 71
Willard, Samuel, 113, 121
Williams, Jim, 29
Williams, John, 129
Williamsburg (Virginia), 164(fig. 4), 166(fig. 7), 167
Wilson, Andrew, 148
Wilson, George, 148
Wilson, Hiram, 148
Wilson, James, 148
Wilson, John M., 147–48
Wilson, Wallace, 148
Wilson Brothers Pottery, 148
Wingard, Phil, 4
Winterthur Museum, 192*n*3
The Wonderful Wheel (Earle), 161*n*7
Wood, Enoch, 129
Woods, Michael E., 47
Working Cures (Fett), 7
World's Columbian Exposition, 156–57, 158
World's Industrial and Cotton Centennial Exposition, 156, 157
Wythe County (Virginia), 55, 68

X-ray fluorescence (XRF), 91, 108, 109, 194*n*42

Yam Shinqua, 182
Yorktown (Virginia), 174
Young, Jennie J., 137
Yount, Andrew, 52
Yronwode, Catherine, 10

Zimmerman, Hans, 51, 52, 87*n*4
Zimmerman, Salome, 51
Zordan, Joseph, 91–92
Zug, Charles G., III, 76, 85, 86

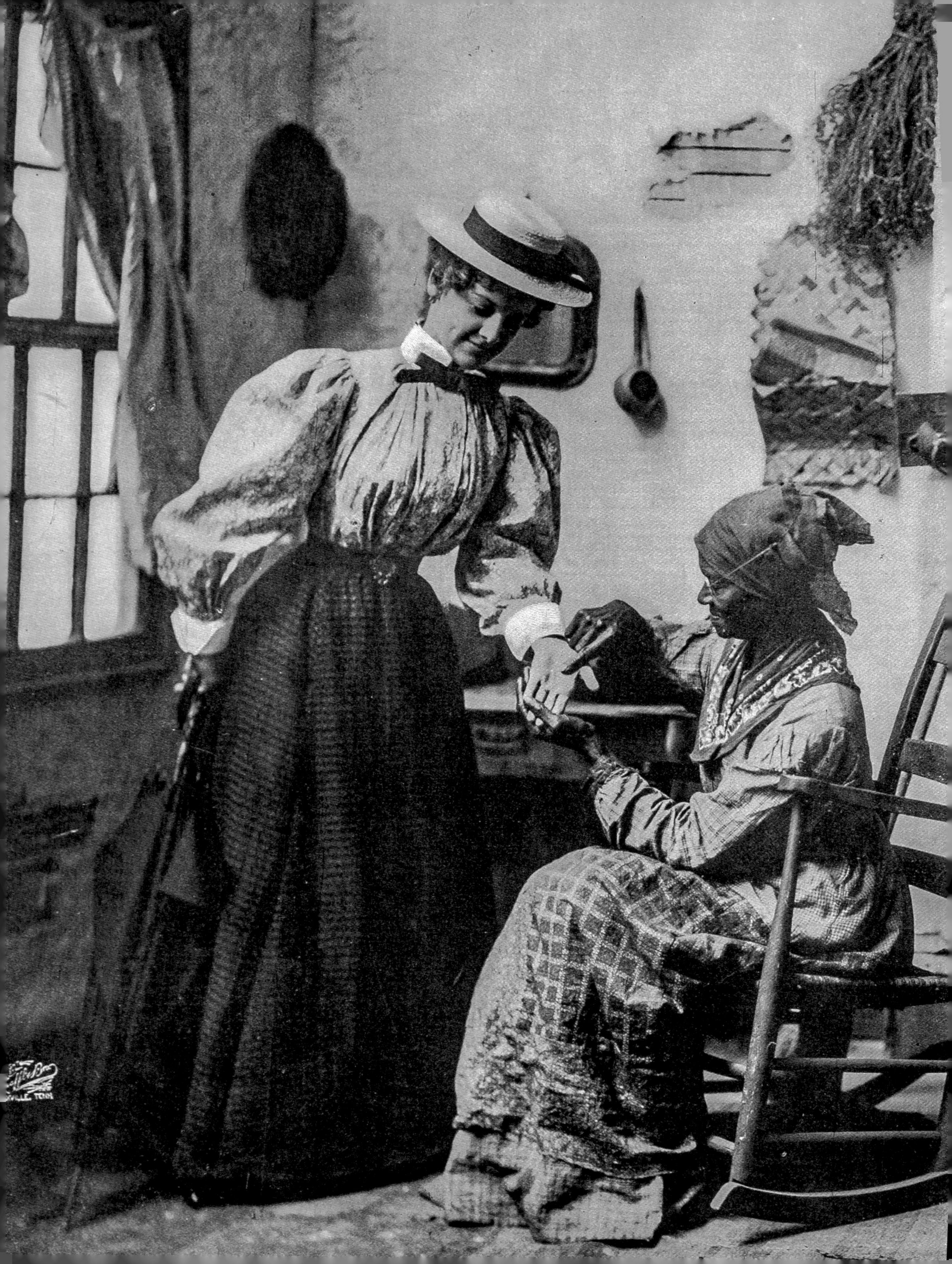